DATE DUE

FE 26 '92			

DEMCO 38-296

THE
METHODISTS

**Recent Titles in
Denominations in America**

The Unitarians and the Universalists
David Robinson

The Baptists
William Henry Brackney

The Quakers
Hugh Barbour and J. William Frost

The Congregationalists
J. William T. Youngs

The Presbyterians
Randall Balmer and John R. Fitzmier

The Roman Catholics
Patrick W. Carey

The Orthodox Church
Thomas E. FitzGerald

THE
METHODISTS

JAMES E. KIRBY, RUSSELL E. RICHEY, AND KENNETH E. ROWE

Denominations in America, Number 8
Henry Warner Bowden, *Series Editor*

Greenwood Press
Westport, Connecticut • London

under the auspices of
"United Methodism and American Culture," a program funded
through a grant by Lilly Endowment, Inc.

Library of Congress Cataloging-in-Publication Data

Kirby, James E.
  The Methodists / James E. Kirby, Russell E. Richey, Kenneth E.
Rowe.
      p.   cm.—(Denominations in America, ISSN 0193–6883 ; no. 8)
  Includes bibliographical references and index.
  ISBN 0–313–22048–4 (alk. paper)
      1. United Methodist Church (U.S.).   2. Methodist Church—United
States.   I. Richey, Russell E.   II. Rowe, Kenneth E.   III. Title.
  IV. Series.
  BX8382.2.A4K57   1996
  287'.6—dc20   96–536

British Library Cataloguing in Publication Data is available.

Library of Congress Catalog Card Number: 96–536
ISBN: 0–313–22048–4
ISSN: 0193–6883

First published in 1996

Greenwood Press, 88 Post Road West, Westport, CT 06881
An imprint of Greenwood Publishing Group, Inc.

Printed in the United States of America

The paper used in this book complies with the
Permanent Paper Standard issued by the National
Information Standards Organization (Z39.48–1984).

10 9 8 7 6 5 4 3 2 1

Copyright Acknowledgments

Scattered excerpts from Russell E. Richey, *The Methodist Conference in America: A History*
(Nashville: Kingwood Books, 1996). Copyright © 1996 by Abingdon Press. Used by permission.

The following essays: " 'And Are We Yet Alive': A Study in Conference Self-Preoccupation," 33
(July 1995):249–61; "From Quarterly to Camp Meeting: A Reconsideration of Early American
Methodism," 23 (July 1985):199–213; "The Southern Accent of American Methodism," 27 (Oct.
1988):3–24; and "The Four Languages of Early American Methodism," 28 (April 1990):155–71
are used with permission from *Methodist History*.

CONTENTS

SERIES FOREWORD

The Greenwood Press series of denominational studies follows a distinguished precedent. These current volumes improve on earlier works by including more churches than before and by looking at all of them in a wider cultural context. The prototype for this series appeared almost a century ago. Between 1893 and 1897, twenty-four scholars collaborated in publishing thirteen volumes known popularly as the American Church History Series. These scholars found twenty religious groups to be worthy of separate treatment, either as major sections of a volume or as whole books in themselves. Scholars in this current series have found that outline to be unrealistic, with regional subgroups no longer warranting separate status and others having declined to marginality. Twenty organizations in the earlier series survive as nine in this collection, and two churches and an interdenominational bureau have been omitted. The old series also excluded some important churches of that time; others have gained great strength since then. So today, a new list of denominations, rectifying imbalance and recognizing modern significance, features many groups not included a century ago. The solid core of the old series remains in this new one, and in the present case a wider range of topics makes the study of denominational life in America more inclusive.

Some recent denominational histories have improved with greater attention to primary sources and more rigorous scholarly standards. But they have too frequently pursued themes for internal consumption alone. Volumes in the Greenwood Press series strive to surmount such parochialism while remaining grounded in the specific materials of concrete ecclesiastical traditions. They avoid placing a single denomination above others in its distinctive truth claims, ethical norms, and liturgical patterns. Instead, they set the history of each church in the larger religious and social context that shaped the emergence of notable denomination features. In this way the authors in this series help us understand the interaction that has occurred between different churches and the broader aspects of American culture.

Each of the historical studies in this current series has a strong biographical focus, using the real-life experiences of men and women in church life to highlight significant elements of an unfolding sequence. The first part(s) of every volume singles out important watershed issues that affected a denomination's outlook and discusses the roles of those who influenced the flow of events. The last part consists of biographical sketches, featuring those persons and many others who contributed to the vitality of their religious heritage. This format enables authors to emphasize the distinctive features of their chosen subject and at the same time recognize the sharp particularities of individual attributes in the cumulative richness that their denomination possesses.

The collaborative authors of this volume are associated with three of the most vigorous universities and divinity schools that stem from Methodist beginnings: Russell E. Richey with Duke University, Kenneth E. Rowe with Drew University, and James E. Kirby with Southern Methodist University. These scholars have known each other for decades and have cooperated on numerous conferences, study groups, and planning sessions regarding Methodist experience and history. Thus their backgrounds and professional activities qualify them eminently for exploring new avenues in this denomination's historical development. The cumulative result of their separate contributions amount to more than a simple sum of three parts. Their ideas mutually reinforce each other, and (because carefully constructed to do so) their topics highlight facets of distinctive Methodist growth through interconnected cross-references. In trying to add new verve and insight to denominational narrative, they have chosen original themes and congregational emphases that view somewhat familiar patterns from fresh angles of vision. The results are gratifying to specialists who think they know the church's whole history as well as to those encountering Methodists for the first time. This new blend of the oft-mentioned and the unique will add substantially to the value of this series, and it will profit readers of every level as they sample the treasures that follow.

HENRY WARNER BOWDEN

INTRODUCTION

Through the construal of its past, Methodism has sought the reconstruction of its present. Motives or mandates to construct or reform have governed many of the Methodist histories. Sometimes self-consciously and explicitly, more often indirectly and with asides, Methodism's historians have told the story so as to shape or reshape the present.[1] Recent narrations have come from academic arenas, honored the reigning protocols of historical interpretation, and exercised reticence about setting program for the church. Yet even those have typically come from persons with some significant connection, current or not, with the denomination and have not been entirely free of constructive dimensions.

Doubtless future interpreters will pounce on the constructive agendas in this effort and ferret out the program(s) that we three would advance. We are clearly conscious of our endeavor to reconstruct the past and of Methodism's continuous efforts at reconstructing itself. Indeed, we have chosen to focus our attention on three ways in which Methodism has continuously constructed and reconstructed itself—under a superintending authority, in conference, and as a people disciplined in holy living. To each of these constructive capacities of Methodism we devote a major section of this book. The first treats bishops, the second conferences, the third members. Each topic we essay from the days of John Wesley to the present, the focus after Wesley falling exclusively on the American experience. Each section examines one of the important aspects of Methodism's structuring of itself. ''Bishops'' explores the evolution of the superintending, episcopal power and authority charismatically lodged in John Wesley, given American monarchical expression in Francis Asbury and transmitted (less successfully) to their episcopal successors; ''Conferences,'' the character of and changes in quarterly, annual, and general conferences that gathered Methodism's aristocracy; ''Members,'' the Methodist populace, with special attention to processes and structures through which persons were initiated into and sustained in the connection.

We do not, simply could not, treat all aspects of Methodist structuring and structures. To the boards and agencies, for instance, we give but passing attention. Nor do we examine all important dimensions of local Methodism and of congregational life. The three structuring capacities might not be those selected were one to look around at present-day United Methodism and ask, "What now gives it form?" We have instead asked, "What initially gave American Methodism form and shape and how have those structuring powers evolved?" Three formative impulses, we argue, characterized early Methodism: being in connection with Mr. Wesley; working under his superintendency and under that of his appointees; and struggling, with the guidance of others along a way of discipline, to "flee from the wrath to come" and toward holiness. The three impulses are implicit in the question and answer that defined the movement, a statement rendered by Wesley, carried over into the first American Discipline and reiterated in Disciplines thereafter:

Q. 4. What may we reasonably believe to be God's Design in raising up the Preachers called *Methodists?*

A. To reform the Continent, and to spread scriptural Holiness over these Lands.[2]

The putting and answering of the question evidenced the superintending authority, which initially was Wesley; the question itself evidenced the conviction that God was agent in connecting these preachers into a revivalistic and reforming force; and the answer evidenced the expectation that Methodist discipline and nurture would raise a holy people.

The first three parts cover these formative influences. We might have focused the discussion on the principles—superintendency, connection, and discipline— or on the implementing actions—leading, gathering, and training.[3] We chose instead to examine the formal structures through which the principles were put into action—bishops (superintendents), conferences, and members—structures that have left an easily followed trail of evidence. Although the three of us have worked over the whole, each part was drafted by a single hand—"Bishops" by James E. Kirby, "Conferences" by Russell E. Richey, and "Members" by Kenneth E. Rowe.

EPISCOPAL METHODISM: A RATIONALE

In putting for ourselves the question, "Initially what gave it form and how have those structuring powers evolved?" we have also elected to write about one narrow strand of the movements that trace themselves back to Wesley, the strand of episcopal Methodism. This is not a history of the present denomination, the United Methodist Church and its antecedents, a very legitimate endeavor that would take us to points of origin other than Wesley and knit the stories of United Methodism's several denominational predecessors into a common story.[4] Nor does it trace all the strands characterized by episcopacy, connectionalism, and discipline; for instance, we make mention of but do not focus upon the African Methodist denominations. We also only allude to other movements that share Wesleyan origins and in one way or another comment in their own history upon these structuring powers, for example, Republican Methodism, the Methodist Protestants, and the movements influenced by the Holiness cause. We focus upon the Methodist Episcopal Church (MEC), after 1844 also on the Methodist Episcopal Church, South (MECS), and after 1939 on the Methodist Church. And we effectively conclude the story with the uniting of the Methodist Church and the Evangelical United Brethren Church in 1968, although in a few instances we comment about more recent developments. This is, then, not a conventional denominational history—not conventional in refusing to let the present denominational boundaries control our focus, not conventional in our choosing to pursue constitutive or constructive powers in thematic fashion over the course of American Methodist history. In so reading the Methodist saga from the point of view of origins rather than the present denominational situation, we do, however, provide a perspective on the ways that these three structuring capacities have produced this present, and the reader will doubtless note that the three of us are very interested in precisely that point.

By limiting our purview to the Methodist Episcopal traditions and specifically to conferences, bishops, and members, we do gain a fresh perspective on the evolution of denominationalism, on the changing dynamics by and through which this particular denomination held itself together, took direction, and nurtured its members. We attempt to disabuse the reader of the prevalent notion that Methodist polity fell intact from Wesley's hands and remained relatively unchanged thereafter. The three parts each study continuity and change. In Methodism's evolution, we are mindful of the force of character, of human willing, of intentionality, of theological and ethical principle. We also credit accident, experience, praxis, experimentation, and compromise. So we show the gradual, often unintended evolution of patterns, the trial-and-error process of change, the importance of praxis in Methodist policy, the way the church borrowed from the culture and from other denominations, the play of dissent and reform, the importance of competing visions.

The structure and approach of this volume does, then, differ from conventional estimates of Methodism's past. It differs in its trifold structure. Further, we endeavor to find an unplowed furrow in each major section and to expose features of Methodism not salient in other accounts. And we attend in a fresh way to familiar topics. The accent falls on the lived history of Methodism, even where familiar constitutional or polity aspects are under view.

THE BIOGRAPHIES

A distinctive aspect of the Greenwood Press denominational studies series is its narrative/reference character. Each volume offers a narration of that denomination's history and features a biographical section with fresh treatment of figures important to the communion's story. This volume follows the pattern, but biographical coverage is limited primarily to individuals who figure in the narrative. Asterisks are used throughout the narrative to indicate individuals to whom a biography is devoted.

NOTES

1. See Russell E. Richey, "History as a Bearer of Denominational Identity: Methodism as a Case Study," *Beyond Establishment: Protestant Identity in a Post-Protestant Age* (Louisville, KY: Westminster/John Knox, 1993), 270–95, and "Methodism and Providence: A Study in Secularization," *Studies in Church History*, 26: 51–77.

2. *Minutes of Several Conversations Between the Rev. Thomas Coke, LL.D., the Rev. Francis Asbury and Others . . . in the Year 1784. Composing a Form of Discipline . . .* (Philadelphia, Charles Cist, 1785), 4.

3. Or perhaps on the three books that defined early Methodism, exemplified its principles, and were carried by the preachers—the Bible, the Discipline, and the hymnbook.

4. For a recent illustration of that approach and one of which Kenneth E. Rowe was co-author, see *United Methodism in America: A Compact History*, ed. John G. McEllhenney (Nashville: Abingdon Press, 1992).

ABBREVIATIONS USED IN THIS VOLUME

AAP	*Annals of the American Pulpit*, ed. William B. Sprague, 9 vols. (New York, 1857–69; 1969).
ACJ/___	Annual Conference Journal/conf. name/church if not a MEC conf., date, page.
BAME	*The Bishops of the A.M.E. Church*, by Richard R. Wright, Jr. (Nashville, 1963).
BS	*Biographical Sketches of Eminent Itinerant Ministers . . . Pioneers of Methodism within the Bounds of the Methodist Episcopal Church, South*, ed. Thomas O. Summers (Nashville, 1858).
CA	*Christian Advocate* (New York).
CCA	*Central Christian Advocate.*
CB	*Cyclopaedia of Biblical, Theological, and Ecclesiastical Literature*, ed. John McClintock and James Strong, 12 vols. (New York, 1883–87).
CM	*Cyclopaedia of Methodism*, by Matthew Simpson, rev. ed. (Philadelphia, 1880).
DAB	*Dictionary of American Biography*, ed. Allen Johnson and Dumas Malone, 20 vols. (New York, 1828–37; seven suppls. 1944–65).
DANB	*Dictionary of American Negro Biography*, ed. Rayford W. Logan and Michael R. Winston (New York, 1982).
DARB	*Dictionary of American Religious Biography*, by Henry W. Bowden (Westport, CT, 1977).
DCA	*Daily Christian Advocate.*
DCA/M	*Daily Christian Advocate*/Methodist Church.
DCA/S	*Daily Christian Advocate*/MECS.
DCA/UM	*Daily Christian Advocate*/United Methodist Church.

DCIA	*Dictionary of Christianity in America*, ed. Daniel G. Reid et al. (Downers Grove, IL, 1990).
DEM	*Dictionary of the Ecumenical Movement*, ed. Nicholas Losskey et al. (Geneva, 1991).
[ ]	*Discipline*, date. In place of brackets church abbrev. [MEC, MP, MECS, M, UM, AME, etc.]
EAAR	*Encylopedia of African American Religion*, ed. Larry G. Murphy et. al. (New York: Garland Pub., 1993).
EAME	*The Encyclopedia of the African Methodist Episcopal Church*, ed. Richard R. Wright, Jr., et al., 2d ed. (Philadelphia, 1947).
EBA	*Encyclopedia of Black America*, ed. W. Augustus Low and Virgil A. Clift (New York, 1981).
EM	*Evangelical Messenger.*
ERS	*Encyclopedia of Religion in the South*, ed. Samuel S. Hill (Macon, GA, 1984).
EWM	*The Encyclopedia of World Methodism*, ed., Nolan B. Harmon et al., 2 vols. (Nashville, 1974).
HAM	*History of American Methodism*, ed. Emory Stevens Bucke, 3 vols. (New York and Nashville, 1964).
HDM	*The Historical Dictionary of Methodism*, ed. Charles Yrigoyen, Jr., and Susan Warrick (Lanham, MD, 1996).
JGC	*Journal of the General Conference* (MEC).
JGC/MP	*Journal of the . . . General Conference of the Methodist Protestant Church.*
JGC/S	*Journal of the General Conference* (MECS).
JLFA	*The Journal and Letters of Francis Asbury*, ed. J. Manning Potts, 3 vols. (London and Nashville, 1958).
LMB	*Lives of Methodist Bishops*, ed. Theodore L. Flood and John W. Hamilton (New York, 1882).
MB	*Methodist Bishops: Personal Notes and Bibliography*, by Frederick D. Leete (Nashville, 1948).
MH	*Methodist History.*
Minutes	*Minutes of the Annual Conferences (MEC).*
Minutes/MC	*Minutes of the Annual Conferences (MEC) [General Minutes 1948–].*
Minutes/S	*Minutes of the Annual Conferences (MECS).*
Minutes/UMC	*General Minutes of the Annual Conferences (UMC).*
MQR	*Methodist Quarterly Review.*
MQRS	*Methodist Quarterly Review, South.*
MUC	*Methodist Union Catalog: Pre-1976 Imprints*, ed. Kenneth E. Rowe, multivolume series (Metuchen, NJ: Scarecrow Press, 1975–).

NAW   *Notable American Women, 1607–1950: A Biographical Dictionary*,
                 ed. Edward T. James et al. (Cambridge, MA, 1971); vol. 4, *The Mod-
                 ern Period*, ed. Barbara Sicherman et al. (Cambridge, MA, 1980).

NCA   *Nashville Christian Advocate.*

NCAB   *National Cyclopedia of American Biography*, 62 vols. (New York/
                 Clifton, NJ, 1892–1984).

NCE   *New Catholic Encyclopedia*, 16 vols. (New York, 1967, 1974).

NWCA   *Northwestern Christian Advocate.*

NYT   *New York Times*, 1851 to present.

PGC/EA   *Proceedings of the General Conference of the Evangelical
                 Association/Church.*

PGC/EUB   *Proceedings of the General Conference of the Evangelical United
                 Brethren Church.*

PGC/UB   *Proceedings of the General Conference of the United Brethren in
                 Christ.*

POAM   *Perspectives on American Methodism*, ed. Russell E. Richey, Kenneth
                 E. Rowe, and Jean Miller Schmidt (Nashville, 1993).

QR   *Quarterly Review.*

RIL   *Religion in Life.*

RLA   *Religious Leaders of America*, ed. J. Gordon Melton (Detroit, MI:
                 Gale Research, 1991).

RT   *Religious Telescope* (UB).

SH   *New Schaff-Herzog Encyclopedia of Religious Knowledge*, ed. Sam-
                 uel M. Jackson et al., 13 vols. (New York, 1908–14).

UBR   *United Brethren Review.*

WCA   *Western Christian Advocate.*

Y/EA   *Year Book of the Evangelical Association/Church.*

Y/EUB   *Year Book of the Evangelical United Brethren Church.*

Y/UB   *Year Book of the General Conference of the United Brethren in
                 Christ.*

ZH   *Zion's Herald.*

Part One
BISHOPS

1
AMERICAN EPISCOPACY

Expansive, popular, explosive, participatory, Methodism might easily have yielded to its centripetal energies. That it did not but remained largely united owed to remarkable cohesive forces, chief among them its Arminian doctrine, its disciplined piety, its conference structure, and its peculiar episcopal leadership. To the latter, in particular, itinerant general superintendency, modeled after the leadership style of John Wesley, Methodism has ascribed its unity. The form and practice of episcopacy were established and personified in the life and work of Francis Asbury.* He more than any other single individual worked to establish and defend the itinerant principle, appointive authority, and connectional system. He did so countering impulses of localism, democratic reform, and sectionalism, impulses that would ultimately divide the movement. American Methodism and American Methodist episcopacy bore his stamp.

Francis Asbury offered himself for service in America at the British conference that met in Bristol, England, in August 1771.[1] Traveling to the colonies with Richard Wright, he landed in Philadelphia on 27 October 1771.[2] A year later Wesley named Asbury "assistant in America."[3] This status was, however, quickly reduced upon the arrival of Thomas Rankin,* senior to Asbury in years and service and designated by Wesley as "General Assistant." Rankin, shortly after his arrival in 1773, convened the first conference held in America.[4]

During the American Revolution all the preachers sent by Wesley returned to England except for Asbury, who despite persecution, seclusion, and inability to travel retained, even increased, his influence. In 1779 two conferences were held. The first, an "irregular" session convened at Thomas White's, Asbury's sanctuary in Delaware, recognized Asbury's leadership and resolved "that brother *Asbury* ought to act as *general assistant* in America."[5] The 1779 minutes gave the following reasons why he should hold the position: "1st, on account of his age [34]; 2nd, because originally appointed by Mr. Wesley; 3rd, being joined with Messrs. Rankin and Shadford, by express order from Mr.

Wesley."[6] The "regular" session met later on 18 May, at the Broken Back Church in Fluvanna County, Virginia,[7] without Asbury. It did not affirm his leadership, proceeding instead to acts symbolizing the American movement's independence from the church, Wesley, Asbury, and established practice— namely, ordinations by a committee (effectively presbyterial) and authorization of those ordained to administer the sacraments.[8]

The seriousness of this initiative was clear. "There was," as Jesse Lee,* a participant, affirmed, "great cause to fear a division, and both parties trembled for the ark of God, and shuddered at the thought of dividing the Church of Christ."[9] The decision of the southern preachers was condemned by their northern brethren, and when once again free to travel, Asbury was delegated to arrange a compromise.[10] The following year, 1780, he traveled with Freeborn Garrettson* and William Watters to the session of the Virginia conference and proposed that they "suspend the measures they had taken for one year."[11] Whether due to Asbury's power of persuasion, the gracious and conciliatory spirit of his Virginia colleagues, or, as Asbury claimed, the power of prayer, the Virginia preachers consented.[12] Shortly thereafter the conferences reunited and in 1782 gave an affirmative answer to the question, "Do the brethren in conference unanimously choose brother Asbury to act according to Mr. Wesley's original appointment and preside over the American conference, and the whole work?"[13]

Writing from Bristol in October 1783, Wesley also reaffirmed Asbury's position of leadership: "I do not wish our American brethren to receive any who make any difficulty of receiving *Francis Asbury* as the General Assistant."[14]

WESLEY'S ORDINATIONS FOR AMERICA

At least by early 1784 Wesley was convinced that the American church had to be given separate and independent status: "In the American Societies there already existed two marks of a Christian Church, (1) congregations of faithful men, and (2) the preaching of the pure word of God. Mr. Wesley designed to add the other two, (3) orders, or an ordained ministry; and (4) the sacraments instituted by our Lord, thus completing the organization of a Christian Church."[15] His reasons were practical and specific: (1) The Revolution had separated England and America forever. (2) The Episcopal establishment was abolished. (3) The Methodist societies were in a deplorable condition. (4) Asbury had appealed to him to provide a form of church government suited to their needs.[16] He might also have added, as he did in his 10 September 1784 letter to the brethren in America, that he had without success approached Robert Lowith, Bishop of London, who had jurisdiction over the colonies, to provide it.[17] Thomas Coke,* who was already a priest in the Church of England and whom Wesley intended to ordain a superintendent, was at first lukewarm to the idea but gradually warmed to it.

The more naturally I consider the subject, the more expedient it appears to me, that the power of ordaining others should be received by me from you, by the imposition of your hands; and that you should lay hands on brother Whatcoat[*] and brother Vasey, for the following reasons: (1) It seems to me the most scriptural way, and most agreeable to the practice of the primitive churches. (2) I may want all the influence, in America, which you can throw into my scale.[18]

Wesley's influence might serve Coke well in relation to Asbury, who apparently wanted no competitor. Coke wrote: "Mr. Brackenbury informed me at Leeds that he saw a letter from Mr. Asbury, in which he observed that he would not receive any person deputed by you with any part of the superintendency of the work invested in him, or words which evidently implied so much."[19] Concerns about Asbury did not long deter either Wesley or Coke, for on 1 and 2 September 1784 the ordinations took place. On 18 September Wesley's three ordained and commissioned emissaries—Bishop Coke and elders Richard Whatcoat* and Thomas Vasey—sailed from Bristol for America.

Practical necessity and compelling urgency had their role in Wesley's ordinations, but so also did Wesley's theological conviction that he, as a presbyter in the Church of England, could exercise the power of ordination normally reserved to bishops, a judgment long in the making. In his 10 September 1784 letter to "Our Brethren in America," Wesley says, "Lord King's *Account of the Primitive Church* convinced me many years ago—at least as early as 1746— that bishops and presbyters are the same order, and consequently have the same right to ordain."[20] For one who considered himself a loyal member of the Church of England, of the "high church" persuasion, and who had defended apostolic succession, this was a radical transformation.

He was further reinforced in his thinking after reading Bishop Edward Stillingfleet's *Irenicum, or Pacificator: Being a Reconciler as to Church Differences* (London, 1659). Stillingfleet, following the Puritans, argued that church government should be structured under principles of prudence, apostolic precedent, and liberty and that no form was required by Scripture.[21] With respect to ordination, Stillingfleet posited two powers—one of order and the other of jurisdiction, a distinction crucial in the formation of Wesley's position. On the basis of that distinction, Stillingfleet (and Wesley) recognized bishops and presbyters as sharing one order, the former being elders (presbyters) consecrated to a higher "office."[22]

Wesley was concerned, above all else, to meet the needs of his flock in the new American nation, whose mission was to "spread scriptural holiness in the land and reform the nation" and, at the same time, to adhere as closely to the practice of the early church as possible. Viewing himself as ordained to exactly that mission and by an extraordinary call, Wesley thought he enjoyed a presbyter's right and a scriptural *episcopos*'s mandate to ordain. "Both in *ordine* and *gradus* he was a scriptural *episcopos*," says Frank Baker.[23] Luke Tyerman suggests that Wesley might also have been influenced by the decision of the

Countess of Huntingdon Connection, on the same grounds, to move ahead with ordinations.[24]

At any rate, although what Wesley did in the ordinations was irregular, he stood firmly on a tradition of practice and scholarship which gave him defensible grounds for his decision.

AMERICAN EPISCOPAL METHODISM

Coke and his newly ordained traveling companions arrived in New York on 3 November 1784 and met Asbury on the 14th at Barratt's Chapel in Delaware. Asbury expressed surprise at Whatcoat's participation in the administration of the Lord's Supper but knew that Coke was coming on an important mission and was, in fact, quite prepared to receive them.[25] Rather than simply acquiesce in Wesley's ordinations at Coke's hands, Asbury had gathered several preachers "in case Dr. Coke should have anything of importance to communicate from England."[26] They "being convened in a kind of council . . . were made acquainted with the authority with which Dr. Coke was empowered, and with the outlines of the plan with which he was intrusted. In this council it became a question, whether it would not be prudent to appoint a conference, as soon as the preachers could be informed of their intention, and collected together from the various states."[27]

There was unanimous agreement that it would. Asbury's comment confirms that he was convinced the power and the choice properly belonged to the body of preachers: "if the preachers unanimously choose me, I shall not act in the capacity I have hitherto done by Mr. Wesley's appointment. The design of organizing the Methodists into an independent Episcopal Church was opened to the preachers present, and it was agreed to call a general conference, to meet at Baltimore the ensuing Christmas."[28]

Perhaps the most important single step taken by Asbury in shaping the nature of American Methodism and its episcopacy was calling the preachers together and agreeing in advance to abide by their decision. It was significant personally and constitutionally: Personally, it balanced Coke's prior ordination, superior education, power in the movement, and closeness to Wesley with the consent of the governed. Constitutionally, as Jno. J. Tigert says, "Wesley never intended to originate an American General Conference," and "it was the unexpected organization of the Christmas Conference . . . that gave the American Church autonomy; i.e., independence of Mr. Wesley and the English Conference."[29] Or as Bishop Neely writes, the act "conceded power to the Conference such as it never possessed before . . . , destroyed personal government and placed the governing power in the Conference."[30]

THE CHRISTMAS CONFERENCE, 1784

Asbury summoned the preachers to meet in Baltimore near the end of 1784. Of this gathering Jesse Lee wrote, "We formed ourselves into a regular church, by the name of *The Methodist Episcopal Church*; making at the same time the Episcopal office elective, and the elected superintendent amenable to the body of ministers and preachers."[31] All the preachers in the connection were eligible to attend; Coke reported "nearly sixty" of eighty-one were actually present.[32] Among its first acts of business was a pledge of loyalty to Wesley.

Quest. 2. What can be done in order to the future union of the Methodists?

Ans. During the life of the Rev. Mr. Wesley, we acknowledge ourselves his sons in the gospel, ready in matters belonging to church government to obey his commands.[33]

This "binding Minute" was soon to create considerable problems for the Americans and sour their relation to Methodism's founder.[34] "The second action taken was to form ourselves into an Episcopal Church, under the direction of superintendents, elders, deacons and helpers, according to the forms of ordination annexed to our Liturgy, and the Form of Discipline set forth in these Minutes."[35] They took the name the Methodist Episcopal Church (MEC), thus settling the form of government following the directive of Wesley.[36] Then they proceeded to elect Coke and Asbury superintendents, thirteen preachers, elders, and three deacons.

On the 27th Coke, assisted by Reformed pastor William Otterbein,* "and other ministers," "set apart" Francis Asbury "for the office of a superintendent."[37] Asbury was quick to adopt the trappings of his new office. In the latter part of January, at the first meeting after the formal organization of the new church, Jesse Lee expressed his surprise "and no little mortification" to see Asbury "in full canonicals, gown, cassock, and band."[38]

Having created an episcopal organization, the conference, through the Discipline, outlined the duties of a superintendent and established the lines of accountability.

Quest. 26. What is the office of a Superintendent?

Ans. To ordain Superintendents, Elders, and Deacons; to preside as a Moderator in our Conferences; to fix the Appointments of the Preachers for the several Circuits; and in the Intervals of the Conference, to change, receive or suspend Preachers, as Necessity may require; and to receive Appeals from the Preachers and People, and decide them.[39]

A note is added that "no person shall be ordained a superintendent, elder, or deacon without the consent of a majority of the conference, and the consent and imposition of the hands of a superintendent," giving the superintendent veto power over all persons elected to ministerial orders or office.[40] The general superintendents were made amenable to the conference for their conduct, and the conference given "power to expel [them] for improper conduct, if they see it necessary."[41] The power of the body of preachers in conference and that of the bishops counterpoised uneasily.

MR. WESLEY AND HIS BISHOPS

Wesley named Coke and Asbury to oversee the work in America and gave them full authority to do it, including the power to organize into a church, to ordain and appoint the preachers, and to manage its business affairs; but he assumed they would remain subject to him. Crisis came in September 1786 when Wesley wrote Coke: "I desire that you would appoint a General Conference of all our Preachers in the United States, to meet at Baltimore on May the 1st, 1787. And that Mr. Whatcoat may be appointed Superintendent with Mr. Asbury."[42] Lee observed, "When this business was brought before the conference, most of the preachers objected, and would not consent to it. The reasons against it were, 1, That he was not qualified to take the charge of the connection. 2, That they were apprehensive that if Mr. Whatcoat was ordained, Mr. Wesley would likely recall Mr. Asbury, and he would return to England."[43] Coke insisted that the commitment made to Wesley in 1784 obligated them to accept Whatcoat. The body of preachers responded by removing the "binding Minute" and taking Mr. Wesley's name out of the Discipline. Lee says, "They had made the engagement of their own accord, and among themselves, and they believed they had a right to depart therefrom, when they pleased."[44]

Having settled matters with Mr. Wesley, the conference set the record straight with Dr. Coke. Coke, while in Europe, in obedience to Wesley's directive, had changed the agreed-upon date for the next meeting of the conference, a right the preachers had never given to him. As a consequence, they obliged Coke to sign a certificate saying he would not, as a superintendent, "exercise any government whatever in the said Methodist church during my absence from the United States." He further agreed to limit his work as a superintendent when in the country to ordination, presiding in the conferences, and traveling through the connection.[45] He conceded formally the supreme Methodist prerogative, to station the preachers, leaving Asbury the sole episcopal leader with the full powers of the office.

Wesley was displeased by the action of the conference in removing his name from the Discipline and blamed Asbury for their decision.[46] He wrote Whatcoat: "It was not well judged of Brother Asbury to suffer, much less indirectly encourage, that foolish step in the late Conference. Every preacher present ought, both in duty and in prudence, to have said: 'Brother Asbury, Mr. Wesley is your father, consequently ours, and we will affirm this in the face of all the world.' "[47] The conference eventually elected Whatcoat a bishop and returned Wesley's name to the Discipline in 1789, listing him with Coke and Asbury as one of the persons who "exercise the episcopal office in the Methodist Church in Europe and America." They never, however, replaced the "binding Minute."[48]

In 1787, assisted by John Dickins,* Asbury and Thomas Coke revised the form of the Discipline and without the consent of conference changed their title from "superintendent."[49] The new designation was "bishop."[50] The most obvious explanation for the change is that for Asbury the terms were scriptural and synonymous. He used them interchangeably in his "Valedictory Address to William M'Kendree,"[51] in "the Last Will and Testament,"[52] and in his long letter to Joseph Benson.[53]

Wesley, however, responded angrily to the change of title and the similarly aggrandizing decision to name a new college Cokesbury, for Coke and Asbury, dispatching a "Dear Franky" letter:

But in one point, my dear brother, I am a little afraid both the Doctor and you differ from me. I study to be little: you study to be great. I creep; you strut along. I found a school; you a college! nay, and call it after your own names . . . !

One instance of this, of your greatness, has given me great concern. How can you, how dare you suffer yourself to be called Bishop? I shudder, I start at the very thought! Men may call me a knave or a fool, a rascal, a scoundrel, and I am content; but they shall never by my consent call me Bishop! For my sake, for God's sake, for Christ's sake put a full end to this![54]

The title, however, never concerned Americans as much as practical questions of power and practice. Neither the name nor the form mattered, but the substance did. And it would be on the substantive level that the greatest changes in the Asburian model of episcopacy would be effected. That was to be the American Methodist pattern, to concede, even protect the name, the doctrine, the office, while transforming it utterly.

THE COUNCIL AND THE GENERAL CONFERENCE

As the number of annual conferences increased—there were eleven held in 1789 scattered from Charleston to New York—so did the impracticality of a theory and practice of governance that involved presenting every issue to every annual conference for approval.[55] In response to this situation Asbury created "The Council" and presented it to the conferences for their approval in 1789. The Council was to be composed of the bishops and the presiding elders, leaders appointed, not elected.[56] It was quickly opposed by influential preachers like Jesse Lee* and James O'Kelly,* the latter a member.[57] Among their objections were that (1) Asbury's power was enhanced because he had full authority to select the members of the Council, (2) the provision requiring unanimous assent to matters brought before the Council assured Asbury of a veto on all proposed legislation, and (3) acts of the Council had the force of law only in the conferences that affirmed them.[58] Lee saw that this had the potential to divide the connection: "If then, one district should agree to any important point, and another district should reject it; the union between the two districts would be broken: and in process of time our *United Societies* would be thrown into disorder and confusion."[59]

Lee wrote the Council immediately to complain and urged the creation instead of a general conference.[60] O'Kelly's reservations were of a more personal nature, for he suspected Asbury's real motive in creating the Council was to consolidate his power. He wrote Asbury threatening to use his influence against him if he did not "stop for one year."[61] The Council met for the first time Thursday, 3 December 1789, and attempted immediately to amend some of its most glaring faults. Twelve persons, including Asbury, were present. The requirement that all items must pass unanimously was amended to require only a two-thirds majority and the consent of the bishop; resolutions presented to the annual conferences were made binding on all if passed by a majority of the conferences.[62] The modifications were presented to the conferences meeting in 1790, and Asbury reported trouble in several of them. In Virginia, "all was peace until the Council was mentioned."[63] The amendments passed in a number of conferences, however, and the second meeting of the Council convened on 1 December 1790. Despite the fact that Asbury described the meeting as one in which "we had great peace and union in all our labours," he noted that "for the sake of union, we declined sending out any recommendatory propositions."[64] The climate never improved, and Asbury was finally convinced the idea was lost and urged that it not be mentioned again; the church moved on to the next significant phase in its development, the General Conference.

The credit for this change belongs to Coke, James O'Kelly, and Jesse Lee.[65] O'Kelly decided not to attend the second session of the Council, persuaded the preachers in his district not to name a delegate to his place, and convinced Coke by letter into opposition. The problems for which the Council had been created did not abate but grew worse. The growth of the connection, now containing eighteen annual conferences, made it increasingly difficult for each annual conference to act on general church matters. Moreover, their veto power had the potential to destroy the connection. Buckley writes that the separate and independent conferences "had the power to revoke anything that had been done, either by any preceding General Conference, by the Annual Conferences, or by the convention which organized the Church."[66] Although there were two bishops in the connection, only one of them effectively functioned in America. Asbury attended all eighteen conferences held in 1792, and he stationed all the preachers. It took eight months and required him to travel in nearly every state in the union.[67] The lack of episcopal supervision enhanced the status and power of the presiding elders throughout the connection, and they became, in reality, an extension of episcopal presence. Although their office was present from the beginning of the church, it was not officially recognized and its duties defined until the General Conference of 1792. Chosen by, accountable to, and serving at the pleasure of the bishop, they were the load-bearing points of the system, and they remain so today.[68] In the absence of a bishop, presiding elders were able to assume all episcopal duties save that of ordination, including the power to preside at conference and to assign the preachers.[69]

One solution to such diffusion and delegation of power was to convene the body of preachers in plenary session. The first such General Conference convened in Baltimore on 1 November 1792. It was the only gathering since the organizing conference in 1784 to which all the preachers were invited and can properly be described as a "general" conference. A large number attended. Lee says the preachers came both because they believed something important might happen and because they "generally thought that in all probability there would never be another conference of that kind, at which all the preachers in the connection might attend."[70] William McKendree's* journal records that Coke and Asbury presided at the sessions "cojointly," and that he himself shared a room with James O'Kelly that became the center of much activity during the session.[71]

FRANCIS ASBURY: DEFINING EPISCOPAL POWER AND PRACTICE

The preachers who came expecting something to happen did not have long to wait. On the second day of the Baltimore General Conference O'Kelly offered a resolution to curtail the greatest single episcopal power, that of making appointments: "After the Bishop appoints the preachers at Conference to their several circuits, if anyone think himself injured by the appointment, he shall have liberty to appeal to the Conference and state his objections; and if the Conference approve his objections, the Bishop shall appoint him to another circuit."[72] The debate raged "for two or three days."[73] Asbury, who "felt awful at the General Conference," relinquished the chair but drafted a masterful letter to the preachers which said in part, "I am happily excused from assisting to make laws by which myself am to be governed: I have only to obey and execute. I am happy in the consideration that I never stationed a preacher through enmity, or as a punishment. I have acted for the glory of God, the good of the people, and to promote the usefulness of the preachers."[74]

When the O'Kelly resolution was brought to a final vote, it lost by a large majority, and O'Kelly, along with a few loyal followers, left the conference. Ironically, one who went with him was destined to be the first native born son of American Methodism to be elected to the episcopal office, William McKendree.[75] O'Kelly withdrew from the MEC and in 1793 organized the Republican Methodist Church, which later became the Christian Church. Although the Baltimore General Conference did not rein in episcopacy on O'Kelly's terms, it did act to establish its relationship to the office. The Baltimore General Conference determined that the general conference, rather than annual conferences, would elect bishops and make them amenable to it for their conduct. To that end it adopted procedures to govern a trial if needed and decided that should a bishop cease his duties without permission of the conference, he "shall not thereafter exercise any ministerial function whatsoever in our Church."[76]

There were no models of episcopacy in America for Coke and Asbury to follow when the church was organized in 1784. But in the newly established nation, there was the spirit of fresh beginnings ripe with excitement and promise.

Everything was open and possible. As John Locke described it, "In the beginning, all the world was America."[77] The earliest Puritans came to this "New World," determined to create in it nothing less than God's "new Israel," free from the mistakes and accretions of the past. In the same spirit, the Methodists believed they were free in America to reintroduce the government of the Primitive Church and to follow the apostolic model. Presbyters and bishops were of the same order; bishops, like the apostolic evangelists of the early church, were to itinerate throughout the connection and give oversight to it. In every way but one, American episcopal government was formed after the pattern Wesley devised for the societies in England; in America the government of the bishops was relational. The bishops' power was derived and shared with the conference; its locus was not in the episcopacy but in the body of preachers and in the conferences where they functioned. They, in turn, delegated specific powers to the bishops. These powers changed little between the organization of the church in 1784 and the adoption of a constitution twenty-four years later. From the beginning bishops were to travel throughout the entire connection.[78] They were to preside in the conferences; choose presiding elders, ordain deacons, elders, and general superintendents; withhold ordination from any they believed to be unsuited; appoint the preachers at annual conferences as well as between sessions when necessary; receive and suspend preachers between sessions of conference; and interpret the law of the church.[79]

Since the Methodist Church was changing rapidly to adjust to life in the new nation and to expand into the West, these episcopal duties were subject to constant interpretation and modification through practice. Yet through it all there remained a firm commitment to the basic Wesleyan plan: "The episcopacy had the same essential characteristics all the way down from its inauguration in 1784 to the General Conference of 1808."[80]

Francis Asbury was a powerful individual, and as a bishop he had control over the lives of every preacher in the connection. His power made the two issues raised by O'Kelly continuing ones: How would others in power, particularly other bishops, relate to Asbury, and how would Asbury and General Conference define their relationship?

Coke was out of the country most of the time, and when present had but limited powers, leaving Asbury as the undisputed leader of the American church. Even after others joined him in the episcopal ranks, Asbury continued to exercise unique influence.[81] As long as he lived, he was never simply one among equals. Then, as now, knowledge was power, and Asbury's experience in all parts of the church coupled with the sheer force of his personality and his extensive knowledge of the individual preachers gave him immense influence. "That he administered the affairs of the Church with an iron hand and an indomitable will, is unmistakably true," writes his biographer; "but that it was for his own advantage or the advancement of his personal interests, all the evidence is against this."[82]

Asbury became ill in the summer of 1797 and was unable to travel or exercise his responsibilities; Lee was designated by the New York Conference to assist and travel with him. In this capacity Jesse Lee, when necessary, took his place in the conferences. Lee reports that the "conference at Wilbraham [in New England] made choice of me to preside in that meeting, and to station the preachers."[83] In 1800 Asbury let it be known that he planned to resign because "he was so weak and feeble both in body and mind, that he was not able to go through the fatigues of his office."[84] About the same time, the British Conference requested the return of Coke, and after considerable debate permission was granted for him to go. It was clear another bishop needed to be elected.[85]

Whatcoat narrowly defeated Jesse Lee to be elected the third bishop of the Methodist Episcopal Church.[86] It is certainly likely that Asbury's choice was Lee, his traveling companion and assistant. Why the preachers did not finally choose him is a mystery, but one might wonder if their decision could have been a reaction to his close association with the bishop.

Prior to the election of Whatcoat, "there was . . . a lengthy debate respecting the powers the new bishop should possess. Some were of the opinion that he ought to act under the direction of the old bishop, and be governed by him; but it was finally determined that they should be on an equal footing, and be joint superintendents."[87] Although the equal status of bishops was officially declared as the position of the conference, and Asbury accepted the authority of the preachers acting in the general conference to determine the matter, their ruling did little to change his mind or modify his practice.[88] Whatcoat, nor any of the others elected to the episcopacy during Asbury's lifetime, was never his equal. Despite the fact that Whatcoat was nine years older than his colleague, Asbury was always "senior." When they held conferences together, as they often did, Asbury made the appointments.[89] Whatcoat's *Memoirs* do not say what happened with respect to them when he functioned alone.[90]

The business of clarifying the relationship between the bishops and General Conference changed as the understanding of the conference itself evolved. Some changes were simple but had implications for episcopal practice. The General Conference of 1792, which established the office of Presiding Elder in the Church, also placed a limit of four years on the term of service.[91] This effectively placed restrictions on episcopal power, too. In 1796 the number of "yearly" conferences was limited to six.[92] The power of the bishops to add to this number was described and defined. The journal of the conference reflects the presence of movements to establish eligibility requirements for election to the episcopacy, to elect presiding elders, to create an advisory group to counsel the bishop in the making of appointments, and to establish a delegated general conference.[93] Although all these amendments were eventually withdrawn or defeated, they were not forgotten and would appear again in succeeding General Conferences. In 1804, the time a preacher might stay on the same circuit was limited to two years and the bishops were required to allow each annual conference to sit as long as a week.[94] Both decisions restricted episcopal power.

Innovators continued to be present as well. Jesse Lee reports that in 1806, a plan originated in the New York Conference "to call a delegated conference of seven members from each conference chosen by the conference, to meet in Baltimore on the fourth of July 1807, to choose superintendents." He goes on to say that Asbury "laboured hard to carry the point, but he laboured in vain."[95] Had this scheme been adopted, it would have changed Methodist episcopacy from an itinerant, general superintendency into the diocesan form. The attempt was thwarted by the Virginia Conference after being passed by the New York, New England, Western and South Carolina Conferences.[96]

Seeing the weakness of Asbury and Whatcoat, in 1805 Thomas Coke offered to return permanently to the United States on the condition that "the seven Conferences should be divided betwixt us, three and four, and four and three, each of us changing our division annually; and that this plan at all events should continue permanent and unalterable during both our lives."[97] In January of the following year, Thomas Coke wrote a circular letter to the New York Conference, defending his action and making a case for his return. In it he complained of Asbury's unwillingness to allow him to function as a "Coadjutor in the Episcopacy." He notes, "I was not consulted in the least degree imaginable concerning the station of a single Preacher." When present in Georgia, he asked for a list of the appointments after it had been given to every preacher present— and was denied that. When Asbury was too ill to attend the South Carolina Conference, Coke offered to go, "but he refused me & appointed Brother Jackson to station the Preachers, & Brother Jesse Lee to sit as Moderator in the Conference."[98]

Coke was never to function in America with the full powers of a general superintendent. He was granted permission to return to England with the proviso that if needed in America he would return, but the call never came, and he devoted his remaining years to missions and to the work in Europe. Circumstances over which Asbury had no control, however, were changing the nature of the episcopacy. One of these was the rapid increase in membership along with the geographic expansion of the connection. In 1803 there were 383 preachers and more than 104,000 Methodists in America.[99] Although the number of conferences had been reduced, their size had so increased that it was sometimes necessary for preachers to travel long distances to attend, necessitating their being away from their work for weeks at a time.[100] It became impossible for any superintendent to cover all the territory, and meeting the need required increasing the number of bishops and dividing the territory. As the work of the bishops was divided, each had to share equally in the powers of the office. By the end of the first decade of the nineteenth century, the church had considered and rejected a variety of alternative models of episcopacy such as fixing the number of bishops, creating a diocesan episcopacy with a bishop for every conference and providing a senior bishop with assistant bishops.[101]

NOTES

1. "On the 7th of August, 1771, the Conference began at Bristol, in England. Before this, I had felt for half a year strong intimations in my mind that I should visit America. ... At the Conference it was proposed that some preachers should go over to the American continent. I spoke my mind, and made an offer of myself. It was accepted by Mr. Wesley and others, who judged I had a call." *JLFA*, 1: 3.

2. *JLFA*, 1: 6. Also Jesse Lee, *A Short History of the Methodists in the United States of America* (Baltimore: Magill & Clime, 1810; reprint of 1810 edition also available), 38. (Hereafter cited as Lee, *Short History, 1810,* whether as original or reprint.)

3. *JLFA*, 1: 46. "Saturday, 10. (1772) I received a letter from Mr. Wesley, in which he required a strict attention to discipline; and appointed me to act as assistant." Nathan Bangs, *A History of the Methodist Episcopal Church,* 4 vols. (New York: T. Mason & G. Lane, 1838), 1: 74.

4. Lee, *Short History, 1810,* 45. Lee says there "were six or seven travelling preachers at it, most of whom were Europeans." Buckley, more specific, writes, "All in attendance were natives of Europe; they were Thomas Rankin, Richard Boardman, Joseph Pilmoor, Francis Asbury, Richard Wright, George Shadford, Thomas Webb, John King, Abraham Whitworth, and Joseph Yearby." James M. Buckley, *Constitutional and Parliamentary History of the Methodist Episcopal Church* (New York: Methodist Book Concern, 1912), 16.

5. Ibid., 67. The conference began on April 28. Asbury reported that all seventeen northern preachers were present. *JLFA*, 1: 300. Bishop Neely says that "for a time there was no person actually bearing the title of General Assistant," and he reminds us that Asbury had not been reappointed by Wesley after the departure of Rankin. Thomas B. Neely, *The Bishops and the Supervisional System of the Methodist Episcopal Church* (New York: Eaton & Mains, 1912), 45.

6. *Minutes,* 1 (1779, 1840): 10. In answer to "Quest 4, 'What preachers act as assistants?' " the name of Francis Asbury heads the list. Ibid., 9. (Hereafter cited as *Minutes.*)

7. Ibid., 67.

8. Norman Spellman, *The General Superintendent in American Methodism, 1784–1870* (unpublished Ph.D. diss., Yale University, 1960), 85.

9. Lee, *Short History, 1810,* 70. "As we had great reason to fear that our brethren to the southward were in danger of separating from us, we wrote them a soft, healing epistle." *JLFA* 1 (Wednesday, 28 April, 1779): 300.

10. Samuel Drew, *The Life of the Rev. Thomas Coke, LL.D.* (New York: Lane & Tippett, 1847), 64. Drew says that Asbury was released from his confinement because of John Dickins of Pennsylvania. "From Mr. Dickins he received such letters of recommendation as enabled him to appear in public, and finally to travel through the states without molestation." (Hereafter cited as Drew, *Life of Coke.*)

11. *JLFA*, 1: 350. He continues, "After an hour's conference, we were called to receive their answer, which was, they could not submit to the terms of the union. I then prepared to leave the house, to go to a near neighbors to lodge, under the heaviest cloud I ever felt in America."

12. Ibid. Thomas B. Neely, *A History of the Origin and Development of the Governing Conference in Methodism, and Especially of the General Conference of the Methodist Episcopal Church* (New York: Hunt & Eaton, 1892), 171.

13. *Minutes* 1 (1782): 17; Lee, *Short History, 1810*, 80; *JLFA*, 1: 402.

14. *The Letters of the Rev. John Wesley, A.M.*, ed. John Telford, 8 vols. (London: Epworth Press, 1931), 7: 190–191. (Hereafter cited as Wesley, *Letters*.) On 3 October 1783 Wesley wrote through Jesse Lee to the Americans. His letter was a response to an enquiry from them about preachers coming to work in America without Wesley's authority. In addition to the proviso with respect to being subject to Asbury, he also stipulated that anyone coming should have a recommendation from him and agree to submit to the American Conference. See also *JLFA*, 1: 450; Neely, *Governing Conference*, 211.

15. Jno. J. Tigert, *The Making of Methodism: Studies in the Genesis of Institutions* (Nashville: Publishing House of the Methodist Episcopal Church, South, 1898), 139.

16. Buckley, *Constitutional and Parliamentary History*, 39. Wesley's willingness to innovate in the face of necessity as the movement grew in England had caused him to organize societies, to use lay preachers, to preach out of doors, to build meeting places, and to issue a Deed of Declaration to secure this property to the Methodists. See also Drew, *Life of Coke*, 71–72.

17. Frank Baker, *John Wesley and the Church of England* (Nashville: Abingdon Press, 1970), 259–60.

18. Thomas Coke to John Wesley, 9 August 1784. Luke Tyerman, *The Life and Times of the Rev. John Wesley, M.A., Founder of the Methodists*, 3 vols. (New York: Harper & Brothers, 1872), 3: 429.

19. Ibid.

20. Wesley, *Letters* (Telford), 7: 238. Wesley first read Peter King's *Inquiry into the Constitution, Discipline, Unity, and Worship of the Primitive Church* (London, 1691) on 20 January 1746. "Mon. 20. I set out for Bristol. On the road I read over Lord King's Account of the Primitive Church. In spite of the vehement prejudice of my education, I was ready to believe that this was a fair and impartial draught. But if so, it would follow that bishops and presbyters are (essentially) of one order, and that originally every Christian congregation was a church independent on all others!'' *The Works of John Wesley: Journal and Diaries III (1743–54)*, ed. W. Reginald Ward and Richard P. Heitzenrater (Nashville: Abingdon Press, 1991), vol. 20: 112.

21. Edward Stillingfleet, *The Irenicum, or Pacificator: Being a Reconciler as to Church Differences* (Philadelphia: M. Sorin, 1842), 438–40.

22. Ibid., 222–23. He goes on to say, "Ordination doth not belong to the power of order but to the power of jurisdiction, and therefore is subject to positive restraints, by prudential determinations. By this we may understand how lawful the exercise of an episcopal power may be in the church of God, supposing an equality in all church officers as to the power of order." Ibid., 233. Compare Wesley, *Letters* (Telford), 3 (3 July 1756): 182 (twenty-eight years before his ordinations for America):

"As to my judgment, I still believe 'the Episcopal form of Church government to be both scriptural and apostolical': I mean, well agreeing with the practice and writings of the Apostles. But that it is prescribed in Scripture I do not believe. This opinion (which I once heartily espoused) I have been heartily ashamed of ever since I read Dr. Stillingfleet's *Irenicum*. I think he has unanswerably proved that neither Christ nor his Apostles prescribed any particular form of Church government, and that the plea for the divine right of Episcopacy was never heard of in the primitive church."

23. Baker, *John Wesley and the Church of England*, 263.

24. Tyerman, *Life and Times of the Rev. John Wesley*, 431–32.

25. See *JLFA*, 1: 471, and Drew, *Life of Coke*, 99.

26. Drew, *Life of Coke*, 99.

27. Ibid., 99–100.

28. *JLFA*, 1: 471–72. The meeting was held in the home of Mrs. Philip Barratt with eleven preachers present in addition to Asbury and Coke.

29. Jno. J. Tigert, *A Constitutional History of American Episcopal Methodism*, 3d ed., rev. and enl. (Nashville: Publishing House of the Methodist Episcopal Church, South, 1908), 191–92.

30. Neely, *Governing Conference*, 251–52.

31. Lee, *Short History, 1810*, 94.

32. Drew, *Life of Coke*, 102. The number eligible to attend varies in virtually every source but is somewhere between eighty and ninety.

33. *Minutes of Several Conversations between the Rev. Thomas Coke, LL.D., the Rev. Francis Asbury, and Others, at a Conference Begun in Baltimore in the State of Maryland on Monday, the 27th of December, in the Year 1784. Composing a Form of Discipline for the Ministers, Preachers, and Other Members of the Methodist Episcopal Church in America* (Philadelphia: Charles Cist, 1785), 3. (Hereafter cited as *Minutes, 1784.*)

34. Lee, *Short History, 1810*, 95.

35. *Minutes, 1784*, 3.

36. Thomas Ware credits John Dickins with suggesting the name. See Buckley, *Constitutional and Parliamentary History*, 49. Asbury wrote, "It was agreed to form ourselves into an Episcopal Church, and to have superintendents, elders and deacons." *JLFA*, 1: 474.

37. *JLFA*, 1: 474. Wording from his ordination certificate. He was also ordained deacon on the 25th and elder on the 26th.

38. Leroy M. Lee, *The Life and Times of the Rev. Jesse Lee* (Richmond: John Early, 1848), 149. He also wrote in his history that "some of the elders," in addition to the superintendents, "introduced the custom of wearing gowns and bands, but it was opposed by many of the preachers, as well as private members, who looked upon it as needless and *superfluous.*" Lee, *Short History, 1810*, 107.

39. *Minutes, 1784*, 10.

40. Ibid.

41. Ibid.

42. Wesley *Letters*, (Telford), 7: 339. To Dr. Coke, 6 September 1786.

43. Lee, *Short History, 1810*, 126.

44. Ibid., 127. They concluded the matter by writing Mr. Wesley "a long and loving letter" in which they requested him to come to America.

45. Text of the certificate, signed by Coke and witnessed by three members of conference, in Lee, *Short History, 1810*, 125.

46. Wesley, *Letters* (Telford), 8: 183. On 31 October 1789 Wesley wrote of Asbury, "He quietly sat by until his friends voted my name out of the American Minutes. This completed the matter and showed that he had no connection with me." A dozen years after the incident Asbury remembered, "I never approved of that binding minute . . . [and] at the first General Conference I was mute and modest when it passed; and I was mute when it was expunged." *JLFA*, 2, 106, 28 November 1796.

47. Wesley, *Letters* (Telford) 8: 73. Wesley to Whatcoat, 17 July 1788.

48. *Minutes*, 1 (1789): 32.

49. The Disciplinary question had read "Who are the superintendents of our church?" In 1787 the question was modified slightly to read, "Who are the superinten-

dents of our church for the United States?'' The answer is also modified to read, ''Thomas Coke (when present in the States) and Francis Asbury.'' *Minutes* 1 (1785, 1786, and 1787): 22, 24, 26.

50. Lee, *Short History, 1810*, 128. Lee reports that at the next conference ''they asked the preachers if the word *Bishop* might stand in the minutes; seeing that it was a scripture name, and the meaning of the word *Bishop*, was the same with that of *Superintendent*.''

51. *JLFA*, 3: 477. ''Mr. Wesley ordained Thomas Coke, bishop, or general superintendent, and Francis Asbury was elected by the General Conference held in Baltimore, Md., December 1784, general superintendent; was first ordained deacon and elder; on December 27, bishop, or general superintendent.''

52. Ibid., 3: 472. ''Francis Asbury . . . Superintendent and Bishop of the Methodist Episcopal Church in America.''

53. *JLFA*, 3: 544–45. ''With us a bishop is a plain man, altogether like his brethren, wearing no marks of distinction, advanced in age, and by virtue of his office can sit as president in all the solemn assemblies of the ministers of the gospel; . . . raised to a small degree of constituted and elective authority above all his brethren.'' Asbury to Benson, 15 January 1816. Neely, *Bishops and the Supervisional System*, 58, says that in Wesley's vocabulary ''Superintendent was the same as bishop, but he preferred Superintendent, possibly to avoid the appearance of prelatical episcopacy.''

54. Wesley, *Letters* (Telford), 8: 91. Wesley to Asbury, 20 September 1788. Asbury wrote in his journal on 15 March 1789, ''Here I received a *bitter pill* from one of my greatest friends. Praise the Lord for my trials also—may they all be sanctified.'' *JLFA*, 1: 594. It was the last letter Asbury ever received from Wesley.

55. Abel Stevens, *History of the Methodist Episcopal Church in the United States of America*, 4 vols. (New York: Phillips & Hunt, 1884) 3: 11–12.

56. Tigert, *Constitutional History*, 243, and *Minutes* 1 (1789): 33. It is in this plan that the title ''Presiding Elder'' appears for the first time, and also in the *Minutes*.

57. Lee wrote, ''This plan for having a council, was entirely new, and exceedingly dangerous.'' Lee, *Short History, 1810*, 150. O'Kelly began systematic opposition to the idea immediately upon his return from the first session. Tigert, *Constitutional History*, 248.

58. Tigert, *Constitutional History*, 244.

59. Lee, *Short History, 1810*, 151.

60. Ibid., 158–59.

61. *JLFA*, 1: 620.

62. Tigert, *Constitutional History*, 246.

63. *JLFA*, 1: 642.

64. Ibid., 657.

65. Tigert, *Constitutional History*, 253.

66. Buckley, *Constitutional and Parliamentary History*, 123.

67. Bangs, *History of the Methodist Episcopal Church*, 1: 338.

68. Asbury later wrote, ''I wish the most perfect union to subsist between the Episcopacy and the presiding eldership, and at least a circumstantial account by letter at least every half year; that they may be eyes, ears, and mouth, and pens, from the Episcopacy, to the preachers, and people; and the same from the preachers and people, to the Episcopacy.'' *JLFA*, 3: 196. Asbury to Stith Mead, 20 January 1801.

69. *Minutes*, 1792, 6–7.

70. Lee, *Short History, 1810*, 177.

71. Robert Paine, *Life and Times of William M'Kendree, Bishop of the Methodist Episcopal Church* (Nashville: Publishing House of Methodist Episcopal Church, South, 1869) 1: 138.

72. Lee, *Short History, 1810*, 178.

73. Ibid., 179.

74. *JLFA*, 1: 733–34.

75. Paine, *Life of M'Kendree*, 1: 139. "The latter part of the trip, Mr. McKendree was the only companion of his late Presiding Elder. He unfolded his plan to his young *protege*. It was, to have '*a republican, no slavery, glorious Church!*' Bishop Asbury was a pope; the General Conference was a revolutionizing body; the Bishop and his creatures were working the ruin of the Church to gratify their pride and ambition." McKendree did not take an appointment when the Virginia Conference met in November, nor did he follow O'Kelly into his new organization. Ibid., 140.

76. *Minutes*, 1792, 9–10.

77. Quoted in R.W.B. Lewis, *The American Adam* (Chicago: University of Chicago Press, 1955), 42.

78. Travel they did: "Our circuit through the continent since we left Baltimore, 21st of May, 1801, is about four thousand one hundred and eighty-four miles." William Phoebus, *Memoirs of the Rev. Richard Whatcoat, Late Bishop of the Methodist Episcopal Church* (New York: Joseph Allen, 1828), 34.

79. Neely, *Bishops and the Supervisional System*, 94–96. The situation with respect to episcopal "veto" power over ordinations is interesting. It was included in the *Disciplines* of 1785 and 1786. The revision done in 1787 by Asbury removed it, but the *Notes to the Discipline*, prepared by Coke and Asbury, make it appear that in their minds the change was editorial in nature. Speaking of the bishops, they say, "They have, indeed, authority to suspend the ordination of an elected person, because they are answerable to God for the abuse of their office, and the command of the apostle, 'Lay hands suddenly on no man,' is absolute"; *Notes to the Discipline by Dr. Coke and Bishop Asbury*, quoted in Robert Emory, *History of the Discipline of the Methodist Episcopal Church* (New York: Carlton & Porter, 1843), 391. This would appear even a higher power than any General Conference was able to grant.

80. Neely, *Bishops and the Supervisional System*, 130.

81. Tigert, *Making of Methodism*, 10. "Despite his legal parity with Asbury, Whatcoat was practically little more than an 'assistant bishop.' " When Coke proposed in 1805 to divide the conferences with Asbury, he failed to mention Whatcoat at all.

82. Ezra Squire Tipple, *Francis Asbury: The Prophet of the Long Road* (New York: Methodist Book Concern, 1916), 261.

83. Lee, *Short History, 1810*, 251. Lee also went with Asbury to three other conferences at which he conducted the business, took the minutes, but did not station the preachers. Ibid., 252.

84. Ibid., 265. Asbury was granted the right to continue as a bishop "as far as his strength will permit." "This was the first case of partial cessation from traveling, by permission of the General Conference." Tigert, *Constitutional History*, 288.

85. *Minutes*, 1800, 59. The fact that Coke acknowledged by his action that he was subject to the American Conference is important. Moreover, the Americans did not quickly agree to let him go.

86. Lee reports—and it is likely he remembered correctly—that there was no election on the first ballot, he and Whatcoat were tied on the second, and Whatcoat was elected on the third by four votes. Lee, *Short History, 1810*, 266.

87. Ibid. There was a resolution "that the Conference determine, before the votes be canvassed, the powers of the new bishop, whether he shall be equal to Bishop Asbury or subordinate to him," which was withdrawn by consent. See *JGC*, 1800, 35.

88. Tigert makes reference to a now lost communication sent to the New England Conference in 1797 in which Asbury nominated Lee, Poythress, and Whatcoat to be "assistant bishops." "The Conference wisely declined to act, in view of the requirements of the Discipline, and his proposal appears not to have been laid before any other conference." It seems unlikely, however, that Asbury would have ceased to favor the idea if he thought it could be passed. Tigert, *Constitutional History*, 283.

89. Despite the fact that Whatcoat's *Memoirs* contain many references to conferences, including the number of persons ordained deacon and elder, there is never any mention of his stationing the preachers.

90. See Phoebus, *Memoirs of the Rev. Richard Whatcoat,* 39. Bishop McKendree accurately described Asbury's unique place in his impromptu response to Asbury's criticism of his address to the General Conference in 1812. He said, "You are our father; we are your sons. You never had need of it. I am only a brother, and have need of it." Paine, *Life of M'Kendree*, 1: 264.

91. *Minutes*, 1792, 7.

92. Lee, *Short History, 1810*, 233–34.

93. See *Minutes*, 1800, 34–36, 60.

94. Lee, *Short History, 1810*, 298. See *JGC*, 1804, 52, 56.

95. Lee, *Short History, 1810*, 344–45.

96. Ibid.

97. *JLFA*, 3: 319. It is interesting that Whatcoat is not considered at all in this proposal.

98. Coke's long letter is contained in *JLFA*, 3: 334–39.

99. Bangs, *History*, 2: 143. Of these members, 22,453 were "colored."

100. Ibid., 2: 20. "In consequence of reducing the number of annual conferences to seven, (in 1795) some of the preachers, who labored in the frontier circuits, had to come from two to four hundred miles to attend the conferences, which obliged them to leave their regular work from three to six weeks, during which time the people were unsupplied with the word and ordinances of the gospel."

101. Asbury probably never gave up the idea of assistant bishops. Reporting on the actions of the General Conference of 1808 in his journal, he said, "We have done very little except making the rule for representation hereafter, one member to the General Conference for every five members of the annual conferences; and the electing dear brother William M'Kendree assistant bishop." *JLFA* 2 (6 May 1808): 569–70.

2
CONSTITUTIONAL
METHODISM

A motion to establish a delegated general conference had been soundly defeated in 1800. The presenting concern—equal and fair representation—did not go away. At the General Conference of 1804, 70 of the 112 ministers present came from the Philadelphia and Baltimore Conferences. The New England, Western, and South Carolina Conferences had but 13 ministers together; Virginia had 17.[1]

GENERAL CONFERENCE AND EPISCOPACY

In 1807 the New York Annual Conference passed a memorial proposing a delegated general conference "composed of a specific number on principles of equal representation from the several annual conferences."[2] The three conferences that met after New York concurred but Baltimore, Philadelphia, and Virginia, which constituted a decided majority when General Conference convened in 1808, were opposed.[3] When the memorial was presented, General Conference referred it to a committee. In a stroke of political genius Francis Asbury,* who favored the change, proposed that the committee should be composed of an "equal number" of persons from each annual conference, thereby ensuring that those favoring the memorial would be equally represented.[4] A distinguished group was elected, including two persons who would later become bishops.[5] The committee established a drafting subcommittee of Ezekiel Cooper,* Joshua Soule* and Philip Bruce—all proponents of the delegated conference.[6] Cooper and Soule prepared written documents. With the exception of the section on the episcopacy, there was general unanimity. Cooper favored the creation of a form of diocesan episcopacy and earlier had seconded a motion to elect a bishop for each annual conference.[7] His version of one of the constitutional safeguards the subcommittee deemed requisite for a delegated conference read thus: General Conference "shall not do away Episcopacy, nor reduce our ministry to a presbyterial parity."[8] Soule, by contrast, was specific and concrete: General Conference "shall not change or alter any part or rule of our government, so as to do away episcopacy, or destroy the plan of our itinerant general superintendency."[9] The model ("plan") Soule assumed was the Asburian form of episcopacy, "which plan for the last quarter of a century had been operated by three bishops, and which, for the next quarter of a century was to be operated by five other bishops, all of whom had seats in the General Conference of 1808."[10] Soule's version passed the committee and then went to the conference.[11]

The subcommittee's report is a remarkable document that, with little modification, has regulated the form of General Conference to the present. It recommended the creation of a conference with delegates from the various annual conferences, delegates chosen by ballot without debate in the year previous to its meeting. It determined the number of delegates, and set the date of meeting as May 1 every four years. It stipulated the number needed for a quorum, and designated the bishops as presiding officers. General Conference was given "full powers to make rules, regulations and canons for our Church," with six restrictions: General Conference shall not "(1) revoke, alter, or change our Articles of religion, nor establish any new standards of doctrine"; (2) change the number of delegates provided for in the report; (3) "change or alter any part or rule of our government so as to do away episcopacy, or to destroy the plan of our itinerant general superintendency"; (4) "revoke or change the General Rules of the United Societies"; (5) deny the right of preachers and members to a trial before an appropriate body, and of appeal; (6) allocate the proceeds of the Book Concern and the Charter Fund to any purpose except the support of "traveling, superannuated, supernumerary, and worn-out preachers, their wives, widows and children." Finally it provided that upon the recommendation of all the annual conferences with concurrence of two-thirds of General Conference, the restrictions could be altered.[12]

The process leading to the adoption of the committee report in the conference was long and complex. Jesse Lee,* an early proponent of a delegated conference, led the opposition, pressing for selection by seniority, not election.[13] At the other extreme Ezekiel Cooper fought for further elective rights. Cooper successfully managed to postpone discussion of the entire report by making a motion once again for election of presiding elders.[14] It was a brilliant strategy that, if successful, would reduce the power of the bishops and be protected forever under the Third Restrictive Rule as part of the "plan."[15] After an extended discussion, Cooper's motion was defeated by a majority of twenty-one.[16] The ordination of William McKendree,* who had been elected a week earlier, took place immediately afterward.

When business resumed in the afternoon, the conference took up the first resolution of the committee report—to create a delegated general conference. It was defeated by seven votes, sixty-four to fifty-seven.[17] Eight disappointed delegates, six from New England and two from the Western Conference, prepared to leave the conference; once again the possibility of division threatened the body. Asbury and McKendree met with the eight disaffected preachers and encouraged them to remain in the conference in order to see if a reconsideration of the question were possible.[18]

The strategy to produce this reconsideration, undoubtedly worked out in the interim, unfolded on Monday, 23 May beginning with a motion made by Leonard Cassell and seconded by Stephen G. Roszel "that the motion for considering when and where the next General Conference shall be, lie over until it be determined who shall compose the General Conference."[19] It passed. Immediately Enoch George,* who was later to become a bishop, moved "that the General Conference shall be composed of one member for every five members of each Annual Conference."[20] After it, too, was adopted, Soule sought to silence the objections of Jesse Lee and his supporters by moving that "each Annual Conference shall have the power of sending their proportional number of members to the General Conference, either by seniority or choice, as they shall think best." Lee's biographer says that after being defeated by the move, Lee walked up to Soule, "poked him in the side with his finger and whispered, 'Brother Soule, you've played me a Yankee trick.' "[21] Soule's motion passed, and the first meeting of a delegated general conference was set for 1 May 1812 in New York. The restrictive rules were adopted in order, with Lee making the motion to adopt Soule's third rule.[22]

A watershed in the government of the Methodist Church in America had been reached. The powers of the body of preachers had been transferred to a delegated assembly with clearly defined and sharply limited powers. "The old General Conference could create a new Constitution and a new kind of General Conference, but the new kind of General Conference could not of itself and by itself do such things."[23] The role of the episcopacy vis-à-vis the new delegated body was also redefined. Whereas in the old General Conferences bishops enjoyed all the powers of any member of the body of preachers, in the delegated conference they presided but did not vote or speak as delegates. Moreover, they lost their power to interpret church law. Under the new constitution, they were limited "to act as presidents, with power to rule on points of parliamentary law, but not to decide points of ecclesiastical; for the General Conference was to be the interpreter as well as the maker of church law."[24]

One other matter concerning the episcopacy was reiterated in the case of Dr. Coke (it is interesting that he is rarely, if ever, given the title of "Bishop" Coke). Acceding to the request of the British Conference and Coke's own preferences, it was once again decided that he could continue to reside outside the United States, subject to the call of the General Conference or annual conferences, but "was not to exercise the office of superintendent or bishop . . . in the United States until he be recalled by the General Conference, or by all the annual conferences respectively."[25] Bishops were clearly elected for service in the United States and not for missions.

THE MANTLE FALLS: DEFINING EPISCOPACY

William McKendree's election to the episcopacy brought changes in the practices of the bishops. Robert Whatcoat,* always regarded by Asbury as a "junior" bishop, served only six years and died in July 1806. McKendree, however, was a native son of America, had recognized standing because of his service in the Western Conference, and was destined to continue in the office for twenty-seven years. From the beginning he had the courage to modify Asbury's practice in order to accommodate it to his own sense of order and propriety. The first evidence, which appeared only three years after his election, concerned the role of the presiding elders in the stationing of the preachers. Asbury had always made appointments alone; McKendree felt more comfortable sharing the task with the elders and wrote Asbury on 8 October 1811 proposing a "council of the Presiding Elders in stationing the preachers."[26] McKendree's determination to work with a cabinet of presiding elders in making the appointments was moot, however, since the bishops traveled to the conferences together and Asbury stationed the preachers until 1815, when failing health required him to relinquish the responsibility to McKendree.[27]

The second innovation came at the first delegated General Conference, held in 1812. "Previous to the first delegated General Conference, May 1, 1812, Bishop McKendree drew up a plan of business to be brought before the General Conference."[28] The address was read on Tuesday afternoon, 5 May.[29] It obviously came as a surprise to Asbury, who rose and confronted McKendree: "I never did business in this way, and why is this new thing introduced?" Facing the venerable Asbury, McKendree replied: "You are our *father*, we are your sons; you never have had need of it. I am only a *brother*, and have need of it." Asbury sat down with a smile, and the Episcopal Address became a feature of General Conference.[30]

The conference accorded McKendree's address a mixed review. John Early's motion to record it in the *Journal* lost; Jesse Lee's to include it with the conference papers carried. During the afternoon session it was referred to the conference acting as a committee of the whole.[31] In this manner its various parts established an agenda for business and were brought to the conference separately as items for action, most of which were referred to select committees appointed for the purpose.[32] One of these was the Committee on Episcopacy.[33]

Laban Clark of the New York Conference reintroduced the subject of allowing annual conferences to choose presiding elders by election. After a lengthy debate and unsuccessful attempts to amend, his motion lost by a margin of only three votes, forty-two to forty-five, an omen of things to come.[34] McKendree thought that with the bishop's power to choose presiding elders removed, "there will remain with them no power by which they can oversee the work, or officially manage the administration; and therefore the Conference must in justice release them from their responsibilities as Bishops."[35] He believed also that "therefore, the office of a Presiding Elder is not separate or distinct from that of a General

Superintendent, but is inseparably connected with a part of it, and included in it. They are deputized by the Bishops, who bear the whole responsibility of the administration, as their assistants in the Superintendency."[36] McKendree's certainty and resolution, however, could not keep the matter off the agenda.

PLURALIZING EPISCOPACY

The General Conference of 1816 as well as the year itself marks a turning point in the history of American Methodism. The delegated general conference was a reality. Coke and Asbury were dead, and for the first time, the episcopal office was held entirely by American-born clergy. Although "personal" government in the style of John Wesley and Francis Asbury was over, Asbury's spirit hovered. During the thirty-two years of Asbury's episcopacy, he presided in 234 annual conferences and ordained about four thousand persons in the traveling or local ministry."[37] The church bore his stamp. William McKendree, the only bishop in the church when the General Conference of 1816 convened in Baltimore on 1 May 1816, was ill. Asbury spoke through a "Valedictory" addressed to McKendree and written in 1813. He advised: "there may be only three effective Bishops, as from the beginning, traveling through the whole continent—each one to preside alternately in the Annual Conferences; one to preside during the sitting of the same Conference, the other two to have charge of and plan the stations and perform ordinations, assisted by the Elders in both branches."[38] General Conference concurred and elected two additional bishops, Enoch George* of the Baltimore Conference and Robert Roberts* of the Philadelphia Conference.[39]

The advocates of an elected presiding eldership tried once again to limit the power of the bishops but with a new tack—nomination by the bishops and election by the annual conference.[40] It was further moved that the presiding elders should constitute a council to assist the bishop in the stationing of the preachers.[41] The conference formed itself into a "committee of the whole" to discuss the motion, and Bishop McKendree relinquished the chair during the debate, which went on for a week. One of the issues raised was whether the motion was constitutional. Late in the conference the original motion's maker, Samuel Merwin, proposed a resolution that "the motion relative to the election and appointment of presiding elders is not contrary to the constitution of our church."[42] The motion failed by a large majority, but the matter was far from settled.[43]

In other action bearing on the episcopacy, the delegates made it the duty of the bishops, or of a committee appointed by them, to devise a course of study to be followed by candidates for the ministry who before being received into full connection "shall give satisfactory evidence respecting his knowledge of those particular subjects."[44] This was a first in the history of the church, a new responsibility for the bishops.

McKendree's journal reports that he met with the two new bishops and all agreed to attend the first three conferences in order to allow the newly elected superintendents to learn the "peculiarities and difficulties of the Episcopal duties"; afterward they would follow a plan that made it unnecessary for every bishop to attend each annual conference. "Thus was begun the practice of *dividing the work of superintending the Conferences by the Bishops themselves, and also of alternating*—a method which, it is hoped, will be perpetuated as most consistent with the genius of our Church-constitution, and best calculated to promote union and perpetuate the itinerancy."[45]

McKendree's hopes were not to be realized. With the death of Asbury the old pattern of a true itinerant general superintendency was abandoned, the movement toward a sectional and diocesan episcopacy was begun, and the church set on the road to division.

BISHOPS AND PRESIDING ELDERS

The movement to elect presiding elders resurfaced in the General Conference of 1820. Timothy Merritt* of the New England Conference made a motion seconded by Beverly Waugh, that presiding elders were to be elected in the annual conference.[46] This proposal was shaped by Ezekiel Cooper and John Emory* to call for the bishop to nominate three persons for each vacancy, and for the annual conference to choose the proper number from among them.[47] It retained the provision that these elders were to constitute a council to advise the bishop in stationing the preachers. First laid on the table, after lengthy debate it was determined that a committee composed of an equal number of persons opposed to and favoring the change should confer with the bishops. Ezekiel Cooper, John Emory, and Nathan Bangs,* proponents, S. G. Roszel, Joshua Wells, and William Capers,* opponents, were named.[48] A compromise was reached that had the support of Bishop George. Capers says, "It met with his (the Bishop's) approbation, and, if I am not mistaken, . . . was the bishop's motion."[49] Drafted by John Emory, the committee report clarified that "when there is more than one wanted not more than three at a time shall be nominated, nor more than one at a time elected."[50] The committee's resolutions each passed by a large majority.

Joshua Soule, who had been elected a bishop a week earlier but had not yet been ordained to the office, left the conference and drafted a letter to the bishops.[51] In it he declared that "the constitution of the Methodist Episcopal Church . . . [was] violated . . . by a transfer of executive power from the Episcopacy to the several Annual Conferences." Further, he emphasized:

I cannot, consistently with my conviction of propriety and obligation, enter upon the work of an itinerant General Superintendent.

I was elected under the *constitution and government of the Methodist Episcopal Church* UNIMPAIRED. . . .

. . . I cannot act as Superintendent under the rules this day made and established by the General Conference.[52]

Soule's act had dramatic force because he was the author of the constitution in question. McKendree, as adamantly opposed to the action as Soule, acted with similar force, writing to the conference, "I extremely regret that you have, by this measure, reduced me to the painful necessity of pronouncing the resolution *unconstitutional, and, therefore destitute of the proper authority of the Church.*"[53]

When the bishops met, each was asked to express his opinion on the constitutionality of the resolutions. Bishop Roberts "was of the opinion that the resolutions of the Conference were an infringement of the constitution." Bishop George "chose to be silent." McKendree "considered them unconstitutional."[54] Should they proceed with the ordination of Soule? They decided to do it, as did General Conference, though not without considerable criticism of Soule, charging that he had refused to submit to the authority of the conference and deadlocked a ballot on a key motion. A time was set for the ordination service, but Soule responded by announcing his resignation from the episcopacy.[55] Technically, it is difficult to see how he could resign because ordination is required for the episcopal office, but he was only the first of a number of persons who through the years have refused to accept the office after their election but before consecration.[56] The resignation was promptly laid on the table where it remained until it became clear that Soule was firm in his intention to resign and it was accepted.[57]

General Conference then resolved that the "rule passed in this conference respecting the nomination and election of presiding elders be suspended until the next General Conference."[58] Advocates of the measure to elect the presiding elders correctly saw that the real issue "was now merged in the more important one whether the episcopacy or the General Conference was to be supreme."[59] On the last day of conference, a motion to elect a bishop was defeated and one adopted advising the annual conferences to pass the necessary resolutions to enable the superintendents to determine the constitutionality of any measure brought to the General Conference. It read:

If they [the superintendents], or a majority of them, shall judge it unconstitutional, they shall, within three days after its passage, return it to the conference with their objections to it in writing. And whenever a resolution is so returned, the conference shall reconsider it, and if it pass by a majority of two-thirds it shall be constitutional and pass into a law, notwithstanding the objections of the superintendents.[60]

Thus General Conference passed to the annual conferences two issues for consideration: whether presiding elders should be elected and whether General Conference should be the judge of the constitutionality of its own actions. Both actions recognized that constitutional questions required the affirmation of the annual conferences.[61] The latter resolution failed in the annual conferences and was reintroduced in 1824, only to fail again.[62] A satisfactory solution was not found until the Judicial Council was organized by the Methodist Church in 1939.

The fate and divisive force of the other constitutional question, election of presiding elders, was indicated in an 1824 General Conference motion by the illustrious Peter Cartwright:* "a majority of the annual conferences have judged them unconstitutional, and . . . six of the annual conferences have recommended their adoption."[63] The issue had roiled the conferences in politics.[64] Nor could General Conference make up its divided mind. Instead it acknowledged its own and the annual conference's indecision, by a vote of only sixty-three to sixty-one resolving that the resolutions concerning the election of presiding elders "not [be] of authority and shall not be carried into effect."[65] However, "the Senior Bishop had prosecuted to a successful issue his appeal from the action of a General Conference to the tribunal of the Annual Conferences; and the Delegated General Conference, acting under a constitution, formally recognized the supremacy of the primary bodies which had called it into existence."[66]

On Wednesday, 26 May the conference proceeded to the election of two bishops. Joshua Soule was elected on the second ballot with sixty-five votes and Elijah Hedding* on the third with sixty-six.[67] Each party had managed to elect a champion. The action taken earlier with respect to the presiding elders resolutions was challenged because not all the annual conferences had voted on the measure, and so theoretically it could still pass. William Winans* wanted them to be considered as "unfinished business," and finally a motion, introduced by Robert Payne and William Capers, passed: "It is the sense of this General Conference that the suspended resolutions, making the presiding elder elective, etc., are considered as unfinished business, and are neither to be inserted in the revised form of the Discipline nor to be carried into operation before the next General Conference."[68] This was a significant act, since the conference had, in a sense, agreed with the principle stated by Bishop Soule during the debates: "The General Conference is not the proper judge of the constitutionality of its own acts. . . . If the General Conference be the sole judge in such questions, then there are no bounds to its power."[69] The restrictions had been imposed by the adoption of a constitution, and it, too, had been protected. But the events were ominous in other ways less obvious to most. The conferences had divided on the constitutional issue, with the South and West supporting the existing policy of episcopal appointment of presiding elders and the North and East favoring their election. "In our Church, as in our nation, the division was along the line of strict construction of the powers delegated by the constitution, on the one hand, and a loose and broad interpretation of those powers, on the other."[70] American Methodism was now on the road to division. McKendree grasped the seriousness of the situation. "The course I took relative to the suspended resolutions was not to defeat them, but to bring them into operation conformably to the constitution, and thereby confirm the '*peace-measure*' and to harmonize the preachers. To this the preachers who prefer the old system are willing to submit for the sake of peace."[71]

The reformers wanted more. Some of them, in fact, wanted to introduce laypersons into the conferences. Emory's biography makes it clear that the advocates of lay representation and electing presiding elders were not united as a party. John Emory himself favored electing presiding elders but was opposed to lay representation.[72] The outspoken advocates for lay delegation, associated with the *Wesleyan Repository*, saw themselves as a "third party." "As we courted neither party [those for and those against the election of presiding elders], so *have we not identified ourselves with either party: we have spoken of you both, on all occasions, as an independent or a third party would speak.*"[73] The reasons for this were interesting. H. D. Sellers, who favored lay delegates, wrote: "The advocates of a lay delegation, however, were not all favourable to the election of presiding elders. Some of us held very firmly to the opinion, that the power of the episcopacy was conservative against the body of preachers, and were disposed to believe that any accession of power to them would obstruct the introduction of a lay delegation."[74]

Subsequent events proved him right. The General Conference of 1828 declared the suspended resolutions void and the reformers walked out. They formed the Methodist Protestant Church (MPC) in November 1830 as a democratic church. It featured lay representation and abandoned the episcopacy.

Another threat to the unity of the connection loomed. When the General Conference of 1824 ended, there were but five bishops, four of whom were active, McKendree being ill. They had to divide the work among themselves in seventeen annual conferences. The conference had encouraged them by resolution to constitute a council in order "to form their plan of traveling through their charge."[75] Although the advice was not mandatory, the bishops met immediately following the close of the conference and agreed to divide the work in such manner that Roberts and Soule would oversee the Southern and Western Conferences while George and Hedding would attend to the Northern and Eastern. They were to exchange conferences after two years.[76] Their next meeting was held in April 1826, when they gathered in Philadelphia, where George and Hedding were holding the Philadelphia Conference.[77] Roberts did not attend. They needed to appoint a delegate to the British Conference and arrange a new schedule of conferences. William Capers of South Carolina was nominated by McKendree, supported by Soule and Roberts; George and Hedding objected to Capers because he owned slaves and would likely be offensive to the British and to the North. Hedding and George suggested Wilbur Fisk.* Unable to name the delegate, McKendree, as the senior bishop, then turned to the matter of conference assignments. Bishop George, however, protested that he was in a hurry, and so the question was postponed to another meeting held five days later, on 18 April, at six in the morning in McKendree's rooms. After failing a second time to reach agreement on a delegate, once again they took up the assignment of conferences.[78] George was opposed and "pronounced it inadmissible! Said he was hurried by a press of business and must go. . . . Thus ended our official interviews, on various business of the Church.''[79] The proposed exchange of conferences was never made, and for more than twenty years George and Hedding continued to serve in the North. ''Bishop Hedding in twenty years, from 1824 to 1844, made but a single tour of the Southern Conferences, and that in 1831, seven years after he became a Bishop; in the same year Bishop Soule made his first episcopal visitation in the North!''[80] The Asbury-McKendree model of itinerant general superintendency no longer existed, and regionalized episcopacy became the norm in the church, a monumental change in the form of simple and seemingly inconsequential modifications of practice, a line of division, constitutional and sectional, ran through the church, separating it, in all but name, into two sharply contrasted Episcopal Methodisms.[81]

THE ROAD TO DIVISION

The General Conference of 1832 elected James O. Andrew* and John Emory* to the episcopacy.[82] Having made a final appearance in a general conference, McKendree died on 5 March 1835. Emory served only until December 1835, when he died from injuries suffered in a carriage accident.[83] The conference conceded to the bishops to ''leave them now at liberty on their joint and several responsibility to make such arrangements among themselves for the entire administration, and for the visitation of the annual conferences as they shall judge most conducive to their general good.''[84] In 1836 Beverly Waugh, the book agent from New York, Thomas A. Morris,* editor of the *Western Christian Advocate*, and Wilbur Fisk, president of Wesleyan University, were elected,[85] Fisk refusing the office.

Increasingly affected by sectional interests and the presence of slavery, the bishops played key roles in the church's return to the issue. From 1820 until 1836, General Conferences found it easier to ignore than to address the issues related to slaveholding within the church. No significant legislation on the subject was enacted at any of these conferences. By 1836, however, antislavery sentiment had risen sufficiently that inattention became itself an issue. The bishops, however, sought to make silence a principle:

From every view of the subject which we have been able to take, and from the most calm and dispassionate survey of the whole ground, we have come to the solemn conviction, that the only safe, Scriptural, and prudent way for us, both as ministers and people, to take, is wholly to refrain from this agitating subject, which is now convulsing the country, and consequently the Church, from end to end, by calling forth inflammatory speeches, papers and pamphlets.[86]

The bishops could not, however, avoid battles being fought in some annual conferences over the moral issue of slavery and the practical question of who had the power to regulate conference agenda, a prerogative traditionally belonging to the episcopacy. The sharpest challenges to episcopal authority came in the northeastern conferences and to Hedding. The New England Conference met in July following the General Conference. Orange Scott,* who had served during the General Conference as the spokesperson for the abolitionist movement, raised the subject and commanded the support of most of his colleagues. Hedding felt obligated to follow the directive of the General Conference to refrain from discussing the topic.[87] That conviction led him to remove Orange Scott from his appointment as presiding elder of the Providence District and to refuse to allow consideration of a report from the conference "Committee on Slavery."[88]

The New Hampshire Conference followed immediately afterward, and once again Hedding found himself in trouble. This time he refused to appoint abolitionist George Storrs to a district unless there was "some assurance that he would cease to distract the Church by active participation in the ultra measures of the day." Storrs replied that he felt himself under "no such obligation," read a paper to the conference expressing his conviction "that he could not take an appointment under an officer of the General Conference in view of the action of that body on the subject of slavery" and asked to be located.[89] Hedding also rejected a motion which condemned an action taken in the Baltimore Conference interpreting the General Rule on slavery. His decision was based on the premise "that it was not competent . . . for one annual conference to pass judgment upon the acts of another, each annual conference being amenable to the General Conference only for its individual action.[90] Defending himself in a speech to the New Hampshire Annual Conference, he discussed the rights of an annual conference and the duties of its president. Citing the provisions in the Discipline giving the bishops responsibility to set the day for ordinations and to meet the conference for at least a week, Hedding argued that they conveyed the right and responsibility to arrange the business in such a manner that both could be done. The real crux of his argument, however, was his contention that "an annual conference is not a primary, independent body. Although it was so originally, when there was but one annual conference . . . it is not so now."[91] He refuted the claim to conference "rights" by saying: "An annual conference is constituted by the General Conference; it is dependent on, and responsible to it. And the General Conference has told the annual conference what to do; its duty and rights are laid down in the Discipline. That is its charter, and it has no other rights as a conference, only those which are granted either by statute or by fair inference in that charter."[92]

The bishop then speculated that in conferences located in parts of the country where slavery existed a discussion of it might well be in order and allowed. But in places where it did not exist, "where you have no jurisdiction over slaves or slave owners, it is impossible to make it appear that you have any authority in the case."[93]

These stances earned Hedding great opposition and vilification. To answer his critics and exonerate himself, Hedding filed charges in 1838 against Orange Scott and LaRoy Sunderland,* editor of *Zion's Watchman*, but both were acquitted by their annual conferences.[94] Hedding then appealed the decision to the General Conference of 1840, but he withdrew the complaint before it could be considered. Other bishops took a similar and consistent line, and each suffered criticism because of it.

BISHOPS AND SLAVERY, 1844

Whereas, the Discipline of our Church forbids the doing of anything calculated to destroy our itinerant general superintendency, and whereas, Bishop Andrew has become connected with slavery by marriage and otherwise, and this act having drawn after it circumstances which, in the estimation of the General Conference, will greatly embarrass the exercise of his office as an itinerant general superintendent, if not in some places entirely prevent it; therefore, Resolved, That it is the sense of this General Conference that he desist from the exercise of this office so long as this impediment remains.[95]

There is, noted Hamby Barton, "no question that the real issue of the Conference of 1844 was slavery. But the point of attack was one of the bishops of the church."[96] The bishop was James O. Andrew* of Georgia, who had become entangled with slavery through inheritance and marriage. And the above motion by James B. Finley* framed the debate. Finley's motion had displaced one by Alfred Griffith, of the Baltimore Conference, "that the Rev. James O. Andrew be, and he is hereby affectionately requested to resign his office as one of the Bishops of the Methodist Episcopal Church."[97] Speaking in support of his motion, Griffith said, "We are here concerned exclusively with an officer of the General Conference," and the issue is "whether the General Conference . . . has power to regulate her own officers—that is the question."[98]

The question before the conference was not solely the moral issue of slavery, or even a bishop's relation to it, but also the constitutional powers of General Conference with respect to the episcopacy. Did General Conference have the right to demand the resignation of a bishop without charges and a trial? The power of General Conference to bring charges against Andrew was undisputed, but he was not accused of wrongdoing, only with being associated with slavery and benefiting from the labor of slaves. Moreover, the Discipline of the church no longer barred slaveholders from membership in the church or election to its episcopacy. The General Conference of 1840 had, in fact, ruled

that the simple holding of slaves, or mere ownership of slave property, in States or Territories, where laws do not admit of emancipation, and permit the liberated slave to enjoy freedom, constitutes no legal barrier to the election or ordination of ministers, to the various grades of office known in the ministry of the Methodist Episcopal Church, and cannot, therefore be considered as operating any forfeiture of right, in view of such election and ordination.[99]

This conference was of a different mind, as it showed early on with Francis A. Harding who had been "deprived of ministerial character" by the Baltimore Conference. Harding appealed his case to the General Conference, which upheld the decision of the annual conference. This vote took place prior to the debate over Bishop Andrew and was prelude to the final disposition of his case.[100]

The drama of this conference had begun before it began. On his way to the conference Andrew learned there would be trouble in New York. Having no special love for the episcopal office, he met the southern caucus and announced his willingness to resign. They refused to allow it, believing the act to be a "fatal concession" to their northern colleagues.[101] Indeed, they resolved: "Whereas in a meeting of said delegates to consider this matter, after solemn prayer and much deliberation, it appears to us that his resignation would inflict an incurable wound on the whole South and inevitably lead to division in the Church, therefore we do unanimously concur in requesting the Bishop . . . not to allow himself for any consideration to resign."[102]

At no time was Andrew's character questioned. His treatment of the slaves was humane. As a matter of fact, he maintained that it was because of his Christian commitment that he had kept the slaves belonging to his wife under his care. Addressing the conference he said:

I might have avoided this difficulty by resorting to a trick—by making over these slaves to my wife before marriage, or by doing as a friend who has taken ground in favour of the resolution before you suggested: "Why," said he, "did you not let your wife make over these negroes to her children, securing to herself an annuity from them?" Sir, my conscience would not allow me to do this thing. If I had done so, and those negroes had passed into the hands of those who would have treated them unkindly, I should have been unhappy. Strange as it may seem to brethren, I am a slaveholder for conscience' sake.[103]

Speaking to the conference out of frustration and with strong feelings, Andrew put the matter squarely before the delegates. "The conference can take its course," he declared, "but I protest against the proposed action as a violation of the laws of the Discipline, and an invasion of the rights secured to me by that book."[104]

The maker of the substitute motion, James B. Finley, rose immediately to reply to the bishop.

There are two great principles to be determined in this resolution which have not been decided in the Methodist Episcopal Church. One is this: Has the General Conference a right, or has it the power, to remove from office one, or all of the bishops, if they, under any circumstances, become disqualified to carry out the great principles of our itinerant general superintendency? The second is: Will the Methodist Church admit the great evil of slavery into the itinerant general superintendency?[105]

The bishops in their Episcopal Address had collectively conceded their accountability to General Conference. That was never in dispute. A bishop was, as Jesse T. Peck observed, "an officer of the whole Church, responsible to the General Conference."[106] The bishops declared:

The office of a Bishop or Superintendent, according to our ecclesiastical system is almost exclusively executive; wisely limited in its powers, and guarded by such checks and responsibilities as can scarcely fail to secure the ministry and membership against any oppressive measures. . . .

So far from being irresponsible in their office, they are amenable to the General Conference, not only for their moral conduct, and for the doctrines they teach, but also for the faithful administration of the government of the Church, according to the provisions of the Discipline, and for all decisions which they make on questions of ecclesiastical law.

In all these cases this body has original jurisdiction, and may prosecute to final issue in expulsion, from which decision there is no appeal.[107]

The bishops surprisingly acknowledged that even the power to ordain did not belong exclusively to their office: "The Bishop can ordain neither a Deacon nor an Elder, without the election of the candidate by an Annual Conference: and in case of such election he has no discretional authority; but is under *obligation* to ordain the person elected, whatever may be his own judgment of his qualifications."[108]

Nonetheless, the basic question remained: Could General Conference depose a bishop without formal charges or a trial? Was slaveholding a sufficient "impediment" to the exercise of episcopal functions to warrant summary removal by General Conference? Was expediency sufficient ground for removal in itself? Soule thought not and said so:

I wish to say, explicitly, that if the superintendents are only to be regarded as the officers of the General Conference of the Methodist Episcopal Church, and consequently as officers of the Methodist Episcopal Church liable to be deposed at will by a simple majority of this body without a form of trial, no obligation existing growing out of the constitution and laws of the Church, even to assign cause, wherefore—I say, if this doctrine be a correct one, everything I have to say hereafter is powerless, and falls to the ground.[109]

The bishop reminded his hearers that he had been present at the first General Conference, but he spared them the obvious additional fact that he was the author of the constitution in question. He made it clear that the provisions for the trial of a bishop were essential because bishops alone in the church had no right of appeal.[110]

The definitive, contrary position was taken by an Ohio Conference delegate, Leonidas Hamline,* who later in the conference was elected a bishop. His speech describing the relationship of the episcopacy to the General Conference and his understanding of the nature of episcopacy in a "Croton River" argument informed the practice of the Methodist Episcopal Church throughout its existence.[111] He began by asking, first, "Has the General Conference constitutional authority to pass this resolution," and second, "is it proper or fitting that we should do it?"[112] Arguing the first point, he noted that throughout its history "strict amenability in Church officers, subordinate and superior, is provided for in our Discipline."[113] In a variety of relationships—pastor to class leader, presiding elder to pastor, or bishop to pastors—there is the power to exercise summary removals. "It is a ministerial, rather than a judicial act. . . . It is for no crime, and generally for no misdemeanor, but for being 'unacceptable.' "[114] He then argued that the power to "depose a bishop summarily for improprieties morally innocent" is derived from "*the relations of the General Conference to the Church, and to the episcopacy.*"[115] The General Conference is supreme in its legislative, judicial, and executive authority, and it "is the *fountain* of all official executive authority. It is the '*Croton River*' of that system of executive ministrations which flow in healthful streams throughout our Zion."[116] It has been given full power to make rules and regulations, and the latter includes electing and empowering a bishop. Moreover, "all that this conference can confer, it can withhold." "Our Church constitution recognizes the episcopacy as an abstraction, and leaves this body to work it into a concrete form in any hundred or more ways we may be able to invent."[117] Moreover, with its full powers, General Conference is not limited by what has been passed into legislation: "Whatever this conference can constitutionally do it can do without first resolving that it has the power to do it—without passing a rule into the Discipline declaring its authority. . . . Is there anything in the restrictive articles which prohibits the removal or suspension of a bishop?"[118]

Continuing to follow the analogy of others in the church, Hamline agreed that bishops cannot be removed from the ministry without trial, but the episcopacy is an office that can be taken away.

We have seen that when clerical orders or membership in the Church is concerned, crime only, or obstinate impropriety, which is *as* crime, can expel. This is Methodism. We have seen, on the other hand, that as to office, removals from it may be summary, and for anything unfitting that office, or that renders its exercise unwholesome to the Church . . . the General Conference, under certain restrictions, is the depository of all power.[119]

Coming to his conclusion, Hamline urged the delegates never to lose sight of the fact that "the General Conference is '*the sun of our system.*' "[120]   As interpreted by Hamline and those who agreed with him, the Finley motion required executive rather than legislative or judicial action. Their view prevailed on 1 June when the substitute was adopted by a vote of 110 to 68.[121]

The position of the minority was fully articulated in the "Protest," which was entered near the end of the conference and after the decision in Bishop Andrew's case was final. It described the understanding of the southern view of episcopacy as a "co-ordinate" branch of Methodist church government.

As the Methodist Episcopal Church is now organized, and according to its organization since 1784, the Episcopacy is a co-ordinate branch, the executive department proper of the government. A Bishop of the Methodist Episcopal Church is not a mere creature— is in no prominent sense an officer of the General Conference. . . .

In a sense by no means unimportant the General Conference is as much the creature of the Episcopacy, as the Bishops are the creatures of the General Conference.[122]

The "Protest" argued that if bishops did not exercise their authority to call meetings of the annual conferences, there would be no elections and no delegates to meet in General Conference. As a result, General Conference has no power to remove them. Following the analogy of the relationship of appointed officials to legislative bodies, they concluded the power of removal does not follow the power to appoint. In both the instances of judges and bishops "who, instead of being the officers and creatures of the General Conference, are de facto the officers and servants of the church, chosen by the General Conference . . . and no right of removal accrues, except as they fail to accomplish the aims of the church in their appointment, and then only in accordance with the provisions of law."[123]

By the time Hamline spoke, there was open discussion of secession, if not division. As a matter of fact, early in the session Thomas Bond,* editor of the Christian Advocate, rose to deny a report that "a plan has been formed by northern members of the conference, to force the south into secession."[124] There were also many attempts to preserve the union. On 14 May, William Capers and Stephen Olin* offered a joint resolution to create a "Committee of Pacification," composed of three delegates each from the North and the South to confer with the bishops in hopes of formulating a compromise.[125] Bishop Soule reported four days later on behalf of the committee that "after a calm and deliberate investigation of the subject submitted to their consideration, they are unable to agree upon any plan of compromise to reconcile the views of the northern and southern Conferences."[126] The bishops tried to buy time but were also powerless to influence the outcome. A peace measure drafted by them urging postponement of any action in the case of Bishop Andrew was tabled; Bishops Hedding and Waugh quickly disassociated themselves from it after it was presented.[127]

The position of the southern delegates was clear and firm. They made no secret of the fact that they believed any action against Bishop Andrew would leave them no choice but to leave the connection. So divide they did. William Capers offered the resolutions to create separate General Conferences on 3 June. They were referred to a committee that was unable to agree on a report favorable to the conference. Later J. B. M'Ferrin* of Tennessee, moved on behalf of delegates from fourteen conferences that the body "devise, if possible, a constitutional plan for a mutual and friendly division of the Church."[128] The Plan of Separation resulted.

Bishop Andrew left the conference immediately after the vote on the Finley substitute. He did not, therefore, know all that finally transpired in his case. In response to a request from the bishops for a ruling on the practical implications of the action taken in Bishop Andrew's case, the conference agreed that Andrew's name could continue to stand in the minutes, the hymnbook, and the Discipline; his salary and family support would be continued; and he would be free to determine in what work he would engage.[129] Waiting for him to reveal what he would do, the bishops did not include him in their published plan of episcopal visitation. Learning what they had done, Andrew wrote to his friend William Wightman, "I see the bishops have interpreted the action of the Genl. Conference and I presume have acted out the true intent and will of their masters in giving me *no work*."[130] The matter was quickly moot, since Andrew, at the invitation of Bishop Soule, began to accompany him to the southern conferences. This later resulted in charges being brought against Soule that he, by not waiting for a written request from Andrew, had abused his authority and defied the conference.

Meeting in New York, following the adjournment of the General Conference, southern and southwestern delegates decided to hold a convention to determine their future in the church but to allow time for the sentiment of clergy and laypersons to be obtained in the interim. It convened in April 1845 in Louisville, Kentucky, and acted to create a new church following the guidelines laid down in the Plan of Separation. A year later the first General Conference of the Methodist Episcopal Church, South (MECS) met in Petersburg, Virginia.

"In the South, the episcopacy was an aristocracy providing independent leadership for the church. In the North, the republican sentiments of a great middle class church culminated in the General Conference which employed the episcopacy as the chief administrative instrument."[131] These differences, germinating, in a climate of social unrest and sectionalism, had finally separated the family of Methodists just as later they were to separate the nation itself.

NOTES

1. *JGC*, 1804, 71–72.
2. *Minutes*, 1807, 77.
3. Jno. J. Tigert, *A Constitutional History of American Episcopal Methodism*, 3 ed., rev. and enl. (Nashville: Publishing House of the Methodist Episcopal Church, South, 1908) 300.
4. *JGC*, 1808, 78–79.
5. The committee was composed of Ezekiel Cooper, John Wilson (New York); George Pickering, Joshua Soule (New England); William McKendree, William Burke (Western); William Phoebus, Josias Randle (South Carolina); Philip Bruce, Jesse Lee (Virginia); Stephen G. Roszel, Nelson Reed (Baltimore); and John McClaskey, Thomas Ware (Philadelphia). McKendree was elected to the episcopacy at this conference, and Joshua Soule some years later. *JGC* 1 (1808): 79.
6. Charles Elliott, *The Life of the Rev. Robert R. Roberts* (New York: G. & Lane C. B. Tippett, 1844), 157–58.

7. *JGC* 1 (1808): 80.

8. Tigert, *Constitutional History*, 303.

9. *JGC* 1 (1808): 82–83.

10. Tigert, *Constitutional History*, 303.

11. Elliott, *Life of the Rev. Robert R. Roberts*, 157–58.

12. *JGC* 1 (1808): 82–83.

13. Leroy M. Lee, *Life and Times of the Rev. Jesse Lee* (Richmond: John Early, 1848), 442.

14. *JGC* 1 (1808): 83; Tigert, *Constitutional History*, 306.

15. Bishop McKendree's "Essays on our Church-Government," Robert Paine, *Life and Times of William M'Kendree, Bishop of the Methodist Episcopal Church* (Nashville: Publishing House of the Methodist Episcopal Church, South, 1869), 2: 368.

16. *JGC* 1 (1808): 84.

17. Ibid., 84. Lee's biographer says, "The defeat was a source of surprise and sorrow to the friends of the measure," and he credits Lee with its defeat. See Lee, *Life and Times of the Rev. Jesse Lee*, 442.

18. Paine, *Life of M'Kendree*, 1: 191; Elliott, *Life of the Rev. Robert R. Roberts*, 158–59.

19. *JGC* 1 (1808): 88.

20. Ibid.

21. Lee, *Life and Times of the Rev. Jesse Lee*, 442–43.

22. *JGC* 1 (1808): 89; Paine, *Life of M'Kendree*, 1: 191.

23. Thomas B. Neely, *The Bishops and the Supervisional System of the Methodist Episcopal Church* (New York: Eaton & Mains, 1912), 139.

24. Thomas B. Neely, *A History of the Origin and Development of the Governing Conference in Methodism, and Especially of the General Conference of the Methodist Episcopal Church* (New York: Hunt & Eaton, 1892), 376–77.

25. *JGC* 1 (1808): 76.

26. Paine, *Life of M'Kendree*, 1: 260–261. No record of this exists in Asbury's journal or letters.

27. "My eyes fail. I will resign the stations to Bishop M'Kendree—I will take away my feet." *JLFA* 2 (22 October 1815): 794.

28. Henry Smith to Robert Paine, quoted in Paine, *Life of M'Kendree*, 1: 263.

29. *JGC* 1 (1812): 100.

30. Paine, *Life of M'Kendree*, 1: 264. Although the address was a surprise to Asbury, McKendree had, in fact, consulted a committee of delegates and sought advice before presenting it. Ibid., 270–71. For McKendree's Episcopal Address see Paine, *Life of M'Kendree*, 1: 265–70.

31. *JGC* 1 (1812): 101.

32. Ibid., 102.

33. Ibid., 103.

34. Ibid., 114.

35. Paine, *Life of M'Kendree*, 2: 356.

36. Ibid., 364.

37. The number is based on an estimate by Nathan Bangs that Asbury held an average of seven conferences each year. Nathan Bangs, *A History of the Methodist Episcopal Church* (New York: G. Lane, 1839), 2: 400.

38. Paine, *Life of M'Kendree*, 1: 311. It appears in a number of other places.

39. *JGC* 1 (1816): 142.

40. Ibid., 135.

41. Ibid.

42. Ibid., 164.

43. Ibid., 140. The vote was forty-two in favor and sixty against. This was the largest majority ever recorded against the measure.

44. Ibid., 161.

45. Paine, *Life of M'Kendree*, 1: 361–62.

46. *JGC* 1 (1820): 207.

47. Ibid., 213.

48. Paine, *Life of M'Kendree*, 1: 409.

49. Ibid.

50. *JGC* 1 (1820): 221. See also Paine, *Life of M'Kendree*, 1: 410–11.

51. *JGC* 1 (1820): 222.

52. Quoted from the original letter in the possession of Paine, *Life of M'Kendree*, 1: 420–21.

53. Ibid., 418.

54. Ibid., 422.

55. Ibid., 427–29; *JGC* 1 (1820): 232.

56. The next one was Wilbur Fisk, who was elected in 1836 while out of the country and refused after his return to accept ordination because of his work and reasons of health.

57. *JGC* 1 (1820): 236–37, Paine, *Life of M'Kendree*, 1: 429–30.

58. *JGC* 1 (1820): 235.

59. Robert Emory, *The Life of the Rev. John Emory* (New York: G. Lane, 1841), 147.

60. Ibid., 238.

61. Bishop McKendree believed that the precedent of bringing such issues before the annual conferences had been established in 1809 when the Virginia Conference protested the initiative taken by the bishops to form the Genesee Conference, which was to meet between meetings of the General Conferences. In response to Virginia's appeal the question was submitted to the annual conferences, and "by this act, the Bishops and the Annual Conferences tacitly declared the Annual Conferences to be the proper judges of constitutional questions." Paine, *Life of M'Kendree*, 1: 426.

62. Tigert, *Constitutional History*, 353–63.

63. *JGC* 1 (1824): 27; Paine, *Life of M'Kendree*, 1: 458.

64. McKendree had in one conference urged adoption for the sake of peace in the connection only to see "a resolution pronouncing the suspended resolutions unconstitutional . . . indefinitely postponed by a large vote." Emory, *John Emory*, 148n., Paine, *Life of M'Kendree*, 1: 440, 444–58.

65. *JGC* 1 (1824): 281. D. W. Clark, *Life and Times of Rev. Elijah Hedding* (New York: Carlton & Phillips, 1855), 300, illustrates the fervor of the struggle.

66. Tigert, *Constitutional History*, 384.

67. *JGC* 1 (1824): 285.

68. Ibid., 297. See also Paine, *Life of M'Kendree*, 2: 39–40.

69. Paine, *Life of M'Kendree*, 2: 37. This agreement in principle, however, did not resolve the question of who should make such judgments.

70. Tigert, *Constitutional History*, 371.

71. Paine, *Life of M'Kendree*, 2: 49.

72. Emory, *John Emory*, 151.

73. Ibid., 152.

74. Ibid., 164.

75. *JGC* 1 (1824): 301.

76. Paine, *Life of M'Kendree*, 2: 48.

77. Hedding's biography says that the meeting was held in Baltimore, not Philadelphia. Clark, *Elijah Hedding*, 324. M'Kendree was in Philadelphia for the conference which opened April 12. Paine, *Life of M'Kendree*, 2: 89.

78. Ibid., 325; *JGC* 1 (1828): 339.

79. Quoted in Tigert, *Constitutional History*, 390–91.

80. Ibid., 392.

81. Ibid., 398.

82. *JGC* 1 (1832): 401.

83. Emory, *John Emory*, 288.

84. *JGC* 1 (1832): 419–20.

85. *JGC* 1 (1836): 478.

86. Reprinted in Bangs, *History of the Methodist Episcopal Church*, 4: 260.

87. Clark, *Elijah Hedding*, 493.

88. Ibid., 494–96.

89. Ibid., 496–97.

90. Ibid., 505.

91. Ibid., 507.

92. Ibid., 508.

93. Ibid., 509.

94. Ibid., 525–26.

95. *JGC* 2 (1844): 65–66. The argument that Andrew was unable to function as an itinerant general superintendent because he would not be welcome in certain conferences ignored the fact that by 1844 there was no superintendent who itinerated through all the conferences.

96. Jesse Hamby Barton, Jr., *The Definition of the Episcopal Office in American Methodism* (unpublished Ph.D. diss., Drew University, 1960), 108.

97. *JGC* 2 (1844): 64.

98. *Report of Debates in the General Conference of the Methodist Episcopal Church, 1844* (New York: Carlton & Phillips, 1855), 83.

99. Quoted in the Pastoral Address of the General Conference of the Methodist Episcopal Church, South, 1846, in *History of the Organization of the Methodist Episcopal Church, South, with the Journal of Its First General Conference* (Nashville: Publishing House of the Methodist Episcopal Church, South, Lamar & Barton, Agents, 1925), 494. It is also contained in Charles Elliott, *History of the Great Secession from the Methodist Episcopal Church in the Year 1845* (Cincinnati: Swormsteadt & Poe, 1855), 228. Elliott adds an important editorial comment: "The resolution was passed without reference to any but traveling and local preachers, or members, having no reference, as it has no pertinency, to the Episcopacy. At a future day this became the stronghold in favor of a slaveholding Episcopacy."

100. Donald G. Mathews, *Slavery and Methodism: A Chapter in American Morality, 1780–1845* (Princeton, NJ: Princeton University Press, 1965), 254. Mathews notes that in deciding the Harding case, "for the first time in the history of the Methodist Episcopal

Church, Southerners had lost an important vote." The Baltimore Conference voted as a bloc in favor of its own decision, but the rest of the South voted against it. The border conferences divided, and only one delegate from Texas and one from Missouri actually voted with the North.

101. Mathews, *Slavery and Methodism*, 258.

102. George G. Smith, *Life and Letters of James Osgood Andrew* (Nashville: Southern Methodist Publishing House, 1883), 342–43.

103. *Report of Debates in the General Conference*, 1844, 148–49.

104. Ibid., 150.

105. Ibid.

106. Jesse T. Peck, "The General Conference of 1844," *MQR* 52 (April 1870): 184.

107. "Episcopal Address," *JGC* 2 (1844): 154.

108. Ibid., 155.

109. Soule speaking to the conference on 29 May 1844, *Report of Debates in the General Conference*, 1844, 2: 169.

110. Ibid. "It seems to me that the Church has made special provision for the trial of a bishop, for the special reason that the bishop has no appeal."

111. The Croton River provided drinking water for New York City, where the conference was meeting. It was in a real sense "the fountain" that flowed "in healthful streams."

112. *Report of Debates in the General Conference*, 1844, 2: 128.

113. Ibid.

114. Ibid., 129.

115. Ibid.

116. Ibid., 131.

117. Ibid., 131–32. This was exactly the position which was rejected in 1808 in the controversy over the shape of the Third Restrictive Rule of the constitution.

118. Ibid., 132.

119. Ibid., 133.

120. Ibid., 134.

121. *JGC* 2 (1844): 83.

122. Ibid., 194.

123. Ibid., 195.

124. *Report of Debates in the General Conference*, 1844, 74.

125. Ibid., 54.

126. *JGC* 2 (1844): 54.

127. Ibid., 2: 81. In an article later published in *MQR* (April 1871), James Porter, a New England Conference delegate, explained that after a caucus it was decided that if Bishop Andrew were allowed to remain in place, the New England Conferences would secede in a body and invite Bishop Hamline to preside over them. Hamline could not be reached with this information before he signed the document. See Holland N. McTyeire, *A History of Methodism* (Nashville: Publishing House of the Methodist Episcopal Church, South, 1910), 636.

128. *JGC* 2 (1844): 109, 111.

129. Ibid., 117–18.

130. Bishop Andrew to William Wightman, 6 July 1844, quoted in Barton, *Definition of the Episcopal Office*, 112. The bishops actually made two plans. In the one they published, he was given no work. Morris wrote in February 1845 to explain that since

he was not present and they did not know his wishes, not wishing to infringe on his freedom, they had omitted him. See George G. Smith, *Life and Letters of James Osgood Andrew* (Nashville: Southern Methodist Publishing House, 1883), 364.

131. Barton, *Definition of the Episcopal Office*, 122.

3
TWO PATTERNS OF EPISCOPACY

Bitterness created by the division, heightened by a war of words in the church press and intensified by the civil conflict that later swept the country, kept the two episcopal Methodisms apart for almost a century. The separation allowed the two churches to develop their own unique practices and styles of episcopacy.

DEFENDING THE ASBURIAN ARK: THE SOUTHERN PATTERN

In theory the Methodist Episcopal Church, South (MECS) adopted the earlier, Asburian notion of episcopacy as a separate but co-equal branch of the government of the church. William McKendree* years earlier had supported this interpretation because he believed that "from the preachers *collectively* both the General Conference and the General Superintendents derive their powers."[1] Bishop Horace M. DuBose wrote that Joshua Soule,* the author of the Third Restrictive Rule, entered the MECS because "as he saw it, the Asburian ark, with the scroll of the law and the staff that budded, went with the minority rather than with the majority."[2]

What was this Asburian episcopal form? Bishop Thomas B. Neely* summarized it years later when listing powers now lost to the episcopacy:

In the early days the bishop acted as a superior court and decided appeal cases;
   The bishop could receive a preacher into the ministry, . . . suspend a preacher from the ministry; . . . prevent a preacher putting anything into print and circulating the same; . . . veto the election of any preacher to clerical orders and refuse to ordain any one so elected by a Conference; . . . veto the election of a minister to the bishopric, and refuse to consecrate him to that office.
   But all these powers have disappeared from the episcopacy.[3]

The MECS maintained the clear distinction of episcopacy as a coordinate branch of church government, protected by its constitution,[4] that of 1808.[5] Indeed, southern bishops were granted additional authority in 1820 and 1824. The third General Conference (1854) of the MECS empowered the bishops to object to any action of General Conference that they deemed unconstitutional, "and, if after hearing the objections and reasons of the Bishops, two-thirds of the members of the Conference present shall still vote in favor of the rule or regulation so objected to, it shall have the force of law—otherwise it shall be null and void."[6] This veto Norman Spellman judged "the historic act which marked the peak of episcopal power in the MECS—indeed, in any branch of Methodism."[7]

In 1870 the General Conference created a special committee to review this legislation. Chaired by Leroy M. Lee, it reported that "the veto power does not inhere in the Episcopal office, and does not belong to it by any legitimate act or authorization of the church."[8] The committee also concluded the action of 1854 was defective "in authority as a law, and that it is not, and of right cannot be either received or maintained as a part of the Constitution of the Church."[9] Despite this conclusion, the committee affirmed that similar legislation was needed and proposed the 1870 substitute that was adopted. It read thus:

That when any rule or regulation is adopted by the General Conference, which, in the opinion of the Bishops is unconstitutional, the Bishops may present to the Conference which passed said rule or regulation, their objections thereto, with their reasons; and if then the General Conference shall, by a two-thirds vote, adhere to its action on said rule or regulations, it shall then take the course prescribed for altering a restrictive rule [sent to the annual conferences for ratification], and if thus passed upon affirmatively, the Bishops shall announce that such rule or regulation takes effect from that time.[10]

The principal reaffirmed by this action defined and limited both General Conference and the episcopacy—the final authority in the church resided, as it always had, in the body of preachers. If they had allowed either General Conference or the bishops to determine "the constitutionality of the acts of a delegated body,"[11] they would have relinquished that primary authority, and they did not do it.[12]

The southern "style" of episcopacy nevertheless encouraged and permitted a power of individual authority that went beyond anything bestowed on the office formally by the Discipline.[13] The church elected to the post aristocratic individuals—college and university presidents, editors of church papers, leaders of its boards, princes of the pulpit—and through them established a kind of aristocracy of the pastor. Not surprisingly, they sometimes exercised power in autocratic fashion.

CHANGING THE FORM: NORTHERN STYLE

The Methodist Episcopal Church also altered episcopacy, albeit in a direction different from that taken by the South. The Third Restrictive Rule of the 1808

Constitution requires that "General Conference shall not change nor alter any part or rule of our government so as to do away episcopacy, nor destroy the plan of our itinerant General Superintendency." Much change came through practice rather than by statute.[14] This was a pattern formally recognized by the MEC Committee on Judiciary in 1928, when it recognized as valid a decision based on "custom and practice."[15]

The Church proved willing, however, to amend the Third Restrictive Rule when the need demanded, as instanced in the creation of the office of "missionary bishop" in the mid-nineteenth century, thus creating another form of episcopacy. The legislation had far-reaching and unexamined implications that were to trouble the church for the better part of a century.

The problem facing the church was how to provide episcopal supervision for its foreign missions. Beginning in 1836 and in each succeeding General Conference, the Liberia Annual Conference requested episcopal supervision.[16] In 1836 it was judged "inexpedient," but a recommendation was adopted directing the bishops to "select one of their number to visit our work in Western Africa, in the course of the ensuing four years."[17] Nobody went. Practical considerations alone—only six bishops for the entire church; a trip at best dangerous, expensive, and requiring months away from the United States; and an episcopacy thought without sufficient strength to do all the work at home—militated against deployment abroad.

Both precept and precedent also suggested that general superintendents were elected by General Conference exclusively for service in the United States. It had been so since 1787, when Thomas Coke* was prohibited from acting as a bishop when outside the country. Nevertheless, the appeals for episcopal supervision from Methodists overseas continued and intensified as the church increased the number of its missions. In 1852 and again in 1856 General Conference sought to address the issue by recommending the amendment of the Third Restrictive Rule to allow for the establishment of a new order of bishops "to be exclusively devoted to our missions in foreign countries respectively, as the General Conference may direct." Their service would be limited to the overseas conference to which they were assigned.[18] The 1852 legislation also provided that in the absence of an elected bishop for Liberia, one of the regular bishops should visit twice during the quadrennium.[19] Newly elected Bishop Levi Scott made the first episcopal visit to Africa after the General Conference in 1852. His report spurred the General Conference of 1856 to further action.

In their Episcopal Address the bishops described the situation in Liberia and affirmed that episcopal authority "on the spot is very desirable," but they conceded, "It cannot be regularly furnished from this country without embarrassing our home work."[20] The conference delegates accepted the recommendation and again sent a proposed amendment to the Third Restrictive Rule to their annual conferences for ratification.[21] They also adopted a provision allowing for the election of a missionary bishop during the interim of the General Conference if the amendment was ratified in the annual conferences. The conferences did ratify the amendment, and Francis Burns,* an African-American pastor with ten years' service in Liberia, was duly elected and ordained by Bishops Janes* and Baker in the October 1858 Genesee Annual Conference. He was the first of his race to be elected a bishop in the Methodist Episcopal Church.[22]

Regulations governing the work of missionary bishops, proposed by John P. Durbin,* missionary secretary, were also adopted in 1856. They required the missionary bishop to live "in the particular mission field assigned," enabled bishops to perform all their duties while residing in that area, but barred them from exercising any episcopal powers outside of it. All bishops were equal, but now some were clearly more equal than others. Missionary bishops were not general superintendents. In fact, missionary bishops were fully comparable to the general superintendents only in being amenable for their conduct to the Investigating Committee of the General Conference.[23]

In its desire to meet the needs of the missionary conferences, the church not only created a new form of episcopacy but in so doing raised significant new questions about the nature of the episcopal office. Does General Conference in the United States have the right to elect persons for service outside the United States? Early Methodists had refused to do it. Does General Conference have the power to limit episcopal service to a single area without violating at least the spirit of a "general, itinerant, superintendency" protected in even the amended form of the Third Restrictive Rule? And by implication, then, could a general superintendent be assigned to a particular area in the United States, as well as overseas, and limited to serve within it—a clear step away from an itinerant superintendency in the direction of the long-feared local or diocesan form of episcopacy?[24]

The MECS sent its first missionaries to China in 1848 (Charles Taylor, M.D., and the Rev. Benjamin Jenkins). It never adopted the missionary episcopate but evolved a practice of assigning general superintendents to live and work in specific conferences overseas. Eventually it created central conferences in its foreign missions with power to elect indigenous leadership.[25] The MEC, on the other hand, had for a time both missionary bishops and general superintendents serving overseas assignments under the same limitations. Isaac W. Joyce became the first bishop assigned by the MEC to an overseas area. From 1896 to 1898 he supervised the church's mission work in Japan, China, and Korea. He was a general superintendent, elected in 1888, who had full powers to itinerate throughout the church but who, nevertheless, was given a specific overseas location in which to serve.[26] Although the church had been very clear since 1888 about the difference between the two forms of episcopal leaders, in practice the distinctions blurred.

Further blurring and another major turning point came for the northern church in 1920. In that year and after quadrennia of requests by the black conferences for an election of one of their own, General Conference elected two African-Americans, Matthew Wesley Clair* and Robert Elijah Jones,* on a separate ballot. It was understood at their election that they were to serve exclusively in the black annual conferences. Ironically, General Conference that year also elected twelve other bishops, several of whom were given overseas assignments. No missionary bishops were elected.[27] Bishop Neely, who opposed the stationing of general superintendents in missionary conferences, argued that this election "transformed all the effective missionary bishops into general superintendents and left them in their foreign mission fields."[28]

By 1924 overseas missions in the MEC were organized into central conferences. The General Conference of 1928 proposed to amend the Third Restrictive Rule to enable the central conferences to elect their own bishops, thereby giving the church yet another form of the episcopal office. The General Conference of 1932 brought the era of specialized episcopacy to an end, although "by custom" black bishops were assigned only to black conferences and the church continued to elect missionary bishops for Africa. The remaining missionary bishops were elected general superintendents.

The decision to allow central conferences to elect their own bishops raised questions that took the church years to answer: What was their relationship to the Council of Bishops? their status vis-à-vis the general superintendents? their relationship to the General Conference? the implications of the special provisions assigned to their office for other branches of the episcopacy, especially their election for a fixed number of years rather than for life? and their status when no longer bishops?

LOCALIZING THE GENERAL SUPERINTENDENCY: NORTH AND SOUTH

A localized "general" superintendency came gradually through sincere attempts to serve the needs of the church better, often with little real intent to change the form of Methodist episcopacy. For instance, the MEC General Conference in 1872 determined that it had the power to designate cities in which the eight newly elected bishops were to reside.[29] Earlier, bishops were free to select their place of residence.[30] The MECS took similar action in 1882, recommending that "the Bishops should be distributed by the College of Bishops in such manner, if practicable, that every great section of our work may have a Bishop residing in some one of the Conferences embraced in said section."[31] Four years later it reaffirmed this request to the bishops but determined that no "official" action was needed to organize the annual conferences into permanent episcopal districts.[32]

The MEC General Conference in 1884 asserted its power to assign the bishops to a specific location.[33] That authority was based on the equality of all bishops and the precedent of the appointment of missionary bishops to a locale.[34] And four years later, as noted already, the first general superintendent was designated to serve overseas. "Thus was the theory of general superintendency . . . for all practical purposes laid aside; there was no real distinction now between the work of missionary bishop and general superintendent. The general superintendent could still itinerate, but his assigned residence represented a serious restriction of his freedom."[35] The MEC began in 1900 to assign its bishops to their residences, "subject to the approval of the General Conference."[36]

Despite a ruling in 1904 by the Committee on the Judiciary that localized episcopacy with an assigned term of four years was unconstitutional, the northern church continued in its efforts to create it.[37] In 1908, however, General Conference acknowledged at least the spirit of the prohibition by requesting the Board of Bishops to organize annual conferences into districts and to assign bishops to them. This took General Conference out of the role of mandating the change and reaffirmed a practice followed since 1816 by which the Board of Bishops exercised responsibility to assign its members to their conferences. The conference did urge the bishops to plan their work in such manner to "make at least two visits during the year in each Annual Conference within the United States which is assigned to them respectively."[38] Taking a step beyond its 1908 "recommendation," in 1912 General Conference created an area system of episcopal administration, a system on which the bishops commented favorably in 1916: "The plan of residential supervision and presidential administration has given general satisfaction."[39]

Southern Methodism followed a similar path to a localized episcopacy but did so mindful of its constitutive commitment to the power of its bishops, their co-equality as a branch of government, their unity as a body, their role as general itinerant superintendents for the whole church, and the importance of having change in the appointive office.[40] The usual pattern adopted by the College of Bishops in the South and not unknown with the Board of Bishops in the North was to designate two or more bishops to serve the same conference during a quadrennium. There were instances when one bishop would preside in an annual conference for three years of the quadrennium and a second would be assigned for the fourth. The question finally to be resolved, however, was whether a general conference had the power to send its bishops to a specific area for a fixed amount of time. The resolution in the affirmative created the modern form of Methodist episcopacy.

LIMITING EPISCOPAL POWER

From its earliest days American Methodists have been concerned about episcopal power (and its perceived abuse) and have regularly taken action designed to limit or restrict it. Over the years these attempts have generally fallen into three categories: (1) to change the bishop's power to select and station the presiding elders (later district superintendents); (2) to limit power by challenging the life tenure of bishops and establishing a term episcopacy (a model implicit in the office of missionary bishop and explicit in other Methodist bodies);[41] (3) to assign bishops to episcopal areas and impose limits on the number of years a bishop may reside in one episcopal area.[42]

A fourth limitation has been related to the creation of regulations that make retirement mandatory at a specified age. Joined to it, when once they were in place, has been an informal practice of electing persons whose age will allow them only a few years of service before retirement. It is not infrequently heard today that a candidate is too young to be elected. This is usually not so much an assessment of ability as it is an expression of discomfort about the number of years to serve. The MEC in 1912 made retirement for bishops mandatory "at the close of the General Conference nearest his seventy-third birthday."[43] In 1932 the age was reduced to seventy, setting the mandatory age at seventy-two.[44] The MECS enacted similar legislation in 1930.[45]

In neither branch of Methodism did bishops gladly itinerate into the twilight of retirement. Bishop James Cannon, Jr.,* who had prior to his own election played an active role in forcing the retirement of Bishop A. W. Wilson in 1914, was himself forced to retire in 1934. Bishop Wilson was eighty and Cannon seventy-seven when the action was taken. Bishop Cannon appealed his case to the General Conference, as did Bishop Thomas B. Neely in the MEC. Both were defeated. Cannon later wrote that "I would never have agreed to accept the election with an age limit attached."[46]

Even while defending life tenure for bishops, John M. Moore* acknowledged, "It is an admitted fact that the appointive power is autocratic, and has always been so—and has been considered best so—by the express will and requirement of the Church."[47] Episcopal power and its abuse have always been a concern of the body of preachers and laity. The source of this power was and is found in the authority of the bishops to station the preachers and to appoint the district superintendents. It cannot be disputed that the exercise of the authority to station the preachers has sometimes led to autocratic practice, particularly in the MECS.[48]

The rule of seniority has also had an influence. In the MECS, according to custom, the presidency of the College of Bishops went to the senior bishop. This created problems from time to time, especially when strong bishops like Candler held the post for years at a time. In 1927 the change was made, perhaps as much directed by dissatisfaction with Candler as by a new sense of democracy. At their spring meeting the College of Bishops voted to rotate the chairmanship and also replaced Bishop Collins Denny,* who had served as secretary continuously since his election to the episcopacy in 1910.[49] This is not to suggest, however, that the MEC has not had its share of strong and autocratic leaders, too; but from time to time some have received the honor with refreshing modesty and good humor. Bishop Earl Cranston wrote in his diary on 26 May 1896: "This day Charles C. McCabe and I, having been duly elected thereto after many ballots by General Conference were solemnly set apart and no less democratically infected with 'hotocratic tendencies' in the presence of the General Conference in a large assembly of reverend observers."[50]

Although not all attempts have been successful, real and significant limits to episcopal power have been imposed through the years. The bishops, with some justification, frequently protested the erosion of their powers. Speaking in the Episcopal Address to the MEC General Conference of 1912, they declared:

As president of the General Conference the bishops are governed by rules adopted by the delegates, and their decisions in the chair may be reversed by the house on appeal. Formerly they had a discretionary voice as to the ordination of persons elected general superintendents, elders, or deacons. Now they have no such voice. Once the bishops could receive and suspend preachers; he could hear and decide all law questions and appeals, thus virtually holding power to exclude members. Now he has no such powers. Formerly the bishops nominated the most important standing committees. These are now elected by the district representatives. Once they chose their own residences, like other circuit riders. Now they are assigned to designated cities. All these modifications are proper safeguards against abuses of power, but in effect they leave our episcopacy weakened in administrative efficiency.[51]

Although the understanding of the episcopacy generally afforded bishops in the southern church more authority than was granted their northern counterparts, the truth is that the changes in the office in both branches, often decried by the bishops as a loss of power, is more accurately a reflection of the changing nature of the church and society than a result of organized efforts to limit power.[52] The presence of laypersons in the government of the church, especially in the delegations of General Conference, and as member of boards and agencies made a significant difference. They demanded a greater role in the affairs of the church and a more democratic style of leadership.

The greatest modification in episcopal authority to appoint the preachers came in 1976 after the formation of the United Methodist Church (UMC). Here the presence of the Evangelical United Brethren and its practices were influential. The General Conference of 1972 authorized yet another "Study Commission on the Episcopacy and the District Superintendency." It recommended that the assigning of clergy to their stations require a consultative interaction among bishop, cabinet, district superintendent, clergy, and congregation.[53] Since 1976 bishops commonly make and announce appointments prior to the meeting of the annual conference. This has eliminated the suspenseful moment in every annual conference when clergy, members, and kin once sat with bated breath awaiting the reading of the appointments, which, until the announcement, were known only to the bishop and the district superintendents. Although the process outlined in 1976 is cumbersome and works to a greater or lesser degree in the various contexts to which it is applied—bishops have since the middle of the nineteenth century lamented in various Episcopal Addresses the propensity for larger churches to influence the appointment process, and smaller congregations believe that no matter what is said, they will get whomever the bishop and cabinet decide to send—it has reduced the temptation to arbitrariness and imposed limits on unquestionable judgments in the appointive process. Francis Asbury* would not have been at home in such a situation, nor would hosts of his successors, especially in the MECS during the late nineteenth and early twentieth centuries.

This, of course, also raises the question of episcopal accountability. Although formally the bishops are subject to the Committee on Episcopacy in the Jurisdictional Conference and finally to the General Conference for their conduct and administration, the study commissioned by the General Conference in 1972 revealed considerable ambiguity on the part of the bishops themselves. The question was raised to every active bishop, and the writers reported, "Probably on no score was there greater disagreement among the bishops. It almost looked like utter confusion."[54] The report also asked bishops about their sense of accountability to the Council of Bishops: "There seems to be a tendency that bishops do not hold each other accountable for the work they do, each in his own area. And when they are together, they are reluctant to police themselves."[55]

SELECTING THE BISHOPS

Modifications in the understanding and expectations of episcopacy have brought new kinds of persons to fill the office. Prior to 1845 only fourteen men had been elected bishops. Francis Asbury, Thomas Coke, and Richard Whatcoat* were missionaries, born in England; William McKendree,* the first native son of America; Robert Roberts,* the first to be married and at thirty-eight one of the youngest persons ever elected.[56] Joshua Soule* was the first to be elected and decline to serve, Leonidas Hamline,* the forceful advocate of limited episcopacy subject to General Conference, was elected as the northern candidate in 1844 because of his role in the deliberations on the case of Bishop Andrew* and was the first to resign the office (in 1852).[57] Six of the first nine bishops elected were presiding elders; only Bishop Soule was a pastor at the time of his election; Bishop Janes, thirty-seven and a medical doctor, was secretary of the American Bible Society and was not a member of the General Conference of 1844, which elected him "to balance the ticket."[58] These persons carried the responsibility for supervising the entire denomination for six decades. Under their leadership the church grew from a small and isolated sect to the largest Protestant denomination in the United States. Bishops were, if ever the term could apply, Methodism's "general superintendents," although as has already been noted, McKendree was the last itinerant, general superintendent actually to preside in all the conferences.

After the 1844 division until reunion created the Methodist Church in 1939, the Methodist Episcopal Church elected ninety-three general superintendents, two of whom (Clair and Jones) were African-Americans allowed to serve only in black conferences and fourteen of whom were missionary bishops. Two of the missionary bishops, William F. Oldham and John W. Robinson, were later elected general superintendents. John M. Springer in 1936 was the last person ever to be elected a missionary bishop, an exception made for African service. The MECS elected fifty-six bishops in the same period of time.

During these years laypersons took their places in the various conferences, boards, and agencies of the church. The boards themselves took on increasing significance, and the general secretaries and their staff rose to power and prominence in the life of the church. Often they exercised a more general supervision than that of the bishops, reducing "the general superintendency of the episcopacy almost entirely to the general supervision of the ministry," as one Episcopal Address put it.[59] Other arrangements have also limited episcopal power. The creation of the Committee on the Judiciary early in the life of the MEC, and the Judicial Council in the MECS in 1934 (which also was carried into the reorganized Methodist Church) removed from the bishops the authority to determine the constitutionality of legislation and put them under its direction. Episcopal decisions are now routinely reported to and reviewed by the Judicial Council.

The practical results of these changes in the responsibilities and nature of the episcopal office are reflected in the selection of persons who would and could serve effectively as managers. Prior to 1900 few pastors were elected to the episcopacy. In order to be elected a bishop in both branches of Episcopal Methodism prior to 1939, one had to gain visibility and prominence, in addition to possessing skills and experience that would seem to prepare a person for the work. Connectional appointments were the surest ways to the episcopacy. Of the persons elected in both branches of Methodism in this period, five were publishing agents, fifteen were missionary secretaries, twelve held other connectional posts, and twenty-two (fifteen in the MEC and seven in the MECS) were editors of church papers at the time of their election. Fifty-five were serving in educational institutions, often as presidents, when elected, and another thirteen had previously been connected with a school or college.[60] The contrast between this and the pattern that after reunion created the jurisdictional structure is striking. One hundred nine persons were elected bishops by the Methodist Church from 1939 to 1968. Of these, only thirteen were employed in boards or agencies at the time of their election; seven editors were chosen; one was a district superintendent at the time of his election.[61] The number of pastors elected jumped sharply, and an already localized episcopacy became regional. The road to the episcopal office since 1939, at least, ran through the great pulpits of the connection.

Nothing has altered the face of the episcopacy in Methodism's long history more than the organization of the jurisdictions in 1939. No longer elected by their peers, "itinerant general superintendents" now presided in an area often composed of three annual conferences or less; they served their entire career in one jurisdiction, but with the responsibility to promote and interpret the programs of the general church. Only an individual who was acceptable in the region could be elected. As a pattern, the bishops have seldom been educated or served outside the jurisdiction in which they were elected. Few persons have ever been elected by jurisdictions other than their own, and seldom is a bishop transferred from one jurisdiction to another after election, although it is permitted.[62] Those who created the Plan of Unification were certainly not unaware of what they were doing. In the Joint Commission on Unification meeting in 1918, Bishop Richard J. Cooke, a delegate from the MEC, affirmed "that the kind and character of Methodist episcopacy is hereby changed. Is that understood, that the fundamental character and the nature of Methodist episcopacy is hereby changed from an itinerant general superintendency to diocesan episcopacy limited to the jurisdiction from which he comes?"[63]

In their attempt to settle the question of the place of black members and to reunite the church, the planners of church union changed the nature of its superintendency.[64] After the creation of the jurisdictional structure, three things became essential to election to the episcopacy: (1) Since candidates now are nominated, they need strong support from an annual conference. The most advantageous position from which to run is leader of the delegation to the General and Jurisdictional Conferences.[65] (2) All persons who agree to be candidates must campaign and be interviewed by the delegates from the various annual conferences. An aspiring bishop must do well in these interviews to be elected. And (3) some area within the jurisdiction must indicate its willingness to receive the bishop if elected. The candidate must have a place to go.

The profile of persons elected under the new system in the United Methodist Church (1968–present) is striking, important, even ground-breaking. Of special note are the election of women and ethnic persons to episcopal office. In 1972 the United Methodist Church elected Wilbur Choy, the first Asian-American bishop; in 1984, Elias Galvan, the first Hispanic, and Leontine T. Kelly, the first African-American woman; in 1988, Joseph B. Bethea, the first African-American elected in the Southeastern Jurisdiction; and in 1992, Hae Jong Kim, the first Korean-American bishop. The denomination elected its first woman to the episcopacy (Marjorie Matthews*) in 1980, the first major denomination to do so. Since then, a total of eight have been elected. Four of the eight were in connectional assignments: two pastors, two district superintendents. (In selection of women bishops, the church's recent preference for pastors does not seem to pertain, suggesting perhaps that not enough women have reached the type of pastoral appointment that would enable them to be elected.)

Through the Jurisdictional Conferences of 1992, ninety-three persons had been elected for service in the United States. More than half (fifty) were pastors at the time of their election; fifteen were district superintendents, and of the total number elected to the episcopacy an additional forty-one had been district superintendents at one time during their career.[66] The UMC obviously regards the superintendency as providing relevant experience for persons entering the episcopacy but, as was even more the case in the Methodist Church, not a likely place from which one may be elected. Eleven were in educational institutions and sixteen were in connectional assignments. Of these sixteen, six were directors of the Conference Council on Ministry, a new position created after the merger with the United Evangelical Brethren. James L. Armstrong, Sharon Brown Christopher, and Joseph H. Yeakle were the youngest ever elected in the UMC, all age forty-four. The oldest person was Don Holter, who was sixty-eight when elected, followed closely by J. Chess Lovern, who was sixty-seven. The average age of those elected in the United Methodist Church since 1968 was just over fifty-seven.[67]

One of the most dramatic recent changes in the episcopacy in the UMC is the tension and political maneuvering that surrounds the stationing of the bishops. The responsibility to assign them belongs to the Jurisdictional Committee on Episcopacy, but for the first time in our history, a general superintendent must be received by those to be served. Areas can refuse to accept a bishop. It would have been unthinkable at any time prior to the creation of the UMC in 1968 for any annual conference to express its unwillingness to receive a bishop even though conferences have obviously had preferences. Bishops, like clergy, were, in the words of Bishop McFerrin Stowe, "called to be sent." With this change ceremonial occasions have been created in which new bishops are "received and welcomed" into their areas. Often a part of the ceremony involves the presentation of symbols of the episcopal office—the shepherd's crook, or a stole, for example—and various groups within the area are represented. This is more fitting to the installation of an Episcopal bishop than to the installation of an "itinerant, general superintendent," elected to an office and appointed to an area for service. It is difficult to imagine how a unique, "cause oriented," controversial, and colorful candidate like Gilbert Haven,* "Chaplain" C. C. McCabe,* Atticus Haygood,* or James Cannon, Jr., could be successful in a bid for election today.

The issue that has now come to the fore is how regional bishops can provide leadership for the entire church. The UMC has no general superintendency. The Council of Bishops, organized after the Uniting Conference in 1939, is headed by a president whose term of office is one year.[68] The significant power in the Council of Bishops is the office of secretary, who serves a four-year term and may be reelected; Bishop G. Bromley Oxnam* served for sixteen years.[69] He, more than any other person, shaped the manner in which the Council of Bishops does its business. The only official voice of the denomination is the General Conference.

Nevertheless, through the years Methodist bishops have addressed themselves in pastoral letters to the church on a variety of issues—on the eve of World War II (1939) a "Message on the World Situation," and recently on peace and ecology, "In Defense of Creation," and church renewal, "Vital Congregations, Faithful Disciples." Between 1939 and 1978 they addressed the denomination in this manner twenty-two times.[70] These comments, however, have only the force of respect United Methodists are willing to afford the Council of Bishops. They do not have the power to direct legislation in either the church or society. Bishops have become personnel, promotional, and program officers who work almost exclusively with clergy and laypersons in their areas. The most recent study of the episcopacy indicated that bishops have little involvement in the communities in which they live. The days in which strong bishops like A. Frank Smith or Fred Pierce Corson* are so connected in the communities where they lived that a word from them has broad and significant influence have passed. Today even the episcopal leaders who reside in centers of power and influence like Washington, D.C., or New York City appear to have little real influence on government or commerce. If the church itself has lost power to speak to society, so also its bishops have lost their ability to use their influence to speak through it.

Nevertheless, the office retains great significance within the church and in the lives of clergy. Despite the reforms that have transformed the system of appointing the preachers, bishops still determine who goes and who stays. And the bishops do lead by precept and by example. Their example, in particular, we surmise, sets the terms for ministerial behavior as a whole. Their self-consciousness about the teaching role suggests that Methodism might recover something of the dimensions of John Wesley's own exercise of superintendency. And on the other side, episcopal desire for stability, longer tenure, sabbaticals, and single conferences seem to reinforce overall patterns in ministry that radically change the itinerant system. In episcopal hands, we suggest, lies the future of the connection. More than any other office, the bishops have emblemed and defended the itinerant principle, appointive authority, and connectional system against the impulses of localism, democratic reform, and sectionalism.

NOTES

1. Robert Paine, *Life and Times of William M'Kendree, Bishop of the Methodist Episcopal Church* (Nashville: Publishing House of the Methodist Episcopal Church, South, 2 vols., 1869) 1: 456.

2. Quoted in Norman Spellman, *The General Superintendency in American Methodism, 1784–1870* (unpublished Ph.D. diss., Yale University, 1960), 213.

3. Thomas B. Neely, *The Bishops and the Supervisional System of the Methodist Episcopal Church* (New York: Eaton & Mains, 1912), 228–29.

4. Norman Spellman refutes the idea that the South's adherence to the Asburian tradition of co-equal episcopacy was sectional and associated with the larger concern over slavery by noting that the Methodist Protestant Church was far more radical in its anti-Asburian stance, was primarily a southern movement, and was both anti-bishop and pro-slavery. See Spellman, *General Superintendency in American Methodism*, 242.

5. "It came to be accepted as the doctrine of the Methodist Episcopal Church, South that the formal establishment of the constitution in 1808 did in fact establish the episcopacy as a co-ordinate office." Herbert Stotts, "History of the Episcopacy," *Study of the General Superintendency of the Methodist Church*, 1963, pt. 1, 39. Authorized by General Conference, 1960.

6. *JGC/S*, 1854, 356.

7. Spellman, *General Superintendency in American Methodism*, 318.

8. *JGC/S*, 1870, 282.

9. Ibid., 286.

10. Ibid., 287.

11. Ibid., 285.

12. Paine, *Life of M'Kendree*, 2: 37. Spellman, *General Superintendency in American Methodism,*, 216.

13. See Mark K. Bauman, *Warren Akin Candler: The Conservative as Idealist* (Metuchen, NJ: Scarecrow Press, 1981), 67.

14. "The role of the bishop in the Methodist Church has historically been shaped more by the acts of the men after election than by formal legislation." *The Study of the General Superintendency of the Methodist Church: A Report to the General Conference of 1964*, presented by the Co-Ordinating Council of the Methodist Church, 40.

15. "A custom," they said, "is a usage which has obtained the force of law. In other words, it is a law established by long usage." Report 18, Committee on Judiciary, *JGC*, 1928, 509.

16. The Liberia Annual Conference was organized in 1834. For a brief summary of its history see Prince A. Taylor, Jr., *The Life of My Years* (Nashville: Abingdon Press, 1983), 93–113.

17. *JGC*, 1836, 473.

18. *JGC*, 1852, 67; Neely, *Bishops and the Supervisional System*, 164.

19. *JGC*, 1852, 68.

20. "Episcopal Address," *JGC*, 1856, 198.

21. The amendment added the words "but may appoint a Missionary Bishop or Superintendent for any of our foreign missions, limiting his episcopal jurisdiction to the same respectively." It passed by a margin of 159 to 27. *JGC*, MEC 1856, 145. This legislative (as opposed to constitutional) act established a precedent allowing the form of episcopal government to be modified by amending the Third Restrictive Rule. The implication is that the church can have whatever kind of episcopacy it desires, so long as it does not do away with episcopacy entirely. The episcopal form is protected by the church constitution. This matter has, over the years, been tested in the various judicial forums, especially with regard to "term" episcopacy.

22. *JGC*, 1856, 184. See "Episcopal Address," *JGC*, 1860, 373; also see Thomas B. Neely, *The Methodist Episcopal Church and Its Foreign Missions* (New York: Methodist Book Concern, 1923), 125. Burns was followed by another African-American, John Wright Roberts, who was consecrated in New York City, on 20 June 1866. The first Anglo to be elected a missionary bishop was William "Father" Taylor, who was assigned to supervise the entire continent of Africa.

23. *JGC*, 1856, 177. See Neely, *Methodist Episcopal Church*, 126–31; see also his subcommittee report and speeches to the General Conference of 1888, which clarified the status of missionary bishops. *JGC*, 1888 [19 May 1888].

24. This concern runs through Episcopal Addresses. In 1844, the bishops insisted that superintendency is "*general embracing the whole work in convectional order, and not diocesan, or sectional.*" *JGC*, 1844, 156. In 1852 they worried over any modifications that "would be likely to result in the introduction of Diocesan Episcopacy," particularly any "restricting Episcopal labours to a definite and limited sphere," which would "lead to the introduction of Diocesan Episcopacy," "destroy the itinerant General Superintendency, and in this way change the essential character of our economy." "Episcopal Address," *JGC*, 1852, 182–83.

25. Bishop E. M. Marvin made the first episcopal visit to the Orient in 1876. See

James Cannon, III, *History of Southern Methodist Missions* (Nashville: Cokesbury Press, 1926), 94. One must at least consider that they may have been motivated by an overriding concern to avoid electing persons of color.

26. Wilbur F. Sheridan, *The Life of Isaac Wilson Joyce* (Cincinnati: Jennings & Graham, 1907), 92. Moreover, on several occasions missionaries from North America were elected to the episcopacy by central conferences. John William Tarboux was elected the first bishop of the Methodist Church in Brazil after forty-seven years of missionary service.

27. Ten missionary bishops were elected between 1884 and 1916: Taylor,* Thoburn,* Parker, Warne, John E. Robinson, Oldham, John W. Robinson, Hartzel, Harris, and Johnson. Oldham and John W. Robinson were eventually elected general superintendents. Bishops Clair and Jones were more like missionary bishops than general superintendents, but no challenges were lodged. The MEC had few African-American members after the end of the Civil War. In 1870 the Colored Methodist Episcopal Church was established, two of its members were elected bishops and ordained by the bishops of the MECS.

28. Neely, *Methodist Episcopal Church*, 255.

29. *JGC*, 1872, 321.

30. From the organization of the church until 1872, in the MEC the bishops selected the site of their residences. Bishop Matthew Simpson, for example, decided to live in Evanston, Illinois, because of his friendship with John Evans, for whom it is named. From 1872 until 1900 they chose on the basis of seniority from a list created by General Conference. From 1900 until 1939 General Conference stationed the bishops. After the organization of the jurisdictional system, the decisions were made by the Jurisdictional Committee on the Episcopacy.

31. *JGC/S*, 1882, 165–66.

32. *JGC/S*, 1886, 105.

33. *JGC*, 1884, 369. Surprisingly, the Committee on Judiciary ruled in 1904 that assignment for a specific period of time would threaten the itinerant general superintendency. *JGC*, 1904, 517. Bishop Neely supported the theory that location per se does not threaten the "itinerant" episcopacy, since "a residence does not and never was understood to confine the bishop to the particular point or its precincts." Neely, *Bishops and the Supervisional System*, 298.

34. *JGC*, 1884, 369.

35. Gerald F. Moede, *The Office of Bishop in Methodism* (New York: Abingdon Press, 1964), 142. Thomas B. Neely wrote and presented the 1888 report on the missionary bishopric. As adopted, it determined that a missionary bishop (1) is elected for service in a "specified foreign mission field" with full episcopal powers and limited jurisdiction, (2) is not a general superintendent, (3) is coordinate with general superintendents in authority in the field to which appointed, (4) cannot be made a general superintendent unless elected to the office, and (5) is supported by the Episcopal Fund. Neely, *Methodist Episcopal Church*, 128–31. *JGC*, 1888, 392–96. Neely never abandoned the premise articulated in this report that general superintendents are elected for work only in the United States. Neely, *Methodist Episcopal Church*, 133.

36. *JGC*, 1900, 424–25.

37. *JGC*, 1904, 517.

38. *JGC*, 1908, 456–57. In their action the Committee on Episcopacy acknowledged the need to modify the present plan of episcopal supervision, the ruling of the Committee on the Judiciary in 1904 against localized episcopacy, and the right of the Board of

Bishops under the constitution "to assign individual Bishops to preside over Conferences in contiguous territory for a period of several years." It was a shrewd move within the letter, but outside the spirit of the protection of "itinerant General Superintendency."

39. "Episcopal Address," *JGC*, 1916, 161, 481.

40. See Bishop Collins Denny in the 1918 Episcopal Address, *JGC/S*, 1918, 322. Compare later "Episcopal Addresses," *JGC/S*, 1922, 340, and *JGC/S*, 1930, 384.

41. Proposals for the creation of a "Term Episcopacy" have come before many General Conferences. Proposals surfaced in the MEC in 1856 for a term of four years and in 1884 for twelve years. See Stotts, "History of the Episcopacy," *General Superintendency of the Methodist Church*, 1: 46–48. In the MECS proposals to limit episcopal tenure came as early as 1888 and were renewed in years following. A strong push was made in 1924, and again at the 1930 and 1934 General Conferences. In the southern church, such legislation came as a response to autocratic episcopacy. John M. Moore devoted a substantial portion of the Episcopal Address in 1934 to refute the idea. The creation of the UMC in 1968 brought into play the traditions of the Evangelical Association, an episcopacy limited to two four-year terms from the beginning. Discussions with the Free Methodists, who also had an elected district superintendency, have also encouraged those who advocated term episcopacy.

42. A limit of twelve years was imposed in 1956 and reduced to eight in 1976. See Par. 507, UMC *Discipline*, 1976, 215.

43. Par. 210.2, MEC *Discipline*, 1912, 149. There was no similar provision for ministers.

44. Par. 245.2, *Discipline* MEC, 1932, 218.

45. Par. 120, MECS *Discipline*, 1930, 72.

46. James Cannon, Jr., *Bishop Cannon's Own Story* (Durham, NC: Duke University Press, 1955), xiii.

47. "Episcopal Address," *JGC/S*, 1934, 384.

48. Warren Candler's biographer says of the MECS episcopacy:

"During his youth and early manhood [Candler was born in 1857 and lived to be eighty-five] it was expected that bishops should be autocratic, and not often did the strong bishops of that period—and sometimes the feebler ones, which was worse—fail to rise to the occasion. . . . Democracy was slow in making its way into the Methodist Episcopal Church, South. . . . The prerogatives of this body were almost absolute. The most arbitrary bishop, in his most arbitrary moment, did not strain his authority; he rather restrained himself from using his authority to the limit. These prerogatives Bishop Candler inherited but did not create; he simply exercised what had been handed down to him with no connivance on his part. He was a strong man, with great confidence in his own judgment, with no excessive fondness for opposition, and with vast constitutional prerogatives. The stage was set for him to play the autocrat, and sometimes he acted the part remarkably well." Alfred M. Pierce, *Giant against the Sky* (New York: Abingdon-Cokesbury Press, 1943), 98.

49. See Robert W. Sledge, *A History of the Methodist Episcopal Church, South, 1914–1939* (unpublished Ph.D. diss., University of Texas at Austin, 1972), 140. The bishops still honor this principle in the selection of the president of the Council of Bishops. Although the presidency is largely ceremonial and rotates through the jurisdictions, it is the senior bishop who is elected. The College of Bishops in the South Central Jurisdiction also elects its president on the basis of seniority.

50. Quoted in Stotts, "The History of the Episcopacy," *General Superintendency of the Methodist Church*, 92.

51. "Episcopal Address," *JGC*, 1912, 186–87.

52. "The forces . . . had hewn out a new type of bishop in Methodism, a bishop fully responsive to the checks and balances of democratic government . . . but also localized, that is sensitive and sympathetic with the local needs of particular areas . . . a bishop whose influence has been drastically curtailed in both sectors of the church by his steady descent to *Promotor inter pares*, but, at the same time, following unique Methodist tradition, a bishop whose position represented what the church in its age felt would be most useful to the church." Moede, *Office of Bishop in Methodism*, 156–57.

53. The constitution of the United Methodist Church has since 1968 stipulated, "The bishops shall appoint, after consultation with the district superintendent, ministers to the charges." Article X. See UMC *Discipline*, 1976, sec. 8, pars. 527–29, 228.

54. Egon W. Gerdes and Ellis Larsen, *Sharing a Royal Priesthood: First Report to the Study Commission on Episcopacy and District Superintendency in Joint Session with the Council of Bishops of the United Methodist Church Meeting in Los Angeles, April 16-19, 1974*, 2: 53.

55. Gerdes and Larsen, *Sharing a Royal Priesthood*, 2: 55. It is interesting in the light of this to recall that McKendree was prepared to file formal charges in the General Conference against Bishops Hedding and George for their failure to itinerate through the southern conferences.

56. Bishop Janes was thirty-seven, Roberts was thirty-eight, and Asbury and Soule were thirty-nine when elected. Roberts started a trend, for the next person never to have been married at the time of election was William R. Cannon in 1968.

57. Although the first to resign, he was by no means the first to consider seriously leaving the office. Throughout the history of the church there has never been any doubt that one could resign. In 1799 Asbury announced his intention to resign because poor health was keeping him from his duties, but he was encouraged by the General Conference of 1800 to continue "as well as his strength will permit." *Minutes*, General Conference of 1800 quoted in Nathan Bangs, *A History of the Methodist Episcopal Church* (New York: T. Mason & G. Lane, 1838), 88. Bishop Roberts offered his resignation in 1836 because of poor health, but it was not accepted; T. A. Morris indicated his intention to resign in 1840 because he said he was not suited to the office and was uncomfortable presiding in the conferences. (See John F. Marlay, *The Life of Thomas A. Morris* [Cincinnati: Hitchcock & Walden, 1875], 140, 165.) Bishop Janes in 1855 cited stress on his family: "But painfully as I regret this, I know of but one way to relieve the affliction, namely to resign my office." See Henry B. Ridgaway, *Life of Edmund S. Janes* (New York: Phillips & Hunt, 1882), 154. Many of the bishops have found the office difficult for the same reason. Bishop Candler indicated his intention to resign in 1922 and 1926. Bishop James Armstrong resigned in 1983.

58. See Ridgaway, *Life of Edmund S. Janes*, 50, 86. Despite being from the North, Janes was presented for his consecration by William Capers and George Pierce, both of whom were later to be elected bishops in the MECS.

59. Bishop John M. Moore, "Episcopal Address," *JGC/S*, 1934, 378. See also Robert W. Goodloe, *The Office of Bishop in the Methodist Church* (unpublished Ph.D. diss., University of Chicago, 1929), 178, and Gerdes and Larsen, *Sharing a Royal Priesthood,*, 2: 49.

60. See Roy H. Short, *Chosen to Be Consecrated* (Lake Junaluska, NC: Commission

on Archives and History of the United Methodist Church, 1976), 76. Also see Frederick DeLand Leete, *Methodist Bishops* (Nashville: Parthenon Press, 1948).

61. See Short, *Chosen to Be Consecrated*, 17–18. Bishop Short is incorrect in his assertion that no person was a district superintendent at the time of election. H. Bascom Watts of the Oklahoma Conference was serving on a district when elected in 1952. See Leland Clegg and William B. Oden, *Oklahoma Methodism in the Twentieth Century* (Nashville: Parthenon Press, 1968), 297. Short is correct in his general conclusion that district superintendents had been out of favor as candidates since 1832. The MECS elected only one during its existence (Bishop Robert K. Hargrove), and only seven were elected in the MEC.

62. Gerald Kennedy was elected a bishop in the Western Jurisdiction in 1948 while serving as pastor of a congregation in Lincoln, Nebraska in the South Central Jurisdiction. The African-American bishops serving in the Central Jurisdiction were transferred to previously white annual conferences after its dissolution. Bishop Prince A. Taylor (New Jersey area) and Bishop James S. Thomas (Iowa area) were the first to be assigned. Bishop Taylor's previous service had been in Liberia. In point of fact, no bishop has actually been transferred to another jurisdiction after serving in an area.

63. *Joint Commission on Unification of the Methodist Episcopal Church and the Methodist Episcopal Church, South*, Vol. 2, *Proceedings at Savannah, GA, 23 January–6 February 1918* (New York: Methodist Book Concern, 1920), 574. (Herafter cited as *Proceedings of the Joint Commission on Unification*.) Bishop Edwin Mouzon followed Cooke's comment by asking how the bishops elected in the central conferences would be related to those elected in the jurisdictions—also a pertinent question.

64. The "racist" tone of these deliberations is offensive today. In a response to the proposed plan, J.W.E. Bowen, elected a bishop in the Central Jurisdiction of the Methodist Church in 1948, wrote, "We have even consented to constitutional limitation of that episcopacy, lest we disturb the ungrounded fears of many in our Church that they would lose social preeminence were one lone black bishop placed in the position of leadership among his own people." Quoted by Edgar Blake in the *Proceedings of the Joint Commission on Unification*, 2: 351.

65. The study of the episcopacy done in 1964 noted that delegates to the General Conference, both clerical and lay, do not fit the profile of the denomination as a whole. They "are older, better educated, and come from larger churches, paying larger salaries, located in larger towns and cities." *Study of the General Superintendency of the Methodist Church: A Report to the General Conference of 1964*, presented by the Co-Ordinating Council of the Methodist Church, 102.

66. A survey taken in the Council of Bishops in 1982–83 produced seventy-six responses. On average the bishops had spent 19.8 years in the local church pastorate and 4.73 years as district superintendents. Results of the survey can be found in James K. Matthews, *Set Apart to Serve: The Role of the Episcopacy in the Wesleyan Tradition* (Nashville: Abingdon Press, 1985), Appendix B, 297–305.

67. Trends are difficult to determine, but the average age of the sixteen persons elected in 1992 was fifty-four. However, the youngest was forty-five (Susan Morrison), and this would skew the average. The oldest was sixty. Eleven were pastors, four were district superintendents, and one (Alfred Norris) was a seminary president.

68. In November 1989 Bishop Jack M. Tuell presented a proposal to the Council of Bishops to bring legislation before General Conference to create the office of "Presiding Bishop in the United Methodist Church" by amending the constitution. The individual

selected would be assigned to serve a four-year term, and along with fulfilling other responsibilities, the individual would have to "serve as spokesperson for the United Methodist Church within the context of the positions of the General Conference." The first rationale given for the change was to provide more unified leadership in the face of urgent national and international issues; the second was to meet the request of the denomination for its bishops to provide greater leadership; the third was to enable the UMC to become a "more effective participant in the long range strategies of ecumenism." The measure failed to pass the Council of Bishops. Confidential document to the Council of Bishops, November 1989.

69. The secretary controls the agenda of the Council of Bishops and names persons to its committees. The "lock" of seniority that dominated for years was broken by a group of younger bishops, led by Kenneth Goodson, McFerrin Stowe, and Dwight Loder, who after their election in 1964 "sat on the back row" and lobbied for equal status for all members of the council. In 1971–72 the Council was re-organized into standing committees.

Bishop Prince Taylor recalls Council protocol: "The time had not come when the church was willing to accept the black bishops as representatives of the whole church. They would be heard on matters pertaining to the Central Jurisdiction, but were not expected to contribute to the solution of the larger problems of the church. . . . Theoretically, the black bishops had every right the white bishops had in the Council, but this did not prevail in practice." Taylor, *The Life of My Years*, 93.

70. Bishop James K. Matthews, secretary of the Council of Bishops, compiled these under the title "Messages of the Council of Bishops of the Methodist Church, The United Methodist Church during Its First Forty Years, 1939–1978." Typescript, n.d.

Part Two
CONFERENCE

4
THE METHODIST CONFERENCE

Like so much else in Methodism, conference bore the personal stamp of the Wesleys. The conference began as an extension of John Wesley's own deliberative processes.

In June, 1744, I desired my brother and a few other Clergymen to meet me in London, to consider how we should proceed to save our own souls and those that heard us. After some time, I invited the lay Preachers that were in the house to meet with us. We conferred together for several days, and were much comforted and strengthened thereby.

The next year I not only invited most of the Travelling Preachers, but several others, to confer with me in Bristol. And from that time for some years, though I invited only a part of the Travelling Preachers, yet I permitted any that desired it, to be present.[1]

The name given to the record of these endeavors, "Minutes of Some Late Conversations between the Rev. Mr. Wesleys and Others," suggests accurately the dominant role played by the Wesleys.[2] Wesley posed questions, and discussion followed; Wesley framed the conclusion, and he then reworked the raw minutes into publishable form. To these annual affairs Wesley and his preachers brought the fundamental issues generated by the movement. These concerns took permanent form as a series of questions that defined the order of business. The conference quickly emerged as the basic and characteristic structure of Methodist governance, and the published minutes something of a constitution.

MR. WESLEY'S CONFERENCE

In conference John Wesley eventually placed his hope for Methodism after his death and his plan for an orderly transference of authority. He recognized the conference as the heir to his authority, identified its membership in terms of signed adherence to "the *old Methodist doctrines* . . . contained in the minutes of the Conferences" and "the whole *Methodist discipline*, laid down in the said minutes," and constituted it as a legal entity, initially by planning for election of an executive committee and moderator. Compacts were signed and minuted in 1769, 1773, 1774, and 1775. Later Wesley sought more precise legal identity of conference by actually enumerating a hundred individuals who constituted the conference.[3] This endowed conference, according to Neely, "with the supreme power which had been centered in Mr. Wesley."[4]

The vital political function of conference was but one of its several dimensions. Indeed, assent to conference's normative and constitutional prerogatives probably derived from conference's other competencies. It was a family of preachers headed and governed by John Wesley; it was a monasticlike order held together by affection, by common rules, by a shared mission, and by watchfulness of members over one another; it was a brotherhood of religious aspiration and song; it was a quasi-professional society that concerned itself with the reception, training, credentialing, monitoring, and deployment of Wesley's lay preachers; it was a community of preachers whose commitment to the cause and to one another competed with all other relationships; it was a body that pooled its resources to provide for the wants and needs of its members; when one of its members died, it was the agency of memorial and memory; and it was the spiritual center of Methodism.[5]

A query put in 1747 clearly conveys the spiritual dimensions of conference:

Q. How may the time of this Conference be made more eminently a time of prayer, watching, and self-denial?

A. 1. While we are in Conference, let us have an especial care to set God always before us. 2. In the intermediate hours, let us visit none but the sick, and spend all our time that remains in retirement. 3. Let us then give ourselves unto prayer for one another, and for the blessing of God on this our labour.[6]

The religious development of its members, the spiritual well-being of the immediate community, and the care of the overall connection concerned conference during its sittings. Fittingly, in "The Large Minutes" Wesley recognized conference as one of five "instituted" means of grace. That designation and the character of the other four—prayer, searching the Scriptures, the Lord's Supper, and fasting—suggest how very central to the Christian life and the Methodist movement Wesley placed conference.[7] By the reference Wesley intended not specifically annual or quarterly conferences but, rather, the mode of engagement, discipline, purpose, and structure that they shared with all serious Christian encounter. Conference was the way Wesley sought to conduct his affairs with his people.

The conference in British and American Methodism—quarterly conference, annual conference, and general conference—was the spatial *and* temporal outworking of a set of religious impulses, never fully integrated into theory, but nevertheless characteristic of a peculiar Wesleyan style of organization, unity, mission, reform, and spirituality. Constituting the Wesleyan economy, these structural features bore the Wesleyan spiritual and religious impulses, the accent on the priesthood of all believers, and the insistence on the mutual interdependence of all parts of the body of Christ. The several structurings of the Wesleyan spirit had emerged in stages and in relation to entities named as the occasion suggested—societies, bands, classes, stewards, trustees, circuits, connexion, conference, quarterly meeting. They cohered because Methodism cohered, because they belonged together in the religious experience and administrative style of John Wesley, because they possessed a center in him, because Wesley envisioned Methodism as an integrated connection. In treating the coherence and multidimensionality of conference we will consider conference as fraternity, conference as revival, and conference as polity—three rubrics representing its social, spiritual, and constitutional dimensions.

THE FIRST AMERICAN CONFERENCES

Throughout this organizational period Americans followed English blueprints but found that the resultant structures and practices took on an American appearance. The sheer size of American society made it difficult, from the very start, to replicate British order; the distance from final authority necessitated local decisions; the relative equality of all the preachers militated against the concentration of all authority in a Wesley appointee or Wesley-like figure.

The first preachers appointed by Wesley arrived on American shores in 1769 to find that local and lay initiatives in New York and Maryland had spread the work sufficiently to make plausible the oversight and organization developed in the British conference system. The structures of governance and common life grew as Methodist numbers and Methodist territory demanded: first through quarterly meetings (1769–73), then through a single annual conference (1773–79), next through multiple sessions of a theoretically single annual conference (1779–92), and finally (1792 and after) through a general conference meeting every four years, overarching geographically conceived annual conferences, which in turn overarched circuit-based quarterly conferences.[8] In the midst of that development occurred the irregular Christmas Conference of 1784 by which American Methodism achieved its independence and stature as a church.

The first quarterly conference for which records exist (1772) was chaired by Francis Asbury,* newly appointed as Wesley's assistant, succeeding Richard Boardman and to be quickly succeeded by Thomas Rankin.* The six questions that defined its business disclose an American conference already searching for its own way. After "What are our collections?" and "How are the preachers stationed?" the conference asked, "Will the people be contented without our administering the sacrament?" The query tested the unity and authority for the little movement. Should Robert Strawbridge,* the planter of American Methodism, set policy by conniving at sacramental authority? And could English Methodist assumptions, particularly about the accessibility of the sacraments, apply to the colonial situation where the scarcity of Anglican churches and the infrequent availability of the eucharist in those few made conformity much less possible? Asbury's minuted answer indicated a divided house and divergent policy: "I told them I would not agree to it at that time, and insisted on our abiding by our rules. But Mr. Boardman had given them their way at the quarterly meeting held here before, and I was obliged to connive at some things for the sake of peace." Here already Asbury exercised authority (polity), putting a premium on the inner bonds within the conference, on the relationship between and among the preachers, and on the unity of the preachers. He captured the fraternal aspects of conference with a summary remark: "Great love subsisted among us in this meeting, and we parted in peace."[9] Asbury would exercise power in a fashion different from that of Wesley. He might pose the questions, but the answer as well as the discussion came from the entire fraternity.

The tensions between authority and fraternity surfaced more sharply under Wesley's next assistant, Thomas Rankin.[10] Rankin gathered the preachers in July for the first annual conference. He understood his charge and purpose as safeguarding Methodist discipline. Asbury had greeted his replacement with the notation, "He will not be admired as a preacher. But as a disciplinarian, he will fill his place."[11] Indeed, Rankin took his reading of the American situation and judged that "our discipline was not properly attended to, except at Philadelphia and New York; and even in those places it was upon the decline."[12] The first three questions of that first conference disclose Rankin's effort to bring the American Conference fully into conformity with British practice and fully subordinate to its authority and that of Wesley:

Ought not the authority of Mr. Wesley and that conference to extend to the preachers and people in America . . . ?

Ought not the doctrine and discipline of the Methodists, as contained in the minutes, to be the sole rule of our conduct . . . ?

If so, does it not follow, that if any preachers deviate from the minutes, we can have no fellowship with them till they change their conduct?[13]

Applying such principles to the divisive issue of the sacraments, conference decreed: "Every preacher who acts in connection with Mr. Wesley and the brethren who labor in America, is strictly to avoid administering the ordinances of baptism and the Lord's Supper."[14] By legislating on what might have been presumed to be beyond its legislative competence, conference set important precedents for itself and stumbled toward political competence, in some independence of Wesley's or the British Conference's will. Conference connived a competence that it had no right to. It did so on the strength of emerging bonds of fraternity.

Reinforcing the inertial pressures toward political competence were empowering bonds developing among the preachers, bonds both fraternal and spiritual in character. Such feelings Asbury noted for the annual conference of 1775:

"From *Wednesday* till *Friday* we spent in conference with great harmony and sweetness of temper."[15] Freeborn Garrettson,* admitted on trial at this conference, spoke of the company of preachers as "this happy family." He fainted and awoke in an upper room surrounded by preachers. They "appeared more like angels to me than men." Recalling the event some fifteen years later, he claimed to have "blessed my dear Lord ever since, that I was ever united to this happy family."[16] Asbury epitomized a quarterly conference early the next year in this fashion: "With mutual affection and brotherly freedom we discoursed on the things of God, and were well agreed."[17] William Watters put a similar construction on the annual conference of the following year: "We were of one heart and mind, and took sweet counsel together, not how we should get riches or honors, or anything that this poor world could afford us; but how we should make the surest work for heaven, and be the instruments of saving others."[18] In these intense gatherings, powerful currents of spirituality interplayed with the deepening affections among the preachers and the common obedience they accepted to the Methodist cause and its authority.

In its work, and particularly in the maintenance of its boundaries, conference wedded Methodist purpose and authority (polity) to fraternity and revival. Beginning with the 1774 conference, the minutes pose the questions that marked those initiated into probationary status, those being received into full connection with Wesley, and those to serve as his assistants. By these commitments the preachers bound themselves to the rules spelled out in the British minutes, rules that defined both order and mission. In that year and in every subsequent conference, a further question was put which obliged the conference to the scrutiny of each member. It read, "Are there any objections to any of the Preachers?" It was answered, "They were examined one by one."[19] This careful attention to one another's religious development was, and would continue to be, a powerful stimulant, heightening the spiritual character of conference proceedings, a censer that suffused the room with an infectious spirituality. Ideally then, the religious, fraternal and polity aspects of conference reinforced one another.

REVOLUTION

Under pressure of the Revolution and suspicions of Toryism that haunted the Methodist movement, a number of the English preachers, including Rankin, returned home. Asbury and several other preachers gathered prior to conference, "drew a rough draught for stationing the preachers the ensuing year," and decided on "a committee . . . to superintend the whole."[20] Both the extraordinary preparatory session and these actions can be understood as emergency measures necessitated by the Revolution; they nevertheless instanced fraternity usurping polity, conference as a fraternity of preachers claiming authority that belonged to Wesley or his assistant. American Methodist independence rode as much on the authority that this fraternity of preachers had connived, this spiritual declaration of independence, as it did on the prerogatives conferred on it later by Wesley. Indeed, a single line in Asbury's journal captures the dynamics of American Methodist independence. After this preparatory session, Asbury reported, "And on *Monday* we rode together to attend the conference at Deer Creek."[21] Conference was to be a cavalry that rode together.

That conference had to wrestle with the future of American Methodism without its deputized leader, Rankin. It found interim solutions in fraternal authority—the supervising committee and a plan for "a future union" based on "some articles of agreement" pledging devotion to God, adherence to "the old Methodist doctrine," and commitment to "observe and enforce the whole Methodist Discipline."[22]

The implications of such fraternal authority became evident in the conferences of 1778 and 1779. In 1778, the chair of the supervising committee, William Watters presided. (The Wesley-appointed preacher, former "assistant," and second in rank to the departed Rankin, might have logically taken leadership but had gone into hiding.[23]) The matter of the sacraments resurfaced and was again, but with great difficulty, deferred.[24]

The following year American Methodism fought its first schism. Two conferences were held. The first was an illegal, or at best irregular, gathering around Asbury in Delaware; the second, the regular conference, was called at Fluvanna, Virginia. The continuity of leadership and the historiographical tradition of Methodism run through the first, that specially convened by Asbury. Despite its irregularity, it has been treated as that year's link in the sequence of Methodist conferences. However, far more of the thematic agenda of Methodism flows though the second, that at Fluvanna, than Methodism's historians have been willing to concede.[25]

The first, ostensibly "considered . . . as preparatory to the conference in Virginia," was held for "the convenience of the preachers in the northern stations." It clearly acted to preempt and forestall decisions pending in Virginia. It reasserted Wesley's and Methodism's commitment to avoid "a separation from the church, directly or indirectly"; it proclaimed Asbury the general assistant for America, largely because he had been appointed by Wesley; and it lodged a Wesley-like authority in that position. "How far," it asked, "shall the power of the General Assistant extend?" "Ans. On hearing every preacher for and against what is in debate, the right of determination shall rest with him according to the Minutes."[26]

The Fluvanna Conference proceeded, in quite contrary directions, toward the establishment of an American Methodist church. Making the fraternity of conference the fount of its religiosity and authority, Fluvanna reaffirmed the authority lodged in a committee with administrative and appointive powers and vested it also in a presbytery to be elected by conference. The latter was now empowered to ordain, and those ordained empowered to administer the sacraments in a simple, scriptural mode.[27] With the ordaining presbytery itself unordained and obliged to ordain itself, Fluvanna proceeded in a fashion theologically suspect but consistent with the principles of 1776, to assert conference's authority. Clear lines extend from this act to the church constructed in 1784, to African-American assertions of similar rights, and to later schisms that would more dramatically champion the competence of conference over and against episcopacy—those of James O'Kelly,* of the Methodist Protestants, of the Wesleyan Methodists, and of the Free Methodists.

The two conferences went their separate ways. Each reconvened the next year, although only the Northern Conference was to be represented in the (subsequently) printed minutes. That body's privileged posture was asserted in a series of queries posed by Asbury. They functioned to establish Asbury's leadership and that conference's sole legitimacy. Notably the Northern Conference answered yes to these questions:

Quest. 20. Does this whole conference disapprove the step our brethren have taken in Virginia?

Quest. 21. Do we look upon them no longer as Methodists in connexion with Mr. Wesley and us till they come back?[28]

The conference also prescribed conditions and procedure for unity, namely, suspension of the sacraments and meeting together in Baltimore.[29]

Acting to brake the declaration of conference independence, this meeting nevertheless took several other actions that in the long run worked on behalf of conference authority. One was a seemingly straightforward administrative decision to make the smaller conference unit, the quarterly conference, a two-day event, "to be held on Saturdays and Sundays when convenient." As we shall see, this created possibilities for the spiritual or revivalistic use of conference that were to be of immense importance.

Second, it legislated against slavery, declaring the institution "contrary to the laws of God, man, and nature, and hurtful to society," and it urged the preachers to convey "our disapprobation." It also required the "travelling Preachers who hold slaves, to give promises, to set them free." This significant legislative action added "non-slave holding" to the many Wesley-given expectations of a preacher. Of members of the fraternity, much could be expected. Thereafter, slavery and race were to function in complex, highly ambiguous ways throughout Methodist history in setting and maintaining the boundaries of conference, in determining what it meant to be a part of that fraternity, in identifying those who belonged and those who did not, and finally in tearing the Methodist fraternity asunder.

The next year, as we have seen, the schism was healed and the two branches rejoined. In this accord, the preachers established, or we should say reestablished, the foundations of American Methodism—a confraternity of preachers whose shared affections, mutual support, and unity (under superintendence) gave the movement both its political and its religious coherence.

SPACE AND TIME

Conference would increasingly serve also to define space and time—Methodist space and time. The principle had already been established by Wesley as a way of relating people (societies, classes, and bands) to preachers. Each quarter the preachers of a specific area and Methodist work, a circuit, gathered to care for discipline, business, and the religious needs of the movement. American Methodists adhered to the quarterly meeting design, thereby dividing Methodist land into quarterly conferences. As Methodism expanded, it added to itself by such quarterly units, the circuits. Jesse Lee charted Methodist expansion by the circuits taken in. For instance, in 1781 he noted the adherence of six new circuits.[30]

That same year, Methodism gave the annual conference a geographical meaning as well. In their brief schism over the sacraments, Methodist preachers had come to recognize the value of a division of the land by annual conference. While meeting in two conferences, the preachers apparently found the "convenience" of this arrangement to their liking. So in 1781 the now reunited body chose to meet in two sessions. They had not solved the conceptual problem of how two sessions could be politically and legislatively one. Consequently, they sought to explain the division to themselves.[31] They construed the two meetings as one conference. This style of governance, leaving the final determination of legislation to the meeting of the Baltimore session, permitted the elaboration of other conferences. It continued through and beyond the organizing 1784 Christmas Conference to 1787. Thus began the process by which conferences would be identified with specific terrain and conference (annual as well as quarterly) would become place. Eventually preachers as well as people would become affiliated with a specific conference.[32] Conference then would become a polity of place.

Conference had been and would always be a fraternity of time. In the conference of that same year, question 13 asked, "How are the Preachers stationed this year?" The answer began, "West Jersey—Caleb B. Pedicord, Joseph Cromwell," and then followed with twenty-four other circuit places and the preacher(s) appointed to them.[33] From the earliest minutes down to those of today, conference has, at each gathering, so connected preacher to place. And at quarterly meetings, and between them on the circuits, adjustment would be made and the actual appointments of each preacher laid out. Quarterly meeting also regulated the rhythms of the lower echelons of Methodist leadership—local preachers, exhorters, stewards. Quarterly meetings were the minute hand; conference served as the hour hand on the Methodist clock. At conference, the preacher was connected to place. That appointment stood until the next conference. Appointments lasted from conference to conference or until discipline, the pull of other responsibilities, ill health, or death claimed a preacher from his traveling.[34] Such claims were experienced as genuine losses to the fraternity, for preachers existed—they remained in time—only while active in the fraternity.

When preachers could not accept an appointment, they "located," thereby dropping out of conference time (and space). Death, of course, registered the most telling blow to conference's time. As the early preachers began to die, conference addressed itself to time's finitude. It did so explicitly for the first time in the regular (not the Christmas) conference of 1784. In that year the fraternity asked a new question: "What Preachers have died this year?"[35] That question became an important and regular feature of conference sessions and minutes. Conference marked time as well as space.

THE CHRISTMAS CONFERENCE

The events of late 1784 that, as we have seen already, established an independent episcopal church solidified the governing power of conference.[36] Key to that was Asbury's insistence upon confirmation of his selection for superintendency through election. A richly symbolic act, this gesture defined Asbury's relations with Thomas Coke,* with Wesley, and with the conference. President of the American Conference by Wesley's appointment, by default at Rankin's departure, by resolution of the Fluvanna schism, and by formal conference action in 1782,[37] Asbury established a constitutional principle by insisting on election to the episcopacy. Episcopacy would rest on conference's assent (as on Wesley's).

The gathering to which Asbury made this significant declaration—a quarterly meeting at Barratt's Chapel—took a second act of similar symbolic proportions. "It was agreed," reported Asbury, "to call a general conference, to meet at Baltimore the ensuing Christmas."[38] Several points about this call deserve remark: (1) A conference seemed requisite for establishing an independent episcopal church. (2) No such conference had been intended. (3) The call for it was effected by another conference, specifically a quarterly conference.[39] As for Asbury the bishop, so also for the Methodist Episcopal Church (MEC) as a whole, power and authority would derive both from Wesley and from the existing American Conference.[40]

No minutes apparently survive from the conference that met at Christmas 1784,[41] nor a full roster of those in attendance. German Methodism was symbolically present in the person of William Otterbein,* who participated in Asbury's ordination to the episcopacy, and tradition places one or more of the black Methodist preachers there.[42] The journal entries and memoirs of key participants were surprisingly spare, but they clearly indicate that conference acted to constitute the church. Asbury noted, "We then rode to Baltimore, where we met a few preachers: it was agreed to form ourselves into an Episcopal Church, and to have superintendents, elders, and deacons. . . . We spent the whole week in conference, debating freely, and determining all things by a majority of votes."[43] In "determining all things by a majority of votes," conference claimed supremacy for itself. It proclaimed its supremacy also by its production of the Discipline—by editing "The Large Minutes," which Wesley had so single-handedly and guardedly constructed—so exercising its authority to establish a governing manual for the church.[44] Conference granted to itself supreme electoral, disciplinary, and legislative power formally in the act of and through the letter of legislation. For instance, it reserved to itself the power already exercised of electing the bishops or superintendents (question 26). It made the bishop "amenable for his Conduct" to "the Conference" (question 27). It did not, however, define its own powers or limit its powers, save (1) in recognizing the authority of the bishops elected and (2) in prescribing a continuing oversight to Wesley. Conference symbolized its sense of political self-confidence by publishing its own minutes, which, as Jesse Lee* noted, it had not previously done but did thereafter.[45]

THE BALTIMORE CONFERENCE SYSTEM[46]

Conference's political competence was tested in the years after 1785 as it strove to exercise authority over a rapidly growing and far-flung work; to clarify its relation to the superintendents and particularly to Bishop Coke, who moved back and forth across the Atlantic; and to find the appropriate way of honoring the debt to and immense influence of Wesley without jeopardizing American jurisdiction and authority.

The premium on conference's political function increased the tension with conference's other values—fraternity and revival. An immediate issue pitted polity against fraternity. How could a conference, which had already divided itself into three sessions so that all the brothers could conveniently attend, act in unity? How could it legislate as one body when it was—as in 1785—an April conference at Green Hill's, North Carolina, May in Virginia, and June at Baltimore. Lee noted that in earlier years conference had simply adjourned from one site to another but "Now there were three, and no adjournment." The resolution was awkward: "The business of the three conferences was all arranged in the minutes as if it had all been done at one time and place."[47] Unity was achieved by granting preeminence to the last conference held, that in Baltimore. Baltimore enjoyed the final say on legislation, rules, and the Discipline. That resolution had preceded the Christmas Conference, dated from 1780, and reflected the victory in the Fluvanna division of the northern preachers. The arrangement Jno. J. Tigert termed "the Baltimore Conference system of government in American Methodism."[48] It lasted only until 1787.

In that year Wesley claimed the authority over the American movement that he regarded as his, ordering the calling of a general conference and the appointing of Richard Whatcoat* and Freeborn Garrettson as superintendents.[49] The first conference that met, that in South Carolina, apparently acceded to Wesley's wishes and elected Whatcoat. In Virginia, however, James O'Kelly objected strenuously to this exercise of British authority.[50] O'Kelly voiced concerns about Wesley's relationship to and authority over the American bishops and American Methodism and more abstractly, the power of superintendency—whether that of Wesley or of Coke and Asbury—vis-à-vis conference. Would conference permit the sort of superintendency exercised by Wesley of proposing and disposing? O'Kelly tested the limits of conference power; he also tested the political integrity and unity of this brotherhood, the conference as fraternity. Could the fraternity, when in fact divided into more than one conference, act sufficiently in unity to exercise the authority it had claimed in the Discipline? The Virginia crisis was Baltimore's to resolve.

The Baltimore Conference rejected Wesley's proposal of Whatcoat as bishop, ignoring Coke's appeal to the rubric of the Discipline that pledged the fraternity to be his (Wesley's) "Sons in the Gospel, ready in Matters belonging to Church-Government, to obey his Commands."[51] It put conditions on Garrettson's nomination that led him to reject the office. It stripped the above binding rubric from the Discipline. It exacted from Coke a signed affidavit pledging not to exercise his superintendency while absent from the United States and limiting that office while in America to ordaining, presiding, and traveling. It also unceremoniously dropped the name of John Wesley from the designated superintendents.[52] These actions vindicated Asbury as well as the conference and were partially motivated by apprehension that the election of Whatcoat might permit Wesley to recall Asbury.[53] Yet they did indeed, and in the face of formidable exercises of authority by both Wesley and Coke, reassert conference's political competence. These acts did not resolve the *how* question—how an expanding Methodism could sustain political cohesion and integrity. And conference actually exacerbated the problem by appointing six conferences for 1788. Seven were held according to Lee, the last of which was in Philadelphia, not Baltimore. And for 1789, eleven conferences met, Baltimore falling near the middle of the schedule. The Baltimore system was the first of many casualties of Methodist growth.

MULTIPLE CONFERENCES AND COUNCIL

The division of conference, though undermining the unity of the fraternity, had preserved the size and intensity of conference that made fraternity possible, that made conference's many specified functions possible. A large conference could simply not devote the careful attention to the religious state and progress of both probationer and member that the Discipline and the minutes prescribed. The divided conference permitted that scrutiny. Conference continued to be a time in which each preacher's gifts and graces were carefully sifted and weighed in the ore-detecting system devised by Wesley. The minutes record the decisive question and answer:

Quest. 9. Are all the preachers blameless in life and conversation?

Ans. They were all strictly tried, one by one, before the conference.[54]

By this exercise of discipline by the fraternity over itself, the ministerium shed its ineffective members, rejected those not fit, physically and spiritually, for the rigors of itinerancy, and dealt with theological heterodoxy. Discipline defined fraternity. It did so judicially by determining who was to be elder, who deacon, who in full connection, who on trial, who to desist from traveling, who died.[55] It did so psychologically and socially by defining and maintaining boundaries of the Methodist fraternity. It did so spiritually and emotionally by heightening the commitment of those sustained to one another. Submitting to and going through these annual trials bound brother to brother. The hearing of one another's spiritual pilgrimage, the recounting of spiritual struggles, the probing of each other's soul, and the description of conversion and narrative of perfection functioned to establish familial bonds, to mark the brother and mark off the brotherhood. On this spiritual level, especially, discipline delineated the contours of fraternity.[56]

A fraternity so constituted nourished revival among the people who attended its preaching. The spirituality within the fraternity readily spilled outward, and conferences, both annual and quarterly, became revivalistic occasions. Jesse Lee, Methodism's first historian, reported in 1787 a considerable revival in southern Virginia in connection with quarterly meetings:

At one quarterly meeting held at Mabry's chapel in Brunswick circuit, on the 25th and 26th of July, the power of God was among the people in an extraordinary manner: some hundreds were awakened; . . . one hundred souls were converted. . . . Some thousands of people attended. . . .

The next quarterly-meeting was held at *Jones's* chapel in *Sussex* country, on Saturday and Sunday the 27th and 28th of July. This meeting was favoured with more of the divine presence than any other that had been known before. . . .

Soon after this, some of the same preachers who had been at the quarterly-meetings mentioned above, held a meeting at Mr. F. Bonners, ten miles from *Petersburg*, where a large concourse of people assembled; and the Lord wrought wonders among them on that day. As many as fifty persons professed to get converted. . . .

They had another meeting at *Jones-Hole* church; about twelve miles from *Petersburg*, and many people assembled. . . . On that day many souls were brought into the liberty of God's children.[57]

The following year Lee reported more general and extensive revivals, particularly in Virginia, North Carolina, and Maryland. That in Maryland culminated at the conference held in Baltimore, at which time Lee noted, "We were highly favoured of the Lord, and souls were awakened, and converted."[58] Methodists expected conference, both the annual gatherings and the quarterly meetings, to deepen the spirituality of the movement, to revive. And their way of doing business made provision for this expectation. In particular, they allowed the probationary, disciplinary, and judicial trying of one another's spiritual state its natural spiritual force. The unity of spirituality and business, actually of all three ideals—polity (business), spirituality (revival), and unity (fraternity)—is tersely captured by Asbury's (1791) typical entries for conference meetings:

[W]e opened conference in great peace. Many of the preachers related their experience, and it was a blessed season of grace. . . . Several of our brethren expressed something like the perfect love of God. . . .

The business of our conference was brought on in peace; and there was a blessing attended our speaking on our experiences, and in prayer.

Our conference began, and was conducted in much peace and harmony amongst preachers and people. Our meetings in public were attended with great power.

We had a tender, melting account of the dealings of God with many souls; and settled our business in much peace.

. . . We had a fast day; and in the afternoon a feast of love. It was a time to be remembered: some precious souls were converted.

We attended to the business of the conference with a good spirit. In the course of our sitting we had some pleasing and some painful circumstances to excite our feelings.

Our conference came together in great peace and love. Our ordinary business was enlivened by the relation of experiences, and by profitable observations on the work of God.[59]

Conference's spiritual intensity, exercise of discipline, and tightening of fraternal bonds proved favorable to revival. Fraternity's bonds and boundaries had a less favorable and pleasant aspect as well. To this traveling brotherhood, some who felt called were not elected—African-Americans, local preachers, the laity, women. The first who offered themselves only to be repudiated were African-American Methodists. Already in 1787 the color line around conference had been faintly etched by Richard Allen and black Methodists of Philadelphia who had by that time taken as much racial affront as they could stand. Their separation prefigured a later delineation of conference's boundaries. This fraternity would observe the color line.[60] Black Methodists would have to form their own conference to achieve what all American Methodists had sought in the years leading up to the 1784 Christmas Conference and to which, ironically, Allen may have been a witness.[61] Methodist fraternity was not achieved, then, without cost. The personal costs have always been noted—the terrible toll on the preachers that itinerancy exacted. Its social costs—the lines drawn and the classes excluded thereby—were no less severe.

The eleven conferences of 1789—through all of which legislation had to pass—established the unwieldiness of Methodism's political apparatus and prompted a short-lived and, as we have seen, unpopular solution, a council. The council possessed features well devised to doom it—its appointed rather than elected composition, the provision that all decisions required unanimity,[62] and the stipulation that legislation would be binding only if concurred in by each conference, a "dangerous clause," Lee thought, prone to divide the connection.[63]

Although in its first meeting the council addressed itself to and adopted a constitution that remedied these three glaring defects, it continued to be an affront to the fraternity of preachers, particularly to those portions thereof influenced by O'Kelly. The second meeting of the council did not stem the tide of opposition. O'Kelly had, in fact, rallied Coke to that side. Lee also played an important oppositional role. Nevertheless, as its minutes attest, the council did show a capacity to act, to initiate, to address itself to the connection's needs, a political capacity that had been missing. Methodism wanted for that administrative and legislative ability, for a body to frame policy.

NOTES

1. John Wesley, "Thoughts Upon Some Late Occurrences," [1785] in *The Works of John Wesley*, ed. Thomas Jackson, 14 vols. (London, 1872; Grand Rapids, Michigan: Zondervan, 1958), vol. 8. Neely observed, "But let it not be supposed that the Conferences which Mr. Wesley called had any governing power. The members discussed, but Mr. Wesley decided. They debated, but he determined. Mr. Wesley was the government; and, though he invited the preachers to confer with him, he did not propose to abandon any of his original power. They had a voice by his permission, but he reserved the right to direct." Thomas B. Neely, *A History of the Origin and Development of the Governing Conference in Methodism, and Especially of the General Conference of the Methodist Episcopal Church* (New York: Hunt & Eaton, 1892), 9–10.

2. Frank Baker, "The People Called Methodists—3. Polity," *A History of the Methodist Church in Great Britain*, ed. Rupert Davies and Gordon Rupp (London: Epworth Press, 13: 1965), 1: 211–55, p. 242.

3. *Works* (Jackson), 13: 243. Wesley had earlier selected John Fletcher to succeed him. See Richard Heitzenrater, *Wesley and the People Called Methodists* (Nashville: Abingdon Press, 1995), 253–59, 282–84, 305–8; Baker, "The People Called Methodists," 244–45; Jno. J. Tigert, *A Constitutional History of American Episcopal Methodism*, 3d ed., rev. and enl. (Nashville: Publishing House of the Methodist Episcopal Church, South, 1908), 27–44. This 1784 document, known as the *Deed of Declaration*, was a legal instrument entered in the Chancery that formally transferred Wesley's authority and rights to Methodist property to a conference of individually named persons. See also Henry W. Williams, *The Constitution and Polity of Wesleyan Methodism* (London: Wesleyan Conference Office, [1880?]), 14–19.

4. Neely, *Governing Conference*, 70.

5. W. L. Doughty, *John Wesley: His Conferences and His Preachers* (London: City Road, 1944), 27.

6. "John Bennet's Copy of the Minutes of the Conferences of 1744, 1745, 1747 and 1748; With Wesley's Copy of Those for 1745," *Publications of the Wesley Historical Society* 1 (1896): 39.

7. See Tigert, *Constitutional History*, 575–76. This section of Tigert's work parallels "The Large Minutes" with the first Discipline of the American church. The five means of grace were taken over intact into the Discipline.

8. Frederick A. Norwood in *The Story of American Methodism* (Nashville: York: Abingdon Press, 1974), 70, breaks the development of Methodist structure at the Christmas Conference (1784) and therefore discerns three periods prior to that, 1769–73, 1773–79, and 1779–84.

9. *JLFA*, 1: 59–60, entry for 22 December 1772. For the next quarterly meeting (conference) Asbury minuted this summary: "The whole ended in great peace." *JLFA*, 1: 75.

10. Neely, *Governing Conference*, 99.

11. *JLFA*, 1: 80. For 3 June 1773.

12. "The Life of Mr. Thomas Rankin," in *Lives of Early Methodist Preachers*, ed. Thomas Jackson, 4th ed., 6 vols. (London, 1872), 5: 193.

13. *Minutes of the Methodist Conferences, Annually Held in America from 1773 to 1813, Inclusive* (New York: Daniel Hitt & Thomas Ware for the Methodist Connexion in the United States, 1813), 5. Cited also by Nathan Bangs in *A History of the Methodist Episcopal Church*, 12th ed., 4 vols. (New York: Carlton & Porter, 1860), 1: 78–79.

14. Ibid.

15. *JLFA*, 1: 156. For 16 May 1775. For conference see *Minutes of the Methodist Conferences, Annually Held in America; From 1773 to 1813, Inclusive*, 9–10.

16. The Experiences and Travels of Mr. Freeborn Garrettson (Philadelphia, 1791). Reprinted in *American Methodist Pioneer: The Life and Journals of the Rev. Freeborn Garrettson, 1752–1827*, ed. Robert Drew Simpson (Rutland, VT: Academy Books, 1984), 55. Compare Jesse Lee on his first conference as reported by Minton Thrift, *Memoir of the Rev. Jesse Lee, with Extracts from His Journals* (New York: N. Bangs & T. Mason for the Methodist Episcopal Church, 1823), 42.

17. *JLFA*, 1: 178. For 5 February 1776.

18. Cited by Tigert, *Constitutional History*, 85.

19. *Minutes of the Methodist Conferences, Annually Held in America; From 1773 to 1813, Inclusive*, 7.

20. *JLFA*, 1: 239. For 12 May 1777. For official gathering, see *Minutes of the Methodist Conferences, Annually Held in America; From 1773 to 1813, Inclusive*, 13–15.

21. *JLFA*, 1: 239.

22. Both doctrine and discipline carried the stipulation "as contained in the Minutes." "Minutes of a Conference held in Baltimore, May, 1777," a version kept by Philip Gatch and originally printed in the *WCA* (19 and 26 May 1837) and reproduced in Frederick A. Norwood, ed., *Sourcebook of American Methodism* (Nashville: Abingdon Press, 1982), 56.

23. Asbury's rank among the American preachers is indicated in his placement on the list of "assistants." During Rankin's tenure, Asbury's name came second. See the minutes of 1774, 1775, 1776, and 1777, *Minutes of the Methodist Conferences, Annually Held in America; From 1773 to 1813, Inclusive*, 7, 9, 11, and 13.

24. Tigert, *Constitutional History*, 94.

25. The most notable exception to this historiographical tradition is the great historian of the Methodist reformers Edward J. Drinkhouse. See his *History of Methodist Reform*, 2 vols. (Baltimore: Board of Publication of the Methodist Protestant Church, 1899), 1: 212–25. Tigert, *Constitutional History*, also evidences great sympathies for the southern or Virginia side. See chap. 7. Consult also Norwood, *The Story of American Methodism*, 91.

26. *Minutes of the Methodist Conferences*, 19–20.

27. Portions of the manuscript minutes are reproduced in *The Life and Times of the Rev. Jesse Lee* by Leroy M. Lee (Charleston: John Early for the Methodist Episcopal Church, South, 1848), 79–81, and also by Tigert, *Constitutional History*, 106–7. A fuller version can be found in the *WCA* 4 (26 May 1837): 18. Jesse Lee reported that for the

most part the Methodist people received the sacraments happily. Jesse Lee, *A Short History of the Methodists* (Baltimore, 1810; Rutland, VT: Academy Books, 1974), 69–70. This facsimile edition, hereafter cited as Lee, *Short History, 1810*.

28. *Minutes of the Methodist Conferences*, 26.

29. Ibid, 26. The Northern Conference also reaffirmed Asbury's position as general assistant, requiring his signature on licenses, thereby warranting good standing in the Methodist connection. It also reasserted its intention to remain within the Anglican Church. (Questions 8, 9, 12, 13) 24–25.

30. Lee, *Short History, 1810*, 75. The next year two circuits were taken in; and in 1783, eleven. Ibid., 79, 82.

31. *Minutes of the Methodist Conferences, Annually Held in America; From 1773 to 1813, Inclusive*, 28–29, for 1781. The title of that conference specified "Held at Choptank, State of Delaware, April 16, 1781, and Adjourned to Baltimore the 24th of Said Month." Quest. 2 asked, "Why was conference began at Choptank?" The answer: "To examine those who could not go to Baltimore, and to provide supplies for the circuits where the Lord is more immediately pouring out his Spirit." Tigert termed this development "the germ of the modern American Annual Conference." *Constitutional History*, 122. See also his discussion of "The Baltimore Conference System of Government," ibid., 523–31.

32. Tigert, *Constitutional History*, 123–24, observed: "To this day, according to the language of the Discipline, a preacher is 'admitted on trial,' not into a particular Annual Conference, but 'into the traveling connection.' The Annual Conferences arose and continue to arise from subdivisions of the Church, its territory, and its one body of ministers, who form what is technically called the 'travelling connection.' The Church did not arise from the amalgamation of Annual Conferences. The Annual Conference is thus a unit of administration, created first by the Superintendents for their convenience and that of the preachers, and later by the authority of the General Conference. This unit of administration is territorial, for, within its prescribed boundaries, every Annual Conference, great or small, exercises precisely the same powers, under the same rules and regulations."

33. *Minutes of the Methodist Conferences, Annually Held in America; From 1773 to 1813, Inclusive*, 30–31.

34. Beginning with 1779, the question would be posed thus: "Who desist from travelling?" *Minutes of the Methodist Conferences, Annually Held in America; From 1773 to 1813, Inclusive*, 18.

35. Ibid., 48. The next year, conference began a practice still honored of entering a biographical sketch of the "brother" who had died. Initially each sketch was no more than a sentence. Lee observed of the initiation of the notice: "This was a new plan, and it was a very proper and profitable one. By it we might know when our preachers left the world. Previous to this we had taken no account in our minutes of the death of any of our travelling preachers." *Short History, 1810*, 87.

36. This is the title and theme of Thomas B. Neely's volume, *A History of the Origin and Development of the Governing Conference in Methodism*.

37. A question that year asked: "Do the brethren in conference unanimously choose brother Asbury to act according to Mr. Wesley's original appointment, and preside over the American conferences and the whole work?" *Minutes of the Methodist Conferences, Annually Held in America; From 1773 to 1813, Inclusive*, 37, Quest. 19. The answer was yes. This formulation warranted Asbury's authority on two grounds: (1) appointment

by Wesley and (2) selection by conference. See Tigert, *Constitutional History*, 136. Its twofold derivation was reasserted in the (regular) annual conference of 1784 in the formula by which European preachers were to be deemed acceptable. They were to have standing if, among other qualifications, they would "be subject to Francis Asbury as General Assistant, whilst he stands approved by Mr. Wesley, and the conference." *Minutes of Several Conversations between the Rev. Thomas Coke, LL.D., the Rev. Francis Asbury, and Others at a Conference Begun in Baltimore, in the State of Maryland, on Monday, the 27th of December, in the Year 1784. Composing a Form of Discipline for the Ministers, Preachers, and Other Members of the Methodist Episcopal Church in America* (Philadelphia: Charles Cist, 1785), 48, Quest. 21.

38. *JLFA*, 1: 427.

39. Jno. J. Tigert, *The Making of Methodism: Studies in the Genesis of Institutions* (Nashville: Publishing House of the Methodist Episcopal Church, South, 1898), 86.

40. Frank Baker, *From Wesley to Asbury* (Durham, NC: Duke University Press, 1976), 162.

41. Journals and memoirs of participants provide the detail. See especially that of Bishop Thomas Coke excerpted in *The Arminian Magazine* 1 (1789): 290–92.

42. See Norman W. Spellman's discussion in *The History of American Methodism*, ed. Emory S. Bucke, 3 vols. (New York: Abingdon Press, 1964), 1: 215–16. (Hereafter cited as HAM.)

43. *JLFA* (18 December 1784). Compare the account in *The Life and Travels of Rev. Thomas Ware* (New York: G. Lane and P. P. Sandford for the Methodist Episcopal Church, 1842), 105–7.

44. The handiwork of the Christmas Conference can best be observed in Tigert's parallel reproduction of "The Large Minutes" and first Discipline, in *Constitutional History*, 532–602. On preparatory work toward that editing, see P. P. Sandford, *Memoirs of Mr. Wesley's Missionaries to America* (New York: G. Lane & P. P. Sandford for the Methodist Episcopal Church, 1843), 365–66.

Whether American Methodism had a constitution at this stage and, if so, in what it consisted is a matter of some debate. See, for instance, James M. Buckley, *Constitutional and Parliamentary History of the Methodist Episcopal Church* (New York: Methodist Book Concern, 1912), 121–27. It is instructive that the second Discipline carried this title: "The General Minutes of the Conferences of the Methodist Episcopal Church in America, forming the Constitution of the said Church." *The Sunday Service of the Methodists In the United States of America* (London, 1786).

45. Lee, *Short History, 1810*, 89, 100.

46. This is Tigert's formulation and the title of a chapter in his *Making of Methodism*.

47. Lee, *Short History, 1810*, 118.

48. Tigert, *The Making of Methodism*, 147–57.

49. See Part 1 of this text and *JLFA*, 3: 49.

50. *JLFA*, 3: 53. The letter extends from p. 51 to p. 53.

51. Quest. 2 in Tigert, *Constitutional History*, 534.

52. *JLFA*, 3 (2 May 1787). The minutes for that year reflect Coke's abdication.

Quest. 1. Who are the Superintendents of our church for the United States?

Ans. Thomas Coke, (when present in the States) and Francis Asbury.

Minutes of the Methodist Conferences, Annually Held in America; From 1773 to 1813, Inclusive, 62.

After this, the term "superintendent" is changed to "bishop." See discussion in the first part of this text. Tigert observed: "Thus in 1787—not in 1784—the American Methodist Episcopal Church fully and finally asserted its autonomy." *The Making of Methodism*, 156.

53. Lee, *Short History, 1810,* 126.

54. *Minutes of the Methodist Conferences, Annually Held in America; From 1773 to 1813, Inclusive,* 1787, 64.

55. Ibid., 62–64.

56. See Asbury's directives in this regard. *JLFA,* 3: 100–101. Dated 29 May 1791, New York, New York.

57. Lee, *Short History,* 1810, 129–33.

58. Ibid., 138–40. Compare the accounts by Richard Whatcoat for quarterly meetings the following year in Sandford, *Memoirs of Mr. Wesley's Missionaries to America,* 367–68.

59. These are entries for conferences in North Carolina (March 30), Petersburg (April 20), Duck Creek, MD (May 10), Chester (May 17), Trenton (May 22), and New York (May 26). *JLFA,* 1: 671–75. Asbury took careful measure of the peace and harmony of each meeting because of the lingering controversy over the council. See discussion in Chapter 5.

60. See Carol V. R. George, *Segregated Sabbaths: Richard Allen and the Rise of Independent Black Churches, 1760–1840* (New York: Oxford University Press, 1973), and *The Life Experience and Gospel Labors of the Rt. Rev. Richard Allen,* 2d ed. (New York: Abingdon Press, 1960); Will B. Gravely, "African Methodisms and the Rise of Black Denominationalism," in *Rethinking Methodist History,* ed. Russell E. Richey and Kenneth E. Rowe (Nashville: Kingswood Books, 1985), 111–24; and *POAM,* 108–26.

61. George, *Segregated Sabbaths,* 43, casts doubt on this possibility.

62. Tigert noted that this "virtually gave Bishop Asbury—for Bishop Coke was not present at either of the sessions held—an absolute veto on all proposed legislation." *Constitutional History,* 244. Of course, it gave every member such a veto, but since the elders, "presiding elders" in the language of the plan, served at the bishop's pleasure, the power of the bishop was effectively magnified.

63. Lee, *Short History, 1810,* 150. Tigert used the term "nullification" to describe the potential effect of this provision. *Constitutional History,* 245. Lee excerpts liberally from the minutes of the 1789 and 1790 meetings of the Council of Bishops, 151–59. See also the published versions, seven- and eight-page documents, entitled differently each year: *The Proceedings of the Bishop and Presiding Elders of the Methodist-Episcopal Church, in Council Assembled, at Baltimore, on the First Day of December, 1789* (Baltimore, 1789) and *Minutes Taken at a Council of the Bishop and Delegated Elders of the Methodist Episcopal Church: Held at Baltimore in the State of Maryland, December 1, 1790* (Baltimore, 1790).

5
GENERAL CONFERENCE:
A CONTINENTAL ORDER

1791 proved a momentous year for American Methodism. John Wesley died on 2 March. Late conferences that year took observance of his passing. The Council also died that year. Both deaths resolved important questions about the nature and exercise of authority in American Methodism.

A General Conference had been mooted but dismissed when the plan for a council was initially introduced.[1] Jesse Lee* and James O'Kelly* continued to prefer a conference, the latter persuading Thomas Coke* by correspondence, and the three carried the connection. The first General Conference was called for November 1792. It left its record in the Discipline, which it revised.[2] Several of its actions had long-term consequences for the nature of conference in Methodism. Perhaps most importantly, it decided to convene again in four years in a conference "to which, all the preachers in full connection were at liberty to come."[3] That plenary definition of itself, its claim to a future and its assumption of the authority to legislate, specifically to revise the Discipline—two-thirds majority being required for new actions or total rescission of existing legislation but only a majority to amend—provided what Asbury had sought through the Council, namely, a politically competent and sovereign center to the movement.[4] General Conference also claimed the right to elect and try bishops.[5] Thus, said Jno. J. Tigert, "this body became the permanent organ of connectional government in American Methodism."[6]

The General Conference also gave further impetus toward what would in the future be termed annual conferences by authorizing the uniting of two or more of the districts (the purview of the presiding elders) and between three and twelve circuits (the assignment of the traveling preachers).[7] Here, as in the case of General Conference, annual conference is defined, in the Discipline, by its membership—the traveling preachers in full connection. Its leadership was also given formal definition by recognizing presiding elders and assenting to the bishops' authority to select, station, and change them.[8] It also limited the term of presiding elders in one place to four years. In this action, the fraternity of preachers expressed its apprehension over the growing power and independence of this potentially aristocratic office. It was a worry dramatized in the style of a specific presiding elder, James O'Kelly, an individual with a penchant for autonomy.[9]

FRATERNITY CHALLENGED

That worry had already proved itself well placed. The second day of General Conference, O'Kelly had placed a motion giving preachers who thought themselves "injured" by the bishop's appointment the "liberty to appeal to the conference" and the right, if the appeal was sustained, to another appointment.[10] A long and eloquent debate followed. O'Kelly and his partisans made appeal to the language or ideology of republicanism—the rhetoric of the Revolution and the American Republic—that powerful strain of radical Whiggery that bifurcated social reality into a people with real but fragile rights versus authority whose natural tendency was to tyranny and usurpation of rights. The liberties of the people demanded collective resolve on the part of the people, a unity founded in virtue, watchful monitoring of authority, forceful response against authority's inducements, and resistance to luxury. Liberty and virtue were easily corrupted and the people's resolve dissipated; authority was ever encroaching; freedom's hope demanded vigilance; unless liberty were defended, the people would be reduced to slavery. So taught the history of republics.[11]

Republicanism gave forceful and meaningful expression to those powerful but inchoate tendencies that we have termed "fraternity," those bonds that bound preacher to preacher, member to member. And there was much in the preachers' experience that found resonance in O'Kelly's republican motion. Had they not been injured by appointments? Did not Coke and Asbury connive to increase their power? Had they not had to check episcopal tyranny already? Was not the preachers' liberty in danger? Would it not be better safeguarded in conference rather than in episcopal hands?[12] The rhetoric had appeal. The motion might have passed but for the spirit with which the campaign was led and the radical character of the argument.[13] The motion failed.[14] O'Kelly walked out with a party of supporters to form a rival movement that took the republican banner into its name.[15] O'Kelly's was not the first Methodist fracturing of fraternity. The controversy over the sacraments and ordination had earlier more completely divided the young movement. Black Methodists under Richard Allen* had initiated a break in Philadelphia that would be imitated across the church by the creation of separate African congregations and would lead in the decades ahead to full-fledged separate denominations.[16] And at roughly the same time that O'Kelly rallied opposition in Virginia and North Carolina, William Hammett took a course toward independence in Charleston. There, too, the authority of Asbury was challenged. However, O'Kelly was at this juncture perceived to be the greatest threat, in part because he mounted a Republican cause.

The Republican language captured the powerful egalitarian sentiments of the fraternity of preachers.[17] The Republicans emblemed that egalitarianism with the antislavery banner. They did so at a point when the Methodist Episcopal Church was already finding antislavery problematic. The Republican schism, then, drained off antislavery sentiment from the church. In so doing, it may well have opened a less egalitarian door for the larger Methodist body. So also the Republican Methodist departure represented the loss to the connection—at least to that generation in the connection—of this very significant intellectual expression to and interpretation of fraternity. Methodism would face other challenges from within that appealed to fraternity with Republican imagery—African-Americans, the Methodist Protestants, the Wesleyans, the Free Methodists.

CHAPTERS

With the two creations of 1792—annual conferences and general conferences—Methodism now ordered itself through conference: general conferences every four years for the entire connection, annual conferences for each region, quarterly conferences for the circuits, and weekly conferencelike structures in society and class in communities across the new nation. The three explicitly named conference structures, quarterly, annual, and general, each had a turn in the overall governance of the movement. The succession of these efforts, the search for political stability, and the untidy evolution of governance had distributed certain functions at one level, others at another. It would be tempting to conclude that the three ideals of conference had lodged themselves successfully in the three conference levels: polity in general conference, fraternity in annual conference, and revival in quarterly (conference) meeting. In fact, each level of conference sought to preserve all three ideals, each continued important aspects of the conference structure that had previously guided American Methodism, and each found it difficult to resist polity's tendency to encroach on fraternity and revival.

Polity's ascendancy came as Methodists faced perplexities in living out their ideals in a new and rapidly expanding society. Their struggles were gargantuan: the testing of limits and possibilities under the emerging rules of voluntarism and toleration; the pressures of religious competition; the demands put on religious structure for social, political, and legal services, especially under frontier conditions; the opportunities and burdens presented groups willing to assume responsibility for order in American society as a whole. Growth alone proved more than Methodists could handle. In coping with growth, Methodists struggled to make General Conference more politically accountable, finally following civil precedent to a delegated or representative model; they put boundaries on annual conferences, thereby stabilizing their membership; and they found a new vehicle for the revivalistic force of quarterly meetings. In the first decade of the new century, growth wrought subtle changes in polity, fraternity, and revival; it wrought subtle changes in all three levels of conference. Its effects on the annual conference level were most immediate and obvious.

The number of annual conferences had continued to expand—seventeen in 1792 according to Lee,[18] and nineteen in 1793. Lacking fixed membership or boundaries, they went year round, throwing the Methodist sense of both time and place into chaos. Lee viewed the multiplication of conferences and length of the conference season as damaging to the fraternity's rhythms, as fragmenting the once unified brotherhood into bodies out of touch with one another, as frustrating fraternal communication.[19] The evidence suggests that these men who quite often rode together, who called each other yoke-fellows, who shared the adversities of the itinerancy, who coached each other on ministry—that these men did indeed cherish their time together and when apart cherished whatever communication was possible.[20] James Meachem made this entry in his journal: "May 26, 1792 rode to Hanover Town to meet with my Elder bro J. E. who brought in several Letters from Sundry Brothers, we had sweet union while Together, my soul thinks it a great blessing to be with the Elder Brethren & Preachers."[21]

Sentiments like these lend some plausibility to Lee's construction. The fraternity had become genuinely perplexed by its own fragmentation. So in 1796 the General Conference legislated both the number and the boundaries of the conferences, establishing on the North American landscape six geographically defined conferences. The fraternity sought the reduction in number and increase in conference size.[22] It was the specification of boundaries that would in time both give new life to fraternity and most alter its character. That produced the notion, enunciated in 1804, that a preacher actually belonged to one conference, a view foreign to a collegium that had been deployed across the entire connection. Conference membership came into Methodist thought.[23]

Henceforth, Methodism's fraternity would be divided into relatively cohesive regional bodies. Movement between conferences would continue, though lessening as the years passed, but even that movement underscored the new walls that had been established within, for thereafter redeployment of preachers amounted to more than just a new episcopal appointment; it involved the changing of membership. Methodism's fraternity had acquired internal boundaries. Determining the boundaries of conferences would be the work of successive General Conferences; in 1816 the task deserved the creation of the Committee on Temporal Economy; and by 1820 a general conference structuring itself with standing committees established the Committee on Boundaries.[24]

Another item of legislation in 1796 also increased the cohesion of annual conferences. That was a social boundary for conference. In answer to a question posed in the Wesleyan manner, "Who shall attend the yearly conferences?" General Conference decreed:

Those who are in full connexion, and who are to be received into full connexion.

N.B. This regulation is made that our societies and congregations may be supplied with preaching during the conferences.[25]

Though ostensibly motivated by the concern to keep those on trial and local preachers back on the circuits, the effect was to return conference to the more closed affair established by Wesley. This decision, too, would strengthen the fraternity—of traveling preachers—by delineating its social boundaries, reinforcing those drawn by region, by status, and by race.

What made Methodism open, expansive, and inclusive in one respect closed it in others. Whether so intended or not, this 1796 legislation served to make conference an all-white affair.[26] Three years later Richard Allen was ordained a deacon. Though under the supervision of the Philadelphia Conference, he as a deacon would not be a member of it. The next year, in 1800, General Conference gave formal authorization to such "African" ordinations but set the ceiling for African leadership to deacon only and chose not to print the legislation, in deference, Lee reported, to the preachers from the southern states. "This rule is at present," in 1810, when Lee wrote, "but little known among the Methodist preachers themselves, owing to its having never been printed; yet it is a regular rule which has been standing for nine years."[27]

By the time that Lee wrote, annual conferences symbolized and exercised the boundary-keeping function by establishing an office—that of doorkeeper.[28] The doorkeeper did not, in fact, watch to keep out African-Americans or to discourage German attendance, but the office stood for the exclusive character of the fraternity.

A more decisive doorkeeping, as we noted earlier, constituted the main business of conference: assessing those who presented themselves to be admitted on trial and ordained deacon, reviewing the character and process of those on trial, and determining who would be admitted into full connection and ordained elder. The boundary maintenance work of the conference becomes more visible after 1800 when General Conference mandated that each annual conference appoint a secretary to keep its records.[29] Entries from the New England Conference indicate how seriously this work was taken and how deeply invested in it the entire conference became: Joshua Soule,* "a man of great tallents, so called, he being absent was examined, and tho' brother Taylor, who spoke concerning him tho't him in great danger of highmindness, Yet he with others judged that if brother Soule continued humble and faithful, he would become a useful Minister in our Church, and Connection. He, sustaining a good moral character, is continued on trial."[30] In such reviews, the conference did not mince words or spare feelings.[31]

In determining its membership, conferences showed a decided preference for the unmarried. In 1806, New England reviewed twenty-one candidates for admission on trial, accepting only two married men, rejecting three candidates, two of them married, the only single person rejected being of "doubtful; or singular character."[32] Asbury certainly shared the conference's preference for single preachers. He viewed marriage as inimical to Methodist ministry. At the Virginia Conference in 1809, he found only three married men, apparently of the eighty-four present, noted that marriage to a Methodist preacher was socially disdained, and celebrated the singleness that disdain produced.[33] So Methodism drew boundaries around its ministry; so it found boundaries drawn; so groups of largely young, white males in each region of the country shared their intense religious experiences, committed themselves to go where sent, and bound themselves into a fraternity they called conference.

Methodists still desired that conference serve the revivalistic purposes that it had previously. So they found places within conference rhythms to make space for public events: "On Saturday Conference closed by singing and prayer, after which the ordination of the Deacons took place & on Sabbath, a Lovefeast was held, five sermons were preached, the Eucharist administered to about 230 communicants, & Epaphras Kibby, Comfort C. Smith, Asa Heath, Daniel Webb, & Reuben Hubbard, were ordained Elders, in the presence of nearly 3000 people, as it was judged."[34] Reports of this sort would continue for several decades. Even at General Conference, where the political function was paramount, the preachers sought to sustain the revivalistic ideal of conference by preaching on the side. Indeed, the General Conference of 1800 produced something of a revivalist wildfire that spread out from Baltimore, where conference sat to the Delmarva Peninsula.[35] Yet the primary revivalistic function of conference took another form, through quarterly meeting and increasingly through camp meeting.

QUARTERLY AND CAMP MEETINGS

Just when the new boundaries and the attention to prerogatives made conference less accessible to the Methodist people and less conducive to revival, Methodists discovered the camp meeting.[36] Despite its novelty, it looked familiar, a continuation of the established tradition of revivalistic quarterly meetings and annual conferences. The camp meeting proved to be ideally structured for the revivals that had been, in a sense, incidental to the business of the quarterly or annual conference and was unencumbered with the obligations to do church (conference) business.

Very quickly the Methodist connection took up the institution and began to promote it zealously. By late 1802 Asbury had taken the step that made manifest Methodism's recognition of itself in the camp meeting. He wrote to the preachers directing that they establish camp meetings in connection with conference. George Roberts of the Baltimore Conference was informed: "The campmeetings have been blessed in North and South Carolina, and Georgia. Hundreds have fallen and have felt the power of God. I wish most sincerely that we could have a campmeeting at Duck Creek out in the plain south of the town, and let the people come with their tents, wagons, provision and so on. Let them keep at it night and day, during the conference; that ought to sit in the meeting."[37]

Camp meetings become standard practice, and in just the way that Asbury specified. It became customary for Methodists to hold camp meetings in connection with conference.[38] Bishop McKendree* distinguished such a "campmeeting Conference" from other conferences.[39] Camp meetings became most affixed to the quarterly conference and especially to the quarterly meeting held typically in late summer.[40] The conjunction extended what had long been a great two-day Methodist festival and put a premium on the planning, preparation, attention to grounds and layout, provision for order, and liturgical staging that guaranteed success. Camp meetings stylized the conference revival, established revival and conversions as an expectation, and made what would otherwise have been an intra-Methodist and perhaps even intra-leadership occasion into a great annual public display.[41] Their promotion became a Methodist business and a central preoccupation of the person essential to any quarterly meeting, the presiding elder.[42] Indeed, the quarterly camp meeting became, particularly in the summer, the primary work of that official.[43]

The camp meeting then institutionalized conference as revival. And in the short run it preserved the revivalistic dimension of conference itself because camp meetings so frequently were held in conjunction with conference and particularly quarterly meetings. In the long run, this institutionalization and externalization of conference's revivalistic dimension permitted conferences themselves to become less revivalistic. The changes that altered conference's revivalistic substance came slowly and piecemeal and in what seemed like Methodist interest. It is curious, nevertheless, that they took the camp meeting so much to heart and saw no need to incorporate it into the body. It remained outside the polity and outside the Discipline.[44]

CONFERENCE BY DELEGATION

General Conference suffered no such exclusion. In sessions of 1800, 1804, and 1808 it acted to define itself and the church. Its political supremacy, as we have seen, was immediate and plenary. Gone were the days in which Asbury and Coke could huddle with a hand-picked few to rewrite Methodist polity. Polity and therefore politics would now be the business of General Conference. But like the other levels of conference, it yielded the other ideals—revival and fraternity—unwillingly and gradually. The revival associated with the conference of 1800 was not readily duplicated, but preaching for the larger community continued. Methodists struggled also to sustain General Conference's fraternal character. The early secretaries (up through 1808) did their part by minuting actions by brother this or that. But the so-called brothers found themselves divided on important issues.

One such question vexing these early General Conferences, as we have already seen, was the matter of membership. The principle "all in full connection" did not anticipate expanding territory and an expanding ministry nor did it put a premium on experience, wisdom, political savvy—the "gifts" sometimes guaranteed by seniority or office.[45] In 1800, General Conference restricted its membership, to those who "have travelled four years." That reduction and guarantee of some maturity did not address an equally serious matter, the misrepresentation of the several conferences. That misrepresentation led, as our earlier discussion indicates, to agitation for and finally the legislation of a delegated general conference. Soule's version of that legislation, that adopted, with this set of Restrictive Rules at its heart, came eventually to be regarded as the constitution of the church. From its introduction it was recognized as a critical turn in the denomination's history, granting the General Conference "full powers to make rules and regulations for our Church," subject to but six restrictions.[46]

Delegation made General Conference *the* political forum, the arena within which differences and disputes would be settled, and also the political prize. Thereafter, Methodism sent its leadership to General Conference. Election proved to be a highly significant and sought-after recognition. In addition, the delegates to General Conference would elect, typically from among their ranks, the bishops. The church has not been especially eager to recognize the political character of its life and the politicizing of General Conference. That oversight has served to obscure also the subtle but important changes that the politicizing of General Conference worked in the other levels of conference, but that is to anticipate the story.

COLOR AND LANGUAGE LINES

The same General Conference cast the "fraternity" of annual conferences "free" to deal separately with the matter of slavery, authorizing "each annual conference to form their own regulations relative to buying and selling slaves."[47] This was a major retreat from its forthright Wesleyan antislavery stance and from a racially inclusive fellowship.[48] On local levels, also, Methodists drew the color line, particularly in the North. Black local deacons, among them Richard Allen and Daniel Coker, took charge of the African classes and congregations. Functioning restively under white elders, the African-American leaders and congregations pressed for the prerogatives that would give them ecclesial legitimacy and standing, particularly ordination as elders and conference membership.[49] Frustrated, congregations in Baltimore, Philadelphia, Wilmington, and New York took steps toward establishing their own conferences.

One such in 1816 brought together delegates from Philadelphia; Salem, New Jersey; Baltimore; and Attleborough, Pennsylvania. The convention called itself the African Methodist Episcopal (AME) Church.[50] It ordained Richard Allen as bishop, created two conferences, and structured itself along Methodist lines.[51] A similar break of fraternity had already occurred in Wilmington. The leader of the "African chapel" there, Peter Spencer, though apparently present at the AME conference threw his efforts into making his African Union Church an alternative denomination.[52] So also in New York, although a few years later black Methodists gravitated hesitatingly toward independence, their situation complicated by involvement with William Stillwell, an elder who led a biracial schism. Eventually the New York–based movement stabilized as the African Methodist Episcopal Zion (AMEZ) Church.[53]

So Methodism segregated by conference, indeed, in totally separate denominational conference structures.[54] By these actions—black overtures for membership, white conference refusal, and black initiative to establish separate conferences (churches)—conference fraternity drew the color line. This boundary, once drawn, would prove very difficult to erase. Slavery, antislavery, and race would however continue to be conference issues.

Conferences drew other ethnic boundaries at this time, most notably that between German-speaking and English-speaking Methodists.[55] Here, too, prejudice, disdain for other peoples, and unwillingness to accommodate difference nullified initial efforts at unity and comity. Among the German-Americans, William Otterbein* and Martin Boehm* exercised leadership for the scattered Reformed and Mennonite peoples. The early developments were quite distinct from the Methodists, roughly contemporaneous but stylistically similar, owing to shared Pietist principles. Just prior to the Revolution, Otterbein convened other traveling preachers in a series of semiannual meetings held in and around Frederick and Baltimore. Again after the war—in 1789 and 1791—larger groups, including Boehm and other Mennonites, met. Both sets of gatherings concerned themselves with the order and discipline of German-speaking classes and congregations, tied together primarily by the bonds among their leadership. These bonds remained highly informal, however; formal conference structures were not established.

During this period Otterbein, Boehm, and others became familiar with the Methodists and the two groups recognized each other as kindred, a relationship symbolized by Otterbein's role in Asbury's ordination and Boehm's son's later extensive traveling with Asbury. In 1800 Otterbein and Boehm were elected bishops (or superintendents) in another conference in Frederick. Calling themselves the United Brethren in Christ, these thirteen or fourteen preachers, apparently at Asbury's urging, moved toward discipline along Methodist lines. They agreed, on a motion put by Otterbein, to have the Methodist Discipline translated into German. That translation came too late to be followed precisely; instead, Christian Newcomer* drafted a simpler set of rules (1808) accommodating established patterns of structure and belief; disagreements over discipline continued. Still, on both sides efforts were and would be made to bring the movements closer.

Newcomer intended his Discipline to serve as a basis for union not only with the Methodists but also with the other Methodistlike German denomination, the Evangelical Association. The latter, a movement among Lutherans led by Jacob Albright,* had closer Methodists ties. In its first formal conference in 1807, it had called itself the "Newly-Formed Methodist Conference" and charged Albright to draft articles of faith and a discipline.[56] Like Otterbein and Boehm, Albright came to appreciate Methodist structure and discipline through German Pietist religious experience. Soon after his conversion Albright was drawn by a neighbor and Methodist class leader into active leadership among Methodists. As a class leader and then a licensed exhorter, Albright began itinerant preaching among German-speaking communities in Pennsylvania, Maryland, and Virginia in the late 1790s. He apparently never broke formally with the Methodists but found it necessary to create structures to sustain himself and others who joined him in caring for the newly formed German classes and societies, an initiative necessitated by Asbury's disinterest in sustaining German-language work. At a conference in 1803, Albright was ordained and recognized as leader.[57] After the 1807 conference, age and health left him unable to carry through on the mandate to prepare a discipline, and so Albright left that task to his associate George Miller. Miller took advantage of the translation into German of the Methodist Discipline (of 1804) and "compiled Articles of Faith and Discipline, partly out of the Word of God, and partly according to the Episcopal form of church government."[58]

The Discipline was adopted by the annual conference of 1809, by which time the movement was terming itself "Those Designated as Albright's People."[59] Both Methodists and United Brethren made overtures for unity, some formal, some informal. Each group wanted accord on its own terms. In 1816 a general conference met and selected the name the Evangelical Association, both acts symbolizing that this fraternity would go its own way.

Language, race, ethnicity, ecclesial ancestry, polity differences, creedal matters, separate episcopal leadership—all provided legitimacy for broken brotherhood, for separate organization. Conference as polity served to give ecclesial integrity to divisions within the Methodist fraternity, indeed, to establish separate fraternities. Though separate, the several bodies shared the conference way of structuring the church. Quarterly, annual, and general conferences defined space and time; deployed and changed itinerants' circuits; committed each movement to revivalistic expansion; and provided the structural grammar in terms of which new territory would be conquered. Each of these denominations saw its mission in continental and world terms.

CONFERENCING THE CONTINENT

Beginning in 1796 when it established specific annual conference boundaries, General Conference directed the bishops "to appoint other yearly conferences . . . if a sufficiency of new circuits be anywhere formed," thus establishing a new pattern.[60] Conferences would march west with overall American settlement. Religious territories would emerge on the landscape much as political ones, indeed, in advance of the latter. So after reducing the number of conferences in the interest of communication, efficiency, and fraternal authority, the preachers authorized their increase as the church exploded west, north, and south: six in 1796, seven in 1800, nine in 1812, eleven in 1816, twelve in 1820 along with three provisos, seventeen in 1824, twenty-two in 1832, and twenty-nine in 1836.[61]

Much of the drama occurred on the circuit level as local preachers and itinerants blazed a Methodist path to isolated cabins and settlements.[62] That penetration began a pattern that culminated with the formation of conference—

settlement and lay witness, local preacher initiatives, formation of class(es), extension of existing circuits to incorporate them, visitation by the presiding elder or even the bishop, the division of the new area into a new circuit, erection of preaching houses, quarterly meetings and annual conferences in the region, and the establishment of a regional annual conference.[63] Knitting frontier folk into both church and society were the classes, quarterly meetings and camp meetings, in the movement westward continuing their function of consolidating those gained into the Methodist orbit.[64] The Methodist economy and the conference system—with its balanced ideals of revival, fraternity, and polity—functioned effectively to carry the Methodist message and mission west.[65] Having now given conferences specific geographical meaning, the church cared for expansion by cellular addition—new conferences—each of which would be a fraternity in its own right.

This expansive mission, this spirituality, required order. Indeed, spirituality and order, the freedom Methodists found through conversion and the discipline to which they subjected themselves and others, represent two sides of the evangelical impulse.[66] So conferences began to devote more exacting attention to their own political structure, to polity. Until the first decade of the nineteenth century, conferences depended on the questions of the Discipline for structure and procedure to their sessions. So in 1808, conferences attended closely to the following queries, minuted actions, and reported the results:[67]

1. Who are admitted on trial? 2. Who remain on trial? 3. Who are admitted into full connexion? 4. Who are the deacons? 5. Who have been elected and ordained Elders this year? 6. Who are the Bishops and Superintendents? 7. Who have located this year? 8. Who are the Supernumerary Preachers? 9. Who are the superannuated and worn-out Preachers? 10. Who have been expelled from the connexion this year? 11. Who have withdrawn from the connexion this year? 12. Were all the Preachers characters examined before the Conferences? 13. Who have died this year? 14. What numbers are in society? 15. Where are the preachers stationed this year? 16. When and where shall our next conferences be held?[68]

These questions continued, indeed, continue to this day, to shape conference workings.

By the first decade of the century, conferences wanted more structure and procedure. They established committees, charged typically with handling preachers' financial claims, business, or communication.[69] Gradually the practice developed of constituting those and adopting formal rules in the organization. This formalization took place on the populist edge of the movement, in the West, as early as in the East. For instance, by 1810 the Western Conference in organizing itself "proceeded to elect by Ballott a Committee of Appropriations" and "a Committee to adjust the book accounts."[70] It voted seriatim on nineteen rules: governing parliamentary order and procedure, mandating the election of a secretary on organization, and covering the keeping, safeguarding, and reporting of proceedings. The next year the Western Conference "adopted sd. Rules without amendment."[71]

By rules, committees, and routinized behavior, conferences undertook the business of ministry. New roles emerged, leadership requirements changed, and assignments increasingly went to expertise. The secretary, for instance, came to be an important and powerful position. He kept the memory, fashioned into coherent sentence and paragraph the torrent that flowed from these men of the word, sustained the agenda, and gave mood and texture to the occasion—and did that one day so that it could be approved the next. The role has that potentiality in any organization. The special power in the Methodist conference secretary derived from two peculiarities of the system: (1) The presiding officer, the bishop, was absentee and as the century wore on, was frequently rotated;[72] (2) The secretary stayed in the conference and, more strikingly, stayed in the office. For instance, seven secretaries served the New England Conference for most of the nineteenth century: Ralph Williston, 1800–1803; Thomas Branch, 1806–10; Daniel Fillmore, 1813–37, interrupted by a two-year interim for Martin Ruter and a year for Timothy Merritt;* C. Adams, 1842–52; W. R. Bagnall, 1853–59; E. A. Manning, 1860–89; and thereafter James Mudge, 1889–1918. It was the secretary, Mudge himself noted, who knew the political complexion of the conference, who was who, and how the body operated. The bishop depended upon the secretary.[73]

The business of conference had begun, but only begun, to take business form. Earlier Methodism was just the explosive, popular movement so well described by Nathan O. Hatch, Jon Butler, and others.[74] The spread of circuits, the march of conferences west, evidenced that. But it is important to take note that the growth entailed the organization that would yield later bureaucratic structure and procedure. The organizational and the spiritual impulse went hand in hand.[75] Polity served revival, revival required polity, and the conference fraternity kept the two together.

NOTES

1. Jesse Lee, *A Short History of the Methodists in the United States of America*, (Baltimore: Magill & Clime, 1810; reprint of the 1810 edition also available), 149. (Hereafter cited as Lee, *Short History, 1810*.)

2. A reconstruction of the minutes was later effected and published by Thomas B. Neely as *Journal of the General Conference of the Methodist Episcopal Church, 1792* (Cincinnati: Curts & Jennings; New York: Eaton & Mains, 1899) and can be found in Lewis Curts, ed., *The General Conferences of the Methodist Episcopal Church from 1792 to 1896* (Cincinnati: Curts & Jennings; New York; Eaton & Mains, 1899) and can be found in Lewis Curts, ed., *The General Conferences of the Methodist Episcopal Church from 1792 to 1896* (Cincinnati: Curts and Jennings; New York: Eaton & Mains, 1892). For a recent analysis of the conference, see Frederick A. Norwood, "A Crisis of Leadership: The General Conference of 1792," *MH* 28 (April 1990): 195–201.

3. Curts, *General Conferences*, 193.

4. Jno. J. Tigert, *The Making of Methodism: Studies in the Genesis of Institutions* (Nashville: Publishing House of the Methodist Episcopal Church, South, 1898), 145.

5. James M. Buckley, *Constitutional and Parliamentary History of the Methodist Episcopal Church* (New York: Methodist Book Concern, 1912), 68–69.

6. Ibid., 263.

7. Lee, *Short History, 1810*, 181; Jno. J. Tigert, *A Constitutional History of American Episcopal Methodism*, 3d ed., rev. and enl. (Nashville: Publishing House of the Methodist Episcopal Church, South, 1908), 263–64; Tigert, *The Making of Methodism*, 123.

8. Lee, *Short History, 1810*, 183.

9. Tigert, *Constitutional History*, 264–65.

10. Lee, *Short History, 1810*, 178. See discussion in the first part of this text.

11. For discussion of this ideology and its play in American Methodism, see Russell E. Richey, "The Four Languages of Early American Methodism," *MH* 28 (April 1990): 155–71. The literature on republicanism is extensive. See helpful delineations of earlier phases of the debate by Robert E. Shalhope, "Republicanism and Early American Historiography," *The William and Mary Quarterly*, 3d ser. 39 (April 1982): 334–56, and "Toward a Republican Synthesis," *The William and Mary Quarterly*, 3d ser. 29 (January 1972): 49–80. See also Isaac Kramnick, "Republicanism Revisionism Revisited," *The American Historical Review* 87 (June 1982): 629–64, and the various essays in *Three British Revolutions: 1641, 1688, 1776*, ed. J.G.A. Pocock (Princeton, NJ: Princeton University Press, 1980).

12. See O'Kelly's letter to a local preacher, *JLFA*, 3: 114, "To Jesse Nicholson."

13. *The Life and Travels of Rev. Thomas Ware*, (New York: G. Lane and P. P. Sandford for the Methodist Episcopal Church, 1842), 220–21. Ware affirmed: "Had Mr. O'Kelly's proposition been differently managed it might possibly have been carried. For myself at first I did not see any thing very objectionable in it." See also Robert Paine, *Life and Times of William M'Kendree, Bishop of the Methodist Episcopal Church* (Nashville: Publishing House of Methodist Episcopal Church, South, 1869), 1: 64.

14. Critical to the change in sentiment was the adroitly crafted letter that Asbury, sick in bed, sent to the conference. See Part 1 of this text and *JLFA*, 1: 734 for Thursday, 8 November 1792.

15. William Warren Sweet estimates that the overall losses suffered in the 1790s to the Republicans, to William Hammett, and to other causes amounted to some 10,000. *Methodism in American History*, rev. ed. (New York: Abingdon Press, 1953), 134. The Hammett movement, centered in Charleston and taking the name Primitive Methodists, made less of an impact on the movement. Buckley regarded the loss as only that shown in the minutes, some 7,352, which he too spreads over various causes. *Constitutional and Parliamentary History*, 76.

16. For an analysis of that process, see Will B. Gravely, "African Methodisms and the Rise of Black Denominationalism," in *Rethinking Methodist History*, ed. Russell E. Richey and Kenneth E. Rowe (Nashville: Kingswood Books/United Methodist Publishing House, 1985), 111–24; see also *POAM*, 108–26.

17. Buckley, *Constitutional and Parliamentary History*, 76.

18. Lee, *Short History, 1810*, 174–75. Lee actually said eighteen but numbered the General Conference among them.

19. Ibid., 194–95.

20. Entries from Freeborn Garrettson's manuscript journal illustrate the "traveling together." See *American Methodist Pioneer: The Life and Journals of the Rev. Freeborn*

Garrettson, 1752–1827, ed. Robert Drew Simpson (Rutland, VT: Academy Books, 1984) 282–88.

21. *Journals*, 4, for 26 May 1792, in James Meachem Papers, 1788–97. Manuscript Department, Duke University Library, Durham, NC. Used with permission.

Two rather remarkable collections of letters attest the general character of Meachem's sentiments and the legitimacy of Lee's concern: the Dromgoole papers at the Southern Historical Collection and the Hitt letters at Ohio Wesleyan University. See especially "The Letters Written to Daniel Hitt, Methodist Preacher, 1788 to 1806." Given by the Stevenson Family to Ohio Wesleyan University. Transcript made by Miss Annie Winstead, Upper Room. Footnotes and introduction by Raymond Martin Bell, 1967. Copy in the Drew University Library.

22. See the rationale General Conference gave in legislating the change: *JGC*, 1796, 11–12.

23. Wallace Guy Smeltzer, *Methodism on the Headwaters of the Ohio: The History of the Pittsburgh Conference of the Methodist Church* (Nashville: Parthenon Press, 1951), 73.

24. For these boundary actions, beginning with 1796, see *JGC* 1, 1796, 12; 1800, 43; 1804, 52–53; 1812, 107–9; 1816, 152–54; 1820, 215–17; 1824, 273–75; 1828, 304, 324; 1832, 364, 388–90; 1836, 428, 458, 460, 465, and 469–72. The 1808 journals suggest there was little or only minor change.

25. Ibid., 1 (1796): 12.

26. And, of course, also an all-male affair. A less open conference moved women farther from the political center of the movement.

27. Lee, *Short History, 1810*, 270–71. For discussion of efforts by African-American congregations to obtain ordination of their leadership and the church's resistance to that, see Gravely, "African Methodisms," 113 ff.

28. The New England Conference appointed such an officer in 1812. *Minutes of the New England Conference of the Methodist Episcopal Church . . . 1766 to . . . 1845*, 2 vols. Typescript prepared by George Whitaker for New England Methodist Historical Society, 1912), 1: 161–62. The mss. of early New England Conference minutes are at Drew University.

29. Appealing to Philip Gatch's *Journal* and minutes of the South Carolina Conference, Tigert hypothesized that annual conferences had already initiated the office and General Conference standardized the practice. *The Making of Methodism*, 93, 93 n.

30. *Minutes of the New England Conference*, 1 (1800): 29–31.

31. See ibid., 1801, 36–37.

32. Ibid., 1806, 94.

33. "The high taste of these southern folks will not permit their families to be degraded by an alliance with a Methodist travelling preacher; and thus, involuntary celibacy is imposed upon us: all the better" *JLFA* 2 (1 February 1909): 591.

34. *Minutes of the New England Conference* 1 (1802): 50.

35. See Lee, *Short History, 1810*, 271–73; "Memoirs of the Rev. Richard Whatcoat," in P. P. Sandford, *Memoirs of Mr. Wesley's Missionaries to America* (New York: G. Lane & P. P. Sandford for the Methodist Episcopal Church, 1843), 372–73; and Gordon Pratt Baker, ed., *Those Incredible Methodists: A History of the Baltimore Conference of the United Methodist Church* (Baltimore: Commission on Archives and History, Baltimore Conference, 1972), 88–90.

36. See Russell E. Richey, "From Quarterly to Camp Meeting," *MH* 23 (July 1985): 199–213; Kenneth O. Brown, "Finding America's Oldest Camp Meeting," *MH* 28 (July

1990): 252–54; and the standard treatment, Charles A. Johnson, *The Frontier Camp Meeting* (Dallas: Southern Methodist University Press, 1955).

37. *JLFA*, 3: 255, dated 30 December 1802. Zachary Myles of Baltimore wrote Coke (11 January 1803), "Mr. Asbury wrote word to our preachers, to make preparation for the erection of a Camp within two miles of this City, at our next Conference in April." *Methodist Magazine* 26 (1803): 285.

38. The emergence and continuation of the pattern can be seen in J. B. Wakeley, *The Patriarch of One Hundred Years; Being Reminiscences, Historical and Biographical of Rev. Henry Boehm* (New York: Nelson & Phillips, 1875; reprinted Lancaster, PA: Abram W. Sangrey, 1982), 128–36, 147–54, 163–69, 210, 213, 255, 282, 290, 302, 312–13, 315, 317, 363, 417, 460–61, 467; *The Journal of the Reverend Jacob Lanius, An Itinerant Preacher of the Missouri Conference . . . from 1831* A.D. *to 1841* A.D., ed. typescript Elmer T. Clark, 1918, 6–7; and "The Journals of the Illinois Conference," in William Warren Sweet, *Religion on the American Frontier 1783–1840: The Methodists* (New York: Cooper Square Publishers, 1964; first published 1946), 261–366.

39. Paine, *Life of M'Kendree*, 2: 380.

40. Johnson dates the practice from 1806 (*The Frontier Camp Meeting*, 86–87). For an illustration see Sweet, *Religion on the American Frontier,* "Journal of Benjamin Lakin," 230, 252–54; "Journal of James Gilruth," 440, 442–43, 447; references to camp meetings in Ohio, 172, 179, 183–85, 193, 197, 198–99. For conjunctions of conference and camp meeting, see 266, 279, 337.

41. *JLFA*, 3: 380–81. For 14 December 1807.

42. Ibid., 452–53. For 1 September 1811. See also entry for the next day, 3: 455.

43. John F. Wright, *Sketches of the Life and Labors of James Quinn* (Cincinnati: Methodist Book Concern, 1851), 109.

44. Johnson, *Frontier Camp Meeting*, 6, 82; compare Lee, *Short History, 1810*, 362. Methodists did, of course, legislate on and regulate the phenomenon. See Baker, *Those Incredible Methodists*, 54, 96.

45. Buckley, *Constitutional and Parliamentary History*, 93.

46. See part 1 of this text and *JGC*, 1808, 88–89, 95.

47. *JGC* 1 (1808): 93.

48. On this see Donald G. Mathews, *Slavery and Methodism* (Princeton, NJ: Princeton University Press, 1965); Gravely, "African Methodisms"; and H. Shelton Smith, *In His Image, But . . .* (Durham, NC: Duke University Press, 1972). The church had, as we have noted, already in 1804 printed separate Disciplines for the South minus the antislavery rubric. See Mathews, 30 ff.

49. Considerable tension occurred over property, title, access to the pulpit, and other intracongregational matters treated elsewhere in this volume.

50. See Carol V. R. George, *Segregated Sabbaths: Richard Allen and the Rise of Independent Black Churches, 1760–1840* (New York: Oxford University Press, 1973); Howard D. Gregg, *History of the African Methodist Episcopal Church* (Nashville: AMEC Sunday School Union, 1980).

51. *Discipline of the African Methodist Episcopal Church,* 1817.

52. Lewis V. Baldwin, *"Invisible" Strands in African Methodism: A History of the African Union Methodist Protestant and Union American Methodist Episcopal Churches, 1805–1980* (Metuchen, NJ: Scarecrow Press, 1983).

53. David H. Bradley, *A History of the A.M.E. Zion Church 1796–1968*, 2 vols. (Nashville: A.M.E. Zion Publishing House, 1956, 1960); William J. Walls, *The African Meth-*

odist Zion Church: Reality of the Black Church (Charlotte: A.M.E. Zion Publishing House, 1974).

54. At one stage African congregations proposed the establishing of black conferences if ordination and the measure of authority and integrity that entailed would be granted. Even that had been denied.

55. The label of "Methodist" perhaps overstates the unity existing at this point but serves to suggest the possibility that events would frustrate. For the developments that brought the German movements into being, see Part 1 and J. Bruce Behney and Paul H. Eller, *The History of the Evangelical United Brethren Church*, ed. Kenneth W. Krueger (Nashville: Abingdon Press, 1979).

56. R. Yeakel, *Jacob Albright and His Co-Laborers*, trans. from the German (Cleveland: Publishing House of the Evangelical Association, 1883), 102.

57. Ibid., 83. Behney and Eller, *History of the Evangelical United Brethren Church*, 75–76.

58. Yeakel, *Jacob Albright and His Co-Laborers*, "Life Experience and Ministerial Labors of George Miller," 244–45. Behney and Eller, *History of the Evangelical United Brethren Church*, 78–79. Using the 1804 Discipline rather than that of 1808, Miller and company did not put the Restrictive Rules into their constitutive order.

59. "Die soggenannten Albrechtsleute." Another phrase used was "Die sogenannten Albrechts." Behney and Eller rightly prefer the translation given to the more frequently seen "The so–called Albright's people" or "The so-called Albrights." *History of the Evangelical United Brethren Church*, 91.

60. *JGC*, 1796, 11.

61. The last included "an annual conference on the western coast of Africa, to be denominated The Liberian Mission Annual Conference." See Robert Emory, *History of the Discipline of the Methodist Episcopal Church* rev. ed. (New York: Carlton & Porter, [1856]), 246–60.

62. "An Appeal to the Methodists, in Opposition to the Changes Proposed in Their Church Government" (1827), in Thomas E. Bond, *The Economy of Methodism Illustrated and Defended* (New York: Lane & Scott, 1852), 9–56, p. 19.

63. Wallace Guy Smeltzer, *The History of United Methodism in Western Pennsylvania* (Nashville: Parthenon Press, 1975), 69–83.

64. For examples, see *Journal of The Reverend Jacob Lanius*, ed. Elmer T. Clark, 1918, 270, 275, 277–80; and James B. Finley, "Autobiography of Rev. William Burke," *Sketches of Western Methodism* (Cincinnati: Methodist Book Concern, 1854), 22–92.

65. See Theodore L. Agnew, "Methodism on the Frontier," *HAM*, I, 488–545; Nathan O. Hatch, *The Democratization of American Christianity* (New Haven, CT: Yale University Press, 1989).

66. See Daniel Walker Howe, "The Evangelical Movement and Political Culture during the Second Party System," *Journal of American History* (March 1991), 1216–39, and "Religion and Politics in the Antebellum North," in *Religion and American Politics*, ed. Mark Noll (New York: Oxford University Press, 1990), 121–45.

67. These annual or general minutes have been aggregated, a practice begun when the conference was one or considered one, but continues to this day, a further indication of the unity of this fraternity. See for 1808 *Minutes of the Methodist Conferences, Annually Held in America; From 1773 to 1813, Inclusive* (New York: Daniel Hitt & Thomas Ware for the Methodist Connexion in the United States, 1813), 1810, 405–35.

68. Often this structure governed proceedings but remained implicit in the minutes.

Sometimes, however, the secretary would indicate the movement of business: "The Conference proceeded to take up & answer the 3rd Question. Who are to be admitted into full connection." William Warren Sweet, *The Rise of Methodism in the West, Being the Journal of the Western Conference* (New York: The Methodist Book Concern, 1920), 192. "Took up the second question, " 'Who remain on trial?' " *Minutes of the New England Conference* 1 (1819): 272.

69. In 1802, the Western Conference elected "A Committe of Claimes," then a committee "to waite on the next Assembly, at Frankfort, in Kentucky, to attend to the business of Bethel Academy." By 1804 the former had been renamed "Committe of Appropriations" and remained the only such committee established at the organization of the conference. In 1805 the organization also involved the "Committee of Address." Conferences created ad hoc committees as needed. Sweet, *The Rise of Methodism in the West*, 81, 92, 101.

70. Ibid., 174.

71. Ibid., 175, 192. Baltimore also adopted rules in 1810. James Edward Armstrong, *History of the Old Baltimore Conference* (Baltimore: Printed for the author, 1907), 160. The New England Conference, on the other hand, established in 1808 a committee of business, along with "a committee to examine a manuscript collection of hymns" and "a committee for examination of publications." In 1814 stewards were established. Apparently only in 1819 did New England move to rules. *Minutes of the New England Conference*, 1: 118, 122, 153, 271–72. The General Conference of 1812, the first delegated conference, constituted a committee of rules and various other committees in organizing. *JGC* 1 (1812): 98–104.

72. James Mudge, *History of the New England Conference of the Methodist Episcopal Church, 1796–1910* (Boston: Published by the Conference, 1910), 158.

73. For the entire list see the *Minutes of the New England Conference* and particularly the section frequently included, "Sessions of the New-England Conference," which identified both bishop and secretary. See also Mudge, *History of the New England Conference*, 159–68. For the Baltimore Conference pattern, though of terms of only five to ten years, see Baker, *Those Incredible Methodists*, 491–94 (MEC conferences). Patterns of other contributory conferences follow. Brief discussion of the role can be found on pp. 112–13 and p. 271.

74. Nathan O. Hatch, *The Democratization of American Christianity* (New Haven, CT: Yale University Press, 1989); Jon Butler, *Awash in a Sea of Faith* (Cambridge, MA: Harvard University Press, 1990).

75. A history of Methodism makes the point in its title, *Organizing to Beat the Devil*. Charles W. Ferguson (Garden City: Doubleday & Company, 1971).

6
CONFERENCE POLITICIZED

After Francis Asbury's* death, William McKendree* chose to lead in a new fashion—by method, by rule, by law, and by proposal. As we have seen, he put items on the church's agenda. Others did as well, including topics focused on episcopal prerogative or that of conference, among them, election of presiding elders, inclusion of local preachers, lay representation, Canadian independence, abolition, and antimasonry. These issues were fought out in conference— increasingly politicized conference, enhancing polity at the expense of both fraternity and revival; divided conferences; eventuated in new conferences (denominations).

A REFORM AGENDA

In the 1820s, controversy over the first three matters and particularly over the election of presiding elders divided the church. The office, which intruded itself into Methodist community at its most basic levels, proved an ideal lightening rod for tension between episcopacy and the fraternity, for built-up static over authority and its exercise. The presiding elders, "coeval with the Church itself," were gradually distinguished from the larger population of elders by the oversight they exercised over districts.[1] They were formally defined by rubric in the Discipline, in 1792, and their appointment specified:

Quest. 1. By whom are the presiding elders to be chosen?

Ans. By the bishop.[2]

Thus the office became an extension of the episcopacy, indeed, the extension of episcopacy into the affairs of every preacher and member and an appointive position of great power. The presiding elders never left the fraternity but for the

interim of their tenure in that office functioned within and as part of the episcopacy.

The ambiguity of the office made it controversial, perhaps from the start.
Suspicions deepened and sensitivities heightened as the church internalized the
republican or democratic ethos of the country but also formalized the office and
gave geographical definition to conference boundaries. Whereas the bishops
were initially elected by conference and accountable to it, the presiding elders
were neither elective nor accountable, reporting only to the bishop(s). As conference boundaries and membership stabilized and presiding elders were appointed from within and to their own conferences, the exercise of their authority
over their brethren took on a different feel. Issues of power and authority, previously diffused by movement of presiding elders, preachers, or whole circuits
from conference to conference, were now bottled up within the conference. The
presiding eldership became very much a conference issue.

Those who raised the banner of election—for instance, Ezekiel Cooper* and
Jesse Lee* in 1808, like William McKendree earlier—were leaders of the
church. Proponents at the General Conference of 1812 included Lee and Nicholas Snethen,* both of whom had traveled with Asbury and had exercised the
office of presiding elder. In 1816 Nathan Bangs,* a rising star and to be every
bit as luminous in the middle decades of the nineteenth century as Lee had been
in the church's morn, offered a motion for election of presiding elders.[3] With
Asbury's spirit hanging over it, the conference soundly defeated Bang's motion
and a later motion interpreting election of presiding elders as not contrary to
the constitution. It also rejected a petition by local preachers for representation.[4]

By 1820 when General Conference again assembled, the church had established tract and missionary societies, had launched *The Methodist Magazine*,
and was showing greater seriousness about higher education—structural indi-
cations of engagement with the larger Protestant community on behalf of a
Christian America. Further accommodation with slavery, adherence by middling
and even upper-class persons, flourishing women's organizations, and improved
church properties—the signs of respectability—increased. Deeper engagement
with American society meant, of course, communication in its language. Dominant then in the American idiom were strains of republicanism. Republicanism
heightened suspicion of authority and intensified democratic aspirations.[5]

In the Episcopal Address, McKendree both celebrated and worried over such
"progress." In the same sentence, he acknowledged the "desirable intimacy
which subsists among different denominations" but warned of "the danger of
being injured by the influence of men—especially of men of the world professing religion." Doubtless concerned that some of that worldliness might be
present and voting, he reminded the conference that the 1808 General Conference had settled the constitutional issues. "It is presumed that no radical change
can be made for the better at present."[6]

Undeterred by this admonition, Timothy Merritt* of New England and Beverly Waugh of Maryland put the issue of an elective presiding eldership again

before General Conference.[7] The proposal passed but divided the bishops. The dissenting resignation by the newly elected Joshua Soule* led to the suspension of the legislation (and the acceptance of his resignation).[8]

To the subsequent round of annual conferences McKendree submitted a letter setting forth the unconstitutionality of elective presiding elders and asking that the annual conferences concur in that judgment.[9] Seven did, but the five northern and eastern conferences did not.[10] Other hands also conveyed the issue to wider audiences, notably the connection of "reformers" who now created their own medium of expression, the *Wesleyan Repository and Religious Intelligencer*. Appearing first in April 1821 and edited by William Stockton,* a New Jersey printer and lay member, the semimonthly spoke on behalf of election of presiding elders, but also about a constellation of reform measures. Included were rights of local preachers, lay representation, procedures in church trials, and check on episcopal tyranny—in short, the reform of the church. Such advocacy involved risk for the preachers under appointment; in consequence, articles appeared under pseudonyms.[11]

One of several spokespersons, Nicholas Snethen—former traveling companion of Asbury's, secretary of the 1800 General Conference, antislavery advocate, chaplain to the House of Representatives, and unsuccessful candidate for Congress—framed the reform cause in Republican terms. In one early piece he identified himself as "one of those theorists, who conceives that the love of power is so general among men, that in any order of society, civil or religious, those who yield the principle of liberty will never want a master."[12] An essay entitled "On Church Freedom" argued that "the very essence of church freedom, consists in having a voice personally, or by our representatives, in and over the laws by which we are to be governed, and in being judged by our peers."[13] So Snethen defended the liberties of the fraternity of preachers against encroachments by episcopacy, encroachments most effectively made through appointment of presiding elders and the constitution of 1808.

CONFERENCE FOR LOCAL PREACHERS?

Snethen spoke not only on behalf of the fraternity of preachers but also for preachers outside the fraternity, the local preachers. He had been one. Local preachers constituted a diverse but large population that did not enjoy membership or representation in conference. Outnumbering the traveling preachers three to one, they, with class leaders, constituted the mainstay of Methodist local ministry at this period. The office itself derived from Wesley. It was exercised under the authority of the traveling preacher and quarterly conference. By 1796 the Discipline devoted a distinct paragraph to it. Ordination to deacon's orders had been legislated in 1789 and to elder's orders in 1812.[14] The office served as the entry into itinerancy for some, a permanent status for others, and the station to which traveling preachers resorted for family, health, or financial reasons. The minutes annually asked, "Who have located this year?" and then identified by name those who had left the traveling fraternity.[15] Lee and Bangs cited the number each year, again sounding a somber note.[16] The General Conference Committee of Ways and Means reported in 1816 on loss to church through locations of its experienced, trained, and pious "ornaments."[17] Included among the ranks of this population, quite literally left out of the fraternity, were some of its brightest stars, persons who had exercised conference and national leadership. Many continued active ministries but were excluded from the associations, activities, and authority of annual conference. Snethen was but one among this rank of the disenfranchised, of the fraternity outcasts.[18]

What was the church, what was the conference, to do with the gifted persons who remained in ministry but did so outside the traveling ranks? The 1820 General Conference made a stab at the problem, providing district conferences for local preachers, transferring to it authority previously vested in the quarterly conference, and giving it some of the character of an annual conference.[19] Separate and very unequal, this experiment was doomed, though lasting as disciplinary provision until 1836, when its functions and authority were restored to quarterly conference.

Snethen and the reformers wanted real incorporation into the political life of the denomination.[20] The same political principles that pointed toward the rights of local preachers could be invoked on behalf of the laity. Ought they also to be included in annual conference? General Conference? Ought they to be involved in the body or bodies that acted legislatively on, for, and over them? Snethen thought so and compared the system to "Popery," which makes "laws for the laity without their consent" and lodges all power in the bishops.[21] So the agenda was expanded; so the ring fixed for yet another round, the General Conference of 1824.

No revivals were associated with the General Conference of 1824. It was a heated gathering and particularly heated over the suspended legislation. The decisive motion interpreted the votes taken in the conferences as deeming "the resolutions making presiding elders elective . . . unconstitutional."[22] The measure passed sixty-three to sixty-one. Similar split votes came on elections to the episcopacy, the constitutionalists putting in Soule and the reformer Elijah Hedding.* Presiding elders would not be elected. Nor, at this stage, would laity or local preachers be brought into the assembly.

The debate had exposed and reinforced significantly different Methodist self-understandings, different sets of political analogies, different views of church and of conference. One spoke for responsibilities invoking Tory, court, or Federalist principles on behalf of the connection (the fraternity as a whole) and episcopacy. The other appealed to rights and liberties invoking whiggish, country, or Republican principles on behalf of a decentralized political structure in which power devolved from below and authority was vested in the fraternity of annual conference.[23] The contest over rights, the debate over the meaning of the constitution—in a new nation whose new constitution was itself contested—the exchanges between the two sides, made conference gatherings, both annual and general, very political affairs. By politicizing conference, the contestants changed dramatically what both had wished only to preserve. And the contest, by its invocation of constitutional and political analogy, added to the pressures for acculturation.

THE METHODIST PROTESTANTS AND OTHER DIVISIONS

While General Conference met but with defeat looming, a number of reformers, including seventeen members of the conference, convened to constitute the Baltimore Union Society.[24] They encouraged the formation of other such societies "whose duty it shall be to disseminate the principles of a well balanced church government, and to correspond with each other" and disseminated a circular setting forth these principles.[25] Symbolizing their appeal, the reformers renamed their journal *The Mutual Rights of Ministers and Members of the Methodist Episcopal Church* and proclaimed, "What scripture authority can you produce to authorise you to govern Americans otherwise than as free men?"[26] Snethen, Asa Shinn, Alexander McCaine,* and others voiced the reform cause, other union societies emerged, the agitation spread, and the church plunged into confusion. The Baltimore Annual Conference, rent with the controversy, sought to suppress the movement. In 1827 it denied Dennis B. Dorsey an appointment for refusal to address questions about his involvement. It then passed a motion of censure against members who circulate or support "any works defamatory of our Christian, and ministerial character, or in opposition to our Discipline and Church Government."[27]

At this juncture Alexander McCaine fanned the flames with a blast on episcopacy, *History and Mystery of Methodist Episcopacy*, arguing that the present form of government was surreptitiously introduced and that it was imposed upon the societies under the sanction of Wesley's name.[28] Immediate responses came from John Emory,* *Defence of "Our Fathers,"* and Thomas Bond,* "An Appeal to the Methodists, in Opposition to the Changes Proposed in Their Church Government."[29]

The debate turned on two Republican stratagems: (1) primitivism, the appeal to Wesley's intentions and provisions, and (2) "rights," rights of conference, rights of the preachers, rights of local preachers, and rights of the laity. Emory spoke especially to the former, showing that episcopacy was indeed Wesley's original design. The character and quality of fraternity itself was Bond's worry. He probed the effect the proposed changes, notably the inclusion of local preachers and laity, would have on the fraternity, on conference. He thought the reformers struck the very genius of Methodism, itinerancy itself, the principle of sacrifice inherent in it, and the localization of ministry implicit in the reformers' scheme.[30] Bond defended a national itinerancy—"the different conferences contribute to the supply of each other's necessities."[31] He feared that among the "brothers," "parties and caucuses will be formed, which will necessarily alienate their affections from each other; brotherly love no longer continuing, strife, and envy, and malice, evil-speaking, misrepresentation, and slander, will take the place of those fruits of the Spirit.'' He saw and foresaw the politicizing of conference, citing as evidence the positions, slander, and misrepresentation in the *Wesleyan Repository* and *Mutual Rights*.[32]

Damage to conference, politicizing of conference, came as much from Bond's side. Presiding elders in the Baltimore Conference levied charges and initiated trial proceedings against twenty-five laity and eleven local preachers, expelling the former and suspending the latter, Alexander McCaine included, and charging them with ''1st. Becoming a member of the Union Society. 2d. Directly or indirectly supporting the *Mutual Rights* . . . 3d. Approving the 'History and Mystery' written by Alexander McCaine.''[33] In that climate, the union societies, now some twenty-four in number, met in a general convention (November 1827).[34] The convention elected officers, established a committee of vigilance and correspondence, and drafted a memorial to General Conference.

The General Conference of 1828 declared the (suspended) presiding elder legislation void, dismissed the memorials from the reformers' convention (rejecting lay representation), confirmed the suspensions, and offered relief from these decisions only if the union societies were dissolved and *Mutual Rights* suspended.[35] Having faced this challenge to its polity and constitution, the conference also initiated the first amendment. Henceforth a majority of three-fourths of the members of annual conferences rather than all the conferences must concur in a change to a restrictive rule. By this action, General Conference restored to the entire fraternity of preachers the decisive political and constitutional prerogative. Hereby, Jno. J. Tigert noted, ''the Annual Conference rightfully ceased to be in any sense a constitutional unit.''[36]

With expulsions continuing and new congregations forming, the second General Convention of Methodist Reformers met in Baltimore and laid plans for new conference, the formation of a new denomination. They adopted Articles of Association (to be worked into a Discipline two years later) providing for equal lay and clergy representation in annual and general conferences and an elective presidency, but retaining the ''Articles of Religion, General Rules, Means of Grace, Moral Discipline, and Rites and Ceremonies in the main of the Methodist Episcopal Church.''[37] The convention deputized agents, including Nicholas Snethen and Alexander McCaine, to travel on behalf of the cause. By the 1830 General Convention, they had organized twelve annual conferences. That convention met also in Baltimore, where the movement had its greatest strength.[38] There the new constitution and Discipline were ratified.[39] Francis Waters, ordained but functioning as an educator, was elected president, and at his prompting the convention chose the name the Methodist Protestant Church, appointed a book committee, and authorized the transformation of *Mutual Rights* into an official church weekly.[40] The new entity accomplished two of the three major reformers' aims, an elective superintendency and lay representation; local preachers were not granted conference membership. The president would station preachers, though subject to revision by an annual conference committee.

In Methodist Protestantism, conference fraternity was enlarged. Its political authority vis-à-vis superintendency was defined and strengthened. Indeed, in the Methodist Episcopal view, superintendency was destroyed.[41] But revival? In their several gatherings the Reformers had taken care to provide amply for services, including nightly preaching (featuring Snethen). However, temperatures ran too high at these conventions, they were too devoted to polity, for revival to take place. No, revival would be the future test, the measure of the religious integrity, the scriptural character, the fidelity to Wesley of the systems, the polity of Methodist Protestants (MP) and Methodist Episcopals (MEC). Both sides would look at the numbers, at conversion, at revival to assess their own and the other side's faithfulness—an appeal to the Spirit amid the contentions, fights over property, and mutual recriminations that thereafter divided the once-united fraternity.[42]

Similar conference breeches, similar recriminations, and similar appeal to the test of revival had occurred in Charleston and environs with William Hammett's Primitive Methodist Church (the 1790s); the Reformed Methodist Church led by Pliny Brett, in the northern United States and Canada (the mid-1810s); the New York–based movement led by William Stillwell* (the early 1820s); and the English "Primitive Methodists," a movement precipitated by the American Lorenzo Dow and then exported to the United States (in 1829).[43] A less acrimonious but every bit as political a line was drawn between U.S. and Canadian Methodism. The 1828 General Conference acknowledged the desire on the part of "the brethren" in "the province of Upper Canada" to "organize themselves into a distinct Methodist Episcopal Church in friendly relations with the Methodist Episcopal Church in the United States" and established the procedures for amicable separation.[44] Less friendly would be another division of Methodism within the United States.

SECTIONAL CRISIS

The Methodist Protestant Church (MPC), though committed to liberty, made an exception when it came to "colored members," denying them vote and membership in General Conference and permitting each annual conference to form its own rules "for the admission and government of coloured members within its district; and to make for them such terms of suffrage as the conferences respectively may deem proper."[45] The church expressed its ambivalence in its constitution with this qualification: "But neither the General Conference nor any Annual Conference shall assume powers to interfere with the constitutional powers of the civil government or with the operations of the civil laws; yet nothing herein contained shall be so construed as to authorize or sanction anything inconsistent with the morality of the holy scriptures."[46] Methodist ambivalence on slavery betokened its growing "respectability," the adherence to it in North and South of the propertied (and slaveholding) class, the church's coming to terms with culture, and its concern for and investment in the social order.[47] Methodist Protestants, strong in what would become border states, evidenced the "doubleness" of Methodist acculturation—adjustment to society's values, symbolized in acceptance of the slaveholder into communion and efforts to transform society, manifested in educational endeavor, particularly the founding of colleges.[48] The Methodist Episcopal Church showed the same pattern, finding other vehicles than antislavery for the gospel of social transformation and adopting with respect to slavery what Mathews terms strategies of "compromise," namely, the mission to the slave and the commitment to the American Colonization Society.

Methodists participated in the revived antislavery of the 1830s. The controversy animated conference life. Two changes in Methodism made conferences particularly susceptible or hostile to the antislavery gospel. Of great importance were the media then available, newspapers and magazines, which we have already seen proved important in the spread of the reformers' cause. In the Methodist Episcopal Church, one national paper, the *Christian Advocate and Journal* (New York), competed with six regionals for Methodist Episcopal attention, the *Western Christian Advocate* (Cincinnati), *Zion's Herald* (Boston), the *Pittsburgh Christian Advocate*, and three southern papers—the *Southwestern Christian Advocate* (Nashville), the *Richmond Christian Advocate*, and the *Southern Christian Advocate* (Charleston). The *Methodist Magazine* reached the ministers.[49] A second factor was the increased sectional character of the church, reflected in the clergy's deployment of themselves on a regional basis—the bishops' sectional itineration but also the transformation of the fraternity from a national to a conference affair.[50] Preachers increasingly lived out their careers in a single conference. The minutes, beginning in 1824, were structured on a conference-by-conference rather than unified basis.[51] The reward structure, including election to General Conference, presupposed close annual conference ties and support. And General Conference came to structure itself in accordance with such regional patterns. The latter established committees "one from each annual conference,"[52] so honoring region and representation, a formula for political activism.

Sectional media, sectional ministry, and sectional episcopacy reinforced the powerful sectional currents at work among the people. The MEC divided along regional lines, in various ways, on various issues, including the already knotty constitutional problems posed by the reformers.[53] The battles embroiled the papers and the conferences. In May 1835 a New England Wesleyan Antislavery Society was established. In June abolitionists gained six of the seven delegates to the following General Conference. They failed to pass antislavery resolutions, the questions not being put by the presiding bishop, Elijah Hedding, but did beat back motions of censure.

The bishops suppressed abolition, endeavoring to see that the following annual conferences take a "safe, Scriptural, and prudent way." The New York Conference welcomed this posture and condemned *Zion's Watchman*, launched the prior year by LaRoy Sunderland,* to "defend the discipline of the Methodist Episcopal Church against the SIN OF HOLDING AND TREATING THE HU-

MAN SPECIES AS PROPERTY."[54] The 1836 New England Conference followed suit, at least to the extent of charging Sunderland with slandering Nathan Bangs, editor of the *Christian Advocate* and a particular target of the abolitionists. Hedding, who presided, stripped Orange Scott* of his presiding eldership and reassigned him to a church. In the next session, Hedding brought charges against both Sunderland and Scott; the bishop also denied that abolitionists had the right to introduce memorials or the committee to publish its report. Analogous to the suppression of petition and debate in the Congress, this episcopal stance gave to abolition a second cause, "conference rights." Thereafter Scott and another reformer, George Storrs, went from conference to conference in the North preaching abolition and raising the conference rights banner.[55] The bishops attempted to inhibit this abolitionizing and employed the annual review of the character of the preachers to press charges against those who "agitated" the issue.

The church's papers generally followed the bishops' practice of muzzling the controversy, led in that cause by Nathan Bangs and the New York-based *Christian Advocate*. Abolitionist ferment, however, drew active response in southern papers and conferences, where tacit acceptance of slavery turned into an explicit pro-slavery rationale,[56] as in the prospectus (1837) for the *Southern Christian Advocate*, William Capers,* editor.[57] Southern conferences issued resolutions condemning abolition, denying that slavery was sin, and insisting that the institution ought, as a civil matter, to be beyond the church's attention.[58] Bishops saw fit not to muzzle these southern defenses of slavery and attacks on abolition as their episcopal counterparts had muzzled the abolitionists. They saw the problem as abolition not slavery, as they made clear in their address to the next (1840) General Conference.[59] However, much of the church, including some of its strongest conferences, like Baltimore, found themselves torn between the two poles, fighting both explicit pro-slavery sentiment and abolition.[60]

Pro-slavery and antislavery agitation, efforts to keep both out, and struggles to maintain the unity of the church each increased the political aspect of conferences, damaging those dimensions we have termed fraternity and revival.[61] Memorials, resolutions, and legislation on slavery, elections of slates to General Conference, trials and other "political" use of the annual reviews turned conferences into political forums, political forums seemingly persuaded and possessed of their own sovereignty. The politicizing of conference increased through the "moral" passion or righteous indignation that led conferences to judgments on other parts of the church and particularly on other annual conferences or members thereof.[62] In the 1840 General Conference, southerners won the key battles. Conservatives won key elections—to the helm of the northern papers—Thomas Bond over the *Christian Advocate*, Abel Stevens over *Zion's Herald*, and Charles Elliott* over the *Western Christian Advocate*.[63] Conceding defeat and its message, "The M. E. Church, is not only a slaveholding, but a slavery defending, Church," Orange Scott and Jotham Horton withdrew, the first stage in the formation of yet another Methodist body, the Wesleyan Methodist Connection.[64] The movement viewed itself as it titled its paper, *True Wesleyan*; it pledged in its organizing convention at Utica in 1843 to uphold Wesleyan principles on slavery; and it committed itself specifically to holiness.[65]

These "come-outers" appealed to and recruited among northern Methodists with sympathies for the slave, solicitations that ironically had more transforming effect on the Methodist Episcopal conferences when outside than inside. Northern conferences increasingly reclaimed their antislavery heritage, passing resolutions to that effect in preparation for the 1844 General Conference.[66] Southern conferences and papers intensified their defenses, proclaimed slavery to be no moral evil, insisted that the institution itself lay beyond the church's purview, proposed the election of a slaveholding bishop, and prepared for division, should that be necessary.[67] In the General Conference of 1844 the church clashed against itself.

DIVISION, NORTH AND SOUTH

Prior divisions had yielded fresh nuances in Methodism's understanding of itself and of conference and institutionalized those nuances as "the Wesleyan standard." And 1844 would prove no exception.[68] The questions posed by slavery were quite fundamental: the nature of sin, the relation of the church to the social and political orders, the real meaning of church membership, constraints to be placed on officeholding for classes of people (African-Americans),[69] the nature and unity of the ministerial fraternity, the relation of episcopacy and conference, the location of sovereignty, and the exercise of authority. The church put the questions to itself in memorials and petitions that poured in to General Conference from conference and quarterly meeting. The presentation of them went on for two weeks, as day after day the roll call of annual conferences dramatized the concern of the church (North).[70]

Particularly striking were the concurrences in resolutions that had gone, annual conference to annual conference, testing for common conference resolve:

[May 4] Black River Conference.—G. Baker presented six resolutions of this Conference: 1. On the Genesee Conference resolution on slavery; 2. On the New-York Conference resolution on temperance; 3. On the New-York Conference resolution on slavery; 4. On the New-Jersey Conference resolution on the trial of local preachers; 5. Asking the General Conference to rescind the resolution upon coloured testimony; 6. Asking the General Conference to define the "evil of slavery."[71]

The fraternity in annual conferences had acted in concert, albeit on a regional basis. The new fraternal consensus showed itself in tactics and leadership. At this General Conference, the conservative middle and particularly the Baltimore Conference, not the abolitionists and New Englanders, tackled slavery, the result apparently of a deal struck between the parties just prior to conference.[72]

So, instead of suppressing the issue, the conference responded to the first slavery resolution by constituting a committee "to be constituted by one member from each Annual Conference," defeated a proposal from Capers and the South "to lay this on the table."[73] It next went on to deal with the appeal from the Baltimore Conference by Francis A. Harding, who "had been suspended from his ministerial standing for refusing to manumit certain slaves which came into his possession by his marriage."[74] It then took up the case of the bishop entangled with slavery, that of Bishop James O. Andrew.* As we have seen, the different parties to the dispute framed the issue in different ways.[75] The Finley motion called for Andrew to "desist from the exercise of this office so long as this impediment remains."[76] The constitutional framing of the issue would prove to have long-term significance in both regions (churches), serving to resolve into political philosophy the host of issues posed by racism and slavery.[77]

After over a week of intense debate, the other four bishops submitted a letter proposing that the matter concerning Andrew be held over till the next General Conference, arguing that a decision "whether affirmatively or negatively, will most extensively disturb the peace and harmony of that widely-extended brotherhood which has so effectively operated for good in the United States of America and elsewhere during the last sixty years, in the development of a system of active energy, of which union has always been a main element."[78] The New Englanders thought fraternity need no longer be bought at the price of slavery, gathered the delegates of those conferences, agreed to "secede in a body, and invite Bishop Hedding to preside over them," and conveyed that resolve to Hedding.[79] Hedding then withdrew his signature from the bishops' initiative,[80] effectively collapsing what Tigert concluded was the only "hope of harmonizing the difficulties of the Conference."[81] The motion "to desist" then passed.

Long debate followed Capers's resolutions to divide the church.[82] The resolutions, the carefully worded southern "Protest,"[83] and the ensuing clash set forth understandings of the impending division, of the nature of the church, of slavery, of episcopacy, and of conference that would define and characterize the southern church. Among those points were that (1) "the episcopacy is a coordinate branch, the executive department proper of the church"; (2) a "bishop of the Methodist Episcopal Church is not a mere creature—is in no prominent sense an officer—of the General Conference"; (3) "the General Conference is as much the creature of the episcopacy, as the bishops are the creatures of the General Conference"; and (4) the "General Conference is in no sense the Church, not even representatively. It is merely the representative organ of the Church, with limited powers to do its business, in the discharge of a delegated trust."[84]

As if calculated to put on record the emerging northern understanding of General Conference supremacy, the Committee on Slavery reported resolutions rescinding the proscription in church trials of testimony by "persons of colour," stipulating that no slaveholding bishop be elected, urging that conference take measure "entirely to separate slavery from the church," but proposing no change in the General Rules on slavery.[85] The fuller and also carefully honed northern understanding of conference and episcopacy came in "The Reply to the Protest."[86]

The Committee of Nine on the Division of the Church followed the design outlined by Capers and reported plans for an amicable division of the church. It provided for measures to assure peaceful delineation of a boundary between the church and to divide property. A key provision, an enabling constitutional revision of one of the restrictive articles, required three-fourths majorities in annual conferences and thereby assured that the debates and concerns of General Conference would become those of the following annual conferences. Peter Cartwright, who spoke immediately on the introduction of these resolutions, "thought the proposed arrangements would create war and strife in the border conferences."[87]

The resolutions nevertheless passed. After adjournment, the delegates from the slaveholding states met.[88] They called a convention to be held in Louisville on 1 May 1845 for the annual conferences "within the slaveholding States" and issued an explanatory address "To the Ministers and Members of the Methodist Episcopal Church, in the Slaveholding States and Territories."[89] Methodist conference would now define a new relationship to the American landscape, a new vision of itself as new creation. Conference would take regional form, a fraternity of place (and race), its boundaries drawn by slavery and attitudes held thereunto.

NOTES

1. See the second Discipline, entitled, *The General Minutes of the Conferences of the Methodist Episcopal Church in America, forming the Constitution of the Said Church* (London, 1786), 11. See also Robert Emory, *History of the Discipline of the Methodist Episcopal Church* (New York: Carlton & Porter, 1843), 137; Jno. J. Tigert, *The Making of Methodism: Studies in the Genesis of Institutions* (Nashville: Publishing House of the Methodist Episcopal Church, South, 1898), 34–37; Jesse Lee, *A Short History of the Methodists in the United States of America* (Baltimore: Magill & Clime, 1810; reprint of 1810 edition also available), 120–21. (Hereafter cited as Lee, *Short History, 1810.*)

2. *The Doctrines and Discipline of the Methodist Episcopal Church . . . 1792* (Philadelphia, 1792), 18. See *The Doctrines and Discipline of the Methodist Episcopal Church, in America, with Explanatory Notes, by Thomas Coke and Francis Asbury* (Philadelphia, 1798. Reprinted in facsimile, ed. Frederick A. Norwood, Rutland: Academy Books, 1979), 46–53, for the legislation, a description, and the bishop's interpretation of the office.

3. *JGC* 1 (1816): 140.

4. On this matter, see Edward J. Drinkhouse, *History of Methodist Reform: Synoptical of General Methodism 1703 to 1898 with Special . . . Reference to the History of the Methodist Protestant Church*, 2 vols. (Baltimore: Board of Publication of the Methodist Protestant Church, 1899), 1: 525. Drinkhouse provides a distinctively "reform" perspective on the whole issue before us.

5. See *HAM*, 1: 636ff. Also see the discussion on James O'Kelly and the Republican Methodists.

6. Robert Paine, *Life and Times of William M'Kendree*, 2 vols., 1: 397–404.

7. For narrative of the conference, see Nathan Bangs, *A History of the Methodist Episcopal Church* 4 vols. (New York: T. Mason & G. Lane, 1838), 3: 100–57; *HAM*, 1: 642ff.; Jno. J. Tigert, *A Constitutional History of American Episcopal Methodism*, 3d ed. rev. and enl. (Nashville: Publishing House of the Methodist Episcopal Church, South, 1908), chap. 20; James M. Buckley, *Constitutional and Parliamentary History of the Methodist Episcopal Church* (New York: Methodist Book Concern, 1912), chaps. 41 and 42; and Edward J. Drinkhouse, *History of Methodist Reform*, 2 vols. (Baltimore: Board of Publication of the Methodist Protestant Church, 1899), vol. 2, chap. 1.

8. See part 1 of this text. For a vivid and passionate firsthand account of the proceedings, see the paper drafted by Ezekiel Cooper but published only later by his biographer, Geo. A. Phoebus, *Beams of Light on Early Methodism in America* (New York: Phillips & Hunt; Cincinnati: Cranston & Stowe, 1887), 298–308. A comparable perspective but on the other side of the debate is Stephen Roszel's, found in Paine, *Life M'Kendree*, 1: 408–14.

9. Among his arguments, McKendree advanced a point revelatory of the episcopacy's view of the growing regional character of annual conferences. He suggested that an effective general superintendency, supported by an appointive presiding eldership, protected "our itinerant plan of preaching the gospel," which "by removing preachers from District to District, and from Conference to Conference, (which no Annual Conference nor Presiding Elder can do) perpetuate and extend missionary labors for the benefit of increasing thousands, who look unto us as teachers sent of God." Paine, *Life of M'Kendree*, 1: 444–58. Cf. Nathan Bangs, *A History of the Methodist Episcopal Church*, 4 vols. (New York: T. Mason & G. Lane, 1838), 341–42.

10. For the text of two of these quite varying interpretations of the constitution, namely those of Philadelphia and South Carolina, see Tigert, *Constitutional History*, 370–71.

11. *HAM*, 1: 646–52.

12. "Remarks and Observations Addressed to Travelling Preachers," *Wesleyan Repository* 2 (August 1822). Initially printed in December 1820, it was circulated among traveling preachers. Reprinted by Nicholas Snethen in *Snethen on Lay Representation* (Baltimore: John J. Harrod, 1835), 37–58, p. 37.

13. "On Church Freedom," *Wesleyan Repository* 1 (20 December 1821). Reprinted in Snethen, *Snethen on Lay Representation*, 75–78, p. 75.

14. Emory, *History of the Discipline*, 191–202. Lee had calculated the number and proportions of local preachers to traveling: In 1799 there were 850 local to 269 traveling; in 1809 there were 1,610 local to 589 traveling. Lee, *Short History, 1810*, 255, 359, 362. McKendree gave the same proportions for 1812: 2,000 to 700. See also James Mudge, *History of the New England Conference of the Methodist Episcopal Church, 1796–1910* (Boston: Published by the Conference, 1910), 239–40.

15. See *Minutes of the Methodist Conferences, Annually Held in America; From 1773 to 1813, Inclusive* or minutes for any subsequent year.

16. See Lee, *Short History, 1810*, 354, or the year-end tally for any prior year. Bangs took a similar "body" count. See his *History of the Methodist Episcopal Church*, 3: 183, for the 1820 accounting.

17. *JGC*, 1816, 148–52, 166–69.

18. For another see Mudge, *History of the New England Conference,* 241.

19. Emory, *History of the Discipline,,* 193–96.

20. "Letters from a Local Preacher to a Travelling Preacher," *Wesleyan Repository* 3 (June 1823): 184–93. Reprinted in Snethen, *Snethen on Lay Representation,* 184–93, p. 186. One complaint was that annual conferences pass on the character of the local preachers: "These travelling preachers cannot be called to account—a local preacher can have no redress. No matter what is said to injure him, he may neither hear nor reply." See *Wesleyan Repository* (September 1823), reprinted in Snethen, *Snethen on Lay Representation,* 216.

21. "Letters to a Member of the General Conference," *Wesleyan Repository* (November 1823), reprinted in Snethen, *Snethen on Lay Representation,* 233–34. Snethen continued: "3dly, The right of presentation to livings, which is sometimes in the bishops, or the governments, or the lay patrons, is wholly in our bishops. 4th. The generals or heads of the orders of friars or travelling monks, can send them where they please—so our bishops can send travelling preachers."

22. *JGC,* 1828, 278–79.

23. For discussion of the complex intertwining of these two ideological constellations, see J.G.A. Pocock, ed., *Three British Revolutions: 1641, 1688, 1776* (Princeton, NJ: Princeton University Press, 1980), particularly the essay by John A. Murrin.

24. Drinkhouse, *History of Methodist Reform,* 2, 62–63; *HAM,* 1: 650–51.

25. *Mutual Rights,* August 1824, 3.

26. Often considered a continuation of the *Wesleyan Repository and Religious Intelligencer.* See "Matters worthy of the serious reflection of Travelling Preachers," *Mutual Rights* 2 (April 1826), in Snethen, *Snethen on Lay Representation,* 316–20, p. 317.

27. "Journal of the Baltimore Conference," 18 April 1827, 202, as cited in *HAM,* 1: 653.

28. Baltimore 1827, 74.

29. Both appeared in 1827. Emory's bore the full title, *A Defense of "Our Fathers," and of the Original Organization of the Methodist Episcopal Church, against the Rev. Alexander McCaine, and Others* (New York: N. Bangs & J. Emory, for the Methodist Episcopal Church, 1827). Bond's was reprinted in Thomas E. Bond, *The Economy of Methodism Illustrated and Defended* (New York: Lane & Scott, 1852), 9–56.

30. "An Appeal to the Methodists, in Opposition to the Changes Proposed in Their Church Government," in Bond, *The Economy of Methodism,* 20.

31. Ibid., 48.

32. Ibid., 39–40.

33. Cited by Drinkhouse, *History of Methodist Reform,* 2: 128. See also "A Narrative and Defence of The Proceedings of the Methodist Episcopal Church in Baltimore City Station, Against Certain Local Preachers and Lay Members of Said Church," in Bond, *The Economy of Methodism,* 57–136.

34. Attenders were listed by Drinkhouse, *History of Methodist Reform,* 2: 137–39.

35. Bangs reproduced the committee report on the Reformers' memorial and the resolutions on trials in *History of the Methodist Episcopal Church,* 3: 413–30.

36. *JGC* 1 (1828): 346. See Tigert, *Constitutional History,* 400–403, for analysis and interpretation. See also discussion under "Episcopacy."

37. See Drinkhouse, *History of Methodist Reform,* 2: 211–12, for a summary of the seventeen articles.

38. On the leadership provided by and the centrality of Baltimore, see Gordon Pratt

Baker, ed. *Those Incredible Methodists: A History of the Baltimore Conference of the United Methodist Church* (Baltimore: Commission on Archives and History, Baltimore Conference, 1972), 165.

39. For the text see Drinkhouse, *History of Methodist Reform*, 2: 257–67.

40. It bore the name *The Mutual Rights and Methodist Protestant* from 1831 to 1834 and then continued only the latter designation.

41. Bangs observed, "The offices of bishop and presiding elder were abolished." *History of the Methodist Episcopal Church*, 3: 435.

42. See Drinkhouse, *History of Methodist Reform*, 2: 287, 293, 296, 298, 315, 343, 349, 371–72. Compare Nathan Bangs, *The Present State, Prospects, and Responsibilities of the Methodist Episcopal Church, with an Appendix of Ecclesiastical Statistics* (New York: Lane Y. Scott, 1850).

43. See *HAM*, 1: 617–35.

44. *JGC*, 1828, 338; Bangs, *History of the Methodist Episcopal Church*, 3: 389–90, reproduced the text of the enabling resolution and discussed the division, its rationale, and its results. See also Tigert, *Constitutional History*, 405–9.

45. *Constitution and Discipline of the Methodist Protestant Church* (Baltimore: Published for the Book Committee of the Methodist Protestant Church, 1830), 21. This had been the posture of the MEC from 1808 until 1820, when rescinded by General Conference at the prompting of the bishops and in the face of continued antislavery activity in northern and western conferences. For the MEC's "Missouri Compromise," see Donald G. Mathews, *Slavery and Methodism: A Chapter in American Morality, 1780–1845* (Princeton, NJ: Princeton University Press, 1965), 46–52; for the successive legislation on slavery see the appendix in Mathews, 293–303, and/or Emory, *History of the Discipline*, 17, 20, 372–79.

46. *Constitution and Discipline of the Methodist Protestant Church*, Articles VII and XII, 21–22 and 29. See also Drinkhouse, *History of Methodist Reform*, 2: 261, 265.

47. See Mathews, *Slavery and Methodism* and *Religion in the Old South* (Chicago: University of Chicago Press, 1977); and for the North, see A. Gregory Schneider, *The Way of the Cross Leads Home: The Domestication of American Methodism* (Bloomington: Indiana University Press, 1993). For transformations in evangelicalism as a whole, see Leonard I. Sweet, ed., *The Evangelical Tradition in America* (Macon, GA: Mercer University Press, 1984).

48. On the Methodist relationship to society, see Richard M. Cameron, *Methodism and Society in Historical Perspective*, vol. 1 of *Methodism and Society*, undertaken by the Board of Social and Economic Relations and the Boston University School of Theology (New York: Abingdon Press, 1961).

49. See James Penn Pilkington and Walter N. Vernon, *The Methodist Publishing House*, 2 vols. (Nashville: Abingdon Press, 1968–88), vol. 1, chap. 5.

50. See part 1 of this text. The church continued to cling to the notion that the ministry was deployed nationally, as we have seen in the controversy over reform. A further illustration of that occurred in 1840, when General Conference voted down a memorial from New England to add to the Discipline a stipulation that "a bishop shall have no authority to transfer a member of one Conference to another Conference, in opposition to the wishes of said member, or in opposition to the wishes of a majority of the members of the Conference to which it is proposed to transfer said member." *JGC*, 1840, 56.

51. See *Minutes of the Annual Conferences of the Methodist Episcopal Church . . . 1773–1828* (New York: T. Mason & G. Lane, 1840).

52. *JGC* 1 (1816): 126, 128–29; 2 (1820): 246; 1 (1828): 304; 1 (1832); 364; 1 (1836): 428.

53. See part 1 of this text and Tigert, *Constitutional History*, 398.

54. Cited by Mathews, *Slavery and Methodism*, 138.

55. Ibid., 148–57; Mudge, *History of the New England Conference*, 283–86.

56. On the evolution of southern evangelicalism and its conscience, see Mathews, *Religion in the Old South*, 136–84.

57. *Southern Christian Advocate* 1 (21 June 1837): 1.

58. "It is the sense of the Georgia Annual Conference that slavery, as it exists in the United States, *is not a moral evil*." Reported in *Southern Christian Advocate*, 5 January 1838, 114; cited by Mathews, *Slavery and Methodism*, 181.

59. *JGC*, 2 (1840): 134–37. Bangs reproduced the entire Episcopal Address in *History of the Methodist Episcopal Church*, 4: 336–71.

60. See Homer L. Calkin's chapter in Baker, *Those Incredible Methodists,* 192–228.

61. Mathews divides the church, circa 1840, into three parties: abolitionists pressing for recommitment to the church's antislavery tradition, southerners threatening secession if such were done, and conservatives attempting to hold the church together. *Slavery and Methodism*, 192 ff. Contemporaries also recognized three parties. For instance, in 1844 a southerner spoke of "three parties: the ultraists of the north, the antislavery men, and *what they call* the pro-slavery men. These antislavery men had assumed to be conservatives." Robert T. West, reporter, *Report of Debates in the General Conference of the Methodist Episcopal Church . . . 1844* (New York: G. Lane & C. B. Tippett, 1844), 16.

62. See "Episcopacy" for the discussion of such activity.

63. On these developments and their implications, see Mathews, *Slavery and Methodism*, 225–28. They declared their intention to be antislavery, but not radical.

64. Frederick A. Norwood, *Sourcebook of American Methodism* (Nashville: Abingdon Press, 1982), 255–58. That was the first reason for their withdrawal. The second was "The government of the M.E. Church contains principles not laid down in the Scriptures, nor recognized in the usages of the primitive Church—principles which are subversive of the rights both of ministers and laymen." They had in mind the "power which our bishops claim and exercise, in the Annual Conferences" (256). On the initial stages of the movement, see *HAM*, 2: 39–47.

65. See "Pastoral Address," reproduced by Norwood, *Sourcebook*, 258–61.

66. *ZH*, 7 December 1842, 190; cited by Mathews, *Slavery and Methodism*, 233.

67. See *HAM*, 2: 33; Mathews, *Slavery and Methodism*, 235–40.

68. Fulsome discussions of this conference can be found in *HAM*, 2: 47–85; Mathews, *Slavery and Methodism*, 246–82; Tigert, *Constitutional History*, 435–59; and part 1 of this text.

69. The limits placed on women and laity would be issues at later conferences.

70. "[May 4, New Hampshire,] C. D. Cahoon presented . . . memorials, on the subject of slavery, from Claremont and Athens, which were referred to the Committee on Slavery. Also a memorial of the New Hampshire Conference on slavery, which document he asked to have read. A. B. Longstreet moved to dispense with the reading. This motion was lost; and the document was then read, and referred to the Committee on Slavery. Also certain resolutions of the New-Hampshire Conference, on the appointment of slaveholders to the office of Missionary Secretary, or missionaries, under the direction of the Parent Board, which were read and referred to the Committee on Slavery. Also resolutions on the subject of coloured testimony: read and referred to the same committee"

(*JGC*, 1844, 20). References to their presentation and reception abound. See 18–22, 25–27, 35–37, 39–41, 42–43, 44, 47–48, 54. They came from conferences and individual circuits. For examples, see Charles Elliott, *History of the Great Secession from the Methodist Episcopal Church in the Year 1845* (Cincinnati: Swormsteadt & Poe, 1855), 971–73. Mathews observes, "Almost every Northern annual conference petitioned the General Conference to take more decisive action against slavery." *Slavery and Methodism*, 240.

71. *JGC*, 1844, 20–21.

72. HAM, 2: 56–57; Baker, *Those Incredible Methodists*, 207.

73. West, *Report of Debates*, 5. Capers "hoped to hear no more of a Committee on Slavery. It never did and never could do any Good. It had done much evil and always would do."

74. *JGC*, 1844, 29. For narrative, see Baker, *Those Incredible Methodists*, 207–10; Mathews, *Slavery and Methodism*, 251–54; *HAM*, 2: 51–54. For text of arguments, see West, *Report of Debates*, 18–52.

75. For details of his situation and the conference's handling of the case, see part 1 of this text.

76. *JGC*, 1844, 65–66.

77. Samuel Dunwody of South Carolina objected to the resolution "for three grand reasons": "First, it was unscriptural; second, it was contrary to the rules and constitution of the Church; and, thirdly, it was mischievous in a very high degree." West, *Report of Debates*, 164.

78. *JGC*, 1844, 75. The letter extends to 76. Also in West, *Report of Debates*, 184–85.

79. See James Porter, "General Conference of 1844," *MQR* 53 (April 1871): 234–50.

80. *JGC*, 1844, 81; also West, *Report of Debates*, 188–89.

81. Tigert, *Constitutional History*, 445.

82. "Be it resolved by the delegates of all the Annual Conferences in General Conference assembled:

"That we recommend to the Annual Conferences to suspend the constitutional restrictions which limit the powers of the General Conference so far, and so far only, as to allow of the following alterations in the government of the church, viz.:

"That the Methodist Episcopal Church in these United States and territories, and the republic of Texas, shall constitute two General Conferences, to meet quadrennially, the one at some place, *south*, and the other *north* of the line which now divides between the states commonly designated as free states and those in which slavery exists.

"2. That each of the two General Conferences thus constituted shall have full powers, under the limitations and restrictions which are now of force and binding on the General Conference, to make rules and regulations for the church, within their territorial limits respectively, and to elect Bishops for the same." *JGC*, 1844, 86.

Four more enabling resolutions followed. *JGC*, 1844, 86–87. See also West, *Report of Debates*, 192, or Elliott, *History of the Great Secession*, 1008–9.

83. "The Protest of the Minority in the Case of Bishop Andrew," in West, *Report of Debates*, 203–12; Elliott, *History of the Great Secession*, 1017–29, or *History of the Organization of the Methodist Episcopal Church, South with the Journal of Its First General Conference* (Nashville: Publishing House of the Methodist Episcopal Church, South, 1925), 102–23. (Latter hereafter cited as *History of MECS Organization*.)

84. West, *Report of Debates*, 209.

85. *JGC*, 1844, 112. Conference took action passing the first item.

86. West, *Report of Debates*, 229–37; Elliott, *History of the Great Secession*, 1030–41; and *History of MECS Organization*, 142–45.

87. West, *Report of Debates*, 220.

88. On the propriety and legality of this gathering, see Tigert, *Constitutional History*, 450–51.

89. *History of MECS Organization*, 147–52, or Elliott, *History of the Great Secession*, 1045–48.

7
FRATRICIDE

The annual conferences, North and South, set off the first volleys in what would be a war within "our beloved Zion," pitting section against section, conference against conference, church against church.[1] A Methodism that once conferenced the continent now divided the people of God into a northern and southern kingdom. A Methodism that once had viewed its purposes in eschatological and biblical terms now reduced Zion to its own tribal ends and contested borders. Judah and Israel looked each to its own interest.

THE POLITICAL CONFERENCE

The Kentucky Conference, the first in the South to meet after separation, set the pattern by establishing a committee of division, condemning the actions of General Conference and approving the holding of the Louisville Convention.[2] So the conference structured and choreographed itself for politics.[3] Other conferences in the slaveholding states followed suit with formal expressions of disapproval over the 1844 General Conference, the establishment of committees on separation or division, approval of the convention, passage of the amendment to the Sixth Restrictive Rule that would permit the division of property, and provision for dissemination of actions in the southern papers.

The editors of the northern papers (*Zion's Herald*, the New York *Christian Advocate and Journal*, the *Western Christian Advocate*, the *Pittsburgh Christian Advocate*, and the *Northern Advocate*) entered countercriticisms.[4] The first MEC conferences to meet voted before this *Advocate* warfare was felt and acted favorably on the key constitutional issue in the division of the church, the amendment of the Sixth Restrictive Rule, so as to permit proportional division of the Book Concern and the Chartered Fund. By August when North Ohio met, MEC resentment was building. Insisting that the MEC "having always been considered a unit, can not . . . be divided into separate and distinct organizations, unless it be by a secession of one party,"[5] it defeated the amendment, as did most of the following conferences. Ohio voted 132 to 1 against the change. Ohio expressed pain over "the *politico-religious* aspect which the question of division has assumed at the south."[6] In truth, MEC (northern) conferences assumed an equal, if not more intense, *politico-religious* aspect. Conferences North and South roiled with politics. And each controversial act seemed to stimulate others. The property issue alone, defeated by the votes of the northern conferences, festered for years, drawing attention from conferences as well as *Advocates.* Even its resolution ten years later, by the Supreme Court, did not end the comment.

And the boundary issue excited conferences, particularly the border conferences, from 1844 to the Civil War and beyond. The Louisville Convention, voting that "it is right, expedient, and necessary to erect the Annual Conferences represented in this Convention, into a distinct ecclesiastical connexion,"[7] requested its bishops when presiding in border conferences to incorporate "any societies or stations adjoining the line of division when said societies or stations" "request such an arrangement."[8] This act challenged the line between conferences that divided the two churches, a line crossing state lines and separating peoples often sharing history, sentiments, and loyalties. In the border skirmishes that ensued, each side accused the other of deceit, intrigue, and misconduct. Such warfare turned conference membership from fraternal and missional into political and "military" purposes.[9]

Fittingly, the 1848 MEC General Conference, though hearing from the Methodist Episcopal Church, South (MECS), fraternal delegate, Lovick Pierce* that the MECS wanted "warm, confiding, and brotherly, fraternal relation" and acceptance "in the same spirit of brotherly love and kindness," instead noted the "serious questions and difficulties existing between the two bodies" and considered it improper "at present, to enter into fraternal relations with the Methodist Episcopal Church, South."[10] The General Conference then undid the work of 1844, declaring the constitutional amendment failed, deeming "null and void" the Plan of Separation, and judging that the General Conference (1844) could not legally divide the church.[11] It authorized the formation of the Western Virginia Conference, prompting the MECS General Conference (1850) to organize its own West Virginia Conference.[12]

On the eve of secession and during the Civil War, conference politicization further intensified. In the late 1850s the Genesee Conference found itself embroiled in controversy over slavery, holiness, choirs, pew rent, and secret societies—all touchstones for accommodation to the social order.[13] The conference divided itself politically between Nazarites, who called for return to the fraternal, revivalistic old standards, and those characterized as "New School Methodists" or the Buffalo Regency. Forced from editorships and from pulpits, the critics founded their own paper, *The Northern Independent*, held laymen's conventions, garnered support for ousted ministers, and in 1860 founded the Free Methodist Church.

To stem defections, the MEC General Conference passed in 1860 a "new chapter" on slavery explicitly declaring that "the buying, selling, or holding of human beings, to be used as chattels, is contrary to the laws of God and nature."[14] Border conferences meeting thereafter were deluged with petitions and resolutions calling for its repeal.[15] Secession and war brought similar political disruption in the MECS.

During the war, conferences passed patriotic resolutions, administered oaths to themselves and to their probationers,[16] brought the flag into their sessions, encouraged the war effort and Methodist participation therein, supported chaplains, demanded stronger national action on slavery, and denounced the secessionists.[17] Southern conferences, perhaps somewhat more circumspect in their declarations, were no less politicized by the events, particularly after Bishop Edward Ames secured from Secretary of War Stanton a directive ordering officers to turn over to the MEC churches belonging to the MECS "in which a loyal minister, who has been appointed by a loyal Bishop of said Church does not officiate."[18] Would the MECS simply cave in to a northern takeover? Ministers and laity in the Missouri Conference gathered in 1865 and issued a redeclaration of independence: "Resolved, That we consider the maintenance of our separate and distinct ecclesiastical organization as of paramount importance and our imperative duty." This Palmyra Manifesto grounded continuation of the MECS on "our Church doctrines and discipline" and on opposition to "the prostitution of the pulpit to political purposes."[19] So was sounded an antipolitical political creed, a refrain that would politicize the MECS and its conferences under the guise of eliminating politics from the church, a refrain that established purity (southern) by contrast to prostitution (northern):[20] "Preach Christ and him crucified. Do not preach politics. You have no commission to preach politics."[21]

The politically fervid atmosphere of Southern Conferences continued into Reconstruction sustaining (or criticizing) MEC efforts on behalf of the freed slaves. In this new warfare between the churches for souls to save and organize, the fights to establish borders and claim constituency gradually extended from the border states proper to the entire nation. Northern conferences in southern territory and southern in northern made for a continuous state of warfare.

DIVIDING FRATERNITY FROM BELOW

Easily lost sight of, amid the sectional strife, nationwide controversy over slavery, warfare, and reconstruction were the dramatic changes, slow but gradual, affecting Methodism from below and also fundamentally altering conference "fraternity and revival." Perhaps best illustrating those shifts was quarterly conference. Once the only gathering of the circuit and the occasion for camp and protracted meetings, the quarterly meeting in small town and city stations competed now with the weekly Sunday service and with the plethora of other fraternal and spiritual bodies—missionary, Sunday school, Bible. As early as

1844 the bishops complained that the emergence of the station and the erosion of the circuit gave quarterly meeting conferences "scarcely . . . an existence except in name" and sought the recovery of the institution, so that "members of the Church, as in former days of Methodism, would come together from the different appointments to improve their spiritual state, and strengthen their Christian fellowship, by mutual attendance on the means of grace, and by religious intercourse in conversation and prayer."[22] Why the loss of this means of "revival"? The same address complained of that engine that slowly changed quarterly meeting as it changed Methodism—the "stationing" of the itinerant, "locality in our traveling ministry," and "preachers with local views."[23] Both itinerancy and quarterly conferences yielded to "locality," to the settling of the itinerant into stations, and to the reduction of circuit gatherings into station oversight.

Fraternity and revival were pulled into new forms and contexts, as we shall see. They were pushed from conference by other tribalisms and by the inability of now respectable congregations to be as open as the quarterly meetings had been. Who could and should share a pew and the means of grace? Congregations, quarterly conferences, and conferences increasingly embraced only their own. The 1844 General Conference established the Indian Mission Conference, capitalizing on several decades of efforts with Native Americans.[24] The bishops that year also proposed the creation of a "German Missionary Conference,"[25] recognizing the fruits of a decade of effective mission work with the German-Americans, and conference did make provision for presiding elders' districts.[26] The 1856 MEC General Conference set aside separate German districts. The 1864 General Conference established German annual conferences and also segregated African-Americans into separate annual conferences.

Racial segregation and the exclusion of African-Americans from leadership were old patterns. The sectional crisis just gave racism fresh structural expression. The MECS in its first General Conference (1846) dealt with African-Americans through its Committee on Missions. The committee proposed and conference adopted a ten-point plan for the mission to the slave, endorsing missionary efforts where circuits did not embrace the black population but prescribing separate sittings when African-Americans remained in a congregation, galleries for buildings, accommodations "at the back of the stand, or pulpit" in camp meetings, and distinct class meetings for oral catechetical instruction—with all efforts to be reported to quarterly conference.[27]

And the MEC, with the end of the Civil War and the abolition of slavery in sight, acted to segment African-Americans into separate districts. The 1864 Philadelphia Conference passed such a resolution, calling for the bishops and presiding elders to organize "our colored people into district Circuits . . . with a view of furnishing them with ministerial service by preachers of their own color." The MEC General Conference of that year authorized the bishops to organize distinct black "Mission Conferences."[28] Accordingly, they established the Delaware and Washington Conferences. The southern church proceeded in the same direction (motivated by northern and AME and AMEZ missions among the freedmen) and cooperated in the release of congregations and properties and the ordinations that would set up the Colored Methodist Episcopal Church.[29]

Conferences had once embraced the people called Methodist and given structural and dramatic expression, albeit imperfectly, to an egalitarian gospel. Now distinct peoples were structurally differentiated and made the objects of missionary attention.

LAY CONFERENCING

Laity had opinions on the fundamental social issues on which the church was then speaking. Quarterly conferences had permitted laity a voice. However, the erosion of quarterly conference—its reduction to congregational oversight, its transformation into a business meeting, its reduced importance—damaged the one forum in which the laity could be heard. As annual conferences increasingly embroiled themselves politically and spoke on national questions, the laity felt restive at having their opinions and influence confined to quarterly conference. So in episcopal Methodism the issue that had animated Methodist Protestants resurfaced, lay representation. A politicized episcopal Methodism faced but defeated resolutions for lay representation, the MEC in 1852 and the MECS in 1854. The issue would return, necessitated by the increasing 'locality' of quarterly conference and the divisive issues before the church. The controversy in the Genesee Conference had widened to division through the holding of a succession of Laymen's Conventions, the first in 1858, the second in 1859, the third in 1860, each of them functioning politically. They issued resolutions, circulated petitions, gathered money, organized "Bands." In 1859 the Ministers' and Laymen's Union was formed within the New York Conference, a body dedicated to preserving the status quo on the slavery issue within the MEC. In response, a rival group, the Anti-slavery Union of the New York East Conference, also composed of ministers and laity, pressed for change.

In 1860, Baltimore Conference laity at a camp meeting at Loudoun took matters into their own hands.[30] They called a laymen's conference for December. Other lay or public meetings followed, each expressing itself, with resolutions on the sectional crisis and recent MEC General Conference actions. An important laymen's convention sat concurrently with the annual conference of 1861 at Staunton and nudged it into an act of secession. The first item of business for this annual conference was the memorial from the "Convention of Laymen which assembled in Baltimore in December last, relating to the action on Slavery by the General Conference . . . 1861." This conference voted to break with the MEC.[31]

The next (1862) Baltimore annual conference met in Baltimore rather than in Virginia, that is, outside the Confederacy, and recognized the actions of the previous conference as an act of severance and those not present as withdrawing. This annual conference entertained but voted down lay delegation, thirty-four against twenty-two.[32] It had seen the power of lay initiative. So had the southerners. The MECS approved lay representation in 1866. Laity belonged in politicized and businesslike conferences that legislated on social issues and stated the church's position and set policy for the whole. And with the collapse of quarterly meeting into station or small circuit, laity demanded a role on more effective conference levels, that is, annual and general. The MEC conceded the issue in 1872, but only on the General Conference level. Women's rights to representation and ordination lay ahead. Quarterly meeting without revival and annual conference without fraternity but business and politics galore!

BUSINESS

In the period after the Civil War, Methodist conferences found themselves scurrying to adjust to the organizational revolution then sweeping American society. Many Methodists experienced the new organizational processes and structures as congenial, successful, providential, and "Methodistic."[33] Some, though, like the Free Methodists took such accommodation to the social order to be a violation of everything for which Methodists had stood. Each had a point. Methodism wanted to have it both ways. It understood itself providentially guided, dynamic, pragmatic, transformative, with a mission to spread scriptural holiness and reform the continent. So it adapted and adopted as it found itself more and more invested in and invested with American societal leadership. Also, since the time of Wesley himself, Methodism had been abjured to heed our doctrines and discipline. And so from the start it had worried about "our Zion" and its preservation. Conferences betrayed both the change and the efforts to hold the ancient landmarks, or at least, to remember them.

Conferences treasured the Methodist past by inviting members with fifty years of service to deliver semicentennial sermons. They created new rituals, including the singing as an opening hymn of "And Are We Yet Alive?" which celebrated the Wesleyan fraternity.[34] They continued the pattern of drafting, approving, and minuting the biographies of deceased members. Indeed, some even created a special office for that purpose. Conferences now published their minutes and used the minutes to represent themselves, both in present activity and in the past. They employed elaborate charts and lists galore to recall the fraternity's past.[35] For instance, in the mid-1860s New England produced and published lists of deceased members of the New England Conference; the sessions of the New England Conference; delegates to the General Conference from the New England Conference, by years, 1804 to 1864; and a "Retrospective Register of N.E. Conference." The latter provided a history for each living member, charting the successive appointments of each. Another table gave the members alphabetically, indicating addresses, present relation to the conference, year and admission, and years in present appointment.[36]

Although conferences sustained the sense that its fraternity remained what it had been, they did business by the rituals and protocol of the new organizational world, particularly through committees. Conference's first order of business was constituting the nominations committee and putting it to work staffing the standing committees, the most important of which would require representation from every district.[37] In the mid-1860s the standing committees were Stewards, Necessitous Cases, Education, Bible Cause, Tract Cause, Temperance, Public Worship, "To receive Moneys for Benevolent Operations," Memoirs, Statistics for the General Minutes, Statistics for Conference Minutes, Missions, "To Nominate Officers for Conference Societies," Preachers' Aid, Benevolent Operations, Observance of the Sabbath, Church Aid, Ministerial Support, Relief Society, Sunday Schools, "Slavery and the State of the Country," and Conference Minutes. Conference would constitute other committees as it worked.

The committees represented the agency of conference in managing and directing the denomination's work. Committees connected annual conference with the national agents, editors, and corresponding secretaries, all of whom would typically be present to make reports. Annual conference implemented and gave oversight to ongoing denominational enterprises through permanent conference societies—the Conference [Foreign] Missionary Society, the Domestic Missionary Society, the Tract Society, and the Sabbath School Society. These were auxiliary to national counterparts but had a lively sense of their own agency, met during annual conference, heard reports and sermons, gave direction to the local auxiliaries, and rendered fulsome reports to their members. Most of the denominational dollar was under conference control. Conference trustees and stewards took fiscal responsibility. Aside from the publishing efforts and the Advocates, aside from the large publishing business, the national agencies or societies—Sunday school, missions, temperance, tracts, Bible—were quite modest endeavors, typically an individual secretary who encouraged activity at conference level. Each secretary was accountable to an annual conference and "his" agency was effectively under the supervision of that conference or that one and those immediately contiguous.[38] Annual conferences had been the workhorse of the denomination, and the New England Conference reflected that. Its sessions were devoted to reports and actions through which it attempted to take responsibility for the institutions of the church, including its own institutions and particularly both secondary and higher education, the latter including oversight of Wesleyan University and of the church's venture in theological education, the Biblical Institute (late in the decade moved to become part of Boston University).[39] Oversight was exercised through trustees on the institution's board and also visiting committees.

Conferences ran the business of Methodism and perforce devoted annual sessions to annual reports. Each agency and each committee reported, in some cases, at great length. Minutes bristled with complex statistical tables and exhibits. And conference did not respect conference boundaries. It looked on the nation, indeed, the whole world, as its domain. New England, for instance, concerned itself in 1865, as it had for years, with what was happening in the South, guided by its standing committee "On Slavery and the State of the Country," and appointed an additional committee to think about reconstruction.[40] Accordingly, conference heard a long report on "Reconstruction of the Church."[41] News came during its sitting of the capture of Richmond, eliciting the singing of "Mine Eyes Have Seen the Glory" and the Hallelujah Chorus. The attention to the South went hand in hand with concern for the whole nation and, in particular, the Methodist connection. Conferences thought for the whole church, vying to set its agenda, formulating resolutions that could be passed to other annual conferences, and knowing that through their actions would be carefully covered by the Advocates (and for New England, *Zion's Herald*). So New England did not imagine that problems of race relations were just confined to the South. It objected to the action at the recent MEC General Conference authorizing the drawing of the color line within the conference structure, segregating by conference, using polity to divide fraternity.[42]

As conference fraternity and polity showed marked changes, so did its spirituality, so did revival. This session of the New England Conference opened with the Lord's Supper, an innovation for American conferences. But was traditional, revivalistic, class meetinglike spirituality gone? The conference did not want it to be. It devoted the afternoon of the first day to a conference prayer meeting. However, the one ceremony may have been as unusual as the other, or so the secretary's remark would suggest: "The blessing of God rested upon the Assembly. Why might we not have more such meetings, where we can join our prayers and songs, and offer our testimonies? Oh that the day may come when our Conferences shall prove spiritual Jerusalems, and each minister receive the baptism of the Holy Ghost!"[43] Yet there were ample sermons, and even on Sunday, a love-feast at 9:00, prior to the ordination sermons and ordinations. In the evening conference celebrated the anniversary of the New England Missionary Society. Celebration of such a dynamic institution and celebration of the sacrament and celebration through addresses and celebration in reports produced a spirituality quite distinct from that of earlier Methodism. Indeed, conference itself found difficulty in holding that new spirituality within its bounds.

NEW BOUNDARIES, NEW FRATERNITIES

Two years later this same New England Conference took up an issue that would trouble it for several sessions and was then troubling much of Methodism: boundaries. How big could and should conferences be? And should conference boundaries follow the lines that the world drew; specifically, should they heed state lines? New England thought so, as long it could be done "without injuring our work." For the rest of the century Methodism worked at "right-sizing" its conferences and bringing them into closer proximity to political boundaries. So also the church dwelt on the size of districts and the proper ordering of the presiding elders' work in relation to urban and economic patterns. Correspondingly, the district and district conference displaced the quarterly conference as the significant unit below the annual conference, the working "conference" for program purposes. It became especially important in the southern church. And on the local level, the quarterly conference itself, though still named as the operative authority, was given an alter ego, an executive body, the Leaders' and Stewards' Meeting, and later an official board (the MECS established a comparable local entity, the church conference, in 1866).[44] The first duty delegated by the MEC to this new local executive body was that once carried by the classes and class leaders, the screening of persons for church membership.[45] An official board at the local level and boards up and down the conference structure took over the roles that had once fallen to conferences.[46]

Similarly, conference time gave way to program time. Setting the rhythms for the Methodist year was the Sunday school. Its new quarterly uniform lessons and *Sunday-School Teachers' Quarterly*, the interdenominational standard time, displaced quarterly conferences as the de facto timepiece of Methodist life.[47] And the Sunday school superintendent rose to prominence and power, was symbolically and grudgingly given a seat on quarterly conferences, and assumed great significance nationally.[48] John H. Vincent,* prominent in the interdenominational effort but also as head of the new department of Sunday school instruction and corresponding secretary of the Methodist Sunday School Union, provided the interdenominational Sunday school cause, Methodist rhythms, with the quarterly publications, the periodic great national conventions, and the annual teachers' institutes on state and county levels.[49] As well, Methodism's other institutions and activities—colleges and schools, church extension, temperance, and missions—made their own claims on Methodist time and intruded their own rhythms into conference life. Time no longer ran solely on conference patterns. Or perhaps we should say that Methodist life had spilled out beyond the Disciplinary conferences into new conferences, each with its own definition of Methodist time and space.

Sunday school teachers' institutes and conventions were but one of an array of new conferences that had emerged by the time of the Civil War. Women and men, preachers and people met in Tuesday Meetings for the Promotion of Holiness. Preachers meetings stabilized in major cities.[50] Businessmen gathered weekly in special men's only affairs (out of which came both revival and petitions for lay representation). Indeed, the "businessmen's revival" of the late 1850s had invigorated and Methodists had participated in a number of important institutions, including the YMCA and Moody and Moody-type revivals. During the war the Christian Commission had mobilized clergy and laity in channeling support, supplies, and medicine to the front.

The Free Methodists had, as we have noted, organized with meetings of preachers and laity. Both the MEC and the MECS in approving lay delegation provided for lay electoral or district conventions, which found other things to do than just vote. Camp meetings, notably Martha's Vineyard, Massachusetts, Round Lake, New York, and Ocean Grove, New Jersey, had metamorphosed into summer retreats.[51] In the early 1870s Vincent would transform one of them, Chautauqua, into a summer training institute and thereafter a model, a program, and a national scheme for similar gatherings across the country. Other camp

meetings moved decidedly away from nurture and endeavored to reclaim historic
camp meeting religiosity and the holiness that went with it. A. E. Ballard,
George C. M. Roberts, Alfred Cookman, and John Inskip called the National
Camp Meeting for the Promotion of Holiness for Vineland, New Jersey, in
1867.[52] Its success led organizers to establish a National Camp Meeting Association for the Promotion of Holiness and to call a second national conference
for Manheim, Pennsylvania, the next year, a gathering that produced an attendance of some 25,000, including 300 preachers, and that featured preaching by
Bishop Matthew Simpson.* Early support from Methodism's leadership mod-
erated as this venture generated other associations; spawned, encouraged, and
sanctioned a new style of supraconference holiness itineration; and reinvigorated
specifically holiness camp meetings that functioned as a preservation of earlier
patterns and as a prophetic judgment against an Israel that had abandoned its
covenant. Eventually the tension between these new associations and the
church's leadership led to explicit breaks and the founding of new holiness
denominations.

Also testing the conference system were the new organizations for women.
Some, like the Ladies' and Pastors' Union, formally recognized in 1872, would
work within existing conference and congregational networks. Others like the
Woman's Foreign Missionary Society (MEC), approved the same year, founded
1869, and their counterparts in the MECS (1878) and MP (1879), developed
patterns of independence, networks of women's conferences paralleling those of
the denomination, their own publications (particularly *The Heathen Woman's
Friend*), separate itinerancy (women missionaries), and highly successful fund-
raising techniques.[53] Out of such networks, specifically the WFMS but also the
Sunday school institutes and temperance crusades came in 1874 the Woman's
Christian Temperance Union, yet another highly complex system of "alternative" Methodist conferences.[54]

As erosive of the sufficiency of conference were the variety of institutions
established by conferences for their work but now demanding more than yearly
oversight and therefore necessitating trustees or a board. For instance, in addition
to its array of committees, the Philadelphia Conference in 1870 listed officers
and, as appropriate, lay and clergy members of the Conference Church Extension
Society, Managers, the Conference Missionary Society, the Conference Tract
Society, the Trustees of Education Fund, the Philadelphia Conference Education
Society, the Trustees of Ministers' Burying Ground, the Trustees of Centenary
Fund, the Preachers' Aid Society, and the Historical Society.[55] Such bodies,
including the lay and women's organizations, might hold an anniversary meeting
in connection with conference but would in addition meet separately to transact
business.[56] More distinct, of necessity, were the boards for the many secondary
schools (male and female seminaries), the colleges, and the theological seminaries, which conferences staffed but then operated to suit educational rather
than ecclesial patterns.

And then for the MEC there were the new missionary conferences created abroad through foreign missions and in the South through the Freedmen's Aid Society and the educational and missionary efforts there. The church would be perplexed from the start as to how to treat these new conferences, their delegates, and their episcopal leadership.[57] Also new but more immediately suited to the overall conference pattern were district conferences, formed in each presiding elder's district, and in the MECS charged with electing the lay delegates to annual conference. These found more of niche, at least initially, and effectively took over the revivalistic functions once the feature of quarterly conferences. These conferences, noted one contemporary commentator, "give prominence to preaching, prayer-meetings, love-feasts, and revival exercises."[58]

In one sense the district conferences and the new holiness camp meeting associations did reinvigorate conference revival, just as the new men's organizations (clergy and lay) found fresh meaning to fraternity and women's organizations balanced fraternity with sorority, and just as the new boards, nationally and regionally, discovered new vehicles for polity. But in each instance the prerogative that had once been conference took new form and assumed new boundaries. Methodism had simply become too big, too complex, too institutionalized, and too wealthy to run itself by conferences that met only periodically. Conference had once embraced the continent and everything Methodist therein. Conference had once defined time and all Methodism that transpired. Conference had been a new creation, a miracle on the American landscape. Conference, annual conferences in particular, had indeed conferenced the continent. Their sheer number, seventy-six in the MEC in 1872, plus those in the MECS and the MP, attested that conferencing conquest. That number radically divided Methodist agency and gave it a highly regional orientation. Provincial clerical gatherings had administered Methodism life and work a generation earlier. Now Methodism began the centralization and nationalization and bureaucratization through which American society as a whole was tending.[59]

NOTES

1. From resolutions by the North Ohio Conference in August 1844. Cited in Charles Elliott, *History of the Great Secession from the Methodist Episcopal Church in the Year 1845* (Cincinnati: Swormsteadt & Poe, 1855), 402. Michigan spoke of slavery's causing a "deep affliction of our beloved Zion" (407). North Indiana pledged "to the best of our ability, to heal the wounds of Zion" (408). Compare the statement from Holston, on the southern side: "In common with our brethren all over our widely extended Zion, our hearts are exceedingly pained at the prospect of disunion." In "Report of the Committee on Separation," 1844 Holston Annual Conference, in A. H. Redford, *History of the Organization of the Methodist Episcopal Church, South* (Nashville: A. H. Redford, for the Methodist Episcopal Church, South, 1871), 179–81, 179. See "Report of the Committee on Division," 1844 Mississippi Annual Conference, in *History of MECS Organization*, 190–92, and an encomium to Bishop Soule by the Committee on Episcopacy at the 1850 MECS General Conference as "this strong pillar and bright light of our Zion." *JGC/S*, 1850, 179.

2. See *History of MECS Organization*, 153–75, for its resolutions and the text of a long, closely argued "Address. To the Members of the Methodist Episcopal Church within the bounds of the Kentucky Annual Conference." The Kentucky actions and those of other conferences are conveniently gathered also in *History of MECS Organization*, Appendix B, 594–628.

3. *HAM*, 2: 99.

4. The easiest access to this warfare, albeit from an MEC perspective, is through Elliott, *History of the Great Secession*. Himself editor of the *Western Christian Advocate*, Elliott collected clippings from these MEC (northern) papers and from their southern (MECS) counterparts, the *Southern Christian Advocate* (Charleston), the *Richmond Christian Advocate*, and the *South-Western Christian Advocate* (Nashville). From what came to eight volumes and a total of 6,727 fourteen-inch columns, he produced his *History*, which cites liberally from these papers, includes full statements of various conference actions, and represents a companion to the southern *History of MECS Organization*. Reading the two together puts one into the fray.

5. Elliott, *History of the Great Secession*, 402.

6. Ibid., 405.

7. *History of MECS Organization*, 262.

8. Ibid., 264–65.

9. Frederick A. Norwood, *The Story of American Methodism* (Nashville: Abingdon Press, 1974), 207–9; Gordon Pratt Baker, ed., *Those Incredible Methodists: A History of the Baltimore Conference of the United Methodist Church* (Baltimore: Commission on Archives and History, Baltimore Conference, 1972), 214–15; *HAM*, 2: 127–28, 159–67.

10. *JGC*, 1848, 16, 21-22. Also Redford, *History of MECS Organization of the Methodist Episcopal Church, South*, 533–34, 535–38. Pierce responded that his communication was "final on the part of the M.E. Church, South."

11. *JGC*, 1848, 80–85, 154–64.

12. *JGC/S*, 1850, 130–43.

13. *HAM*, 2: 339–60.

14. *JGC*, 1860, 260.

15. An easy access to this political character, albeit only on the northern side, is through Rumsey Smithson's *Political Status of the Methodist Episcopal Church*, 2d ed. (Canton, IL: H. S. Hill, 1868). Smithson excerpted the "political" resolutions passed by MEC annual conferences from 1861 to 1866 (see pp. 11–54). He argued that since the 1844 division, "the Methodist Episcopal Church, has maintained a non-secular character, while the M.E. Church (north) has boldly entered the arena of political agitation" (3).

16. See *ACJ*/Philadelphia, 1862, 7.

17. William Warren Sweet, *The Methodist Episcopal Church and the Civil War* (Cincinnati: Methodist Book Concern Press, 1912); *HAM*, 2: 206–56. Donald G. Jones, *The Sectional Crisis and Northern Methodism: A Study in Piety, Political Ethics, and Civil Religion* (Metuchen, NJ: Scarecrow Press, 1979).

18. See James E. Kirby, "The McKendree Chapel Affair," *Tennessee Historical Quarterly* 25 (winter 1966): 360–70; Sweet, *Methodist Episcopal Church and the Civil War*, 98–99.

19. "The Palmyra Manifesto, June 1865," in Frederick A. Norwood, ed., *Sourcebook of American Methodism* (Nashville: Abingdon Press, 1982), 330–32. Palmyra was the community in which the gathering met.

20. See, for instance, Smithson, *Political Status of the Methodist Episcopal Church*.

He extracted ninety-seven political platforms from forty-six annual conferences covering the years 1861 to 1867, followed a given conference (e.g. New England) through that period and provided then a very handy summation of the political statements for that and other conferences. See pp. 12–14 and 52–53.

21. *ACJ/MEC/S*/Mississippi, 1865, 25–29. Cited in *HAM*, 2: 269.

22. *JGC*, 1844, 158.

23. Ibid., 157.

24. Wade Crawford Barclay and J. Tremayne Copplestone, *History of Methodist Missions*, 4 vols. (New York: Board of Missions, Board of Global Ministries, 1949–73), 1: 257–79, 2: 171–72.

25. "Address of the Bishops," *JGC*, 1844, 162–63. The bishops detailed the benefits thereof.

26. David Sherman, *History of the Revisions of the Discipline of the Methodist Episcopal Church*, 3rd ed. (New York: Hunt & Eaton, 1890), 48.

27. *Journal of the General Conference of the Methodist Episcopal Church, South* (1846), in *History of MECS Organization*, 436–39.

28. *JGC*, 1864, 485–86.

29. For a recent discussion that accents African-American rather than white agency in this church's establishment, see Katharine L. Dvorak, *An African-American Exodus: The Segregation of the Southern Churches*, preface by Jerald C. Brauer (Brooklyn: Carlson Publishing, 1991).

30. For treatment of this and the following see Baker, *Those Incredible Methodists*, 218–28.

31. *ACJ*/Baltimore, 1861, 5, 18 (printed under reports, 44–47), 49; "Preamble and Resolutions," 47–50.

32. *ACJ*/Baltimore, 1862, 22–23.

33. For the flavor of such approbation see the sermon preached by Bishop Morris before the 1864 MEC General Conference on "the *Spirit of Methodism*." *JGC*, 1864, 281–91. See also Abel Steven, *The Centenary of American Methodism: A Sketch of Its History, Theology, Practical System, and Success. Prepared by Order of the Centenary Committee of the General Conference of the Methodist Episcopal Church* (New York: Carlton & Porter, 1865).

34. See the Russell E. Richey essay of that title in *MH* 33 (July 1995): 249–61.

35. See, for instance, *ACJ*/New England, 1864, 1865.

36. Such recollecting demanded the efforts of a specialist and New England had created one, a conference biographer or personal statistician and necrologist, William Bridge, a person who also held the position a long time, for twenty years. Mudge noted that two years later: "He and Secretary Manning, sent out, February 9, 1867, to all the preachers a circular asking them to fill in answers to twenty-seven questions, covering all the important points of their biography, for preservation in the archives and as contributions to the Conference annals." James Mudge, *History of the New England Conference of the Methodist Episcopal Church, 1796–1910* (Boston: Published by the Conference, 1910), 168.

37. The next year New England would achieve another efficiency by preconstituting the Nominations Committee so that it could bring the nominations to conference instead of spending a day or so in making the nominations. *ACJ*/New England, 1866, 4.

38. On the regional character of American society and American institutions, see Peter Dobkin Hall, *The Organization of American Culture, 1700–1900: Private Institutions,*

Elites, and the Origins of American Nationality (New York: New York University Press, 1984), 240–42; and Thomas Bender, *Community and Social Change in America* (Baltimore: Johns Hopkins University Press, 1978), 108–20.

39. This conference heard a sermon on ministerial education.

40. *ACJ*/New England, 1865, 3.

41. *ACJ*/New England, 1865, 42–43.

42. "We deplore the organization of colored Conferences at the last session of the General Conference." Ibid., 45.

43. Ibid., 6.

44. *JGC/S*, 1866, 96, 99–100.

45. The 1868 General Conference made provision for a "Leaders' and Stewards' Meeting," a substitution for sec. II, chap. ii, sec. 17, no. 8, pp. 96–97, of the 1864 *Discipline* (MEC *Discipline*, 1860, 84–85), which had provided for a leaders' meeting. The original report had used the phrase "Official Board" but J. McClintock had moved to amend and substitute "Leaders' and Stewards' Meeting." *JGC*, 1868, 252–54, 539.

46. The same 1868 General Conference provided for the creation of "The Board of Education of the Methodist Episcopal Church" as "a General Agency of the Church in behalf of ministerial and general education." It also reconstructed the Church Extension Society. *JGC*, 1868, 320–22.

47. Later renamed *The Sunday-School Teacher* and made a monthly. See Marianna C. Brown, *Sunday-School Movements in America* (New York: Fleming H. Revell, 1901), 78–79. See extended discussion in part 3 of this text.

48. The 1852 General Conference (MEC) had passed a resolution giving "male superintendents of our Sunday schools . . . a seat in the Quarterly Conferences having supervision of their schools with the right to speak and vote on questions relating to Sunday schools, and on such questions only." *JGC/S*, 1852, 116.

49. See further discussion in part 3 of this text. Anne M. Boylan indicates that the convention system showed Methodist organizational traditions "highly structured and enormously effective at mobilizing large numbers of people. The similarities between the Methodist system—congregationally based class meetings supplemented by local, regional, and national conferences—and the Sunday school conventions was not accident: the conventions had adapted the structure through the influence of their Methodist leaders. Likewise, it was Methodists like Vincent who championed the type of interdenominational cooperation exemplified by the conventions, cooperation based on educational method and technique, not theology." Anne M. Boylan, *Sunday School: The Formation of an American Institution, 1790–1880* (New Haven, CT: Yale University Press, 1988), 92–93. J. M. Freeman, "Growth of the Sunday-School Idea in the Methodist Episcopal Church," *MQR* 53 (July 1871): 399–413. Robert W. Lynn and Elliott Wright, *The Big Little School: 200 Years of the Sunday School*, 2d ed. (Birmingham: Religious Education Press; Nashville: Abingdon Press, 1980), 94–116.

50. Sweet referred to meetings in 1861 of the Boston Methodist Preachers' Meeting and to minutes of the same, a meeting held with some frequency, perhaps monthly. See *Minutes of the Boston Methodist Preachers' Meeting* as cited in Sweet, *Methodist Episcopal Church and the Civil War*, 67, 68.

51. This was already noted in Matthew Simpson, ed., *Cyclopaedia of Methodism,* 5th ed. (Philadelphia: Louis H. Everts, 1883), 162.

52. See Melvin E. Dieter, *The Holiness Revival of the Nineteenth Century* (Metuchen, NJ: Scarecrow Press, 1980), 103–55.

53. See Hilah F. Thomas, Rosemary Skinner Keller, and Louise L. Queen, *Women in New Worlds*, 2 vols. (Nashville: Abingdon Press, 1981, 1982), and specifically Keller, "Creating a Sphere for Women," 1: 246–60. Also see Ethel W. Born, *By My Spirit: The Story of Methodist Protestant Women in Mission, 1879–1939* (New York: Women's Division, General Board of Global Ministries, United Methodist Church, 1990).

54. See Ruth Bordin, *Woman and Temperance: The Quest for Power and Liberty, 1873–1900* (Philadelphia: Temple University Press, 1981) and *Frances Willard: A Biography* (Chapel Hill: University of North Carolina Press, 1986).

55. *ACJ*/Philadelphia, 1870.

56. See *ACJ*/New England, 1873, 5, and 1897, 6.

57. See *JGC*, 1864, 138, 384–85; and *JGC*, 1868, 23–24, 12.

58. Hilary T. Hudson, *The Methodist Armor; or, A Popular Exposition of the Doctrines, Peculiar Usages, and Ecclesiastical Machinery of the Methodist Episcopal Church, South*, rev. and enl. (Nashville: Publishing House of the Methodist Episcopal Church, South, 1892), 146. See also *HAM*, 2: 295–97.

59. See Bender, *Community and Social Change in America*, and Hall, *The Organization of American Culture*..

8
FORMALIZATION

In 1872 the MEC General Conference assembled with laypersons as full dele-gates and took action to make the boards of national Methodist societies elective and thus accountable to the church, that is, to General Conference.[1] The MECS had anticipated the MEC on lay delegation and made boards accountable in 1874.[2] Lay participation and denominationally controlled agencies brought to a culmination the long process by which conferences regularized and formalized administrative duties, established societies or standing committees to execute and implement its affairs, and in effect transferred to agencies the visions and ideals that it had once summarized and embodied in its own life. The 1872 actions completed that process by centralizing denominational agency, thus moving to national boards what had previously been of necessity effected through annual (and to some extent quarterly) conferences.[3] At the expense of annual conferences, General Conference and general boards acquired executive prerogative and initiative and power.

In these once-societies, now national, corporate, and denominational boards or agencies, Methodist individuals and communities increasingly found common interest, labored, invested themselves, channeled their monies, took pride, de-fined denominational loyalty, expressed Methodist identity, and exercised their corporate will.[4] And from them Methodists received program, publications, di-rection, and guidance. Fittingly, the MEC bishops in 1876 recognized the gen-eral agencies as expressions of Methodism's connectional unity: "The great agencies of the Church are bonds of union."[5]

Another change checked the formal authority of General Conference by pro-viding for judicial review. Here the southern church took the initiative and in 1854 empowered the bishops, acting collectively and in writing, with the pre-rogative of challenging a rule or regulation and thereby obliging General Con-ference to muster a two-thirds majority on the question. This action, consonant with its high doctrine of episcopacy, the MECS confirmed and clarified in 1874.[6]

Consonant with its understanding of conference and episcopacy, the northern church proceeded in a different fashion, namely, by generating from out of conference itself and conference procedure a body with judicial authority. Both this committee and the southern College of Bishops would thereafter render "court" decisions, thereby leaving a body of *national* law.[7]

"FORMAL FRATERNITY"[8]

The creation of judicial structures, the structuring of what were once conference prerogatives into national agencies, the admission of laity into General Conference, and the further testing of conference boundaries (by women, African-Americans, missionary structures, and new ethnic populations) focused the church's work at the national level.

Ironically, at this time when the meaning and boundaries of fraternity were being tested from seemingly every side, the term itself acquired increasingly formal force and limited application. Formal expressions of fraternity and exchange of fraternal delegations characterized church gatherings, particularly at national and regional levels. The MEC typically reciprocated with Canadian, Irish, and British Methodists, with the separate German-American denominations, with the African Methodists, and with other American communions. These formal gestures took enough General Conference time to warrant an enquiry into their importance and the appointment of the Committee on Fraternal Relations, which in 1872 recommended that in the future a specific day be set aside for reception of fraternal delegations and the speeches and sermons confined therein and to as many evenings as needed.[9]

In the 1870s white Methodists increasingly applied the phrase "fraternal relations," already possessed of a formal, technical force,[10] especially to the two largely white episcopal bodies, the MEC and MECS, and to international Methodism. The reestablishing of MEC-MECS relations ironically came out of efforts at union between the AME and AMEZ, which broadened to include an overture to the MEC.[11] The overture of the AMEZ to the MEC came to nought. However, MEC legislation authorizing conversations with the AMEZ or "any other Methodist Church that may desire a like union" became the pretext for an overture by Bishops Matthew Simpson* and Edmund Janes* in 1869 to the MECS College of Bishops. Janes also participated in a visit to the 1870 MECS General Conference. The 1872 MEC General Conference appointed, for the first time, a fraternal delegation to the MECS. In response, the 1874 MECS General Conference empowered a fraternal delegation to carry the proposal of a joint commission to "adjust all existing difficulties" standing in the way of fraternal relations.[12] The MEC reciprocated and a Joint Commission on Fraternal Relations met at Cape May, New Jersey, in August 1876. The first southern demand and the first action recalled the overture made by Lovick Pierce in 1848 and a staple in MECS self-understanding, that "there is but one Episcopal Methodism . . . our two General Conference jurisdictions being each rightfully and historically integral parts of the original Methodist Episcopal Church constituted in 1784." Further, "each of said Churches is a legitimate Branch of Episcopal Methodism in the United States, having a common origin in the Methodist Episcopal Church organized in 1784."[13]

The southern commissioners convened separately and kept their own record. They noted that "the form of statement in a certain connection would exclude several colored organizations from the classification of Episcopal Methodisms of this country" and concluded that "the omission of reference to them could not be properly construed as an oversight."[14] The larger Methodist fraternity would be bracketed out by careful attention to constitutional, jurisdictional, and connectional concerns.[15] A formula for fraternity had been defined that would privilege the relationship between the MEC and MECS and keep relations with the AMEZ at very formal levels, the mere exchange of fraternal regards. The joint commissioners then went to deal with the contests over property and territory between the two churches, setting out rules and procedures for adjudication of disputes.[16]

Further gestures of fraternity followed in what would be more than a half-century effort at reunion.[17] Both churches thereafter appointed fraternal delegations, both participated in the first international Methodist Ecumenical Conference of 1881.[18] Both also cooperated in the 1884 centennial of American Methodism.[19] To be sure, these larger gatherings and events, including a second Methodist Ecumenical Conference in Washington, D.C., in 1891, and the many descriptive publications of the churches, exhibited the larger family of Methodist churches. And in the 1890s the MECS and MEC would appoint commissions on federation that seemingly had open agenda.[20] But, in fact, they treated with the AME, the AMEZ, and Colored Methodist Episcopal (CME) Church by encouraging their separate unification. Formal fraternity had taken on an all-white aspect.

FRATERNAL BORDERS

During the 1870s and 1880s the MEC especially faced questions about gender boundaries as well; such questions also troubled the MECS, MPC, Evangelical Association, and United Brethren.[21] One resolution, as we have noted, was to form or give formal recognition to women's organizations. But women's initiatives and experience in running those quickly raised issues of governance, accountability, and representation. Given the established principle among Methodist Protestants and the new opening to lay representation in Episcopal Methodism, could and should the latter permit women to stand as candidates for the lay electoral conferences? Could and should women be elected as delegates to General Conference? Could and should women hold offices in Sunday school and in quarterly conferences?

In certain areas congregations and conferences answered yes to all the above and even to yet another question—Could and should women's call to ministry be recognized and women accepted as local pastors?—and recommended them for ordination as deacon and elder? As early as 1880 the MEC General Conference faced this test in the case of Anna Oliver,* a 1876 recipient of the bachelor of sacred theology from Boston University School of Theology, briefly a pastor in Passaic, New Jersey, until displaced by the Newark Annual Conference, and by 1879 exercising leadership over a Brooklyn congregation.[22] Having obtained a quarterly conference recommendation, she was presented as a candidate to the New England Conference, as was Anna Howard Shaw,* another graduate of Boston. The presiding bishop ruled their recommendations out of order, holding that the law of the church did not authorize the ordination of women. The matter came to General Conference on appeal, with an accompanying resolution from the New England Conference instructing its delegates "to use their influence to remove all distinctions of sex in the office and ordination of our ministry," with the backing of Boston alumni and via a petition from the Willoughby Avenue M.E. Church of Brooklyn petitioning the conference "to make such alteration or alterations in the Discipline as they may consider necessary to remove the disability or disabilities in the way of the *ordination* of our Pastor."[23] On recommendations of its Judiciary and Itinerancy Committees, the conference sustained the bishop's ruling and rejected appeals for a change in the Discipline. Full conference membership and ordination would be a twentieth-century accomplishment, some seventy-five years later.

Also tested in the 1880s was the issue of whether women might, as laity, be conference members.[24] Women involved in missionary organizations and the temperance cause exercised leadership, garnered resources, and demonstrated competence in matters of concern to the denomination as a whole. Should they not be represented where issues of articulation, coordination, and authority were resolved? A particularly important test occurred with the 1888 General Conference to which five women were elected, including one with high visibility across the church, Frances Willard.* The bishops in their Episcopal Address acknowledged their presence and the constitutional issue it raised.[25] The conference refused to seat them, ruling them ineligible under the constitution.[26] Then in a close vote it referred the matter to the annual conferences by proposing a change to the Restrictive Rule applying to lay delegation—"and the said delegates may be men or women."[27] Both laity and clergy voted majorities in favor, but the latter not with the three-quarters required. In response in 1892, the Judiciary Committee unanimously ruled that women were ineligible, but on an amendment another construction of the Restrictive Rule was proposed—"and said delegates must be male members." The strategy was for this to fail in the annual conference votes, thus entailing the opposite reading of the word *laymen*. The proposal failed decisively, but in a quite partial vote, the consequence of some conferences' simply not balloting the question, not an outcome that gave conclusive force to the alternative reading.

Women delegates appeared again in 1896 but withdrew amid the ensuing controversy and did not actually take their seats under a compromise. Only with the adoption of a new constitution in 1900 were equal laity rights for women accepted. With the 1904 General Conference, women could then sit in general conference and in the new lay annual conferences, bodies parallel to the ministerial bodies. Methodist Protestants, long experienced with lay participation, granted lay rights to women about the same time, in 1892, though permitting them roles in annual conference somewhat earlier.[28] Full lay rights for women in the MECS came later, with approval by General Conference in 1918.[29]

The new MEC constitution was driven by lay demands for equal representation in General Conference, demands that animated annual conferences and General Conference sessions from the 1870s on.[30] A 1888 proposed change to allow for no more "lay delegates than there may be ministerial delegates," failed decisively in annual conference votes. But further memorials and requests prompted yet another proposal out of the 1892 General Conference, this one providing that ministers and laity would vote "as one body." It too failed, largely owing to that language.[31] The offensive language was stripped in 1896, but the measure again went down to defeat in annual conference ballots. Later in that quadrennium a similar resolution (from the Rock River Conference) circulated and passed 9,258 to 1,524. During that same period General Conference had put the Constitutional Commission to work on giving greater precision and clarity to "the organic law of the Church" and the procedures for amendment. The 1900 General Conference concurred on the proposition of equal lay representative, and enabling language was therefore incorporated into a new constitution, which was thereafter submitted to annual conferences and passed. Once again the church had been pressed, by both procedure and substance, toward thinking of itself, particularly in General Conference, in political terms. Here, too, as in the case of the general boards and with regard to race, the church would work out its problems at the national level. There, lay men and women would focus their energy and attention.

PROFESSIONALIZING CONFERENCE

By permitting laity, men and women, roles on the national and local levels, in general and quarterly conferences, but not in annual conference, the church reconfigured that regional fraternity, making it the primary clerical entity. Efforts to introduce lay representation into annual conferences recognized that this body, in particular, had special ministerial roles and recommended that laity, if included, have power to speak or vote on all questions "except those affecting the conduct, character, and relations of traveling elders, and the election of ministerial delegates to the General Conference."[32] Increasingly, especially during the twentieth century, annual conferences would take on the character of professional organizations. That development occurred slowly. But already in the late nineteenth century, changes in ministerial preparation occurred that laid the foundations for the later professionalization.

In particular, the church put incredible energy into institution building and made the church colleges and the new theological seminaries important contexts for ministerial preparation.[33] Because conferences invested themselves in these enterprises and viewed them as extensions of their own life and work; because they heard lively annual reports and sent visiting committees; because bishops appointed conference members to presidencies and to the chairs in Bible (college) and theology (seminary), conferences did not, by and large, experience formal theological education as a loss of their prerogative in preparation of persons for conference membership and ordination.[34] At this stage the numbers going to seminary remained small, and the church had to work to remove the disincentives from attendance; for instance, only in 1884 did the MEC make it possible for a person to attend seminary "under appointment" and thus not suffer the loss of time earned "on probation."[35] But formalizing theological education into a seminary program represented a dramatic change in the way that conference had brought persons into ministry.

Previously, ministerial preparation had been solely a conference affair. In two decisive ways the conference and its members had formed new members. First, candidates were brought along through the stages of local leadership into itinerancy through an informal but highly effective mentoring process. The latter preparatory stages included a "traveling with," a supervised apprenticeship while on trial as the junior preacher, yokefellow under a more seasoned itinerant.[36] Second, during this preparatory phase the young preacher read from the conference course of study—by the late nineteenth century a denominationally approved, four-year program of disciplined study.[37] To work effectively the course of study needed the mentoring or apprenticeship relationship; it needed someone to travel with the neophyte in his theological journey; it needed a teacher.

Changes in the itinerancy, as well as heightened appreciation for what formal theological education might achieve, pointed to increased reliance upon institutionalized instruction. Conferences began to put a higher premium on collegiate and seminary preparation for ministry.[38] They also legislated and spoke on the variety of issues having to do with the status, well-being, care of, remuneration for, and number of ministers. Conferences thus began to take on aspects of a professional organization. Conferences would then increasingly traffic with seminaries as one professional agency with another. The MEC conferences did so under guidelines issued by General Conference and, after 1892, of a University Senate, Methodism's venture into national accrediting and standard setting. But each conference came to have its own board of examiners. And these bodies, in the last decade of the nineteenth century and the early decades of the twentieth, exercised exacting oversight over candidates, both those qualifying under the course of study and those pursuing formal schooling, the former often transformed by the conferences into schooling, a quasi-seminary—with a regimented program, with clear classes, assignments, and examinations for each year, with heightened expectations about growth and learning, and with some provisions for direct instruction and a faculty. Persons entering the ministry chose, not between school and the no school, but between the conference cor-

respondence course-of-study school and the residential academic year seminary.[39]

New ministers received the more exacting and more uniform attention than
in earlier days, but they received it from an institution or a committee. Gone
were the linking of junior to senior preacher on circuit and the oversight by the
conference as a whole over the process. Conference dealt with its probationers
through committees. To be sure, it so dealt with virtually everything that way.
By the turn of the century the journal needed ten pages to describe the structure
of conference—officers, commissions, boards, managers and trustees, women's
societies, standing committees, visiting committees, and special committees.[40]
Conference had become a forum for committees and institutions to provide year-
end statements; conference sessions featured a series of reports, votes, resolutions, recognitions, certifications, introductions, addresses, sermons—the annual
missionary sermon, punctuated by the Disciplinary questions—ordinations, a
memorial service, and the reading of appointments.

Complexity and expertise and delegation and specialization and differentiation
were drawing new lines, lines that connected, lines that distinguished, lines that
compartmentalized, lines that unified. Conferences busied themselves tracking
the variety of institutions that now served them, including quite large institutions
like colleges; attending to initiatives that increasingly flowed out of the new
agencies; dealing with local churches themselves becoming wealthy, powerful,
and complex. Minutes, as we have noted, registered the myriad responsibilities
and activities conferences faced. Everything remained connected through conference. Yet the new situation mismatched authority and power. The conferences, which met annually or quadrennially, "oversaw" entities exterior to
themselves that worked day to day with strong executive leadership, large budg-
ets, and responsibilities that intruded into the life of the church, into conference
and congregational affairs. Colleges, seminaries, and especially boards, denominational and women's, though not constitutional and merely creatures of conference, exteriorized work that by polity belonged to conference.

And in other ways, rights and prerogatives that belonged to conference were
exteriorized. The various new gatherings—clergy and lay, male and female—
including those specifically committed to holiness, exteriorized revival from
conference. Even fraternity had come to have an exteriority as it applied less to
relations among brothers than to relations among church bodies. Is it surprising
that conference, annual conference in particular, threw up and defended the
boundaries around maleness and whiteness and language and clerical prerogative? What, otherwise, was brotherhood to mean? What would be left of fraternity, revival and polity?

FROM CONFERENCE TO LOCAL CHURCH

The church found it difficult to let go of the quarterly meeting. As early as
1896 the bishops proposed and as late as 1920 the MEC General Conference
took up again a proposal to concede power to official boards and district con-

ferences and provide only for semiannual church or local conferences.[41] Instead, General Conference would agree, as it did in 1908, not only to displace quarterly meetings as the bishops had proposed but to permit a charge to combine or omit the second and third quarterly meetings.[42] Rather than to change the district conference radically, General Conference gave the presiding elder a new name, district superintendent, a name that distanced and dissociated "him" from the local gathering, a name that accented the supervision of the whole rather than the presidency of the local, a name that gave "him" more organizational than sacramental aura.[43]

Quarterly conference lived on through the twentieth century, but its revivalist and fraternal ideals continued to flag. Increasingly, Methodism put its focus, not on conference, but on the local church. The combined quarterly conferences for the MEC came increasingly to resemble what the MECS knew as the annual church conference, and both churches ran their business monthly with an official board, the MEC formally, the MECS more informally.[44] By the 1920s, "the local church" had become a new norm. Indeed, in their 1928 address, the bishops of the MEC structured the entirety of their remarks in relation to "the local church."[45] By conceptualizing the church in terms of its tasks and the local church, the bishops had made irrelevant, or perhaps better, made "subservient," the entire conference fabric of Methodism: The tasks belonged to the boards and agencies; ministry belonged in the local church. What, then, of quarterly, district, annual, and general conferences? The bishops would never have conceded the irrelevance of conference, nor could they. The denominational tasks and local ministry were tied together by the layers of conference, and through them tasks were distributed, resources garnered, and ministry defined and deployed. Nevertheless, the bishops had recognized a new norm at the bottom that went readily with the new bureaucratic norm at the top. Increasingly, the official board at one end and the boards and agencies at the other defined the operative polity of Methodism. Polity had become organizational. Conferences adjusted accordingly.

The Disciplines reflect the change. The 1928 MEC Discipline indexed "The Local Church" but had treated it under various rubrics. The 1930 MECS Discipline included a subsection entitled "The Local Church," but it appeared under "Christian Education." The first Discipline of the Methodist Church, that of 1940, devoted a section to "The Local Church" but positioned it last under Part IV, "The Conferences." It belonged still to the conference order of Methodist reality.[46] By 1944 and from 1944 to 1960, "The Local Church" became Part II of the Discipline, following immediately after "The Constitution" and preceding Part III, "The Ministry," and Part IV, "The Conferences." Within "The Local Church" were embraced treatments of the quarterly conference and the church conference, as well as the official board. Within that section as well was placed "Church Membership," once a major rubric in its own right. In the 1968 Discipline of the United Methodist Church (UMC) (the union of the Methodist and Evangelical United Brethren Churches), "The Local Church" stands first, constitutes a major section, and even is made to incorporate the church's calendar. And by 1976 Wesley's ministry, once itinerating and connectional and continental and worldwide, had been embraced by, or collapsed into, the local church. "The Local Church" demands fifty-two pages of text and follows immediately upon a short theological statement about ministry. Ministry is characterized as local, and the Discipline recognizes nonlocal ministry under a new rubric, "Appointments beyond the Local Church." Soon thereafter the norm at the top, that defined by boards and agencies, was in deep trouble. Increasingly, Methodists thought not in connectional but in local and parish terms; they spoke of parish ministry and reflected the overall therapeutic and professional changes through which American ministry was passing. By 1990 when the bishops produced a "Vision for the Church," they rendered it in congregational terms: *Vital Congregations—Faithful Disciples.*[47]

JURISDICTIONS

The dynamics of professionalization produced activity at the center—in the general conferences or through the MEC University Senate or MECS College of Bishops—where standards were set, new selections made for the courses of study, regulatory action or oversight undertaken, resources garnered, and rules and definitions made. Professionalization also produced activity at the periphery—on the local and conference level—where, as we have just noted, boards or committees took charge of implementing, interpreting, and applying the standards and where congregations made their own application of standards. Professionalization thus reinforced national standards and, ironically, by their implementation at the conference level, also reinforced longstanding patterns of regionalization and localization, walling up the Methodist fraternity ever more within separate fraternal conference units.

Also to stimulate and reinforce inertial movement toward regionalization of ministry within conferences and within regions were the efforts at unification of Methodism—those conversations between the MECS and the MEC, eventually involving the MPC, that brought the 1939 reunion. They aimed at making Methodism a more national church and, indeed, would have that effect particularly insofar as the boards and agencies were concerned. Ironically, the effect on conference and on episcopacy was not centralizing and nationalizing but fragmenting by region and race. A constitutional regionalization came with the 1939 union by the addition of yet another conference, the jurisdictional, to the great iron organizational wheel—quarterly, district, annual, jurisdictional, general— by locating all white annual conferences within regional jurisdictions and placing all African-American conferences into a new central jurisdiction, and by empowering the jurisdictions with important authority, including that of electing bishops and of the members of national boards. The effect was a far more regionalized and fragmented fraternity than had existed with the three uniting denominations, each of which had been, in its own way, a national body.

The aspiration for jurisdictions came from the MECS, which in conversations that extended over half a century, held out for a minority power (by minority they understood "southern white").[48] They insisted on a conference arrangement that would accord the southern minority within a united church "the power to control its own affairs."[49] In addition, the arrangement would place another minority, namely, the African-American members of the MEC, many of whom gathered in conference in southern territory, into some separate ecclesial structure, preferably one as distinct as the CME Church.[50] The proposed solution surfaced in a 1911 round of discussions of a Joint Commission on Federation, comprised by representatives of the MEC, MPC, and MECS and held at Chattanooga.[51] On this proposal the MPC General Conference deferred action pending action of the episcopal bodies. The MECS in 1914 recognized the agreement as containing the "basic principles of a genuine unification . . . by the method of reorganization" but insisted that African-American Methodists be "formed into an independent organization holding fraternal relations with the reorganized and united church."[52] The MEC, meeting in 1916, also embraced the plan "as containing the basic principles of a genuine unification" but called for additional "Quadrennial or Jurisdictional Conferences" and conceded that its "colored membership" should be reorganized "into one or more Quadrennial or Jurisdictional Conferences."[53]

These actions led to the constitution of a joint commission on unification representing the two episcopal bodies that met from 1916 to 1920 and left on record three volumes and over fifteen hundred pages of debates and speeches. Central in these negotiations was the racial complexion of any "unified" Methodist fraternity.[54] On this issue, the southern commissioners were consistent in insisting on the segregation of African-Americans into some distinct conference, either within or without the new church. The jurisdictional scheme gradually emerged through the discussions as a structure that would (1) provide regional configurations among white Methodists, thus protecting the southern (white) minority from domination by the northern majority, and (2) establish a "compromise" between the southern desire for a CME-like solution and northern resistance to a unification that would further divide the church and expel its black membership. Supporting such a compromise were the two African-American MEC commissioners, I. G. Penn and R. E. Jones, who viewed jurisdictions as much preferable to excision, who did not aspire to union with the other black Methodist bodies, and who welcomed a plan that would, at last, provide for black episcopal leadership. They resisted what became another southern stratagem in the discussions, namely, a conference embracing both Africa and the United States,[55] a scheme for six white regional conferences, one for the "colored people in the United States," and four for membership in foreign countries.[56] African-American Methodists would be represented in General Conference, though not in the same proportions as would the white regional conferences and the foreign representation was even more reduced. To these regional conferences were conferred the rights of episcopal election.[57] In addition, provision was made for a judicial council and for a brake on General Conference action by vote of two regional delegations.[58]

The 1920 MEC General Conference found the plan troubling, and while reaffirming its commitment to unity, it continued its commission and called for the convening of a joint general convention of the MEC and MECS to iron out problems.[59] Where the MEC saw problems, the MECS experienced crisis. Virtual warfare broke out in the South over unification, warfare that badly divided the College of Bishops, that roiled annual conferences, that became the consuming passion of certain papers, and that politicized the entire church. Progressives supported the commission's plan; to oppose it, conservatives formed organizations like the League for the Preservation of Southern Methodism. The lines were clearly drawn and honored over a variety of controversies during the 1920s and 1930s, touching reorganization, the Klan, prohibition, fundamentalism, evolution, and Al Smith.[60] Each of the issues seemed to entail the others, and unification certainly served to emblem conservative fears of the Negro, the North, change, modernism, and secularism.

By its temporizing action of 1920, the MEC took the MECS (1922) off the hook of action on the plan. The MECS rejected the notion of such a joint general convention but also continued a commission and authorized the calling of a special session of its General Conference if the commissions were able to work out a viable plan.

This new Joint Commission met in early 1923 and adopted a new plan, which continued some features of the 1916–20 proposal, but it addressed southern racial and regional concerns by establishing only two jurisdictions, one embracing the MEC, the other the MECS. The MEC General Conference adopted it with little fanfare, as did its annual and lay conferences. By contrast, the MECS General Conference experienced a tense special session, marked by prolonged debate over a procedural amendment proposed by A. J. Lamar and supported by four of the bishops challenging the legality of the special session and calling for a year's delay.[61] The southern church eventually defeated the Lamar Resolution and passed the plan, but not before the opposition to unification had scored its points, many of them detailed in a twenty-five-page Minority Report that insisted that the issues of 1844 were not dead, that the plan surrenders the liberty and independence of the church, that it "practically strips the Annual Conferences of all power in the government of the Church" and confers it on "the Super-General Conference," and that "it established a relation with the negro race not best for him, not possible for us."[62]

Such sentiments carried the day when the plan was submitted, as such fundamental constitutional changes required, to the MECS annual conferences. New organizations emerged, the "Friends of Unification," and the "Association to Preserve the Methodist Episcopal Church, South by Defeating the Pending Plan of Unification," each with its backing within the church press and its patrons on the College of Bishops. The southern Advocates, twenty for unification, six against, hoisted the battle banners and the bishops in their teaching office and as the appointive power weighed in for the two causes. Presiding bishops used and abused their power to sway the annual conference votes. As leaned the presiding bishop so voted the conference, with but one exception.[63] The plan went down to defeat, 4,528 for, 4,108 against, far short of the required 75 percent and indicative of how badly divided the southern church found itself. Convening again two years later in regular session, the MECS accepted the recommendation of its Committee on Church Relations "that there be no agitation, discussion, or negotiation concerning unification during the ensuing quadrennium."[64]

The MECS found further reason for reticence in the 1928 action of the MEC in resolving that it would hold General Conference only where its white and black delegates could be entertained on the same basis.[65] In response, Bishop Edwin D. Mouzon (MECS) proclaimed that this action "postponed the union of the Church South and the Church North indefinitely."[66] The MEC and MPC did continue conversations in the late 1920s and early 1930s, and the MECS rejoined in 1934, the resumption preceded by national youth gatherings, informal meetings of interested leaders, and exploratory sessions of standing commissions on union. The three churches formally authorized negotiations in general conferences of 1932 and 1934. Yet another Joint Commission met in 1934 and 1935, accepted the principles of jurisdictional governance and full lay representation, and appointed a drafting subcommittee.

The plan produced reverted to the 1916–20 conception of multiple white regional jurisdictions and one central black jurisdiction; equal representation of laity and clergy in annual, jurisdictional, and general conferences; retention of bishops and establishment of the Council of Bishops; establishment of a judicial council related to General Conference and the Council of Bishops; and a new name, The Methodist Church. This plan passed in general and annual conferences in all three churches, again eliciting opposition in the South, and this time producing considerable anguish in African-American conferences and among others committed to more genuine Methodist fraternity.[67] African-Americans contributed thirty-six of the eighty-three "no" votes in the 1936 MEC General Conference, eleven others abstaining, and sat in silence while the conference sang "We're Marching to Zion." Seven of the nineteen black conferences defeated the proposal, a few others refusing to vote, the remainder resigning themselves to the inevitable.[68] Just as the nation was becoming more sensitive to its racial inequalities and to segregation as a blight on democracy, Methodism had made more visible and constitutional the color line it had long drawn within its fraternity.

NOTES

1. See MEC *Discipline*, 1872, 164, and the "Report of Committee on Benevolent Societies," *JGC*, 1872, 295–98.
   2. *JGC/S*, 1874, 445, 533.

3. For a discussion of the import of this change, see the "Report of the Board of Church Extension after the change to the General Conference of 1876," by A. J. Kynett. *JGC*, 1876, 602–4.

4. On the import of 1872 and these changes, see William McGuire King, "Denominational Modernization and Religious Identity: The Case of the Methodist Episcopal Church," *POAM*, 343–55; also in *MH* 20 (January 1982): 75–89.

5. "Address of the Bishops," *JGC*, 1876, 393–405. See especially, 400–401.

6. The 1854 measure had been passed with a majority vote and was judged in 1870 to be of constitutional significance, therefore requiring both a two-thirds majority and concurrence of the annual conferences. The constitutional corrective action conveying such judicial review on the College of Bishops was achieved in 1874. See P. A. Peterson, *History of the Revisions of the Discipline of the Methodist Episcopal Church, South* (Nashville: Publishing House of the Methodist Episcopal Church, South, 1889), 38, and Nolan B. Harmon, *The Organization of the Methodist Church*, 2d rev. ed. (Nashville: Methodist Publishing House, 1962), 189–213.

7. Holland N. McTyeire's *A Manual of the Discipline of the Methodist Episcopal Church, South, Including the Decisions of the College of Bishops.* (Nashville: Southern Methodist Publishing House, 1870). In 1903 Bishop Richard J. Cooke produced *The Judicial Decisions of the General Conference of the Methodist Episcopal Church*, the third edition of which was "published under a resolution adopted unanimously by the General Conference of 1916." 3rd ed. (New York: Methodist Book Concern, 1918), xiii.

8. This is the title of the volume that documents the formal fraternity between the MEC and the MECS: *Formal Fraternity: Proceedings of the General Conferences of the Methodist Episcopal Church and of the Methodist Episcopal Church, South, in 1872, 1874, and 1876, and of the Joint Commission of the Two Churches on Fraternal Relations, at Cape May, New Jersey, August 16–23, 1876* (New York: Nelson & Phillips, 1876).

9. *JGC*, 1872, 387–88.

10. See "Early Efforts at Reunion," *HAM*, 2: 660–706.

11. Charles Spencer Smith, *A History of the African Methodist Episcopal Church* (Philadelphia: Book Concern of the A.M.E. Church, 1922), 371–72, 491; *HAM*, 2: 672. David H. Bradley, *A History of the A.M.E. Zion Church*, 2 vols. (Nashville: Parthenon Press, 1956, 1970), 2: 314–18; William J. Walls, *The African Methodist Episcopal Zion Church* (Charlotte: A.M.E. Zion Publishing House, 1974), 460–64; John J. Moore, *History of the A.M.E. Zion Church in America* (York, PA: Teachers Journal Office, 1884), 235–36; *HAM*, 2: 675. William J. Walls, *African Methodist Episcopal Zion Church* (Charlotte: A.M.E. Zion Publishing House, 1974), 464–66; Bradley, *A.M.E. Zion Church*, 2: 319, 321, 332; Moore, *History of the A.M.E. Zion Church*, 262–63; *HAM*, 2: 677. See also *JGC*, 1868, 199, 227, 238, 264, 471–76.

12. *JGC/S*, 1874, 560. That southern delegation included the aged Lovick Pierce,* the fraternal representative not received in 1848 and able to convey his sentiments only by letter.

Fraternal gestures occurred on less official and juridical bases as well. Attesting something of the genuinely "fraternal" aspects of fraternal relations was a camp meeting in the summer of 1874. See *Fraternal Camp-Meeting Sermons. Preached by Ministers of the Various Branches of Methodism at the Round Lake Camp-Meeting, New York, 1874. With an Account of the Fraternal Meeting* (New York: Nelson & Phillips).

13. "One Methodist family, though in distinct ecclesiastical connections." *Formal Fraternity*, 60–61, 67.

14. Journal of the Proceedings of the Board of Commissioners of the Methodist Episcopal Church, South, 1876, 112.

15. *HAM*, 2: 667.

16. *Formal Fraternity*, 69–70.

17. *HAM*, 3: 407–78; James H. Straughn, *Inside Methodist Union* (Nashville: Methodist Publishing House, 1958), 52–55.

18. *Proceedings of the Oecumenical Methodist Conference . . . 1881* (London: Wesleyan Conference Office, 1881). See *HAM*, 2: 696–701.

19. See H. K. Carroll et al., eds., *Proceedings, Sermons, Essays, and Addresses of the Centennial Methodist Conference . . . 1884* (New York: Phillips & Hunt, 1885), and W. H. DePuy, ed., *The Methodist Centennial Year-Book for 1884* (New York: Phillips & Hunt; Cincinnati: Walden & Stowe, 1883).

20. *HAM*, 2: 683–89.

21. See Elaine Magalis, *Conduct Becoming to a Woman* (Women's Division, Board of Global Ministries, United Methodist Church, 1973?); and in Hilah F. Thomas, Rosemary Skinner Keller, and Louise L. Queen, eds. *Women in New Worlds*, 2 vols. (Nashville: Abingdon Press, 1981, 1982), vol. 1, the following essays: Virginia Shadron, "The Laity Rights Movement, 1906–1918: Woman's Suffrage in the Methodist Episcopal Church, South," 261–75; William T. Noll, "Laity Rights and Leadership: Winning Them for Women in the Methodist Protestant Church, 1860–1900," 219–32; Donald K. Gorrell, " 'A New Impulse': Progress in Lay Leadership and Service by Women of the United Brethren in Christ and the Evangelical Association, 1870–1910," 233–45; Rosemary Skinner Keller, "Creating a Sphere for Women: The Methodist Episcopal Church, 1869–1906," 246–60.

22. Kenneth E. Rowe, "The Ordination of Women: Round One; Anna Oliver and the General Conference of 1880," *POAM*, 298–308.

23. Ibid., 302–4.

24. *HAM*, 3: 56–58; Harmon, *Organization of the Methodist Church*, 121–23.

25. "Address of the Bishops," *JGC*, 1888, 33–63, 51.

26. The report as adopted asserted that the church in amending the Second Restrictive Rule "contemplated the admission of men only as lay representatives" and therefore "1. That under the Constitution and laws of the Church as they now are women are not eligible as lay delegates in the General Conference."*JGC*, 1888, 463.

27. Ibid., 95; James M. Buckley, *Constitutional and Parliamentary History of the Methodist Episcopal Church* (New York: Methodist Book Concern, 1912), 307–9.

28. Noll, "Laity Rights and Leadership," 219, 226–30.

29. Shadron, "The Laity Rights Movement, 1906–1918," 270–74.

30. Buckley, *Constitutional and Parliamentary History*, 314–26; Harmon, *Organization of the Methodist Church*, 114, 122.

31. Buckley, *Constitutional and Parliamentary History*, 315.

32. *JGC*, 1880, 92–93, 276, 310, 311.

33. *JGC*, 1888, 248, 287, 355. See Russell E. Richey, "Ministerial Education: The Early Methodist Episcopal Experience," in *Theological Education in the Evangelical Tradition*, ed. D. G. Hart and R. Albert Mohler, forthcoming; also Glenn T. Miller, *Piety and Intellect: The Aims and Purposes of Ante-Bellum Theological Education* (Atlanta: Scholar's Press, 1990); L. Dale Patterson, "The Ministerial Mind of American Meth-

odism: The Course of Study for the Ministry of the Methodist Episcopal Church, the Methodist Episcopal Church, South and the Methodist Protestant Church, 1876–1920" (Ph.D. diss., Drew University, 1984); J. Bruce Behney and Paul H. Eller, *The History of the Evangelical United Brethren Church*, ed. Kenneth W. Krueger (Nashville: Abingdon Press, 1979), 158–59, 192–93; Gerald O. McCulloh, *Ministerial Education in the American Methodist Movement* (Nashville: United Methodist Board of Higher Education and Ministry, 1980), 11–15.

34. William F. Warren, "Ministerial Education in Our Church," *MQR* 54 (April 1872): 246–67, 260.

35. *JGC*, 1888, 354–56.

36. As late as 1931, *A Manual of the Discipline of the Methodist Episcopal Church, South, Including the Decisions of the College of Bishops*, by Holland N. McTyeire, rev. and enl. by Collins Denny, 19th ed. (Nashville: Publishing House of the Methodist Episcopal Church, South, 1931), carried a section entitled "Of the Junior Preacher," 95–96.

37. Warren, "Ministerial Education in Our Church," 246–51.

38. See, for instance, the statement by the Education Committee of the Philadelphia Conference: "We recommend all candidates for admission to our traveling ministry to seek a classical and theological education as a qualification for the duties of the same." *ACJ*/Philadelphia, 1889, 88–89, 41.

39. See *ACJ*/Philadelphia, 1897, 174–76; 1898, 173–80; 1898, 173.

40. Ibid., 1901, 4–13.

41. *JGC*, 1920, 1457, 424–25.

42. *JGC*, 1908, 493, 439.

43. Ibid., 1908, 519–20, 432–33.

44. Harmon, *Organization of the Methodist Church*, 157–63.

45. "The Episcopal Address," *JGC*, 1928, 148–208, 152. "The local church is taken as the unit in our study of denominational progress, for it is there that we are to test the value of our organization and polity. It is the point of Methodism's contact with humanity. It is our recruiting office for the King's service. It is for us the institute of religious technology, our workshop, our training camp, our spiritual hospital, our home."

46. The MECS had, really from 1870, treated "Church Conferences."

47. Council of Bishops of the United Methodist Church, *Vital Congregations—Faithful Disciples: Vision for the Church*, Foundation Document (Nashville: General Board of Discipleship, 1990).

48. See *A Record of All Agreements Concerning Fraternity and Federation between the Methodist Episcopal Church and the Methodist Episcopal Church, South . . .* (Nashville: Publishing House of the Methodist Episcopal Church, South, 1914); Thomas B. Neely, *American Methodism: Its Divisions and Unification* (New York: Fleming H. Revell, 1915); *A Working Conference on the Union of American Methodism, Northwestern University* (New York: Methodist Book Concern, 1916); Paul N. Garber, *The Methodists Are One People* (Nashville: Cokesbury Press, 1939); John M. Moore, *The Long Road to Methodist Union* (Nashville: Methodist Publishing House, 1948); Straughn, *Inside Methodist Union*; Frederick E. Maser, "The Story of Unification, 1874–1939," *HAM*, 3: 407–78; Walter G. Muelder, *Methodism and Society in the Twentieth Century*, vol. 2 of *Methodism and Society* (New York: Abingdon Press, 1961), 251–71; Harmon, *Organization of the Methodist Church*, 167–82; Robert Watson Sledge, *Hands on the Ark: The Struggle for Change in the Methodist Episcopal Church, South, 1914–1939* (Lake Jun-

aluska, NC: Commission on Archives and History, United Methodist Church, 1975), 90–123; Grant S. Shockley, ed., *Heritage and Hope: The African-American Presence in United Methodism* (Nashville: Abingdon Press, 1991); William B. McClain, *Black People in the Methodist Church* (Cambridge: Schenkman Publishing, 1984); James S. Thomas, *Methodism's Racial Dilemma: The Story of the Central Jurisdiction* (Nashville: Abingdon Press, 1992).

49. The language is that of A. J. Lamar, one of the southern commissioners in the Joint Commission on Unification of the Methodist Episcopal Church, South and the Methodist Episcopal Church. The commission's proceedings appeared in a work of that title in 3 vols. (Nashville: Publishing House of the Methodist Episcopal Church, South; New York: Methodist Book Concern, 1918–20), 2: 274. (Hereafter cited as *Joint Commission on Unification.*)

50. By 1916, the MECS had made the creation of a Supreme Court-like judicial body a third concern. *Joint Commission on Unification*, 1: 46.

51. This plan also provided, as would subsequent proposals, for fuller lay representation in annual conferences, a concession to the Methodist Protestants and to advocates of lay rights within the MEC and the MECS. See *A Record of All Agreements Concerning Fraternity and Federation between the Methodist Episcopal Church and the Methodist Episcopal Church, South, and the Declaration in Favor of Unification Made by the General Conference of the Methodist Episcopal Church, South* (Nashville: Publishing House of the Methodist Episcopal Church, South, 1914), 38–39, 43–44. *HAM*, 3: 415–23. This joint commission and round of discussions had been stimulated by a conference of Methodist Protestant and MEC laity in Baltimore and out of that lay conference by a spirited address to the MEC General Conference of 1908 by the Methodist Protestant college president Thomas H. Lewis of Western Maryland.

52. *Joint Commission on Unification*, 2: 42–43; *JGC/S*, 1914, 263–64.

53. *JGC*, 1916, 710–15, 711, 712.

54. See the statements by A. J. Lamar. *Joint Commission on Unification*, 2: 24, 368.

55. See ibid., 100–103, 438–40.

56. For a summation thereof, see *HAM*, 3: 423–34. For the "Report Submitted by the Ad Interim Committee, Richmond, VA., November 7, 1919," see *Joint Commission on Unification*, 3: 561–67.

57. Some saw and bemoaned the effect of these plans on both conference and episcopacy. Said Bishop R. J. Cooke: "We were sent here to unify the Church, not to divide it; but with these Regional Conferences with such regional powers we are dividing the Church again. We may deny it, and keep on denying it; but you do not do away with the thing. Where is your episcopacy? Were we sent here to destroy the itinerant general superintendency?"

Retorted E. C. Reeves: "That is what we are doing."

Responded Bishop Cooke: "Of course, and we know it, no matter what we say to the contrary. You know very well you have not got itinerant general superintendency in regional superintendency as localized in your regions. We all know that. And we were not sent here to do that." *Joint Commission on Unification*, 3: 41.

58. Ibid., 3: 565–67.

59. *JGC*, 1920, 701–4.

60. Sledge, *Hands on the Ark*, 90–123.

61. *Journal of the Special Session of the General Conference of the Methodist Episcopal Church, South*, 1924, 20, 22, 52–54.

62. Ibid., 114–17. The entire Minority Report is pp. 96–120.

63. Sledge, *Hands on the Ark*, 104–7.

64. *JGC/S*, 1926, 161–63.

65. On matters of race see *JGC*, 1928, 257, 259–60, 262, 271, 276, 296.

66. Moore, *Long Road to Methodist Union*, 183.

67. After the MECS College of Bishops declared the plan's adoption, Bishop John M. Moore, president of the College, submitted a written request for a declaratory opinion about the adoption and its legality to the southern Judicial Council, a maneuver calculated to stave off a future legal challenge to unification. See Moore, *Long Road to Methodist Union*, 200–207.

68. Shockley, *Heritage and Hope*, 115; *HAM*, 3: 456–57.

9
PLURALISM

1939 brought unity and division, unity in a larger general conference, now combining the three branches of Methodism into a truly national church, and division into jurisdictions of region and race. That story line—of mergers producing ever-larger fraternities and of new institutions for division and diversity—also defined the drama for annual conferences from 1939 to the 1990s.

JURISDICTIONED FRATERNITY

Jurisdictions divided Methodist fraternity by race, gathering all the African-American conferences into one Central Jurisdiction. Jurisdictions also divided the white fraternity by region. Within the jurisdictions were located critical connectional powers, namely, the election and deployment of bishops and the election of the governing board members of the national agencies. One other connectional power was stripped from General Conference at the Uniting Conference of 1939—the election of the general secretaries of the national agencies.[1] The proposal honored professionalism—Election of agency staff by its own board was, as one proponent put it, in accordance with "the usual practice when you are seeking experts as these boards will require to perform an expert job." Would the nearly 800 members of the new General Conference have the competence, leisure, and judgment to choose as wisely?[2] A few thought that staff professionalism sacrificed important denominational values.

The Uniting Conference was in a festive, celebrative, even revivalistic mood, not in the mood to test elements of the new bond of fraternity, jurisdictionalism, and professionalism, even in the name of what had been essentials of Methodism—connectionalism and accountability to conference (polity and fraternity). The consequence of so defusing authority was to leave the boards and agencies as *the* connectional principle in the church. If the plan did not exactly "ensmall" the church, it did decentralize both conference and episcopacy so as to "enlarge" bureaucracy.[3]

In the churches produced by the 1939 union and another in 1968, jurisdictions functioned as electoral colleges in the Methodist polity. Three of them evolved in significant fashion into genuine conferences, developed an ongoing apparatus, and played key roles in conference economy. The two southern jurisdictions, the Southeastern and South Central, did so by design, effectively carrying into their operations the personnel, relationships, papers, schools, camps, style, and ethos of the southern church. The Southeastern owned the Lake Junaluska Assembly and Emory University, developed a kind of axis between Junaluska and Atlanta, employed two executive secretaries, established program committees covering the major areas of the church's life, and carried on promotional campaigns within the jurisdiction.[4]

The Central Jurisdiction was symbolically problematic from the start, dissociated black Methodists from their white counterparts across town or countryside, created some large and unwieldy conferences, forced leadership to cover great distances, and did not garner the resources nor claim the denominational attention that its proponents had envisioned. It did, nevertheless, connect African-American Methodists in ways that they had not been previously connected; it provided for the identification, development, selection, and exercise of black leadership and did so particularly among black women through the Central Jurisdiction's Women's Society of Christian Service. It also guaranteed black representation on national boards and committees (denominational and women's), produced national leadership for the church, continued as the *Central Christian Advocate* a denominational paper with a significant black readership, gave sustained national attention to the denomination's black colleges, and from the start witnessed prophetically against the very racism that it emblemed.[5] Working with white counterparts and through the Board of Missions, the Women's Society played particularly important roles, from the early 1940s, in promoting interracial concord, campaigning for African-American staffing and representation in denominational missions, and protesting segregation.[6]

The campaign to end the Central Jurisdiction began, then, from within and virtually with its constitution and continued as a quest for a fuller affirmation of Methodist fraternity in the 1950s and 1960s. The church made slow progress, in 1944 expressing a commitment to "the ultimate elimination of racial discrimination in The Methodist Church," in 1948 redrawing some western boundaries to make easier the voluntary transfer of black churches out, in 1952 easing such transfer in 1952, and in 1956 establishing a constitutional principle (Amendment IX) of voluntary transfer of entire conferences or parts of conferences as well as congregations. In 1960 the church embroiled itself in a major debate over elimination of the Central Jurisdiction but failed to agree on a deadline, studying the matter in commissions over the 1960–64 quadrennium and resolving in 1964 with respect to projected unity with the Evangelical United Brethren that "no racial structure[s] be carried over into the Constitution of the new United

Church.'' The Central Jurisdiction met last in a special session in 1967, and the final transfers and mergers were completed by 1973. Some of its energy and vision live on in Black Methodists for Church Renewal (BMCR), a caucus expression to jurisdictional life and yet another form of Methodist fraternity and conference.[7]

Jurisdictions did not create Methodism's racial and regional divisions. Racial divisions survived the elimination of the Central Jurisdiction on a congregational level and in appointment patterns. Jurisdictions did give such divisions constitutional and conference expression. They legitimated a fraternal exclusivism that had been in Methodism from the start and that yielded grudgingly at admission of laity, local preachers, women, and people of color. They also put in place a principle of representation by category (by region and race) that would, as it came to be applied to more and more self-identifications, build division into denominational workings.

CONFERENCE BROTHERHOOD?

The 1939 Uniting Conference did not really debate the Central Jurisdiction and its racial boundaries of Methodist fraternity. Nor was it willing to address another boundary issue, namely, full clergy rights for women. It ''grandfathered'' women already ordained in the MPC;[8] other women would wait until 1956 for full clergy rights and admission as clergy to annual conference. Lay women, however, retained rights of annual conference membership in the new church, as they had in the MPC and MECS (the latter only since 1918).

For former conferences of the MEC, both the admission of laity and the inclusion therein of lay women represented changes to what had once been an intimate *brother*hood. Bodies into which clergy were ordained for life now welcomed lay representatives, with membership only for that one session, and with nothing like the clergy's sense of belonging to the body. Another change, less recognized, was its increased size.

Conference growth had been gradual up to that point, as can been visualized through the opening roll calls of two of the older MEC bodies:

	Baltimore[9]		**Philadelphia**	
	Clergy	*Laity*	*Clergy*	*Laity*
1860	73	0		
1870	115	"	118	0
1880	146	"	155	"
1890	144	"	156	"
1900	160	"	240	"
1910	178	"	215	"

| 1920 | 217 | " | 254 | " |
| 1930 | 202 | " | 217 | " |

Unification doubled both groups by the admission of laity to what were already quite large bodies:[10]

	Baltimore		Philadelphia	
	Clergy	Laity		Clergy	Laity
1940	294	233		258	232

Although only former MEC conferences experienced doubling merely through the admission of laity (by the uniting of the lay conference and the annual conference), even the former MPC and MECS conference members found themselves in bodies of much larger size. Many of the MPC conferences had been small, and the MECS had not accorded the laity parity.[11] Conferences from all three traditions felt the change in scale from being put together with bodies of the other two churches. The Virginia Conference of the new church grew dramatically over its primary predecessor body, that of the MECS. In 1939 it convened with 269 ministers and 127 laity in attendance. The new (MC) conference that same year experienced difficulty in opening, determining its new membership and adjusting lists from the MEC, MPC, and MECS. It boasted 401 clergy and 276 laity.[12] The new West Virginia Conference of the Methodist Church exceeded predecessor conferences even more dramatically. Its first two sessions gathered, respectively, 353 clergy and 224 laity and 415 clergy and 286 laity. The predecessor conferences had been fraternities of roughly 150: MEC conference, 156 ministers plus 23 supplies; MECS conference, 109 clergy and 44 laity; MPC conference, 69 each, clergy and laity.[13] Roll calls for such a crowd were out of the question, and conferences that had not already done so abandoned yet another fraternal ritual. They resorted to registration cards. Clergy complained about conference size.[14]

Although conferences away from the overlap of the predecessor churches did not grow so dramatically and some conferences remained small, new social definitions of conference had been established.[15] Smallness was no longer prized, and a new pattern of conference unifications was set, reversing what had been the nineteenth-century policy of dividing conferences. Over the next decades clergy and bishops sought to enlarge conferences—to increase the appointment options for ministers; to reduce, preferably to one, the number of conferences over which a bishop had to preside; to develop stronger conference programs; to increase the financial base for pension programs; and to achieve efficiencies and savings by merging conference staffs.[16] By 1970 when yet another merger had taken place—this time with the Evangelical United Brethren—the ministerial membership of the Baltimore Conference had reached 662, of eastern Pennsylvania (Philadelphia) 559, of West Virginia 541, and of Virginia 887.

Texas was by then 657, southern California–Arizona 828, East Ohio 799, Iowa 813, West Ohio 1,190, western North Carolina 834 and Florida 854.[17] With roughly equal numbers of laity present, such conferences were outgrowing the sanctuaries and even the college chapels in which they had often met and resorting to gymnasiums and civic centers.

IDENTITY IN UNITY

With a premium now on inclusion, with representation as a constitutive principle, and with conferences of such size as to make exclusion anomalous, the church struggled after 1939, as we have noted, with the segregation that it had institutionalized in the Central Jurisdiction. Other conference particularities and "conferenced" particularity had given way with less resistance. Notable was the decline of the ethnic-language conference. In the 1920s the MEC had divided itself ethnically—ten German conferences, six Swedish, two Norwegian-Danish, two Hispanic, a Japanese, a Chinese, and twenty African-American, plus missions and mission conferences abroad. The MECS lacked the African-American conferences but did feature Native American, Hispanic, and German mission conferences. This older conference ethnicity succumbed to the integrating and unifying tendencies.

German Methodism (within the MEC and the MECS) had suffered in the anti-German fervor of World War I. Churches gave up language particularities, and German conferences merged with overlapped English-speaking counterparts—for the MECS in 1919, for the MEC over the next decade. Also in the 1920s some Swedish, Norwegian, and Danish conferences united with English conferences. Others continued through unification but merged among themselves and then with English-speaking counterparts in the 1940s. A distinct Chinese conference remained until 1952, and a Japanese one until 1964. The major exception to this pattern of ethnic merger were those of the Native Americans and the Hispanics, who though merged with English conferences elsewhere, in the Southwest and Puerto Rico had sufficient territorial rootedness as well as ethnolinguistic staying power to survive the unifications of 1939 and 1968 and the abolition of the Central Jurisdiction. The Rio Grande Conference, the Puerto Rico Conference and the Oklahoma Indian Missionary Conference remain as emblems of bygone conference particularity.[18] A powerful statement of the church's commitment to end conference particularity came in the 1968 unification of English-speaking Methodism with a former German-speaking denomination, the Evangelical United Brethren, itself the product of complex mergers including particularly the Evangelical Church and the Church of the United Brethren in Christ. The 1968 unification entailed the abolition of the Central Jurisdiction and the uniting of the remaining black and white conferences. The process was again one of aggregation and absorption, with the smaller language or racial conferences and churches integrated into the larger and existing Anglo or English-speaking entities. A notable exception was South Carolina, where white and black conferences were of similar size. African-American congregations and ministers were but the last to be absorbed in a church that had put unity in its name.

Ironically, inclusion bred new anti-types. African-Americans were among the first to establish a new, members-only form of conference, the caucus, and were to be among the intended beneficiaries of a new modality of connectionalism, the monitoring or regulatory agency. Black Methodists for Church Renewal (BMCR) dates from a national organizing conference in February 1968, which in the mood of black power, called for self-definition, self-determination, and black solidarity.[19] In that same year, General Conference established the Commission on Religion and Race as a general agency for the new church. Both the caucus and the regulatory commission continued and gave fresh expression to the conference and connectional life that African-Americans had experienced in the Central Jurisdiction. These entities functioned in relation to the whole, though, in a different fashion, not as fellow conferences in the larger fraternity but as monitoring, watch-dogging, advocacy, special-interest agencies. The religious counterpart to the political action group, they operated with a hermeneutic of suspicion, powers or presumptions of investigation and report, a mandate to correct and the warrant of official church policy.

Other groups and commissions, with similarly particularized agenda and membership, emerged about the same time—some like the 1966 Good News Movement to remain an association, others like the 1970 Commission on the Status and Role of Women (COSROW) to gain agency status. In the same year as COSROW was established there emerged the Native American International Caucus.[20] In 1971 come Methodists Associated Representing the Cause of Hispanic Americans (MARCHA).[21] Then in 1974 the National Federation of Asian American United Methodists was formed.[22] In 1975 there followed Affirmation, a gay and lesbian caucus. The caucuses have functioned as political action groups in identifying and developing leadership and urging its recognition by the church as a whole, in representing the interests of their membership, in demanding the resources requisite for effective ministry and mission, and in serving as spokespersons for their membership. The caucuses have also been Methodist conferences, with conference's revivalistic, fraternal, and organizational roles. National and regional gatherings feature fervent, celebrative worship and especially singing; individuals network with brothers or sisters sharing the cause, culture, heritage, or language, and publications sustain those networks between meetings; collectively the members dream, plan, and labor in building effective institutions, both within the caucus and between the caucus and United Methodism as a whole, and they typically garner resources to institutionalize and staff for such programming. Caucuses have become among the most obvious and effective expressions of Methodist connectionalism (though obviously they divide as well as unite). The principles of inclusion and pluralism, and particularly inclusion of diverse populations into conferences of a large, impersonal size, have their costs, among which are fraternity, revival, and order.

THE UNCONFERENCING OF MINISTRY

From the days of Wesley, ministry had been an annual conference affair. Conference determined the conditions and expectations for admission on trial and full connection in the traveling ministry. It decided who would be admitted and ordained. Every year it examined the characters of all in connection. It tried and disciplined any who strayed from the path to holiness. It did the business of the church. It also spent its sessions in preaching and worship, in conversation and dialogue, renewing and reviving fraternity and spirituality. And with the concluding reading of appointments by the bishop, its members accepted or reaccepted a place of ministry in the Methodist connection.

In the late twentieth century, annual conferences were neither capable of exercising nor expected to exercise these offices. Definitions became the office of General Conference, which dealt with ministry directly in a series of studies.[23] Admission and other matters of ministerial relations belonged to a committee that reported to an executive session, a session programmatically and emotionally divorced from annual conference as a whole. Discipline turned into counseling and counseling out, an affair for the conference psychologist and a subcommittee of a committee. The conference's business became the province of a professional conference staff, working out of conference headquarters and bringing to meetings the agenda and actions to be taken. Dialogue and conversation could be found away from the conference floor, in the crowded meal halls or around the bookstalls, but fraternity had become not the one with the whole but the one with his or her tribe or kin. Preaching and worship, confined to the conference itself and no longer regional in its outreach, struggled against the tide of business, reports, appearances, promotions, and elections and struggled in buildings often ill suited to the worship occasion. Logistics and liturgical sensibilities fought to control how communion would be celebrated and other services "staged." Fraternity booked special meals for each caucus and cause to convene and for seminaries to gather their own. Appointments were made long before conference itself, by elaborate, increasingly mandated procedures of consultation, and were widely known before conference convened. Bishops gave up the reading of appointments, a convention imparting no information and lacking drama. Conferences still opened with the singing of "And Are We Yet Alive?" It was a good question. And conferences as a means of grace?

NOTES

1. See *Doctrines and Discipline of the Methodist Church*, 1940, 350–51, for stipulations for staffing of the Board of Education and elsewhere for other boards.

2. See *DCA*, 1939, 181, 183–84.

3. The term "ensmall" was Harold Paul Sloan's. See *DCA*, 1939, 179, 181, 182.

4. *HAM*, 3, 482–83.

5. Grant S. Shockley, ed., *Heritage and Hope: The African-American Presence in United Methodism* (Nashville: Abingdon Press, 1991), 117–72. This really is the motif

of *Methodism's Racial Dilemma: The Story of the Central Jurisdiction* (Nashville: Abingdon Press, 1992), by Bishop Thomas.

6. Shockley, *Heritage and Hope*, 131–37; *To a Higher Glory: The Growth and Development of Black Women Organized for Mission in the Methodist Church, 1940–1968* (Cincinnati: Women's Division, Board of Global Ministries, United Methodist Church, 1978).

7. Major J. Jones, "The Central Jurisdiction: Passive Resistance," in Shockley, *Heritage and Hope*, 189–207; James S. Thomas, *Methodism's Racial Dilemma: the Story of the Central Jurisdiction* (Nashville: Abingdon Press, 1992), 84–147.

8. *DCA*, 1939, 454–58. *Journal of the Uniting Conference of the Methodist Church*, 1939, 509.

9. The Baltimore Conference had been split in 1857 into Baltimore and East Baltimore in consequence of having grown to 363 traveling preachers, the largest conference in Methodism, too large. Hence the division, but only one of many that Baltimore had experienced over the years.

10. For these figures I have used the first roll call vote rather than the opening call of the roll.

11. Illustrative of MPC conferences were Indiana and Ohio:

Indiana	Clergy	Probationers	Laity
1937	51	5	36
1938	48	8	36
1939	56	12	50
Ohio			
1937	53	7	48
1938	58	7	50

ACJ/MPC/Indiana, 1937, 12; 1938, 13; 1939, 14. *ACJ*/MPC/Ohio, 1937, 8; 1938, 22.

12. In the absence of a reliable roll call, this count of those voting indicates how many were on the floor. The next year (1940) the roll call was answered by 477 clergy and 179 laity. In future years the laity would turn out in better proportions. The pattern in the Virginia Conference (MECS) had been

	Ministers	Laity
1936	251	115
1937	275	115
1938	247	94
1939	269	127

ACJ/MECS/Virginia, 1936, 31; 1937, 28; 1938, 21; 1939, 23. *ACJ*/MC/Virginia, 1939, 39–41; 1940, 32.

13. The 1939 MEC conference had included laity (in anticipation of unification) and the numbers had been 170 clergy, 33 supply, 41 laity. *ACJ*/West Virginia, 1938, 17; 1939, 31. *ACJ*/MPC/West Virginia, 1936, 9–12. *ACJ*/MECS/Western Virginia, 1938, 25–26. *ACJ*/MC/West Virginia, 1939, 368–69; 1940, 15. The actual number of effective ministers for 1940 for West Virginia was 369 and the number of pastoral charges 470, 357 of which were filled by episcopal appointment. *Minutes*/M(E)C, spring 1940, 259.

14. For complaints about size, see Nolan B. Harmon, *The Organization of the Methodist Church*, 2d rev. ed. (Nashville: Methodist Publishing House, 1962), 137.

15. West Virginia's experience did not typify those of conferences more remote from the swath across the country where the MEC and MECS competed or where episcopal Methodism overlapped with Methodist Protestant strongholds. Some conferences remained small. In the Northeastern Jurisdiction, in fact, only West Virginia and Baltimore were of this scale. New York East, Newark, Philadelphia, New Jersey, Central Pennsylvania, and Pittsburgh had ministerial membership of 200 or so. And two New England conferences, New Hampshire and Vermont, were under 100. The East German, Eastern Swedish, and Porto Rico Conferences were even smaller, each having about 20 effective ministers. In the Western Jurisdiction, Southern California had 285 ministers in effective relation and California had 225, with other conferences, including the Japanese, Hawaiian, and Latin-American, being quite small.

16. For a charting of conference mergers, see *EWM*, I, Albea Godbold, "Table of Methodist Conferences (U.S.A.)" 2656–75; John H. Ness, Jr., "Table of E.U.B. Conferences," 2676–85.

17. *Minutes/UMC*, 1970, 36–57. The comparable figures for total ministerial membership and pastoral charges were Baltimore, 770/541; eastern Pennsylvania (Philadelphia), 624/467; West Virginia, 617/598; Virginia, 1,040/768; Texas, 718/527; southern California–Arizona, 934/495; East Ohio, 908/689; Iowa, 905/575; West Ohio, 1,402/1,014; western North Carolina, 961/687; and Florida, 953/585.

18. The Porto Rico Conference is now an autonomous Methodist Church in affiliated relationship with the UMC.

19. Shockley, *Heritage and Hope*, 209–10, 225–28.

20. Homer Noley, *First White Frost: Native Americans and United Methodism* (Nashville: Abingdon Press, 1991), 225–30.

21. Justo L. Gonzalez, ed., *Each in Our Own Tongue: A History of Hispanic United Methodism* (Nashville: Abingdon Press, 1991), 60–61, 155–59.

22. Artemio R. Guillermo, ed., *Churches Aflame: Asian Americans and United Methodism* (Nashville: Abingdon Press, 1991), 135–53.

23. Richard P. Heitzenrater, "A Critical Analysis of the Ministry Studies since 1948," in *POAM*, 431–47, and as *Occasional Paper*, 76 (September 1988), United Methodist General Board of Higher Education and Ministry.

Part Three
MEMBERS

10
MAKING MORAL CHRISTIANS
AND LOYAL METHODISTS

'Scrap'd from the world, redeem'd from sin,
   by friends pursued, by men abhorred,
Come in, poor fugitive, come in
And share the portion of thy Lord.[1]

Charles Wesley's 1740 hymn "On the Admission of Any Person into the [Methodist] Society" sounded distinct notes of openness and closedness. In England the Methodist societies were not, nor did John Wesley ever consider them to be, a church but supplementary associations to increase piety. Wesley expected Methodists to retain membership in the Church of England (or other church body).[2] Baptism by an episcopally ordained priest was understood as the sacrament that incorporated persons into the church; confirmation by a bishop was formally necessary before such members could receive Holy Communion. However, many eighteenth-century Anglican clergy attached more importance to baptism than confirmation as the prerequisite for communion—John Wesley included. Since Wesley regarded the Lord's Supper as a converting as well as a sustaining ordinance, he welcomed to the Lord's Table all baptized persons who sincerely sought God's grace and were honest seekers after faith. Only one additional condition was required of those who desired admission into a Methodist Society: "a desire to flee from the wrath to come, and to be saved from their sins."

CLASS MEETINGS, TICKETS, AND TRIALS FOR ADULTS

The openness of Wesley's society was something in which he gloried. But within this openness there was a "closed shop." No particular faith statement was required.[3] The open invitation was almost immediately glossed with the corollary that the members would meet "in order to pray together, to receive the word of exhortation, and to watch over one another in love, that they might help each other work out their salvation."[4] Under the direction of Wesley and his preacher assistants, women and men class leaders watched over those committed to their care as those who must "give an account." The class meeting became the heart of the Methodist fellowship for a century.[5]

The wide range of religious experience and Christian practice that the societies had to accommodate as a consequence of their rapid growth made necessary new measures of supervision. To guard against "disorderly walkers" in the Bristol and Kingswood societies, forty of whom were expelled in February 1741, Wesley borrowed the practice of issuing membership tickets from the early church. Seeing the effectiveness of the measure, similar disciplinary action was taken in London the following April (1742). Thereafter he ordered them for all the societies, combining the issue of tickets with a quarterly examination of the classes by himself or one of his preachers. Those who were keeping the society rules were provided with a visible means of encouragement, and those who were "disorderly" could be removed in a quiet and inoffensive manner simply by withholding their new ticket.[6] To prevent any complaint on the ground of ignorance of what was required of them, the General Rules of the society were read to them the first time they met in class. To remain within a Methodist society, persons had to lead a holy life and offer quarterly proof for review by preacher and peers. Admission itself took place after a period of probation, was recorded in a register, and was marked by the gift of a membership ticket. The right hand of fellowship was used as a visible sign of admission; the context was a society meeting.[7]

In his 1749 *Plain Account of the People Called Methodists* Wesley says that every ticket implies "as strong a recommendation of the person to whom it was given as if I had wrote at length, 'I believe the bearer hereof to be one that fears God and works righteousness.' "[8] As visiting lists became class books, the quarterly class ticket became a kind of passport. Its withdrawal was the sign of exclusion from membership. The discipline was strict, though it must always be remembered that what was involved was removal from the membership of society, and not excommunication from the church.

From the beginning Wesley required prospective members to first complete a period of probation in order to prevent the casual acceptance of "unworthy persons." Prospective members required the recommendation of a class leader with whom they had met. On the formation of the Methodist Episcopal Church (MEC) in 1784 this regulation passed into American Methodist disciplines. In the beginning the probationary period was fixed at two months; five years later (1789) it was extended to six months. Upon recommendation by a class leader the preacher issued new converts a probationary ticket. Although several minor changes were made through the years, a six-month period of probation remained standard in the MEC throughout the nineteenth century. Full members continued under the spiritual and disciplinary supervision of a class leader and an episcopally appointed preacher who issued tickets quarterly to members in good standing. Having already enjoyed the means of grace and the fellowship of the society, probationers were admitted simply by the preacher, upon vote of the Leaders' and Stewards' Meeting, later by the Official Board. Becoming a Methodist meant admission to a class or a particular local church that was part of a connectional system under a common discipline.

The period of probation required before full membership was in some respects comparable to the concept and practice of the catechumenate in the early church, and participation in class meetings may have served as the equivalent of the old scrutinies of baptismal candidates, but a very important difference is that Methodist "catechumens" were persons already baptized.[9]

Although American Methodism organized its revival or society movement into an independent church in 1784, no liturgy for reception of members was provided. In his revision of the Book of Common Prayer for American Methodists, Wesley omitted the office of confirmation. Not until 1864 and 1866 did the MEC and the Methodist Episcopal Church, South (MECS), respectively, adopt their first liturgies for reception of members. Of course, countless persons had "joined" or become members of the MEC long before these liturgies were adopted: through conversion and/or nurture in a class, transfer from other "orthodox" churches, and a public declaration of faith before the congregation. New members were admitted into the classes at the love-feast following the quarterly meeting, and into the local church on the Sunday following the quarterly meeting.

Admission into the Methodist society (later, church) was not permanent. The preacher regularly checked the rolls, and those who did not live up to their profession were excluded. In this sense early Methodists were always on probation. Qualification for membership in Methodist churches was basically moral and disciplinary rather than sacramental, not a sacramental state to be received or attained, but a style of discipleship to be maintained according to stipulated rules and responsibility. (By 1789 some preliminary rules were devised to deal with those members accused of serious lapses of discipline.)

The local church was a society of classes that by disciplinary procedure could receive *and* expel members. From the beginning preachers were required four times a year to read the names of members received and members removed. After 1800 the responsibility shifted from the pastor to a committee. Church trials were always regarded as an expedient of last resort in the Methodist tradition, after every reasonable effort had been made to correct a wrong. The Fifth Restrictive Rule of the constitution of 1808 provided a right to a fair trial for both clergy and laity.[10]

Throughout Methodism's first century members who were unwilling to stick to the Discipline of the church were expelled after a trial by their peers. Preachers generally took the initiative in filing charges. Most expulsions were due to improper conduct or failure to attend class meetings, public worship, and Holy

Communion, seldom for doctrinal deviations.[11] Expelled members who subsequently showed penitence were welcome to return to the fold.

HEAVENLY HOMES, SAINTLY MOTHERS, AND
MEMORABLE CATECHISMS

Training the young, Methodists agreed, belonged in the private sphere of life. This was a sphere that Methodists, along with other Evangelicals, shaped and sacralized as the realm of heavenly homes, saintly mothers, and impressionable children.[12] Methodist leaders assumed that children would be taught the Bible and Christian attitudes by their parents. The home was to be "a little church" in which children and young people learned the moral values of Christian citizens.[13]

To help parents teach their young people the faith into which they had been born, Wesley and early Methodists employed the catechetical method and produced and sold in large numbers a steady stream of catechisms.[14] In the largely bookless homes of the late eighteenth and early nineteenth century Methodists the little summaries of doctrine called catechisms stood out. Although Methodists did not understand themselves to be a confessional church, one finds repeated references to the need to teach the catechism so as to keep children and youth from doctrinal error and build denominational loyalty. Parents, especially mothers, were enlisted to teach the catechism to their children and servants. To counter their argument that they lacked the time, preachers and bishops reminded parents of the long winter evenings and the proper use of Sunday, sometimes threatening them with Christ's judgment if they neglected this responsibility and appealing to the joy they would have in knowing that they had contributed to their children's salvation.

Almost from the beginning (1787) American Methodist books of discipline ordered the preachers to teach Wesley's "catechism" to the children in every charge.[15] Titled *Instructions for Children* and first published in 1745, Wesley created lessons easier for young children to understand than the prayer book catechism.[16] Part one, a sixty-question catechism adapted from Abbe Claude Fleury, was arranged under nine lessons. Lessons 1 and 2 explained the nature of God. Lessons 3 and 4 taught the Creation and Fall. Redemption was treated more expansively in lessons 5 through 7, illustrating the evangelical nature of Wesley's catechism. Lessons 8 and 9 taught the means of grace—the Lord's Supper, prayer, searching the Scriptures, fasting, and Christian conference. The second part of Wesley's *Instructions* shifted from the question-and-answer format to short, pithy lessons on God and the human soul, and how to "regulate" passions and practice borrowed from Pierre Poiret.[17] Wesley's thirty-nine-page catechism became one of his most popular works and was never absent from his publications lists.[18] Throughout his life Wesley continued to urge its use by families, educators, and preachers. Charles Wesley's 1763 collection of *Hymns for Children* contained at least five hymns that were paraphrases in verse of sections of his brother's catechism.[19] For older youth Wesley published *Lessons for Children* in four parts from 1746 to 1754, more an abridged Bible than a catechism.[20] For adults Wesley relied on the standard catechism of the Church of England, which was published in the English Book of Common Prayer. Although Wesley deleted the church catechism when he revised the Prayer Book for American Methodists in 1784, his *Instructions for Children* continued to be available in the United States through successive British and American printings into the 1840s. As early as 1785 Ezekiel Cooper* had been teaching Wesley's catechism to the children of Wesley's Chapel in New York City on Wednesday afternoons:

Wednesday [September] 28, 1785. At three o'clock P.M. I met thirteen or fourteen children in order to catechise them. The Lord met us, and powerfully wrought on the dear children. I believe there was not more than one of them who was not in a flood of tears; the most of them felt a desire to have an interest in Christ. I do not recollect that I ever saw a number of children so wrought upon before. I found my soul unspeakably blessed, and was very happy all the evening.[21]

Within months of establishing a publishing business of their own, in December of 1790 the Council of Bishops and Presiding Elders put Wesley's *Instructions for Children* at the head of their list of titles that needed to be published as soon as possible.[22] Three months later, in the spring of 1791, Wesley's catechism was available from their Philadelphia press at six pennies a piece.[23]

In practice, parents and preachers found Wesley's *Instructions* too advanced for young children and asked for a simpler text "to teach them learning and piety." Preachers carried their plea to the 1790 conference, which requested the Bishops' Council to commission a new "junior" catechism.[24] In response, John Dickins,* a member of the Council who headed the publishing operations for the new denomination in Philadelphia, compiled and published *A Short Scriptural Catechism Intended for the Use of the Methodist Societies* in 1793.[25] The "principal design" of his catechism, Dickins informed parents and schoolmasters in his preface, was to introduce young children to the Bible. "Therefore every answer is as nearly as possible in the language of Scripture."[26] Its thirty-four lessons were heavy on duty (to God, pastors, parents, and neighbors) and harsh on derelicts—the final seven lessons warn about God's judgment! The Lord's Prayer, the Apostles' Creed, and the Ten Commandments concluded the little catechism.

It was Dickins's new catechism rather than Wesley's old one that was "particularly recommended" by Bishops Asbury* and Coke* in their 1798 annotations on the Discipline.[27] Church publisher Ezekiel Cooper's* record book indicates large printings thereafter: 4,000 copies in 1799, 5,000 copies in 1801, and 10,000 copies in 1802.[28] By 1816 Dickins's catechism had been reprinted fifteen times; the latest documented printing is 1847. Freeborn Garrettson,* reminiscing about Methodism's founding era in his semicentennial address to the

New York Conference in 1826, praised Dickins's "most excellent *Scripture Catechism*, which has been [used] so long and so very usefully in the church."[29] Many of the preachers, as they had opportunity, taught the catechism from house to house and urged parents to do the same. Circuit riders routinely carried copies in their saddlebags for sale along the way. Benjamin Lakin, for example, sold fifty-seven catechisms on his Limestone circuit in Ohio in 1817.[30] The new senior preacher on the New York City circuit in 1810, Nathan Bangs,* proposed to his colleagues a plan for catechising the children of the Methodist churches of the city: "Accordingly I gave notice that on a given afternoon I would meet all the children who would attend, furnish them with our "Scriptural Catechism", and give them, lessons to learn. At the time appointed there were no less than three hundred children assembled in the Forsyth-Street Church, to whom I gave the Catechism, and pointed out the method by which they should study it." Bangs continued this practice during the two years he was appointed to the city, and some of his colleagues followed his example. When he returned to the city a decade later as an executive of the denomination, he found many of those children, grown to maturity, members of the church, and "eminent for piety, living witnesses for our highest doctrines of holiness."[31]

More systematic measures were taken by the Tennessee Conference in 1818, which instructed preachers, in a three-part program, to catechize themselves "as often as may be practicable" and to select "in each class of his charge" a person or persons "to keep a record of the names of the children baptized in that neighborhood" and "to meet and catechize the children of the neighborhood who have been baptized by us, or any others put under our care, at least once a month."[32]

SUNDAY SCHOOLS FOR THE POOR

While children of Methodist families received their basic instruction in the home, schools were started to provide Christian nurture and knowledge of the Bible for poor children, servants and slaves who lacked the advantages of Methodist family life. Created in England around 1780, the schools provided rudimentary instruction to working people on their only free day. These schools had the additional purpose of controlling children's behavior, providing an alternative to Sunday rowdiness. By the middle 1780s there were several such "Sunday" schools supported by the Methodists in North America.[33]

The Christmas Conference of 1784 strongly emphasized the importance of religious instruction of "children whose parents are in Society" and enforced upon the preachers the obligation of meeting them an hour every week for religious instruction.[34] Ensuing conferences renewed and enlarged upon these rules. Bishop Asbury led the way by teaching children himself when he could find time to do so. In 1783 he is said to have established a Sunday school for African-American children that was conducted in the home of Thomas Crenshaw in Hanover County, Virginia.[35] Another early Methodist Sunday school was said to have begun in 1785 by William Elliott,* a Methodist lay convert, in his home in Accomac County, Virginia. On Sunday afternoons Elliott taught white boys who had been ''bound out'' to him, together with his own children and some young girls. At another hour he conducted a school for slaves and servants.[36]

Although rules for the instruction of children were incorporated into the first Disciplines of the new church, the term *Sunday school* appears nowhere. Not until 1790 do we find the first recorded conference action on the subject. The first of the fourteen regional conferences of preachers to meet that year (in Charleston, South Carolina, 15–17 February) resolved to establish Sunday schools:

Quest. 17. What can be done for the instruction of poor children (whites and blacks) to read?

Answ. Let us labour, as the heart and soul of one man, to establish Sunday schools, in, or near the places of public worship. Let persons be appointed by the bishops, elders, deacons or preachers to teach (gratis) all that will attend, and have a capacity to learn; from six o'clock in the morning till ten; and from two o'clock in the afternoon till six, where it does not interfere with public worship.[37]

The following year (1791) Bishop Francis Asbury issued a pastoral letter in which he encouraged lay leaders to work with the preachers to found ''in, or near every place of worship'' a Sunday school for boys and a separate one for girls where the fundamentals of learning and religious life would be taught. Evangelism as well as education was on his mind: ''We have but small hope of coming properly at the lambs of the flock,'' he wrote, ''till you have schools of your own founding, and under your direction.''[38] He republished the letter in the 1792 minutes and added a reinforcing postscript dated Philadelphia, 7 September 1792:

I am fully persuaded that the minds of many of our brethren and sisters have been impressed with the propriety of establishing Christian schools on this continent.

We have already had some powerful instances of a gracious work in those schools, where the order of God has been introduced. . . . If preachers, parents and trustees, with schoolmasters and mistresses, would be diligent in this matter, the point would be carried.[39]

Bishops Asbury and Coke continued to press the case for Sunday schools in notes on the 1798 Discipline. Methodists, they said, would be held accountable before God if they neglect ''about one half of the human race [which] is under the age of sixteen.'' After speaking of the difficulties of finding lay teachers of proper piety, the bishops urged the preachers themselves to supply the defects. ''If we can with love and delight condescend to their [the children's] ignorance and childishness, . . . we shall be made a blessing to thousands of them.''[40]

In the years that followed few Methodist Sunday schools were formed and even fewer were successful. Some stout and noisy opponents of Sunday schools attacked them as desecrations of Sabbath. Even more serious was the objection of others to the presence of large numbers of poor and black children in Methodist Sunday schools, a policy Bishop Asbury stressed. Thomas Ware of New Jersey attributed the failure of Methodism's early Sunday schools to their being confined "chiefly to the poor."[41] Jesse Lee* of Virginia highlights racial tensions in his 1809 history:

After this [conference action of 1790], Sunday schools were established in several places, and the teachers took nothing for their services. The greater part of the scholars were black children, whose parents were backward about sending them; and but few of them were regular in attending, and in a short time the masters [teachers] were discouraged, and having no pay, and but little prospect of doing good, they soon gave it up, and it has not been attended to for many years.[42]

Nine winters before, in 1800, George Dougherty, the Methodist preacher stationed in Charleston, South Carolina, was beaten by a mob and had water pumped on him at a public cistern for conducting a Sunday school for the African-American children of that southern city.[43]

By the early 1800s Methodists had founded Sunday schools in the principal seaport cities of New York (1812),[44] Philadelphia (1814),[45] and Baltimore (1816).[46] These early Sunday schools were not attached to a particular local church but were housed in their own buildings and supported by citywide Sunday school societies. The morning and afternoon sessions on Sundays, avoiding public worship hours, included lessons in reading and spelling alternating with periods of religious instruction and hymn singing.[47] Early Methodist Sunday school leaders, following Asbury, emphasized religious instruction over reading and writing, although most schools taught the latter subjects as a means of inculcating the former. (Only later did Sunday schools become institutions primarily for the teaching of the Bible.) As late as the 1820s the Sunday school book list of the Methodist publishing house included books on grammar, mathematics, and history. In the early decades of the nineteenth century many Sunday school organizers began lobbying for a system of free daily schools so that they would be free to teach religion alone on Sundays.[48]

But these early Methodist Sunday schools in urban centers appear to be exceptions. John B. McFerrin* states that previous to 1818 "no move have been made in the [Tennesee] Conference for the organization of Sunday-schools" and that he was not aware of the existence of any up to that time "west or south of Pittsburgh."[49] Not until 1824 did the Discipline emphasize the responsibility of pastors for religious education, and not until 1828 did the Discipline specifically recommend Sunday schools in every pastoral appointment.[50]

NOTES

1. Hymn "On the Admission of Any Person into the [Methodist] Society," Charles Wesley, *Hymns and Sacred Poems* (London: W. Strahan for James Hutton, 1740), 169–

70, stanza 2. Stanzas 3 and 4 read: "Welcome from earth! lo! the right hand, of fellowship to thee we give; With open arms and hearts we stand, And thee in Jesu's name receive! Say, is thy heart resolv'd as ours? Then let it burn with sacred love; Then let it taste the Heavenly Powers, Partaker of the joys above."

2. Principal resources for this part are Ole E. Borgen, "Baptism, Confirmation and Church Membership, Part 1," *MH* 27/2 (January 1989): 89–109; Frederick A. Norwood, *Church Membership in the Methodist Tradition* (New York: Methodist Publishing House, 1958); Paul S. Sanders, *An Appraisal of John Wesley's Sacramentalism in the Evolution of Early American Methodism* (unpublished Th.D. thesis, Union Theological Seminary, 1954); M. Lawrence Snow, "Confirmation and the Methodist Church," *Versicle* 13/4 (Christmastide 1963): 3–17.

3. The General Rules make no reference to the Methodist Articles of Religion or the ancient creeds.

4. "Plain Account of the People Called Methodists," John Wesley, *The Works of John Wesley* (bicentennial ed.), 9: 256.

5. The basic story is told in David Lowes Watson, *The Early Methodist Class Meeting: Its Origins and Significance*, rev. ed. (Nashville: Discipleship Resources, 1987).

6. For more extended accounts of the origin of membership tickets, see Watson, *Early Methodist Class Meeting*, 104–5 and 208–11, and John C. Bowmer, *The Sacrament of the Lord's Supper in Early Methodism* (London: Dacre, 1951), 116–17.

7. Stuart A. Bell, "Reception into Full Membership: A Study of the Development of Liturgical Forms in British Methodism," *Wesley Historical Society Proceedings* 48 (February 1991): 1–40.

8. *Works* (bicentennial ed.), 9: 265.

9. Charles Hohenstein, *The Revisions of the Rites of Baptism in the MEC 1784–1939* (Unpublished Ph.D. diss., Univ. of Notre Dame, 1990), 148.

10. *JGC*, 1808, 89.

11. See James L. Lubach and Thomas L. Shanklin, "Arbitrations and Trials of Members in the Methodist Episcopal Church, 1776–1860," *MH* 9/4 (July 1971): 30–49. A partial list of charges discovered in the pre–Civil War records of John Street Church, New York, and Lovely Lane Church, Baltimore, included "hypocrisy, buying and selling slaves, marrying a wicked man, quarreling and brawling, non-attendance, cock fighting, habitual neglect of family proper, trifling, disorderly walking, immoral conduct, marrying a second wife while first wife was still alive, drinking, fathering a child, swearing, unChristian-like conduct, singing war songs, desertion of a family, non-penitent, adultery, living with husband before marriage, illegitimate child, playing dominoes" (40).

12. On the evangelical sacralizing of the home, see Mary P. Ryan, *Cradle of the Middle Class: The Family in Oneida County, New York, 1790–1865* (Cambridge: Cambridge University Press, 1981); A. Gregory Schneider, *The Way of the Cross Leads Home: The Domestication of American Methodism* (Bloomington: Indiana University Press, 1993); Janet Fishburn, *Confronting the Idolatry of Family: A New Vision for the Household of God* (Nashville: Abingdon Press, 1991); and Colleen McDannell, *The Christian Home in Victorian America, 1840–1900* (Bloomington: Indiana University Press, 1986).

13. Describing pastoral visitation on the Baltimore circuit in 1788, Ezekiel Cooper wrote in his journal: "Time passed delightfully; every friend's house was like a church."

Geo. A. Phoebus, *Beams of Light on Early Methodism in America* (New York: Phillips & Hunt; Cincinnati: Cranston & Stowe, 1887), 92.

14. Protestant catechization blossomed in the Evangelical Revival. The revival's leaders agreed with sixteenth-century Reformers that catechisms of the church, stamped with its authority, should be used in instruction. In the sixteenth century Protestant reformers had revived catechetical instruction. Luther used a question-and-answer form, although the answers tended to be quite long, following the form of questions on the Creed, the Lord's Prayer, the Ten Commandments, and the "Hail Mary," which had developed in the Middle Ages. Later, material on the sacraments was included. Other reformers, including John Calvin and Thomas Cranmer, favored the short-question-and-answer form for their catechisms, which became the prevailing Protestant model.

15. *A Form of Discipline for the Ministers, Preachers, and Members of the Methodist Episcopal Church in America* (New York: William Ross, 1787), 38. Section VIII, "On the Instruction of Children," was added that year.

16. The English catechism appeared in the first prayer book in 1549 and was much shorter than catechisms in use on the Continent. The text was essentially complete by 1604 when its use to prepare persons for confirmation was imposed by canon law. The young Wesley faithfully conducted classes for children and adults using the prayer book catechism during his Georgia mission. Wesley, *Works* (bicentennial ed.), vol. 18; *Journals*, 1:176 and 512. Forty years later, in 1777, Wesley told Mary Bishop, "Our Church Catechism is utterly improper for children of six or seven years old. . . . I should imagine it would be far better to teach them the short Catechism, prefixed to [my] 'Instructions for Children.' " Wesley, *Letters* (Telford), 6:258.

17. John Wesley, *Instructions for Children* (London: Printed for M. Cooper, 1745). Wesley's high opinion of the catechetical works of Fleury and Poiret may be seen in his *Short Account of the Life and Death of the Rev. John Fletcher* (London: J. Paramore, 1786), 160, n.*. Also in *Works* (Jackson), 11:339, n.+. For essential background on Wesley's catechism, see Frank Baker, *The Heart of True Spirituality*, vol. 2, *John Wesley's Own Choice* (Grand Rapids, MI: Francis Asbury Press of Zondervan Publishing House, 1986).

18. Ten separate editions (i.e., printings) were issued during his lifetime and as many afterward.

19. Charles Wesley, *Hymns for Children* (Bristol: Farley, 1763).

20. There are no known U.S. printings of Wesley's *Lessons*, but British printings may have been used in the United States.

21. Phoebus, *Beams of Light on Early Methodism*, 32.

22. *Minutes Taken at a Council of the Bishop and Delegated Elders of the Methodist-Episcopal Church Held at Baltimore in the State of Maryland, December 1, 1790* (Baltimore: W. Goodard & J. Angell, 1790), 4.

23. Wesley's "Children's Instructions" is included in the list "Books published by John Dickins, No. 182 Race Street, near Sixth Street, Philadelphia, for the use of the Methodist Societies in the United States of America, . . . sold by the Publisher and the Ministers and Preachers in the several Circuits," appended to the first U.S. printing of John Wesley's funeral sermon by John Whitehead: *A Discourse Delivered in the New-Chapel in the City-Road on the Ninth of March, 1791, at the Funeral of the Late Mr. John Wesley* (Philadelphia: Joseph Crukshank for John Dickins, 1791). No known copies survive of the early U.S. printings of Wesley's *Instructions*. At least three nineteenth-century American printings survive: New York: Published by Daniel Hitt and Thomas

Ware for the Methodist Connexion in the United States, 1814; New York: Mason & Lane for the Sunday School Union of the Methodist Episcopal Church, 1837; and New York: Lane & Scott for the Sunday School Union of the Methodist Episcopal Church, 1849.

24. The directive to the Council of Bishops to prepare a "proper school book" is included in Jesse Lee's text of the resolution but is not included in the 1795 collected minutes of the conferences. See Jesse Lee, *A Shory History of the Methodists in the United States of America* (Baltimore: Magill & Clime, 1810). (Hereafter cited as Lee, *Short History, 1810.*)

25. *Minutes of the Methodist Conferences, Annually Held in America; From 1773 to 1794, Inclusive.* (Philadelphia: Henry Tuckniss for John Dickins, 1795), 147.

26. *A Short Scriptural Catechism Intended for the Use of the Methodist Societies* (Philadelphia: Parry Hall for John Dickins, 1793). Fifteen documented "editions" (i.e., printings) were issued through 1815; the last documented printing is 1892.

27. *The Doctrines and Discipline of the Methodist Episcopal Church in America, with Explanatory Notes by Thomas Coke and Francis Asbury* (Philadelphia: Henry Tuckniss for John Dickins, 1798), 105.

28. "Account of Books, Pamphlets &c Published for the Methodist Connection by E. Cooper, 1799–1804," Ezekiel Cooper Papers, Drew University Library; see also Ezra S. Tipple, "Ezekiel Cooper: His Pocket Book," *CA,* 17 April 1919, 496.

29. Freeborn Garrettson, *Substance of the Semi-centennial Sermon before the New-York Annual Conference at Its Session May 1826* (New York: N. Bangs & J. Emory for the Methodist Episcopal Church, 1827), 35.

30. For numerous records of catechism sales see "The Preacher as Book Agent in the West" in William Warren Sweet, *The Methodists: A Collection of Source Materials,* vol. 4, *Religion on the American Frontier, 1783–1840* (Chicago: University of Chicago Press, 1946), 698–709. Record of books sold by [Benjamin] Lakin 1807–8, p. 705.

31. Nathan Bangs, quoted in Abel Stevens, *Life and Times of Nathan Bangs* (New York: Carlton & Porter, 1863), 188 f.

32. John B. M'Ferrin, *History of Methodism in Tennessee* (Nashville: Southern Methodist Publishing House, 1873), 3: 18.

33. For the history of American Methodist Sunday schools see John Q. Schisler, *Christian Education in Local Methodist Churches* (Nashville: Abingdon Press, 1969); Cawthon A. Bowen, *Child and Church: A History of Methodist Church School Curriculum* (Nashville: Abingdon Press, 1960). The two-volume *Methodist Publishing House: A History* by James Pilkington and Walter Vernon (Nashville: Abingdon Press, 1968–88) documents the development of Sunday school publications. An older but still useful work because of elaborate documentation is Addie G. Wardle, *History of the Sunday School Movement in the Methodist Episcopal Church* (New York: Methodist Book Concern, 1918), upon whom Schisler and Bowen depend. For the larger context and interpretation see Anne M. Boylan, *Sunday School: The Formation of an American Institution, 1790–1880* (New Haven, CT: Yale University Press, 1988); Robert W. Lynn and Elliott Wright, *The Big Little School: Sunday Child of American Protestantism,* 2d ed., rev. and enl. (Birmingham: Religious Education Press, 1980); and Marilyn Hilley Pettit, *Women, Sunday Schools, and Politics: Early National New York City, 1797–1827* (unpublished Ph.D. diss., New York University, 1991).

34. *Minutes of Several Conversations between the Rev. Thomas Coke, the Rev. Francis Asbury, and Others at a Conference Begun in Baltimore . . . in the Year 1784, Composing*

a Form of Discipline for the Ministers, Preachers, and Other Members of the Methodist Episcopal Church in America (Philadelphia: Charles Cist, 1785), 19. These were, of course, rules Wesley drafted for the Methodist societies in England.

35. "Sunday School Union of the Methodist Episcopal Church, Extract from the First Annual Report," *MQR* 11/9 (September 1828): 350. See also *JLFA*, 1: 349, n. 35, quoting William W. Bennett, *Memorials of Methodism in Virginia* (Richmond, VA: The author, 1870), 127, 297. The 1783 date is based on evidence uncovered in the 1950s by the editors of *JLFA*.

36. Addie Grace Wardle, *History of the Sunday School Movement in the MEC* (New York: Methodist Book Concern, 1918), 46 f.

37. *Minutes of the Methodist Conferences*, 147; *JLFA*, 1: 625.

38. *JLFA*, 3: 102–3. The earliest printing found was in the first collected minutes of the denomination: *Minutes of the Methodist Conferences*, 162–64. The author could not locate a 1791 printing of the minutes.

39. *Minutes Taken at the Several Conferences of the Methodist-Episcopal Church in America for the Year 1792* (Philadelphia: Parry Hall for John Dickins, 1792), 16–19. *JLFA*, 3: 102–3, includes the full text of the 16 September 1791 letter but without the 1792 postscript.

40. Notes on Section XVI, "Of the Instruction of Children," *Doctrines and Discipline*, 104 f. Five biblical texts were cited in support of religious education of children.

41. Thomas Ware, *Sketches of the Life and Travels of Rev. Thomas Ware, an Itinerant Methodist Preacher for More than Fifty Years* (New York: T. Mason & G. Lane for the Methodist Episcopal Church, 1839), 183.

42. Lee, *Short History, 1810*, 163.

43. "Biographical Recollections of the Rev. George Dougherty," by P. P. Sandford, *Wesleyan Repository* (Philadelphia) 3/5 (September 1823): 162 f. The incident is highlighted in "Sunday School Union of the MEC, Extract from the First Annual Report," *MQR* 11/9 (September 1828): 350–51. See also Francis Asbury Mood, *Methodism in Charleston: A Narrative* (Nashville: A.H. Redford for the Methodist Episcopal Church, South, 1875), 89–91.

44. The first Sunday school in New York was established at John Street Church in 1812 by Mary Mason. See G. S. Disosway, "First Methodist S. School in New York," *CA*, 25 May 1865, 162, and *Consecrated Talents: or, The Life of Mrs. Mary W. Mason* (New York: Carlton & Lanahan, 1876; New York: Garland, 1987).

45. *Pioneering in Penn's Woods: Philadelphia Methodist Episcopal Annual Conference through One Hundred and Fifty Years* (Philadelphia: Philadelphia Conference Tract Society, 1937), 169 f.

46. Gordon Pratt Baker, ed., *Those Incredible Methodists: A History of the Baltimore Conference of the United Methodist Church* (Baltimore: Commission on Archives and History, Baltimore Conference, 1972), 123 f.

47. The Methodists had not yet begun to produce Sunday school literature. The Bible and catechism along with the hymnal were the principal texts in the early period.

48. Anne M. Boylan, *Sunday School: The Formation of an American Institution, 1790–1880* (New Haven, CT: Yale University Press, 1988), 19 f.

49. John B. M'Ferrin, *History of Methodism in Tennessee* (Nashville: Publishing House of the Methodist Episcopal Church, South, 1895), 3: 20.

50. *JGC*, 1824, 1:295; MEC *Discipline*, 1824, 58; MEC *Discipline*, 1828, 58.

11
CLASS MEETING AND
SUNDAY SCHOOL, 1816–1866

At the beginning of the nineteenth century, Methodism was a marginal church associated with religious fervor, cultural poverty, and social dispossession. By the 1820s the Methodists were a rapidly growing church and began to climb the ladder of social respectability. They had as many churches, if not as many members, as the Baptists. By 1830 they were reported to be the largest denomination in the United States. By 1850, in a nation where only 25 percent of the population claimed any religious affiliation, almost one out of fifteen Americans claimed affiliation with the Methodists. Each year more Americans were joining the Methodist family.[1]

ADULTS ON PROBATION

What standards did the growing denomination have for new members, what training was required, what kind of rite marked their entry into the church? Critics in other denominations, alarmed by Methodism's growth, scoffed that Methodists had no standards, required no training, and with a simple handshake welcomed all comers. Press reports of a Cincinnati revival in the spring of 1840 insinuated that "irreligious persons who are unfit members of any Church" were cordially received among the Methodists. In a stinging editorial, the editor of the Cincinnati-based *Western Christian Advocate*, Charles Elliott,* retorted that Methodists require prospective members, including those from revivals, to undergo a rigorous, six month period of probation and demand Christian practice as well as profession; but they do not require conversion for admission and do not "pronounce" a probationer or member as "truly regenerated" unless he or "she has plain proofs in the life and conversation" and on membership rolls carry after each name one of two designations *S* for seeker or *B* for believer. Further, Methodists require "the exhibition of Scriptural tests" not just at reception but during a member's whole life as a Methodist: "In the Methodist

Church, it is not required as a condition of membership, that the person *must* have a knowledge of salvation by the remission of sins. But it is required that he be resolved to *forsake all sin, do all the good in his power*, and *use all the means of grace.*'' Finally, Elliott noted, those who reproach the Methodists receive the same kind of persons as full members of their own churches. The only difference, he said is ''what we call *seeking*, they call religion or faith.'' He closed by saying that the critics are simply jealous that the number of Methodists in Cincinnati had grown so large so fast.[2]

During the period of probation candidates were not only under pastoral oversight but also required to meet weekly in small groups called classes under the care of a leader whose duty it was to instruct, exhort, and reprove. Class leaders were to report weekly to the preacher and monthly to the Leaders' and Stewards' Meeting, whether any of the probationers ''walk disorderly, and will not be reproved.'' If, after the lapse of six months, probationers live up to the conditions on which they were admitted and promise to lead a Christian life, they are admitted into full membership. Persons who do not live up to the required standards are dismissed. In doubtful cases persons could be continued on probation for several additional months.

Until 1848 these rules for reception and entry into the church were included in the section of the Discipline dealing with class meetings and came as the answer to the question ''How may we prevent improper persons from insinuating themselves into the society [after 1816 church]?'' Baptism was presupposed but not stipulated explicitly until 1836. The provision that those who were admitted as probationary members should meet at least three or four times in class changed in 1836 to two or three times. The Discipline of 1840 introduced further provisions, also presupposed in earlier days, that the candidates should be examined by the minister in a service of public worship and give satisfactory assurances both of the correctness of their faith and their willingness to keep the rules of the church.[3] Members in good standing from other mainline churches who sought to join the Methodists had to undergo the same six-month probationary period until 1840, after which they could be admitted at once by giving satisfactory answers to the usual enquiries.

Bishop Osmon C. Baker, who wrote the influential *Guide-Book in the Administration of the Discipline* in 1855, expounded these provisions carefully.[4] He quoted Lord King, Bishop Stillingfleet, and Origen to the effect that the early church was very careful concerning the training of church members. Baker made it clear that the preacher in charge had sole authority concerning admission of persons on trial.[5] The acceptance or rejection of an applicant was never submitted to the vote of a congregation. The probationary period, said Baker, provided ample time for lay members to express their opinion to the class leaders and pastor. Baker emphasized that attendance at class meetings was not of itself admission on trial. Candidates for membership had to give evidence of their understanding of the faith and willingness to abide by the General Rules of the church. Baker also cautioned that six months was the *minimum* period for probation. At the end of probation the approval of the leaders and stewards had to be given before reception into full membership by the pastor, which beginning in 1864–66 was marked by a prescribed liturgy in the presence of the congregation. New members were generally received at quarterly meetings or communion Sundays. Since conduct of new converts and old pros alike continued to be monitored by class leaders and pastors, Baker devoted a full third of his companion to church trials.

CONVERT'S GUIDES AND RITES FOR RECEPTION OF MEMBERS

To guide the growing number of converts along the Methodists membership path, the church began to issue survival manuals. Timothy Merritt* wrote one of the earliest convert's guides in 1838 at the request of the New England Conference.[6] A second edition revised by the book editor and published on behalf of the whole denomination in 1841 had much wider circulation in the church.[7] The first half of Merritt's large 260-page guide described the marks of conversion; the second half set forth the convert's duties to God, neighbor, and self. At the request of the Virginia Conference that same year the church's publishing house issued a second guide for converts by Leroy M. Lee.[8] Lee's themes were temptation, watchfulness, prayer, fasting, self-examination, life of faith, and Christian holiness. Both guides found a ready market among would-be Methodists in decades of considerable expansion.

In 1852 Charles R. Lovell of the Ohio Conference published a manual for Methodist families giving a "systematic plan" for studying the doctrines and the Discipline of the MEC along with a guide for Bible study, rules for Christian families, and a "brief catechism upon experimental religion."[9] Other popular guides for northern Methodists-in-training of the period were John Bakewell's *Admonitory Counsels* (1842), Charles Adams's *Portraiture of New Testament Church Members* (1851), John S. Inskip's *Methodism Explained and Defended* (1851), and Augustus C. George's *Counsels to Converts* (1864).

Thousands of Methodists-in-training in the South relied on a series of guides written by Josephus Anderson of the Florida Conference. Thomas O. Summers,* influential book editor for southern Methodists, issued Anderson's first 350-page guidebook for "Bible Christians" in 1855.[10] Five years later, in 1860, Summers urged southern Methodist pastors to use a second manual specifically designed to train members and probationers.[11] Roughly half of Anderson's 1860 work centers on the duties of membership.

Methodists inherited no concept or rite of Confirmation from Wesley. The Methodist's progress in faith was long thought to begin with infant baptism, to continue in catechetical training at home and in church, and to be marked decisively by a conversion experience.[12] Special prayers and thanksgivings were offered on Sundays when new members were welcomed long before formal rites were approved.[13] Disciplines of the several churches required the General Rules to be read quarterly in local churches and especially on occasions when new members were publicly admitted. By 1840 the Book of Discipline of the MEC added a public examination to probation. After the six-month probationary period new members were required to "give satisfactory assurances both of the correctness of their faith and their willingness to observe and keep the rules of the Church."[14]

SUNDAY SCHOOLS AS NURSERIES OF PIETY

After 1820 the status and role of Sunday schools in Methodism changed. Schools increasingly shifted to exclusively religious education, since more of their pupils came under the orbit of local public schools. Their clientele, originally restricted to poor, neglected, often black children, came to include the children of the middle class. With the inclusion of middle-class children, congregations incorporated Sunday schools into their life and denominational leaders gave growing support. Women, particularly middle-class women, found the Sunday school one of the earliest of Christian programs receptive to their services; schools profited from the talents of women as teachers. Methodism applied its Wesleyan-Arminian theological framework and its revivalistic program to theories of children's spiritual development and to the schools' curricula, organization, and goals. Presuming that salvation was offered free and that proper training in early childhood would ease the transition to regenerate adulthood, Methodists assumed that their primary task was to impart religious knowledge to children who lacked it and thereby to bring children to conversion.[15] The program and theory worked well. Religious conversions occurred in striking proportions among Sunday school pupils.

The schools' curricula reflected its new purposes. Children were organized into classes according to reading skills, not by age, and boys and girls customarily attended separate classes. One began in the alphabet class and finished in the reading class. In the latter, students busied themselves memorizing prescribed portions of the Bible and vying with each other for weekly prizes awarded to those who memorized the largest number of verses.

Early Sunday school boosters seemed to believe that truth lodged in the mind could not fail of good effects. Emphasizing the importance of understanding what one learned, Methodist Sunday school teachers began actively to discourage random memorization of Bible verses and to experiment with new lesson schemes.[16] Each lesson contained ten to twenty selected Bible verses for students to memorize and teachers to explain. The lessons were logically organized to take students through whole portions of the Bible in a specified time. Limiting the lessons, suggested the authors, enabled the children to receive explanations from their teacher, calculated to drive home the intended moral or spiritual lesson.

Both the random memorization method and the selected lesson method had the same purpose: to instill basic knowledge of biblical truths. Yet the move to selected lessons seems to have been precipitated by the teachers' recognition that in dealing with children they could not use the methods they employed with adults. Children's Bible reading had to be guided; they had to be shown what the Bible was telling them to do. So Methodists blended theological concepts with psychological concepts. The child's mind was not merely an empty receptacle into which one poured useful facts but a working mechanism that processed and organized information. Similarly, the child's soul was less like a glass clouded by original sin than like a piece of soft wax, shaped by impressions received in the experiences of daily life. The impressions conveyed by Sunday school lessons might spark a realization of a child's depraved state (a realization that preceded conversion) and in later life bear fruit in regeneration. The new emphasis on helping the child understand and feel the lessons indicated growing acceptance of the notion that the child's heart as well as mind was capable of being shaped. By 1830 most teachers were no longer content merely to teach students to read, or simply to listen to their recitation of lessons. They had come to expect conversion as the end result of Sunday school instruction.[17]

PROMOTING SUNDAY SCHOOLS

The spread of these new theological and psychological ideas among Methodist Sunday school teachers in turn precipitated reorganization of the schools. In April 1827 the Sunday School Union of the Methodist Episcopal Church (SSU) was organized in New York City, with Nathan Bangs,* head of the Methodist publishing house since 1820, as corresponding secretary.[18] Bangs's leadership of the church's publishing house served the new society well. Books and tracts on Sunday school work poured forth—Bibles and hymnals,[19] lesson books and teacher manuals,[20] and the denomination's first periodical for young children, *The Child's Magazine*.[21] To wean Methodists away from publications of the rival American Sunday School Union (perceived to be tainted with Calvinist heresy[22]), Bangs added a regular Sunday school column in the church's widely circulated weekly newspaper, the *Christian Advocate*, which mixed Sunday school book promotions with Sunday school news and teacher training. The workload demanded an assistant and a second editor specifically assigned to Sunday school publications. John P. Durbin* was appointed in 1832.

In fall 1827 the *Advocate* announced the publication of the first in a series of question books, *Scripture Questions*, part 1(on the Gospels and Acts), compiled by John P. Durbin to meet the need for selected lessons.[23] Designed primarily for teachers who, often having little training aside from their own religious experience, were not able to ask questions and interest the scholars by any instruction connected with the lesson, *Scripture Questions* represented a new, more direct approach to Bible study.[24] With the aid of the books, teachers could ask their students the types of questions that would excite the mind to a careful and thorough examination of the Scriptures. The "Scripture Question" for July 1829 was "How do you prove that the saving grace of God is free in all?"[25]

The books contained no answers; students and teacher had to deduce the answer from the memorized text. Aimed at stimulating religious conversion, questions books served to drive home the doctrines of sin, repentance, and regeneration as the Bible illustrated them. Age-grading replaced crude division by reading skill. Small classes of six to ten pupils per teacher, previously considered desirable, became a necessity. Bible classes came into being to accommodate adolescents of conversion age. After completing the Bible class and experiencing conversion, older adolescents could return to the school as teachers, and many did. The best-developed schools thus had a series of three or four classes through which students passed from around seven years of age to about sixteen. Methodists appear to have pioneered "infant classes" for four- to six-year-olds.

The new Sunday school society was welcomed by a majority of Methodists. Within four months it had received the sanction of the Philadelphia, New York, New England, and Genesee (upstate New York) conferences. The 1828 General Conference of the church gave its approval to the new society, formed a general committee on Sunday schools and tracts, and added to the Book of Discipline the first formal directive to organize Sunday schools in every pastoral appointment (circuit or station).[26] That year Ebenezer F. Newell reported:

In Kennebunk Port we organized for the purpose of raising a [Sunday] school. The enemies tauntingly remarked, "The Methodists can't get up a Sunday School and sustain it." But we selected our teachers—gave them class papers—advised them to go through the whole place—search out all the little children and youth, and advise with their parents and guardians to send them to some Sabbath school. . . . The next Sabbath more than 30 united with us in a school. . . . [27]

Gathering up reports from Maine to Missouri, the SSU claimed a rapid growth in the number of Sunday schools and pupils, both doubling in the first year.[28] After 1830 the growth was steady and constant until the schism of 1844. In the fourteen-year period there was a gain of over 2,000 schools and 100,000 students.[29]

Further efforts to support Sunday schools took place in the 1830s. The 1832 General Conference made it the duty of the presiding elder to promote Sunday schools, and it added statistics on Sunday schools to reports of preachers to the annual conferences. The General Conference also ordered the publication of a manual on Sunday school teaching.[30] In 1833 three struggling Methodist societies—the Bible Society (formed 1828), the Tract Society (formed 1817), and the Sunday School Union—were united into one organization. By the late 1830s the Sunday school division of the new organization had become administratively ineffective, and by 1840, according to Nathan Bangs, the SSU was "defunct." His explanation is that the attempt at "amalgamation" had proved "injudicious."

In response the General Conference of 1840 enacted legislation marking a new era in the relation of the church to children and youth. Reorganized preceding the general Conference on lay initiative, the General Conference gave official sanction to the SSU, required Sunday schools in all congregations, placed them under the control of the quarterly conference, and expanded their mandate to include young people as well as children. Pastors were required to visit Sunday schools regularly, to give a progress report at each quarterly conference, and to preach on their benefits twice each year. Bishops were requested to appoint Sunday school agents to travel through the conferences promoting Sunday schools.[31] The publishing house was instructed to launch a new Sunday school paper. Begun in 1841, the *Sunday School Advocate* became the church's first successful Sunday school periodical which soon overtook the adult *Advocate* in the number of subscribers.[32]

The effect of this legislation was to make the Sunday schools an integral part of the church, its curriculum officially planned, each separate school no longer a law unto itself. The 1840 General Conference had taken the first step toward making Sunday schools *church* schools. John M'Clintock bragged: "There is no other [church], we believe, which has distinctly recognized the Sunday school in its legislation, and has so closely incorporated it with the whole system of its ecclesiastical and pastoral work."[33]

Lack of a full-time executive and sufficient funds for the promotion of its program handicapped the reorganized SSU in its first quadrennium (1840–44). The next General Conference (1844) remedied the situation by providing a source of income—each Sunday school was asked to contribute one cent per pupil per quarter—and by electing as "editor of Sunday School Books and Tracts" Daniel P. Kidder,* widely known through the church as a person of energy, of administrative skill, and with literary gifts.[34] The next month, elected "corresponding secretary" of the SSU, Kidder made the Sunday School Union the central agency for education of children and youth in the church.

As editor of the three-year-old *Sunday School Advocate*, Kidder boosted its circulation to 200,000 subscribers. To stock the growing number of Sunday school libraries, Kidder began the "Sunday School and Youth's Library," a series of cheap (prices ranged from ten cents to twenty-five cents apiece) cloth-bound books on all sorts of subjects, which by 1846 had run to some 570 titles and a series of even cheaper "Juvenile books" of stitched paper (from eight cents to seventy-seven cents a dozen).[35] He arranged reprint rights with the prestigious Religious Tract Society of London and enlisted the aid of many American writers. In his tenure at the SSU, Kidder is said to have compiled and edited more than eight hundred Sunday school books.[36] Besides selling books through ministers and by mail, the Book Concern established retail outlets in six cities for its Sunday school and other publications.[37]

CATECHISMS GO TO SUNDAY SCHOOL

Throughout the early decades the Sunday school session seems usually to have consisted of the memorization and recital of Bible verses, songs, and the catechism.[38] Successive Disciplines instructed Methodist parents and preachers to teach their children to read and commit to memory "our catechisms." By the 1820s as Sunday school leaders began to take up the catechetical task, they longed for a new catechism to replace the aging catechisms drawn up by Wesley and Dickins.* In his Episcopal Address to the 1820 General Conference Bishop William McKendree's* final appeal was for greater attention to training of the children of the denomination and for "an enlarged and doctrinal catechism . . . to train the children of the Methodists so as to establish them in the religion of their fathers."[39] The next General Conference (1824) responded to the bishop's appeal to save the children. It required preachers in charge to introduce the catechism into Sunday schools and commissioned a new catechism.[40]

The General Conference of 1824 appointed a committee "to compile a larger Catechism for the use of Sunday Schools and of children in general."[41] Instead of drafting a whole new set of catechisms, the American committee simply revised a set of three catechisms recently published by Methodists in England.[42] Richard Watson, the most influential Methodist theologian on both sides of the Atlantic during the second and third quarters of the nineteenth century, drafted the series of catechisms while systematizing Wesley's thought into his famous *Theological Institutes*, published 1823–29. Watson's series of three graded catechisms designed for the use of Sunday schools and families had been commissioned by the British Methodist conference as the authorized catechisms of the church. They were first published by the Methodist Book Concern in New York in 1826.[43]

The first and second catechisms made considerable use of the catechisms of the Church of England and the Westminster divines, as well as Wesley's *Instructions for Children*. Catechism 1, designed for children under seven years of age, was arranged under five topics: God, Creation, the Fall and humankind's sinful state, Redemption, and Heaven and Hell. Then follows a section devoted to prayers for little children, a morning prayer, a prayer for evening, and a young child's prayer for the Lord's Day. Children were to learn these prayers while they were mastering the catechism and follow each with the Lord's Prayer.

Catechism 2 was arranged under nine headings—God; Creation; Fall; redemption through Christ; the Holy Ghost, the law of God, the sacraments, the Word of God; and prayer, death, and judgment. The content is similar to that of Catechism 1, with the addition of a number of scriptural texts for each theme. An appendix contains a short catechism of scriptural history and additional prayers. The scriptural history covers the main facts and events of both the Old Testament and the New Testament set forth in catechetical fashion. In the section on prayer, examples are given of morning and evening prayers along with table graces.

Catechism 3 was Watson's own original work. Intended for use by older youth, it aimed to guard young minds against the snares of skepticism and infidelity by stating with clearness and force the leading "evidences of revealed religion" and by refuting the most plausible and popular objections to the Christian faith. The strictly catechetical method shifts to the form of a dialogue between young people and their pastor or teacher: Therein are shown proper questions for youth to ask and proper answers for the pastor to give.

Watson's senior catechism, a miniversion of part 1 ("Evidences of Christianity," i.e., apologetics) of his famous *Institutes*, covered (1) "Definitions and Explanations," (2) "A Revelation from God highly probable and necessary," (3) "The Evidence by which a revelation may be satisfactorily proved to be divine," (4) "the Antiquity, genuineness and authenticity of the books of Scripture," (5) "Internal evidence of the truth of Scripture," and (6) "Objections answered."

Methodism's new catechisms, like those of the Westminster divines and the Church of England, stated their truth dispassionately in terms of formal doctrines and used precise language. They lacked the warm, personal character of Luther's *Small Catechism* or the Reformed *Heidelberg Catechism*, whose style and phraseology possess a degree of warmth and beauty and appear to late-twentieth-century readers to be difficult, abstract, and beyond the comprehension of the average young person.

Nevertheless, beginning in 1840 Methodist pastors were required by their Discipline to use the catechisms "as extensively as possible, both in our Sunday-schools and families" and to "faithfully enforce upon parents and Sunday-school teachers the great importance of instructing children in the doctrines and duties of our holy religion."[44] The annual report of the Sunday School Union of the denomination for 1845 reported: "Two textbooks, the Bible and our church Catechism, with the auxiliary of suitable question books, commentaries, etc., constitute the sum total of the books to be incorporated into its course of study."[45] Watson's catechisms along with Wesley's *Instructions for Children*[46] continued in use more or less regularly among northern Methodists until 1852.

Public examinations of candidates in the Sunday school became a standard part of Methodist practice in the early nineteenth century. The pastor who failed to catechize the children in the presence of the congregation lost one of the most important means of Christian education within church life. Such examinations were accompanied by suitable hymns, prayers and sermon by the pastor. Certificates indicated that the holder had completed the course of instruction, had learned the rudiments of the Christian faith, and fortified by these, was all the more prepared for the hoped-for conversion and holy living. Only after the Civil War would the concluding event for older youth and adults in a catechism class be reception into church membership, now called confirmation.

CATECHISMS FOR SLAVE MISSIONS

When Methodists in the South organized themselves into a separate church in 1845, they continued the use of Watson's Wesleyan catechisms for older white youth and young adults. For African-American children and adults, they had already a separate catechism prepared and published by William Capers* as early as 1833.

A system of plantation missions was begun by the South Carolina Conference in 1829.[47] It prospered under the direction of Capers, veteran missionary among the Creek Indians and then presiding elder of the Charleston District.[48] By 1843 seventeen missionaries were preaching to 6,000 (6,556) slave members and giving instruction to 25,000 (25,025) slave children.[49] The missionary on the Savannah River Mission in the Georgia Conference in 1835, W. P. Harrison, described his work: "The work . . . embraces [nine] plantations. . . . I visit each plantation every week, catechize orally 165 children, divided into 9 classes, and pray with the old and sick in their houses or hospitals. . . . On each plantation a house is provided by the owner in which the slaves assemble to receive my instruction and worship. I have lectured or preached every night, and three or four times each Sabbath, beginning at sunrise."[50] On some of the plantations African-American local preachers assisted the white missionaries in their catechetical duties.

By 1840 Capers had become secretary of the southern department of the church's missionary society, and from that position he inspired much enthusiasm, support, and action on behalf of plantation missions throughout the South. Other slave or plantation missions were maintained by the entire denomination, but most of their financial support came from Methodists and other friends (notably Episcopal plantation owners) in the South.[51]

Missionaries, like frontier circuit riders, traveled from plantation to plantation, meeting with the slaves on conditions laid down by the white planters. The plan was usually class meeting and preaching followed by catechizing of the children. The greatest handicap that confronted the missionaries was the ban on the use of written materials, including the Bible and catechisms, in the instruction of slaves, a response, in part, to the 1831 Nat Turner slave rebellion. By the 1850s nine of the fifteen slave states restricted the instruction of slaves to oral means. Although northern critics were certain that religious instruction without books would fail, southern missionaries like Capers resigned themselves to the slave code. Missionaries soon found oral instruction worked well because of the remarkable memory of many of the slave children whom they catechized.

To meet the requirements of oral instruction, southern clergy had to devise special materials designed for learning by rote.[52] In 1833 Capers published in Charleston one of the earliest catechisms designed with the oral instruction of slaves in mind.[53] The tiny three-by-five-inch *Catechism for Little Children* combined lessons on salvation with lessons on duty.[54] Each of the four untitled lessons on salvation is followed by a summary that could be sung responsively by the girls and boys. The Lord's Prayer follows the second lesson, and the whole is followed by three hymns.[55] Four years later Capers expanded the children's catechism to twelve lessons.[56] He added an appendix of selected passages of Scripture on duty to God and master.[57] Two passages taught obedience and servitude as a religious duty (Ephesians 5:22–26:4 and I Timothy 6:1–2). Others forbade sins slaves were believed most likely to commit: sexual immorality (Matthew 5:27–28), lying and false witness (Zechariah 5:3 and James 5:12), Sabbath breaking (Nehemiah 13:17–18 and Numbers 15:32–36). I Corinthians 5:9–10 and Revelation 21:7–8 condemned drunkenness and stealing. With one exception, Romans 4:2–3, which treats justification by faith, the basic themes of God's love are notably absent. Capers chose Bible verses not for general instruction in Christian faith and conduct but for the indoctrination of slaves, making them submissive to their masters and moral in their outward conduct. Capers also added the Ten Commandments and twenty hymns that reinforced the same themes.

By the middle 1830s Methodists throughout the South employed the little booklets to instruct their slaves in their homes and on their plantations. The catechism reflects the growing moral sentiment in the South that sanctioned the "Christian" patriarchal family and fostered gender, parental, and slaveholding control.[58] The following was a note struck in Capers's report on the work of the South Carolina Conference Missionary Society to the 1836 South Carolina Conference:

Our missionaries inculcate the duties of servants to their masters, as we find those duties stated in the Scriptures. They inculcate the performance of them as indispensably important. We hold that a Christian slave must be submissive, faithful, and obedient, for reasons of the same authority with those which oblige husbands, wives, fathers, mothers, brothers, sisters, to fulfill the duties of these relations. We would employ no one in the work who might hesitate to teach thus; nor can such a one be found in the whole number of the preachers of this Conference.[59]

Two years after Methodists in the South were organized into an independent pro-slavery church and one year after he had been elected a bishop, in 1847, Capers published a third edition of his catechism.[60] The MECS kept Capers's black catechisms in print well after slavery was abolished.[61]

NEW CATECHISMS ALL AROUND

For a generation Methodists North and South had relied on catechisms borrowed from the Wesleyan Methodist Church in England. Mid-century parents, pastors, and educators found them "correct in doctrine" but "not well adapted to the use of our people, chiefly on account of containing many hard words and phrases not easily remembered by children."[62] Both the MEC and the MECS took steps in the next few years to commission, publish, and promote new catechisms.

The 1848 MEC General Conference directed its SSU to prepare "one principal Catechism for general use on Christian doctrine, ordinances, and duties, to be accompanied with Scripture proofs" and a new elementary catechism "in shorter and plainer words, adapted to the capacities of young children." The job of drafting the new catechisms went to Daniel P. Kidder, editor of Sunday school publications since 1844, who welcomed the assignment and relished the task of reinstating the catechism into the growing numbers of Sunday schools of the denomination.[63] Kidder's drafts were approved by the Book Committee in 1851 and submitted to the General Conference of 1852. The conference unanimously approved the two catechisms and authorized the development of a third for older youth and adults that would have additional study materials attached.[64]

Kidder planned one catechism covering basic concepts as God, Creation, salvation, the means of grace, death, and judgment, but he offered it in three graded versions. In the basic or starter catechism, No. 1, the answers are "generally short, and the words easy."[65] From such a beginning Kidder promised easy progress from the Scripture proofs of the second to the enlarged instructions of the third. To the starter catechism were added a selection of liturgical materials designed to prepare children for public worship—the Lord's Prayer, the Ten Commandments, the Apostles' Creed, the Beatitudes, and "the Baptismal Covenant"—along with a collection of "Prayers for the Young," including the famous "Now I Lay Me down to Sleep" and the still familiar Wesley table grace "Be Present at Our Table Lord."

Kidder planned that young children would commit the basic catechism to memory to be able to repeat it verbatim when asked, either in numerical order or at random. The next step would invite children to commit to memory the Scripture proofs of the several answers as furnished in Catechism 2. More mature scholars were then ready for the instructions of Catechism 3, which expands the answers of No. 1 and the proofs of No. 2 into something like a minisystematic theology. Each question with proofs is followed by an explanatory essay, a number of practical questions, and a set of definitions. "The design of this catechism throughout," Kidder argued, "is not only to exercise the memory, but to discipline the mind, to enlighten the understanding, and to improve the heart."[66] Kidder succeeded on all counts except the last. His catechism gave greater prominence to the intellectualist moral psychology lurking behind Watson's catechisms he intended to replace. Following his mid-century theological colleagues, Kidder significantly narrowed Wesley's interest in means that awaken, strengthen, and shape Christian character. Instead instruction focused on formal doctrines and apologetics.

Kidder and other church leaders hoped that the study of the new catechisms would "become universal in our Sunday-schools and in our families."[67] Minor revisions of Kidder's Catechism 1 occurred in the years following the Civil War, probably by Bishop Vincent: The first was the addition in 1876 of an appendix titled "The Church," which acknowledged the newly reorganized boards and agencies.[68] The second came in 1884, Bishop Vincent's "Ten Doctrines of Grace."[69] Catechisms 2 and 3 remained unchanged from 1852 to 1905. To accommodate Methodism's non-English-speaking pastors and congregations, Kidder's catechisms were translated into Swedish in 1854,[70] into German and Norwegian in 1857,[71] into Danish in 1870,[72] into Spanish in 1879,[73] into Korean in 1885,[74] into Italian in 1887,[75] and into French in 1893.[76]

At the same time, catechisms became a focal point of the southern Methodism's mission to the slaves; the 1854 General Conference recommended "a more systematic use of catechisms in our [white] Sunday Schools."[77] This was in part the work of Thomas O. Summers, book editor for the denomination, who favored catechetical training centered in the Sunday school. The previous year, in 1853, Summers wrote a small book tracing the history of catechetical instruction from the primitive church through the Reformation to the Evangelical Revival. Modern Methodism and its Sunday schools, he concluded, were "not incompatible with the Catechumenical System."[78] The next MECS General Conference (1858) called for a new set of catechisms for Sunday school and family instruction and invited Summers to draft them and seek the bishops' approval.[79]

Before the year was out, in November 1858, Summers published a two-part *Scripture Catechism* that blended biblical scholarship and liturgical sensibilities.[80] Each part contained sixty-plus question-and-answer lessons on the books of the Old or New Testaments. Part 1 also featured versions of the Apostles' Creed, the Lord's Prayer, the Ten Commandments, and Jesus' Summary of the Law designed to be "chanted" in Sunday school or church service.[81]

Two years later, in 1860, Summers published a comprehensive, 460-page book of catechisms for the use of his church. To his own new *Scripture Catechisms* Summers added another newly commissioned catechism: S. L. Farr's *A Manual for Infant Schools*, a 16-page catechism for young children first published that year.[82] Two other older sets of catechisms still in use were also included: the three catechisms of the Wesleyan Methodist Church prepared by Richard Watson in 1823–24 and Capers's two-part *Catechism for the Use of Missions*, essentially the enlarged catechisms prepared for slave missions in 1837 and revised in 1847.[83]

Bishop George F. Pierce gave high praise for the impressive collection.[84] Nonetheless, after the Civil War the southern bishops preferred catechisms which "shall indoctrinate the children under our religious tuition in *Wesleyan theology*."[85] So an abridged version of Watson's Catechism 2 was printed as an appendix to the 1866 Book of Discipline,[86] although the practice of including a catechism in the Discipline did not continue. Requests for new catechisms at the 1870 and 1874 General Conferences were deemed "inexpedient." Instead, the 1874 General Conference instructed pastors and Sunday school teachers to "see that our infant classes are faithfully instructed in Caper's Catechism No. 1 and that the Wesleyan series be used after that by the different classes, according to their advancement."[87] Southern Methodist pastors and Sunday school teachers continued to use Watson's catechisms until a new series of "common catechisms," produced jointly by the MEC and MECS, were published in 1905.[88]

Immigration in the years following 1840 swelled Methodism's German population. Both the MEC and the MECS formed German districts within many English conferences. By 1864 northern Methodism's ministry among German-

Americans was reorganized into four separate annual conferences. German-language editions of the hymnals and Disciplines, along with weekly newspapers, followed. Additional resources in German were sought, including a catechism.[89] William Nast,* principal organizer of German-American Methodism and long-time editor of the MEC's German Methodist newspaper, produced two graded catechisms for review by the 1868 General Conference.[90] Nast's "Smaller" and "Larger" catechisms were published with the blessing of the General Conference that year (1868).[91] They were so good that within a year they were translated and printed for use in English congregations.[92] A revised edition of the Larger Catechism appeared in 1892, and the last documented printings in English appear to be 1896. Methodism's mission conferences in Germany and Switzerland kept them in print well into the new century.[93]

Nast drew generously upon the pattern of Luther's smaller and larger catechisms and on fellow German-American Philip Schaff's recently published catechism, sources he gratefully acknowledged.[94] The purpose of the catechism, said Nast in the preface, was not a mere drill in Methodist doctrine; it was much more to develop attitudes of confidence in God and in God's love. For example, God's providence was stressed in comforting words: "What application should you make of the fact that God is the creator, preserver, and ruler of the World? This, that I, myself, owe my life and all that I enjoy to the special providence of a gracious, all-wise, and Almighty God."[95] The warm pastoral spirit communicated through a profusion of personal pronouns marks off Nast's catechism from the cool, dispassionate definitions of Watson's, Kidder's and Summers's then widely used by English-speaking congregations.

FADING USE OF CATECHISMS

In the years that followed the publication of this new family of Methodist catechisms, interest in and use of catechisms waned as the influence of the Sunday school movement crested in American Methodism. Still bishops, church executives, and conferences regularly admonished pastors and Sunday school teachers to use the new catechisms and steadily bombarded them with creative pedagogical and promotional packaging. Kidder, Summers, and Nast all hoped to revive catechetical instruction by making it central to the mission of the Sunday school. Kidder sponsored a new rule in the northern Methodist Discipline, added in 1852, which required preachers to "publically catechise the children in the Sunday-school."[96] A monthly recitation of the whole catechism was recommended in every Sunday school. To make the task interesting a variety of exercises were suggested, including recitation in unison, by classes, by gender, and by individuals.

In addition to drafting a new rule for the Discipline, Kidder wrote in 1871 one of the most influential books on pastoral theology. Revised in 1881, Kidder's *Christian Pastorate* became a standard textbook in Methodist theological seminaries on the practice of ministry for the rest of the century. Kidder's text urged pastors to implement the disciplinary directive to use the catechism in the Sunday school and publicly catechize the children in special and in general exercises, "thus making sure that they all understand the great principles of Christian doctrine, and can vindicate them by Scripture proofs."[97] Kidder also recommended that pastors question children on the catechism during pastoral visitation in homes.

To add interest a *Pictorial Catechism*, large in size and lavishly illustrated, was published by northern Methodists beginning in 1855. One reviewer called it "the best [catechism] now extant in any of the Churches," which "should be a household book in every Methodist family."[98] To aid pastors in leading public recitations the catechism was set to music. The Oxford League, an early fellowship for Methodist youth formed in 1884, published a book of choral services that mixed hymns and catechism in the middle 1880s.[99] John O. Foster produced a catechism "in concert exercise form" in 1891. Twelve leaflets designed to be used as a complete program or serially on twelve Sundays intermingled hymns and prayers with the catechism's questions and answers.[100] In the early 1870s Bishop Vincent produced an expanded version of the standard catechism for Sunday schools, *The Church Teacher*, which added lessons for young people in the history, doctrines, and usages of the MEC.[101] Sunday school hymnals also played a role. In 1879 the standard *Hymnal of the Methodist Episcopal Church* was issued with Catechism 2 plus the Baptismal Covenant, the Lord's Prayer, the Ten Commandments, the Apostles' Creed, and the Beatitudes for use of Sunday schools.[102] A completely new Sunday school hymnal, at the direction of the General Conference of 1884, contained the liturgical portion of the catechism: the Baptismal Covenant, the Lord's Prayer, the Ten Commandments, the Apostles' Creed, and the Beatitudes.[103]

To stimulate plummeting sales of the catechism in 1882, the MEC Sunday School Union reduced the already low price of the catechisms. To reward those who completed the course of catechetical study, "Catechumen's Certificates" were rushed into print. By the 1890s MEC's top-of-the-line certificates were printed in two colors on heavy enameled cardboard, bound in white satin, and enclosed in a "neat" envelope with printed blank for the inscription of presentation. "Just what is needed to emphasize and make interesting this important branch of home and Church training" said the Book Concern's advertising.[104]

Parents, too, were regularly reminded of their duty to teach the catechism at home. After 1864 the revised Methodist Episcopal rite for baptism of infants reminded parents and guardians of their duty to teach the catechism along with the Lord's Prayer, the Ten Commandments, and the Apostles' Creed to newly baptized infants "as soon as *he* shall be able to learn."[105] Bishop Vincent in his 1872 book on the Sunday school tried to persuade heads of families "every Lord's Day, at night, [to] cause all his family to repeat the Catechism to him, and give him some account of what they have learned in public that day."[106]

Perseverance is the key to success in catechetical instruction, but mid-century

Methodism's commitment to basic training wavered. Despite admonitions, directives, price cuts, retitling, and promotional efforts, Methodists showed little interest in the new catechisms either at home or in Sunday schools. The MEC Sunday School Union, in its 1872 annual report, reluctantly conceded that the church catechism was "frequently overlooked."[107] Although the SSU continued to offer the catechism as an official alternative curriculum,[108] and printed selections from the catechism in the popular new uniform-lesson series (Berean Leaflets),[109] Methodists had discovered a better way to form Christians than drilling children in denominational theology. The way to teach children, and by implication adults, they increasingly thought, was to recognize the futility of catechetical rigidity and to present the truths of biblical religion in a more pleasant manner. Only German-American Methodists continued to take catechetical training of children seriously.[110]

NOTES

1. Roger Robins, "Vernacular American Landscape: Methodists, Camp Meetings, and Social Respectability," *Religion and American Culture* 4/2 (summer 1994): 166.

2. Charles Elliott, ed., "Receiving Persons into the Church," *WCA*, (1 May 1840), 6, cols. 4–5.

3. MEC *Discipline*, 1840, 91; *JGC*, 1840, 124. See also David Sherman, *History of the Revisions of the Discipline of the Methodist Episcopal Church* (New York: Nelson & Phillips, 1874), 123. Public examination by the pastor before the congregation was dropped in the 1908 MEC *Discipline*.

4. Osmon C. Baker, *Guide-Book in the Administration of the Discipline of the Methodist Episcopal Church* (New York: Carlton & Phillips, 1855), 28 ff. Baker's guidebook was updated each quadrennium through 1884–88.

5. The propriety of maintaining the duty of receiving members as a pastoral function, in opposition to its surrender to the laity as a whole or to a committee, had been defended by Bishops Coke and Asbury in their 1798 notes on the Discipline: *The Doctrines and Discipline of the Methodist Episcopal Church in America, with Explanatory Notes by Thomas Coke and Francis Asbury* (Philadelphia, Henry Tuckniss for John Dickins, 1798), 147 f.

6. Timothy Merritt, *The Convert's Guide and Preacher's Assistant* (Boston: D. S. King, agent for the New England Conference, 1838).

7. Timothy Merritt, *The Convert's Guide and Preacher's Assistant*, 2d ed., rev. (New York: G. Lane for the Methodist Episcopal Church, 1841).

8. Leroy M. Lee, *Advice to a Young Convert in a Series of Letters on Practical Christianity* (New York: G. Lane for the Methodist Episcopal Church, 1841).

9. Charles R. Lovell, *Methodist Family Manual Containing the Doctrine and Moral Government of the Methodist Church* (Cincinnati: Applegate & Co., 1852).

10. Josephus Anderson, *The Bible Christian: A View of the Doctrinal, Experimental, and Practical Religion*, ed. Thomas O. Summers (Nashville: E. Stevenson & J. E. Evans for the Methodist Episcopal Church, South, 1855). Six additional printings were issued through 1884.

11. Josephus Anderson, *Our Church: A Manual for Members and Probationers of*

the Methodist Episcopal Church, South, ed. Thomas O. Summers (Nashville: Southern Methodist Publishing House, 1860). A second printing was issued in 1874.

12. For British Methodist practice see Stuart A. Bell, "Reception into Full Membership: A Study of the Development of Liturgical Forms in British Methodism," *Proceedings of the Wesley Historical Society* 48 (February 1991): 1–40.

13. Nolan B. Harmon makes the case for an informal equivalent to confirmation in his *Rites and Ritual of Episcopal Methodism* (Nashville: Publishing House of the Methodist Episcopal Church, South, 1926), 57. Charles Hohenstein doubts the practice was widespread in his *The Revisions of the Rites of Baptism in the MEC, 1784–1939*, unpublished doctoral diss., Univ. of Notre Dame, 1990, 143. However, at least one pastor, D. W. Clark, chair of the Ritual Revision Committee, 1860–64, and later a bishop, confessed that since the mid-1840s he had been using a rite he prepared on his own: *DCA*, 13 May 1864, 2–3. Josephus Anderson included a proposed "Form to Be Used in the Reception of Persons into Full Connection" as an appendix to his 1860 book *Our Church: A Manual*, 301–4.

14. MEC *Discipline*, 1840, 84.

15. Anne M. Boylan, *Sunday School: The Formation of an American Institution, 1790–1880* (New Haven, CT: Yale University Press, 1988), 22–59.

16. See in the next section a discussion of *Scripture Questions*, a series of Sunday school texts launched by the Methodists in 1827.

17. Boylan, *Sunday School*, 14 ff.

18. "Constitution Adopted April 2, 1827, Sunday School Union of the Methodist Episcopal Church," *MQR* 10/8 (August 1827): 367.

19. The first of a long line of hymnals specially designed for Methodist Sunday schools was issued in 1827. Its publication was announced in the *CA*, 17 August 1827, 198, col. 3. The hymnal was priced at $1.50 per dozen or $12.00 per hundred. *Selection of Hymns for the Sunday-School Union of the Methodist Episcopal Church* (New York: N. Bangs & J. Emory for the Methodist Episcopal Church, 1827). The little hymnal contained 174 hymns without tunes. Revised and enlarged Sunday school hymnals were issued in 1832?, 1841, and 1849.

20. In its first annual report the Sunday School Union reported, "Already they have published for the use of our schools 111 editions of 38 different and appropriate books, besides 10,000 copies of the Sunday school hymn book, 3,500 copies of the Holy Bible, 18,000 copies of the New Testament, and 6,000 of the *Scripture Questions on the Evangelists and Acts*. . . . It is estimated that 773,000 books have been printed for the use of our sabbath schools since our organization, besides 154,000 numbers of the *Child's Magazine*, and several hundred thousand tickets for rewards. . . . Upwards of 60 depositories have been established in various parts of the country for supplying the schools with greater convenience." *MQR* 11/9 (September 1828): 351. The Union did not print its own literature but bought at cost from the Methodist Book Concern.

21. *The Child's Magazine*, a sixteen-page monthly ornamented with a woodcut, cost 37 and 1/2 cents per year plus postage, reduced to 25 cents per year plus postage for persons who took eight or more copies. By 1828 its circulation reached twelve thousand. Nineteen volumes were published from 1827 to 1845. For older youth the denomination had been publishing *Youth's Instructer [sic.] and Guardian* since 1823, nine volumes of which were published from 1823 through 1832. James P. Pilkington, *Methodist Publishing House: A History* (Nashville: Abingdon Press, 1968), 1: 209 f.

22. See Nathan Bangs, "Sunday School Library Books," *MQR* 13/3 (July 1831): 352–53.

23. *CA*, 19 October 1827, 26, col. 3. Parts 2 and 3, containing questions on the historical books of the Old Testament and the Epistles respectively, were published early in 1828. See "Extract of the first annual report of the SSU," *MQR* 11/9 (September 1828): 351.

24. See James C. Wilhoit, *An Examination of the Educational Principles of an Early Nineteenth Century Sunday School Curriculum: The Union Questions* (unpublished Ph.D. diss., Northwestern University, 1983).

25. "Scripture Questions" were included in each monthly issue of *The Child's Magazine*. This example is taken from 3/1 (July 1829): 14.

26. *JGC*, 1828, 357; MEC *Discipline*, 1828, 57–58.

27. Ebenezer F. Newell, *Life and Observations of Rev. E. F. Newell, Who Has Been More than Forty Years an Itinerant Minister in the Methodist Episcopal Church New England Conference* (Worcester, MA: C. W. Ainsworth, 1847), 230.

28. Early annual reports were published in full in the *CA*: the first was 23 May 1828, 151; the second, 3 July 1829, 174; the third 21 May 1830, 150. Extracts were included in the *MQR*, e.g., the first, September 1828, 349–53.

29. *HAM*, 1: 585.

30. *JGC*, 1832, 410–11.

31. *JGC*, 1840, 127 f.; MEC *Discipline*, 1840, 65.

32. *The Sunday School Advocate* continued to be published for eighty-one years, from 1841 until 1921.

33. John M'Clintock, "The Sunday School in Its Relation to the Church," *MQR* 3/49 (October 1857): 515.

34. *JGC*, 1844, 140.

35. *Annual Report of the Sunday School Union of the MEC (1846)* (New York: Lane & Scott, 1847), p. 22. For description of these series see Pilkington, *Methodist Publishing House* 1: 282–85.

36. Addie Grace Wardle, *History of the Sunday School Movement in the MEC* (New York: Methodist Book Concern, 1918), 83.

37. Pilkington, *Methodist Publishing House* 1: 214.

38. The McKendrean Female Sabbath School Society of Baltimore in its *Seventh Annual Report* (1824) states that in the Lombard Street School, with a regular attendance of fifty to sixty, "of Scripture, Catechism, and Divine Songs, twenty-eight thousand nine hundred and fifty-six verses have been rehearsed, and eight hundred and fifty-six words, with their definitions." *The Youth's Instructor and Guardian* 2/2 (February 1824): 45 ff.

39. William McKendree, *To the General Conference to Be Held in Baltimore, May 1820* (Baltimore: John D. Toy, 1820), 10–11.

40. MEC *Discipline*, 1824, 58; *JGC*, 1824, 295.

41. *JGC*, 1824, 295.

42. For Watson's authorship of the Wesleyan catechisms, see Thomas Jackson, *Memoirs of the Life and Writings of the Rev. Richard Watson* (New York: G. Lane for the Methodist Episcopal Church, 1844), 285. In 1830 Watson also produced a companion to his series of slight catechisms, a hefty 300-page introduction to the Bible titled *Conversations for the Young, Designed to Promote the Profitable Reading of the Holy Scrip-*

tures. By 1832 copies of Watson's *Conversations* were available through the Methodist Book Concern in New York, which kept it in print for thirty years.

43. Wesleyan Methodist Church, *The Catechisms of the Wesleyan Methodists Compiled and Published by Order of the British Conference, Revised and Adapted to the Use of Families and Schools Connected with the Methodist Episcopal Church* (New York: N. Bangs & J. Emory for the Methodist Episcopal Church, 1826), No. 1, "For Children of Tender Years," with an appendix containing a short catechism of scripture names, and prayers for little children (16 pp.); No. 2, "For Children of Seven Years of Age and Upwards," with an appendix containing a short catechism of Scripture history and examples of prayers (72 pp.); No. 3, "For the Use of Young Persons, on the evidences of Christianity and the Truth of the Holy Scriptures" (70 pp.).

44. MEC *Discipline*, 1840, 62.

45. Methodist Episcopal Church Sunday School Union, *Annual Report*, 1845, 87–90.

46. Wesley's *Instructions for Children* was kept in print by the Methodist Episcopal Sunday School Union until at least 1849: John Wesley, *Instructions for Children, Intended for the Use of the Methodist Societies* (New York: Lane & Scott for the Sunday School Union of the Methodist Episcopal Church, 1849). Watson's series of Wesleyan catechisms were regularly reprinted from 1826 through 1854.

47. A convenient and perceptive short account of Methodism's slave missions is Donald G. Mathews, "The Methodist Mission to the Slaves, 1829–1844," *Journal of American History* 51/4 (March 1965): 615–31. See also his "The Southern Compromise of Conscience: The Mission to the Slaves, 1824–1844," *Slavery and Methodism: A Chapter in American Morality, 1780–1845* (Princeton, NJ: Princeton University Press, 1965), 62–81.

48. See Duncan A. Reily, *William Capers: An Evaluation of His Life and Thought* (Ph.D. diss., Emory University, 1972). The older standard biography of Capers is still useful for the large number of original documents included: William M. Wightman, *Life of William Capers, D.D., One of the Bishops of the Methodist Episcopal Church, South, Including an Autobiography* (Nashville: J. B. M'Ferrin, Agent, Southern Methodist Publishing House, 1858).

49. Joseph C. Hartzell, "Methodism and the Negro in the United States," *Journal of Negro History* 8 (July 1923): 304.

50. W. P. Harrison, letter, *CA*, 9/40 (29 May 1835): 40.

51. William P. Harrison, ed., *The Gospel among the Slaves: A Short Account of the Missionary Operations among the African Slaves of the Southern States, Compiled from Original Sources* (Nashville: Publishing House of the Methodist Episcopal Church, South, Barbee & Smith, Agents, 1893); Milton C. Sernett, *Black Religion and American Evangelicalism, White Protestants, Plantation Missions, and the Flowering of Negro Christianity, 1787–1865* (Metuchen, NJ: Scarecrow Press, 1975), 63–81; Grant S. Shockley, ed., *Heritage and Hope: The African-American Presence in United Methodism* (Nashville: Abingdon Press, 1991), 36–37, 67–68.

52. Catechetical instruction of servants and slaves had a long history before the 1830s, in particular among Anglicans. See Albert J. Rabateau, *Slave Religion: The "Invisible" Institution in the Antebellum South* (New York: Oxford University Press, 1978), chap. 4.

53. Benjamin Morgan Palmer published a slave catechism for use in Presbyterian missions in 1828: *A Plain and Easy Catechism, Designed Chiefly for the Benefit of*

Coloured Persons, to which are annexed suitable prayers and hymns. (Charleston, S.C.: Observer Office Press, 1828). Presbyterian Charles Colcock Jones published another in 1834: A Catechism for Colored Persons (Charleston: Observer Office Press, 1834). John Francis Hoff, rector of Christ Church (Episcopal), Millwood, VA, published a large catechism for slaves in 1852: *Manual of Religious Instruction, Specially Intended for the Oral Teaching for Colored Persons* (Philadelphia: King & Baird, 1852). A revised edition was published in 1857.

54. William Capers, *A Catechism for Little Children (and for Use on) the Missions to the Slaves in South-Carolina* (Charleston, SC: Printed by J. S. Burges, 1833), 16 pages.

55. Lesson 1 concerns the Creation and human nature and destiny, lesson 2 teaches about God, lesson 3 sets forth sin and its consequences, and lesson 4 offers penitent believers salvation through Jesus Christ.

56. Section 1, God; 2, Creation of Man; 3, Fall of Man; 4, Promise of a Savior; 5, Ministry of Christ; 6, Death and Resurrection of Christ; 7, Christ Seen by the Disciples, His Ascension and Intercession; 8, Judgement; 9, Who Are Righteous, How We Become and Continue So; 10, Particular Duties; 11, The [Apostles'] Creed; 12, The Sacraments.

57. The revised version of Capers's catechism for children was printed in full in the *Southern Christian Advocate* (Charleston), which he edited: "A CATECHISM for the use of the Methodist Missionaries in their Godly Work of Instructing the Negroes," 1/17 (21 October 1837): 69–70.

58. These views were developed by four prominent southern Methodists in the 1850s: (1) Holland N. McTyeire, *Duties of Christian Masters* (Nashville: Southern Methodist Publishing House, 1859), a prize-winning essay first published by the Southern Baptists in 1851 as *Duties of Masters to Servants: Three Premium Essays* (Charleston, SC: Southern Baptist Publication Society, 1851). (2) James O. Andrews, "Four Letters on the Religious Instruction of Negroes," *New Orleans Christian Advocate* (1856), republished in McTyeire's 1859 *Duties of Christian Masters*, 219–66. (3) William A. Smith, *Lectures on the Philosophy and Practice of Slavery* (Nashville: Stevenson & Evans, 1856). (4) Richard H. Rivers, *Elements of Moral Philosophy* (Nashville: Southern Methodist Publishing House, 1859). For the larger context see H. Shelton Smith, *In His Image But . . . Racism in Southern Religion, 1780–1919* (Durham, NC: Duke University Press, 1972), esp. 129–65.

59. William Capers, "Report of the South Carolina Conference Missionary Society" quoted in William M. Wightman, *Life of William Capers* (Nashville: J.B.M. Ferris, 1858), 296.

60. William Capers, *Catechism for the Use of the Methodist Missions, First Part* (Louisville, KY: John Early for the Methodist Episcopal Church, South, 1847). Preface designated "third edition." Part 2 was published the next year: *Catechism for the Use of the Methodist Missions, Second Part, Comprehending a Brief Outline of the History of Redemption* (Richmond, VA: John Early for the Methodist Episcopal Church, South, 1848). The second part, "Comprehending a Brief Outline of the History of Redemption" for older slave children and adult slaves, was published in the same year. Questions, answers, and comments were arranged in nine chapters: (1) The Creation, Adam & Eve, Good Angels, Evil Angels, Heaven and Hell; (2) More about the First Transgression, the First Promise of a Saviour, and Primitive Worship; (3) More about the First Age of the World, Abraham, Covenant with Him, His Faith; (4) Israel Brought out of Egypt, the Law Given; (5) From Joshua to Christ; (6) Christ and the Apostles; (7) The Crucifixion

of Christ; (8) The Burial and Resurrection of Jesus, Ascension, and Prophecies concerning Him; (9) Pentecost.

61. Thomas Summers revised and reissued Capers's two-part catechism in 1860. As late as 1874 the General Conference of the MECS ordered the continued use of the Capers catechisms (*JGC/S*, 1874, 431–32). The latest documented printings by the Publishing House of the Methodist Episcopal Church, South, for part 1 is 1918 and for part 2 is 1900.

62. *JGC*, 1848, 113.

63. Methodist Episcopal Church Sunday School Union, *Annual Report*, 1848, 36–39; *JGC*, 1848, 113.

64. John McClintock reviewed the catechisms as they were published—*MQR* 34/4 (October 1852): 633 and *MQR* 35/3 (July 1853): 476—and later described the process and product in his *Lectures on Theological Encyclopaedia and Methodology* (Cincinnati: Hitchcock & Walden, 1873), 136.

65. *Catechism of the Methodist Episcopal Church No. 1* (New York: Carlton & Phillips, Sunday School Union, 1852), 3.

66. *Catechism No. 3*, 1852, 5.

67. Ibid.

68. *Catechism No. 1 and the Church Teacher; or, Lessons for Young People in the History, Doctrines, and Usages of the Methodist Episcopal Church* (New York: Nelson & Phillips; Cincinnati: Hitchcock & Walden, 1876), 24.

69. *Catechism No. 1; with Other Lessons for Young People in the History, Doctrines, and Usages of the Methodist Episcopal Church* (New York: Phillips & Hunt; Cincinnati; Cranston & Stowe, c1884), 30–31.

70. *Methodist-Episcopal Krykans Kateches* (New York: Carlton & Phillips, 1854). 3 pts.

71. *Katechismus der Bischofl. Methodisten-Kirche* (Cincinnati: Swormstedt & Poe, 1857), *Den Methodist-Episkopallke Kirkes Catechismus* (Frederikshald: Chr. Olsen, 1857).

72. *Den Biskoppelige Methodist-Kirkes Catechismus* (Kiobenhavn: C. J. Elvius' Bogtrykkeri, 1870).

73. *Catechismo Iglesia Metodista Episcopal*, Segunda Edicion (Mexico City: Imprenta Metodista Episcopal, 1879). 3 pts.

74. "Report on the Tract Society," *Manual of the Methodist Episcopal Church* 6 (January 1886): 40.

75. *Catechismo della Chiesa Metodista Episcopale* (Roma: Tipografia Popolare, 1887).

76. *Catechismo de L'Eglise Metodiste Episcopale* (Manchester, NH: Thomas A. Dorion, Editeur, 1893–1894). 3 pts.

77. *JGC/S*, 1854, 283.

78. Thomas O. Summers, *The Sunday-School Teacher; or, The Catechetical Office* (Richmond, VA/Louisville, KY: John Early for the Methodist Episcopal Church, South, 1853), 134.

79. *JGC/S*, 1858, 404, 520.

80. Summers's contributions to biblical scholarship included a four-volume *Commentary on the Gospels* (1869–72) and a *Commentary on the Acts of the Apostles* (1874), and in 1867 he republished Wesley's revision of the Anglican Book of Common Prayer

(*The Sunday Service of the Methodists in North America*) for use in the churches of southern Methodism (1867).

81. Thomas O. Summers, *Scripture Catechism*, vol. 1, *The Old Testament* (Nashville: Southern Methodist Publishing House, 1858). Some of the liturgical material was borrowed from *Divine Songs* by Isaac Watts.

82. S. L. Farr, *A Manual for Infant Schools*, ed. Thomas O. Summers, (Nashville: Publishing House of the Methodist Episcopal Church, South, 1860). The sixteen-page manual was reprinted in 1863 by the Richmond-based Soldiers' Tract Association of the MECS. The last documented printing by the MECS Publishing House is 1894.

83. The whole volume has its own title page: *Catechisms of the Methodist Episcopal Church, South*, rev. by T. O. Summers, with intro. by Bishop Pierce (Nashville: Southern Methodist Publishing House, 1860). Separate title pages with the same imprint are included for each part: (1) *Catechisms of the Wesleyan Methodists Compiled and Published by Order of the British Conference, Adapted to the Use of Families and Schools Connected with the Methodist Episcopal Church, South*, no. 1, "For Children of Tender Years"; no. 2, "For Children of Seven Years of Age and Upward"; no. 3, "For the Use of Young Persons." (2) Thomas O. Summers, *Scripture Catechism*, vol. 1, *The Old Testament*; vol. 2, *The New Testament*. (3) William Capers, *Catechism for the Use of the Methodist Missions and Infant Classes in Sunday Schools, Part First, Comprehending the Elements of Christianity*, rev. by T. O. Summers. (4) William Capers, *Catechism for the Use of the Methodist Missions, Part Second, Comprehending a Brief Outline of the History of Redemption*, rev. by T. O. Summers. (5) S. L. Farr, *Manual for Infant Schools*, ed. Thomas O. Summers.

84. George F. Pierce, "Introduction," in *Catechisms of the Methodist Episcopal Church, South*, 4.

85. *JGC/S*, 1866, 80, 118.

86. MECS, *Discipline*, 1866, 289–327.

87. *JGC/S*, 1870, 213–14, 264; 1874, 431–32.

88. Separate southern printings of Watson's series of three Wesleyan catechisms were available through 1924, which meant they were in use by some Methodists for almost a century! A number of unofficial catechisms were produced, including one in 1895 by editor of Sunday school publications William G. E. Cunnyngham, *A Catechism for Infant Classes*, which continued to be used in Sunday schools until 1933.

89. *JGC*, 1868, 334.

90. For Nast's life and thought see Carl Wittke, *William Nast, Patriarch of German Methodism* (Detroit: Wayne State University Press, 1959).

91. *Der Kleinere Katechismus fur die deutschen Gemeinden der Bisch. Methodisten-Kirche mit Genehmignung der General-Conferenz* (Cincinniati: Verlag von Hitchcock & Walden, 1868). 92 pp.; *Der Grossere Katechismus fur die deutschen Gemeinden der Bisch. Methodistischen-Kirche* (Cincinnati: Verlag von Hitchcock & Walden, 1868). 156 pp. Nast's *Larger Catechism* was meant for older youth able to memorize all the Scripture proofs and it was designed for pastors and Sunday school teachers using the *Smaller Catechism* to aid in explaining the latter according to the capacity of pupils.

92. See "Publishers' Preface," William Nast, *The Smaller Catechism*, English ed. (Cincinnati: Hitchcock & Walden; New York: Carlton & Lanahan, 1869); *The Larger Catechism* (Cincinnati: Hitchcock & Walden; New York: Carlton & Lanahan, 1869). Revised editions of both were published in 1892. A reviewer of Nast's catechism in the *Advocate* in 1870 predicted, "All other catechisms in our Church will go into disuse,

and this will go forth to instruct millions for many generations in the grandest truths open to the mind of man." B. F. Rawlins, "Structure and Theology of the New Catechism," *CA*, 20 January 1870.

93. William Nast, *Grossere Katechismus fur die deutschen Gemeinden der Bischoflichen Methodistenkirche* (Bremen: Verlag des Tractathauses, 1869).

94. Nast lifted whole passages from Philip Schaff's catechism, first published in 1862: *A Catechism for Sunday-Schools and Families; or, An Exposition of the Lord's Prayer, the Creed and the Ten Commandments* (Philadelphia: Lindsay & Blakiston, 1862). Many times reprinted.

95. Nast, *Larger Catechism*, 34, 36.

96. MEC *Discipline*, 1852, 86. The new rule required pastors to report to each quarterly conference to what extent they had publicly or privately catechized the children of their charge. To reinforce the new plan the next General Conference (1856) rewrote the section on duties of preachers in charge of a circuit or station. MEC *Discipline*, 1856, 84; *JGC*, 1856, 186.

97. Daniel P. Kidder, *The Christian Pastorate: Its Character, Responsibilities, and Duties* (Cincinnati: Hitchcock & Walden; New York: Carlton & Porter, 1871), 368.

98. "Short Reviews and Notices of Books," *MQR*, January 1855, 141. *The Catechism of the Methodist Episcopal Church, Numbers 1, 2, and 3 in One Volume Designed for Consecutive Study in Sunday Schools and Families* (New York: Carlton & Phillips, 1855).

99. *The Choral Services of Doctrine Embodying the Church Catechism* (New York: Phillips & Hunt, 1885?), Oxford League Service Series no. 3.

100. John O. Foster, *The Catechism of the Methodist Episcopal Church with Scriptural Proofs, Baptismal Service, Apostles' Creed, Ten Commandments, and the Beatitudes in Concert Exercise Form, with Music and Hymns Selected from Standard Authors, Designed for Consecutive Study in Families, Sunday-Schools, and Churches* (Cincinnati: Cranston & Stowe; New York: Hunt & Eaton, 1891).

101. *The Church Teacher; or, Lessons for Young People in the History, Doctrines, and Usages of the Methodist Episcopal Church, Including the Catechism, the Beatitudes, the Lord's Prayer, the Apostles' Creed, etc. etc.* (New York: Nelson & Phillips; Cincinnati: Hitchcock & Walden, Sunday School Department, between 1872 and 1879), 16 pp.

102. *Hymnal of the Methodist Episcopal Church, with Catechism No. 2, Baptismal Covenant, the Lord's Prayer, the Ten Commandments, the Apostles' Creed, and the Beatitudes for the Use of Sunday-Schools* (New York: Phillips & Hunt; Cincinnati: Hitchcock & Walden, 1879).

103. *JGC*, 1884, 360; *Epworth Hymnal* (New York: Phillips & Hunt, 1885), 14–16.

104. *Catechism of the Methodist Episcopal Church, Number 1* (Cincinnati: Curts & Jennings for the Sunday School Union of the Methodist Episcopal Church, [between 1896 and 1900]), outside back cover.

105. MEC *Discipline*, 1864, 133–34.

106. Vincent, in Wardle, *History of the Sunday School Movement*, 115 f.

107. Methodist Episcopal Church Sunday School Union, *Annual Report*, 1872, 18.

108. Methodist Episcopal Church Sunday School Union, *Year Book for 1872*, 54.

109. Philip G. Gillett, "The Catechism in Sabbath School," *Sunday School Teacher*, 3/4 (Chicago, April 1868), 98. See also "Methodist Doctrines in Sunday-Schools," *Manual of the Methodist Episcopal Church* 2 (1882): 414–15: "Not only have the doctrines

of Methodism been emphasized in the Berean Lesson, through blackboard symbols and sentiments, in golden texts, in doctrinal statements, in direct Scriptural exposition, but we have reduced the cost of the Catechism.''

110. Paul F. Douglass, *The Story of German Methodism* (New York: Methodist Book Concern, 1939), 213–32. Thorough drill in the catechism was a venerable German tradition dating back to Martin Luther. Nast's catechisms made the Germans of the Methodist Episcopal Church its best-trained members. Just as German Methodists mastered their songs, so they knew the doctrines of their faith. Next to the Bible and hymnal, Nast's catechism ranks as one of the major formative influences on German-American Methodists.

12
SUNDAY SCHOOL FOR ALL, 1866–1915

In the years following the Civil War few Methodists could have imagined their churches without a Sunday school and all recognized them as a key means of recruiting new members. Who could quarrel with success? A Methodist editor's 1854 estimate that Sunday schools accounted for "half the entire net of increase of the membership of the Church" was probably conservative, but it testified to the Sunday school's importance.[1] By 1890 the Methodist Episcopal Church alone had more Sunday schools than churches (27,000 Sunday schools to 23,000 churches), with 300,000 teachers instructing 2.5 million students; since 1866 the number of Sunday schools had doubled.[2] As Sunday school scholars swelled the ranks of church members, clergy and laity alike agreed that the Sunday school had become the nursery of the church.

SUNDAY SCHOOL FOR ALL AGES

In the previous era the class meeting was the residential complement of the itinerant ministry; in the post–Civil War era it was the Sunday school. In 1869 John Vincent* openly talked of merging the class meeting with the Sunday school. "To the study of Scripture truth (the chief thing in the best Sunday-school classes as now conducted) we should add the element of personal experience (the main thing in the Church class)."[3]

Efforts of the MEC to reinforce the connection between the church and the Sunday school at denominational and local level are apparent in these years. The 1856 General Conference made Sunday school superintendents voting members of local church governing bodies (the quarterly conference).[4] By 1864, General Conference gave local church quarterly conferences power to remove "unworthy or inefficient" superintendents and mandated a Sunday school committee in each local church to recruit teachers, promote attendance, and raise money. Eight years later, in 1872, the voluntary Sunday school unions, along with other general agencies, became boards whose elected managers were accountable to the whole church. Annual conference Sunday school unions (later boards of Sunday schools) were recommended in 1868 in the MEC and mandated in 1882 in the MECS.[5]

Taking the place of the class meeting, the Sunday school had also changed. When Methodist educator, later novelist, Edward Eggleston reviewed recent changes in Sunday school work in 1869, he pronounced them nothing less than "a revolution." During the brief span of a decade between 1859 and 1869, Eggleston contended a new professionalism (new leaders, new organizations, new curricula, even a call for new buildings) had reinvigorated and transformed Sunday school work. Older concerns—the need for punctuality and order in schools, the importance of visiting students and encouraging their early conversion, and congregational support for the schools—had been replaced by a preoccupation with system, method, and order in Sunday school work and the use of convention-style meetings and teach-training magazines to achieve these goals.[6] By adding the one word *adults* to the regulations concerning the Sunday school, the MEC General Conference of 1860 expanded the Sunday school's mandate to include training adults.[7]

"GROWTH NOT CONQUEST"

The new understanding of the Sunday school's function derived in large part from changing conceptions of conversion, of emotion in religious life, of the rhetoric of sensation, and of the nature of the child. The MEC SSU in 1857 asked the church to "*have a hearty faith in the feasibility of childhood conversion. The history of this institution affords the evidence. Children can feel. They can weep tears of genuine gospel sorrow when they have transgressed the divine law. They can feel the agony of conviction, and they can exercise saving faith in Jesus Christ.*"[8]

Pastors and church leaders came to realize that there were greater numbers of unconverted souls in the Sunday school than in any other branch of the church. Further, children were at a favorable age for receiving and understanding the saving power of the Word. Moreover, a large supply of church workers existed to serve as agents for joining the child and the message to effect salvation. Conversion soon became the great refrain of Sunday school workers. The Decision Day was instituted by the Sunday schools as the annual event for encouraging the spiritual redemption of young scholars.

By the 1850s discussions of children turned less and less frequently on the question of whether they were "by nature children of wrath." Instead, new theological ideas, best exemplified by Congregational pastor Horace Bushnell's *Christian Nature* (1847), along with the growth of romantic ideals of childhood, increasingly gained currency. The shift from conversion to nurture led teachers to downplay or reject entirely the belief that one life-defining experience should be the focus of Sunday school instruction. Instead they hoped to encourage the child's gradual growth into an adult Christian. With the shift in goals, teachers found their work easier as well as harder: easier because they now had a rationale for keeping children in school indefinitely; harder because they bore a heavier burden of responsibility for the children's religious destiny.[9]

As Sunday school workers turned away from older notions of childhood, they found it necessary to remodel the antebellum Sunday school. Major alterations in the schools' curricula and goals took place during the 1860s and 1870s. In the remodeling process the old goal of preparing students for conversion gave way to the new goal of "Growth not Conquest." Sunday school leaders came to see children as more capable than adults of religious sentiment and began to incorporate new pedagogical techniques from public schools. New types of lessons replaced the old question-and-answer books. Teachers learned Pestalozzi's seven laws of teaching and their practical application. "Never tell a child what he can discover for himself," counseled the Swiss educator's followers; proceed step by step from the simple to the complex, the known to the unknown. Through institutes, conventions, and teachers manuals, object teaching and the art of questioning became standard tricks of the Sunday school trade.

JOHN VINCENT AND SARA JANE CRAFTS

Foremost among the Sunday school reformers was John Heyl Vincent, who led the SSU for twenty years beginning in 1868. Born in 1832, Vincent became a minister in the circuit-riding system, receiving his first pastorate in 1853. From that position in New Jersey Vincent went on to a church in Joliet, Illinois, in 1857 and there rose quickly to prominence, taking successive Illinois pastorates before being assigned to Trinity Methodist Episcopal Church in Chicago in 1864. Despite his rapid ascent to the pastorate of a big-city church, Vincent was bored by his pastoral duties and found an outlet for his considerable energies in the Chicago Sunday School Union. He began to address Sunday school assemblies, publish model lessons, and organized teacher-training institutes. In 1865 he brought out a new journal, a forerunner of the *National Sunday School Teacher*, which breathed new life into the concept of a magazine for teachers. He also introduced the system of uniform Sunday school lessons with lesson leaves for each student.

Vincent's reforms were a smash hit in Chicago, and within a year, in 1866, he was called to New York to help the SSU move Methodist Sunday schools everywhere in the same direction. Two years later Vincent became corresponding secretary, not only running the SSU but also editing its magazine for teachers, the *Sunday School Journal*. Under his management subscriptions to the *Journal* increased tenfold, while his lesson leaves had a circulation of nearly 2.5 million. With fellow Methodist Lewis Miller he went on to found the Chautauqua Assembly, a kind of people's college, in 1874, helped organize a new fellowship for Methodist youth, the Epworth League, in the 1880s, and eventually (1888) became a bishop.[10]

For the MECS, Dr. Thomas O. Summers* was the first Sunday school editor, beginning his work in Charleston, South Carolina, in 1851 on the *Sunday School Advocate*, afterward changed to the *Visitor*. In 1854 the Methodist Publishing House was established in Nashville, where the erudite Englishman took up his duties. Summers continued his duties until 1870, when Atticus Green Haygood* (afterward bishop) was elected. Haygood began the publication of *Sunday-School Lesson Leaves* for adults, and *Our Little People* for young people, and the *Sunday School Magazine* for teachers. Haygood resigned in 1875 and was followed in the post by W.G.E. Cunnyngham, who adopted the international lesson system and a series of lesson quarterlies replaced the older lesson leaves.

The importance of Vincent's position and an indication of the significance of Sunday schools is revealed by the Sunday School Union's statistical reports to the General Conferences. When Vincent took charge in 1868 there were fifteen thousand Sunday schools in the denomination.[11] Twenty years later when Vincent left leadership of the Sunday schools to become bishop, the number of Sunday schools had grown to twenty-five thousand. By then these schools involved nearly 278,000 teachers and officers and over a million "scholars" for the MEC alone. Two-thirds of the "scholars" were children under the age of fifteen; the other third were teenagers and adults.[12]

Two themes dominated Vincent's life—self-education and a distaste for revivalism. Throughout his life Vincent expressed regret that he never attended college. To compensate he spent much of his life studying, teaching, and devising self-education schemes for himself and others. He never tired of likening the church to "a school with many departments" where "what is generally taught in detail only in theological schools ought to be taught in outline at least."[13] Vincent's distaste for revivalism had personal as well as intellectual roots. Not only had he little success at rousing revivals in his pastoral work, he also associated revivalism with the gloomy religion of his childhood, with excessive emotionalism, with deprivation, and with emphasis on the irrational at the expense of rational understanding. As a pastor he preferred the stability of the Sunday school to the upheaval of revival and worked hard to encourage church members of all ages to be involved in the Sunday school. "Calm, rational unremitting endeavor for twelve months of every year" was preferable, Vincent believed, to occasional superficial excitements.[14]

In systematizing Sunday school training, encouraging the convention system, and regularizing the Sunday school curriculum, Vincent undercut the revivalistic basis of Methodist Church membership and replaced it with a staged process of religious growth. Relying on the "Christian nurture" ideas of Horace Bushnell, Vincent stressed the gradual religious development of children.[15] Vincent's anti-revival, pro-nurture stance did not, however, completely displace conversion as the main goal of Methodist Sunday school instruction. The two goals existed side by side for some time.

Although the Sunday school convention leadership was overwhelmingly male, women gradually emerged as leaders by entering two new areas of activity—

teacher training and temperance education—rather than threatening male baili-
wicks. Many were graduates of state teachers colleges whose expertise in new
teaching techniques gave them special status at the conventions. Typical of these
women leaders was Sara Jane Timanus (later Sara Jane Crafts*), a teacher at
Minnesota State Normal School.[16] Timanus, who was one of the first women to
conduct convention sessions, became well known through her articles in the
National Sunday School Teacher and other periodicals as well as her books on
the teaching of young children. The northern Methodist publishing house kept
her 1876 *Open Letters to Primary Teachers* in print for twenty-five years. After
her marriage in 1874 to fellow Methodist Sunday school worker, Wilbur F.
Crafts, she became a full-time Sunday school leader, lecturing widely on child
psychology, disseminating Pestalozzian principles, and campaigning for the
adoption of kindergartens (primary departments) in Sunday schools.[17]

Sara Jane Crafts was neither an agitator nor a feminist. She did not press for
her right to participate in conventions but became a participant because she was
expert in the new pedagogy. Believing that evangelical women should defer to
male, and especially clerical, authority, yet convinced that women possess innate
qualities that suited them for work with small children, she accepted contemporary ideas about women's "sphere" as mothers and teachers. Her achievement was to extend the boundaries of the sphere by establishing a beachhead
in the conventions from which she and others could push forward as Sunday
school leaders.

Another group of women stretched those boundaries further as they used the
convention movement to promote the cause of temperance. Methodist women
had been active in temperance work since the early nineteenth century, and
advocacy of temperance was not in itself controversial within Methodist Sunday
school circles. Sunday school literature had for decades extolled the virtues of
total abstinence. Still, the issue of whether women should act publicly to promote any cause remained divisive. When a group of Methodist women began
teaching temperance in Sunday schools in the 1860s, arguing that teachers could
win the battle against demon rum by converting children to total abstinence,
they often faced criticism.

Jennie Fowler Willing,* Methodist temperance worker and suffragist, took
the crusade to the first Chautauqua meeting in 1873, where she received the
moral support of John Vincent. Despite his own temperance beliefs, however,
Vincent required that Willing follow custom and address only separate women's
meetings. There, and again at the following summer's Chautauqua gathering,
Willing organized women teachers and held training sessions on temperance
work in Sunday schools. Out of these meetings came a call for a national wom-
en's temperance convention, which met in November 1874, with Willing as
president. Here she helped organize the Woman's Christian Temperance Union
(WCTU), which quickly established committees on juvenile temperance and
Sunday school work. Because so many WCTU organizers, including Francis
Willard,* had Sunday school experience, the work seemed a natural focus for

their organization. The WCTU organized Sunday school students into the Juvenile Temperance Union, complete with banners and pledges of total abstinence, and lobbied for the adoption of temperance lessons in Sunday school curricula. The lessons written by Sara Jane Crafts and others were in widespread use by 1880.[18]

In the Sunday school movement women worked alongside men in church activities, spoke in Christian gatherings, and at most of the conventions voted on issues facing the delegates. Although women were the majority of Sunday school teachers, women's numerical preponderance did not translate into greater power within the schools. When women's Sunday schools and Sunday school unions merged with men's, as became common during the course of the century, women were relegated to secondary status. Whereas in 1820, for example, Philadelphia women ran almost half of the city's Sunday schools, by 1859 all 219 Sunday schools had male superintendents; and in Baltimore, when the McKendrean Female Sabbath School Society merged with the male-led Asbury Sunday-School Society in 1845, women surrendered leadership positions to the men.[19] Improvement came slowly. An 1893 survey indicated that only 10 percent (350) of the church's 3,500 Sunday schools were superintended by women. Of that number none were found in any conference east of the Allegheny Mountains and none south of Mason and Dixon line.[20]

The experience of women Sunday school teachers illustrates the possibilities and the limitations that Methodist women encountered in the nineteenth century. From the standpoint of the teachers, Methodism offered a positive image of womanhood, useful and engaging work, and opportunities for social interaction beyond the family circle. Many women looked on Sunday school work as liberating and ennobling, providing an appealing vision of themselves as useful and significant individuals. At the same time, however, their acceptance of the evangelical idea of womanhood restricted the autonomy and independence of women teachers and limited their ability to challenge nineteenth-century gender-role prescriptions. Only in the late nineteenth century, through the convention movement, did women teachers begin to reclaim some of the authority they had exercised in the Sunday schools' early history. Women were successful as convention participants and leaders, however, only insofar as they observed established codes of behavior. Ironically, in teaching Sunday schools, Methodist women helped both to enlarge women's sphere and to perpetuate the notion of separate gender spheres.

CONVENTIONS AND MAGAZINES

Women teachers, along with their male cohorts, embodied the tradition of the amateur at its best. The amateur is not one who does things poorly but, rather, one who cares about the activity and is intelligent in the way in which he or she cares. In the latter half of the nineteenth century, church leaders like Vincent encouraged the development of caring and intelligent mentors. Vincent established a system of "normal schools," where Sunday school teachers could study the latest in pedagogy, Bible geography, and other topics. He founded Chautauqua as a national Sunday school university and eventually, from Chautauqua, launched a nationwide system of local reading groups that in turn encouraged local adult education. The Chautauqua Literary and Scientific Circle sparked the first "book of the month" club, sending out books each month in response to the hunger for culture and religion on the part of teachers in Sunday schools across the land. Trained amateurs was the goal.

One innovation, the interdenominational Sunday school convention, was not entirely new in the 1860s. It had originated on the local level in the 1850s when teachers decided to follow the lead of their public school counterparts. To encourage mutual self-improvement, Sunday school teachers began to organize city-, county-, and statewide conventions once a year to boost morale and disseminate new methods adapted from public school teaching. From 1869 to 1914 national conventions of Sunday school teachers and leaders from all the evangelical denominations were held every three years. Methodists, who had usually remained aloof from interdenominational causes, became especially active in local and national Sunday school meetings.[21]

The conventions served two purposes: inspiration and instruction. Inspiration took the form of oratory, slogans, music, parades, banners, and other forms of "boosterism." Instruction was fostered in the division of the delegates into areas of interest, for reports, addresses, question-and-answer sessions, demonstrations, and discussions.

Two Chicago pastors-turned-convention-planners, John Vincent and Dwight L. Moody, shaped the new institution. Vincent aimed the conventions at training Sunday school teachers. In Vincent's words, they were designed to banish "the false and injurious notion that *anybody* is competent to teach in a Sabbath school." Instead, like public schools, Sunday schools should employ "a regular system of teacher training."[22] So convention planners regularly added practical sessions on the model teacher and superintendent, the need for teachers' meetings, and new teaching methods—the use of blackboards, illustrations, objects, and music in teaching, for example. Along with sessions on missionary work and extension work, teacher training quickly became a regular part of Sunday school conventions on the local and national levels. Pastors with experience in revivalism made the Sunday school convention an important focus of their evangelistic activities. Moody made the Sunday school conventions an important focus of his evangelistic activities. Moody's prayer sessions at Chicago Sunday school conventions helped convention leaders discover the appeal of revival-style gatherings.

The alliance between Vincent and Moody contained paradoxes. The same conventions that enabled Moody to develop his revivalistic skills offered Vincent a chance to promote his anti-revival goals. Vincent saw teacher training and curriculum development as a means of undercutting the role of revivals in the churches and encouraging staged religious growth throughout life. Differing purposes occasionally led to conflict between Sunday school workers who sided with Vincent and those who sided with Moody. Generally the conventions accommodated the needs of both groups. Because his revivals were conducted outside of congregational settings in the context of large public gatherings, Moody served Vincent's purpose by eliminating the pressure on pastors to cultivate revivals in their churches. Pastoral energy could be focused on improving the Sunday school and expanding its reach to all members of the congregation. Participants at Sunday school conventions went home fired by the religious zeal the mass meetings encouraged and ready to put into practice the teaching techniques learned in the workshops.[23]

Later Sunday school conventions reflected these twin interests: After training sessions planned by Vincent, delegates participated in mass meetings that were led by Moody and orchestrated by the Chicago-based Methodist hymnist Phillip Phillips. The Illinois mold was so influential in other states that later Sunday school historians referred to Vincent and Moody and other colleagues like Eggleston as "The Illinois Band" and attributed to them the success of the convention movement.

Another means of disseminating the new Sunday school methods were magazines for teachers. Although the SSU had been publishing a magazine for teachers since the 1820s, these magazines proliferated and took on a new look in the 1860s. Emphasizing teaching techniques over religious content, they offered detailed instructions on how to teach Sunday school classes using the techniques borrowed from the new state teachers colleges. In addition they supported the convention movement by providing information about local and national meetings. The most popular postwar Methodist journals—the *Sunday School Journal* (MEC), *Haus und Herd* (German-speaking MEC), and the *Sunday School Magazine* (MECS)—reflected the strong influence of Sunday school reformers. Teaching guides and advice books for teachers also proliferated in this period. Among the most representative Methodist ones were Wilbur Fisk Crafts's *The Ideal Sunday School* (1880) and Vincent's *The Modern Sunday-School* (1887). Both reflected the new emphasis on system and order, teacher training, and pedagogy.

Young MEC Sunday school scholars had been subscribing to their own newspaper, the *Sunday School Advocate*, later *Sunday School Classmate*, for years. By the 1880s circulation had climbed to 350,000.[24] When the MECS resumed its publishing program after the Civil War, the *Sunday School Visitor*, "a sweet little messenger of truth and grace sent monthly to the children of the Church," was revived almost as soon as its *Christian Advocate*.[25] Methodist Protestant youth had the *Sabbath School Recorder* and German-speaking Methodist Sunday school children had *Der Kinderfruend* to read.

The new Sunday school conventions and magazines succeeded because the new generation of Sunday school workers shared new goals and aspirations. Their vision directed them toward the reformation of American society through efficiency and training. They sought less the immediate conversion of the individual and the society—the utopian visions of the 1820s and 1830s—than a perfected world on Christian principles to be reached gradually. They aimed to establish Sunday schools, staff them with trained teachers, provide them with systematic lesson plans, encourage the religious development of each student, and lead them to become faithful church members—and thereby bring in God's kingdom.

THE UNIFORM LESSON PLAN, 1872

For years Sunday school teachers followed their own whims in choosing lesson materials, at first from church catechisms, later from the Bible. The result was a state of casual chaos, the "Babel Period" of Methodist Sunday schools.[26] John Vincent's reforms ordered this babel, drawing on the pedagogical ideas and techniques of Pestalozzi, which meshed nicely with the new goal of nurture. The lessons that emerged to take the place of old question books—sequential in character—emphasized the students' steady growth in religious knowledge through orderly week-by-week, year-by-year study of the Bible. Unlike the old question books, which combined Bible study with preparation for conversion, the new lessons focused on the Bible but downplayed conversion. The first successful new-style lesson book was Orange Judd's *Lessons for Every Sunday in the Year* published by the Sunday School Union of the MEC in 1864. A successful newspaper man and agricultural expert, Judd was appalled by the lack of order and system in the Methodist Sunday schools in New York City and later in Chicago, which he superintended. With guidance from Methodist biblical scholar James Strong, Judd provided four year-long lesson sequences "adapted to scholars of all ages," each built around a specific part of the Old or New Testament. In one sequence, for example, students went through fifty-two lessons on the historical sections of the Old Testament, studying biblical history, memorizing selected verses, and using their Bibles to answer questions posed in the lessons. Two million copies were sold![27]

Chief promoter of the uniform-lesson system was John Heyl Vincent, who as a young pastor in Irvington, New Jersey, had experimented with a similar approach during the summer of 1855: To his "Palestine class" he invited persons of all ages and denominations to join in singing and learning the facts of biblical geography.[28] At an institute conducted by the Chicago Sunday School Union in 1865 Vincent asked whether it was practicable to introduce a uniform plan of lessons into all Sunday schools. A year later he was largely responsible for the preparation and publication of the first uniform-lesson system, the National Uniform Lessons, published in Chicago. Entitled *Two Years with Jesus: A New System of Sunday School Study*, the lessons featured all sorts of innovations such as helpful hints for teachers and a weekly "Golden Text" memory selection for pupils. When Vincent moved to New York in 1866, he helped the Methodists launch a similar lesson system, which he named the Berean Lessons in honor of the Christians at Berea in the apostolic period who were considered more diligent scholars than their contemporaries, studying the Scriptures every day.[29] The name Berean became a synonym for Methodist Sunday school literature for the next seventy years.

A problem remained for making the new lessons truly uniform and truly national. Two rival uniform-lesson systems were being promoted, the Chicago-based National series edited by Edward Eggleston and the New York–based Berean series edited by Vincent. On the eve of Sunday school leaders' 1872 national meeting, thirty Sunday school publishers agreed on one lesson system for all Sunday schools in the country. This limited competition to publication of lesson guides and teacher manuals designed to accompany the prescribed texts. The publishers appointed a committee, including the two rival editors Eggleston and Vincent, to select the Scripture lessons. In the meantime several denominations and publishers balked at the decision, but victory for the plan was assured at the National Sunday-School Convention in Indianapolis in spring 1872 when rank-and-file Sunday school teachers from across the country overwhelmingly voted in favor of a uniform-lesson system.[30]

The so-called international uniform lessons were published beginning in 1873. The plan was to read through the entire Bible in the course of a seven-year period, alternating between the Old Testament and the New Testament each quarter or half year. At first only the lesson title and Scripture text, consisting of from six to fourteen verses, was specified. Teachers and superintendents at the local level were free to expand upon the text and approach its teaching as they saw fit. In 1874 a Golden Text was added to each week's lesson. Six years later, in 1880 verses were suggested for memorization by the children.[31] The lessons were pitched to an adult level and adapted to the capacities of children and youth. This principle of adaptation, that adult concepts of religion and life cannot be brought within the range of understanding and experience of young pupils simply by shortening words and simplifying sentences, was later to be questioned. Vincent aimed to bring a spirit of unity and fellowship between classes and ages by establishing a common lesson text for all class, yet keeping enough flexibility for teachers to approach the text and expound its meaning as she or he saw fit.

Methodist publishing houses were among the first to adopt the uniform system for their curricula. To supplement the texts, they published helps or additional material that gave the desired denominational slant to each subject. The MEC *Sunday School Journal*, for teachers and superintendents, featured a regular section "Methodism in the Lesson" by Dr. Daniel D. Whedon, editor of the *Methodist Quarterly Review* from 1856 until 1888. For each lesson there were sections on printed Scripture, home readings, lesson hymns, questions for senior, intermediate, and younger scholars, explanatory and practical notes, critical notes, the lesson council, analytical and biblical outline, thoughts for young people, lesson word pictures, orientation of the lesson, the lesson catechism, and the church catechism. By the 1880s Vincent's Berean lesson system included two magazines for teachers (*The Study* and the *Sunday-School Journal*) and a commentary on the Bible lessons.[32] In addition, there were four series of weekly lesson leaflets for students (the *Senior Leaf*, the *Berean Leaf* for scholars ten to sixteen years of age, the *Beginner's Leaf*, and the *Picture Lesson Paper* for infant classes), along with a set of pictures and maps of the holy land. Secular newspapers joined church publishers by printing each week's lesson as well.

The switch first to new-lesson series like Judd's and then to uniform lessons reflected the Sunday schools' changing goals. Whereas the old question books contained varying numbers of lessons, combined Bible study with basic Methodist theology, and assumed a relatively short student tenure in school, the new lessons were predicated on the assumption that students would remain in school for many years, that they should grow gradually in religious knowledge, and that conversion would be a minor aspect of the overall experience. Individual schools and teachers, of course, continued to place greater or lesser stress on conversion.

The alterations were not universally welcomed. Old-timers questioned whether the new lessons might lessen the spiritual results of teaching. They were reassured when annual report after annual report of the Sunday school Union showed that Sunday school conversions had increased. By 1880 the new lessons had permanently changed the Sunday school. The uniform-lesson triumph in the 1870s has been called the ''second birth'' of the Sunday school movement, after Robert Raikes's own pioneering work a century earlier. For most Methodists the ''way to the promised land was paved by uniform lessons.''[33]

The Sunday school session was organized, controlled, and led by a superintendent often drawn from executive officers of business and industry.[34] The best-known Sunday school superintendents of the period included Lewis Miller, the inventor and industrialist, John D. Rockefeller, the oil magnate, and John Wanamaker, the Philadelphia department store tycoon. The superintendents were responsible for leading the opening and closing exercises, when all doors or partitions between classrooms and the assembly area were pushed aside. During the instruction period—the heart of the session—they sat at their desk or wandered about the halls to ensure that no class was disturbed. Aiding the superintendent was a large group of officers and assistants—secretary, treasurer, and librarian—along with departmental superintendents.[35]

Schools were divided into grades roughly equivalent to public school practice, incorporating preschool ages through adolescents, with separate classes for adults. In larger schools the grades were grouped into departments each headed by a superintendent, usually including a primary or infant department for children averaging from five to eight years of age, an intermediate department for children ages eight to ten, a junior department for ages ten to fifteen, and a senior department for children from fifteen to twenty years of age. Supplementing these basic departments could be several others, including a preschool department or nursery school, a home department for those who could not attend the school sessions at the church, and various other Bible or adult classes. The school session was usually preceded by instrumental music, consisting of a full orchestra when possible or simply a coronet or violin if the school was small. Pianos and small organs were increasingly used after the Civil War, although Sunday school orchestras continued to serenade Sunday schools well into the twentieth century. The last musical number would be perfectly timed to finish precisely at the moment the session proper was to begin. The commencement was signaled by the stroke of a bell.

Opening exercises. A period of silence was followed by a brief introduction and the singing of a hymn. The previous weeks' lessons would be reviewed by the superintendent, the titles, topics, and Golden Texts recited in unison by the entire school. Some schools asked for a show of Bibles by those having brought theirs from home; classes whose entire membership brought Bibles were "star classes." The school's motto and memory verses were recited. Following the singing of another hymn or two and a brief prayer, opening exercises closed with the reading of the lesson.

Lesson study period. The study period, though only thirty to forty minutes long, made up the heart of the Sunday school session. At this point teachers closed the doors to their individual rooms and began to impress upon young minds the meaning of the day's lesson and Golden Text.

Closing exercises. The last few minutes featured a review for the entire school of the day's lesson, which reemphasized its main points and provided a sense of united effort and coordinated study for the whole school. This was the occasion for reports by the secretary on attendance and by the treasurer on the collection, additional hymns and prayer, a few words from the minister if present, and a benediction.

Ideals are not reality. At any time during the mid-nineteenth century years a visitor could have found Sunday schools that came close to the ideal and those that were far removed from it. In most rural and frontier areas, for example, Sunday schools met only for the summer months and closed during the winter season. For many local churches the practical difficulties of organizing and maintaining a Sunday school program overshadowed any sustained effort at age-grading or the latest methods and curricula. Urban Sunday schools sometimes had such difficulty controlling rowdy children that teachers focused their efforts on simple, repetitive lessons. Even the best-financed and organized urban church schools had problems, frequently suspending their programs during the summer months, when heat and teacher vacations took their toll.

AKRON-PLAN BUILDINGS

The inclusion of the Sunday school within the church, its rapid growth, the expansion to multiple age groups each needing space, the new pedagogy, and especially the new organization of the Sunday school demanded more than the simple buildings of early Methodism. By the 1850s church architects were advocating a combination lecture room–Sunday school room alongside of, or to the rear of, the sanctuary. This plan meshed nicely with the growing popularity of Gothic designs. When placed to the rear of the pulpit wall, the room usually appeared on the outside as a chancel; if to the sides of the nave, the areas appeared as transepts. If placed at the front of the church, they could easily be disguised beneath a tower. In effect the newly emerging Methodist church complex was disguised in traditional Gothic garb. A less expensive and more popular alternative was to raise the sanctuary, thus providing for a full basement in which to house the Sunday school.

A new building design to match the new curriculum came from Lewis Miller, a Methodist businessman in Akron, Ohio, who had grown rich by inventing and manufacturing superior farm machinery and famous by helping found the Chautauqua Association. He turned his inventiveness and philanthropy toward the Sunday school.[36] Shortly after moving to Akron, Miller became Sunday school superintendent of the First Methodist Episcopal Church, a position he retained for over thirty-five years until his death in 1899. He grieved that the Sunday schedule (church and school meeting at the same time) deprived children of the experience of worship. So he guided them to plan and lead worship for their peers using part of the Sunday school hour. He also saw the wisdom of dividing the school into grades based on age using a uniform-lesson plan. When Akron Methodists decided to build a new church, Miller saw his chance to plan and build the most efficient Sunday school building possible for the growing congregation.

Tradition says Miller found his inspiration at a Sunday school picnic held in a park that contained a natural amphitheater or geological punch bowl.[37] Observing how children naturally grouped in ascending curves, all facing the central spot at the flat base of the incline, he sketched a building to match in fall 1866. Advice from Sunday school leader John Vincent—''Provide for togetherness and separateness; have a room in which the whole school can be brought together in a moment for simultaneous exercises, and with the minimum of movement be divided into classes for uninterrupted work''[38]—matched Miller's emerging conception of the Sunday school plan. Akron architect and fellow church member Jacob Snyder helped Miller perfect the Sunday school plan and designed the adjoining sanctuary.

The Sunday school building, erected at the rear of the church sanctuary, was dedicated in 1870, two years before the rest of the church was completed. The brick-faced exterior of the Sunday school wing and the sanctuary remained in Gothic style. The Sunday school building was two storeys capped by a nine-sided, windowed, semicircular dome. Inside, two tiers of classrooms framed a large, open semicircular space dominated by a wide superintendent's platform on the side wall, which later would adjoin the sanctuary. On the platform was a lectern and table; in front was a piano; behind was a blackboard. Chairs were grouped in semicircles for the youth classes held in the main room.[39] Classrooms were separated by brick partitions and from the central space by windowed doors. When folded open, they gave each class member and teacher a clear view of the superintendent without their leaving their seats. The transition from worship to learning could be made quietly and quickly, as Vincent's maxim suggested.

Aesthetic considerations tempered the pragmatic in the decoration of the building's interior. The ceiling of the main room was painted sky blue with wisps of white clouds. Frescoes of *Faith*, *Hope*, and *Christ Blessing Little Children* were added to the wall above the superintendent's platform. The motto adopted by the school, ''And they searched the Scriptures daily whether those things were so,'' was painted on the wall above the classrooms. At the center of the main room was a large fountain that squirted water on a statue of a boy hugging a fish. The stained-glass windows of the dome above cast a rosy glow on the green carpets that covered the floors of the main room and classrooms.[40]

Delegations from all sections of the country visited Akron to see and be convinced. Considered by most visitors to be a functional and aesthetic success, the plan was much discussed in the religious press. Vincent promoted it as the model Sunday school in his *Sunday School Journal* and later in his 1887 book *The Modern Sunday School*.[41] He supervised construction of a Sunday school modeled after it for his home church in Plainfield, New Jersey, in 1888.[42] Standard church-building books soon promoted the Akron plan. Denominational architectural catalogues of the period incorporated the plan into their larger, more costly church designs. No one asked whether children should worship without their parents, their pastor, or their choir. No one asked whether the assembly hall was a good space for worship. No one asked whether cubicles made good classrooms, nor why half the space stood empty much of the time.

Architects and builders, prominent and obscure, rushed to accommodate the demand. Bruce Price's design for the First Methodist Episcopal Church in Wilkes-Barre, Pennsylvania (completed in 1877), is said to have been the first use of the Akron plan in the eastern United States.[43] Akron plans were prominent in Stanford White's First (now Lovely Lane) Methodist Episcopal Church in Baltimore (completed 1887), Sydney R. Badgley's Epworth Memorial Methodist Episcopal Church in Cleveland (1893), and George W. Kramer's Christ Methodist Episcopal Church in Pittsburgh (1895).

The Akron plan evolved into a standard type that was fitted with an increasingly sophisticated array of furnishings and equipment—seating designed for each age group, blackboards, sand tables for replicating biblical geography, cabinets for curios from the Holy Land, and a multitude of maps, charts, and pictures. The most remarkable feature of the Sunday school was the partitions. Although curtains placed on horizontal rods were sometimes used to save cost, only wood partitions provided soundproofing. By the 1890s a number of manufacturers produced doors that folded, rolled up, or slid to one side. Rolling partitions, resembling roll-top desks then in vogue, were the most popular and practical for large openings. Partitions in some churches, like those in Epworth Memorial M.E. Church, Cleveland, were so large and so heavy that four hydraulic engines were used to lift them.[44]

Credit for popularizing the Akron plan belongs not to John Vincent or Lewis

Miller but to architect George Washington Kramer. In the early 1880s Kramer joined Jacob Snyder's Akron firm, which designed the Akron Sunday school, and quickly became the firm's specialist in church design. His work was so highly regarded that in 1894 he withdrew from the Akron firm to open his own firm in New York City, where he devoted himself exclusively to designing churches until his retirement in 1924. Kramer published his own theories and plans in an 1897 book, *The What, How and Why of Church Building*, which was reprinted in 1901. In 1911 Kramer served as architectural consultant and illustrator for Marion Lawrence's definitive work *Housing the Sunday School*, published jointly by the Methodist Episcopal Church and the Presbyterian Church for the International Sunday School Association.[45] Kramer supplied designs and plans for moderately priced churches published by the MECS and had connections to the MEC Board Church Extension in Philadelphia.

Standard Akron-plan Sunday schools by Kramer and others called for two curved tiers of classrooms facing onto a central rotunda. Throughout his long career Kramer experimented with the Akron plan, producing a number of variations on the theme. His major innovation was the "combination church," which placed the Sunday school beside the sanctuary and separated from it by a movable partition. When opened, the Sunday school became an extension of the sanctuary, often doubling its size for special occasions such as lectures, plays, and holiday and revival meetings. The Sunday school could also spill out into the sanctuary for its major extravaganzas. In a combination church the Sunday school could not be placed behind the pulpit wall, as with the original Akron arrangement. Instead, the school was placed to one side of the sanctuary. This arrangement combined with Kramer's pulpit in the corner church would permit the superintendent's platform to be used in the preaching service or revival meeting as an extension of the pulpit platform. Kramer drew out his combination church to its logical conclusion in the building he designed for Bushwick Avenue M.E. Church, Brooklyn, in 1894. To house "the largest Methodist Sunday school in the world," he wrapped its rooms around three sides of a central pulpit and organ.[46]

By the 1890s the Akron plan had become standard for Sunday schools for all medium-sized or large Methodist congregations. Village or rural churches with smaller schools made do with simpler facilities that consisted of a small suite of rooms not unlike the conventional mid-nineteenth-century arrangement. But the height of ambition for pastors and Sunday school teachers at the turn of the twentieth century was to have a building modeled on the Akron plan.

The growing size of the Sunday school and the increasing sophistication of its operation combined to create a building that came to rival the church proper. It represented the first step toward institutional churches of the twentieth century—multipurpose buildings joining sanctuary with Sunday school classrooms, kitchens, fellowship halls, gymnasiums, swimming pools, bowling alleys, and club rooms.

READING, RACE, AND RELIGION

The nation's cities, made "un-American" by immigrant masses, gave the Sunday school its most severe challenge as the century ended. Although the changing city seemed hostile and appeared as an unnatural habitat to many Sunday school workers, others saw the city and its newcomers as a challenge. The Sunday school continued to be a major thrust of home missions and church extension among native Americans and new immigrant communities. In these settings the Sunday school often reverted to the more comprehensive curriculum of a century earlier—reading, writing, and arithmetic and basic English-language training along with Bible study. Following the General Conference of 1876, the Western Methodist Book Concern at Cincinnati created a German Sunday School Department with Dr. Henry Liebhart as editor. Publications for the German Sunday schools included *Der Sonntagschule Glocke*, begun in 1857 and eventually reaching a circulation of thirty thousand. *Der Bibelforscher* was started in 1871 and at one time reached a circulation of forty-four thousand. A weekly paper for children, *Fur Kleine Sente*, began in 1879 and sold for $12 per hundred for the year. *Der Wegeneiser zur Heiligung* was a monthly publication. The Book Concern also issued leaflets for children and youth, tracts, songbooks, and other reading materials in German, totaling over 350 items. Henry Liebhart also helped to develop a German "youth Library" of a hundred titles.[47] By 1893 the MECS started publishing a Spanish edition of *Senior Quarterly* and of the *Illustrated Lesson Paper*.[48]

Late-nineteenth-century Sunday school leaders were no less awkward in their efforts to help African-American Sunday schools. They tried a number of black-oriented experiments in the 1890s and 1900s. The MEC Sunday School Union began to publish special curricula designed for black Sunday schools. The first, called *Good News*, later *Good Tidings*, was published from 1879 until 1908. The uniform lesson was simply presented in large type and with some illustrations. By 1900 it was reaching forty thousand African-Americans in some three thousand churches.[49] The Methodist Episcopal Freedmen's Aid Bureau hired black staff members to develop parallel Sunday school structures among the "colored people." Among the leaders in this movement were M.C.B. Mason, first black clergy executive of the Freedmen's Aid Society (served 1896–1912), and I. Garland Penn, lay founder of the Epworth League among black youth. Later white workers sponsored special programs in black teacher training across the South. These tactics were largely unsatisfactory. That failure reflected the vast chasm between black Methodists and white Methodists.[50]

White Sunday school workers were unable to discern or appreciate the unique contribution of the black Sunday school in those crucial years after the Civil War. In the South, for example, black Sunday schools had to take over the task of teaching reading and writing, serving as the public school for all ages and bringing literacy to the recently freed slaves. After emancipation many blacks were able to do openly what had been possible only covertly before, namely, learn to read and write on Sunday—first learning the alphabet, then learning small words, and finally reading the Bible. The compelling motive, Carter Woodson said, was for a "better knowledge of one's Christian duty and the reward awaiting the faithful. Many of these Negroes often learned more on a single Sunday than the average [white] student acquired in a day school during a week."[51]

Black colleges in the South, organized in considerable numbers by Methodists after the Civil War, sometimes included Sunday schools in which the faculty would teach. The colleges frequently had black congregations as bases, and teachers understood when hired that they had responsibility in both college and Sunday school. The latter were designed to reach youth who could not qualify for the higher academic program. Woodson's theory as well as the links between black colleges and Sunday school teaching indicate that the black Sunday school had its own distinctive work to do in the late nineteenth century. The elaborate paraphernalia of the white Sunday school organizations was mostly irrelevant— a fact Methodist Sunday school reformers did not clearly understand.[52]

NOTES

1. John McClintock, "The Sunday School in Its Relations to the Church," *MQR* 39 (October 1857): 529.

2. Abel Stevens, *Supplementary History of American Methodism* (New York: Eaton & Mains, 1899), 130–31.

3. John Vincent, "The Church School," *MQR* 51 (April 1869): 207.

4. The MECS gave the quarterly conference the duty to elect Sunday school superintendents and made them voting members of it in 1878. Legislation permitted women to be elected Sunday school superintendents beginning in 1898 but not be members of the quarterly conference!

5. A model constitution for annual conference Sunday school unions was first published in *Annual Report of the Sunday-School Union of the MEC*, 1868 (New York: printed for the Union, 1869), 85–87; MECS *Discipline*, 1882, 134.

6. Edward Eggleston, "The National Sunday School Convention of 1869," *National Sunday School Teacher* 4 (June 1869): 161–64.

7. MEC *Discipline*, 1860, 205. David Sherman, *History of the Revisions of the Discipline of the Methodist Episcopal Church* (New York: Nelson & Phillips, 1874), 214. The MECS Discipline changed "children" to "persons" in 1878.

8. Methodist Episcopal Church Sunday School Union, *Annual Report*, 1857, 9. Italics in original.

9. Anne M. Boylan, *Sunday School: The Formation of an American Institution, 1790–1880* (New Haven, CT: Yale University Press, 1988), 131.

10. The best modern study is Edward A. Trimmer, *John Heyl Vincent: An Evangelist for Education* (unpublished Ph.D. diss., Columbia University, 1986); the vintage biography is Leon H. Vincent's *John Heyl Vincent; A Biographical Sketch* (New York: Macmillan, 1925); see also "Autobiography of Bishop Vincent," *NWCA* 58 (13 April, 1 June, 22 June, 29 June, 13 July, 20 July, 3 Aug., and 24 Aug. 1910). For Vincent's role in Methodist Sunday school publishing, see Walter N. Vernon, *The United Methodist Publishing House: A History, 1870–1988* (Nashville: Abingdon Press, 1989), 2: 70–77.

11. *Annual Report of the Sunday-School Union of the Methodist Episcopal Church for the Year 1868* (New York: Printed for the Union, 1869), 81.

12. *Yearbook of the Sunday-School Union and Tract Society of the MEC for 1888* (New York: Hunt & Eaton, 1889), 71.

13. L. H. Vincent, *John Heyl Vincent*, 82, 90.

14. John H. Vincent, "Autobiography," *NWCA* 58 (1910): 846–47.

15. The secretary of MECS Sunday schools at the time came to similar conclusions: Atticus G. Haygood, *Our Children* (Macon, GA: John W. Burke & Co.; New York: Nelson & Phillips, 1876). See also Richard Abbey, *Christian Cradlehood; or, Religion in the Nursery* (Nashville: Southern Methodist Publishing House, 1881), especially 89–104. Abbey was one of the business agents of the MECS Publishing House.

16. At that time, and for many years to come, normal schools were teacher-training schools. The name, derived from the French, meant a model school.

17. Boylan, *Sunday School*, 124; see "Crafts, Wilbur Fisk," in *National Cyclopedia of American Biography* 14 (1917): 172–73. Crafts followed Vincent as pastor of Trinity Methodist Episcopal Church in Chicago, 1877–79. A year later Crafts transferred his clerical membership to the Congregational Church and later to the Presbyterian Church. Sara Jane Timanus of Cincinnati married Crafts in May 1874. She founded the International Primary Union of Sunday School Teachers and was president from its foundation in 1884 to 1899, when she became honorary president. In 1896 she was appointed Sunday school superintendent of the World WCTU.

18. Joanne Carlson Brown, *Jenny Fowler Willing: Methodist Church-Woman and Reformer*, unpublished doctoral diss., Boston Univ., 1983. Willing's "Sunday-School Temperance Work," *National Sunday School Teacher* 4 (October 1869): 293–94, is representative.

19. Boylan, *Sunday School*, 120.

20. Robert Cowden, "A Century of Sabbath-School Work in the United Brethren Church," *Quarterly Review of the United Brethren in Christ* 4/2 (April 1893): 148–49.

21. On the convention movement in general, see Lynn and Wright, *The Big Little Sunday School Child of American Protestantism* (New York: Harper & Row, 1971), 56–60, and Boylan, *Sunday School*, 85–95.

22. "John Vincent's Speech," in Cook County Sunday School Convention, *Proceedings* (Chicago: Goodman & Donnelley, 1864), 10–12.

23. Boyland, *Sunday School*, 94–95.

24. Vernon, *United Methodist Publishing House*, 2: 101.

25. Cawthon A. Bowen, *Child and Church: A History of Methodist Church-School Curriculum* (New York: Abingdon Press, 1960).

26. Ibid., 87.

27. Orange Judd (1822–92), *Lessons for Every Sunday in the Year* (New York: Sunday School Union of the Methodist Episcopal Church, 1864). Judd first printed the lessons in February 1862 in his own journal, the *American Agriculturalist*. They were so popular that they were officially adopted by the Methodist Sunday School Union. See Bowen, *Child and Church*, 100 f.; Frank G. Lankard, *History of the American Sunday School Curriculum* (New York: Abingdon Press, 1927), 179–80, and Vernon, *United Methodist Publishing House*, 2: 70 f. See also brief biographical sketches in *DAB* and Ohio Wesleyan University *Alumni Record*, 3d ed., 1883.

28. Vincent's fascination with the topography of the Holy Land was manifested again at the Chautauqua camp grounds in Chautauqua, New York, where he established a large

Palestine park, which replicated the contours of ancient Israel for the edification of visitors.

29. Acts 17:10–11; for Vincent's rationale for the Berean name, see Methodist Episcopal Church Sunday School Union, *Annual Report*, 1870, 42–43.

30. Lynn and Wright, *Big Little School*, 100–101.

31. Bowen, *Child and Church*, 91–93; Henry H. Meyer, *The Graded Sunday-School in Principle and Practice* (New York: Eaton & Mains, 1910).

32. Predecessor of the current *International Lesson Annual* still published annually by Abingdon Press. Vincent began editing and publishing a *Lesson Compend* in 1872, later named *Lesson Commentary on the International Sunday-School Lessons* and still later *Illustrative Lesson Notes*. In 1889 editorship passed to Jesse L. Hurlbut.

33. Lynn and Wright, *Big Little School*, 65.

34. The best study of the history of curricular changes and the uniform-lesson plan is Lankard's *Sunday School Curriculum*.

35. See Marion Lawrence, *How to Conduct a Sunday School* (New York: Fleming H. Revell Co., 1905), 248.

36. Ellwood Hendrick, *Lewis Miller* (New York: G. P. Putnam's sons, 1925). The best studies of the Akron plan Sunday school are A. Robert Jaeger, *The Auditorium and Akron Plans* (1984), chap. 4, pp. 139–80, and Jeanne H. Kilde, *Spiritual Armories: A Social and Architectural History of Neo-Medieval Auditorium Churches in the U.S., 1869–1910*. Unpublished doctoral diss., Univ. of Minnesota, 1991, Chapter 4, 184–99. See also Lewis Miller's own essay, "The Akron Plan," in *Seven Graded Sunday Schools*, ed. Jesse L. Hurlbut (New York: Hunt & Eaton, 1893), 11–32. An older and briefer study is Marion Lawrence's "The Akron Plan—Its Genesis, History and Development," in his *Housing the Sunday School; or, A Practical Study of Sunday School Buildings* (New York: Eaton & Mains, 1911), 83–92. An abbreviated version of Lawrence's chapter on the Akron plan was reprinted by the MECS Board of Church Extension in its *Thirty-Second Annual Report, 1913–1914*, 268–71.

37. Hendrick, *Lewis Miller*, 144–47.

38. Vincent's oft-quoted maxim became almost as famous as the architecture it inspired. Cited from Marion Lawrence's *Housing the Sunday School*, 84.

39. A brief contemporary description of the Sunday school interior can be readily found in Matthew Simpson, *Cyclopedia of Methodism* (New York: Gordon Press, 1977, reprint of 1877 ed.), 18. A fuller description can be found in First Methodist Episcopal Church's seventieth-anniversary booklet, 1907. A. Robert Jaeger, *The Auditorium and Akron Plans: Reflections on a Half Century of American Protestantism*, unpublished M. A. thesis, Cornell Univ., 1984, 155 f gives the fullest description.

40. For early description and floorplan see "The Model Sunday-School Room," *Sunday School Journal* n.s. 2/1 (October 1869): 11. Jaeger's detailed description is based on a description of the building in the *Akron Daily Beacon* at the time of the dedication, 1870. See Jaeger, *Auditorium*, 150–54.

41. "The Model Sunday-School Room," *Sunday School Journal* n.s. 2/1 (October 1869): 11; John H. Vincent, *The Modern Sunday-School* (New York: Hunt & Eaton; Cincinnati: Cranston & Curts, 1887), 160–61.

42. Architect Oscar S. Teale was also secretary of the Sunday school. See "A Model Sunday School Room," in *Seven Graded Sunday Schools*, ed. Jesse L. Hurlbut (New York: Hunt & Eaton, 1893), 113–20, and "Building of Vincent Chapel," First Methodist Episcopal Church, Plainfield, NJ, *Program of the 100th Anniversary Exercises October*

16–23, 1932 and Historical Sketch (Plainfield, NJ: The Church, 1932), [8–9]. For description and floorplan, see Lawrence, *Housing the Sunday School*, 59–63.

43. For a detailed description of the Sunday school building see George S. Bennett, "The Wilkes-Barre Plan," in *Seven Graded Sunday Schools*, ed. Jesse L. Hurlbut (New York: Hunt & Eaton, 1893), 36–38.

44. *Epworth Memorial Church: A Monument and a Movement, Published on the Tenth Anniversary of the Dedication of the Church* (Cleveland: The Church, 1903), 23.

45. Lawrence, *Housing the Sunday School.*

46. *The Bushwick Avenue Methodist Episcopal Church, Brooklyn, NY, Kramer & Simonson, Architects, 1 Madison Avenue, New York* (Brooklyn, NY: The Church, [1894]), twelve-page brochure. For description see Lawrence, *Housing the Sunday School*, 64–67.

47. Vernon, *United Methodist Publishing House, A History*, 2: 82.

48. Ibid., 168.

49. Ibid., 76, 136.

50. Charles R. Foster, Ethel R. Johnson, and Grant S. Shockley, *Christian Education Journey of Black Americans, Past, Present, Future* (Nashville: Discipleship Resources, 1985), 10–11.

51. Carter G. Woodson, *History of the Negro Church* (Washington, DC: Associated Publishers, 1921), 268.

52. Lynn and Wright, *Big Little School*, 73–75.

13
FROM CLASS MEETING TO PROBATIONER'S CLASS, 1866–1915

Post–Civil War Sunday schools welcomed adults as well as children. Finding the old class meeting monotonous, lacking inspiration and ineffectively led, many mid-century Methodists accepted the invitation. Were faithful members of the women's or men's Bible classes in Sunday school still expected to attend class meeting? Would the class meeting continue to be the key to membership?

DEMISE OF THE CLASS MEETINGS

The transformation of the Methodist ministry from circuit riders to stationed preachers and the rapid development of the Sunday school in the years following the Civil War had imperiled the class meeting. Earlier itinerants needed class leaders as deputies in residence. Now ministers lived in town in the midst of their people. Even circuits might permit services by the minister at each appointment every other Sunday. The position of the class leader shifted from that of an assistant to a rival. Could not the resident increasingly professional minister give more effective pastoral oversight than untrained laypersons?

The disciplines continued the rules for the class meeting, indeed, kept the section on class meetings substantially unchanged through most of the century.[1] In the Pastoral Address of the MECS General Conference of 1858, the bishops argued that the value of the class required that the provisions remain unchanged. A succession of new manuals for class meetings and defenses of the institution appeared before and after the Civil War. Such efforts, however, indicated that the institution was faltering.

Changes came. Relaxation of discipline in class meetings constituted one of the concerns that led to formation of the Free Methodist Church in 1860. The MECS in 1866 made the institution permissive with the qualifier "whenever it is practicable" and changed the section entitled "Classes" to "The Social Church meetings." Permission was also given for two or more classes to meet jointly.[2] In 1870 the MECS separated the section on membership from the "Means of Grace," which included what remained of class meetings. Signs that the old patterns were breaking down may be found in the MEC provisions of the Discipline of 1872, which also permitted two or more classes to meet together, a concession to convenience, a drop in attendance, and a dearth of new leaders. "Let care be observed," the Discipline continued, "that they do not fall into formality through the use of a uniform method." Such exhortations were not necessary in earlier times.[3]

By the 1880s the old Methodist class meeting was faltering. Resident pastors and adult classes in Sunday schools struck the death blow. Older members continued sometimes to meet in class after Sunday worship, but the practice became increasingly meaningless. By 1890 the bishops of the southern church in their address to the General Conference acknowledged that the class meeting "has very generally fallen into disuse," acknowledged that "it cannot be made compulsory again," and longed for "some more thorough and systematic method of pastoral instruction."[4] With the decline of the class came the decline of the leader. A similar fate attended other older lay offices—those of steward, exhorter, and local preacher. Behind the changes lay altered understandings of church, ministry, Holy Spirit, vocation, Christian perfection, and lay leadership. Laity found new roles as trustees, as members of the official boards, in Sunday school leadership, or in one of the new fellowships for women, men, and youth.

RISE OF PROBATIONER'S CLASSES

In the years following the Civil War the probationary system for members was also crumbling in the North and South. In the pre–Civil War days, when the class meeting was gladly attended, candidates for membership were carefully instructed in the essential doctrine and duties of good Methodists. Whereas children were expected to attend Sunday schools, adult converts were to be formed into probationer's classes. The decline of the class meeting in the post–Civil War era made necessary other methods to train members.

The problem was not just structural. Probationary membership seemed oppressive to mid-century Methodists and disadvantageous to the evangelistic task. Pressure mounted to discontinue or ignore practices that blocked access to church membership or gave recruiting advantages to others. Further, probationary membership, the rules of dress and behavior, and the sanction of trials proved offensive to Methodism's increasingly middle-class constituency. In place of "disciplined" probation, Methodists put an educational process.

Seminary professor Daniel Kidder* issued an early call for probationer's classes in his influential 1871 book on pastoral theology. Instead of trying to revive the class meeting, Kidder taught young pastors to form special classes to train probationers in the doctrines of the church and the duties of church membership.[5] Bishop John Vincent* joined Kidder in calling for probationer's classes. In his 1882 book *The Revival and after the Revival*, Bishop Vincent deplored the then common practice of preachers gathering new members. At the close of a revival, said Vincent, pastors would call all who desire to unite with the church upon probation to come forward or to speak to the preacher after the benediction. The pastors would take down the probationers' names and report to the conference a very large addition of members. During the six months of probation little was said to the new candidates. If new recruits showed up for church and Sunday school from time to time, committed no great wrong, and found someone to recommend them, at the end of the six months they became full members. So careless had been many ministers in this part of their work that many thoughtful Methodists doubted the importance of probation. Even worse, probationers by the hundreds drop out during the six months after the excitement of the revival dies down. To Bishop Vincent probation meant preparation, preparation meant classes, and classes meant study books. His book provided a rationale and a plan for conducting "Probationer's Classes."[6] Vincent urged pastors to require probationers to attend such a class monthly; there they would be treated to a lecture on Methodist history, doctrine, or polity, followed by a conversation on the responsibilities of church membership.[7]

Eager to secure the edification of converts and lower the dropout rate of probationers, pastors welcomed the new plan.[8] Beginning in 1872 extracts from the Discipline were made available in booklet form for pastors to use in probationers classes. The booklet included the historical statement, the Articles of Religion, and the General Rules but could be had with or without the Ritual.[9] However, many pastors needed help in interpreting the texts and designing a meaningful training experience.

In 1875 Luke Hitchcock and John M. Walden, book publishers for the MEC in Cincinnati, announced the publication of a "neat, compact, portable" *Probationer's Manual* designed to "be put in the hands of every probationer as soon as his name is enrolled in the Church lists." The eighty-page commentary on the nature of probation, the Baptismal Covenant, the Articles of Religion and the General Rules, rules for marriage, receiving the Lord's Supper, chargeable offenses, and the reception rite was authored by Edward Cary Bass of the New Hampshire Conference.[10] To introduce new members to their "powers, duties and privileges" in the church of their choice, James Porter, retired book editor, published *Helps to Official Members of the Methodist Episcopal Church* in 1878.[11] A decade later a Philadelphia pastor, Stephen Olin Garrison, produced the most widely used probationer's manual of its day. At a dollar a dozen and five times revised, Garrison's *Probationer's Hand-Book*, first published in 1883, was widely used for thirty years. More than a half million were sold.[12] The handbook introduced Methodist history, doctrine, and polity in six chapters, providing a topic and resources for each of the six months of the prescribed probationary period. More than half of the booklet was taken up with extracts from the Discipline: the Articles of Religion, the General Rules, rules relating to amusements, dress, marriage, temperance, and tobacco, the Apostles' Creed, the Baptismal Covenant, the General Confession, the Ten Commandments, and rituals for adult baptism and reception of members. The Methodist Book Concern published several tracts for use in cultivating probationary members. Jonathan T. Crane's *First Words for a Probationer* was one such tract.[13] Another was Bishop Vincent's "Our Own Church Series," a series of nine tracts for young people.[14]

Demand was so great that ten years later the Methodist Episcopal Book Concern published two additional probationer's manuals. In 1893 it had commissioned the Rev. J. Oramel Peck, who had an enviable record of recruiting and training new Methodists in four annual conferences—98 percent of his probationers were brought into full membership—to write *The Probationer's Companion.*[15] Updated in 1909, Peck's *Companion*, along with Garrison's, was widely used until a new membership manual was published in 1914. For pastors who preferred to train their candidates for membership in newly formed Epworth Leagues, the Methodist Book Concern published William W. Martin's *Epworth Catechism of Christian Doctrines as Taught in Methodism* the next year (1894).[16] Missionaries in Methodism's far flung mission enterprise demanded probationer's manuals in many non-English languages. William Burt, superintendent of Methodist work in Italy, produced one of the first in 1890.[17]

Slippage occurred between the number of probationers received and the number of persons received into full membership, mounting up to the tens of thousands. Not all pastors took responsibility for training new members. They were largely on their own to select resources and plan a program.[18] Not until 1903 did the MEC develop a plan and publish a detailed guide for an effective probationer's training program. James E. Gilbert, superintendent of public schools in several Midwestern cities and later secretary of the American Society of Religious Education (1888–1905) based in Washington, D.C., published a manual for pastors, *Preparation for Church Membership: Methodist Probationer's Trained*, along with a series of three inexpensive study books for children and adult probationers on the subjects of religious experience, biblical doctrine, and American Methodism. Gilbert advised pastors to organize probationers into classes, normally a children's class and an adult class, and to meet weekly for six months each year with children at the Sunday school hour and with adults on a weekday evening. The prescribed order of exercises for the adult probationer's class was as follows:

1. Devotional—singing, prayer, Scripture reading; 2. Roll call with opportunity to learn the causes of absence; 3. The lesson in the course conducted thoroughly with the privilege of questions; 4. Reports of standing committees . . . ; 5. Relations of experience, specially of temptations and trials, not in a dry and formal way, but so as to cover the real things of everyday life; 6. Closing prayer; 7. Cordial hand-shaking, each greeting each other in the most friendly manner leaving upon all minds the feeling of mutual regard.

"In harmony with the episcopal character of the denomination," Gilbert urged pastors to appoint a leader, secretary, and treasurer for each class. A model

Probationer's class ought to "introduce the money element at once" and have organized subcommittees on missions and benevolence. Pastors should rotate members through them; plan recreation and social occasions; present candidates who satisfactorily complete the course to the Official Board to be voted upon; then arrange an "impressive" Sunday celebration of reception with Holy Communion and give each candidate a frameable certificate or commemorative booklet.[19]

Such a ceremony gradually displaced the older pattern of admitting adult members each Sunday during what came to be called the "Invitation to Discipleship" following the sermon. By the late nineteenth century many pastors omitted such altar calls on Sundays and admitted new members but four times a year. To add dignity to the event the MEC General Conference of 1896 provided a new rite for public recognition of probationers in the presence of the church.

Not until 1908 did the MEC end the stipulation of a minimum term of probation and then did so in such a way as to retain the provision for probation without defining a specific duration. In the Discipline of 1916 a footnote was added explaining that according to an interpretation by the bishops in 1912, a probationary period was still mandatory. But by then the trial period meant little more than a stipulated period of time; little monitoring of behavior or attendance was undertaken.

By contrast southern Methodists immediately after the Civil War abolished probation and moved to train prospective new members instead. Most popular of all the post–Civil War era membership manuals for southern Methodists was written by combative Hilary T. Hudson of the North Carolina Conference and entitled *The Methodist Armor*. He produced an abridged edition for the young people of southern Methodism in 1883. In revised form, his *Shield of the Young Methodist* remained in print, drilling Methodists until 1924. "Thousands are brought into the Church through revivals annually," Hudson wrote in the preface, "but alas! how many drop out and disappear for lack of intelligent views of Methodism and of being properly drilled."[20] As an alternative, churches could choose St. Louis Methodist editor John E. Godbey's *Methodist Church-Member's Manual*, which went through seven printings from 1886 to 1916.[21] For young people, a compact statement of what southern Methodists "believe, forbid and require" could be had in George G. Smith's *Young Methodist, A Manual*, published in 1881.[22]

Relations with other churches in the North were defined in the provisions of the Discipline for reception of baptized members from other denominations by letter of transfer. Although some problems remained unanswered, the general practice was to accept without question a letter of dismission and even to receive by transfer when no letter was available—as was the case with those denominations that refused to release such letters. Attempts to require certain standards of belief and practice from those who wish to join by transfer did not meet with great success. Many maintained that a letter of transfer should be valid for admission of the prospective member only if it clearly specifies the worthiness of the prospective member, and that otherwise the candidate should be subject to a probationary period of training and trial. Such counsel recalled that under Wesley full membership was never permanent membership; every member was on probation each quarter; folk who failed to live up to the requirements of the discipline were dropped or placed on probation. Methodist discipline had changed, radically.

FROM TICKETS TO RITUALS, 1866–1884

For Methodism's first century quarterly membership tickets symbolized the strength and vigor of discipline. Post–Civil War patterns of church life increasingly did not include regular renewal of membership and issuance of tickets. After 1884 there was no more mention of them in the MEC. The practice of probation was gradually relaxed. Slowly the "society" character of Methodism changed to that of a "church." In practice, baptism, although formally a precondition for membership, and even conversion, were no longer considered the principal rite of initiation. Instead, formal liturgies for the reception of membership were developed.[23]

Methodists inherited no concept or rite of confirmation from Wesley. Progress in faith was long thought to begin with infant baptism, to continue in catechetical training at home and in church, and to be marked decisively by a conversion experience.[24] Beginning in 1864 in the North and 1866 in the South, reception into Methodist churches began to be certified by a public rite of "joining the church."[25] To enable new members to receive Communion, First Communion for some, the new reception rites were often held on Communion Sundays.[26]

Both new rites imply that those already baptized have not yet been fully received into the church.[27] They also emphasize the requirement of holy living. After a lengthy exhortation describing "how blessed are the privileges and how solemn are the duties" of membership, Methodist Episcopal pastors then asked the candidates to "publicly renew your [baptismal] vows, confess your faith, and declare your purpose."[28] The southern rite of 1866 did not have this extended introduction, but it pulled taut the lines of discipline in the formal interrogation adapted from the adult baptism rite of Wesley's *Sunday Service*: "Do you renounce the world, with all its vanities, together with all sinful practices so that you will not follow or be led by them?"[29] The northern ritual was satisfied, after ratification of the baptismal vows, affirmation of faith in Christ, and agreement to the Methodist Articles of Religion, to enquire: "Will you cheerfully be governed by the rules of the Methodist Episcopal Church, hold sacred the ordinances of God, and endeavor as much as in you lies, to promote the welfare of your brethren and the advancement of the Redeemer's kingdom? Will you contribute of your earthly substance, according to your ability, to the support of the Gospel, and the various benevolent enterprises of the Church?"[30] If the congregation did not object, the minister welcomed the new members into "the communion of the Church of God" and extended the symbolic "right hand of fellowship," a Methodist practice that, as we have observed, dates from 1740 or earlier.

By 1870 southern Methodists were willing to take their new rite seriously enough to place it, considerably revised, with the rest of the ritual. Retitled "Reception and Recognition of Members," it began with a new opening address. The interrogation was mitigated and abbreviated, requiring only two affirmations: ratification of the baptismal vows and acceptance of the rules, sacraments, and institutions of the church. Some of the burden of maintaining discipline was shifted to the Lord, as he was beseeched in a long concluding prayer to "help them to perform the promise and vow which they have made, to renounce the devil, the world, and the flesh . . . and to walk in thy commandments and ordinances blameless." Candidates were commended to the assembly with welcoming response.[31] This 1870 southern rite remained essentially unchanged through 1939 and became the principal form for the reception of adult members in the reunited church until 1964.

The impact of the addition of a public ritual to the admission processes in each of the churches was subtle. Was it a tacit admission of the failure of the class meeting as a regulatory agency? Was it a way to tighten discipline, since each new member was required to publically assent to doctrinal and moral standards and then could be held accountable? Or was it simply language that freed pastors to relax standards and admit whomever they wished? The emphasis on public profession, together with excusing converts from probation suggests a shift. Methodists who had viewed initiation into the church as a process were now viewing it as a single event. Church membership was not a privilege granted after completion of an apprenticeship but a right to be claimed by upright citizens. When saving faith and holy living were no longer demonstrated over time but simply affirmed, the vital Wesleyan connection between personal piety and corporate discipline was weakened if not undermined.[32]

The adoption of liturgies for reception of members underlined the growing Methodist reliance upon affirmation rather than demonstration of serious Christian commitment as the key to church membership. Their timing was significant, since their origins correspond with public admission that members in each of the churches habitually ignored the class meeting. Probationary membership without the class meeting was an empty formality.

NOTES

1. In 1872 the whole section in the Discipline was rewritten because the question-and-answer style was abandoned. The "Design of the Origin of Classes and the Appointment of Leaders" now ran: "I. To establish a system of pastoral oversight that shall effectively reach every member of the Church. II. To establish and keep up a meeting for social and religious worship, for instruction, encouragement, and admonition, that shall be a profitable means of grace to our people. III. To carry out, unless other measures be adopted, a financial plan for the raising of money."

2. MECS *Discipline*, 95, 93–99. The specific section on classes, however, was retained until 1934.

3. MEC *Discipline*, 1872,

4. "Episcopal Address," *JGC/S*, 1890, 28.

5. Daniel P. Kidder, *The Christian Pastorate* (Cincinnati: Hitchcock & Walden; New York: Carlton & Lanahan, 1871), 283 f. Kidder suggested that pastors provide probationary members with a copy of the church's Articles of Religion and, when possible, the whole Book of Discipline. Kidder's colleagues at Drew Theological Seminary, John McClintock and James Strong, included long articles on "Catechetics," Catechisms," and "Catechumens" in their *Cyclopaedia of Biblical, Theological and Ecclesiastical Literature*, 12 vols. (New York: Harper & Brothers, 1868 and 1891), 2: 148–54.

6. John Heyl Vincent, *The Revival and after the Revival* (New York: Eaton & Mains; Cincinnati: Jennings & Pye, c1882); See also James E. Gilbert, *Preparation for Church Membership: Methodist Probationers Trained* (New York: Eaton & Mains; Cincinnati: Jennings & Pye, c1903).

7. Vincent, *The Revival and after*, 63–65.

8. Jonas O. Peck, "Introduction" to Stephen Olin Garrison, *Probationer's Catechism and Compendium* (New York: Phillips & Hunt, 1883), 11.

9. *Origin, Articles, General Rules, and Ritual of the Methodist Episcopal Church* (New York: Nelson & Phillips; Cincinnati: Hitchcock & Walden, 1872), 27, 238–336. The 1880 and 1892 printings included only portions of the ritual, i.e., baptism of infants, baptism of adults, reception of members, and the Lord's Supper.

10. Edward Cary Bass, *The Probationer's Manual* (Cincinnati: Hitchcock & Walden; New York: Nelson & Phillips, 1875), 4.

11. James Porter, *Helps to Official Members of the Methodist Episcopal Church, Indicating Their Powers, Duties, and Privileges, Suggesting Sundry Mistakes, Methods and Possibilities with Regard to their Respective Departments of Service; Designed to Render Them More Efficient and Useful* (New York: Nelson & Philips; Cincinnati: Hitchcock & Walden, 1878).

12. Stephen Olin Garrison, *Probationer's Catechism and Compendium: Religious, Historical, Doctrinal, Disciplinary, and Practical*. Revised editions were published in 1885, 1887, 1896, 1904 and 1909. Title was changed to *Probationer's Hand-Book* in 1885. The title page of the 1909 edition included the publisher's note "500th thousand" printing.

13. Jonathan T. Crane, *First Words for a Probationer* (New York: Phillips & Hunt; Cincinnati: Hitchcock & Walden, Tract Department, [between 1879 and 1880]). Latest documented reprinting is 1900. Crane's twenty-four-page tract congratulated probationers for choosing the MEC, gave them a minihistory of the denomination, described its doctrines, rules, and organization and financial needs.

14. John H. Vincent, "Our Own Church" series (New York: Phillips & Hunt; Cincinnati: Cranston & Stowe, [between 1884 and 1889]). A series of nine numbered tracts, "charmingly written, tastily gotten up, compacted with most precious spiritual thoughts for young Christians," at thirty-six cents a set: No. 1, The Holy Catholic Church; No. 2, The Antiquity of Methodism; No. 3, That "Episcopal Church"; No. 4, The Church and the World; No. 5, Broad and Narrow; No. 6, The Classmates' Meeting; No. 7, Our Settled Itinerancy; No. 8, Earnest Christians; and No. 9, True Church Loyalty. In 1890 Vincent's series of tracts was published in book form as *Our Own Church* (New York: Hunt & Eaton, 1890).

15. Jonas Oramel Peck, *The Probationer's Companion, with Studies in Pilgrim's Progress* (New York: Hunt & Eaton, c1893). Revised 1896 and 1909.

16. William Wallace Martin, *The Epworth Catechism of Christian Doctrine as Taught in Methodism* (Nashville: privately printed, 1893; New York: Hunt & Eaton; Cincinnati: Cranston & Curts, 1894).

17. William Burt, *Manuale del Candidate all' Ammissione nella Chiesa Metodista Episcopale* (Roma: Tipografia Metodista, 1890), 4 editions/printings through 1903. Burt's manual was translated into French in 1909: *Manuel du candidat pour l'Admission dans L'Eglise Methodiste Episcopale* (Lyon: Amstein Fils & Richard, 1909).

18. In *The Drillmaster of Methodism* (New York: Eaton & Mains; Cincinnati: Jennings & Pye, 1902), Charles L. Goddell included a brief chapter on the importance of ''The Probationers' Class,'' including testimonials from several leading pastors, 114–24.

19. James E. Gilbert, *Preparation for Church Membership: Methodist Probationer's Trained* (New York: Eaton & Mains; Cincinnati: Jennings & Pye, 1903). The series of three study books for adult probationers was published in 1904 as *Religious Experience: Adult Probationer's First Book*, *Biblical Doctrine: Adult Probationer's Second Book*, and *American Methodism: Adult Probationer's Third Book*. Each book contained eight lessons with review questions, study topics, and bibliography. A series of three study books on the same topics for junior probationer's was planned but of the books appears to have been published, perhaps because of the new junior *Common Catechism*, published in 1905.

20. Hilary T. Hudson, *Methodist Armor; or, A Popular Exposition of the Doctrines, Peculiar Usages and Ecclesiastical Machinery of the Methodist Episcopal Church, South*, designed for adults and first published in 1882, went through twelve revisions until the last in 1927. *The Shield of the Young Methodist; or, The Methodist Armor Abridged and Arranged in the Form of a Catechism for the Benefit of Sunday-Schools, Young Converts, and for Families* (Shelby, NC: Babington & Roberts, 1883). Privately published until 1889 when the Publishing House of the Methodist Episcopal Church, South, issued a revised edition. Hudson's *Shield*, revised again in 1912, was kept in print until 1924.

21. John Emory Godbey, *The Methodist Church-Member's Manual: A Hand-Book for Every Methodist* (St. Louis, MO: South-Western Methodist Publishers, 1886). Beginning in 1903 the manual was reissued by the Publishing House of the Methodist Episcopal Church, South. Godbey's 124–page manual is in large part a commentary on the vows contained in the reception rite. Educated at Emory College, Godbey served as pastor and district superintendent in Missouri and in 1882 was founding editor of the region's weekly Methodist newspaper, *South-Western Methodist*, later the *St. Louis Christian Advocate*. He edited the *Arkansas Methodist* in Little Rock (1894–1905) and taught philosophy at nearby Hendrix College.

22. George G. Smith, *The Young Methodist: A Manual* (Nashville: Southern Methodist Publishing House, 1881).

23. The basic study is Frederick A. Norwood, *Church Membership in the Methodist Tradition* (Nashville: Methodist Publishing House, 1958).

24. For British Methodist practice see Stuart A. Bell, ''Reception into Full Membership: A Study of the Development of Liturgical Forms in British Methodism,'' *Proceedings of the Wesley Historical Society* 48 (February 1991): 1–40.

25. ''Reception of Members: Form for Receiving Persons into the Church after Probation,'' MEC *Discipline*, 1864, 145–49. The 1866 MECS ''Form of Receiving Members into the Church'' was included in a special appendix of the MECS *Discipline*, 1866,

328–31. (An abbreviated and slightly different version was also included in the general section of the *Discipline*, "Of the Reception of Members into the Church," 91–93. The rite was enlarged, retitled, and moved to the section on rituals in 1870: "Form of the Reception and Recognition of Church-Members," MECS *Discipline*, 1870, 202–7. An unofficial "trial-use" reception rite had been proposed for the MECS in 1860 and included as an appendix to Josephus Anderson's *Our Church: A Manual*, "A Form to Be Used in the Reception of Persons into Full Connection," [301]–4.

26. Gilbert, *Preparation for Church Membership*, 156, 164.

27. A confusing problem concerned the relationship of baptized children to the church. They were regarded as members of the realm of God and as subject to catechetical training to bring them to full membership. But the precise nature of probationary membership was a matter of confusion for years. Were baptized children probationers or was it necessary for them to join on probation? This was the question asked in a memorial considered at the MEC General Conference of 1888. Not until the MEC *Discipline* of 1912 do we find a specific statement to the effect that baptized children are probationary or preparatory members. This status was implied and generally assumed in earlier legislation. The term *probationer* as applied to children in the South was omitted after 1858, although ministers were required to keep a roll of baptized children.

28. The reception rite only alluded to the "Baptismal Covenant" but did not state it. The full text, found in the ritual for baptism and in Catechism No. 1 (1852), was in three parts: (1) the renunciation of the devil: "I renounce the devil and all his works, the vain pomp and glory of the world, with all covetous desires of the same, and the carnal desires of the flesh, so that I will not follow nor be led by them"; (2) the Apostles' Creed; and (3) a concluding vow: "Having been baptized in this faith, I will obediently keep God's holy will and commandments, and walk in the same all the days of my life, God being my helper."

29. "Form of Receiving Members into the Church," MECS *Discipline*, 1866, 329.

30. These questions continued to be asked until 1928, when the northern rite was revised.

31. MECS *Discipline*, 1870, 202–7.

32. A helpful discussion of this point is David F. Holsclaw, *The Demise of Disciplined Christian Fellowship: The Methodist Class Meeting in Nineteenth-Century America* (unpublished Ph.D. diss., University of California, Davis, 1979), 73–75.

14
THE SUNDAY SCHOOL RENAISSANCE, 1915–1935

From 1915 to 1935 the modern Sunday school or church school came of age. Methodists led the advance. With Horace Bushnell they prized *Christian Nurture*, magnified the grace of God, envisioned family and church as conjoined, and embraced as principle the growth and enrichment of human life from childhood to maturity. The Sunday schools also felt the influence of modern Methodist theology, typified by two deans of the church's university divinity schools, Wilbur F. Tillett of Vanderbilt and Albert C. Knudson of Boston. Tillett set about reclaiming an ancient Wesleyan landmark of spiritual growth toward perfection. "There are no higher heights in Christian experience," he wrote in 1902, "than those . . . represented in . . . Scripture as possible to every child of God by growth in grace."[1] Northern Methodists were powerfully shaped by "Boston Personalism" popularized by Knudson, for whom salvation was no longer the rescue of helpless persons: It was their free resolve to improve their condition, divinely assisted in their fulfillment, effecting their moral and spiritual transformation.[2] And when George Albert Coe* produced *A Social Theory of Religious Education* in 1917, many Methodist leaders subscribed to his statement that the aim of Christian education was growth of the young toward and into mature and efficient devotion to the democracy of God and happy self-realization therein.[3]

SALVATION BY EDUCATION

Coe, a Methodist professor at Northwestern University and then at Union Theological Seminary and Columbia Teachers College in New York, injected into religious education the notion that there is a scientific way to solve problems—not only the technological problems of industry but the problems of learning, character building, and institutional organization. The new educational philosophy drew on an emerging new psychology pioneered by William James that saw children as, not "little adults," but possessing unique characteristics which could not be disregarded by those who would teach them. Marking the difference between children and adults was a newly defined period of life, "adolescence." For the Sunday school teacher this meant abandoning the old transmissive method of teaching, standard in inherited catechetical patterns. Instead of pouring preselected content into young minds, teachers must discover subjects of interest to students, engage them in activities related to that interest, and then guide them as they reflected on their experiences. Confirmands should state problems, pose alternative solutions, test options, and draw conclusions.

To promote the new teaching and learning styles in the churches and to set standards for the movement, Coe and educator John Dewey founded the interdenominational Religious Education Association. The new association and the hiring by churches of Christian educators marked the professionalization of the field and the prominence of women in leadership roles. By 1906 a new group of professional lay women, directors of religious education, began to replace amateur male Sunday school superintendents in large, progressive churches. By the 1920s the Discipline made provision for local churches to elect a director of Christian education, "whose duty it shall be, together with the pastor, to have general supervision of the entire educational program of the church."[4]

These educational reforms came during a time of unprecedented growth for Sunday schools. In the 1896–1900 quadrennium northern Methodism's Sunday schools grew at the rate of about 22,000 new members a year. The average annual increase between 1900 and 1904 almost doubled (42,000). By 1908 Sunday school membership outnumbered church membership by almost 40,000. From 1908 to 1916 the average annual increase of Sunday school membership was 150,000, and the enrollment in 1915 was 4,600,000. The northern Book Concern happily reported to the General Conference of 1912 that in the eight-year period from 1904 through 1911 sales of Sunday school literature had increased 66.2 percent and amounted to almost $7 million.[5] The publishing houses of both the MEC and the MECS were taxed to the limits of their very considerable facilities for this ever-increasing demand.

GRADED LESSONS ARRIVE

Curricular change, consonant with the new educational philosophy and new professionalism, came in 1910 with graded lessons. The Uniform Lesson Series, created by the International Sunday School Association and in use for thirty-five years, employed the same Scripture as text for all ages, and different lesson treatments and methods were supplied for each of four age groups—primary, intermediate, senior, and adult. For twenty years and more Sunday school leaders longed for what public schools possessed, literature suited to the various age groups.

The male heads of Sunday school boards, Thomas B. Neely* in the North and Howard M. Hamill in the South, opposed any change from the use of

Uniform Lessons. These men failed to reckon with the power of Methodist women. Martha Barnes* (Mrs. J. W.) represented the MEC at a 1906 conference on international elementary graded Sunday school lessons held in New York City. Active in her church in Newark, New Jersey, she had served for several years as elementary superintendent for the World's Sunday School Association. Named chairwoman, Mrs. Barnes enunciated a set of principles for planning to meet the religious needs of children and then guided the conference to adopt them: God's relation to us, our relation to Him, our relation to others, and our duty to ourselves. Within less than a year great progress had been made in outlining and describing graded courses for children and youth.[6] In 1908 she joined the Book Concern's staff of Sunday school editors.

In spite of considerable opposition the graded system was approved by the influential International Sunday School Association in 1908 for use by those churches desiring it. Immediately the Methodists, now under new Sunday school leaders, Henry Meyer in the North and Edwin B. Chappell in the South, began making their plans, and by fall 1910 the new resources were available for beginners, primaries, and juniors.[7] A year later similar materials were ready for intermediates, and the senior graded lessons came in 1913. Each new series was widely accepted, and the circulation figures soared. In the north the new graded lessons competed with the old uniform lessons, which were kept in print for many years, but in the South graded lessons won the day.

Effort was made to get Sunday school teachers trained to take advantage of the new graded lessons. The MECS took the lead in 1902 by requiring pastors to organize teacher-training classes annually in all of their congregations.[8] The large number of trained teachers may explain the degree of acceptance of graded lessons in the southern church, a phenomenon that surprised Sunday school executives and publishing agents alike. By the 1920s the northern church had also created a market of impressive size and potential for teacher training with its Religious Education Texts, issued in two series, the Community Training School Texts, and the Week Day School Series.

SUNDAY SCHOOL IN SPACE AND TIME

The new day in religious education spelled the end to the great symbol of the uniform lesson—the Akron plan church building—revolutionary in the 1870s, dominant in church planning by 1900, an architectural triumph, fitting form to purpose, a statement of upscale Methodist ambitions and aspirations. By the 1920s Methodists were among the first to actively and officially repudiate the Akron plan, promoting instead a multiroom public school–like Sunday school. Dramatizing the change, the congregation of the First Methodist Episcopal Church in Akron, Ohio, tore down their famous Sunday school building in 1914 and replaced it with a freestanding public school–like educational building.

The calendar also changed to reflect the dominance of the Sunday school over

Methodist life. A Children's Day had been a Methodist standard since the 1872 MEC General Conference, which established the second Sunday in June to celebrate the importance of children in the life of the church. It featured active participation of children in the Sunday service and a special offering for a student loan and scholarship fund. Added to the calendar in the twentieth century were Rally and Decision Days. Rally Day in the early fall summoned students to the work of the new church school year. Decision Day was introduced in the spring as the occasion to encourage children and youth to commit their lives to Christ.

Vacation Bible schools had been held in many communities since the 1890s. The concept was developed in 1894 by Mattie Miles, wife of a Methodist pastor in Hopedale, Illinois. With the help of teenage volunteers, Miles taught Bible lessons to children each week for four weeks in the summer, using music, crafts, storytelling, contests, and games. For many years promoted as separate and independent of the Sunday school, vacation Bible schools now became an integral part of the church school.[9] One of the first publications in the Abingdon Religious Education Text series in 1920 was a planbook for daily vacation Bible schools.[10] By the 1930s daily vacation Bible schools were written into the program and organization of the two churches.

During this period churches remodeled adult Sunday school classes by legislation and literature into well-defined departments, in contrast to the independent, casual, and sometimes irresponsible groupings of the nineteenth century. Instituted in the northern church in 1908 and in the southern church in 1910, these adult Bible classes were an immediate success. By 1914, four years after their organization in the southern church, they reached a total of over four thousand classes with a membership of more than ten thousand.[11] For adults as well as children, the Sunday school became the gateway to the church.

LAST HURRAH: THE COMMON CATECHISMS OF 1905

Reflecting their new fraternal accord, the General Conferences of the MEC in 1900 and of the MECS in 1902 established commissions (appointed by the bishops) to prepare new catechisms for use in both churches. The joint commission of two bishops, three clergy, and two lay members from each church planned at its first session for the preparation of two catechisms, a *Junior Catechism* for children of twelve years and under and a *Standard Catechism* for older youth and adults. Pastors Stanley O. Royal (MEC) and John O. Willson (MECS) drafted the *Junior Catechism*.[12] Clergymen John J. Tigert (MECS) and William V. Kelley (MEC) drafted the *Standard Catechism*.

The *Junior Catechism* aimed "to cover the whole range of essential doctrine; to give a large view of the life of our Lord; to guide children to a personal religious experience; and to enforce the practical duties of daily conduct."[13] The *Standard Catechism* differed from the church's previous catechisms, although the question-and-answer format and Scripture proofs were retained. The new catechism began with a formal definition of the Christian Religion: *"What is Christianity?* Christianity is the religion of God's redeeming love, manifested in the incarnate life, the atoning death, and the glorious resurrection of Jesus Christ, the Founder of the Kingdom of God." Implications of that definition were developed, and an exposition of the Ten Commandments, the Beatitudes, and the Lord's Prayer followed. The catechism concluded with a concise fifteen-page doctrinal section focusing on the Bible, the Trinity, the church, and the sacraments and "the Way of salvation" (sin, repentance, saving faith, justification, regeneration, witness of the Spirit, fruit of the Spirit, sanctification, Christian perfection, glorification, heaven!). An appendix reprinted John Wesley's 1742 tract on the *Character of a Methodist.*[14] The aim of the two catechisms, stated the committee, was to produce works "simple, intelligible, sound and compact, expressed in Scriptural language whenever practicable, in order that vital and saving Christian Truth may be easily and quickly apprehended by our young people."[15] Although drafters of the new catechisms questioned some of the old scholastic assumptions, the intellectualist focus of Methodist theology on formal doctrinal instruction and apologetics remained.

Issued with the blessing of the bishops of the two churches and translated to accommodate the church's still expanding ministry to immigrants, the new catechisms did not live up to billing.[16] An early review by a pastor in the church's chief weekly newspaper was not favorable.[17] Nor were the new catechisms welcomed by Sunday school leaders. In the early years of the twentieth century, under the influence of the new educational philosophy of Dewey, Coe, and company and the new psychology of adolescence, Christian educators turned away from catechisms of all kinds. Memory-centered training was out; experience-centered learning was in.[18] A series of manuals for training in church membership largely replaced the catechisms, although the 1905 common catechism was still used by some pastors until the 1950s.

The common catechisms of 1905 were more widely used in the South and over a much longer period. Southern Methodists produced nothing comparable to the competing membership training manual of their northern cousins. Several alternative resources, however, were available. In 1909 Howard M. Hamill, head of MECS Sunday school training, produced the *Manual of Southern Methodism*, which came closest to unseating the senior common catechism.[19] Richard Watson's catechisms, borrowed from the British Methodists a hundred years earlier, continued to be available through 1924.

EDUCATIONALLY CORRECT MEMBERSHIP MANUALS

In the first two decades of the new century Sunday schools outpaced the church. In the MEC alone Sunday school enrollment doubled from 2.5 million to 5 million by 1920. During the eight years from 1911–19 the MEC received on probation 300,000 converts a year from the Sunday schools.[20] How now to train them for church membership?

The MEC General Conference of 1912 authorized a new plan for membership training.[21] The Board of Bishops assigned three of their number, Bishops Anderson, McDowell, and Wilson, to give oversight to the project. The principal author was the Rev. Louis F. W. Lesemann, a District Superintendent from the Chicago Northern District of the Rock River Conference. The new *Probationer's Manual* was an outgrowth of Lesemann's pastoral experience in preparing children for church membership. Lesemann acknowledged making "free use of our Junior Catechism" in his foreword, but also borrowing ideas from Bishop John Vincent* and Methodist Bible scholar Milton Terry.[22] Lesemann's new manual was organized into three main parts, each with two subsections. Part 1, The Christian Truth, was divided into two sections: "Great Truths of the Christian Religion" and "Helps to the Christian Life" (the sacraments and other means of grace). Part 2, The Church, was also presented in two sections: "The Church of the Past" and "The Methodist Episcopal Church." Part 3, Church Membership, unfolded also in two sections: "The Personal Life" ("Your Habits and Character," "Your Church Covenant," and "Your Consecration") and "Covenants, Confessions, Rules and Forms," ranging from the Apostles' Creed and Methodist Articles of Religion to "Special Advice Regarding Amusements."[23] Revised to incorporate changes made at the General Conference of 1916, especially the softening of probationary membership and revised rituals for baptism and reception of members, and given a new name—*Membership Manual*—the new manual largely replaced the common catechism of 1905.[24] An additional section on stewardship was added in 1924. Minor revisions came following the General Conferences of 1928, 1932, and 1936. The manual was adapted by the Rev. C. W. Ports and translated into Spanish for use in Hispanic-American Methodist churches in 1925.[25]

For training older youth an alternative to the *Standard Catechism* (1905) was readied by the Methodist Book Concern as early as 1909: Robert E. Smith's *Methodist Episcopalians*. Twice revised, in 1924 and 1933, each time with a new episcopal foreword, Smith's manual found wide use in local churches.[26] Lesemann's manual and Smith's study guide pre-packaged content with only an occasional nod to the new styles of teaching and learning now on the horizon.

By the 1920s seminary-trained religious educators and pastors vigorously argued for the Sunday school as the proper context for nurturing personal commitment to Christ and to the church and demanded curriculum resources, including membership training materials, which would take into account progressive religious education ideals. "Dogmatic, iron cast, hide-bound instruction is on its way out," wrote one of them (John Versteeg) in 1919. Memory-based education "made us parrots repeating phrases in which dust called unto dust. Through it we were ever learning but never able to come to the knowledge of the truth."[27] Pastors like Versteeg found relief in 1920 when Archie L. Ryan's *When We Join the Church* appeared in Abingdon's popular Religious Education Texts series.

With the new principles in mind, Ryan designed his manual for boys and girls of "confirmation age" (twelve to eighteen). Expository prose replaced the terse questions and answers of the catechism. The cloth-bound, illustrated manual's ten lessons on history, doctrine, and organization of the church made much of the church "as a means through which to serve others, as well as a spiritual home in which to grow in religious experience and usefulness." A few "Things Methodists Should Commit to Memory" were retained as an appendix—the Apostles' Creed, the Ten Commandments, the General Confession (revived in the 1916 revision of the Lord's Supper rite), and the Lord's Prayer.[28] By the early 1930s the field of membership training resources was crowded, a mix of old catechism-style and new experience-centered materials. The Methodist Book Concern offered six competing resources for church membership training.[29]

By the 1920s southern Methodist confidence in the new graded lessons and better-trained teachers made the pastor's catechism classes increasingly old-fashioned. Busy pastors increasingly relied on Sunday school teachers to train the church's new members, often meeting with young candidates only a few times before "Confession Day," a term religious educators preferred to "Decision Day."[30] The number of persons received into the southern church from the Sunday school soared. During the decade of the 1930s the number ranged from a low of 91,285 in 1937 to a high of 115,590 in 1938, doubtless due to the church-aide Aldersgate bicentennial commemoration crusade. Of the total number of persons received into the church "on Profession of Faith" during the decade, 76 percent were Sunday school pupils.[31]

Sunday school membership and attendance faltered during the 1920s and early 1930s as did the number of youth preparing for church membership. At the same time, church leaders worried about the quality of new member training and lack of attention to it among some clergy. In response northern Methodists at their 1924 General Conference added the words "after Required Instruction Has Been Given" to the title of both reception rites.[32] The Committee on Religious Education in the local church of the Board of Education asked the next (1928) General Conference to appoint a commission to review critically the place of children in the church—their baptism, their status as preparatory members, their reception into the church, and the duties of pastors to children during their critical maturing years.[33] The MEC General Conference of 1932 adopted a report of the Committee of Education providing for graded courses of instruction for candidates for church membership. Bugbee's 1919 lessons were replaced in 1932 by a new training program "for adolescents," *Learning to Live for God* by John E. Charlton and Edith M. Jordan, which included a teacher's manual and a twenty-four-lesson pupil's workbook. For the first time a woman religious educator was invited to share in preparing curricular materials. The new plan called for pastors to gather twelve-year-old young people into a "Membership Class" in early fall, plainly state the class's purpose ("to give an opportunity to know what the church stands for and to find the joy of fellowship with Christ"), use the teaching materials creatively, and aim for "the commitment" at Palm Sunday, which may coincide with Decision Day in the church school.

Decisions were to be made "without undue pressure and with the full knowledge and co-operation of parents." To secure this, pastors were urged to call on the homes of all pupils and talk the matter over with parents.[34] Additional church membership resources were written by Mildred Moody Eakin, one of the first women executives in the MEC Board of Education, editor of Sunday School publications in Chicago since 1919, and after 1933 professor of religious education at Drew Theological Seminary.[35]

A new burst of energy around confirmation training blossomed in the 1930s, culminating in the selection in 1938 of a pastor with a successful record of guiding girls and boys into full membership, Karl Quimby of the Newark Conference (New Jersey), to write the denomination's first manual for pastors and religious educators responsible for "confirmation" training. Quimby's *How to Conduct a Church Membership Class for Boys and Girls* set a new standard for "quality" confirmation training.[36] It contained chapters on understanding the needs of girls and boys, what they should know before joining the church, and how to plan an effective training program for church membership. Whether held in after-school hours on weekdays or Sunday mornings as part of the church school, whether led by the pastor alone or with the aid of religious educators, Quimby stressed home visitation and personal interviews with each confirmand.

Fall training sessions aiming toward reception of children on Rally or Promotion Day became standard.[37] But by the late 1930s Lent was the preferred season for instruction, with Palm Sunday the target date for administering the rite. Quimby urged pastors to make "Confirmation" and "First Communion," whether in fall or spring, a memorable occasion. Quimby recommended specific procedures: Have members of the official board meet the children at the door of the church and process with them to their places at the front; ask the Sunday school superintendent to present the candidates; invite parents and teachers to gather with the minister in the chancel to join in the laying on of hands; and encourage church officials to give each a handclasp and a souvenir.[38] He also suggested following the service by a reception or a banquet in the church parlor.[39] First Communion sometimes followed the reception rite on Palm Sunday, but more often was postponed until Holy Thursday, since few Methodist church's celebrated Holy Communion on Easter Sunday—chancels were too full of lilies! While children were generally received into church membership only once a year, on Palm Sunday, adults were usually received three or four times a year depending on the number of candidates who had completed the "required" training.[40]

Quimby's plea to upgrade training of new members met a significant roadblock—the lack of one training manual authorized and required for the entire church. All Quimby could do was to call attention to the more useful materials available.[41] The manual Quimby and others longed for would not arrive until 1942.

CONFIRMATION-STYLE RECEPTION RITES

In the new century, Methodists North and South became more educated, more affluent, more middle class, and more self-conscious. They discouraged emotional displays and relegated spontaneity to the Wednesday evening prayer meeting. Aestheticism dictated efforts at "enriching" public worship. They reprinted Wesley's *Sunday Service* in the 1890s, placed a recommended "Order for Public Worship" in the front of their new common hymn of 1905, and increasingly worshipped in architect-designed buildings. To meet the competition of Episcopalians, Lutherans, Presbyterians, and Roman Catholics, who made much of First Communion and Confirmation for children, Methodists began to develop confirmation style reception rites for their young people.[42]

The MEC General Conference of 1904 ordered the appointment of a commission to revise the ritual, but only in 1916 were its revised set of rituals adopted.[43] Two reception rites were provided: a new rite for children and a revision of the 1864 rite for adults now titled "for Receiving Persons into the Church from Preparatory Membership."[44] In both rites northern Methodists took the first timid steps toward recovering confirmation, a rite Wesley dropped from the Anglican Book of Common Prayer. The change was dramatic. From 1864 until 1916 reception rites focused on an interrogation of the candidates regarding the faith of all Christians, a profession of loyalty to the Methodist branch of the family, and a welcoming handshake. After 1916 candidates were asked to kneel while the pastor read a prayer borrowed from the confirmation rite in the Book of Common Prayer.[45] The new ceremony did not direct the minister to "lay his hand on every one severally," as in the Episcopal rite.

The 1916 order's indebtedness to Episcopal confirmation rites, in terms both of structure and of emphasis on prayers for the Spirit's presence in the lives of the candidates, set them apart from the earlier Methodist reception rites and clearly moved early twentieth-century Methodism toward a full-blown rite of confirmation. However the rite was not called "confirmation" until 1964, nor did the opening address to the congregation employ that word. The formidable interrogation became more candidate friendly. The "Doctrines of the Holy Scriptures as set forth in the Articles of Religion" became "the Christian faith as contained in the New Testament."[46] The "cheerful" question ("Will you cheerfully be governed by the rules of the Methodist Episcopal Church, hold sacred the ordinances of God, and endeavor, as much as in you lies, to promote the welfare of your brethren and the advancement of the Redeemer's kingdom?" asked since 1864) was replaced with a vow of loyalty to the church and its support by prayer, presence, gifts, and service.

Debate around revising the rite for admission of adults centered on the matters of probation and the doctrinal test.[47] The six-month probationary period had been dropped in 1908, but was probation gone? The Council of Bishops, in a 1912 decision that appeared as a footnote in the Discipline, ruled that probation was required as a condition precedent to reception into full membership. The period of probation was no longer of a definite length, but the probationary (preparatory) membership was imperative.[48] This footnote disappeared in 1928 and with it any requirement of preparatory membership, although the Discipline retained the reception rite for preparatory members and continued to classify members as preparatory and full.[49]

Since 1864 adult candidates in the reception rite were required to profess "saving faith in the Lord Jesus Christ" and to affirm "the doctrines of the Holy Scriptures as set forth in the Articles of Religion of the Methodist Episcopal Church." The "saving faith" reference was modified in 1916 to remove the implication that a person must have experienced conversion before being admitted to membership. The subscription to the Articles of Religion was dropped in the rite proposed by the Ritual Revision Committee but reinserted by General Conference. Harris Franklin Rall, seminary professor and secretary of the Ritual Revision Committee (1912–16) complained that Methodism since 1916 had "two doors by which candidates may enter our fellowship—the one for young people, respecting the New Testament position, and that of Wesley and early Methodism, and the other representing the innovation of the General Conference of 1864."[50] Debate continued until 1924, when the vow was rephrased to an affirmation of faith "as contained in the New Testament," as had been done in 1916 in the new children's rite.[51]

Northern Methodists took a further step toward recovery of confirmation when revising liturgies in 1932. It provided for the laying on of hands with prayer in place of the simple 1864 gesture of the right hand of fellowship. The opening address of a now single "Order for Receiving Persons in the Church" (for children, persons coming from other churches, or adult converts) now made it clear that none of these groups was considered to be a member already. The new commendation at the end—"Brethren, I commend to your love and care these persons whom we this day have received as members of our church and call upon you to do all in your power to increase their faith, confirm their hope and perfect them in love"[52]—reminded the congregation of responsibility to be holy examples to the candidates.

The rituals of the southern church underwent revision in 1910 after considerable debate in General Conference, but no changes were made in the reception rite until 1914. A second rite for "the Reception and Recognition of Children as Members" was added to the rituals of the church that year. The southern church did not use the terms *probationer* or *preparatory members* for either children or adults. The opening rubric directed ministers to gather the children into a class, baptize any whose baptism may have been delayed or neglected, and instruct them in "the things necessary for them to know as to the doctrines and rules of the Church" and then invite parents and teachers to stand with them before the congregation. The opening address described the children as "having arrived at years of discretion, and now of *their* own accord appearing before this congregation to take upon *themselves* the vows and enter upon the privileges and duties of the Church.'' The minister then prayed God to grant *''these tender lambs''* grace and wisdom to lead holy obedient and faithful lives and invited "fathers and mothers" to renew the vows they had made at the time of their children's baptism. Unlike the northern rite, the new southern one made explicit the sense of ongoing relationship with the church rather than initial reception into its membership. In a question addressed to the children, the southern rite asked, "Is it your sincere desire, of your own free will and accord, to continue as *members* of the Church of Christ, in the communion of the Methodist Episcopal Church, South?" Following the friendly interrogation, the assembly read the Twenty-third Psalm, heard two lessons from the New Testament (I Timothy 1:5–6) and Luke 2:40–52), welcomed the new members with the right hand of fellowship, and were dismissed with a blessing.[53]

NOTES

1. Wilbur F. Tillett, *Personal Salvation: Studies in Christian Doctrine Pertaining to the Christian Life* (Nashville: Publishing House of the Methodist Episcopal Church, South, 1902), 323–25. For a study of Tillett's theology see Lester H. Colloms, *Wilbur Fisk Tillett, Christian Educator* (Louisville, KY: Cloister Press, 1949).

2. Albert C. Knudson, *The Doctrine of Redemption* (New York Abingdon Press, 1933). On Knudson's theology see Robert E. Chiles, *Theological Transition in American Methodism* (Nashville: Abingdon Press, 1965), chap. 5, and Paul Deats and Carol Robb, eds. *The Boston Personalist Tradition in Philosophy, Social Ethics, and Theology* (Macon, GA: Mercer University Press, 1986), essay 6, "Albert Cornelius Knudson: Person and Theologian," by S. Paul Schilling, 81–104.

3. George Albert Coe, *A Social Theory of Religious Education* (New York: Charles Scribner's Sons, 1917). Coe's earlier influential work, *The Religion of a Mature Mind* (Chicago: Fleming H. Revell, 1902), 293–306 and 322–26, introduced his concept of salvation by education.

4. Provision for directors of religious education to supervise the educational program of local churches appeared in the MEC *Discipline*, 1920, 101, and in the MECS *Discipline*, 1922, 57. For the full story see Dorothy Jean Furnish, *DRE/DCE—The History of a Profession* (Nashville: Christian Educator's Fellowship, 1976).

5. *JGC*, 1912, 1066.

6. Walter N. Vernon, *The United Methodist Publishing House: A History 1870 to 1988* (Nashville: Abingdon Press, 1989), 2: 221 f.

7. Both leaders published key texts for the new lessons: Henry H. Meyer, *The Graded Sunday School in Principle and Practice* (New York: Eaton & Mains, 1910), and Edwin B. Chappell, *Building the Kingdom: The Educational Ideal of the Church* (Nashville: Publishing House of the Methodist Episcopal Church, South, 1914).

8. Walter Vernon estimates that by 1914–15 the MECS had about 20,000 trained teachers and 2,200 training classes—or about one trained teacher for every seventy-five Sunday school students. The MEC, starting its teacher training drive in 1908, had 50,000 trained teachers—or about one for every ninety-two Sunday school students. Vernon, *United Methodist Publishing House*, 2: 224.

9. "Vacation Bible School: Methodist to the Core," *United Methodist Reporter*,

(1 July 1994), 3. Recognition of the movement by the Methodists and other denominations began in 1901. The International Association of Daily Vacation Bible Schools was organized as early as 1907. The number of related schools rose from 102 in 1911 to 2,534 in 1921.

10. Hazel S. Stafford, *The Vacation Religious Day School Teacher's Manual of Principles and Programs* (New York: Abingdon Press, 1920).

11. *JGC/S*, 1914, 52.

12. Willson had been writing a catechetical addenda to each lesson in the *Sunday School Magazine* and the several lesson quarterlies of the MECS for some years.

13. *The Junior Catechism of the Methodist Episcopal Church and the Methodist Episcopal Church, South* (Cincinnati: Jennings & Graham; New York: Eaton & Mains, 1905), iv.

14. *The Standard Catechism of the Methodist Episcopal Church and of the Methodist Episcopal Church, South* (New York: Eaton & Mains, 1905; Nashville: Publishing House of the Methodist Episcopal Church, South, Smith & Lamar, Agents, 1905). Translated into Russian and Spanish in 1909.

15. Ibid., v.

16. The catechisms were quickly translated into Portuguese, Russian, Spanish, and Swedish, though not into German because Nast's catechisms proved so popular for so long.

17. S. E. Quimby, "The New Catechisms," *CA*, 2 April 1908, 539–40.

18. John M. Versteeg, *The Modern Meaning of Church Membership* (New York: Methodist Book Concern, 1919), 129.

19. Howard M. Hamill, *Manual of Southern Methodism, Including Church History, Doctrine, Polity, and Missions* (Nashville: Publishing House of the Methodist Episcopal Church, South, 1909). The next year Hamill published *Methodist Drills for Southern Methodist Young People* (Nashville: Publishing House of the Methodist Episcopal Church, South, 1910), fifty-two memory exercises on Methodist history, doctrine, and polity for use in Sunday schools.

20. John Q. Schisler, *Christian Education in Local Methodist Churches* (Nashville: Abingdon Press, 1969), 80, 92.

21. *JGC*, 1912, 514, 636.

22. Terry, a professor at nearby Garrett Biblical Institute in Evanston, IL, had published several volumes in Whedon's *Commentary*, *Biblical Hermeneutics* (1883), *Methodism and Biblical Criticism* (1904), and *Biblical Dogmatics* (1907), one of the most advanced studies in biblical theology at the turn of the century.

23. *The Probationer's Manual of the Methodist Episcopal Church. Prepared under the Authorization of the General Conference* (New York: Methodist Book Concern, 1914).

24. *Membership Manual of the Methodist Episcopal Church. Prepared under the Authorization of the General Conference* (New York: Methodist Book Concern, 1916).

25. *Manual de Miembros de la Iglesia Metodista Episcopal* (New York: Casa de Publicaciones Metodista Episcopal, 1925).

26. Robert E. Smith, *Methodist Episcopalians: Who They Are, What They Believe, What They Do. Designed for Those Who Contemplate Uniting with the Methodist Episcopal Church* (New York: Eaton & Mains; Cincinnati: Jennings & Graham, 1909).

27. Versteeg, *Modern Meaning of Church Membership*, 129. For context see Arthur Zilversmit, *Changing Schools: Progressive Education Theory and Practice, 1930–1960*

(Chicago: University of Chicago Press, 1993).

28. Archie Lowell Ryan, *When We Join the Church* (New York: Abingdon Press, 1920). Two years later another resource was published for children from nine to twelve years of age: Clyde Lemont Hay, *The Child in the Temple: A Church Membership Training Course for Children* (New York: Methodist Book Concern, 1922), third document printing, 1930.

29. "Church Membership," a Methodist Book Concern advertisement, *CA*, 29 December 1932, hawked books by Anderson, Bugbee, Charlton and Jordan, Lesemann, Ryan, and Smith.

30. See Mary Alice Jones, *The Church and the Children* (Nashville: Cokesbury Press, 1935), chap. 11, "Confession Day in the Children's Department," 202–12.

31. Schisler, *Christian Education*, 155.

32. MEC *Discipline*, 1924, 454, 456.

33. Schisler, *Christian Education*, 98 f. For the impact of ritual revision, see Charles Hohenstein. The Revisions of the Rites of Baptism in the MEC, 1784–1939, unpublished doctoral diss., Univ. of Notre Dame, 1990.

34. John E. Charlton and Edith M. Jordan, *Learning to Live for God: Preparation for Church Membership* (New York: Methodist Book Concern, 1932), 5–6. The third and last documented printing is 1940.

35. Mildred Olivia Moody Eakin, *Exploring the Church* (New York: Abingdon Press, 1934); *Exploring Our Neighborhood* (New York: Abingdon Press, 1936).

36. Karl K. Quimby, *How to Conduct a Church Membership Class for Boys and Girls* (New York: Methodist Book Concern, 1938).

37. Reception of adults occurred more frequently, depending on supply and demand. In 1914 the Rev. Worth M. Tippy, describing his ministry at Epworth Memorial Methodist Episcopal Church, Cleveland, boasted: "We have not failed to receive persons into the Church a single Sunday for now nearly three years." *The Church: A Community Force* (New York: Missionary Education Movement of North America and Canada, 1914), 75.

38. To add dignity to the reception rite in 1930 the Methodist Book Concern released *Christ's Holy Church*, a handsome certificate and souvenir booklet of church membership designed for presentation to confirmands. It was printed in two colors on heavy stock and tied with white silk floss. The booklet contained the ritual for reception, the General Rules of the church, a place for signatures of well-wishers, and counsels on the beauties and duties of church membership written by William K. Anderson. See *Christ's Holy Church. Designed for Presentation by Methodist Episcopal Churches to Those Who Are Being Received into the Fellowship of Christ* (New York: Methodist Book Concern, 1930). In the late 1940s Thomas A. Stafford, MEC Board of Pensions executive, published another souvenir booklet for new church members: *Guide-Marks on the Christian Way: A Devotional Manual with Personal Record of Church Membership*, 4th ed. (Chicago: 740 Rush Street, 1940).

39. Quimby, *How to Conduct a Church Membership Class*, 39.

40. Anderson described this pattern to candidates for the ordained ministry in his *Pastor and Church* (Nashville: Methodist Publishing House, 1943), 161–62.

41. "Every minister is at liberty to chose the best materials for his own purpose. They should meet the standards for any good religious teaching materials for boys and girls. For example, they should not be in catechetical form nor centered in the leader's activity," 33. Carefully avoiding any mention of Lesemann's aging *Membership Manual*

though still in print, Quimby recommends Bugbee's *Preparatory Lessons for Church Membership* (1919), Ryan's *When We Join the Church* (1920), Charlton and Jordan's, *Learning to Live for God* (1932), Mildred Moody Eakin's *Entering the Church* (1934) and *Exploring our Neighborhood*, (1936), and Lovejoy's *The Church We Love* (1935). In addition, Quimby reminds pastors not to neglect material found in the regular curriculum of the church school (*Closely Graded Church School Courses*, course VI, pt. 2, and course XI, pt. 2) and the Epworth League (*Discovering What It Means to Be Christian*, by W. and A. Morgan [Chicago: Dept. of the Epworth League and Young People's Works Board of Education, MEC, 1929]).

42. James E. Gilbert, in his 1903 *Preparation for Church Membership* (New York: Eaton & Mains; Cincinnati: Jennings & Pye, 1903), urges Methodists to follow Roman Catholic, Lutheran, Episcopal, Dutch Reformed, and Scotch Presbyterian practice on this point, 15 f.

43. Full text of the 1908 revised rites for receiving persons into the church "as Probationers" and "after Probation" may be found in the *JGC*, 1908, 967–70.

44. The optional "Form for Receiving Persons into the Church as Preparatory Members," added in 1896, was continued in revised form.

45. "Form for Receiving Children as Members of the Church" and "Form for Receiving Persons into the Church from Preparatory Membership," MEC *Discipline*, 1916, 397, 400. The text of the prayer closely follows that found in the Book of Common Prayer rite of confirmation and the 1906 northern Presbyterian rite.

46. Harris Franklin Rall, seminary professor and chair of the church's ritual revision committee, 1912–16, spoke for many: "Pastors innumerable had felt the absurdity of asking twelve-year-old boys and girls whether they believe in doctrinal statements which it would tax nine preachers out of ten to explain." Rall, "Making a Methodist Ritual II," *CA*, 22 April 1920, 561.

47. After heated debate on these points, on the ninth day General Conference "received and referred [the report of the ritual revision commission] to the Board of Bishops with full power to consider, approve, amend or disapprove, all or any part thereof and to print the Ritual, as they may finally approve it, in the next edition of the Discipline and of the Psalter." Twenty days later, just before adjournment, the bishops presented the new rituals. *JGC*, 1916, 334, 396.

48. MEC *Discipline*, 1916, 51.

49. For comment on these developments, see Gayle C. Felton, *This Gift of Water: The Practice and Theology of Baptism Among Methodists in America* (Nashville: Abingdon Press, 1922), 144–45.

50. Rall, "Making a Methodist Ritual II," *CA*, 22 April 1920, 561.

51. "Form for Receiving Persons into the Church from Preparatory Membership," MEC *Discipline*, 1924, 455.

52. MEC *Discipline*, 1932, 516–18. An "Order for Receiving Persons as Preparatory Members," optional since 1896, was retained in revised form, 514–16. For General Conference discussion, see *JGC*, 1932, 275–76, 431, and 650–51, and *DCA*, 26 May 1936, 656–657.

53. MEC/S *Discipline*, 1914, 316–21. See also *JGC/S*, 1914, 367–70.

15
MAKING METHODIST DISCIPLES, 1939–1968

At the end of World War II the new Methodist Church, a new world order, a baby boom, and a growing economy invited attention once again to basic questions of nurture that had long been neglected. Sunday school attendance took a sharp upturn. Soon children of the postwar boom filled preschool and elementary classes. The Crusade for Christ each year from 1944 to 1948 swelled Sunday school membership, weekly attendance, and number of pupils joining the church. From 1948 to 1952 there were 678,670 church school pupils who joined the church, 7 percent of the total number.[1]

Crowded Sunday schools raised the church's consciousness about religious education. The newly unified Methodist Church Board of Education recruited an increasing number of trained women and men to reorganize all aspects of the educational program in local churches. By 1949 the Board of Education staff, having outgrown offices rented from the Methodist Publishing House, planned a new building of their own in Nashville. The million-dollar building was dedicated in March 1952. From this headquarters an ambitious and comprehensive program of Christian education was launched.

DEVELOPING CURRICULUM

The Curriculum Committee of the church produced a series of documents setting forth the underlying assumptions and philosophy for its work beginning in 1944 titled after 1960 *Foundations of Christian Teaching in Methodist Churches*.[2] Christian education, like public education, now stressed person-centered education. The church's youth were to be understood and then materials adapted to their capacities. Curriculum development in all the churches was stimulated in 1948 with the pioneering Presbyterian *Faith and Life* series. Presbyterian insight, filtered through the 1950s Cooperative Curriculum Project of the National Council of Churches provided the basis for Methodism's new cur-

riculum designs. Accordingly, curriculum writers furnished materials designed
to stimulate young people and their counselors to develop their own programs
and projects. The "ready prepared" lessons of an earlier period were no longer
in favor, and the staid *Classmate* was transformed into a paper that spoke the
high school student's language. Its color, art, and contents whistled to the youth
of the 1960s.

A major task for the reunited church was to decide on a series of curriculum
and enrichment resources. The three predecessor churches had a total of fifty-
five series! Under the leadership of the new editor of church school publications
C. A. Bowen, the staff set to work, in consultation with the publishers, to reduce
the number of publications yet maintain a balanced and comprehensive curriculum. Twenty-four series in four categories were planned—for officers, teachers,
and parents, for children, for youth, and for adults.

Pressure was placed on congregations to use the new materials as they were
produced. The Commission on Education of each local church was instructed
by the Discipline beginning in 1952 to "see that the literature used is appropriate
for each class and group, and that it is selected from the literature approved by
the Curriculum Committee of the General Board of Education." District superintendents were obliged to ask at annual meetings in every charge whether
Methodist church school literature was being used.

Regional and annual conference leadership training institutes were held under
general board sponsorship, and after 1950 came laboratory schools, where teachers learned through participation in actual teaching situations under skilled leadership. During 1959, 248 such schools were held in various parts of the United
States. This project, originally started for teachers of children, was later expanded to include workers with youth and adults. Residential training programs
in the denomination's theological seminaries and Scarritt College in Nashville
produced a steady stream of directors of religious education.

The training of young children was a matter of concern to parents as well as
to Christian educators. Nursery schools and kindergartens set up by local
churches and church-sponsored settlement houses helped care for children of
working mothers. The movement of married women into factory and office
employment created a need the churches could meet only in small part. The
high standards for day nurseries set by state and local laws made such projects
expensive to operate, and not many churches could afford them.

In 1951 a new director of the Department of Christian Education of Children
was appointed, Dr. Mary Alice Jones.* Jones came into the board's service
directly from Rand McNally, where she had been children's book editor. She
herself was the award-winning author of several children's books. Her *Tell Me
About . . .* series, as well as many of her other books, were widely used in Methodist churches. Her previous wide experience in the area of religious education
meant that she was already well known throughout the church both by ministers
and laypersons. She had served as conference director of children's work, editor
of church school materials, and director of children's work for the International

Council of Religious Education. Jones earned the M.A. degree in religious education from Northwestern University and the Ph.D. degree from Yale Divinity School. Her knowledge of theology and her ability to speak the language of clergy was a distinct asset as she and other department staff members sought to improve the church's educational ministry to children.

PROGRAMMING YOUTH AND SENIORS

Unifying the new church's ministry with youth proved a challenge. Programs for youth in local churches and at the denominational level of the three uniting churches differed in significant ways. Methodist Protestants had Sunday schools and Christian Endeavor societies, the latter directed by an interdenominational organization. Methodist Episcopal youth were divided into four different, unrelated organizations: the youth division of the Sunday school, the Epworth League, the Standard Bearer Society, an auxiliary of the Woman's Foreign Missionary Society, and the Queen Esther Circle, an auxiliary to the Woman's Home Missionary Society, each accountable to a different program board at the denominational level. The MECS alone had a unified organization for youth, the Youth Division of the Church School (following a 1930 consolidation at the national level of three separate boards: Sunday Schools, the Epworth League, and Education).

The confusion was not resolved until 1942, when the youth of the newly united church voted on the name, emblem, covenant, benediction, motto, and colors of the proposed new unified youth organization. The Methodist Youth Fellowship (MYF, as it came to be known) was officially born in 1942.[3] Every local church was expected to have such an organization to include all persons between twelve and twenty-three years of age. In 1960 the maximum youth age was dropped to twenty-one, in recognition of the earlier maturing and high mobility of young people and the frequency of youthful marriage. In churches of sufficient size three subdivisions were advised, each with its own Sunday school class, evening meetings, and other projects: junior high youth, senior high youth, and older youth groups.

A special nationwide youth conference under the sponsorship of the Board of Education was held over the year-end 1947–48. Planned as youth's part in the climaxing Crusade for Christ, this brought together about 11,000 youth and adult leaders. Tensions between the autonomous National Council of Methodist Youth (NCMY) and the MEC Board of Education dating from the late 1930s, when two of its leaders were dismissed as economic and social radicals, eased through systematic and patient work by the Board of Education. By 1952 the NCMY became, by action of the General Conference, the youth arm of the Methodist Church Board of Education.

The growing interest in wholesome family relationships and family counseling was reflected in the church's educational program also. In 1945 the Department of the Christian Family was organized in the Division of the Local Church.

Beginning with 1948, each local church was asked to observe National Family Week early in May. A magazine, *The Christian Home*, was published and leaflets and audiovisual materials prepared. Under the leadership of Bishop Hazen G. Werner the first of several national conferences on family life was held in Chicago in 1951.

GONE CAMPING

Since the early days of camp meetings, Methodists linked outdoor experiences with religious instruction and inspiration, so it was not surprising that a camp program came into full swing in the 1950s. By 1960, 222 church campsites were in use, valued at $16 million. Most of them were owned by annual conferences; forty-six had been acquired between 1956 and 1960. There was a rapid rise in attendance by all age groups, and family camps for parents and children became particularly popular. Demand for camping and weekend planning conferences and retreats expanded beyond the summer months, and in response many facilities were winterized and placed on a year-round basis, often with a residential director.

Adult educational work was traditionally stronger in Methodist churches in the South, where the adult department of a church school often had an enrollment as large as the children's department. Two trends in adult education were noticeable during the 1950s. The first was a growing interest on the part of middle-aged and older adults in Bible study and the theological foundations of the Christian faith. A second trend, especially in the larger urban churches, was the increasing awareness of the needs of older persons. The rising number of those past sixty-five years of age and their concentration in older sections of the city created a new opportunity for a specialized ministry. "Golden Age," "Borrowed Time," and "Sunset" clubs met a warm response from retired persons who enjoyed the constructive activity and fellowship.

CONFIRMING CONFIRMATION

As three churches grew together, church leaders sought to improve the preparation of candidates for church membership. Materials of almost every kind were being used in the newly united church, some far outdated, others of dubious quality, some prepared by other denominations.[4] In a number of instances no preparation was given the candidates; the pastors merely "took" the children into the church. Leaders thought the situation serious. Several general agencies of the church surveyed the situation during the early 1940s. They had no authority to prepare membership material but were encouraged to do so because of the seriousness of the situation.

Out of agency cooperation came a series of new graded church membership manuals in 1942. The editors were made responsible for securing writers and getting the manuals published. The new series consisted of a book entitled *My*

Church Book to be given to parents at baptism of their children. Written by Mary E. Skinner, director of children's work of the Board of Education, the little book contained pages to record the date and circumstances of their child's baptism, first visit to the church building, reception into membership, church school promotions, and other church activities. A study book for boys and girls, *Your Church and You* by Dr. Roy H. Short, pastor of St. Paul's Methodist Church in Louisville, Kentucky, later bishop, was designed to be used with the help of the pastor, parents, and Sunday school teacher. A manual for youth entitled *My Church* was written by Dr. James S. Chubb, pastor of First Methodist Church, Baldwin, Kansas; and one for adult candidates, *I Join the Church*, was authored by Karl Quimby,* then cultivation secretary of the Board of Missions and Church Extension. Most important of all was Dr. William K. Anderson's *Church Membership Manual for Methodist Pastors*, published in 1943. Anderson, educational director of Board of Ministerial Training, offered full texts of the children, youth, and adult study books, teaching plans, and suggestions "designed to enrich the experience and to make the service of reception most impressive."[5] The new materials were well received and won approval at the next General Conference, 1944. But by 1948 the five-year-old training materials appeared dated. The General Conference that year set up for the first time a churchwide committee to monitor membership training and plan a fresh set of "official" membership training matters.

The new committee met early in quadrennium (July 1949) and began its work. During the next two years it generated a series of four *Membership Manuals of the Methodist Church—For Boys and Girls*, by Mary Alice Jones; *For Teen-Agers*, by Mrs. Leila Bagley Rumble; *For Young People and Adults*, by James Chubb; and *For Pastors*, by W. Emory Hartman. By December 1955, 641,000 copies had been sold. The committee conferred with pastors of the church by letter and questionnaire and received valuable suggestions. The manual for boys and girls was revised in 1956 to provide questions for study at the head of each chapter and "statements of truths for study and memory" at the end.[6]

While the four approved manuals continued to enjoy wide distribution in the next quadrennium 1956–60, the Joint Committee on Materials for Training in Church Membership enquired how to improve them. The committee decided to combine the "teen-age" and youth and adult manuals, thus making only two age groups instead of three; expand the children's manual to include intermediate ages (twelve to fourteen); begin the youth–adult manual with the senior high group (fifteen to seventeen years of age) to reach all ages upward through adulthood; and rewrite the pastor's manual to support the new plan. Mary Alice Jones, director of the Children's Division, prepared the new children's manual; Dr. Francis E. Kearns, pastor of First Methodist Church, Wauwatosa, Wisconsin, and author of many church school lessons, prepared the youth–adult manual; while Dr. Leon M. Adkins, general secretary of the Department of the Local Church of the Board of Education drafted the pastor's manual.[7] By fall 1960 the new series was ready. Mary Alice Jones introduced them in a special issue of the church school magazine as resources for the pastor to "prepare children, youth and adults for the high privileges and duties of church membership" and as geared to "tie in with church-school learning and build upon it."[8] The new manuals were reissued in 1964 to take into account the new confirmation rite adopted by the General Conference that year.[9] Revised manuals for confirmands and pastors were issued in 1970, 1977, 1981, and 1993. The UMC's evangelical caucus, Good News, dissatisfied with the church's official confirmation and membership training materials, began publishing their own resources beginning in 1976.

In every region pastors were giving more attention to preparing the youth of the church for the full responsibilities of membership. The pastor in some churches took charge of the class of twelve-year-olds each year for a three-month period, making it a membership-training class. Other pastors required the youth seeking admission to the church, and also adults transferring from Methodist and non-Methodist churches, to attend a series of three or four instruction sessions where the meaning of the Christian faith and the significance of church membership were discussed. Church school teachers and directors of religious education also claimed a role.[10] Joining the Methodist Church in most communities was no longer taken as casually as in 1940.

Controversy had yielded to consensus on many points regarding membership training, but numerous ambiguities were carried over into the new united church. Bishop Nolan Harmon told Methodists: "While our Reception of Members [rite] is a close replica of the office of Confirmation in the Protestant Episcopal Church, there are profound differences between the underlying philosophies manifest in those separate rites."[11]

Two orders for reception of members had been provided in the plan of union, one for children and youth and another for adults. The northern confirmation pattern of prayer with laying on of hands was omitted from the children's rite but retained in the adult rite. Except for an introductory admonition concerning Christian fellowship and discipline and a request for loyal support, the new rites said nothing regarding discipline as such. Moreover, all theological interpretations of the principle of the disciplined holy life had long since disappeared.

The "Order for Receiving Persons into the Church" was a condensed form of the ritual from the MEC. The "Order for the Reception of Probationers" was dropped. The order for receiving children was designed for a membership class of youth and stated specifically that the pastor "shall have instructed them in the things necessary for them to know as to the Doctrines and Rules of the Church."[12]

Fine-tuning of the new reception rites occurred at the first General Conference of the new church in 1940. An alternate form at the end of the principal rite restored the southern practice of a congregational greeting: "In token of our brotherly love, we give you the right hand of fellowship, and pray that you may be numbered with His people here, and with his saints in glory everlasting." An optional order for receiving persons as preparatory members based on the

MEC rite of 1896–1939, dropped in the plan of union, was restored. Four years later, in order to have a rite for every conceivable occasion, the 1944 General Conference added an "Order for Receiving Members by Transfer or on Reaffirmation of Faith or in Affiliated Membership," bringing the number of reception rites to four, all featured prominently in the new *Book of Worship* adopted that year.[13]

To bring order out of the confusion a commission began working toward a major revision of the church's rituals as early as 1956. Trial use of some new liturgies began in 1960 with the publication of *Proposed Revisions for The Book of Worship for Church and Home*, accompanied by a commentary by the church's Commission on Worship.[14] For the first time the order for receiving persons into membership was renamed "Order for Confirmation and Reception into the Church." But more than the name had been changed. Two new rubrics were added at the head of the new order: One specified that "All who are to be confirmed as members of Christ's holy Church shall have been baptized, and instructed in the doctrines and duties of the Christian faith" (no mention of Methodist doctrinal standards); the other rubric instructed that "This service shall be conducted in the church in the presence of the people at a stated hour of worship." The opening address described "persons who are to be confirmed" as having "received the Sacrament of Baptism" and "instructed in the teachings of the Church" (not the Methodist Church). The four traditional interrogations of 1939 were retained virtually unchanged, including the renewal of the baptismal vows, except for the pledge of loyalty, which was changed from "The Methodist Church" to "Christ's holy Church." The renewal of vows was followed by a completely new text. The opening rubric dropped the permissive "may" with respect to the minister's laying on of hands. The words that accompany the laying on of hands in the 1964 rite, in use among Anglicans since the second Edwardian prayer book of 1552, include a clear invocation of the Holy Spirit:

N., the Lord defend you with his heavenly grace and by his Spirit confirm you in the faith and fellowship of all true disciples of Jesus Christ. *Amen.*

After the vows and laying on of hands, those confirmed and members of "other communions in Christ's holy Church" were admitted into membership in the Methodist Church, pledged to uphold it by presence, prayers, gifts, and service, commended as new members of the local congregation with welcoming response, and blessed by the minister.[15] Approved by the 1964 General Conference, the new rite found its way into the church's life by being placed in the church's popular new hymnal.[16]

A 1973 study of confirmation education for junior high youth and senior high youth and adults in United Methodist churches in Maryland indicated only a moderate degree of concurrence with the stated polity and policy of the denomination and widespread resistance to using the church's official training materials.[17]

IRONIES

The pattern of growth and expansion established by the Sunday school in the late nineteenth century continued through the early twentieth century. The institution gained a sophisticated organization that manifested itself in a burgeoning variety of curricula, books, and periodicals, a vast network of teacher-training resources, conventions, and institutes, and a proliferating group of denominational and interdenominational agencies. It enjoyed equal prominence in the typical congregation, often commanding a physical plant that rivaled, if not surpassed, the sanctuary. Sunday school became the primary vehicle and community, perhaps even more than the family, for religious indoctrination of Methodist youth. Initially through preparation for conversion, later through nurture, the Sunday school brought young Methodists to membership. But how were those nurtured to become full-fledged church members? Methodism needed some way of understanding and dramatizing the processes of preparation. It found those in confirmation.

Ironically, as Methodists reclaimed the theology and practice of confirmation, the Sunday school engine that brought children and youth to that threshold showed signs of breaking down. The status and role, to say nothing of the size, of Methodist Sunday schools shrank steadily in the latter half of the twentieth century. Further, Methodists recovered confirmation just as liturgical renewalists in the post–Vatican II era called for its elimination, favoring recovery of baptism as the principal rite of initiation. However, the rite of confirmation proved impossible to dislodge even when Methodist leaders came around to the new (old) liturgical views and attempted to remove it in liturgical reforms between 1988 and 1992. Finally, interest in Wesley and the Wesleyan tradition led some to recall and reclaim the preparatory structure and leadership that predated the Sunday school, namely, the class and the class leader. The venerable office of class leader was restored to the United Methodist Church's *Book of Discipline* in 1988 and the functions of the office were clarified in 1992. Although the office of class leaders had virtually disappeared in mainline Methodism, it had remained pivotal in ethnic-minority congregations—such as African-American, Hispanic-American, and Korean-American—where one ordained minister continued to serve circuits composed of several small congregations. Now a variety of new institutions, like Covenant Discipleship, Disciple Bible Study, and Walk to Emmaus reach back for a fresh understanding of discipline, probation, and growth in the faith.

NOTES

1. Clarence W. Hall, *Crusade for Christ Manual for Pastor and Local Church Leaders* (Chicago: Crusade for Christ, [1944]), 57 f; John Q. Schisler, *Christian Education in Local Methodist Churches* (Nashville: Abingdon Press, 1969), 260.

2. *Some Points of Needed Emphasis in Making the Curriculum of Christian Education* (Nashville: General Board of Education, 1947) was developed during the quadrennium 1944–48. A second edition, retitled *Educational Principals in the Curriculum* (Nashville: Curriculum Committee, 1952), was developed during the quadrennium 1948–52. The third edition was titled *Foundations of Christian Teaching in Methodist Churches* (Nashville: Curriculum Committee, 1960). Revised editions were issued in 1965, 1969, and 1979 for use in the United Methodist Church. The most recent set of guidelines for Christian education in the UMC was published in 1993, *Foundations: Shaping the Ministry of Christian Education in Your Congregation* (Nashville: Discipleship Resources, 1993).

3. J. Warren Smith, "Youth Ministry in American Methodism's Mission," *MH* 19/4 (July 1981): 224–30; Schisler, *Christian Education*, chap. 14, "Organizations and Programs for Children and Youth—the Process of Unification," 193–216.

4. To fill the gap two aging manuals were hastily revised and reissued in 1940 one more time: Lesemann's *Membership Manual* and Bugbee's *Preparatory Lessons for Church Membership*. That year the Methodist Publishing House also published Costen J. Harrell's *A Methodist Child's Membership Manual*. Even more confusing was the publication a year earlier of popular Baptist pastor Percy R. Hayward's *Your Life and the Church: A Book for Boys, Girls, and Young People Who Singly or in a Group Seek to Discover What It Means to Choose the Christian Way of Life and Join the Church* (New York: Abingdon Press, 1939). Hayward's book contained the following directive on the title page: "For pastor's classes in church membership."

5. C. A. Bowen, "Preparing for Church Membership," *Church School* 2/1 (January 1943): 7. The back cover of *Church School* 2/2 (February 1943) was devoted to introducing the new materials. In 1948 the Commission on the Preparation of Manuals for Training in Church Membership published a set of two new manuals (for pastors and for pupils) written by Lucius H. Bugbee, *At the Door of the Church*. Cecil Daniel Smith's *I Choose the Church: A Church Membership Course for Intermediates*, was published privately in 1949 but marketed by Cokesbury bookstores. Smith's minister's manual and pupil's workbook was reissued in revised form in 1957.

6. "Report of the Committee on Materials for Training in Church Membership," *Quadrennial Reports of the Boards and Commissions of the Methodist Church to the General Conference, 1956* (Nashville: Methodist Publishing House, 1956), 635.

7. "Report of the Joint Committee on Materials for Training in Church Membership," *JGC/MC*, 1960, 1628–30.

8. Mary Alice Jones, "The Methodist Program for Preparing Children for Church Membership," *The Church School* 15/3 (December 1961): 6.

9. A 1964 Cokesbury flyer "Membership Materials of The Methodist Church," which announced the revised editions of the "official" manuals, promoted five competing manuals: Roy L. Smith's *You're a Member Now* (1954), Costen J. Harrell's *A Methodist Child's Membership Manual* (1940), Mary Skinner's commemorative *My Church Book* (1943, revised 1960), Cecil D. Smith's *I Choose the Church* (1949, revised 1957), and, wonder of wonders, Lesemann's 1914 *Membership Manual of the Methodist Church* in 1940 revised form!

10. "The Church School Prepares Persons for Church Membership," special issue *The Church School* 15/1 (December 1961). See especially Mary Alice Jones, "The Methodist Program for Preparing Children for Church Membership," 4–7, and Dorothy Jean Furnish, "We Share in Membership Training," 2–3.

11. Nolan B. Harmon, *Understanding the Methodist Church* (Nashville: Methodist Publishing House, 1955), 175.

12. *Journal of the Uniting Conference*, 735; *Discipline*, 1939, 554–55.

13. *The Book of Worship for Church and House* (New York: Methodist Publishing House, 1945), 339–408.

14. *Proposed Revisions for the Book of Worship* (Nashville: Methodist Publishing House, 1960), 29–31.

15. For a contemporary description of the rite and its rationale see M. Lawrence Snow, "Confirmation and the Methodist Church," *Versicle* 13/4 (Christmastide 1963); Herbert J. Cook, "Confirmation and Lay Membership of the Methodist Church," in Oxford Institute on Methodist Theological Studies, 1962, *The Doctrine of the Church*, ed. Dow Kirkpatrick (New York: Abingdon Press, 1964) 103–20. Curiously, the official *Companion to the Book of Worship* (1964), ed. W. F. Dunkle and J. D. Quillian, Jr. (Nashville: Abingdon Press, 1970), contained essays on every major rite except confirmation.

16. *The Methodist Hymnal* (Nashville: Methodist Publishing House, 1965), 829.

17. Norman Bruce Kuehnle, *A Study of the Concurrence of the Confirmation-Education Practices of the Pastors of the Baltimore Conference with the Stated United Methodist Polity and Policy* (unpublished Ph.D. diss., American University, 1972).

Part Four
A BIOGRAPHICAL DICTIONARY OF METHODIST LEADERS

A

ALBRIGHT, JACOB (1 May 1759, near Pottstown, Montgomery County, PA–
18 May 1808, Lebanon County, PA). *Career*: farmer and tilemaker, 1785–96;
itinerant preacher in Pennsylvania, Maryland, and Virginia, 1796–1808; founder
of the Evangelical Association; and bishop, 1807–08.

The Albrecht (Albright) family were German-speaking Lutherans, and Jacob
Albrecht was baptized, catechized, confirmed, admitted to the eucharist, and
received as a member in that communion. Schooling was rudimentary. He served
in the Revolution and lost a brother to the American cause. In 1785 he married
Catherine Cope, who was Reformed (Calvinist). They settled in Lancaster
County, where Albright established a brick and tile business, a trade that he
pursued even after taking up ministry and that earned him a reputation as "the
Honest Tilemaker."

The loss of several of his six children in a dysentery epidemic precipitated a
religious crisis, which he resolved under Pietist auspices—particularly in the
prayer meetings and with the counsel of a German neighbor, Adam Riegel,
affiliated with the Pietists, just then coalescing into the German evangelicalism
that would be known as United Brethren; by involving himself with a class of
English-speaking Methodists, led by another neighbor, Isaac Davies; and
through a conversion experience that threw him also into ministry.

Albright found congenial the discipline and doctrine of the people called
Methodists, who licensed him as an exhorter. He began itinerant preaching
among Germans in 1796. Speaking wherever he could get a hearing in Lancaster, Dauphin, and Berks County, Pennsylvania, and in adjacent German areas
of Virginia and Maryland, he threatened and aroused opposition, even persecution, from the existing German denominations. Albright attracted converts,
organized classes (the building block of Methodism), structured his preaching
into circuits, brought those from adjacent areas together periodically for religious
festivals that among German Pietists were termed "big meetings," accepted a

few assistants in his itinerant ministry, gathered them together (in 1803) as a conference, and was there ordained and elected to lead this new association. That conference the later Evangelical Association regarded as its founding.

In 1807 the conference elected Albright bishop, termed itself the "Newly-Formed Methodist Conference," and asked Albright to draft Articles of Faith and a Discipline. These acts pressed the movement in a direction that it trod reluctantly, namely, toward breaking with Methodism and constituting itself a separate denomination. Self-designations capture that hesitancy; in 1809, for instance, the conference called itself "The So-called Albright's People."

His health failing, Albright proved unable to give the movement literary form. However, he had already led it to embrace Methodist discipline and belief (e.g., entire sanctification), and others gave those commitments constitutional and creedal expression. Despite sickness Albright continued to travel, hold conference, and station the preachers and participate in the "big meetings." He died, on the road, at the home of a friend and associate.

Bibliography

A: Albright's journal was lost and apparently nothing else that he wrote survives.

B: *CM* 24; *DAB* 1, 136–37; *DARB* 9–10; *DCIA* 32–33; *EWM* 1, 79–80; *HDM*; *LMB* 631–38; *NCAB* 11, 114; R. Yeakel, *Jacob Albright and His Co-Laborers*, trans. from the German (Cleveland, 1883); J. Bruce Behney and Paul H. Eller, *The History of the Evangelical United Brethren Church* (Nashville, 1979); George Miller, *Jacob Albright*, trans. G. E. Epp (Dayton, 1959).

ALLEN, RICHARD (14 February 1760, Philadelphia, PA–26 March 1831, Philadelphia, PA). *Career*: African-American itinerant preacher in Delaware and Maryland, 1781–86, businessman, community leader, and lay preacher in Philadelphia, 1786–99; deacon, Bethel MEC, Philadelphia, 1799–1816; bishop of the AME Church, 1816–31.

Richard Allen was born in 1760 in Philadelphia, slave of a Quaker master. Allen later passed into the hands of a Methodist farmer near Dover, Delaware. When seventeen Allen converted to Methodism, purchased his freedom and began to travel as a Methodist lay preacher. In 1786 he returned to Philadelphia, where he joined the growing black membership of St. George's Methodist Church.

When racism reared its ugly head, Allen sought to establish a black congregation that would be free of the discrimination experienced in St. George's Church. With Absalom Jones, he formed a Free African Society in 1787, but the society soon became an Episcopal church. Convinced that Methodism best suited the religious needs of African-Americans, Allen worked to establish a black Methodist church in the city. Although Allen's Bethel ME Church was built and dedicated by Bishop Asbury* in 1794, Allen himself was not ordained until 1799, and then only as a special deacon, with no conference ties.

Although committed to preserving the unity of the body of Christ, Allen led sixteen congregations of African Methodists into a separate denomination in

1816 after many years of struggle against white control and failure to ordain black preachers. By 1830 the African Methodist Episcopal (AME) Church had missions in Canada, Haiti, and West Africa; but the church exerted a much greater influence at home on the growing community of free blacks in the North. In 1801 Allen compiled the first hymnbook published by a black for use by blacks, many of the hymns of which became sources for black spirituals. With Daniel Coker and James Champion, Allen also compiled the first official hymnbook of the AME Church in 1818.

In addition to serving as the first bishop of the AME Church, Allen took an active part in promoting the welfare of blacks in Philadelphia. He worked as a shoemaker, teamster, and labor contractor, opened his home to fugitive slaves, assisted fellow citizens during a yellow fever epidemic, and earned the esteem of prominent whites in both religious and political circles. He opposed the colonization movement that proposed to send free blacks back to Africa in the 1820s, and he hosted the first national convention of black religious and political leaders in Bethel AME Church in 1830.

Bishop Allen died on 26 March 1831 in Philadelphia and is buried in the undercroft of Mother Bethel AME Church.

Bibliography

A: *Collection of Hymns and Spiritual Songs* (Philadelphia, 1801); *A Collection of Spiritual Songs and Hymns* (Philadelphia, 1801); *Doctrines and Discipline of the African Methodist Episcopal Church* (Philadelphia, 1817); *The Life Experience and Gospel Labours of the Right Reverend Richard Allen* (Philadelphia, 1833), many times reprinted; with Absalom Jones, *Narrative of the Proceedings of the Black People during the Late Awful Calamity in Phila. in the Year 1793* (Philadelphia, 1794).

B: *CBTEL* 1, 164; *CM* 26–27; *DAB* 1, 204–5; *DANB* 12–13; *DARB* 15–16; *EWM* 1, 90–91; *HDM*; *LMB* 649–56; *NCAB* 13, 200–201; Carol V. R. George, *Segregated Sabbaths* (New York, 1973); Gary B. Nash, *Forging Freedom: The Formation of Philadelphia's Black Community, 1720–1840* (Cambridge, 1988); C. Wesley, *Richard Allen: Apostle of Freedom* (Washington, DC, 1935).

ANDREW, JAMES OSGOOD (3 May 1794, Wilkes County, GA–2 March 1871, Mobile, AL). *Education*: educated at home by a schoolteacher father, and in rural schools. *Career*: joined South Carolina Conference, December 1812; ordained, 1816; itinerant preacher in the Carolinas and Georgia, serving as pastor in such places as Charleston, Wilmington, Columbia, Augusta, and Savannah and as presiding elder, 1812–32; bishop, Methodist Episcopal Church, 1832–44; bishop, Methodist Episcopal Church, South, 1845–71.

James Osgood Andrew's father, John, was the first Georgian ever to enter the itinerant ministry of the Methodist Church. Andrew was later to gain recognition of his own when he became the center of controversy at the 1844 General Conference at which the denomination divided North and South over the issue of slavery.

Although his early education was inferior and he had few gifts as a scholar,

Andrew was converted at the age of fifteen and licensed to preach three years later. He was admitted to the South Carolina Annual Conference in 1812 and ordained four years later. He served with distinction as a pastor in a number of congregations in Georgia and the Carolinas, and as a presiding elder. This service was recognized in 1832 when he was elected to the episcopacy on the first ballot. It is ironic that William Capers,* another southerner, was the favorite for election but declined because he owned slaves. He recommended Andrew, who did not.

Bishop Andrew was usually assigned conferences located in the South, but on occasion he went as far west as Arkansas and Texas and into the Illinois and Iowa Conferences in the Midwest. He exercised his duties in these conferences without criticism. All of this was to change, however, when due to circumstances beyond his control he became a slaveholder. After his election to the episcopacy in 1832, an elderly lady living in Augusta, Georgia, willed him a mulatto girl named Kitty. Under the terms of the will, she was to be cared for until the age of nineteen and then, if she consented, to be sent to Liberia. She reached that age in 1841 and refused to leave. The laws of the state of Georgia would not allow Andrew to set her free. His situation was further complicated in 1842 upon the death of his first wife, who held a slave willed to her by her mother. Because she died intestate, the boy became the property of Bishop Andrew. Then in 1844 Bishop Andrew was remarried to a woman who held a number of slaves inherited from her first husband.

The news of the bishop's situation quickly spread through the connection, which was already greatly agitated by the slavery question, and when he began the journey to New York for the session of the General Conference of 1844, he was well aware there would be trouble. The question was not whether Andrew had done wrong, but whether a slaveholding general superintendent of the church could serve all its conferences. Andrew was enjoined from resigning by his southern brethren, since there was no law in the church that prohibited either members or clergy from holding slaves. Moreover, the delegates understood the question of slavery to be political, social, and economic as well as moral. Andrew's situation was not the cause of the eventual separation, but it became the occasion for it, and the delegates voted in substantial majority for him to desist from the exercise of his office until his connection with slavery had been resolved.

A plan of separation was devised, and Methodism divided North and South. At the first General Conference of the newly formed MECS (Louisville, May 1845), the credentials of Andrew and Joshua Soule were recognized and the two men thus became the MECS's first bishops. Andrew continued his work in the southern church until 1866, when he requested and was granted retirement from active service.

Bibliography

A: *Family Government: A Treatise on Conjugal, Parental, Filial, and Other Duties* (Nashville, 1859); *Miscellanies, Comprising Letters, Essays, and Addresses* (Louisville, 1854).

B: *CM* 36–37; *DAB* 1, 277–79; *DCIA* 61–62; *EWM* 1, 106–97; *LMB* 533–42; *MB* 15. Henry B. Bascom, *Methodism and Slavery* (Frankfort, KY, 1845); Donald G. Mathews, *Slavery and Methodism* (Princeton, NJ, 1965); George Peck, *Slavery and the Episcopacy* (New York, 1845); Cole Vernon Smith, *James Osgood Andrew* (M.A. thesis, Southern Methodist University, 1950); George Gilman Smith, *The Life and Letters of James Osgood Andrew* (Nashville, 1882).

ASBURY, FRANCIS (20/21 August 1745, Handsworth, near Birmingham, England [his own account, *JLFA*, 1: 720]–31 March 1816, at the home of George Arnold, near Fredricksburg, VA). *Education*: little formal education. *Career*: apprenticed to a craftsman for six and one-half years; entered the Methodist connection of John Wesley as a local preacher in 1766. In 1771 he answered the invitation to serve in the American Colonies and spent the remainder of his life in America. He never returned to England. Bishop of the MEC, 1784–1816.

American Methodism rightfully claims Francis Asbury as its founder. More than any other single person, Asbury deserves credit for moving Methodism into the villages and onto the frontier. As one of his biographers put it, "Not only had he the genius to lead, but he had the will to govern" (Tipple, 242). From the time of his ordination in 1784 at the organizing conference of the MEC, Asbury named every preacher in the connection to his station until his death in 1816. It was due in large measure to Asbury's talent and strong will that Episcopal Methodism established and maintained strong central control in an infinitely expandable organization. He governed the connection by himself until 1808, when William McKendree* was elected to the episcopacy.

Asbury came to America in October 1771 and never returned to England again. He found both vocation and home in America. At various times he was named by John Wesley as "assistant in America" and as "general assistant." But in 1784, when Thomas Coke* brought news from Wesley that the Methodists in America were to be provided with ordination and independence from English Methodism, Asbury became Methodism's bishop. Refusing to accept the ordination which Wesley offered through Coke without the approval of his fellow preachers in conference, he effectively shifted power to the body of preachers and established himself as their leader, independent of John Wesley. His power was unsuccessfully challenged by James O'Kelly* in 1792, by Coke in 1805, and his attempt to govern through an appointed council was thwarted, but through it all Asbury was never "one among equals."

Never married, constantly on the road subject to every extreme of weather, danger, and illness, Asbury managed by example to lead the new organization into a period of expansive growth. The itinerant system, with its circuit riders, won the West, and Asbury interpreted and protected the system. In the first twenty years of its existence its membership passed 100,000; by the middle of the nineteenth century it was America's largest Protestant denomination. At the same time Asbury also managed to give Methodism its first college and a publishing establishment. He lived long enough to see power evolve to a delegated general conference defined by a constitution.

And while on the road, he maintained the discipline of keeping a journal that today provides a window into the times in which he lived and worked. No one doubted that Asbury was strong, even autocratic at times, but it cannot be said that he did ought for personal gain.

Bibliography

A: *Journal and Letters*, ed. Elmer T. Clark (Nashville, 1959).

B: *CM* 58–61; *DAB* 1, 379–83; *DCIA* 83; *EWM* 1, 159–62; *LMB* 75–104; *MB* 17–20; the first biography of Asbury is W. P. Strickland, *The Pioneer Bishop* (New York, 1858); the latest is L. C. Rudolph, *Francis Asbury* (Nashville, 1966); also Frank Baker, *From Wesley to Asbury* (Durham, 1976); Thomas Coke, *Substance of a Sermon Preached at Baltimore . . . December 27, 1784 at the Ordination of the Rev. Francis Asbury to the Office of a Superintendent* (New York, 1840); Edward M. Lang, *Francis Asbury's Reading of Theology* (Ph.D. diss., Garrett Theological Seminary, 1972); Wallace Guy Smeltzer, *Bishop Francis Asbury: Field Marshall of the Lord* (s.l., 1982).

B

BANGS, NATHAN (2 May 1778, Stratford, CT–3 May 1862, New York). *Education*: almost entirely self-educated, learned surveying from his father, and taught in rural schools in New York State and Canada. *Career*: Licensed to exhort in the New York Conference of the Methodist Church, August 1801, and served as pastor and presiding elder until 1820. Having worked in Canada until 1812, he is regarded as the father of Methodism in Quebec; book agent and editor of the *New York Advocate*, the *Methodist Magazine*, and the *Methodist Quarterly Review*, 1820–36; secretary, Methodist Missionary Society, 1836–41, which he founded in 1819; president, Wesleyan University, CT, 1841–42; pastor and presiding elder, 1842–52.

Nathan Bangs is one of the great literary figures of American Methodism. At various times he served the denomination as book agent, editor, and college president. He was directly associated with the establishing of the *Christian Advocate*, founded and edited the *Methodist Magazine* (later the *Methodist Quarterly Review*), and led the Missionary Society. His four-volume history of the denomination, the original manuscript of which was destroyed in a fire that burned the Book Concern in February 1836, is well known today.

Bangs was born in Connecticut, the son of a blacksmith. Educated in village schools, he became a tutor at the age of seventeen in the family of a merchant, who, as he said, "treated me with more respect than I deserved"; he then taught in a public school. In 1799 he moved to Canada, where he continued to teach. Converted under the influence of an itinerant Methodist named James Coleman, licensed to preach in 1801, he received his first assignment as assistant on the Niagara circuit. Subsequently he was ordained by Francis Asbury and admitted to the New York Conference, which included Canada (1804). Offering himself for service in the new settlements on the River Thames in an area north of Detroit beyond the northwestern shore of Lake Erie, he extended the scope of Methodist territory. By 1806 he had traveled most of the settled areas of upper

Canada, and went in that year to Quebec. Two years later he was given his first assignment in the United States—the Delaware circuit. A year later he went to Albany, and then to New York City.

Bangs was quickly accepted as a leader in the New York Conference, and through the years he served as presiding elder and pastor in it. He also turned his attention to the operation of the Book Concern and proposed the publication of a monthly magazine in 1812. In addition, he found time for study and writing, producing a polemic volume on *The Errors of Hopkinsianism* (1815) and another, *Predestination Examined* (1817). In 1820 he was appointed book agent of the church.

He found the operation in debt and poorly organized, but Bangs solved the problems by expanding rather than reducing the scope of the enterprise. The *Christian Advocate and Journal* appeared on 9 September 1826, with the majority of its editorial content supplied by Bangs. Bangs also edited the *Methodist Magazine* during his entire tenure as book agent. The *Advocate* was a great success with its circulation of twenty-five thousand exceeding that of any other paper in the United States. The General Conference of 1832 gave Bangs editorial responsibility for the *Methodist Magazine* and all book publishing. Because of his prominence and leadership, he was encouraged to accept election to the episcopacy, but Bangs declined. There is little reason to doubt that he could have been elected.

Throughout his career Bangs urged the support of ministerial education. In 1816 he reported in his role as chair of the Ways and Means Committee in favor of the creation of a course of study; the curriculum was subsequently adopted and became the responsibility of the bishops to prepare. In 1844, it was extended to four years.

The missionary outreach of the denomination reached sufficient size and importance that at the General Conference of 1836 it was determined to appoint someone to oversee its work, and Bangs was named "Resident Corresponding Secretary" of the Missionary Society. He served in the post with distinction for five years before accepting the presidency of Wesleyan University in January 1841. During that time the German missions of the denomination were begun under the supervision of William Nast. The presidency was not a successful appointment, and Bangs resigned a year later to return to the pastorate. The balance of his career was spent in various appointments in the New York Conference. The last years of his life were troubled by poor health, and Bangs died one day after his eighty-fourth birthday.

Bibliography

A: *An Authentic History of the Missions under the Care of the Missionary Society of the Methodist Episcopal Church* (New York, 1832); *The Errors of Hopkinsianism Detected and Refuted* (New York, 1815); *An Examination of the Doctrine of Predestination* (New York, 1817); *A History of the Methodist Episcopal Church*, 4 vols. (New York, 1838–41); *The Life of the Rev. Freeborn Garrettson* (New York, 1830); *An Original Church of Christ: or, A Scriptural Vindication of the Orders and Pow-*

ers of the Ministry of the Methodist Episcopal Church (New York, 1837); A Vindication of Methodist Episcopacy (New York, 1820).

B: CM 85–86; DAB 1, 574–75; DCIA 104; EWM 1, 213–14; MUC 1, 203–7; Richard E. Herrmann, "Nathan Bangs: Apologist for American Methodism" (Ph.D. diss., Emory University, 1973); Abel Stevens, Life and Times of Nathan Bangs, D.D. (New York, 1863); A. H. Tuttle, Nathan Bangs (New York, 1909); Nathan O. Hatch, The Democratization of American Christianity (New Haven, CT, 1989).

BOEHM, HENRY (8 June 1775, Lancaster County, PA–29 December 1875, Staten Island, NY). Career: lay preacher in Lancaster County, 1800; probationary member of the Philadelphia Conference and ordained deacon, 1801, and elder, 1805; itinerant preacher in English- and German-speaking communities in Maryland and Virginia, 1801–08; traveling companion with Bishop Asbury,* 1808–13; presiding elder 1813–20; retired from active ministry in 1839, joined the New Jersey Conference, and settled in Staten Island, 1839–75.

Henry Boehm was the son of Martin Boehm, an expelled Mennonite who became a bishop of the Church of the United Brethren in Christ. Young Boehm received his basic education at the local German school and had the advantage of access to his father's library, which contained English as well as German works. From this library, Henry Boehm later noted, he read "with great pleasure and profit, among others, Wesley's Sermons and Fletcher's Checks" (Reminiscences, 383). Converted at a Methodist quarterly meeting in 1798, Henry two years later accompanied his father on a preaching tour through Pennsylvania, Maryland, and Virginia and agonized over whether to stay with the United Brethren, whose ministry was only to Germans, or to join the Methodists. Henry became an ordained itinerant preacher in the MEC in 1801, traveling circuits in Maryland and Virginia. Because Henry was able to preach fluently in both English and German, Bishop Asbury later appointed him to serve in Pennsylvania, where Henry introduced Methodism into "Pennsylvania Dutch" country from Harrisburg to Reading. To aid the progress of the Methodists among Pennsylvania's growing German community, Bishop Asbury asked Boehm to superintend the translation of the Methodist Discipline into German. The book was printed in January 1808 in Lancaster.

For five years following 1808 Boehm accompanied Bishop Asbury on his episcopal tours, visiting Methodist churches and holding conferences annually not only in the states along the Atlantic seacoast but in the frontier settlements in the mountains and beyond. After ceasing to travel with Bishop Asbury, Boehm was appointed to superintend various important districts of the rapidly growing denomination and then to preach in pulpits of commanding influence in Pennsylvania and New Jersey. He did this until old age compelled him to ask for release from regular ministerial duties in 1839. Boehm continued to preach after his one-hundredth birthday in 1875, and only a few days before his death he gave a formal address.

Ten years earlier in simple, unaffected language Boehm recorded the events, aspirations, and hopes that motivated him and his generation of Methodists in his *Reminiscences*, first published for the denomination's centennial celebration in 1866.

Bibliography

A: *Reminiscences, Historical and Biographical, of Sixty-Four Years in the Ministry* (New York, 1866), republished with additional chapters in 1875 under the title *The Patriarch of One Hundred Years; Being Reminiscences, Historical and Biographical, with Several Additional Chapters, Containing an Account of the Exercises on His One Hundredth Birthday, His Sermon before the Newark Conference and the Addresses Then Delivered, His Centennial Sermon in Trinity Church, Jersey City, and in John Street Church, New York, and the Addresses on Those Occasions, Phonographically Reported*. The Boehm's Chapel Society, Willow Street, PA, issued a facsimile reprint of the 1875 edition with a new index in 1982.

B: *CBTEL* Supp. 1, 540; *CM* 114–15; *DAB* 2, 403–4; *EWM* 1, 289–90; *HDM*; *CA* 6 and 27 January 1876; *ACJ*/Newark 1876, 53–57; sketch by J. N. Good in Alexander Harris, *Biographical History of Lancaster County* (Lancaster, PA, 1872), 49–62; Abram W. Sangrey, *The Temple of Limestone: A History of Boehm's Chapel* (Lancaster, PA, 1991).

BOEHM, MARTIN (30 November 1725, Lancaster County, PA–23 March 1812, Lancaster County, PA). *Career*: Mennonite minister, Pequea, PA, 1756–59; Mennonite bishop, 1759–77; independent itinerant preacher, 1777–1800; bishop of the United Brethren in Christ, 1800–12.

Martin Boehm was the son of Jacob Boehm, one of the Mennonites from the Palatinate who settled in Lancaster County, Pennsylvania, in the early eighteenth century. Jacob married into the Kendig family, early settlers in the county, became a deacon in the Mennonite Church, and prospered as a farmer and a blacksmith. Martin received his early education at home. Although he knew both German and English, he conducted his business and later preached solely in his native German. Like his father, Martin was a farmer, but religion early became the main interest of his life. In 1753 he married Eve Steiner, a woman of Swiss ancestry. Three years later he was chosen by lot as a preacher.

Boehm found his task difficult in part because Mennonite patterns of piety were formal and because he lacked an assurance of his own salvation. A conversion experience in 1758 enabled him to preach thereafter with great power and authority. A year later he was chosen a bishop and began work as spiritual shepherd to area congregations. Martin read the writings of the German Pietists and gradually broke away from the Mennonite ways of worship and began to preach a more vital faith. Later, when Methodist preachers found their way into Lancaster County, they were welcomed into Boehm's home. By the mid-1770s criticism began to mount regarding Boehm's vigorous revival preaching and his association with people of other denominations. Admonitions to conform had no effect, and in 1777 Mennonite clergy excommunicated Boehm for what they perceived to be unorthodox doctrine and fraternizing with outsiders.

Of great significance in Boehm's later life was his connection with William Otterbein. The two preachers met at one of the "big meetings" in 1767. Boehm was preaching to an overflow congregation in Isaac Long's Barn near Lancaster. Otterbein was among the listeners, and at the close of the service he is said to have embraced Boehm in his arms, exclaiming, "We are brothers." Together they began to travel widely through southern Pennsylvania, Maryland, and Virginia, holding services in barns or fields when the regular meeting places failed to accommodate the crowds of Lutherans, Reformed, Mennonites, and Dunkards who flocked to hear him. Annually they organized camp meetings at which German-Americans from a variety of religious traditions gathered in large numbers for spiritual refreshment and fellowship. A small group of sympathetic pastors and lay preachers united with them and began to hold annual meetings. In 1783 the elder Boehm gave supervision of his farm to his son Jacob in order to devote full time to his evangelical ministry. At an organizing conference in 1800, Boehm (then seventy-five years old) and Otterbein were chosen as first bishops of the Church of the United Brethren in Christ.

While playing an important role in the formation of the United Brethren in Christ, Boehm also formed a close connection with the Methodists. A "class" was formed in his home in 1775, and Methodist ministers frequently preached in his father's home until 1791, when the Methodists built a chapel on land donated by the Boehms. Bishop Asbury visited and preached at Boehm's farm each year between 1780 and 1815. Boehm's wife became a Methodist, and his son Henry became a prominent preacher among them. In 1802 Boehm allowed his name to be placed on a class book to comply with Methodist rules, but he never left the United Brethren in Christ. Boehm's ecumenical spirit, which caused his break with the Mennonites, made the dual connection with Methodists and United Brethren possible. In referring to his membership in the Methodist class he said, "For myself, I felt my heart more greatly enlarged toward all religious persons and to all denominations of Christians." Thus affiliated with two churches, the elder Boehm continued to serve as bishop, preaching occasionally, though growing more and more feeble.

Martin Boehm died at his home at the age of eighty-seven. A few days after the burial in the cemetery of Boehm's Chapel, Henry Boehm and Bishop Asbury arrived at Martin's home. The following Sunday, Asbury preached a sermon in tribute to his friend, who was "greatly beloved in life, and deeply lamented in death."

Bibliography

B: *DAB* 2, 405–6; *DARB* 63–64; *EWM* 1, 290; *HDM*; *NCAB* 21, 137–38; J. Bruce Behney and Paul H. Eller, *The History of the Evangelical United Brethren Church* (Nashville, 1979), 39–45; F. Hollingsworth, "Notices of the Life and Labours of Martin Boehm and William Otterbein; and other Ministers of the Gospel among the United German Brethren," *Methodist Magazine* (NY) 6/3 (July 1823): 210–14, 249–56; Stephen L. Longenecker, *Piety and Tolerance: Pennsylvania German Religion, 1701–1850* (Metuchen, NJ, 1994); Kenneth E. Rowe, "Martin Boehm and the Methodists," *Methodist History* 8/4 (July 1970): 49–53; Abram W. Sangrey, *Martin Boehm, Pioneer Preacher in the Christian Faith and Practice, among the First German Speaking Colonists in Pennsylvania, Maryland, Virginia* (Lancaster, PA, 1976); Abram W. Sangrey, *The Temple of Limestone: A History of Boehm's Chapel* (Lancaster, PA, 1991).

BOND, THOMAS EMERSON (February 1782, Baltimore, MD–14 March 1856, New York). *Education:* after primary schooling in Maryland, studied medicine with physicians and at the University of Pennsylvania. *Career:* medical practice in Baltimore; license to preach in the Methodist Church, 1824, but was never ordained; editor, *The Itinerant*, 1830–31; editor, *Christian Advocate and Journal*, 1840–48, 1852–56.

A layman, active and influential in literary endeavors, Thomas Emerson Bond was born to Methodist parents in Baltimore, where he eventually conducted a large medical practice. Described as a "scintillating genius," Bond was one of the most eminent in a distinguished line of editors of the *Christian Advocate*. In 1807 he was offered a professorship at the University of Maryland but declined because of his health.

After being licensed as a local preacher in 1824, he began to write, especially against the reform movement that led to the creation of the Methodist Protestants. His *Appeal to the Methodists* was written in 1827. For a brief period of time he edited an antireform paper, *The Itinerant*, and then served as editor of the New York *Christian Advocate* on two occasions, 1840–48 and 1852–56. He was a man of great ability and talent, and the paper under his editorship had great influence in the affairs of the denomination.

Bond, who was bitterly opposed to the New England abolitionists, followed the policy of General Conference in refusing to allow discussion of slavery in the paper, but he personally advocated African colonization. The antislavery advocates managed to block his reelection to the editorship in 1848. Seeing him as a potent adversary, southern leaders at the General Conference of 1844 believed Bond was a key figure in creating a scenario by which no compromise could be reached to allow southern Methodists to stay in the denomination. Although Bond stoutly denied their accusations, he was against the Plan of Separation and was an active participant in the events at the General Conference. Bond was a "fighting editor," and his writings, following the creation of the MECS, helped to foster a climate of bitterness and nourish the resentment between the two branches. In similar fashion, he found little favor among the Methodist Protestants.

Bibliography

A: *An Appeal to Methodists* (Baltimore, 1827); *The Economy of Methodism Illustrated* (New York, 1852); *Methodism Not a Human Contrivance* (Baltimore, 1839); *A Narrative and Defence of the Proceedings of the ME Church in Baltimore City Station* (Baltimore, 1828); *To the General Conference of the ME Church* (Baltimore, 1852).

B: *CA* 1 May 1856, 70; *CM* 116; *CWM* 1, 295; *MUC* 2, 36–37.

BOWNE, BORDEN PARKER (14 January 1847, Leonardville, NJ–1 April 1910, Boston, MA). *Education*: Pennington Seminary, then University of the City of New York, graduating Phi Beta Kappa and valedictorian in 1871 (A.M. in 1876); studied from 1873 to 1875 in Halle, Gottingen, and Paris. *Career*: taught school after college, then pastor in Whitestone, Long Island (MEC) 1872–73; after his study abroad assistant editor of *The Independent* and assistant professor of modern languages in his alma mater; in 1876 called to the chair of philosophy at Boston University, a position he held for thirty-five years; dean of the Graduate School of Arts and Sciences, 1888–1910.

From a devoutly Methodist antislavery and temperance family (his father was a local preacher), Borden Parker Bowne early took an interest in books and ideas. He excelled in school, producing while in college an essay on Herbert Spencer that was later published. While studying in Europe, Bowne came under the influence of Rudolf Hermann Lotze and Hermann Ulrici, and he returned to the United States and to head the department of philosophy at Boston University, where he wove strands of idealism, neo-Kantianism, biblical criticism, romanticism, and rationalism with those from his heritage (Methodism's moralism, high valuation of freedom, insistence on individual responsibility, optimism of grace, and hope for perfection) into a distinctive modernist Methodist metaphysic. Known as personal idealism, personalism, or transcendental empiricism, this Boston philosophy was to have a major influence on Methodism nationally and in Bowne and his successors—Albert C. Knudson, Edgar S. Brightman, Walter E. Muelder, L. Harold DeWolf, S. Paul Schilling, and Peter Bertocci—to constitute a significant contribution to American philosophy.

Bowne sought a recasting of Wesleyan theology that would respond to materialism and secularism, be credible in a scientific and humanistic world, and hold together monist and pluralist perspectives. Key to this apologetic was a metaphysic that conceived of personality as ultimate. True and full personhood is found in God, a nature revealed in Jesus Christ, a reality in which alone freedom, identity, and unity are realized. Human fulfillment comes from partaking of and realizing the potential of personhood, also made possible through Christ and God's grace. Immanental and optimistic, personalism valued freedom and morality; sought to balance the rational, volitional, and emotional; took religious experience seriously, expecting religious commitment to express itself in life (ethics); accented the individual but also the relationship of persons, one to another and all to God.

In certain areas traditional, in others avant garde, Bowne's immanental theological formulations, his reworking of Christian doctrines, his opposition to intolerance, anti-intellectualism, and fundamentalism, and his support of biblical criticism earned him critics. One of them, George A. Cooke, charged Bowne with heresy, resulting in Bowne's trial by the New York East Conference in 1904. Cooke alleged that Bowne taught doctrines of the Trinity, miracles, inspiration, atonement, and redemption contrary to Methodist Articles and established standards. A distinguished "Select" committee headed by Frank Mason North heard the case, questioned Bowne, deliberated in all some sixteen hours, and voted unanimously to reject the charges.

Termed Methodism's "Last Heresy Trial," it vindicated personalism and discredited the opposition.

Bibliography

A: *The Atonement* (Cincinnati, 1900); *The Christian Life* (Cincinnati, 1899); *The Christian Revelation* (Cincinnati, 1898); *The Essence of Religion* (Boston, 1910); *The Good* (New York, 1895); *The Immanence of God* (Boston, 1905); *Introduction to Psychological Theory* (New York, 1887, c1886); *Kant and Spencer: A Critical Exposition* (Boston, 1912); *A Man's View of Woman Suffrage* (Boston, 189?); *Metaphysics* (New York, 1882); *Personalism* (Boston, 1908); *Philosophy of Christian Science* (New York, [c1908]); *The Philosophy of Herbert Spencer* (New York, 1874); *Philosophy of Theism* (New York, c1887); *The Principles of Ethics* (New York, 1893, c1892); *Studies in Christianity* (Boston, 1909); *Studies in Theism* (New York, 1879); *Theism: Comprising the Deems Lectures for 1902* (New York, 1902); *Theory of Thought and Knowledge* (New York, 1897).

B: *DAB* 2, 522–23; *DARB* 58–59; *DCIA* 179; *EWM* 1, 312; *HDM*; *MUC* 2, 84–87; *NCAB* 11, 180; *NYT* 3 April 1910, 2: 11; *RLA* 56; *SH* 2, 242–43; Thomas A. Langford, *Practical Divinity: Theology in the Wesleyan Tradition* (Nashville, 1983), 119–24; Francis J. McConnell, *Borden Parker Bowne: His Life and His Philosophy* (New York, 1929); Charles B. Pyle, *The Philosophy of Borden Parker Bowne* (Columbus, 1910); Harmon L. Smith, "Borden Parker Bowne: Heresy at Boston," *American Religious Heretics*, ed. George H. Shriver (Nashville, 1966), 148–87.

BUCKLEY, JAMES MONROE (16 December 1836, Rahway, NJ–8 February 1920, Morristown, NJ). *Education*: Pennington School; one year as undergraduate at Wesleyan University, 1856–57; then M.A., 1869. *Career*: taught school, pastor of St. John's ME Church Dover, NH, 1859–61; St. Paul's ME Church, Manchester, NH, 1861–63; abroad, 1863–64; pastor Central ME Church, Detroit, MI, 1864–66; Summerfield ME Church, Brooklyn, 1866–69; First ME Church, Stamford, CT, 1869–72; Summerfield ME Church, Brooklyn, 1872–75; First ME Church, Stamford, 1875–78; and Hanson Place ME Church, Brooklyn, 1878–80; editor, *Christian Advocate* (NY), 1880–1912; lecturer, Drew Theological Seminary, 1912–20.

James M. Buckley was the son of the Rev. John Buckley, a native of Lancashire who emigrated to this country in 1827, became a Methodist preacher, married Abbie Longdale, and soon died of consumption, as had both his parents, leaving behind James, not yet six, and another son still younger. The boys were brought up in the home of their grandfather, Judge Monroe, at Mount Holly, New Jersey, their mother helping to support them by teaching public school. Young James was a bright and energetic boy who early displayed ability as a public speaker, skill in debate, but also a tendency to the family malady. Because of poor health and slender means, his schooling was limited to several years of preparatory work at Pennington School and a year at Wesleyan University, where he enrolled in 1856. After having taught at several schools and preaching from time to time in 1859, he was admitted to the New Hampshire Conference of the MEC and was immediately appointed to the church in Dover, one of the largest in the state. Buckley's ministerial career blossomed quickly: He was ordained deacon in 1861 and elder in 1863. After his pastorates in New Hampshire, Detroit, Michigan, and Stamford, Connecticut, as well as Brooklyn, New York, in 1880 the General Conference elected him editor of the *Christian Advocate*, which office he held for thirty-two years, during which time the paper became one of the best-known religious journals in the country. Buckley soon became one of the most powerful voices in the church and his editorials among the most read features of the *Advocate*.

His meager schooling was no handicap. Possessing a quick mind, a retentive memory, and the ability to speed read, he acquired knowledge of extraordinary extent and variety. He produced ten books, numerous articles, and countless editorials. His most popular book was *Extemporaneous Oratory for Professional and Amateur Speakers* (1898). He wrote an important *History of the Methodists in the US* for the prestigious American Society of Church History series in 1896 and produced an authoritative *Constitutional and Parliamentary History of the MEC* (1912). He attacked both Roman Catholicism and Mormonism in the *Advocate*, but he had a lifelong interest in miracles and spiritual healing that led to his book against Christian Science and other contemporary healing movements, issued in 1892.

A resourceful debater and well-informed on everything pertaining to Methodism, he was a power to be reckoned with in ecclesiastical circles and conferences. In the 1880s, for example, Buckley organized resistance to the ordination of women and their eligibility to be elected lay delegates to General Conference. In addition, on several occasions he effectively blocked the election of men to the episcopacy. Buckley dominated eleven General Conferences of the MEC between 1872 and 1916 and ably represented his church at three ecumenical (world) Methodist conferences: London, 1881; Washington, 1891; and Toronto, 1911. Although a conservative and opposed to many changes that were finally effected, especially the relaxing prohibitions against worldly amusements and the admission of women to the ministry and to the governing conferences of the church, Buckley left his imprint on his beloved church.

After retiring from the *Advocate* in 1912, Buckley joined the faculty of Drew Theological Seminary in Madison, New Jersey, where he lectured on "ecclesiastical law and Philosophy of Christianity" until his death in 1920.

Bibliography

A: *Because They Are Women and Other Editorials from the Christian Advocate on the Admission of Women to the General Conference* (New York, 1891); *Christians and the Theater* (New York, 1875); *Constitutional and Parliamentary History of the MEC* (New York, 1912); *Extemporaneous Oratory for Professional and Amateur Speakers* (New York, 1898); *Faith Healing, Christian Science, and Kindred Phe-

nomena (New York, 1892); *The Fundamentals and Their Contrasts* (Nashville, 1906); *History of Methodists in the US* (New York, 1896), vol. 5 in Schaff's American Church History series; *Oats or Wild Oats? Common-Sense for Young Men* (New York, 1885); *The Theory and Practice of Foreign Missions* (New York, 1911); *Travels in Three Continents* (New York, 1894); *The Wrong and Peril of Woman Suffrage* (New York, 1909).

B: *CM* 140; *DAB* 3, 231–32; *EWM* 1, 347–48; *HDM*; *NCAB* 12, 191; *RLA* 73; *NYT* 9 February 1920, 9:4; *CA* 19 February 1920; George P. Mains, *James Monroe Buckley* (New York, 1917).

BURNS, FRANCIS (15 December 1808, Albany, NY–18 April 1863, Baltimore, Maryland). *Education*: Lexington Heights (NY) Seminary, 1833–34. *Career*: lay preacher, Durham (NY) circuit, 1831–33; missionary teacher and local preacher in Liberia, 1834–44; ordained deacon and elder, 1844; pastor and teacher in Liberia Conference, 1844–49; presiding elder, 1849–51; principal, Monrovia Academy, 1851–58; first missionary bishop of the MEC, assigned to Africa, 1858–63.

Born of poor parents, young Francis Burns was "bound out" at age eight to a Methodist farmer in Greene County, New York. During the winter months he attended the district grammar school. At age fifteen he was converted and joined the MEC. A call to the ministry soon followed, but he was bound to his master until age twenty-one and had a meager education.

When free in 1829, Burns continued his education at the area high school and two years later was licensed to preach and began to hold meetings on the Durham, New York, circuit. His pastor, the Rev. David Terry, called Burns to the attention of the leaders of the Methodist Missionary Society in New York City, who were recruiting African-American teachers for their mission in Liberia. Following a period of intensive training, in September 1834 Burns accompanied the Rev. John Seys as a missionary teacher to that country.

Burns joined the Liberia Mission Conference of the MEC in 1838, and in 1844 he returned to New York, where he was ordained by Bishop Janes.* Back in Liberia Burns taught in the Monrovia Seminary and edited *Africa's Luminary*. He was presiding elder of one of the two districts for ten years, and for six of these he was president of the conference.

In 1856 the General Conference of the MEC made provision for a missionary bishop for Africa. Burns was elected in 1858; he returned to the United States and was consecrated by Bishops Janes and Baker. At once he returned to Liberia and served in the episcopal office there for five years. His new responsibilities differed little from those he had been carrying as presiding elder since 1849, but he was no longer under district limitations. He devoted his energy to recruiting and training native preachers and extending the work of the conference beyond the relocated African-Americans to the masses of Africans themselves. To promote the cause, he edited a conference newspaper in 1859, *Liberia Christian Advocate*. He stretched his small budget to the limit and constantly begged the Missionary Society in New York for more. Death continued to remove the older and more valuable teachers and preachers, and few recruits came from the schools or the mission itself.

Declining health led Bishop Burns to return to the United States in 1863 to regain his stamina. But he died three days after his arrival. Following impressive funeral services in Baltimore's principal black Methodist Episcopal Church, Sharp Street, his body was returned to Liberia and buried at Monrovia.

Bibliography

B: *CBTEL* Supp. 1, 693–94; *CM* 147–48; *EWM* 1, 361; *LMB* 373–90; *NCAB* 13, 373; *CA* 30 April 1863; *Minutes* 1864, Liberia Conference, p. 237; *Missionary Advocate* 19/3 (June 1863): 17; Sylvia M. Jacobs, ''Francis Burns, First Missionary Bishop of the MEC,'' in *Black Apostles at Home and Abroad*, ed. David W. Wills and R. Newman (Boston, 1982); William R. Phinney, *From Chore Boy to Bishop: The Story of Francis Burns, First Missionary Bishop of the MEC* (Rye, NY, 1970).

C

CANNON, JAMES, JR. (13 November 1864, Salisbury, MD–6 September 1944, Chicago, IL). *Education*: B.A., Randolph Macon College, 1884; B.D., M.A., Princeton, 1888. *Career*: admitted to Virginia Annual Conference, 1888; pastor, Charlotte County, Newport News, Farmville, Virginia, 1888–94; principal, Blackstone Female Institute, owner and editor of the *Baltimore and Richmond Christian Advocate*, 1904–18; superintendent of the Anti-Saloon League of Virginia, 1909–19; established the Southern Assembly, Lake Junaluska, NC, 1911–14; bishop, MECS, 1918–44, assigned to areas in TX, AL, the Congo (1921), and Brazil (1926).

A man of prodigious energy and talent, pugnacious and single-minded, James Cannon, Jr., was the center of controversy all his adult life. He rarely avoided confrontation and seldom spared any who chose to oppose him the vitriol of his pen or speech. He was entrepreneurial, and his business dealings made him suspect in the minds of many, too. But this same energy and drive enabled him to rescue the struggling Blackstone Female Academy from economic ruin, to establish the now famous and popular center at Lake Junaluska. It was, however, when he championed the cause of temperance early in his career that he found his life's task. In 1909 he became the superintendent of the Anti-Saloon League of Virginia, which, under his leadership, was successful in gaining a referendum that on 22 September 1914 voted the state dry. His power and influence in the Virginia legislature were crucial to this outcome. He was equally active in the passage of the Eighteenth Amendment.

Cannon was elected over strong opposition to the episcopacy in May 1918 and moved to San Antonio to preside over conferences assigned to him in Northwest Texas, New Mexico, and Mexico. His record as a temperance leader brought him the election. In 1920 he was moved to Washington, D.C., where he remained for more than a decade. He was, in 1921, assigned the Congo Mission and then Brazil. For a number of years these were the only areas assigned to him, but he never lived in any of these foreign conferences. Had he left the country, his political activities would have been severely curtailed. He was chair of the legislative committee of the Anti-Saloon League of America and of the executive committee of the World League against Alcoholism as well as chair of the Board of Temperance and Social Service of the MECS.

The nomination of Alfred E. Smith in 1928 galvanized Cannon into a renewed burst of energy. He would clearly have opposed the governor because of his own views on prohibition, but he also felt compelled to introduce the religious issue. He was so outspoken and anti-Catholic that some fellow bishops publicly disclaimed his statements. Cannon, however, emerged upon Al Smith's defeat as "the most powerful ecclesiastic ever heard of in America," to use H. L. Mencken's words, and the *Christian Herald* gave him a trip to the Holy Land for his efforts.

Just at the time his influence was at its peak, it was disclosed in the press that during 1927–28 the bishop had been trading extensively and speculatively in stocks with a now bankrupt New York firm. The books of the firm showed that in an eight-months period he had been one of its largest customers and had made a profit of $9,000 on an investment of $2,500. To hosts of loyal southern Methodists it was nothing short of gambling. He was then accused of having loaned Board of Temperance funds to the anti-Smith coalition. He denied all charges and issued a manifesto of fifty thousand words titled "Unspotted from the World," submitted to the *Richmond News Leader*. Representative George H. Tinkham of Massachusetts, however, called for the Department of Justice to investigate Cannon's financial activity to see if there were violations of the Federal Corrupt Practices Act.

Charges were filed at the General Conference of 1930 alleging conduct unbecoming a bishop. The Committee on Episcopacy voted to have Cannon tried but later reversed its decision. In an apology to the conference, Cannon admitted "a mistake," but the *Christian Century*, which had defended him against all critics for years, declared him "a lost leader." Cannon appeared before the Lobby Committee of the Senate on 3 June 1930 following the General Conference. He refused to answer most of the questions about his activities in the campaign against Al Smith and finally walked out of the hearing. He came back 11 June and was highly deferential. The committee voted four to one that it could not question him about his anti-Smith activities. In 1931 the Senate Select Committee chaired by Senator Gerald P. Nye began again to look into the bishop's affairs. He was indicted in October by a federal grand jury on charges of violating the Federal Corrupt Practices Act. The Nye Committee report issued in December found that the bishop "had committed numerous apparent violations of the Federal Corrupt Practices Act." The trial did not take place until 9 April 1934, when Cannon was found not guilty.

At the General Conference convened in May following the verdict, the Committee on Episcopacy voted forty-three to twenty-eight to retire Cannon from active service. Once again friends rallied to his defense, and the conference

overruled the decision of its own committee and assigned him to Arizona and
Mexico. He was automatically retired in 1938.

Bibliography

A: James Cannon, *Bishop Cannon's Own Story* (Durham, 1955); *The Present-Day
Whisky Rebellion* (Washington, D.C., 1932); *The Present State of Methodist Unifi-
cation* (Richmond, 1925); *Priest or Prophet?* (Atlanta, 1916).
B: *EWM* 1, 406; *MB* 38–39; *DCIA* 219; *MUC* 2, 294–95; Virginius Dabney, *Dry Messiah*
(New York, 1949).

CAPERS, WILLIAM (26 January 1790, Bull Head Swamp, near Charleston,
SC–29 January 1855, Anderson, SC). *Education*: rural schools, Dr. Robert's
Academy, 1801–05; two separate times (1805, 1807) at South Carolina College
M.A., 1818; studied law with John S. Richardson. *Career*: admitted to South
Carolina Annual Conference, 1808; pastoral service in Fayetteville, NC, Charles-
ton, Orangeburg, and Wilmington, NC, 1810–13; located and taught school,
1814–18; resumed ministry as a pastor in Savannah, 1819–20; superintendent
of the Creek Indian missions in GA and AL, 1821–25; pastor, presiding elder,
Charleston, 1825–31; mission to the plantation slaves in South Carolina, in addition to his duties as presiding elder, 1829–40; pastor, Columbia, Charleston,
and Savannah, and continued mission to the slaves, 1831–36; editor, *Southern
Christian Advocate*, 1836–38; secretary of the Southern Missionary Department
of the MEC, 1840–44; bishop, MECS, 1846–55.

Born near Charleston and admitted to the South Carolina Conference in 1809,
William Capers became one of the premier preachers in the South and prior to
its separation in 1844 provided leadership in the MEC. His biographer described
an exhortation given at a camp meeting by saying, "In this he seemed to drive,
in the chariot of the earthquake, his steeds the storm clouds." He was chosen
by the 1828 General Conference as a fraternal delegate to the British Methodist
Conference. Capers might well have been elected to the episcopacy in the MEC
in 1832, but because he was the owner of slaves, he refused to allow himself
to be considered. Bishop Hamline's* biographer, F. G. Hibbard, wrote, "Dr.
Capers would have been elected to the episcopacy in 1832 had he been free
from slavery." It is ironic that the person he recommended, James O. Andrew,*
was elected because he did not own slaves; and it was Andrew who in 1844
became the center of the great debate on slavery because he had by that time
become himself a slaveholder.

Capers was one of the great missionary leaders of the denomination. When
the mission to the Creek Indians was established in 1821, Bishop McKendree*
selected Capers to lead it. He was successful in establishing schools and continued in the role of superintendent of the mission until 1824, when he was
assigned as a pastor to Charleston. In 1929 two missions to the slaves living on
plantations were begun by the church in the South. Capers was appointed to
administer them in addition to completing his duties as presiding elder. In time
thirty pastors in South Carolina alone served a membership of more than ten

thousand adults. In addition some six thousand children were being taught. Capers's *Catechism for the Use of Methodist Missions* was written for use among the slaves. At various times Capers was offered presidencies of LaGrange College, the University of Louisiana, and Randolph Macon College, Virginia. He declined them all believing that he was not qualified for such a position.

At the 1836 General Conference the publication of the journal that became the *Southern Christian Advocate* was authorized. Capers was elected its first editor. Four years later he became secretary of the southern division of the Missionary Society. He was in this role when he was elected as a delegate to the 1844 General Conference, at which the church was divided. Although siding with the South, at that conference he was a voice of tact and conciliation. When the newly organized MECS convened its first General Conference in 1846, Capers was elected to the episcopacy. He served southern Methodism in that capacity until 1855, when he died following a trip to the Florida Annual Conference.

Bibliography

A: *Catechism for the Use of Methodist Missions* (Louisville, 1847); *Grace Abounding: A Funeral Sermon . . . on the Death of Ann Amelia Andrew, Wife of Rev. J. O. Andrew* (New York, 1842).

B: *AAP* 7, 454–64; *CM* 165–66; *DAB* 3, 483–84; *DCIA* 221; *LMB* 557–72; *MB* 39–40. William May Wightman, *Life of William Capers*, contains a portion of Capers autobiography (Nashville, 1858); Duncan A. Reily, "William Capers: An Evaluation of His Life and Thought" (thesis, Emory University, 1972).

CARTWRIGHT, PETER (1 September 1785, Amherst County, VA–25 September 1872, Pleasant Plains, IL). *Education*: largely self-educated; some at Brown's Academy. *Career*: exhorter, 1802; itinerant, 1803– ; deacon, 1806; elder, 1808; served circuits in Kentucky, Tennessee, Ohio, Indiana, and Illinois; two stints as presiding elder before transferring to Illinois and then continuously from 1823 until 1869 in Illinois; state legislator, 1829–31, 1833–35.

Peter Cartwright, perhaps the most colorful of the Methodist itinerants, earned his reputation by extravagant vignettes told by and about him. *Zion's Herald*, the New England Methodist paper, called him "the greatest man that the first generation of Western Methodism produced." His life was the stuff out of which western myths were forged.

Born in Virginia in 1785, Cartwright moved west with his family about 1790 to settle in Logan County, Kentucky. His father fought in the Revolution, battled Indians on the move west, and joined with other settlers to form "the Regulators" and drive a lawless element from the community. Cartwright inherited that fighting spirit, and also something of his mother's Methodist piety. She played a major part in his early education. Later boarded out for schooling, Cartwright "learned to read, write, and cipher a little" and was, like many of his Methodist contemporaries, largely self-educated.

Despite his mother's influence and pleas, he fell into horse racing, card playing, gambling, and dancing. His recovery from this "gay" life and conversion Cartwright set in the context of Cane Ridge and the great western revival. At sixteen he came home with his father from the frivolity, drinking, and dancing of a wedding condemning himself, convicting himself of sin and seeking divine mercy. A period of agony followed only to be relieved at a joint Presbyterian-Methodist sacramental meeting by an impression "as though a voice said to me, 'Thy sins are all forgiven thee.' " That year, 1801, Cartwright joined the MEC. The next year, the church recognized his talents by licensing him as an exhorter. The family moved about the same time, and Cartwright was commissioned not just to exhort but to travel, hold classes, and form a circuit in that new area. Another short stint of schooling intervened (at Brown's Academy), which Cartwright recalls mainly for the theological conflict he experienced with the Seceder teacher and the wickedness and profanity of classmates, two of whom conspired to throw him in the creek, only to get baptized themselves.

In 1803 Cartwright began "to travel," assuming thereby a junior or apprenticeship relation with another itinerant on circuits that would take a month to six weeks to traverse. He served first on the Red River circuit in Kentucky, then on the Waynesville circuit, which also covered areas of Tennessee; next on the Salt River and Shelby into what would become Indiana and then on the Scioto circuit in Ohio, all then parts of the Western Conference. William McKendree,* later a bishop, his presiding elder in 1804, mentored him and set him on "a proper course of reading and study."

In 1806 Bishop Asbury* ordained him deacon, and in 1808 Bishop McKendree ordained him elder. That same year he married Frances Gaines. The marriage and family life do not figure large in his autobiographical statements, but the union was a fruitful one, leaving nine children, some fifty grandchildren, more than thirty great-grandchildren and even great-great-grandchildren. Family considerations and aversion to slavery did prompt his move in 1824 to Illinois and transfer into that conference.

To that conference Cartwright rendered long and distinguished service, being repeatedly appointed presiding elder, an indication of the bishops' confidence in him, and being repeatedly elected to General Conference, an indication of his brethren's esteem. Cartwright excelled in such public roles—in the give and take of conference life, in committee labors, in the witty but pointed speech, in debate whether with fellow Methodists or with Calvinists, in judging character and making appointments, in framing the church's policy, and in boosting the church's institutions. Cartwright expended effort and energy for missions, education, publications, and fund-raising. He opposed Methodism's ever increasing entanglement with slavery, voiced his opinions in the important 1844 conference that divided the church, and took early and prominent opposition to division and to the property settlement that would have legitimated the southern secession. Such public concerns led him also to dabble in state politics, to win two terms to the Illinois legislature, and to run unsuccessfully against Abraham Lincoln for Congress (1846). His important contributions, however, were to Methodism.

Cartwright's recollection of itinerancy focused especially on camp and quarterly meetings and on the conflict, frequently physical, in and around them. Cartwright's Methodism made its way physically: by manhandling women; by verbal and physical combat with Mormons, Campbellites, Baptists, and Presbyterians; by the bravery of its rustic itinerants, who rode lonely trails from cabin to cabin and suffered the poor lodging and meager fare of frontier homes; by a polity that deployed ministers into every new settlement and into muscular warfare with the powers that haunted the wilderness and with the other armies that contended for dominion; by the boisterous fervor of camp meetings, which brought isolated settlers through conversion into Christian community, enabling them to escape the hard-drinking and riotous life, often visible and audible at camp sites, and contained only by the vigilance and brute force and cunning of Methodist leaders; by an Arminian gospel that elicited the active willing of new life and encouraged the convert into independence, self-reliance, and moral improvement and away from the "gay" life; by classes and love feasts within which the new Christians held one another accountable, encouraged all toward perfection, and prayed for the backslider and hard-hearted; and under leadership whose seminary was in the saddle and whose library consisted in Bible, hymnbook, and Discipline. Cartwright made and imaged himself an exemplar, if an eccentric one, of nineteenth-century Methodism.

Bibliography

A: *Autobiography of Peter Cartwright, the Backwoods Preacher*, ed. W. P. Strickland (New York, 1856); *Dr. Cartwright Portrayed in His Visit to Brooklyn, 1861* (New York, 1861); *Fifty Years as a Presiding Elder*, ed. W. S. Hooper (Cincinnati, 1871).
B: *CM* 170; *DAB* 3, 546–48; *DARB* 91–92; *DCIA* 228–29; *EWM* 1, 420–21; *HDM*; *MUC* 2, 328–31; *NCAB*, 6, 61–62; *NYT* 27 September 1872, 5; SH, 2, 430; Theodore L. Agnew, Jr., "Peter Cartwright and His Times: The First Fifty Years, 1785–1835" (Ph.D. diss., Harvard University, June 1953); S. R. Beggs, *Pages from the Early History of the West and North-West* (Cincinnati, 1868); Helen Hardie Grant, *Peter Cartwright: Pioneer* (New York, 1931); Sydney Greenbie and Marjorie Barstow Greenbie, *Hoof Beats to Heaven: A True Chronicle of the Life and Wild Times of Peter Cartwright, Circuit Rider* (Penobscot, Maine, 1955); Sydney Greenbie and Marjorie Barstow Greenbie, *Hoof Beats in the Canebrake: Being the Second Volume in the True Chronicle of the Life and Wild Times of Peter Cartwright, Circuit Rider* (Penobscot, Maine, 1962); Nancy Veglahn, *Peter Cartwright: Pioneer Circuit Rider* (New York, 1968); Philip M. Watters, *Peter Cartwright* (New York, 1910).

CLAIR, MATTHEW W., SR. (21 October 1865, Union, WV–28 June 1943, Covington, KY). *Education:* B.A., Centenary Bible Institute (Morgan College), 1889. *Career:* admitted to the Washington Conference (one of nineteen black conferences in the MEC), 1889; pastor, Harper's Ferry, WV, 1889–93; pastor, Staunton, VA, 1893–96; pastor, Ebenezer Church, Washington, DC, 1896–97;

presiding elder, Washington (DC) District, 1897–1902; pastor, Asbury ME Church, Washington, DC, 1902–19; presiding elder, Washington, DC District, 1919–20; bishop, MEC, with eight years service in Liberia, then in the Covington, KY, area, in whose bounds were fourteen states, 1920–39.

The first African-American to be elected a general superintendent in the MEC, Matthew W. Clair, Sr., was born to Ollie and Anthony Clair of Union (Monroe County), West Virginia. Reared on the farm, he worked in the hotels of Charleston and as a dishwasher in the Hale House. With support he enrolled in the Centenary Bible Institute in Baltimore and finished his work in theology and classics in 1889.

He was ordained the same year and began his ministerial service in the black congregations of the MEC. His most distinguished assignment was to the Asbury Church (11th and K Streets, Washington, DC), where he served for seventeen years. After one year as a presiding elder, he was elected a delegate to the General Conference of 1920, where he was the first African-American ever elected to the episcopacy in the MEC. At the time of election African-Americans were assigned only to black conferences; Bishop Clair's first eight years were spent in Monrovia, Liberia. While in Liberia he traveled extensively, won the confidence of the president of Liberia, and was subsequently appointed to the national board of education; he also served on the American Advisory Commission of the Booker T. Washington Agricultural and Industrial Institute of Liberia.

His last eight years of episcopal service before retirement were spent supervising black conferences in the Covington, Kentucky, and Atlanta areas. His only son, Matthew Walker Clair, Jr., was also elected to the episcopacy in 1952.

Bibliography

B: *CCA* 1 July 1943, 418; 9 September 1943, 565; *EAAR* 177–78; *EWM* 1, 511; *MB* 43; Margaret B. Ballard, *Bishop Matthew W. Clair: A Biography* (Buckhannon, WV, 1973).

COE, GEORGE ALBERT (26 March 1862, Mendon, NY–9 November 1951, Claremont, CA). *Education*: University of Rochester, 1884; Boston University School of Theology, S.T.B., 1887, and M.A., 1885; University of Berlin, Ph.D., 1891. *Career*: professor, University of Southern California, 1887–93, Northwestern University, 1893–1909, Union Theological Seminary, NY, 1909–22 and Columbia University, 1922–27.

Born in a Methodist parsonage, George Albert Coe was the spiritual child of a religious tradition that valued a conversion experience that could date the day and hour when one was "saved" and that attached much importance to the "assurance" that one had been pardoned and "accepted" by God. Throughout his childhood Coe accepted all this unquestionably, and thus, as he later remarked, he "was a young conformist."

But this spirit of conformity did not last long. As a teenager Coe was unable to experience a conversion in the conventional pattern and underwent a season of stress that numerous revivals could not dispel. During his college years his faith was integrated into a worldview that included evolution, and hence he saw little need for a disjunctive conversion experience. This ended his spiritual turmoil. Referring to this experience in old age, he said, "I settled the question, as far as I was concerned, on a Sunday morning by solemnly espousing the scientific method, including it within my religion, and resolving to follow it wherever it should lead."

Thereafter Coe delighted in pricking the complacency of religious conformists. At Boston University School of Theology Coe quickly shifted his reading from systematic theology to philosophy and world religions. He was impatient with theologians, even the venerable Bowne,* who would not recognize the validity of the empirical method in settling religious problems. Resolving to qualify himself for a professorship in philosophy, he took a doctorate at the University of Berlin, the academic Mecca of all ambitious young American scholars in those days.

Coe returned to the United States, where he held important teaching posts in Los Angeles, Chicago, and New York. Although Coe launched his academic career as a philosopher, he did not abandon his interest in religion. His research and writing centered on religion rather than philosophy. Happily for Coe's interest in the empirical approach to religion, at the opening of the twentieth century psychology was undergoing reorientation. Whereas traditional psychology had preoccupied itself with states of consciousness, the newer psychology sought to investigate human interests and preferences of concrete persons. The problem of adjustment rather than of conscious states became dominant. He believed that such functionalist psychologists as John Dewey were correct when they argued that growth occurred within a network of social relationships. Coe concluded that the aim of religious education was "the growth of the young toward and into mature and efficient devotion to the democracy of God, and happy self-realization therein" (*A Social Theory of Religious Education*, 1917, 55). Only thus, thought Coe, could religious education alter the individual's outlook toward the social good.

By the beginning of the twentieth century, the Sunday school movement had given birth to religious education as a separate discipline concerned with the development of young Christians. In 1903 Coe became one of the founders of the Religious Education Association (REA) and guided its commitment to use contemporary knowledge in the development of religious education programs and curricula. This was the subject of his book *Education in Religion and Morals* (1904). In 1909 Coe's pioneering efforts were recognized when he was named Professor of Religious Education and Psychology of Religion at Union Theological Seminary in New York City and was elected president of the REA. While at Union he wrote his most important books, *The Psychology of Religion* (1916) and *A Social Theory of Religious Education* (1917). In 1922 Coe moved to Teacher's College, Columbia University and authored two more books, *Law and Freedom in the School* (1923) and *What Ails Our Youth?* (1924) before retirement in 1927. During a long retirement in Claremont, California Coe defended liberal Protestantism in the face of neo-orthodox critique and espoused a Marxist social perspective that made him a target for the Un-American Activities Committee of the U.S. Congress.

Coe stood at the forefront of American Protestant thinkers of the first third of the twentieth century. He held top-ranking positions in leading educational institutions, where he taught with a brilliance that fascinated and inspired students from all parts of the world. At the same time he published many pathfinding books, several of which were translated into other languages. Coe's efforts to appropriate the new psychology for the churches contributed not only to a revised appraisal of the traditional Protestant Sunday school but also to a renewed appreciation for methods of pastoral care and counseling that were grounded in psychological research. Many of his views failed to survive the neo-orthodox revolt against liberalism in the early 1930s, but Protestant religious education and pastoral care traditions remain indebted to some of his central insights.

Bibliography

A: *Educating for Citizenship* (New York, 1932); *Education in Religion and Morals* (New York, 1904); *The Motives of Men* (New York, 1928); *Psychology of Religion* (Chicago, 1916); "My Search for What Is Most Worthwhile," *Religious Education* 46/ 2 (March/April 1951): 67–73; *Religion of a Mature Mind* (Chicago, 1902); *A Social Theory of Religious Education* (New York, 1917); *The Spiritual Life: Studies in the Science of Religion* (New York, 1900); *What Is Christian Education?* (New York, 1929).

B: *NYT* 10 November 1951, 17:3; *RLA* 103; *Dictionary of Pastoral Care and Counseling*, 184–85; Helen A. Archibald, *George Albert Coe: Theorist for Religious Education in the Twentieth Century* (Ph.D. diss., University of Illinois, 1975); E. Brooks Holifield, *A History of Pastoral Care* (Nashville, 1983), 225–26; H. Shelton Smith, "George Albert Coe: Revaluer of Values," *Religion in Life* 22/1 (winter 1952–53): 46–57.

COKE, THOMAS (9 September 1747, Brecon, Wales–3 May 1824, at sea in the Indian Ocean). *Education*: B.A., Jesus College, Oxford, 1768; D.L.C., 1775. *Career*: minor political offices, Brecon, Wales, 1768–70; curate, Road and South Petherton, Somersetshire, England, 1770–76; ordained deacon in 1770, priest in 1772; Methodist preacher, 1777–84; bishop of the MEC and founder of Methodism's overseas missions to the West Indies, France, and India, 1784–1813.

Thomas Coke was born the only child of affluent parents in Wales. At age seventeen he entered Jesus College, Oxford, and followed a conventional path: Coke graduated, held minor political offices in Brecon, earned a law degree, and finally became a curate of the Church of England in Somersetshire in 1770.

Here Coke's career began to move away from convention. Some of the members of his congregation began to suspect him of Methodist sympathies. By

1776 he met John Wesley, became increasingly evangelistic, and within a year was dismissed from his church position. After risking a stoning by preaching outside his former parish church, Coke joined Wesley as a preacher on the London circuit in 1778 and soon became one of his most trusted assistants. When Wesley decided to send support to Francis Asbury* and the lay preachers in the former British colonies in North America, he appointed Coke bishop to accompany two newly ordained preachers who would meet with the Americans and discuss the future of the mission. Coke and his companions arrived in 1784, with Coke empowered to ordain additional preachers and take leadership.

Later that year in Baltimore at the Christmas Conference that brought into being the independent MEC, Coke discovered that although he was putatively in charge, Asbury had effective control of the proceedings. When Coke began to ordain Asbury as bishop, Asbury demanded that his colleague first vote approval. Coke's leadership suffered on other counts. A storm of criticism broke upon him when he, with considerable courage, took a firm stand against slavery. In 1789 Coke committed a serious indiscretion when he assisted Asbury in hand-delivering a congratulatory address to George Washington as president of the United States. For this the English conference at Bristol formally rebuked him. His efforts to unite the Methodist and Episcopal Churches in America in 1791 produced great indignation.

Bishop Coke viewed the new denomination as only one of his projects, along with missions to the West Indies, France, and India and, most important, the preservation of Methodism in England after Wesley's death in 1791. In nine voyages to the United States, Coke often quarreled with Asbury, who increasingly saw his fellow bishop as a meddlesome outsider. Coke made his last trip to America in 1803; he died on his way to India a decade later. His conspicuous success in the work of overseas missions gained him a high and enduring place in the history of Methodism.

Bibliography

A: *An Account of the Progress of the Methodist Missions in the West Indies* (London, 1805); *An Account of the Rise, Progress, and Present State of Methodist Missions* (London, 1804); *The Character and Death of Hester Ann Rogers* (London, 1794); *Commentary on the Holy Bible* (London, 1801–03); *Extracts of the Journals, Comprising Several Visits to North-America and the West-Indies, His Tour through a Part of Ireland, and His Nearly Finished Voyage to Bombay in the East Indies* (London, 1816); *The Doctrines and Discipline of the MEC in America, with Explanatory Notes*, with Francis Asbury (Philadelphia, 1798); *Four Discourses on the Duties of a Minister of the Gospel* (London, 1798); *History of the West-Indies* (London, 1808–11); *Life of the Rev. John Wesley*, with Henry Moore (London, 1791); *A Series of Letters Addressed to the Methodist Connection, Explaining the Important Doctrines of Justification by Faith, and the Direct Witness of the Spirit* (London, 1810); *The Substance of a Sermon Preached at Baltimore, in the State of Maryland, before the General Conference of the Methodist Episcopal Church on the 27th of December, 1785 at the Ordination of the Rev. Francis Asbury to the Office of a Superintendent* (Baltimore, 1785).

B: *AAP* 7, 130–42; *CBTEL* 2:403–4; *CM* 233–35; *DAB* 4, 279–80; *DNB* 4, 703–5; *DARB* 122–23; *EWM* 1, 528–32; *HDM*; *LMB* 41–72; *NCAB* 10, 89; Cyril Davey, *Mad about Mission: The Story of Thomas Coke, Founder of the Methodist Overseas Mission* (London, 1985); John A. Vickers, *Thomas Coke: Apostle of Methodism* (London and New York, 1969).

COOPER, EZEKIEL (22 February 1763, Caroline County, MD—21 February 1847, Philadelphia, PA). *Career*: preacher, Methodist circuits from Boston to Baltimore, 1785–99 (ordained deacon in 1788, elder in 1798); head, Methodist Book Concern, Philadelphia, after 1802 New York, 1799–1808; pastoral appointments in the Philadelphia Conference, 1808–13; retired, 1813–20; pastor, St. George's ME Church, Philadelphia, 1820–21; retired again, 1821–47.

Ezekiel Cooper was the son of Richard and Ann Cooper, whom he described as "plain and simple, in easy and plentiful circumstances." Brought up in the Church of England, at fourteen he was converted through the preaching of Methodist Freeborn Garrettson* when evangelizing a company of Revolutionary soldiers who were training in a field near the Cooper home. Not until several years later, however, after experiencing an inner struggle, did he join a Methodist society. Garrettson made him a class leader in Talbot County, but Cooper long hesitated to become a preacher. Finally in 1784, at a conference at Barratt's Chapel, he was brought to the attention of Francis Asbury,* who appointed him "on trial" to the Caroline circuit.

At the conference of 1785 held at Baltimore, Cooper was admitted to the traveling ministry, and two years later at John Street ME Church in New York City he was ordained deacon by Bishop Asbury. Cooper's ministry extended over sixty-four years and covered a wide area. He served churches and led districts from Boston to Charleston. Numerous revivals of religion occurred during his pastorates. He performed heroic service in Philadelphia in the midst of the yellow fever epidemic in 1796. Even when in a slaveholding community he vigorously opposed slavery, publishing a series of letters advocating abolition in the *Maryland Gazette*, the *Maryland Journal*, and the *Virginia Gazette* in 1790 and 1791.

Throughout this long period of the church's formation and growth, Cooper was a recognized leader, effective as a preacher, powerful as a debater, noted for his wide knowledge, and having the confidence of Bishop Asbury until the latter's death. It was his business ability, no doubt, which in 1799 led to his being appointed head of Methodist publishing operations. When he took charge it had no capital, and debts equaled its assets; when he left in 1808, it was on a firm foundation with assets of $45,000.

Cooper retired from the itinerancy in 1821 but was hardly inactive as a preacher. For the next twenty-five years he was appointed eight times to St. George's Church, Philadelphia, once to Newcastle, and twice to Dover in Delaware, as well as nine times as conference missionary. At his own request Cooper was buried at the door of Old St. George's Church in Philadelphia, where a marble slab commemorates his life and ministry.

Bibliography

A: *Beams of Light on Early Methodism in America, Chiefly Drawn from the Diary, Letters, Manuscripts, Documents, and Original Tracts of the Rev. Ezekiel Cooper,* ed. Geo. A. Phoebus (New York, 1887); *A Funeral Discourse on the Death of That Eminent Man, the Late Reverend John Dickins* (Philadelphia, 1799); *The Substance of a Funeral Discourse, Delivered at the Request of the Annual Conference on Tuesday the 23rd of April, 1816, in St. George's Church, Philadelphia, on the Death of the Rev. Francis Asbury, Superintendent of the MEC* (Philadelphia, 1819).

B: *AAP* 7, 108–12; *CBTEL* 2, 499; *CM* 256–57; *DAB* 4, 397–98; *EWM* 1, 582–83; *HDM*; *NCAB* 11, 239; *Minutes* 4, Philadelphia Conference, 1847, 104–5; James P. Pilkington, *The Methodist Publishing House, A History* (Nashville, 1968), 1: 117–28; Lester B. Scherer, *Ezekiel Cooper, 1763–1847, An Early American Methodist Leader* (Lake Junaluska, NC, 1968).

CORSON, FRED PIERCE (11 April 1896, Millville, NJ–16 February 1985, St. Petersburg, FL). *Education*: A.B., Dickinson College, 1917; M.A., Dickinson College, 1920; B.D., Drew Theological Seminary, 1920. *Career*: clergy member of the New York East Conference of the Methodist Church; pastor, Jackson Heights, NY, 1919–24; West Haven, CT, 1924–26; Port Washington, NY, 1926–28; and Simpson Church, Brooklyn, 1928–30; superintendent of the Brooklyn South District, 1930–34; president, Dickinson College, 1934–44; bishop, Philadelphia area, 1944–68.

Fred Pierce Corson graduated with honors from Dickinson College in 1917, prepared for the Methodist ministry at Drew Theological Seminary, and began his ministry in the New York East Conference of the MEC. After serving churches in New York and Connecticut, he became superintendent of the Brooklyn District in 1930. Four years later, at age thirty-eight, when he accepted the presidency of Dickinson College, Carlisle, Pennsylvania, he became one of the youngest college presidents in the nation. During his ten-year college presidency Corson took an active role in church affairs. In 1944 Corson was elected bishop and assigned to the Philadelphia area, which then included the Philadelphia, New Jersey, Wyoming (northeastern Pennsylvania/southern tier of New York), and Puerto Rico Conferences.

In his new role as bishop, Corson favored liturgical worship and introduced clerical garb among the preachers of his area and especially among the bishops. A fund raiser of unusual effectiveness, he also promoted evangelistic programs and opened many new churches in Philadelphia's suburbs. The educator-turned-bishop headed the denomination's general board of education from 1948 to 1960 and was chosen by his fellow bishops to deliver the Episcopal Address to the General Conference of 1956.

Corson welcomed closer contact with other church leaders in the Philadelphia area and took a leading role in many mid-century ecumenical ventures. As president of the World Methodist Council (1960–65) he headed Methodist observers at the Second Vatican Council, 1961–65, and had private audiences with two Popes, John XXIII and Paul VI. In 1967 he accompanied Catholic archbishop Krol of Philadelphia to Rome for the consistory elevating Krol to the College of Cardinals.

Through preaching and writing, Bishop Corson combated communism and supported prayer in public schools. Not an enthusiastic supporter of the ordination of women and cautious on matters of race, he nonetheless appointed one of the first black district superintendents in a newly integrated conference that was created when the all-black Delaware Conference merged with the all-white Philadelphia Conference in 1965.

During a long retirement, Bishop Corson lived in Cornwall Manor Retirement Village in Cornwall, Pennsylvania. He died while vacationing in St. Petersburg, Florida. Two years before his death, he donated his library and memorabilia to the World Methodist Council in Lake Junaluska, North Carolina.

Bibliography

A: *Aldersgate Is for Us* (Nashville, 1960); *Bridges to Unity* (Philadelphia, 1963); *The Christian Imprint* (New York, 1955); *Five Distinctive Marks of Protestantism* (Nashville, 1960); *How Good Is Communism?* (Nashville, 1959); *The Pattern for Successful Living* (Philadelphia, 1953); *The Pattern of a Church* (Nashville, 1946); *Your Church and You* (Philadelphia, 1951).

B: *EWM* 1, 590–91; *Philadelphia Inquirer*, 18 February 1985, 9–D; *Who's Who in America*, 43d ed., 1984–85, p. 679; Lauren B. Meiswinkel, *The Emergence of Bishop Fred Pierce Corson as an Ecumenical Spokesman* (M.A., thesis, Temple University, 1968).

CRAFTS, SARA JANE TIMANUS (1845, Cincinnati, OH–2 May 1930, Washington, DC). *Education*: Wesleyan Female Academy, Davenport, IA; Iowa Women's College, Davenport, IA. *Career*: public school teacher, 1865?–70; teacher, Minnesota State Normal School, 1870–74; full-time Sunday school worker, New Bedford, MA, 1874–77; Sunday school and temperance worker, Chicago, 1877–79; travel in Europe, 1879–80; independent Sunday school, temperance, and anti-opium advocate, New York City, 1880–96; Washington, DC, 1896–1913?; superintendent, Sunday school department, World WCTU, 1896–1913; travel in Orient and Palestine, 1904; in Japan, China, Korea, and Australia, 1907; and in Norway, Sweden, and Iceland, 1910.

Sara Jane Timanus was born and raised in Cincinnati, Ohio. Following training at a Methodist woman's academy and college in Iowa, she became a school teacher and then a teacher of teachers. As a teacher at the Minnesota State Normal School, Timanus was one of the first women to conduct Sunday school institutes and convention sessions. She first presented her methods to the Minnesota Sunday School Teachers' Convention. When reports reached Dwight L. Moody in Chicago, he invited her to give the same presentation at a whole series of Sunday school conventions he had planned. She became well known through her articles in the *National Sunday School Teacher* and other periodicals, as well as through her books on the teaching of young children. After her marriage in 1874 to fellow Sunday school worker Wilbur J. Crafts, she became a full-time Sunday school leader, lecturing widely on child psychology, disseminating Pestalozzian principles, and campaigning for the adoption of kindergartens in Sunday schools. She stressed the importance of women as teachers of Sunday school kindergartens, thus helping to establish kindergarten teaching as a special area of expertise reserved for women.

A Methodist minister in the New England Conference, after graduation from Wesleyan University and Boston University School of Theology Wilbur Crafts served churches in New England until 1877, when the couple moved to Chicago, where Mr. Crafts followed John H. Vincent* as pastor of influential Trinity MEC. After the couple traveled to Europe and Palestine in 1879–80, Mr. Crafts became pastor of important Congregational and Presbyterian churches in New York City (1880–88).

When WCTU leaders systematically began advocating teaching temperance in the Sunday schools, they invited Mrs. Crafts to develop a curriculum. She wrote quarterly temperance lessons for Sunday schools and gave blackboard temperance addresses to children and teachers at Sunday school conventions. Music had long been an important part of Sunday school work, and Mrs. Crafts published several collections of hymns for young children. She founded the International Primary Union of Sunday School Teachers and was president from its foundation in 1884 until 1899, when she became honorary president. She was appointed in 1896 Sunday school superintendent of the World WCTU and frequently addressed gatherings of teachers and children.

Believing that evangelical women should defer to male, and especially clerical, authority, yet convinced that women possess qualities that suited them for work with small children, Mrs. Crafts accepted contemporary ideas about women's proper ''sphere'' as mothers and teachers. Her achievement was to extend the boundaries of that sphere by establishing a position in the Sunday school convention movement, from which she and others could take leadership.

When Mr. Crafts established the International Reform Bureau in 1895, a clearinghouse for Christian reform movements, the Crafts relocated to Washington, D.C. Mrs. Crafts's later work increasingly centered on temperance and substance abuse education for children. In the late 1890s, with her husband she traveled extensively in Japan, China, Korea, and Australia, speaking in aid of the anti-opium movement. Upon their return together they wrote a widely circulated book on intoxicants in all lands and times.

Bibliography

A: *Blackboard Temperance Lessons* (New York, 1875?); *Christmas Chimes for Little Voices* (New York, 1890); *The Infant School: Hints on Primary Religious Instruction* (Chicago, 1870); *Intoxicants and Opium in All Lands and Times*, with Mr. Crafts (Washington, DC, 1900); *The Lesson Handbook for Primary and Intermediate Teachers* (Boston, 1884); *Little Pilgrim Songs* (New York, 1883); *Normal*

Outlines for Primary Teachers (New York, 1883); *Open Letters to Primary Teachers* (New York, 1876); *Plain Uses of the Blackboard and Slate, and Other Visible and Verbal Illustrations in the Sunday-School and Home*, with Mr. Crafts (New York, 1881); *Primary Teachers' Handbook for Mothers and Sunday School Teachers* (Boston, 1882); *Songs for Little Folks* (Chicago, 1875); *Through the Eye to the Heart; or, Eye Teaching in the Sunday School*, with Mr. Crafts (New York, 1873); *World Book of Temperance: Temperance Lessons, Biblical, Historic, Scientific*, with Mr. Crafts (Washington, DC, 1908).

B: *NCAB* 14, 172–73, ''Wilbur Fisk Crafts''; *Standard Encyclopedia of the Alcohol Problem* 2 (1924): 727; *Union Signal* (WCTU) 17 and 24 May 1930; *Who's Who in America* 13 (1924–25): 831–32; Anne M. Boylan, *Sunday School: The Formation of an American Institution, 1790–1880* (New Haven, CT, 1988).

D

DENNY, COLLINS (28 May 1854, Winchester, VA–12 May 1943, Richmond, VA). *Education:* Shenandoah Valley Academy, 1872; B.A., Princeton, 1876; B.L., University of Virginia, 1877; M.A., Princeton, 1879. *Career:* practiced law in Baltimore, 1877–79; admitted to Baltimore Annual Conference, MECS, 1880; pastoral assignments in Maryland, Virginia, and West Virginia, 1880–89; Chaplain, University of Virginia, 1889–91; professor of mental and moral philosophy, Vanderbilt University, 1891–1910; bishop MECS, 1910–34.

Collins Denny was the church lawyer without equal. A learned man with a vast knowledge of church history, the *Discipline*, and parliamentary procedure, he was known throughout the church for his skills as a presiding officer, but he was exact and demanding of those who served under him. His leadership style was autocratic and he seemed at times to be cold and harsh. After his service as secretary of the College of Bishops, from 1910 until 1927, the rules favoring seniority were changed to remove him and Bishop Candler from their positions; he was retired from episcopal service against his will by the General Conference of 1934.

He was also a man of strong convictions. Although a member of the Joint Commission on Federation, organized in 1910, and one of its two members to actually live to see reunification in 1939, he was never able to support any plan of union and became, along with Bishop Warren Candler, the most consistent and dedicated opponent of reunification in the MECS. Having practiced law, and with the assistance of his son, who was also a lawyer, he used every legal means to slow or defeat the movement for unification. So bitter and unchanging was his opposition that when the documents forming the Methodist Church were finally approved in 1939, Bishop Denny was the only bishop who did not sign, declined to become a bishop in the newly created Methodist Church, and refused even to accept a pension from it.

Bishop Denny was a frequent contributor to the *Methodist Quarterly Review* and other periodicals.

Bibliography

A. *MQR*.
B: *EWM* 1, 658–59; *MB* 57; John M. Moore, *The Long Road to Methodist Union* (New York, 1943).

DICKINS, JOHN (24 August 1747, London–27 September 1798, Philadelphia, PA). *Education:* London, Eton. *Career:* came to America before 1774; admitted to the Virginia Conference on trial in 1777; pastorates in North Carolina and Virginia, 1777–80; located, 1781–83; pastor, New York, Bertie circuit, 1783–89; book steward, Methodist Book Concern, Philadelphia, 1789–98.

Coming to America before the Revolution, John Dickins brought a good education and an interest in literature and learning that few of his Methodist contemporaries could equal. He was a good Latin and Greek scholar with some knowledge of Hebrew. Ezekiel Cooper* in his sermon on the death of Dickins described him as a "person of refined sensibilities, great generosity of spirit, and true dignity of character." He preached throughout Virginia for four years and then located in 1781. Two years later Francis Asbury,* his intimate friend, persuaded him to go to New York, where he served historic John Street Church and remained until 1789. He was the first person to meet and talk with Thomas Coke* when he came on his mission from Wesley in 1784 to establish the MEC. He was ordained a deacon at the Christmas Conference, 1784 but did not become an elder until 1786. He and Thomas Morrell were delegated by the Conference of 1789 to deliver the bishop's congratulations to George Washington.

As could be expected, Dickins made valuable contributions to the denominational interest in education. Along with Coke and Asbury he was involved with the founding of Cokesbury College. In 1789 he became book steward of the newly established Methodist Book Concern, where for nine years he oversaw printing and distribution of materials. In that capacity he also published the *Arminian Magazine* (1789–90) and the *Methodist Magazine* (1797–98). During much of the time he also served as pastor of St. George's Church in Philadelphia. His *Short Scriptural Catechism* (1793) was one of the first Methodist publications in America. It was also Dickins who in 1786 prepared the *Discipline* in the form that was used in all subsequent issues. Refusing to leave his charge, he died in the yellow fever epidemic of 1798. Upon his death Asbury wrote, "What I have greatly feared for years hath now taken place. Dickins the generous, the just, the faithful, skillful Dickins is dead."

Bibliography

A: *Friendly Remarks on the Late Proceedings of the Rev. Mr. Hammet* (Philadelphia, 1792); *A Short Scriptural Catechism Intended for the Use of the Methodist Societies* (Philadelphia, 1793).
B: *AAP* 7, 63–65; *CM* 295–96, *DAB* 5, 292–93; *EWM* 1, 680–81; *JLFA*; Ezekiel Cooper,

A Funeral Discourse on the Death . . . of John Dickins (Philadelphia, 1799); J. P. Pilkington, *Methodist Publishing House* (Nashville, 1968).

DURBIN, JOHN PRICE (10 October 1800, Bourbon County, KY–19 October 1876, New York City). *Education*: Miami University, Oxford, OH, 1822; B.A., Cincinnati College, 1825; M.A., Cincinnati College, 1826. *Career*: minister, Ohio Conference, 1820–26 (ordained deacon in 1822, elder in 1824); professor of languages, Augusta College, Augusta, KY, 1825–32; chaplain, U.S. Senate, 1831; editor, *CA*, 1832–34; president, Dickinson College, 1834–45; pastor of Union ME Church and Trinity ME Church, Philadelphia, 1845–49; presiding elder, Philadelphia Conference, 1849–50; corresponding secretary, Methodist Missionary Society, New York, 1850–72.

With no more preparation than a bit of frontier schooling the skills a cabinetmaker could give, John Price Durbin began his public career as a Methodist minister at the age of eighteen. He was a Kentuckian, born in Bourbon County near Paris, Kentucky. Converted at a Methodist revival in 1818, he joined the Ohio Conference in 1820 and managed to work his way through college while serving a circuit of Methodist churches. Upon graduation in 1825 he taught languages at Augusta College, Augusta, Kentucky, the denomination's first college to be founded after Cokesbury College was destroyed by fire in 1796. Fundraising trips on behalf of the college brought Durbin notice in the East. He took a leave of absence in 1831–32 to serve as chaplain of the U.S. Senate. His sermon on the centenary of Washington's birth preached before a joint session of Congress on 22 February 1832 was accounted a masterful deliverance on the providence of God in human history.

Durbin was now launched on a career of national prominence. The next year, 1832, the young educator moved to New York, where he followed the venerable Nathan Bangs* in the editorial chair of the *Christian Advocate*. Although he held the post only two years, he helped mold Methodist opinion in favor of an educated ministry and the refinement of public worship.

Durbin resigned his editorial post to become president of Dickinson College, in Carlisle, Pennsylvania, in 1834, recently reorganized as a Methodist school. During his eleven-year presidency, while continuing to take an active part in church affairs Durbin successfully steered the college through the opening years of its Methodist history. Elected to the General Conference of 1844, he made a long-remembered stand against the southern delegation, supporting the resolution requiring the slaveholding Bishop Andrew* to desist from the office of the bishop. Durbin was not a radical abolitionist; he opposed the expulsion of slaveholders from the church (see his article in *CA* 26 July 1855) and endorsed the colonization as late as 1852. Reelected to the next six General Conferences through 1868, Durbin championed ministerial education and lay representation.

Durbin returned to the parish ministry in 1845, serving two prominent Philadelphia churches and a short term as presiding elder. Durbin's most distinguished service to American Methodism began in 1850 when he was chosen by the bishops to head the denomination's Missionary Society. His travels to Europe and the Near East a decade earlier helped prepare him for the demanding task. His skill in administration and eloquence as an advocate enabled the Missionary Society to expand greatly. Receipts rose from $100,000 to $700,000. New missions were begun in Europe (Denmark, France, Italy, Norway, and Sweden) and Asia (China and India), as well as Latin America.

Generally recognized as one of Methodism's great preachers, Durbin died at age seventy-six in New York City. He was buried in Laurel Hill Cemetery, Philadelphia.

Bibliography

A: *A Letter to Rev. William H. Norris, Rector of St. John's, Carlisle, PA, on the Identity of Fundamental Doctrines in the Church of England, the Protestant Episcopal Church, and the Methodist Episcopal Church* (Philadelphia, 1844); edited *Mosaic History of the Creation of the World*, by Thomas Wood (New York, 1831); *Observations in Europe, Principally in France and Great Britain* (New York, 1844); *Observations in the East, Chiefly in Egypt, Palestine, and Asia Minor* (New York, 1845); *Our Missionary Picture* (New York, 1861).

B: *CBTEL* Supp. 2, 309–10; *DAB* 5, 544–45; *EWM* 1, 732–33; *NCAB* 6, 463; *Minutes Philadelphia Conference, 1877*; *CA* 26 October 1876; *Harper's Weekly* 11 November 1876; *NYT* and *New York Tribune* 20 October 1876; John A. Roche, "John Price Durbin," *MQR* 69 (May 1887): 329–54, and *The Life of John Price Durbin* (New York, 1889); Abel Stevens, "J. P. Durbin," *National Magazine* 6/2 (February 1855): 137–41, and *History of the MEC*, vol. 4 (New York, 1867).

E

ELLIOTT, CHARLES (16 May 1792, Glenconway, Ireland–8 January 1869, Mt. Pleasant, Iowa). *Education:* privately educated. *Career:* licensed to preach in England, 1813; came to America in 1814. Pastor, presiding elder, missionary to the Wyandot Indians, 1818–27; professor of languages, Madison College (Uniontown, PA), 1827–31; presiding elder, Pittsburgh District, 1832–34; pastor, editor, *Pittsburgh Conference Journal,* 1835–36; editor, *Western Christian Advocate,* 1836–48; pastor, presiding elder, Ohio, 1848–52; reelected editor, *Western Christian Advocate,* 1852–56; professor of biblical literature and president, Iowa Wesleyan University, 1856–60; editor, *Central Christian Advocate* (St. Louis), 1860–64; president, Iowa Wesleyan University, 1864–67.

Charles Elliott is best known for his work in the church press, especially during the debate on slavery. He took an active position against slavery and was outspoken and aggressive in its support. A member of the General Conference of 1844, Elliott took an active role in support of the Plan of Separation, which created the MECS. After the plan was adopted, however, he opposed the new church in his writings in the *Western Christian Advocate.* Elliott must bear responsibility for his part in the bitterness that was to keep the churches separated for almost a century.

We are indebted to his historical work and for his writings on the subject of slavery and the division of the denomination. Elliott was appointed by the General Conference of 1848 to write a history of the events leading to the division of the church. This commission resulted in the publication of three significant works: *The Sinfulness of American Slavery* (1850); *A History of the Great Secession from the Methodist Episcopal Church in the Year 1845* (1855); *The Bible and Slavery* (1857). Elliott also wrote of his experiences among the Wyandot Indians, two volumes in opposition to Roman Catholicism, and a biography of Bishop Robert R. Roberts based on a dictated manuscript now located in the Simpson Papers at Drew University.

His service as editor of the *Central Christian Advocate* during most of the Civil War was requested when the church determined the sitting editor to be ineffective in his opposition to the MECS. Elliott's editorials during this time gained him even more enemies in the South.

While president of Iowa Wesleyan University he demonstrated his support of coeducation by allowing the graduation of a woman. In this he was consistent with the views of his good friend Bishop Matthew Simpson.*

Bibliography

A: *The Bible and Slavery* (Cincinnati, 1857); *Delineation of Roman Catholicism* (New York, 1842); *History of the Great Secession from the Methodist Episcopal Church* (Cincinnati, 1855); *Indian Missionary Reminiscences, Principally of the Wyandot Nation* (New York, 1850); *The Life of the Rev. Robert R. Roberts* (Cincinnati, 1844); *Sinfulness of American Slavery* (Cincinnati, 1851); *South-western Methodism: A History of the M.E. Church in the South-west* (Cincinnati, 1868); *A Treatise on the Inspiration of the Holy Scriptures* (Edinburgh, 1877).
B: *CA* 14 January 1869, 12; *CM* 337; *DAB* 6, 95–96; *EWM* 1, 680–81; *MUC* 4, 146–48.

EMORY, JOHN (11 April 1789, Spaniard's Neck, Queen Anne County, MD–16 December 1835). *Education:* private tutors and country schools; Washington College, 1804; studied law, 1805, in the office of Richard T. Earle, afterward chief justice of the Second Judicial District of Maryland. *Career:* admitted to bar and practiced law, 1808–09, in Centreville, MD; joined Philadelphia Conference in 1810, serving various congregations in Maryland, Pennsylvania, and Delaware as pastor, 1810–18; transferred to Baltimore Conference, where he also served pastorates in Washington, DC, Annapolis, Haggerstown, and Baltimore, 1818–24; assistant book editor, 1824–28; book editor and editor of the *Methodist Magazine*, which in 1830 became the *Methodist Magazine and Quarterly Review*, 1828–32; bishop, MEC, 1832–35.

John Emory was yet another of the church's leaders whose legal training and keen mind served the church well. He entered the ministry in 1809 over the strong opposition of his father. His friend, John McClintock, characterized Emory as "a man of great talent. But he was not a man of genius." In 1810 he offered himself for service in the West but was not accepted by Bishop Asbury.* Ten years later General Conference appointed him fraternal delegate to the conference meeting in Liverpool, England, in July 1820. In 1816 he supported the movement to elect presiding elders, and in 1820 he drafted and supported the "suspended resolutions," which empowered the church to elect them. He did not, however, support the introduction of lay representation into General Conference.

Emory gained recognition for his writing on controversial issues. Devoted to accuracy and understanding in his writings and sermons, though not imaginative, Emory began his work as a polemicist with a reply to an essay published by Protestant Episcopal bishop White in 1817. Through the years he distinguished himself in this genre of literature, and he is now best known for his *Defence of Our Fathers and of the Original Organization of the Methodist Episcopal Church* (1827), a carefully reasoned and well-written apology for the episcopal organization of Methodism, a document drafted in response to its critics.

Emory served Foundry Church, Washington, DC, 1818–20, where he continued his controversial writing, this time against the Unitarians. In 1824 he became assistant book agent, with Nathan Bangs* serving as senior agent. Four years later he became the agent with Beverly Waugh as his assistant. Waugh was elected to the episcopacy in 1836. His work as book agent was among the most important of his entire ministry. He originated the Publishing Fund, which supported benevolent causes in the church, and founded the *Methodist Quarterly Review*, for which he wrote the majority of articles in the early years of its existence.

Emory was elected to the episcopacy at the General Conference of 1832, which recognized both his gifts and the influence of editors and book agents in the life of the church. As a bishop he continued his interest in education and had a part in the organization of New York University, Wesleyan University, and Dickinson College. He drew up a course of study for persons wishing to be ordained deacons and elders and drafted a plan for training local preachers. Unfortunately, however, his service in the episcopacy was cut short when he was killed in a carriage accident while on his way to Baltimore.

Bibliography

A: *A Defence of Our Fathers and of the Original Organization of the Methodist Episcopal Church* (New York, 1827); *The Divinity of Christ Vindicated . . .* (Philadelphia, 1819); *The Episcopal Controversy Reviewed* (New York, 1838); *A Farther Reply to the Objections against the Position of Personal Assurance of the Pardon of Sin* (Philadelphia, 1818); Richard Watson, *The Life of Rev. John Wesley*, notes and translations by John Emory (New York, 1840).

B: *AAP* 486–93; *CM* 340–41; *EWM* 1, 773–74; *LMB* 203–22; *MB* 61–65; *MUC* 4, 157–59; Robert Emory, *The Life of the Rev. John Emory* (New York, 1841); William Larrabee, *Asbury and His Coadjutors*, vol. 2 (Cincinnati, 1854); John J. Matthias, "*A Sermon Preached in the Halsey-Street Church . . . on Occasion of the Death of the Rev. John Emory . . .*" (New York, 1836).

F

FINLEY, JAMES BRADLEY (1 July 1781, NC–6 September 1857, Eaton, OH). *Education*: high school, Bourbon County, KY, 1793–96; studied medicine, 1796–1800. *Career*: farmer in Chillicothe, Ohio, 1796–1800; medical doctor, 1800–1802; lay preacher, 1809, on the Scioto circuit; probationary member, Western Conference, 1810–16 (ordained deacon in 1811, elder in 1813); presiding elder, 1816–21; missionary, Wyandot Mission, Upper Sandusky, OH, 1821–27; pastor, Cincinnati, and presiding elder of several Ohio districts, 1827–46; chaplain, Ohio State Penitentiary, 1846–49; pastor, Yellow Springs, Cincinnati, and Dayton, 1850–57.

Son of a Princeton-trained Presbyterian clergyman who started several churches in Kentucky, young James Finley early showed sympathy for Methodists. After receiving a classical education in his father's academy, he studied and practiced medicine until his desire to be a backwoods farmer won out. In August 1801 he visited a previous church of his father's at Cane Ridge, Kentucky, witnessed the great camp meeting, and was converted on the way home. Resisting a call to preach, he reverted to his old life until he nearly shot his brother by accident in 1808. Both soon professed the faith and entered the Methodist ministry.

Finley spent most of his fifty ministerial years in Ohio. In 1816 Bishop McKendree* put him in charge of the Ohio District. Seven years later the bishop appointed him to a highly successful ministry among the Wyandot Indians. Finley favored Indian customs as a boy and found it easy to assimilate himself to them as a missionary. The Indians showed him unusual respect and devotion. That mission ended when the U.S. government forced the tribe to sell its land and move west of the Mississippi. For three years he was chaplain to the convicts in the Ohio State Penitentiary. He was eight times elected to General Conference, and at the tumultuous 1844 session, Finely proposed a motion that called for a southern bishop to ''desist from the exercise of the office so long as the impediment [ownership of slaves] remains.'' That motion passed and became the catalyst for the sectional split of the MEC.

Throughout his career Finley placed a high priority on reaching out to marginalized persons—Native Americans, blacks, prisoners, the struggling settlers he first encountered in his preaching. He made a conscious personal sacrifice to be a circuit rider to the neglect of his health, his family, and his own economic well-being. His wide experience and observation, together with his habit of journalizing the principal happenings of his life, resulted in five best-selling books that give unique information about early Methodism in the West.

Bibliography

A: *Autobiography; or, Pioneer Life in the West* (Cincinnati, 1853); *History of the Wyandot Mission at Upper Sandusky, Ohio* (Cincinnati, 1840); *Life among the Indians* (Cincinnati, 1857); *Memorials of Prison Life* (Cincinnati, 1850); *Sketches of Western Methodism* (Cincinnati, 1854).
B: *AAP* 7, 531–33; *CBTEL* 3, 562–63; *CM* 361; *DAB* 6, 389–90; *DARB* 180–81; *EWM* 1, 844; *NCAB* 12, 557; *WCA* 16 September 1857, 146; Charles C. Cole, *Lion of the Forest: James B. Finley, Frontier Reformer* (Lexington, KY, 1994).

FISK, WILBUR (31 August 1792, Brattleboro, VT–22 February 1839, Middletown, CT). *Education*: University of Vermont, 1812–13; B.A., Brown University, 1815; studied law in Lyndon, VT, 1815–16. *Career*: family tutor, Baltimore, 1817–18; licensed to preach in the New England Conference, 1818 (ordained deacon in 1820, elder in 1822); appointed presiding elder of Vermont District, 1823–26; principal, Wesleyan Academy, Wilbraham, MA, 1826–30; president, Wesleyan University, Middletown, CT, 1830–38.

Wilbur Fisk's father was a judge and a member of the Vermont state legislature. Much farmwork and scant schooling characterized Wilbur Fisk's boyhood, but by independent study and some preparation at a school in Peacham, young Fisk managed to enter the sophomore class at the University of Vermont in 1812. When its buildings were turned into barracks the following year, Fisk transferred to Brown University in Providence, Rhode Island, where he graduated in 1815. Although reared in the fervid atmosphere of early New England Methodism, he was without deep religious feeling and fond of amusements and ambitious for worldly honors. He first prepared for a career in politics by entering the law office of Isaac Fletcher at Lyndon, Vermont. Better entry-level salaries in education led him to take a post as tutor in the home of a wealthy Baltimore family.

Haunted by the religious training of his childhood, he soon turned his back on a worldly career and decided to become a minister. He joined the New England Conference as a probationer in 1818. One of the denomination's first college-trained preachers, he became an ardent champion of an educated clergy. Not only did he lead Methodism in the Northeast in educational enterprises, but his influence was felt throughout the whole church. He chaired the 1828 General Conference Committee on Education, whose report jump-started Methodism's commitment to higher education. With great vigor Fisk also battled Calvinist theology, championed foreign missions, and advocated temperance. Although opposed to slavery, he shunned abolitionism.

Fisk's pastoral work, including three years as presiding elder in Vermont, was brief. His parish was education. In 1824 he was elected principal of Wesleyan Academy, Wilbraham, Massachusetts, which he helped establish. Leaving it in 1830 a thriving institution, he become first president of Wesleyan University in Middletown, Connecticut, which he also helped found and to the development of which he devoted the remainder of his life, saving the university from the fate of similar early Methodist institutions. In 1828 Fisk was elected bishop of the MEC in Canada, but he declined partly because of frail health and partly because he was devoted to his educational work in New England. In 1835 Wesleyan trustees sent him to Europe to rest and to study European educational institutions. While there he was elected bishop by the General Conference of 1836, but upon his return he declined the honor. The results of his trip are incorporated in his book *Travels on the Continent of Europe*. The European trip failed to strengthen his stamina. He died soon after his return, in his forty-seventh year, and was buried in the College Cemetery in Middletown.

Bibliography

A: *Address to the Members of the MEC on Temperance* (New York, 1832); *Calvinistic Controversy* (New York, 1837); *Future Rewards and Punishments* (New York, 1823); *The Science of Education* (New York, 1832); *Substance of an Address Delivered before the Middletown Colonization Society, at Their Annual Meeting, July 4, 1835* (Middletown, CT, 1835); *Travels on the Continent of Europe* (New York, 1838); editor, *Twenty Eight Sermons on Doctrinal and Practical Subjects, Contributed by Different Ministers of the MEC* (Boston, 1832).

B: *AAP* 7, 576–87; *CBTEL* 3, 581–82; *CM* 363; *DAB* 6, 415–16; *DARB* 182–83; *EWM* 1, 847–48; *HDM*; *NCAB* 3, 177; *CA* 1, 8, 15, and 29 March 1839; *ZH* 27 February, 6 and 13 March 1839; Nathan Bangs, *A Discourse on Occasion of the Death of Wilbur Fisk* (New York, 1839); Joseph Holdich, *Wilbur Fisk* (New York, 1842); David B. Potts, *Wesleyan University, 1813–1910* (New Haven, CT, 1992); George Prentice, *Wilbur Fisk* (Boston, 1889); Daniel D. Whedon, *A Tribute to the Memory of President Fisk* (New York, 1839); Douglas J. Williamson, *The Ecclesiastical Career of Wilbur Fisk: Methodist Educator, Theologian, Reformer, Controversialist* (Ph.D. diss., Boston University, 1988).

G

GARRETTSON, FREEBORN (15 August 1752, near mouth of Susquehanna River, MD–26 September 1827, New York, NY). *Education:* above average for the time; tutored by a schoolmaster; left school around 1770. *Career:* joined Baltimore Conference, 1776; preached in Maryland, Virginia, and Delaware, 1775–84; missionary, pastor in Nova Scotia, 1785–86; presiding elder, Maryland Peninsula, 1787; pastor, New York, 1788; presiding elder in district extending from Westchester, NY, to the Canadian border, 1788; presiding elder, Philadelphia District, 1793; presiding elder, pastor, New York Conference, 1794–1806; conference missionary, 1807–10; presiding elder, New York District, 1811–14; conference missionary, 1816, 1821–27 (a complete list of Garrettson's conference appointments can be found in *American Methodist Pioneer*, 411).

One of Freeborn Garrettson's biographers, Ezra S. Tipple, says that during the forty-seven years of his itinerant career Garrettson traveled 275,000 miles, almost all on horseback. Whether the number itself is accurate, following his decision to enter the ministry and become a Methodist, he was on the road most of his life. A decisive man, his first act as a Methodist was to free his slaves. He fought for the abolition of slavery for the rest of his life.

His first assignment was as an assistant to Daniel Rodda, on the Frederick circuit in Maryland. As was the custom, he stayed only six months and was assigned to the Fairfax circuit and then to Virginia. Garrettson's first preaching assignments coincided with the beginning of the American Revolution. During the war a letter written to John Wesley recounts the hardships he suffered at the hands of mobs and individuals bent on silencing him. He was threatened, beaten, and finally imprisoned. Part of this opposition was aroused by his preaching, but it was also created by his refusal to bear arms or take the oath of allegiance to the United States. Because of their ties to Wesley and England, the notion was widely held that Methodists were not loyal. The clergy sent by Wesley to

America were all gone by 1778, with the exception of Francis Asbury,* who fled to Delaware to avoid the oath.

In the decade between 1775 and 1784 Garrettson preached in Maryland, Virginia, Delaware, New Jersey, Pennsylvania, and North Carolina. During 1779, while Asbury was inactive in Delaware, Garrettson managed the connection and played a key role in mediating a dispute regarding the administration of the sacraments. And when in 1784 Thomas Coke* came from Wesley to organize American Methodists into a separate body, it was Garrettson who was sent "like an arrow, from north to south, directing him to send messengers to the right and left and to gather all the preachers together at Baltimore on Christmas Eve." He rode twelve hundred miles in six weeks, but failed to get the notice to all the brethren because of his habit of stopping along the road to preach. He was among those chosen to be ordained elder at the organizing conference. The same conference appointed him to serve as a missionary to Nova Scotia.

In spring 1787 Coke requested Garrettson's return, planning to name him, with John Wesley's approval, a superintendent for Nova Scotia and the West Indies. The conference, however, refused to approve the appointment and expressed displeasure with Wesley by removing his name from the minutes.

Garrettson went back to the familiar territory of the Delmarva Peninsula for a year and then was sent by Asbury to New York with a charge to "extend the march of the Church up the Hudson." His New York District extended from New Rochelle to Lake Champlain and west to Utica. With the exception of one year, 1793, when he was presiding elder in the Philadelphia District, he spent the rest of his career in the New York Conference, living in Rhinebeck at a place Asbury named "Traveler's Rest." This was possible in large measure because of his marriage to a remarkable woman, Catherine Livingston, who was a member of the wealthiest family in New York and generously supported his work. Robert Livingston, her eldest brother, was a member of the committee of five who framed the Declaration of Independence and administered the oath of office to George Washington when he was inaugurated as America's first president.

In the early years Asbury was Freeborn Garrettson's mentor and there was genuine affection between the two. As he did in 1779, Asbury turned to Garrettson for leadership and guidance—Garrettson was named to the Council when it was formed in 1789. But he did not always agree with Asbury and was open in his opposition. He supported the proposal offered by James O'Kelly* in 1792 that would have limited episcopal appointive power, and he advocated the election of presiding elders. Elected to the first delegated General Conference in 1812, Garrettson led the New York Conference delegation every year, with the exception of 1820, until he died.

Bibliography

A: *American Methodist Pioneer* (Rutland, VT, 1984); *A Dialogue between Do-Justice and Professing Christian . . .* (Wilmington, DE, 1810); *The Experience and Travels of Mr. Freeborn Garrettson* (Philadelphia, 1791); *Journal* (microform, Drew University Library), 1752; *A Letter to the Rev. Lyman Beecher* (New York, 1815); *Substance of a Semi-centennial Sermon before the New York Annual Conference* (New York, 1816); *Truth Vindicated* (New York, 1820).

B: *CM* 300; *DAB* 8, 166–67; *DCIA* 474; *EWM* 1, 902–3; *JLFA;* Nathan Bangs, *The Life of the Rev. Freeborn Garrettson* (New York, 1829); J. Theodore Hughes, *An Historical Sketch of the Life of Freeborn Garrettson* (Rhinebeck, NY, 1976); William C. Larrabee, *Asbury and His Coadjutors*, vol. 2 (Cincinnati, 1854); Robert Drew Simpson, "Freeborn Garrettson: American Methodist Pioneer" (Ph.D. diss., Drew University, 1954); Ezra Squire Tipple, *Freeborn Garrettson* (New York, 1910).

GEORGE, ENOCH (1767 or 1768, Lancaster County, VA–23 August 1828, Staunton, VA). *Career:* lay preacher, North Carolina, 1790–92; ordained deacon in 1792, elder in 1794; circuit preacher, North Carolina, 1795–96; presiding elder, South Carolina and Georgia, 1796–97; circuit minister, Virginia, 1797–98; circuit minister, New York, 1798–99; presiding elder, Maryland and Virginia, 1799–1801; health leave, 1801–03; presiding elder, Maryland and Virginia, 1803–16; bishop, MEC, 1816–28.

Enoch George's father was a planter and a staunch Anglican who took his family regularly to the parish church at Bath. The rector, the Rev. Devereux Jarratt, was an Anglican sympathetic to the Methodists in Virginia. When the family moved to North Carolina, finding the Episcopal rector unfriendly, they began to attend a Methodist chapel. About age twenty Enoch experienced a religious conversion and eventually felt called to the Methodist ministry. After a period as a lay preacher, George was admitted on probation into the Methodist Conference in 1790 and appointed by Bishop Asbury* to form a new circuit on the headwaters of the Catawba River in North Carolina. The difficulties were so great that the young preacher asked the bishop for another appointment. Asbury refused, but George persevered and even succeeded.

After only six years as a circuit minister in North Carolina, George was appointed by Bishop Asbury to be presiding elder of a mission district in South Carolina and Georgia. Asbury continued to reappoint him to churches or districts in the Baltimore–Washington area. George was one of two new bishops elected in 1816 upon the death of Asbury and the declining health of McKendree.* Bishop George headed north to hold conferences in New England and New York, taking time to attend quarterly or camp meetings along the way whenever he could. For three quadrennia George kept up a busy pace of preaching and holding conferences from Canada to Georgia. Following the 1828 General Conference in New York City, George headed south to begin presiding at the southern conferences. He died on the way in Staunton, Virginia, and is buried in Mount Olivet Cemetery in Baltimore. Bishop McKendree preached a memorial sermon at the next General Conference in 1832.

Bibliography

B: *AAP* 7, 186–95; *CBTEL* 3, 809–10; *CM* 404–5; *EWM* 1, 989; *HDM*; *LMB* 149–64; *NCAB* 5, 527; "Memoir of the Late Rev. Bishop George," *MQR* 12/1–4 (January-October 1830): 5–16, 128–42, 248–59, 412–35; Benjamin St. James Fry, *The Life of Rev. Enoch George* (New York, 1852); William C. Larrabee, *Asbury and His Coadjutors* (New York, 1853).

H

HAMLINE, LEONIDAS LENT (10 May 1797, Burlington, CT–23 March 1865, Mt. Pleasant, IA). *Education*: Andover Academy, later admitted to the bar. *Career*: taught school, practiced law in Ohio, 1825–29; licensed to preach, early pastorates, 1829–32; admitted to the Ohio Conference, appointed to the Granville circuit, 1832; Athens circuit, 1833; ordained deacon in 1834, elder in 1836; pastor, Wesley Chapel, Cincinnati, 1834–36; assistant editor, *Western Christian Advocate*, with Charles Elliott, editor, 1836–40; founder and editor, *Ladies Repository*, 1840–44; bishop, MEC, 1844–52 (first person to resign from the office).

Leonidas Lent Hamline is best remembered for the role he played in the General Conference of 1844 in which his speech on the floor argued definitively the northern position that Methodist episcopacy is an office rather than an order. Jesse Peck, who was present, remembered, "The last sentence was finished; the speaker quietly resumed his seat; a thousand people drew a long breath; and the great issue was logically settled." Southern delegates, however, did not find it so persuasive. After his election to the episcopacy, Hamline's failing health gave the opportunity to illustrate his conviction about the nature of episcopacy, and he became the first active bishop in the denomination to resign. Hamline's New York speech was timely and formative, since the 1844 discussion was focused on a bishop and illuminated the conflicting views of the nature of the office held in the northern and southern branches of Methodism. Like several others elected to the episcopacy, he had practiced law, and skills learned there served him well. Charles Elliott* said of him: "As a debater . . . he had no superior for logic, argument, or oratory." Having inherited money from his first wife, Hamline donated $25,000 in 1854 to establish the university in Minnesota that bears his name. He gave an equal amount to create the Mount Vernon Institute in Iowa.

He was born in New England but spent the bulk of his ministerial career in the West. Significant portions of this ministry were in assignments with the church press, the *Western Christian Advocate* and the monthly *Ladies Repository*, to which he gave form and character in its earliest years. The first issue appeared in January 1841. He was editor of the *Ladies Repository* when elected to the episcopacy in 1844. At the same time there was a movement to make Hamline editor of the *Christian Advocate* in New York.

There is little doubt that his speech on the conference floor influenced his election—he was elected eleven days afterward, and indication in his own correspondence is that he did not seek the office. Troubled with heart disease, Hamline was advised by his physicians "that you cannot with any degree of safety go to conference as a member." He was ill when he reached the conference, but with the assistance of his host, Dr. Palmer, he improved and was able to function. He ignored the advice of his doctors and continued to be plagued with failing health. He found himself unable to preach or preside in his assigned conference. For over a year he did not preach at all. His physicians continued to urge him to take an extended period abroad in hopes of some improvement, but he could not go. This led to his decision to resign in 1852 and caused the church, once again, to review its understanding of episcopacy. Hamline firmly believed that the powers of episcopacy were entirely derived from the body of preachers, and if they could be given, they could also be laid aside.

Hamline's remaining years were troubled with the increasing ravages of his disease, and much of the time he was confined to his home. The final few years of his life were spent in Mount Pleasant, Iowa.

Bibliography

A: *Address Delivered in Zanesville, Ohio . . . on the 5th July, 1830* (Zanesville, 1830); *Works of Rev. Leonidas L. Hamline,* 2 vols. (Cincinnati, 1869–71).

B: *CM* 424–25; *DAB* 8, 198–99; *EWM* 1, 1063; *LMB* 289–306; *MB* 82–83; F. G. Hibbard, *Biography of Rev. Leonidas L. Hamline* (Cincinnati, 1880); Walter Clark Palmer, *Life and Letters of Leonidas L. Hamline* (New York, 1866).

HAVEN, GILBERT (19 September 1821, Malden, MA–3 January 1880, Malden, MA). *Education*: Wesleyan Academy, Wilbraham, MA, 1840–42; B.A., Wesleyan University, 1846. *Career*: school teacher, headmaster, Amenia Seminary, Amenia, NY, 1846–51; minister, New England Conference, 1851–61; chaplain, U.S. army, 1861–62; on leave in Europe, 1862–63; pastor, Boston, 1863–67; editor, *ZH*, 1867–72; bishop, MEC, 1872–76, assigned to Atlanta and Liberia areas.

From his conversion to Methodism in 1839 while a student at Wesleyan Academy in Wilbraham, Massachusetts, until his death as a bishop of the church, Gilbert Haven struggled to articulate the social consequences of his religious beliefs. As an undergraduate at Wesleyan, Haven chose to teach Sunday school in a black Methodist church in Middletown. Following graduation he taught and later headed a Methodist boarding school in upstate New York. Passage of the Fugitive Slave Law in 1850 potentially implicated the entire nation in the moral contradiction of slavery to American democracy. Only a minority decried this act as intolerable. One of these fearless folk was Gilbert Haven, a churchman who understood as did few white persons in his era the hypocrisy of racism. As an outgrowth of this revulsion, Haven delivered his famous "higher law" sermon, which marked the beginning of his career as a Methodist preacher and an antislavery reformer.

Haven entered the Methodist ministry through the New England Conference in 1851 and pastored several churches in his home state. When President Lincoln issued his first call for troops in the Civil War, Gilbert Haven volunteered as a chaplain. In the years after the war, first as editor of *Zion's Herald* (a name that fits him to a "T"), New England Methodism's influential weekly newspaper, Haven attracted national attention by his firm expression of the belief that if all persons were equal before God, they could not be unequal in society or politics. He was a powerful ally of Charles Sumner and the radical Republicans. Within his church this led him to oppose the tendency to separate churches and conferences on racial lines, a struggle he lost. Haven also championed prohibition, women's suffrage, and lay representation in Methodist conferences.

Bishop Haven's radical egalitarian views shocked his contemporaries. Even though his supporters managed to get enough votes to elect him bishop in 1872, no conference wanted his leadership. Ironically, yet providentially, he was sent to the mission conferences established by the northern Methodists in the south for blacks. Haven's home was in Atlanta, and his people were entirely black. Socially ostracized and threatened with violence because he practiced the racial equality he preached, he energetically pressed the freedmen's cause, gave his own money and solicited gifts to found schools and colleges for them, and enlisted northern college graduates to come South to teach the former slaves and their children.

Haven assisted William Butler in planting Methodism in Mexico in 1873. Reassigned to Liberia in 1876, he contracted malaria, from which he never fully recovered. Haven returned to Boston in 1879 and died early the next year, like Moses, viewing the Promised Land from afar.

Bibliography

A: *An Appeal to Our People for Our People* (New York, 1875); *Christus Consolator; or, Comfortable Words for Burdened Hearts* (New York, 1893); *Father Taylor: The Sailor Preacher* (Boston, 1871); *Lay Representation in the MEC* (Boston, 1864); *The Mission of America* (Boston, 1863); *National Sermons* (Boston, 1869; reprinted New York, 1969); *Our Next-Door Neighbor: A Winter in Mexico* (New York, 1875); *The Pilgrim's Wallet; or, Scraps of Travel Gathered in England, France, and Germany* (New York, 1866); *Te Deum Laudamus: The Cause and Consequence of the Election of Abraham Lincoln* (Boston, 1860); *The Uniter and Liberator of America: A Memorial Discourse on the Character and Career of Abraham Lincoln* (Boston, 1865).
B: *CBTEL* Supp. 2, 526; *CM* 1094; *DAB* 8, 407–8; *DARB* 228–29; *HDM*; *LMB* 483–98; *NCAB* 13, 261; *CA* 8 January 1880; *NYT* 4 January 1880, 1:5; *ZH* 8 January 1880;

William H. Daniels, *Memorials of Gilbert Haven* (Boston, 1880); William B. Gravely, *Gilbert Haven: Methodist Abolitionist* (Nashville, 1973); George Prentice, *Life of Gilbert Haven* (New York, 1883).

HAYGOOD, ATTICUS GREEN (19 November 1839, Watkinsville, Clarke County, Georgia–19 January 1896, Oxford, Georgia). *Education:* educated at home by his mother; entered Emory College as a sophomore; graduated, 1859. *Career:* Licensed to preach, MECS, 1858; joined Georgia Annual Conference, 1859, and was assigned to assist Lovick Pierce in Columbus, Georgia; ordained, 1863; pastor, Sparta, GA, 1860–61; chaplain, Army of the Confederacy, 1861, 1864; pastor, Watkinsville, Rome-Dalton, Atlanta, 1862–66 with time out for military service; presiding elder, Rome District, Atlanta District, 1867–70; Sunday school secretary, 1870–74; president, Emory College, 1875–84 (1878–82, also edited *Wesleyan Christian Advocate*); agent, John F. Slater Fund, established to aid the education of blacks, 1884–90 (1882 elected bishop, but declined to be ordained); 1890, elected bishop in the MECS, moved to California, and served there until 1893.

Bishop, outstanding educator and editor, pioneer in race relations, Atticus Green Haygood was born in Georgia, where, after admission to the Georgia Conference, he served in pastorates until 1870, when he was elected Sunday School Secretary and first editor of Sunday school publications in Nashville. There he created a scheme of uniform lessons, lesson helps, and "illustrative readings." The circulation of *Sunday School Visitor* was increased and the *Sunday School Magazine* and *Our Little People* created. With the help of R. M. McIntosh, he brought out books of music for use in Sunday schools. Because of problems with his wife's health, Haygood resigned his position in 1874 to return to Georgia.

He was elected the eighth president of Emory College in 1875 and continued in that office until 1884. During most of the time he also edited the *Wesleyan Christian Advocate*. Editorials written for the *Wesleyan* formed the basis for a later book, *Our Brother in Black* (1881). Few persons in southern Methodism wrote more widely than Haygood. Throughout his career he was concerned for the education and improvement of the Negro, a position that brought him opposition in many quarters of the South.

His years at Emory brought the college out of debt, doubled its enrollment, and increased the endowment. Old "Sime," as he was known to the students, was an ever present source of help and encouragement. Haygood was elected to the episcopacy at the 1882 General Conference of the MECS but declined to be ordained. He was concerned for the well-being of students who were dependent upon him and wrote the conference that he could not, "with a good conscience lay down the work which I now have in hand."

When the John F. Slater Fund was created to support the education of blacks, Haygood was sought to be its agent. The story is told that Slater agreed to pay off the debt of Emory College if he would accept the position. He served in this role until 1890, when he was once again elected to the episcopacy. This time he accepted ordination. A tragic figure, as well as a gifted and talented man, Haygood was an alcoholic who died in the fifty-sixth year of his life.

Bibliography

A: (selected) *The Case for the Negro* (Nashville, 1874); *Go or Send: A Plea for Missions* (Nashville, 1874); *Jack Knife and Brambles* (Nashville, 1893); *The Man of Galilee* (New York, 1889); *The Monk and the Prince* (Atlanta, 1895); *The New South* (Oxford, GA, 1880); *Our Brother in Black* (New York, 1881); *Our Children* (New York, 1876); *Pleas for Progress* (Nashville, 1889); *Sermons and Speeches* (Nashville, 1883).

B: *CA* 23 January 1896; *CM* 436–37; *DAB* 8, 452–53; *DCIA* 514–15; *ERS*, 319; *EWM* 1, 1100; *MB* 89; Elam Franklin Dempsey, *Atticus Green Haygood* (1940); John E. Fisher, *The John F. Slater Fund* (Lanham, MD, 1986); Harold W. Mann, *Atticus G. Haygood, Methodist Bishop, Editor, and Educator* (Athens, GA, 1965); George B. Winton, *Sketch of Bishop Atticus G. Haygood* (1915).

HEDDING, ELIJAH (7 June 1780, Pine Plains, NY–9 April 1852, Poughkeepsie, NY). *Education:* rural schools, self-educated. *Career:* joined New York Conference, 1801; deacon by Bishop Whatcoat,* 1803, ordained elder by Bishop Asbury,* 1805; various pastoral appointments, New York and New England, 1801–07; presiding elder, New Hampshire District, 1807–08; presiding elder, New London District, 1809–10; pastor in Boston, Lynn Common, and Nantucket and presiding elder in Portland and Boston Districts, 1811–24; bishop, MEC, 1824–52.

Hedding was born in New York but grew up in Vermont. In 1799, having received an exhorter's license, he was called to follow Lorenzo Dow, who had left for Ireland. A year later he was assigned to the Cambridge circuit to fill in for a preacher who became ill, and in 1801 he joined the New York Annual Conference. By 1805 the boundary lines of the conferences had been redrawn and Hedding became a member of the New England Conference, serving in New Hampshire and Vermont. At various times illness forced him to curtail his work. In 1824 he was elected a bishop in the MEC.

The bulk of Hedding's work was in the northern conferences due to a decision by the Board of Bishops in 1826 to send Bishops Soule* and Roberts* to the South and the West while Bishops George* and Hedding worked in the North and East. From this time until his death, Bishop William McKendree* was the only bishop who itinerated throughout the connection. Bishop Hedding's personal sympathies were antislavery, but the rule of General Conference forced him to restrict the abolitionist activities in his northern conferences and brought him great personal discomfort. Charges were filed against him in General Conference, and he was forced to move his residence from Lynn to Lansingburg, New York, in 1837 because of the pressures. Tobias Spicer said of him, "What he believed firmly to be his duty, that he would do, irrespective of consequences."

At the General Conference of 1848 his age and health caused the Committee on Episcopacy to permit him to use his discretion as to the amount of work he might be able to undertake. Although he continued on the active list until his death, his health greatly restricted his labors after that time.

Bibliography

A: *Discourse on the Administration of Discipline* (New York, 1842); *An Address on Duties of the President of an Annual Conference* (Oneida, NY, 1837).
B: *AAP* 7, 354–62; *CM* 440–41; *DAB* 8, 497–98; *EWM* 1, 1104–05; *LMB* 189–200; *MB* 90–91; D. W. Clark, *Life and Times of Rev. Elijah Hedding* (New York, 1855).

J

JANES, EDMUND STORER (27 April 1807, Sheffield, MA–18 September 1876, NY). *Education:* rural schools, taught school, read law for a brief period and then medicine; M.D., Vermont University. *Career:* admitted to the Philadelphia Conference, 1830; Elizabeth, NJ, 1830–31; ordained deacon, 1832, and sent to Orange, NJ, 1832–33; ordained elder and appointed agent for Dickinson College, 1834–36; Fifth Street Church, Philadelphia, studied medicine, 1836–37; Nazareth, 1837–39; Mulberry Street, New York, 1839–40; financial secretary, American Bible Society, 1840–44; bishop, MEC, 1844–76.

Edmund Storer Janes was born in the Berkshires and grew up in Salisbury, Connecticut. He began teaching school in upstate New York when he was seventeen and continued for about five years. At the same time he began the study of law. In about 1829 he moved to New Jersey to continue his teaching career. This career, however, was interrupted the following year when he was admitted to the Philadelphia Annual Conference. In 1830 that conference encompassed eastern Pennsylvania, the Delmarva Peninsula, Delaware, the eastern shore of Virginia and Maryland, and the entire state of New Jersey. His first appointment was to Elizabeth, New Jersey, with Thomas Morrell. In time he served various congregations in New Jersey, Pennsylvania, and New York. He also raised money as agent for Dickinson College, Pennsylvania.

The Methodists merged their Bible Society in 1836 with the American Bible Society, which in 1840 selected Janes to be secretary. These duties took him into the South and increased his visibility in the church. At the last General Conference of the united church in 1844, Janes and Leonidas Hamline* were elected to the episcopacy. He was the southern candidate—a northerner acceptable in the South—and was presented to the conference for ordination by William Capers* of South Carolina and Lovick Pierce of Georgia. Janes had the distinction of being the first person ever elected a bishop who was not a General Conference member and was not present when elected. At age thirty-seven, he also remains one of the youngest persons ever elected. Before his death episcopal travels would take him into every state except Florida. However, he was not able to maintain his cordial relations in the South because of the agitation over slavery leading up to the Civil War. His attempt to convene the Arkansas Conference in Bonham, Texas, in 1859 was interrupted by a mob; but it was Janes, the last surviving bishop elected by the united church, who at the General Conference of 1876 had the honor to present the fraternal delegates from the MECS and to see action taken to reunite the denomination at the Cape May Conference.

Bibliography

A: *Address to Class Leaders* (New York, 1862); *The Opportunity of Doing Good to All Men* (Philadelphia, 1837); *Sermon on the Death of Nathan Bangs* (New York, 1862); *Memorial of Philip Embury: The First Methodist Minister in the New World* (New York, 1888).

B: *CM* 493–94; *EWM* 2, 1256–57; *LMB* 309–24; *MB* 100–103; Charles Henry Fowler, *Memorial Discourse on Rev. E. S. Janes* (New York, 1876); Henry Bascom Ridgaway, *The Life of Edmund S. Janes* (New York, 1882).

JONES, MARY ALICE (23 June 1898, Dallas, TX–23 September 1980, Nashville, TN). *Education*: B.A., University of Texas, 1918; M.A., Northwestern University, 1923; Ph.D., Yale University, 1934. *Career*: editor of children's publications, MECS, 1923–27; director of children's work, International Council of Religious Education, 1929–45; children's book editor, Rand McNally & Co., 1945–51; director, Christian education for children, General Board of Education, Methodist Church, 1951–63.

As a high school student in Dallas, Mary Alice Jones studied *The Pupil and the Teacher* by Luther A. Weigle and entered at once what proved to be her life vocation in the Christian nurture of children. While a graduate student under Weigle at Yale a decade later, she became director of children's work for the International Council of Religious Education, a post she held for sixteen years.

A keen student of child psychology, Jones knew how to present difficult subjects of God, Jesus, and the Bible so they had a vital meaning to children, based on their own interest and experience. She wrote more than thirty books but is best known for her *Tell Me* series published by Rand McNally. The series deal with God, Jesus, the Bible, prayer, and heaven. The publication of *Tell Me about God* in 1943 received instant popularity among children and parents and paved the way for the series. It was translated into many languages and by the mid-1960s over twenty million copies had been sold. Her last contribution to the Methodist church school curriculum was published in 1978. Her books for adults included *The Faith of Our Children, Guiding Children in Christian Growth*, and *The Church and the Children*.

Jones taught numerous seminars and summer schools for pastors and Sunday school teachers across the church. She held visiting professorships at several theological seminaries, including Garrett Biblical Institute, Iliff School of Theology, Pacific School of Religion, Union Theological Seminary (NYC), and Yale Divinity School. She was a frequent lecturer on college and university campuses, including McMurray and Scarritt Colleges and Duke, Emory, and Southern Methodist Universities, the University of Texas, and the University of Colorado.

Internationally known expert on the religious education of children, Jones was active in several education organizations, including conferences and committees of the National Council of Churches (USA), the Religious Education Association, the White House Conference on Children and Youth (1950), and the White House Conference on Education (1955). In the early 1960s she ably represented the Methodist Church on the interdenominational Cooperative Curriculum Project.

Jones retired with honors from the Nashville-based General Board of Education staff in 1963 and lived in a Methodist retirement community in Nashville until her death.

Bibliography

A: *Bible Stories* (Nashville, 1954); *The Christian Faith Speaks to Children* (New York, 1965); *The Church and Children* (Nashville, 1935); *The Faith of Our Children* (New York, 1943); *God Is Good* (New York, 1962); *God Speaks to Me* (New York, 1961); *God's Church Is Everywhere* (New York, 1965); *Guiding Children in Christian Growth* (New York, 1947); *His Name Was Jesus* (Nashville, 1950); *Let the Bible Speak to Children* (Nashville, 1953); *The Lord's Prayer* (New York, 1964); *Membership Manual of the Methodist Church for Boys and Girls* (New York, 1951); *My First Book about Jesus* (New York, 1953); *The Pastor and Christian Education of Children* (Nashville, 1963); *Robert and the Rainbow and Other Stories* (Nashville, 1926); *Stories of the Christ Child* (New York, 1964); *Tell Me about Christmas* (New York, 1956); *Tell Me about God* (New York, 1943); *Tell Me about Heaven* (New York, 1956); *Tell Me about Jesus* (New York, 1944); *Tell Me about Prayer* (New York, 1947); *Tell Me about the Bible* (New York, 1945); *The Ten Commandments for Children* (New York, 1964); *Training Juniors in Worship* (Nashville, 1925); *Winter Is Coming and Other Stories* (Nashville, 1925).
B: *Christian Century* 22 October 1980, 1001; *Contemporary Authors* 118 (1986): 247; *EWM* 1, 1277–78; *Tennessean* (Nashville) 24 September and 14 October 1980; *Who's Who of American Women*, 1st ed., 1958–59; *Yearbook of the Board of Education, The Methodist Church*, 1964.

JONES, ROBERT ELIJAH (19 February 1872, Greensboro, NC–18 May 1960, New Orleans, LA). *Education*: A.B., Bennett College, 1895; A.M., Bennett College, 1898; B.D., Gammon Seminary, 1897. *Career*: joined North Carolina Conference, 1891; ordained, 1893; served pastorates in North Carolina while a student; assistant manager, *Southeastern Christian Advocate,* 1897–1901; field secretary, Sunday School Board, 1901–04; editor, *Southwestern Christian Advocate,* 1904–20; bishop, MEC, 1920–44.

Robert Elijah Jones and Matthew Clair, Sr.,* were the first two African-Americans to be elected bishops by the MEC for service in the United States.

Although itinerant general superintendents, neither was ever assigned to a white area. That was not done until 1964 when Bishop James S. Thomas was assigned to the Iowa Area of the United Methodist Church (UMC).

Bishop Jones was born in North Carolina and lived much of his life in New Orleans, where the *Southwestern Christian Advocate* was published. His only service as a pastor in a local church was during his student years in North Carolina. He was active in civic affairs in New Orleans, serving as president of the black YMCA and trustee of New Orleans University. He was also a member of the board of trustees at Bennett College and Gammon Seminary in Atlanta.

Jones was also the founder and president of the Gulfside Association in Waveland, Mississippi. He served on every commission on unification in the MEC and was a delegate to five General Conferences, 1904–20.

Bibliography

A: *Southwestern Christian Advocate*, 1904–20.

B: *EAAR* 411–12; *EWM* 2, 1279; *MB* 104; Henry N. Oakes, Jr., *The Struggle for Racial Equality in the Methodist Episcopal Church: The Career of Robert E. Jones, 1904–1944* (Ph.D. diss., University of Iowa, 1973).

K

KIDDER, DANIEL PARISH (18 October 1815, South Pembroke, NY–29 July 1891, Evanston, IL). *Education*: Genesee Wesleyan Academy, Lima, NY, 1832–33; Hamilton College, Schenectady, NY, 1833–34; B.A., Wesleyan University, 1836; M.A., 1839. *Career*: school teacher, Genesee County, NY, 1829–31; instructor of languages and mathematics at Amenia Seminary, Amenia, NY; and pastor, Rochester, NY, 1833–37; ordained deacon, 1836, and elder, 1837, in the Genesee Conference; missionary to Brazil, 1837–40; pastorates in Paterson and Trenton, NJ, 1840–44; secretary of the Sunday School Union of the MEC, 1844–56; professor of practical theology, Garrett Biblical Institute, Evanston, IL, 1856–71; professor of practical theology, Drew Theological Seminary, Madison, NJ, 1871–81; secretary, MEC Board of Education, 1880–87.

Although Daniel Kidder was born in rural upstate New York in 1815, he was raised in an uncle's family in Vermont. After attending country academies in Vermont, at age fourteen he began to earn his living by teaching school. While teaching he attended Genesee Wesleyan Seminary at Lima, New York. Although his father was opposed to the Methodists, Daniel Kidder was converted at the Methodist school and decided to prepare himself for the ministry. He began his training at Hamilton College in 1833 as a sophomore but quickly transferred to Wesleyan University in Middletown, Connecticut, where he graduated in 1836. That year he began to teach at Amenia Seminary in Amenia, New York, and began to preach at a church in nearby Rochester. He joined the Genessee Conference the next year, wishing for an overseas missionary assignment. The Missionary Society accepted him for a new mission in Brazil. From Rio de Janeiro he traveled extensively, distributing the Scriptures and tracts in Portuguese and preaching wherever a Protestant could.

In 1840, upon the death of his wife, Kidder returned to the United States. Joining the New Jersey Conference he served churches in Paterson and Trenton. In 1844, when he was barely twenty-eight years old, his denomination elected him secretary of the Sunday School Union and editor of its Sunday school publications. He gave himself with enthusiasm to the work, then quite unorganized. He drafted a new set of catechisms for the church, provided a new Sunday school hymnal, developed a system of raising funds to promote and expand Sunday schools, and systematized the method of gathering the statistics. He organized auxiliary Sunday school unions in all the conferences and planned Sunday school teacher-training conventions and institutes. As editor he upgraded the *Sunday School Advocate* and supervised the publication of hundreds of publications for Sunday school libraries. Substantial profits from Sunday school publishing fattened the publishing house coffers and funded clergy pensions.

After twelve years in the office, in 1856 he entered theological education, first at the church's new theological school (Garrett Biblical Institute) in Evanston, Illinois and later at Drew Theological Seminary in Madison, New Jersey. His textbooks on homiletics (1864) and pastoral theology (1871) became standard in Methodist seminaries for a generation. In 1880 he was elected secretary of the church's Board of Education, where he monitored the church's growing family of colleges, universities, and seminaries until his health failed in 1887. He retired to Evanston, Illinois, where he died four years later.

Bibliography

A: *Annual Reports of the Sunday School Union of the Methodist Episcopal Church* (New York, 1845–56); *Brazil and the Brazilians* (Philadelphia, 1857); *Catechisms of the MEC, No. 1–3* (New York, 1852); *The Christian Pastorate* (New York, 1871); *Demonstration of the Necessity of Abolishing Constrained Clerical Celibacy*, trans. from the Portuguese of Diego Antonio Feijo (Philadelphia, 1844); *Descriptive Catalog of the Sunday School Publications and Tracts of the MEC* (New York, 1850); *Helps to Prayer* (New York, 1874); *Manual of the Sunday School Union for Ministers* (New York, 1855); *Ministerial Education and Training in the MEC* (Andover, MA, 1876); *Mormons and Mormonism* (New York, 1842); *My Little Book* (New York, 1850); *Responsibilities of the Christian Ministry* (Ann Arbor, MI, 1867); *Senior Classes in Sunday Schools* (New York, 1851); *Sketches of Residence and Travels in Brazil* (Philadelphia, 1845); *A Treatise on Homiletics* (New York, 1864; rev. ed., 1868).

B: *CM* 513–14; *DAB* 10, 369–70; *EWM* 1, 1331–32; *HDM*; *NCAB* 11, 144; *CA* 6 August 1891; *Chicago Tribune* 30 July 1891; *Sunday-School Journal* n.s. 2/4 (January 1870): 74–75; *Alumni Record of Wesleyan University, 1833–1899* (Middletown, CT, 1899), 593–96; *Teachers of Drew* (Madison, NJ, 1942), 81–84; George E. Strobridge, *Biography of the Rev. Daniel Parish Kidder* (New York, 1894).

L

LEE, JESSE (12 March 1758, Prince George County, VA–12 September 1816, Annapolis, MD). *Education:* no formal education. *Career:* served briefly in the Continental Army, 1780; admitted to the Virginia Conference, 1873; preaching, Virginia, North Carolina, and Maryland, 1773–89; missionary, preacher, and presiding elder, established Methodism in New England, 1789–97; assistant to Francis Asbury,* 1797–1800; New York, 1800–1801; Virginia, 1801–15; chaplain, House of Representatives, 1809–13; chaplain, Senate, 1814; Baltimore Conference, 1815–16.

The first historian of Methodism and founder of the denomination in New England, Jesse Lee was considered second only to Francis Asbury* in his influence. Lee was born near Petersburg, Virginia, and grew up there on a farm. His early education was limited to a singing school. Converted under the preaching of the Anglican evangelical Devereaux Jarrett, Lee joined a Methodist society in 1774 and preached his first sermon five years later. Lee continued as a local preacher until he was drafted to serve in the Continental Army in 1780. There he refused to bear arms, continued to preach, was eventually assigned to a baggage wagon, made sergeant of pioneers, and was honorably discharged after three months' service.

Urged to preach, Lee finally joined the Virginia Conference in 1783, served there for six years, but refused ordination until 1790, when he was ordained deacon in private by Asbury and elder publicly the next day. Following the Christmas Conference in 1784 (which Lee did not attend), he went with Bishop Asbury into South Carolina. It marked the beginning of a close and enduring relationship. While on this tour Lee met a man from New England and conceived the idea of going there to serve. It took several years to persuade Asbury to appoint him, but in 1789 he went to the Stamford Circuit in Connecticut. Once there he commenced extensive travel and preaching in Rhode Island, Massachusetts, Vermont, and New Hampshire. He paid his first visit to Boston in

1790. He eventually built the first Methodist church in the city. His efforts were so successful throughout New England that in time helpers were sent to assist him in his work. For years he filled the office of presiding elder.

In 1797 he was, once again, called to assist Asbury, who was in poor health. In this role he did all the work of a bishop except for ordinations. One of the mysteries of early Methodist politics is why Lee was not elected a bishop at the General Conference of 1800. He and Richard Whatcoat* were the only candidates. They were tied on the second ballot, and Whatcoat elected by four votes on the third. Various explanations have been offered—he was not considered dignified enough for the office; Asbury opposed his election (a charge Asbury denied on the floor of the conference); he was too independent and aggressive to be trusted. It may, in fact, have been because of his close association with Asbury that his election was seen as an unwanted enhancement of his already powerful position. Following the election Lee was named by Asbury and Whatcoat as assistant at the annual conferences, but he declined and returned to a circuit in New York. He remained there until 1801, when he returned to Virginia, serving as presiding elder in its South District and in other influential posts for the next fourteen years.

Lee's *Short History of the Methodists* was published in 1810. Because the conference refused to underwrite its publication, Lee did it with private contributions. Asbury said of it, "It is better than I expected." Throughout his life he was forthright, visionary, and progressive. As a young preacher in North Carolina, he differed publicly with Thomas Coke* on the denomination's position with regard to slaveholders, opposed Asbury's creation of a council, and gave his reasons in a letter sent to its first meeting. In 1792 he presented Asbury with a plan for a delegated general conference.

Bibliography

A: *Memoir of the Rev. Jesse Lee,* ed. Minton Thrift (New York, 1823); *A Short Account of the Life and Death of the Rev. Jesse Lee* (Baltimore, 1805); *A Short History of the Methodists* (Baltimore, 1810).

B: *AAP* 7, 80–86; *DAB* 11, 112–14; *DCIA* 640; *CM* 535, *JLFA*; *EWM* 2, 1408–9; William Larkin Duren, *The Top Sergeant of the Pioneers* (Atlanta, 1930); William C. Larrabee, *Asbury and His Coadjutors,* vol. 2 (Cincinnati, 1854); Leroy M. Lee, *The Life and Times of the Rev. Jesse Lee* (Richmond, 1848); William Henry Meredith, *Jesse Lee: A Methodist Apostle* (New York, 1909), Geo. A. Phoebus, *Beams of Light on Early Methodism in America* (1887); standard histories of Methodism, e.g., Nathan Bangs* and Abel Stevens.

M

MCCABE, CHARLES CARDWELL (11 October 1836, Athens, OH–19 December 1906, New York, NY). *Education*: Ohio Wesleyan University, 1854–58. *Career*: high school principal, Ironton, OH, 1858–60; lay preacher, Zanesville, OH, 1860–61; ordained deacon in 1862 and elder in 1864, Ohio Conference; chaplain, U.S. army, 1862–64; agent, U.S. Christian Commission, 1864–65; pastorates in Ohio and agent of Ohio Wesleyan University, 1864–68; assistant corresponding secretary, Board of Church Extension, MEC, 1868–84; corresponding secretary of the MEC Missionary Society, 1884–96; bishop, MEC, 1896–1906; chancellor of American University, Washington, DC, 1902–06.

Charles McCabe's parents were devout Methodists in Athens, Ohio. There he experienced his earliest spiritual impressions during quarterly revival meetings. When he was about fifteen, the family moved to Chilicothe and then to Burlington, Iowa. For a short time he took charge of a farm in Mount Pleasant and then became clerk in a store in Cedar Rapids. He early displayed characteristics that later gave him popularity and power—personal magnetism, bold initiative, glowing optimism, good humor, ability as a speaker, and a rich baritone voice he could use in song with great effect. Since he was evangelically religious, people were sure he was called to the ministry. To prepare himself in 1854 he enrolled in Ohio Wesleyan University in Delaware, Ohio, where his prayers, testimony, and singing won him the love and admiration of faculty and students. He had an enquiring mind, but he was not a diligent student. For days, even weeks, he would be away from college assisting in a revival. Although he never graduated, the college later made him an alumnus of the class of 1860.

After two years as a high school principal McCabe joined the Ohio Conference in 1860 and became pastor in Zanesville. By nature and training an abolitionist, McCabe addressed meetings and inspired thousands to volunteer for the Union Army. Largely through his influence the 122d Regiment of Ohio Volunteer Infantry was raised and he was appointed chaplain. He accompanied his regiment to war in 1862. At the battle of Winchester, Virginia, the next year he was captured and sent to Libby Prison in Richmond. For four months his optimism and song made him the hero of Libby Prison. On his release he joined his regiment but was pressed into the service of the Christian Commission, the remarkable YMCA affiliate that acted as a sort of Salvation Army–USO–Red Cross during the Civil War, on whose behalf he raised large collections. His singing did much to popularize the "Battle Hymn of the Republic."

So great was his ability to persuade people to give that it destined him to be a fund-raiser and promoter for much of the remainder of his ministry. After the war McCabe returned to a pastorate at Portsmouth, Ohio, raised money for Ohio Wesleyan, and in 1868 was tapped to assist the head of the church's Board of Church Extension in Philadelphia. He threw himself into the work of writing, traveling, and preaching and raised considerable sums for building new churches across the land, especially in the West. Once, on a train during a fund-raising tour, McCabe read the famous infidel Robert G. Ingersoll's declaration, "The churches are dying out all over the land!" At the next stop McCabe fired off a telegram: "All hail the power of Jesus' name! We are building more than one Methodist church for every day in the year and propose to make it two a day!" "We're Building Two a Day" became a powerful rallying cry and the title of a hymn (1882) that McCabe sang from coast to coast. His *Winnowed Hymns* (1873) had immense circulation.

In 1884, General Conference elected him chief executive of the Missionary Society, headquartered in New York. At once he sounded a slogan "A Million for Missions." The goal reached in one year, a new one was set. Perhaps the most popular of American Methodists, in 1896 he was elected bishop, resided in Philadelphia, and traveled for a time supervising Methodist work in Latin America. Conferences over which McCabe presided took on the air of a revival or songfest. In December 1902 McCabe added to his episcopal chores the chancellorship of American University, Methodism's graduate university in Washington, D.C. Strenuously active to the close his career, he died in New York soon after completing his seventieth year and was buried in Rose Hill Cemetery near Chicago.

Bibliography

A: *The Grand Review: Progress of the Churches for Four Years* (New York, 1887); *Winnowed Hymns: A Collection of Sacred Songs Especially Adapted for Revivals, Prayer, and Camp Meetings*, with D. T. MacFarlan (New York and Chicago, 1873).
B: *CM* 571–72; *DAB* 11, 557–58; *DARB* 321–22; *EWM* 2, 1476–77; *NCAB* 13, 76; *RLA* 301; *CA* 27 December 1906; *NYT* 20 December 1906, 3:4; *Philadelphia Inquirer* 20 December 1906; *ZH* 26 December 1906; Frank M. Bristol, *The Life of Chaplain McCabe* (New York, 1908).

M'CAINE, ALEXANDER (1768?, Tipperary, Ireland–1 June 1856, Augusta, GA). *Career*: admitted on trial to Methodist ministry, 1797; ordained deacon in

1799, elder in 1801; appointed to circuits Broad River, GA, 1797; Washington, GA, 1798; Norfolk, VA, 1799; Huntingdon, VA, 1800; Fell's Point, Baltimore, 1801; Richmond, VA, 1802; and Greensville, VA, 1803; presiding elder, Salisbury District, 1804; Baltimore City, 1805; school teacher, 1806–18; reentered the Methodist ministry, appointed to Trenton, NJ, 1818; Brooklyn, NY, 1819–20; headmaster of a boys school in Baltimore, 1821–183?.

Alexander M'Caine was born and raised in Ireland but educated in England, where he received a classical education and prepared for the Anglican priesthood. When twenty, M'Caine moved to the United States, settling in Charleston, South Carolina. Under the preaching of a Methodist missionary, William Hammett, he was converted and determined to enter the Methodist ministry. Impressed with his training and zeal for ministry, Bishop Asbury* admitted him on trial to the Methodist Conference at a meeting in Charleston in 1797, and two years later was received into full membership. His early preaching circuits were in Georgia and Virginia. In 1806 he withdrew from the active ministry to educate his children. On the death of his wife in 1815 he reentered the active ministry but again withdrew in 1821 and became the headmaster of a boys school in Baltimore. Although not a member of the General Conference of 1820, he was elected secretary of the body, a recognition of his ability and training.

In the years following Bishop Asbury's death in 1816, Baltimore was the center of a movement to make Methodism more democratic by securing lay representation in the conferences, the election rather than episcopal appointment of presiding elders, and conference rights for local preachers. M'Caine became one of the most prominent leaders of the reform party. He offered strong arguments in favor of reform in the reformers' paper called *Mutual Rights*, beginning in 1824, and in his masterful *History and Mystery of Methodist Episcopacy* (1827). His contention was that the Methodist Episcopal organization never had the sanction of John Wesley, and that an imperial episcopacy had been foisted upon the Methodist societies by Bishop Asbury.

When the General Conference of 1828 refused to pass reform legislation, numerous churches split over the issue and in 1830 a convention of reformers was held in Baltimore and there organized the Methodist Protestant Church (MPC). M'Caine was one of the principal drafters of the constitution of the new church. In this new branch of Methodism, M'Caine was active as a writer until the end of his life.

Soon after the formation of the MPC, slavery became a controversial issue among the Methodists. M'Caine, among others, became an advocate of slavery and wrote a pamphlet in its defense in 1842. Whether arguing for slavery or against bishops, M'Caine was bold, if not blunt, a characteristic that often laid him open to criticism.

During his later years M'Caine lived with his children in South Carolina and Georgia. He died at the home of his daughter, Mrs. James M. Brett, in Augusta, Georgia.

Bibliography

A: *An Appeal to the Public* (Baltimore, 1826); *A Defense of the Truth as Set Forth in the History and Mystery of Methodist Episcopacy* (Baltimore, 1829); *History and Mystery of Methodist Episcopacy* (Baltimore, 1827); *Letters on the Organization and Early History of the Methodist Episcopal Church* (Boston, 1850); *Slavery Defended against the Attacks of Abolitionists* (Baltimore, 1842).
B: *CBTEL* 5, 934; *CM* 572; *Daily Constitutionalist* (Augusta, GA), 3 June 1856; *EWM* 2, 1477; *HDM*; Edward J. Drinkhouse, *History of Methodist Reform* (Baltimore, 1899); Harold Lawrence, *Methodist Preachers in Georgia, 1783–1900* (Tignal, GA, 1984), 333; Samuel E. Norton, *Susbtance of a Discourse on the Decease of Rev. Alexander McCaine of the Methodist Protestant Church* (Montgomery, AL, 1856).

MCCONNELL, FRANCIS JOHN (18 August 1871, Trinway, OH–18 August 1953, Lucasville, OH). *Education:* A.B., Ohio Wesleyan, 1894; B.D., Boston University School of Theology, 1897; Ph.D., Boston University, 1899. *Career:* admitted to the New England Annual Conference, 1894; pastor, West Chelmsford, 1894–97; Newton Upper Falls, 1897–99; Ipswich, 1899–1902; Harvard Street, Cambridge; pastor, New York Avenue Church, Brooklyn, 1903–09; president, DePauw University, 1909–12; bishop, MEC, 1912. Served episcopal areas in Denver, 1912–20; Pittsburgh, 1920–28; and New York, 1928–44.

Francis McConnell was born and reared in the home of a Methodist pastor. He was to become a scholar-bishop, university president, author, lecturer, advocate, and leading Methodist spokesperson for the ''Social Gospel,'' learned at the feet of Borden Parker Bowne* at Boston University School of Theology. He and Edgar S. Brightman were Bowne's best-known students.

McConnell had a penetrating mind and was at home in the worlds of theology, history, and ethics. He wrote and lectured extensively in all these areas. For thirty years his articles appeared weekly in the *Church School Journal*, and he was the author of twenty-four books. Eleven institutions, including Harvard and Yale, awarded him honorary degrees. In 1930 he delivered the Lyman Beecher Lectures on preaching at Yale.

His widest reputation was gained, however, as a social prophet. McConnell's writing, speaking, and preaching unfailingly advocated social reform, and he was known to chide his episcopal colleagues when he judged them to be timid or reticent to speak on behalf of causes he thought important.

He attributed his interest in labor questions to his father's influence, his experiences working in the mills while in school, and with the organization of the Methodist Federation for Social Service in 1908. It and he came to national attention during the Pittsburgh steel strike in 1919. McConnell chaired a distinguished committee created by the interchurch movement to investigate the strike and report. The published report featured the twelve-hour day, seven-day week and twenty-four-hour shift common to American labor at the time and was highly controversial. McConnell was the object of much criticism and abuse, but he was a worthy adversary.

  In addition to his interest in labor issues, McConnell served for fifteen years as president of the Old Age Pension Association of New York, later the Social Security Administration, and in 1928 he became president of the Federal Council of Churches. He was president of the Methodist Federation for Social Service (1912–44 and 1950–52).

  McConnell can be credited with typing the social thinking of Methodism for a period of forty years. G. Bromley Oxnam was one of his better-known disciples in the episcopacy and continued the tradition of social action and concern begun by McConnell.

Bibliography

A: (selected) *Aids to Christian Belief* (New York, 1932); *Basis for the Peace to Come* (New York, 1942); *Borden Parker Bowne: His Life and Philosophy* (New York, 1929); *By the Way: An Autobiography* (New York, 1952); *Christian Citizenship* (New York, 1922); *The Christian Ideal and Social Control* (Chicago, 1932); *Christian Materialism* (New York, 1936); *Christianity and Concern* (Nashville, 1933); *The Christlike God* (New York, 1927); *Christmas Sermons* (Cincinnati, 1909); *The Church after the War* (New York, 1943); *Church Finance and Social Ethics* (New York, 1920); *Democratic Christianity* (New York, 1919); *The Diviner Immanence* (New York, 1906); *The Essentials of Methodism* (New York, 1916); *Evangelicals, Revolutionists, and Idealists* (New York, 1942); *John Wesley* (New York, 1939); *The Preacher and the People* (New York, 1922); *Religious Certainty* (New York, 1910); *Doctrines and Discipline of the Methodist Episcopal Church* (New York, 1936).

B: *DCIA* 682–83; *EWM* 2, 1481–82; *MB* 124–25.

MCFERRIN (M'FERRIN), JOHN BERRY (15 June 1807, Rutherford County, TN–10 May 1887, Nashville, TN). *Education:* no formal education. *Career:* joined the Tennessee Annual Conference, 1825; served on circuits in Alabama and Tennessee, 1826; missionary to the Cherokees, 1827–29; circuit work and station churches in Huntsville, AL, and Nashville, TN, 1829–36; presiding elder, Florence (AL) District, 1836; Cumberland District (TN), 1837–40; editor, Nashville *Christian Advocate*, 1840–58; book agent, 1858; in charge of all missionary work to the Army of Tennessee (C.S.A.), 1861–66; secretary of Domestic Missions, 1866–70; secretary, Board of Missions, 1870–78; book agent, 1878–87.

  McFerrin was for years an acknowledged leader in Methodism. The bulk of his career, however, was spent in the MECS. He sat in more General Conferences and held connectional offices longer than any other man of his time. In addition to serving as editor of the Nashville *Christian Advocate* for eighteen years, McFerrin oversaw the work of the church during the Civil War with the Army of Tennessee, later oversaw the missionary work of the entire MECS, and finished his career with eleven years as book agent. Assuming the duties of agent, he found the publishing interests deeply in debt and suffering from poor management. With his considerable business acumen, in a short period of time he raised $350,000 through the sale of bonds to put the enterprise back on its feet.

McFerrin was a large man whose influence was aided by a keen intellect, prodigious memory, and sharp wit. This was especially true at the General Conference of 1844, and in the organization of the MECS in Louisville a year later. He is also the author of a three-volume history of Methodism in Tennessee.

Bibliography

A: *History of Methodism in Tennessee*, 3 vols. (Nashville, 1869).
B: *CM* 575; *EWM* 2, 1487–88; Oscar P. Fitzgerald, *John B. McFerrin* (Nashville, 1888).

MCKENDREE (M'KENDREE), WILLIAM (6 July 1757, King William County, VA–5 March 1835, near Nashville, TN). *Education:* no formal education. *Career:* served for a number of years in the Continental Army; received into the Virginia Conference and assigned to the Mecklenburg circuit, 1788; Cumberland circuit, 1789; Portsmouth circuit, 1790; Amelia circuit, 1791; Greenville circuit, 1792; resigned as part of O'Kelly* protest movement, 1792; traveled with Asbury,* Norfork and Portsmouth Station, 1793; Union circuit, South Carolina, 1794; Bedford circuit and moves to Greenbriar circuit (Allegheny Mountains), 1794–95; Bottetourt circuit, 1795; presiding elder, Richmond District, 1796–99; presiding elder, Baltimore Conference, 1798; presiding elder, Richmond District (briefly), Kentucky District (all of Kentucky), and Cumberland District (IL), 1800–1808; elected bishop of the MEC, 1808.

Third bishop elected by the MEC, the first born in the United States, and the first from the West. After a number of years serving in the Continental Army, McKendree was converted and at the age of thirty-one joined the Virginia Conference. His first presiding elder was James O'Kelly, who had great influence on him during the early years of his ministry. McKendree, in fact, withdrew briefly from the Methodist connection in support of O'Kelly's protest in 1792, but he never united with the church he founded.

His first appointments were in Virginia, but in 1800 he was sent to Kentucky to strengthen the work on the frontier. In his work as presiding elder, he had responsibility for virtually all of Kentucky. In time he was to move his work into Tennessee, Illinois, and Ohio. One of the circuits in the Cumberland District that he served in 1789 was the entire state of Illinois. When McKendree arrived in Baltimore for the General Conference of 1808, he was an unknown to most of its members. An eloquent sermon, however, propelled him into prominence. Francis Asbury* remarked on leaving the church that the sermon could make him a bishop. His words were prophetic for McKendree was quickly elected by a large majority.

McKendree's first year as a bishop was spent in the company of Asbury, who introduced him to the work and to the conferences. Although intimate friends, Asbury and McKendree were very different kinds of individuals. In 1811 he informed Asbury of his intention to make use of the presiding elders in a cabinet to assign the preachers to their work. Asbury had always done it alone and opposed the idea. At the General Conference of 1812, McKendree, with the help and consent of several preachers, delivered the first Episcopal Address, which set the order of business for the conference. After the address was read, Asbury challenged him on the floor. McKendree responded, "You are our *father*, we are your sons; you never have had need of it. I am only a *brother*, and have need of it." The Episcopal Address remains a feature of General Conference today.

For eight years Asbury and McKendree were the only two bishops in the MEC. The rigors of the work, including the extensive travel took their toll on McKendree's health, and by 1816 he, too, was in feeble health. That year, upon the death of Asbury, Enoch George* and Robert Roberts* were elected bishops and the burden was eased somewhat. By 1820, however, McKendree's health was so precarious that General Conference relieved him from active work and allowed him to use his discretion in what he would do. By 1824 he was better and able to be more active, but he still did not carry the full responsibilities of a chief executive. It is ironic in light of his health that McKendree was the only bishop to actually travel throughout the connection. In 1826 Elijah Hedding* and Enoch George determined to serve the North and the East while Soule and Roberts worked in the West and the South. Despite bidding a formal farewell to the General Conference of 1828, McKendree continued limited work until his death in 1835. In 1830 he donated 480 acres of land to Lebanon Seminary in Illinois, which became McKendree College.

Tall and gracious, McKendree preached with power and simplicity and led in the same manner. His skills as a presiding officer and his knowledge of Methodist practice and doctrine enabled him to protect and defend the power of the episcopacy in 1820 from a strong attempt to reduce it by electing presiding elders. It is difficult to imagine how the denomination could have found a more worthy successor to make the transition from the venerable Asbury.

Bibliography

A: *Substance of a Sermon Preached by Rev. William McKendree . . . at Middlebury, (Vermont) . . . on the 6th of June, 1817* (New York, 1817); *To the General Conference to Be Held in Baltimore, May, 1820* (Baltimore, 1820).

B: *AAP* 7, 160–71; *CM* 577–78; *DAB* 12, 85–86; *DCIA* 693; *EWM* 2, 1490–91; *JLFA*; *LMB* 129–48; *MB* 127–29; standard histories of Methodism, e.g., Bangs,* Stevens, and Bucke; Benjamin St. James Fry, *The Life of Rev. William McKendree* (New York, 1852); Elijah Embree Hoss, *William McKendree: A Biographical Study* (Nashville, 1914); William C. Larrabee, *Asbury and His Coadjutors*, vol. 2 (Cincinnati, 1854); Robert Paine, *Life and Times of William M'Kendree,* 2 vols. (Nashville, 1872); Joshua Soule, *Sermon on the Death of the Rev. William McKendree* (Cincinnati, 1836).

MATTHEWS, MARJORIE SWANK (11 July 1916, Onawa, MI–30 June 1986, Grand Rapids, MI). *Education*: B.A., Central Michigan University, 1968;

B.D., Colgate-Rochester Divinity School, 1972; M.A., and Ph.D., Florida State University, 1974, 1976. *Career*: executive secretary, assistant treasurer, Lobdell-Emery Manufacturing Company, Elma, MI, 1946–63; ordained deacon, 1963, and elder, 1965; pastor of small churches in Michigan, New York, and Florida, 1959–76; district superintendent, Grand Traverse District, West Michigan Conference, 1976–80; bishop, Wisconsin area, UMC, 1980–84; retired, 1984–86.

Marjorie Matthews finished third in her high school class in Elma, Michigan. She went to secretarial school because of the family's financial situation. She married soon after finishing and accompanied her husband to various army posts until World War II was over. Divorced after the war and with a young son to support, she obtained an administrative position with an auto parts manufacturer in Michigan.

At age forty-seven she put aside a comfortable way of life as an executive secretary to answer a call to ordained ministry. She first entered the ministry by the back door, as a part-time local pastor, with no seminary training but only the annual conference inservice training course. It was only after ordination that she began an arduous process of higher education that eventually gained her in succession a bachelor of arts, a bachelor of divinity, a master of arts in religion, and finally, in 1976, a doctor of philosophy degree.

Matthews had overcome early educational deprivation resulting from the Depression, a painful marital breakup shortly after World War II, the problems of single parenthood, the bias against women in business, and breast cancer that made her think briefly that her life was over. Her struggles led her to theological answers and to the Book of Job. The theme of suffering became the basis for her doctoral dissertation.

While pursuing her education she pastored a succession of rural parishes and "two-point charges" in New York, Florida, and Michigan that ranged in membership from 80 to 180. Her pastoral record lists names like Pleasant Valley-Leaton, Vermontville-Gresham, Sunfield-Sebawa Center, Ashley-Bannister, and Napoleon. While she was serving such small churches in Michigan, Bishop Dwight Loder took notice of her abilities and appointed her a member of his cabinet and superintendent of West Michigan's Grand Traverse District. The second woman in the denomination to attain that role, she favored pastoral appointment of clergy across racial lines and worked closely with the local pastors' school for Native American ministers.

Her name surfaced as an episcopal candidate at the 1979 national clergywomen's consultation. The next year her election was endorsed by three annual conferences. The diminutive gray-haired sixty-four-year-old grandmother, who had entered the ministry at age forty-seven, was elected a bishop by the North Central Jurisdiction Conference on 17 July 1980 in Dayton, Ohio, in a hotly contested election that ran to thirty ballots.

As bishop Matthews presided over the Wisconsin area of the UMC from 1980 until 1984, which included supervision of 135,000 Methodists, eight districts, 399 ministers, and 522 churches. Her firmness as an administrator was tempered by her warmth and humanness. She became a symbol of the progress made by women in Protestant churches, then the only woman elected bishop of any major denomination in modern times.

In addition to episcopal duties in Wisconsin, Bishop Matthews lectured at Garrett-Evangelical Theological Seminary in Evanston, Illinois, where she was a trustee. As a delegate to the World Council of Churches' Sixth Assembly in Vancouver in 1963, she was the first woman bishop to address a World Council assembly. She retired in 1984 and died two years later after a long battle with cancer.

Bibliography

B: *HDM*; *NYT* 18 July 1980 and 2 July 1986; *United Methodist Reporter* 11 July 1986.

MERRITT, TIMOTHY (October 1775, Barkhamstead, CT–2 May 1845). *Education*: no formal education. *Career:* entered traveling ministry of Methodists, 1796; pastor, New London circuit, 1796–97; Penobscot circuit, 1797; Portland circuit, 1798–1800; Bath and Union circuit, 1800–1801; Bath station, 1802; located, 1803–17; reentered the traveling ministry and served Boston, 1817–18; Nantucket, 1819; Woods-End; 1820–22; Providence, 1822; Bristol, RI, 1823–24; Boston, 1825–26; Springfield, 1827–28; New Bedford, 1829–30; Malden, 1831; assistant editor, *Christian Advocate*, New York, 1832–35; his last assignment was in Lynn, 1835–36, after which ill health forced his retirement.

Merritt was one of the early leaders of New England Methodism. He was preaching as early as 1794 and entered the Methodist Conference two years later. His first assignments were in Maine, where in 1803 he left the ministry for a period of almost fifteen years in order to support his growing family. In all, he and his wife had twelve children, eight of whom grew to maturity. During this period he wrote and spoke in support of the War of 1812.

When he returned to full-time ministry, he served in Rhode Island and Massachusetts. During this time, Merritt wrote in opposition to the Universalists and in support of the doctrine of Christian perfection. Although opposed to slavery, he was not an abolitionist. His intelligence and intellectual discipline earned him approval both as a writer and a speaker. Much of his writing that exists today was done in response to these controversies. He was a regular contributor to the church periodicals. Highly respected for his sound judgment, Merritt was regularly elected to General Conference, and was a leader in his annual conference.

Bibliography

A: *Anabaptism Disapproved* (New York, 1821); *Animadversions on Mr. Elias Smith's Review* (Portland, Maine, 1807); *The Apostles' Commission* (Palmer, CT, 1816); *The Christian's Manual* (New York, 1825); *The Convert's Guide and Preacher's Assistant* (Boston, 1838); *A Discourse Delivered at the Chapel* in Bromfield's Lane (Boston, 1818); *A Discourse on the Unpardonable Sin* (Boston, 1819); *A Discourse on the War with England* (Hallowell, ME, 1814); *A Discussion on Universal Salvation* (New York, 1829); *Evangelical and Pharisaical Righteousness* (Providence,

RI, 1823); *Letters to Rev. James Wilson* (Providence, RI, 1823); *A Vindication of the Common Opinion* (Boston, 1818).
B: *AAP* 7, 273–76; *DCIA* 730–31; *EWM* 2, 1552–53.

MOORE, JOHN MONROE (27 January 1867, Morgantown, KY–1 August 1948, Dallas, TX). *Education:* B.A., National Normal University, Lebanon, OH, 1887; Ph.D., Yale University, 1895; academic year 1894–95, Leipzig and Heidelberg. *Career:* teaching rural schools, 1884–85; teaching in Texas, 1887–91; admitted to St. Louis Annual Conference, 1895; pastor, Marvin Church, St. Louis, 1895–98, Travis Park Church, San Antonio, 1898–1902, and First Methodist, Dallas, 1902–06; managing editor, Nashville *Christian Advocate*, 1906–09; St. John's, St. Louis, 1909–10; secretary, Department of Home Missions, 1910–18; bishop, MECS, 1918, assigned to Brazil (1918–22), Texas-Oklahoma (1922–26), West Texas, (1926–30), Georgia-Florida (1930–34), and Missouri-Arkansas (1934–38).

John M. Moore's early years were spent on his father's farm near Morgantown, Kentucky. His primary and secondary education were in the schools of the community. After a brief period of teaching he entered the National Normal University in Ohio and eventually earned a Ph.D. degree from Yale. The last year of his program was spent in Germany at the Universities of Leipzig and Heidelberg. Teaching school early in his career brought him to Texas, where he was to later serve in the MECS both as pastor and as bishop.

Completing Yale and finding himself without a suitable college or university teaching appointment, Moore, who had been a local preacher since 1887, presented himself for a pastoral appointment and was eventually assigned to Marvin Church, St. Louis. It was an inner-city congregation composed of many German immigrants. Moore, an unlikely choice except for the fact that he spoke German, did well and regarded it later as one of his most satisfying experiences in ministry. From there he was transferred to the West Texas Conference and assigned to Travis Park in downtown San Antonio. He later served First Church, Dallas, in a similar setting.

After a time as managing editor of the Nashville *Christian Advocate,* Moore went back briefly as pastor to St. John's Church, St. Louis, spent eight years as secretary of the Department of Home Missions, and then was elected to the episcopacy in 1918. When he entered the College of Bishops, the MECS had only thirteen active bishops. The same year he wrote the ''Oklahoma Declaration,'' which inaugurated the discussion on church union that twenty years later created the Methodist Church.

The first episcopal assignment carried Bishop Moore to Brazil, which he remembers in his autobiography as ''perhaps my best quadrennium of episcopal service'' (*Life and I*, 132). While there he built fifty-three churches and purchased the campus and buildings for Bennett College in Rio de Janeiro. In total Moore served five areas during his years as a bishop, but he lived in Dallas during four of the five quadrenniums.

Although a leading bishop of the southern church and an author of note, he is perhaps best known for his leadership in the effort to reunite American Methodism. He, along with Bishop Edwin Holt Hughes of the MEC and Bishop James H. Straughn of the MPC, formed a triumvirate that led the final movement that created the Methodist Church in 1939. The story of this effort is chronicled in Moore's *Long Road to Methodist Union* (1943). Short in stature (5'5'') Moore was an outstanding presiding officer, was rarely unprepared at meetings, and had the keen mind, poise, and self-assurance of a genuine scholar. His theological sentiments were liberal.

Bibliography

A: *Brazil: An Introductory Study* (Nashville, 1920); *Episcopal Address to the General Conference of 1934* (Nashville, 1934); *Etchings of the East* (Nashville, 1909); *Life and I* (Nashville, 1948); *The Long Road to Methodist Union* (New York, 1943); *Making the World Christian* (New York, 1922); *Methodism in Belief and Action* (New York, 1946); *The South Today* (New York, 1916).
B: *EWM* 2, 1665–66; *MB* 135–36.

MORRIS, THOMAS ASBURY (28 April 1794, Kanawha County, near Charleston, WV–2 September 1874, Springfield, OH). *Education:* rural schools, self-taught. *Career:* deputy county clerk, Cabell County, 1811–15; began to preach, November 1815, and joined Ohio Conference, 1816; Marietta circuit, OH, 1816–18; Zanesville circuit, 1818–20; Lancaster, OH, 1820–21; transferred to the Christian circuit, Kentucky Conference, 1821–23; Hopkinsville, 1823–24; Red River circuit, TN, 1824–25; presiding elder, Greenriver District, 1825–27; Louisville, 1827–28; Lebanon, OH, circuit, 1828–30; Columbus, 1830–31; Cincinnati, 1831–32; presiding elder, Cincinnati District, 1832–33; editor, *Western Christian Advocate*, 1833–36; bishop, MEC, 1836.

For years the senior bishop of the MEC during the middle of the nineteenth century, T. A. Morris was born in what is now West Virginia and spent his early years on the farm. His education was rudimentary with little time actually spent in school. After four years as his brother's deputy in Cabell County, Morris determined to preach and joined the Ohio Conference. His early assignments were in Ohio, but in 1821 he was transferred to the Kentucky Conference, where he served until 1828. Because of the meticulous records he kept, we know that during the first twelve years of his ministry he earned on the average of $166 a year.

Between General Conferences in 1833, he was named editor of the *Western Christian Advocate*, where he served until elected to the episcopacy in 1836. At the time of his election there were twenty-eight annual conferences and six bishops. A good portion of his work was among the southern conferences, and although he adhered to the northern branch of the denomination in 1844, he attended the organizing conference of the MECS in Louisville in 1845, and he, along with Bishop Janes,* agreed to fill their obligations to Southern Conference assigned to them in the Plan of Visitation set prior to the division. However, a new plan was devised and they were not permitted to go. A formal complaint was lodged against Morris in the General Conference of 1848 for his refusal to appoint a preacher to the minority of members in a congregation in St. Louis whose majority had determined to affiliate with the South. Investigation by the Episcopal Committee found no grounds for the complaint.

By 1864 he was unable to carry the full responsibility of his office but attended the General Conference of 1868 and remained active until the time of his death. He was one of the bishops who favored the addition of lay representatives to the conferences. This was done in 1872, shortly after his death.

Bibliography

A: *A Discourse on Methodist Polity* (Cincinnati, 1859); *Miscellany* (Cincinnati, 1852); *Sermons on Various Subjects* (Cincinnati, 1842).

B: *CM* 630–31; *EWM* 2, 1673–74; *LMB* 265–86; *MB* 136–39; John F. Marlay, *The Life of Rev. Thomas A. Morris* (Cincinnati, 1875); James Madison Mathes, *Letters to Thomas A. Morris* (Indianapolis, 1871).

N

NAST, WILLIAM (Wilhelm Johann) (15 June 1807, Stuttgart, Germany–16 May 1899, Cincinnati, OH). *Education*: Lower Seminary, Blaubeuren, Wurttemburg, 1821–25; University of Tübingen, 1825–27. *Career*: Family tutor, Harrisburg, PA, 1828–30; librarian and instructor in German, West Point, 1830–32; Kenyon College, Gambier, OH, 1833–35; Methodist preacher in Ohio Conference, missionary to Germans in Cincinnati, 1835–36; missionary to Germans in Ohio, 1836–39; editor, *Der Christliche Apologete* and missionary-at-large to German Methodists, 1839–91; president, German Wallace College (later Baldwin-Wallace College), Berea, OH, 1864–89.

William Nast was born in Stuttgart, Germany. His father was a government official and his mother was the daughter of an Austrian military officer. Both parents died in Nast's teenage years and his rearing was left in the hands of an elder sister. He attended Lutheran schools in Stuttgart and after confirmation (1821) entered the Lower Seminary at Blaubeuren to prepare for the ministry. At age eighteen Nast entered the University of Tübingen, where he studied with rationalist professors F. C. Baur and D. F. Strauss. After two years of study he left the university in a whirl of doubt. He wandered around Vienna, Dresden, and Munich but finally took the advice of his brother-in-law and came to America, aiming to teach classics.

Arriving in 1828 he secured a position as a tutor in a Methodist family near Harrisburg, Pennsylvania. There he had a pleasant home, gained his first impressions of Methodism, and became acquainted with several Methodist ministers. In 1830 he went to West Point as a librarian and instructor in German, and here, amidst "the Godless atmosphere of the military academy," he read the works of English Evangelicals (Jeremy Taylor, William Law, and Richard Baxter) and German Pietists (Friedrich August Gottreu Tholuck) and attended a nearby Methodist chapel. Another period of confusion of followed.

Nast returned to old friends in the familiar territory of central Pennsylvania, where he explored teaching at the Lutheran Theological Seminary at Gettysburg and attended Methodist camp meetings. Deciding against teaching Lutherans, he turned to the Episcopalians. Through Bishop McIlvaine of the Episcopal Church he secured a position as teacher of Greek and Hebrew at Kenyon College in Gambier, Ohio. Here he sought out pious Methodists and attended their meetings. Finally, at a Methodist meeting in Danville, Ohio, in January 1834 Nast experienced a spiritual breakthrough and made the decision to enter the Methodist ministry.

At the time Nast was admitted to the Ohio Conference, the denomination was planning ways to expand its ministry among the rapidly growing German-American community in Ohio. Nast was appointed missionary to Cincinnati's large German community. Progress was slow, but Nast was persistent. By 1838 he organized the first German Methodist Church and Sunday School in the city. He succeeded in making a few good friends, among them Cincinnati soapmaker James Gamble, whose support in years to come was a great boon.

Nast soon criss-crossed Ohio and adjoining states visiting German communities and then traveled to the East and West Coasts. German districts were authorized by the General Conference of 1844, and by 1864 the church's ministry to German-Americans was organized into four separate conferences. Missionaries converted by Nast exported Methodism back to Europe and successfully established churches in Germany, Switzerland, and other countries. Nast made several trips to Europe to organize Methodist work there, beginning in 1844. He represented his church at congresses of the Evangelical Alliance in Berlin (1857) and in New York (1873), where he delivered important addresses on Methodist doctrine.

To aid the progress of Methodism among the nation's growing German-speaking community, in 1839 the Methodists founded a German church paper, *Der Christliche Apologete* (*The Christian Apologist*) with Nast as editor, a position he held for fifty-two years. Besides editing the paper, Nast busied himself with extensive writing and translating. In addition to works on doctrine and church history, Nast's writings include a popular series of catechisms, several collections of hymns and prayers, a biography of Wesley in 1852, and in 1847 the first German translation of Wesley's standard sermons. Nast's principal work was his two-volume commentary on the Gospels published in German and English between 1860 and 1872. More open to biblical criticism than most Methodists of his day, Nast suggested that verbal inspiration was not essential to belief that the Bible was a divine revelation.

Nast helped found and became first president of Baldwin-Wallace College at Berea, Ohio (1864), an important training ground for German Methodist preachers. Noted for his learning, industry, and remarkable bilingualism, Nast died in 1899 and was buried in Cincinnati. A substantial collection of Nast family papers are on deposit with the Cincinnati Historical Society.

Bibliography

A: *Der Aufgabe der christlichen Kirche in neunzehnten Jahrhundert* (Cincinnati, 1857); *Das Biblische Christenthum und Seine Gegensatze* (Cincinnati, 1883); *Christologische Betractungen nach Dr. van Oosterzee's "Bild Christi"* (Cincinnati, 1867); *Commentary on the Gospels of Matthew and Mark* (Cincinnati, 1864); "Dr William Nast's Religious Experience as Told by Himself," *NWCA* 31 May 1899, 6–7; *The Gospel Records, Their Genuineness, Authenticity, Historic Variety, and Inspiration, with Some Preliminary Remarks on the Gospel History* (Cincinnati, 1866); *Der Grossere Katechismus fur die deutschen Gemeinden der Bischofl. Methodistenkirche* (Cincinnati, 1868); *Der Hundertjahrige Bestand des amerikanische Methodisumus* (Cincinnati, 1866); *Der Kleinere Katechismus fur die Gemeinden der Bischofl. Methodistenkirche* (Cincinnati, 1868); *Kritisch-practischer Commentar uber das Neue Testament*, 2 vols. (Cincinnati and Bremen, 1860–72); *Das Leben und Wirken des Johannes Wesley und Seiner Haupt-Mitarbeiter* (Cincinnati, 1852); *Philosophie des Erlosungsplanes* (Cincinnati, 1858); *Sammlung auserlesener Predigten von Johannes Wesley*, 2 vols. (Cincinnati, 1847); *Was Ist und Will der Methodismus?* (Cincinnati, 1853).

B: *CM* 994; *Christliche Apologete* (18 and 25 May 1899); *Cincinnati Enquirer* 17 May 1899; *DAB* 13, 393; *EWM* 2, 1702–3; *NCAB* 10, 223; *NWCA* 24 May 1899; *WCA* 10 February 1837; Paul F. Douglass, *The Story of German Methodism* (New York, 1939); Carl Wittke, *William Nast, Patriarch of German Methodism* (Detroit, MI, 1959).

NEELY, THOMAS BENJAMIN (12 June 1841, Philadelphia, PA–4 September 1925, Philadelphia, PA). *Education:* A.M. (honorary), Dickinson College, 1875; Williamsport Dickinson Seminary. *Career:* joined Philadelphia Conference, 1865; served thirteen congregations, Philadelphia Conference, 1865–89 (on leave because of ill health, 1870–74); presiding elder, South District, 1889–94; secretary, Sunday School Union and Tract Society, 1900–1904; bishop, MEC, 1904–12, with service in Buenos Aires and New Orleans.

Author, bishop, and outspoken champion of the position that the episcopacy was an office rather than a distinct order in Methodism, Thomas Neely also opposed the creation of a missionary episcopacy as in violation of the Third Restrictive Rule of the Methodist constitution. Neely equipped himself by intensive study of the history and operation of the denomination. Few could match his knowledge of the doctrines, constitution, laws, and practices of American Methodism, and even fewer could equal him in debate. Elected to General Conference when he was forty-two, he found it to be the arena in which his strengths were most conspicuous. He was without equal as a parliamentarian.

Despite his knowledge of the nature and history of the office and his sincere commitment to the episcopacy, his own episcopal administration was autocratic and arbitrary. This was especially true in his use of the appointive power. On the whole, his episcopal service was not satisfying to him or to those he served in South America or in the United States. His assignment to Buenos Aires was inappropriate because of his age (sixty-three at the time of election); the altitude, which troubled him; the extent of travel required; and his style of administration. Without being given a reason, he was retired against his will after eight years of service by a vote of General Conference. The act was ironic, for Neely had in his own work supported the supreme power of General Conference over the episcopacy.

After his retirement Neely continued to write and speak. Always a conservative, he was against unification and granting autonomy to the church in mission fields. He opposed the interchurch world movement and the League of Nations. But Neely should be recognized not for the things he opposed but for the body of literature he wrote, which examined with care and precision virtually all the organizational and structural issues in Methodism. Seven of his twenty-one publications were published after his retirement.

Bibliography

A: *American Methodism: Its Divisions and Unification* (New York, 1915); *The Bishops and the Supervisional System of the Methodist Episcopal Church* (New York, 1912); *The Church Lyceum* (New York, 1882); *Doctrinal Standards of Methodism* (New York, 1918); *The Evolution of Methodism and Organic Methodism* (New York, 1888); *A History of the Origin and Development of the Governing Conference in Methodism* (New York, 1892); *Juan Wesley, El Gran Reformador Religioso* (New York, 1905); *The League—The Nation's Danger* (New York, 1919); *The Methodist Episcopal Church and Its Formation* (New York, 1923); *The Methodist Episcopal Church in the United States* (New York, 1896); *The Minister in the Itinerant System* (New York, 1914); *Neely's Parliamentary Practice* (New York, 1914); *Present Perils of Methodism* (Philadelphia, 1920); *South America: Its Missionary Problems* (New York, 1909); *Vital Points in the Methodist Episcopal Church* (Philadelphia, 1924).

B: *DAB* 13, 402–3; *EWM* 2, 1707–8; *JGC* 1928, 797–800; *MB* 140–41.

O

O'KELLY, JAMES (c. 1735 in either Ireland or America–16 October 1826, NC). *Education:* unknown. *Career:* seems to have lived in Surrey County, VA; served in two campaigns of the Revolution; appears in Virginia Conference Minutes in 1778 as on trial; New Hope, Tar River, Mecklenburg, Brunswick, and Sussex circuits, 1779–84; presiding elder, in southern Virginia, 1785–92; left the denomination and organized the Republican Methodist Church, 1793.

The leader of a revolt against Francis Asbury's* use of power and a reformer of Methodist practice, O'Kelly left the MEC in 1792 and a year later founded the Republican Methodist Church. Prior to that time he was an influential leader in the connection. He played a leading role in the controversy over the administration of the sacraments in 1779 and was present at the 1784 Christmas Conference, where he was one chosen by Asbury for ordination as an elder. In 1786 he opposed Wesley's appointment of Richard Whatcoat* as a superintendent and so challenged Wesley's authority in America. O'Kelly was chosen to be a member of Asbury's ill-conceived Council in 1789, but he opposed the organization in favor of a general conference. In January 1790, shortly after the meeting of the Council, he wrote to Asbury charging him with the abuse of power and attempted to enlist Thomas Coke* on the side of a delegated conference. Coke, who was also frustrated with the role he had been given to play by Asbury, agreed to support the idea.

At the conference meeting in Baltimore on 1 November 1792 O'Kelly offered an amendment to provide preachers an avenue of appeal directly to the conference if they were displeased with their appointments. If this appeal were sustained, the bishop would then be forced to make another assignment. This proposal was a direct challenge to Asbury personally and a radical departure from the traditional Methodist concept of episcopal power and responsibility. After considerable debate, at which Asbury was not present, the amendment was defeated by a large majority, and O'Kelly withdrew from the connection. William McKendree,* who was serving in O'Kelly's district at the time, left with him and also briefly withdrew. He did not, however, unite with the Republican Methodist Church. The O'Kelly group favored congregational church government without bishops, was strongly antislavery, and maintained the only creed and rule of faith and practice to be the Scriptures. In time the Republican Methodists became known simply as "Christians." This was the first defection in the denomination, and the MEC suffered a considerable loss of members to the O'Kelly faction. The minutes of the 1792–98 conferences show a loss of eight thousand members, some of which must be explained by the presence of the new denomination. Republican Methodism's greatest inroads were in Virginia and North Carolina.

Jesse Lee,* in his *Short History of the Methodists*, charged O'Kelly with heresy, but it is far more obvious that O'Kelly's concern was about power and polity. In 1798 O'Kelly published a tract, *"Christicola," The Author's Apology for Protesting against the Methodist Episcopal Government*, in which he denied that either Asbury or Coke had been elected bishops by the Conference. The tract was answered in 1800 by Nicholas Snethen,* who called the O'Kelly charge a "notorious falsehood"; a further reply was written by O'Kelly in 1801, *A Vindication of an Apology*.

Bibliography

A: *The Author's Apology for Protesting against the Methodist Episcopal Government* (Richmond, 1798); *Divine Oracles Consulted* (Hillsboro, NC, 1820); *Essay on Negro Slavery* (Philadelphia, 1789); *Hymns and Spiritual Songs Designed for the Use of Christians* (Raleigh, 1816); *Letters from Heaven Consulted* (Hillsboro, NC, 1822); *The Prospect before Us by Way of Address to the Christian Church* (Hillsboro, 1824); *A Vindication of the Author's Apology* (Raleigh, 1801).
B: *CM* 678–79; *DAB* 14, 7–8; *DCIA* 840; *EWM* 2, 1803; *JLFA*; Edward J. Drinkhouse, *History of Methodist Reform*, 2 vols. (Baltimore, 1899); David E. Gillingham, "The Politics of Piety" (B.A. thesis, Princeton University, 1967); Charles Frank Kilgore, *The James O'Kelly Schism in the Methodist Episcopal Church* (Mexico City, 1963); Wilbur E. MacClenny, *The Life of Rev. James O'Kelly* (Raleigh, 1910); Milo T. Morrill, *A History of the Christian Denomination in America* (Dayton, OH, 1912).

OLIN, STEPHEN (2 March 1797, Leicester, VT–16 August 1851, Middletown, CT). *Education*: A.B., Middlebury College, 1820. *Career*: teacher, Tabernacle Academy, Abbeville, SC, 1821–26; preacher, South Carolina Conference, 1824; ordained deacon in 1826, elder in1828; junior preacher on the Charleston circuit, 1824–25; professor of ethics and belles lettres, Franklin College (later University of Georgia), 1826–33; president, Randolph Macon College, 1834–37; president, Wesleyan University, 1842–51.

Son of a prominent Vermont lawyer and politician, Stephen Olin was sent to Middlebury College, where he graduated with honors. He secured these honors, however, at the expense of his health. Young Olin moved to a warmer climate in hopes of regaining his strength. For a time he taught at Tabernacle Academy near Abbeville, South Carolina, and there, with the gentle encouragement of the family with which he boarded, he converted to Methodism. In 1824 he was admitted on trial as a preacher in the South Carolina Conference and was appointed junior preacher on the Charleston circuit of four congregations, including three thousand slaves. The rigors of itinerancy were more than he could endure, and he was forced to conduct a settled ministry. College teaching proved to be a more amenable vocation. Shortly after his ordination as elder in 1828, he became president of Randolph Macon College in Virginia.

For more than two decades he did much to strengthen this denomination's interest in education, particularly in ministerial training. Several of his influential articles in the *Christian Advocate* argued persuasively for better intellectual standards among clergy and laity alike. He also took up the task of systematizing Methodism's theological thought and defending her doctrines. Between 1837 and 1841 Olin traveled in Europe and the Near East for health reasons, but after assuming the presidency of Wesleyan University he made that institution the strongest center for higher learning in the MEC.

By the early 1840s controversies over slavery produced crises in several major denominations. In 1844 Olin attended the General Conference in New York, where his church divided on this tragic question along regional lines. Since he had lived in the South, he was asked to serve on the committee charged with reconciling the two opposing parties. The obstacles to reconciliation were insurmountable, however, and no matter how much Olin hoped to prevent rupture, he finally voted on the antislavery side and watched the church split apart. Immediately afterward Olin strove to reunite the separated branches, activity that was not successful until almost a century later. He also pursued wider ecumenical ventures in 1846, helping to establish the Evangelical Alliance in the United States, and he served as one of his church's delegates to the world congress in London. Through these means he helped Methodism to emerge from sectarian origins and to expand into a mature middle-class denomination.

His wife edited his sermons and addresses for publication shortly after his death and also published a biography.

Bibliography

A: *College Life: Its Theory and Practice* (New York, 1867); *Early Piety* (New York, 1853); *Greece and the Golden Horn* (New York, 1854); *Travels in Egypt, Arabia Petraea, and the Holy Land*, 2 vols. (New York, 1843); *The Works of Stephen Olin*, 2 vols. (New York, 1852).

B: *AAP* 7, 685–99; *CA* 27 August 1851; *CBTEL* 7, 346–47; *CM* 680; *DARB* 406; *EWM* 2, 1811–12; *Hartford Daily Courant* 18 August 1851; *NCAB* 14, 13–14; *SH* 8, 236; *ZH* 28 August 1851; *Life and Letters of Stephen Olin*, ed. John M'Clintock, Joseph Holdich and Julia Lynch Olin (New York, 1853); John M'Clintock, "Death of President Olin," *MQR* 33 (October 1851): 652–55, and "Stephen Olin," *MQR* 36 (January 1854): 9–33; David B. Potts, *Wesleyan University, 1831–1910* (New Haven, CT, 1992).

OLIVER, ANNA (Vivianna Olivia Snowden) (12 April 1840, New Brunswick, NJ–21 November 1892, Greensboro, MD). *Education*: A.B., Rutgers Female

College, New York, NY, 1859; M.A., 1860; Oberlin School of Theology, 1872–73; B.D., Boston University School of Theology, 1876. *Career*: school teacher in Connecticut, 1860–68; missionary teacher, AMA school, Georgia, 1868–69; pastor, First MEC, Passaic, NJ, 1876–77; pastor, Willoughby Ave. ME Church, Brooklyn, 1879–83.

Baptized Vivianna Olivia Snowden, Anna Oliver changed her name in the early 1870s so as not to embarrass her family when she decided to enter the ministry. Educated in Brooklyn public schools and Rutgers Female College in New York City, Oliver began her career as a public school teacher in Connecticut. In addition to teaching, she took an active role in temperance work of women in her adopted state for the next eight years.

In 1868 Oliver volunteered to teach black children in Georgia under the auspices of the American Missionary Association (AMA). Inadequate facilities, domineering male supervisors, and hostility from the southern white community tested her commitment. A year later, when she learned that the AMA paid male teachers twice as much as females for the same work, Oliver resigned. She rejoined her family in Connecticut for a time, resumed her temperance work, and took up painting. A year later, 1870, she went to Cincinnati, partly to study landscape painting and partly to join the Ohio women's temperance crusade, then more advanced than Connecticut's.

Oliver's temperance talks in Ohio townhalls and churches encouraged her friends to urge her to think about becoming a minister. She began theological study at Oberlin but found the theological faculty unsupportive. In 1873 she enrolled in Boston University School of Theology, which in its catalogue claimed to be coeducational. Here Oliver found sympathetic mentors and graduated with honors. While in Boston she found support from Methodist women who had recently organized an independent women's missionary society to protest male domination of church affairs. She also found a sympathetic presiding elder on the Boston District who gave her a license to preach. Armed with a B.D. degree in 1876 and a license to preach, Oliver spent the summer after graduation preaching at summer assemblies and camp meetings on the East Coast from Martha's Vineyard to Ocean Grove, New Jersey. In September 1876 Oliver was invited to become the pastor of the First ME Church in Passaic, New Jersey. The church had been left without a preacher that year by the bishop. Here she busied herself in building up her little church and expanding its ministry to meet the needs of a small industrial city. Replaced by a male minister a year later, she looked for another pulpit but found none. Two years later, 1879, she assumed the pastorate of Willoughby Ave. ME Church in Brooklyn, which actively sought a woman pastor.

With the support of her church and a growing women's caucus in the church at large, Oliver led an unsuccessful campaign for the ordination of women at the 1880 General Conference in Cincinnati. But nothing came of it. Without ordination she continued as pastor of the Brooklyn congregation until 1883, when the church experiment was abandoned. Oliver remained in Brooklyn and devoted much energy to temperance and suffrage work, dress reform, and health care for women and children.

By opening her home and pulpit to a growing stream of women who were pioneering ministerial roles in Victorian churches, Anna Oliver became a respected mentor and model. She continued to preach the message of personal holiness and social responsibility wherever she could until her death in 1892.

Bibliography

A: *Test Case on the Ordination of Women* (New York, 1880); *Church Annual, Willoughby Ave. MEC, Brooklyn, NY* (Brooklyn, 1881).

B: *HDM*; Kenneth E. Rowe, "The Ordination of Women Round One: Anna Oliver and the General Conference of 1880," *Methodist History* 12 (April 1974): 60–72, and "Evangelism and Social Reform in the Pastoral Ministry of Anna Oliver, 1868–1886," in *Spirituality and Social Responsibility: The Vocational Vision of Women in the Methodist Tradition*, ed. Rosemary Skinner Keller (Nashville, 1993), 117–36.

OXNAM, GARFIELD BROMLEY (14 August 1891, Sonora, CA–12 March 1963, White Plains, NY). *Education:* B.A., University of Southern California, 1913; S.T.B., Boston University School of Theology, 1915. *Career:* admitted to Southern California Conference, 1913; pastor, Church of All Nations, Los Angeles; secretary, Los Angeles Missionary and Church Extension Society, 1917–27; professor, Boston University School of Theology, 1927–28; president, DePauw University, 1928–36; elected bishop, MEC, 1936; Omaha area, 1936–39; Boston area, 1939–44; New York area, 1944–52; Washington area, 1952–60.

Pastor, university president, and bishop, Bromley Oxnam was the champion of liberal causes and a worthy successor to Francis J. McConnell—his recent biographer has called him "The Paladin of Liberalism." A controversial and outspoken target for Senator Joseph McCarthy's investigation, organizer of the Council of Bishops, president of the Federal Council of Churches (1944–46), Oxnam presided over the organization of the National Council of Churches (1950) and was chair of the planning committee that organized the World Council of Churches in 1948. Modern Methodism has had few leaders the equal of Bromley Oxnam. He began his career in 1917 as pastor of what came to be the "Church of All Nations"—so called because the Los Angeles neighborhood it served contained forty-two nationalities. Oxnam carried on a ministry that understood the Christian proclamation in the context of human need. In 1928 he was elected president of DePauw University, where he served until he was elected to the episcopacy in 1936. His first episcopal assignment was to the Omaha area of the MEC. Following union in 1939, Oxnam served the most prestigious areas on the eastern seaboard, finishing his career in Washington, D.C., where he sought to be a voice and an influence on the government in support of Methodism. He was always, however, dedicated to the idea of the absolute separation of church and state.

An aristocrat in the true sense of the word, Oxnam was sometimes inconsistent in his views but never inactive. Before the beginning of World War II he supported the movement to aid America's allies and encouraged nonintervention once the fighting started; he led the fight to guarantee the rights of conscientious objectors, and during World War II he was an official visitor for the Joint Chiefs of Staff to army and navy chaplains.

Early in his career he championed the cause of organized labor and consistently supported higher education. The encounter with Senator Joseph McCarthy in his infamous hunt for Communists brought Oxnam national attention and criticism in many quarters. The book *I Protest* was his account of his experiences before the McCarthy hearings. While in Washington, D.C., Oxnam was a major influence in the decision to move Westminster Seminary to the campus of American University as Wesley Theological Seminary; the School of International Service was also begun with support from General Conference.

It was Oxnam, a prolific author and traveler, who in the sixteen years he served as its secretary (1939–56) organized the work of the Council of Bishops into committees, set an agenda to govern its meetings, and oversaw the appointment of bishops to a variety of denominational and extraecclesiastical organizations. During these years Oxnam ran the Council of Bishops, no matter who served as its president. He traveled widely at home and abroad and originated the plan whereby every bishop visits a portion of the church's work abroad at least once a quadrennium.

Bibliography

A: (selected) *Behold Thy Mother* (New York, 1944); *By This Sign Conquer* (New York, 1942); *The Church and Contemporary Change* (New York, 1950); *Effective Preaching* (New York, 1929); *Christian's Vocation* (Cincinnati, 1949); *The Ethical Ideals of Jesus* (New York, 1941); *Facing the Future Unafraid* (New York, 1944); *I Protest* (New York, 1954); *Labor and Tomorrow's World* (New York, 1945); *On This Rock* (New York, 1951); *Preaching and the Social Crisis* (New York, 1933); *Preaching in a Revolutionary Age* (New York, 1944); *The Stimulus of Christ* (New York, 1948); *A Testament of Faith* (Boston, 1958).

B: *DCIA* 856; *EWM* 2, 1840–41; *MB* 147–48; David E. Gillingham, *The Politics of Piety* (B.A. thesis, Princeton University, 1967); Robert Moats Miller, *Bishop G. Bromley Oxnam: Paladin of Liberalism* (Nashville, 1990); Rembert G. Smith, *Garfield Bromley Oxnam: Revolutionist?* (Houston, 1953).

P

PIERCE, LOVICK (24 March 1785, Halifax County, NC–9 November 1879, Sparta, GA). *Education:* M.D., University of Pennsylvania, 1816. *Career:* preacher, South Carolina Conference, 1804–09; ordained deacon in 1807, elder in 1809; presiding elder, 1809–12; chaplain to U.S. troops in Savannah, War of 1812, 1812–14; medical student, 1814–16; medical doctor in Greensboro, GA, 1816–23; preacher of important churches in Georgia, 1823–55?.

Lovick Pierce was born in North Carolina but grew up in South Carolina. Baptist by birth, he was converted under the preaching of a Methodist circuit rider in 1803 and soon decided to become a preacher. He joined the South Carolina Conference in 1804 and was assigned to the Great Pee Dee circuit in the eastern part of the state, where for a time he was engaged in teaching. Two years later he went to the Apalachee circuit, and in 1809 was made a presiding elder of the Oconee District in Georgia. The Pierces had eight children, three of whom became Methodist preachers and one of whom, George Foster, was elected a bishop in the MECS.

Drafted for the War of 1812, Pierce was assigned chaplain to the garrison at Savannah. After the war Pierce stopped preaching and earned a medical degree at the University of Pennsylvania. He practiced medicine and managed the family plantation in Greensboro, Georgia, until 1823. Having assured his family's financial security by his medical practice and by farming, Pierce returned to the ministry, serving appointments near his plantation in west-central Georgia.

He was a charter member of the Georgia Conference and South Carolina Conference and was elected to the first delegated general conference (1812) and to fourteen other MEC and MECS general conferences. A leader of the southern caucus at the divisive General Conference of 1844, he was a delegate to the Louisville Convention, which organized the MECS in 1845, and to the new church's first General Conference in 1846.

Hoping to continue cordial relations with northern Methodists, the conference elected Pierce fraternal delegate to the 1848 MEC General Conference. When the 1848 General Conference rebuffed his overture in Pittsburgh, Pierce became the embodiment of the rift in Episcopal Methodism. Pierce lived to see the two churches establish fraternal relations after the Civil War, however. In 1876 he was again elected fraternal delegate to the northern Methodist General Conference. Ill health prevented his presence at the conference in Baltimore, but the acceptance of his written message did much to repair the damage caused by the General Conference action of 1848.

Pierce supported progressive measures, such as lay representation in the conferences and longer pastorates for ministers. More liberal on such issues as education for women and theological education for ministers than his son, the bishop, Lovick Pierce's life bore fruit in another Georgia bishop, Atticus Green Haygood,* whom he taught to love theology and to prepare sermons carefully. When Pierce died in 1879, his life had spanned almost the entire first century of Methodism in America.

Bibliography

A: *A Semi-centennial Discourse* (Nashville, 1857).

B: *CM* 717–18; *NCA* 15, 22, and 29 November, 6 December 1879; *EWM* 2, 1908–9; William R. Cannon, "The Pierces, Father and Son," *Methodist History* 17 (October 1978): 3–15; George G. Smith, *The Life and Times of George Foster Pierce* (Nashville, 1888); Lewis Walker, "Lovick Pierce, D.D.," *MQRS* 44/3 (January/February 1897): 321–31.

R

RANKIN, THOMAS (1738, Dunbar, Scotland–17 May 1810, London, England). *Career*: Methodist lay preacher in England, 1761–73; general superintendent of Wesley's mission in the North American colonies, 1773–78; Methodist preacher in London, 1778–83.

Born in Scotland, Thomas Rankin was religiously trained by his parents and early showed an inclination to become a minister. After the death of his father, however, he led a dissolute youth. When at seventeen the family moved to Edinburgh, he began to take an interest in religion and became associated with a church whose pastor was renewed by the Evangelical Revival then sweeping Scotland and England. On one of evangelist George Whitefield's visits to Edinburgh, young Rankin was converted and resolved to become a minister in the Church of Scotland.

Lacking resources for a university education, in 1758 Rankin became instead an assistant to an Edinburgh merchant and spent a few months in Charleston, South Carolina, as agent for the firm. The next year, while on leave at home, he was converted in a Methodist revival and encouraged by its leaders to become a preacher, but young Rankin hesitated. He heard Wesley preach in Edinburgh and wrote to him for advice, and eventually he agreed to become one of his preachers in 1761. Wesley appointed him to the Sussex circuit and in the following two years to the Sheffield and then the Devonshire circuits. After preaching on circuits in Cornwall, Epworth, and London, he traveled for a time with Wesley on his supervisory tours.

When Wesley grew dissatisfied with leadership of his North American mission, he sent Rankin, then a man of thirty-five who had been an itinerant preacher for eleven years, to oversee Methodist work there in 1773. Within weeks of his arrival he convened the first conference of American preachers at Philadelphia (July 1773), where he appointed them to their circuits but limited himself to none.

Following Wesley's orders, Rankin tightened discipline among the people and imposed even stricter standards on the preachers, which did not endear him to his assistants or his people. The result was on the one hand a remarkably committed body of members and preachers, and on the other a large erosion of the forces. Between 1773 and 1778, of sixty traveling preachers listed, only twenty-eight were left, including ten admitted that year. Friction developed between Rankin and the emerging leader of the Methodists in America, Francis Asbury,* which prompted Rankin to draw a wedge between Wesley and Asbury.

When the war with Britain broke out, Rankin tried not to take sides, but soon he returned to England, where he was appointed to a London circuit. After only five years he retired from active ministry, only to take it up again in 1789, when he was ordained by Wesley. Rankin continued to make London his home, and at his death in 1810 he was buried near the grave of Wesley in the churchyard at Wesley's Chapel. A portion of Rankin's manuscript journal is in the collection of Garrett Evangelical Theological Seminary in Evanston, Illinois.

Bibliography

A: *The Diary of Rev. Thomas Rankin* (Evanston, IL, 1970?); ''The Life of Mr. Thomas Rankin, written by himself,'' in *The Lives of Early Methodist Preachers*, ed. Thomas Jackson (London, 1866), 5: 135–217; ''A Short Account of Mr. Thomas Rankin, in a Letter to the Rev. Mr. John Wesley,'' *Arminian Magazine* (London) 2/4 (April 1779): 182–98.

B: *AAP* 7, 28–34; *CBTEL* 8, 907–8; *CM* 743–44; *DNB* 16, 733; *EWM* 2, 1986; *HDM*; Frank Baker, *From Wesley to Asbury* (Durham, NC, 1976).

ROBERTS, ROBERT RICHFORD (2 August 1778, Frederick County, MD– 26 March 1843, Greencastle, IN). *Education*: no formal education other than one year in a rural school. *Career:* admitted to the Baltimore Conference, 1802; filled various pastoral assignments in western Pennsylvania, Maryland, and Ohio, 1802–08; pastorates in Baltimore, Alexandria, Georgetown, and Old St. George's Church, Philadelphia, 1808–15; presiding elder, Schuylkill District, 1815–16; bishop, MEC, 1816.

Robert Richford Roberts was the first bishop to be married at the time of his election. After 1816, however, all other Methodist bishops were married until William R. Cannon* was elected in 1968. Growing up on a farm in western Pennsylvania, an expert with a rifle, experienced and skilled in the forest, Roberts was a man of the frontier. He was, in fact, apprehensive about his ability to adjust when he was assigned to Baltimore. When he received the letter of appointment from Francis Asbury,* he told his wife, ''This is a great mistake. We are not city people, and I am not fitted for such an appointment'' (Tippy, 94). But he did well.

He also gained the respect of his colleagues, and when it was necessary to elect a moderator to preside over the sessions of the Philadelphia Annual Conference in 1816 after the death of Asbury, Roberts was chosen. At the following General Conference he was elected to the episcopacy on the second ballot. Never far from his roots, he established his episcopal residence on the farm in the Shenango Valley, from which he had been removed to serve in Baltimore eight years earlier. He moved to Indiana in 1819. One of his early duties required him to preside over the organization of the Mississippi Annual Conference. There were only seven preachers present at the conference, but Roberts made the journey which took nine months, during which he contracted malaria. Until three months before his death Roberts was constantly traveling by horseback, steamer, and stage to perform the duties of his office.

Despite his own lack of formal education, Roberts spent the last ten years of his life actively working on behalf of Indiana Asbury University (DePauw today). He had presided over the Indiana Conference in 1810 when it had been organized, and he may even have suggested the original name for the college. Roberts had also presided in the Kentucky Conference when Augusta College was organized.

Bibliography

B: *DAB* 16, 14–15; *CM* 760–61; *EWM* 2, 2032; *JLFA*; *LMB* 167–86; *MB* 158–59; Charles Elliott, *The Life of the Rev. Robert R. Roberts* (New York, 1844); Benjamin St. James Fry, *Life of Robert R. Roberts* (New York, 1852); William C. Larrabee, *Asbury and His Coadjutors*, vol. 2 (Cincinnati, 1854); Marion Worth Tippy, *Frontier Bishop* (New York, 1958).

S

SCOTT, ORANGE (13 February 1800, Brookfield, VT–31 July 1847, Newark, NJ). *Career*: Methodist Episcopal minister in Vermont and Massachusetts, 1821–30; ordained deacon in 1824, elder in 1826; presiding elder in Massachusetts and Rhode Island, 1830–35; minister, Lowell, MA, 1836; agent, American Anti-Slavery Society, 1837; minister, Lowell, MA, 1839–41; convalescent retirement, 1841–42; minister and publishing agent of the Wesleyan Methodist Church and editor, *True Wesleyan*, 1842–47.

Orange Scott was converted at age twenty at a Methodist camp meeting in Vermont and the next year entered ministry. He overcame poor schooling and excelled in several pastoral appointments in his native New England. In 1833 he became absorbed in a cause to which he became devoted and for which he was eventually censured. He was convinced through reading and attending antislavery lectures that slaveholding was sinful. Owners usurped the place of God, he argued, by giving themselves absolute control over other persons. Opposing all colonization schemes as impractical and unjust, he became an ardent abolitionist led by the vision of immediate emancipation, education for freed blacks, and constitutional provisions to protect their civil rights. For the next fifteen years Scott preached repentance from the sin of slaveholding as one of the nations's chief social sins. In 1835 he contributed several articles to *Zion's Herald*, Methodism's chief paper in New England, in an effort to win support for abolition. When negative reaction from some readers closed the paper's pages to further articles by him, Scott and his friends founded a new newspaper for Methodists who favored abolition. Scott lectured widely on the subject and introduced the cause at Methodist conferences whenever he could, but bishops began to impose what Scott and his colleagues called the gag rule, which declared discussion of the matter out of order.

Scott led the abolitionist caucus at the Methodist General Conferences of 1836 and 1840 but lost each time when moderates voted with conservatives to kill debate. Considered a reckless incendiary by many bishops and preachers, Scott was eventually stripped of his position and accused of endangering the unity of the church by overemphasizing the slavery issue.

By 1842 Scott withdrew from the MEC in a protest combining self-righteousness on the abolition question and opposition to episcopal polity. The next year he presided at a convention in Utica, New York, which formed the Wesleyan Methodist Connection, a group of antislavery churches and preachers ranging from Maine to Michigan. He served the new church as editor of its newspaper, the *True Wesleyan*, and publisher of its books. In 1845 he made an extensive tour of western states to spread the abolitionist gospel, and that arduous task sealed his fate. He retired the next year and died two years later.

Bibliography

A: *An Appeal to the Methodist Episcopal Church* (Boston, 1838); *Church Government: A Work for the Times* (Boston, 1844); *The Grounds of Secession from the M.E. Church* (New York, 1848; reprinted 1969); *The Methodist E. Church and Slavery* (Boston, 1844).
B: *AAP* 7, 667–71; *CM* 791; *DAB* 16, 497–98; *DARB* 478–79; *EWM* 2, 2112–13; *HDM*; *NCAB* 2, 315–16; Donald G. Mathews, "Orange Scott, The Methodist Evangelist as Revolutionary," in *The Antislavery Vanguard*, ed. Martin Duberman (Princeton, NJ, 1965), 71–101; Lucius C. Matlack, *The Life of Rev. Orange Scott* (New York, 1847–48; reprinted 1971).

SHAW, ANNA HOWARD (14 February 1847, Newcastle-upon-Tyne, England–2 July 1919, Moylan, PA). *Education*: B.A., Albion College, 1875; B.D., Boston University, 1878; M.D., Boston University, 1885. *Career*: school teacher, 1862–65; licensed to preach in the MEC, 1871; pastor, Hingham, MA, 1878–79; pastor, Wesleyan Methodist Church, East Dennis, MA, 1879–85; ordained by the New York Conference of the Methodist Protestant Church, 1880; lecturer, Massachusetts Woman's Suffrage Association, 1885–88; superintendent for woman's suffrage, National WCTU, 1888–92; vice-president, National American Woman Suffrage Association, 1892–1904; president, 1904–15; chair, Woman's Committee of the U.S. Council of National Defense, 1917–19.

Anna Howard Shaw was born in England. Her father moved to America when she was two, and with her mother she followed two years later. Thomas Shaw established a flour and grain business in Lawrence, Massachusetts, and had become involved with the reform movements of the day. The Shaw home became a station on the Underground Railroad, smuggling African-Americans from slavery to safety. After living in Lawrence, MA, for eight years, Thomas Shaw relocated his family to rural Michigan (now Big Rapids), where they lived in a log cabin on the farm her father was claiming from the wilderness. At age fifteen Anna Shaw became a school teacher, but she was unable to attend high school until after the Civil War.

In her early twenties Shaw joined the Methodists against her Unitarian parents' wishes. She soon found a presiding elder who assisted her in a growing ambition to become a preacher. When she was twenty-four, she was licensed to preach by the Michigan Conference of the MEC and began to work her way through Methodist Albion College, preaching and lecturing on temperance. After graduation in 1875, she attended Boston University School of Theology, the second female to attend the school. After graduation she became pastor of three small churches and in 1880 applied for ordination in the MEC. As a licensed but not ordained pastor, she could not administer the sacraments or baptize or receive members into the church, but she could marry and bury. When the bishop refused to ordain her and her friend Anna Oliver,* Shaw turned to the MPC and later that year became the first woman ordained by that denomination.

During her Boston years Shaw became aware of the appalling conditions in the local slums. To respond to the need, she studied medicine at Boston University, received her M.D. degree in 1886, and threw herself into settlement house work in the city of Boston.

By the middle 1880s Shaw became convinced that both the ministry and medicine were limited in their ability to deal with basic social problems, particularly those of women. She saw but one solution—the removal of the stigma of disenfranchisement. She resigned her pastorate and lectured for a year on behalf of the Massachusetts State Suffrage Association. In 1886 Shaw became the superintendent for women's suffrage of the WCTU, the largest women's organization in America. She soon became a popular lecturer on the Chautauqua circuit on behalf of women, her primary concern. At a rally in 1888 she met Susan B. Anthony, who became her close friend and colleague. Anthony's niece, Lucy E. Anthony, became Shaw's private secretary and companion for the rest of her life. In 1892 when Susan B. Anthony became president of the National Woman Suffrage Association, Shaw was named vice-president-at-large. Shaw became president in 1904. While in office she raised the membership of the association from 17,000 to 200,000. Shaw was the first ordained woman to speak before both houses of Congress and in the major European cities of Amsterdam, Berlin, Copenhagen, London, and Oslo. She retired from suffrage work in 1915, the same year her autobiography, *The Story of a Pioneer*, was published.

Although an ardent advocate of peace, at the outbreak of World War I she was appointed chair of the Woman's Committee of the Council of National Defense. For her work with this committee she earned the Distinguished Service Medal and received letters of commendation from President Wilson, General Pershing, and several European leaders. At war's end Shaw lectured widely on peace. She was on a speaking tour of the United States to rally public support for the League of Nations when she was stricken with pneumonia, from which she never recovered. Shaw lived long enough to know that the suffrage amendment had at last passed both houses of Congress and was on its way to ratification.

Bibliography

A: "My Ordination: Anna Howard Shaw," *Methodist History* 14/2 (January 1976): 125–31; *The Speeches of Anna Howard Shaw*, collected and edited with introduction and notes by Wil A. Linkugel (unpublished Ph.D. diss., University of Wisconsin, 1960); *The Story of a Pioneer* (New York, 1915; reprinted 1929 and 1972).

B: *Chicago Tribune* 27 July 1919; *DAB* 17, 35–37; *EWM* 2, 2132–33; *HDM*; *NCAB* 14, 456; *Notable American Women* 3, 274–77, 456; *NYT* 3 July 1919; *RLA* 419–20; *Standard Encyclopedia of the Alcohol Problem* (Westerville, OH) 5 (1929): 2427; *Who's Who in America, 1918–19*; Wil A. Linkugel and Martha Solomon, *Anna Howard Shaw, Suffrage Orator and Social Reformer* (Westport, CT, 1990); Mary D. Pellauer, *Toward a Tradition of Feminist Theology: The Religious Social Thought of Elizabeth Cady Stanton, Susan B. Anthony, and Anna Howard Shaw* (New York, 1991); Ralph Spencer, *Anna Howard Shaw, the Evangelical Feminist* (Ph.D. diss., Boston University, 1972); Frances E. Willard, ed. *A Woman of the Century* (Buffalo: C. W. Moulton, 1893): 648–49.

SIMPSON, MATTHEW (21 June 1811, Cadiz, OH–18 June 1884, Philadelphia, PA). *Education*: Madison College, fall 1818; read medicine and licensed to practice, 1833. *Career*: brief medical practice; admitted to Pittsburgh Conference, 1833; pastor, Pittsburgh, 1833–37; professor of natural science, Allegheny College, 1837–39; president, Indiana Asbury College (now DePauw University, Greencastle, IN), 1839–48; editor, *Western Christian Advocate*, 1848–52; bishop, MEC, 1852.

Perhaps the most influential bishop in the MEC in the period during and after the Civil War, Simpson was famous at home and abroad as an advocate of the Union cause, orator, and friend of presidents. He was often a visitor in the White House during the Lincoln, Grant, and Hays administrations, officiated at the wedding of Robert Todd Lincoln there, and delivered the eulogy for Lincoln at the graveside service in Springfield. His speeches on behalf of the Union raised thousands of dollars but gained him strong opposition in the South, especially after he and Bishop E. R. Ames arranged to acquire confiscated southern church property through their influence with Secretary of War Edwin M. Stanton.

Liberal in his social thinking, Simpson favored lay representation in the conferences, temperance, education for women, and church extension. He also supported women's right to vote, since he believed, "They will educate the little children on their knees; while they are young they will consecrate them to Christ, and we will have raised up an army of missionaries to go over the earth" (*The Methodist*, "Ladies Centenary Meeting at St. Paul's," 14 April 1866).

In the fashion of his time, Simpson articulated the common mission of the church and the vision of "manifest destiny" propounded in the country. He believed both had been ordained by God to set an example for the world to follow, and he made little distinction between their values.

Bibliography

A: *Cyclopedia of Methodism* (Philadelphia, 1878); *Funeral Address Delivered at Burial of President Lincoln* (Springfield, 1865); *One Hundred Years of Methodism* (New York, 1876); *Lectures on Preaching* (New York, 1879); *Sermons* (New York, 1885).
B: *CM* 801; *DAB* 17, 181–82; *DCIA* 1087–88; *EWM* 2, 2159–60; *LMB* 768–69; *MB* 165–67; *WCA* 1848–52; George R. Crooks, *Life of Bishop Matthew Simpson* (New York, 1890); Robert D. Clark, *The Life of Matthew Simpson* (New York, 1956); James E. Kirby, *The Ecclesiastical and Social Thought of Matthew Simpson* (Ph.D. diss., Drew University, 1963); "Matthew Simpson and the Mission of America," *Church History* (September 1967); E. M. Wood, *The Peerless Orator* (Pittsburgh, 1909).

SNETHEN, NICHOLAS (15 November 1769, Glen Cove, Long Island, NY–30 May 1845, Princeton, NJ). *Career*: joined Methodist ministry, 1794; rode circuits in Connecticut, Vermont, and Maine, 1794–97; Charleston, SC, 1798–1800; ordained deacon in 1798, elder in 1800; Bishop Asbury's* traveling companion, 1800–1802; Baltimore, 1802–03; New York, 1803–06; retired to his farm in Frederick, MD, 1806–09; pastorates in Fells Point, MD, Baltimore, MD, Georgetown, DC, Alexandria, VA, and Frederick, MD, 1809–14; again retired to farm in Frederick, MD, 1814–29; withdrew from the ministry of the MEC and joined the MPC, 1829; preacher and teacher in Sullivan County, IN, Louisville, KY, and Cincinnati, OH, 1829–34; editor, *Methodist Protestant*, 1834–36; head, Methodist Protestant theological college in New York, 1836–37; head, Methodist Protestant Manual Labor Ministerial College, Lawrenceburg, IN, 1837–38; principal, Snethen Seminary, Iowa City, IA, 1838–39.

Nicholas Snethen was of Welsh descent, the son of a man who cultivated a farm and operated a flour mill, sending his product to New York in his own schooner. Nicholas spent much of his youth on the farm and on the schooner. Through private study he acquired a competent basic education. When he was about twenty-one, the family moved to Staten Island, and in 1791 to Belleville, near Newark, New Jersey. Reared in the Episcopal Church, here Snethen came under the influence of the Methodists and professed conversion.

In time he began to speak and pray in Methodist meetings. He entered the ministry of the MEC in 1794 and for four years served circuits in Connecticut, Vermont, and Maine. In 1799 he was appointed to Charleston, South Carolina, and was ordained elder there in 1800. The following year he preached in Baltimore and in 1801–02 was a traveling companion of Bishop Asbury. For the next three years he preached in Baltimore and New York. Between 1806 and 1809 he temporarily retired from active ministry, but then, until 1814, he preached at Fells Point and Baltimore in Maryland; Georgetown, Washington, D.C., and Alexandria, Virginia. While at Georgetown he was elected chaplain of the House of Representatives, commanding large audiences and the intimacy of Henry Clay and other public figures. In 1814 he retired again to his farm in Maryland, and in 1816 he ran for U.S. Congress but was defeated.

During the controversy that followed the complaints of James O'Kelly against the episcopal authority of Bishop Asbury in 1792, Snethen took Asbury's side. At the General Conference of 1812, however, he identified himself with the caucus favoring lay representation in the conferences and limitation of the powers of the bishops, declaring in the course of the debate that he would not again appear on the floor of General Conference until he was sent there by vote of the laity as well as the ministers. When in 1820 the *Wesleyan Respository* was established to further the cause of reform, Snethen was a frequent contributor. His articles were later gathered and published as *Snethen on Lay Representation*. He also contributed to the reform monthly *Mutual Rights*, published at Baltimore beginning in 1824. He prepared the memorial to the General Conference of 1828 asking for reform. When that body turned a deaf ear to the request, in November 1818 he convened the reformers in Baltimore and proposed the establishment of the Methodist Protestant Church. Snethen was the principal drafter of the Articles of Association for the new church and was elected president of the Maryland Conference.

An ardent abolitionist, in 1829 Snethen freed his slaves, sold his farm, and moved to Sullivan County, Indiana. Subsequently he moved to Louisville and later to Cincinnati, where he continued to preach as well as farm. In 1834 he returned to Baltimore to edit *Mutual Rights*. In addition to reforming the government of the MEC, Snethen favored ministerial education. In 1835 he gave up editorship of the church's paper to head a school to train ministers for the new church in New York City. Moving west again in 1837 Snethen became head of another Methodist Protestant ministerial training school founded by the Ohio Conference at Lawrenceburg, Indiana, which survived but a year. His last activities were spent in the territory of Iowa, where he attempted to establish yet another school for ministers in Iowa City. He died at the home of his daughter before the school got under way.

Bibliography

A: *An Answer to James O'Kelly's Vindication* (Philadelphia, 1802); *A Discourse on the Death of Bishop Asbury* (Baltimore, 1816); *A Reply to an Apology for Protesting against the Methodist Episcopal Government* (Philadelphia, 1800); *Sermons*, ed. W. G. Snethen (Washington, DC, 1846); *Snethen on Lay Representation* (Baltimore, 1835).
B: *AAP* 7, 243–53; *CBTEL* 9, 836; *CM* 813; Thomas H. Colhouer, *Sketches of the Founders of the Methodist Protestant Church* (Baltimore?, 1880); *DAB* 17, 382–83; Edward J. Drinkhouse, *History of Methodist Reform* (Baltimore, 1899); Harlan L. Feeman, *Francis Asbury's Silver Trumpet* (Nashville, 1950); *Methodist Recorder* (Baltimore) 12 July 1845; *NCAB* 2, 165.

SOULE, JOSHUA (1 August 1781, Bristol, ME–6 March 1867, Nashville, TN). *Education:* no formal education, *Career:* admitted to Maine Conference, 1799; assistant to Timothy Merritt, Portland circuit; pastor, Union River circuit, Maine; Sandwich circuit, Nantucket, MA, 1799–1804; presiding elder, Maine District,

1804–06; Kennebec District, 1806–08, Portland District, 1808–12; pastor, Lynn, MA, 1812–13; presiding elder, Kennebec District, 1813–16; book agent, 1816–20; elected bishop, 1820, but refused to be ordained; pastor, New York and Baltimore, 1820–24; elected bishop, MEC, 1824–44; bishop, MECS, 1844–67.

First editor of the *Methodist Magazine,* book agent, and bishop in two branches of Methodism, Joshua Soule is best known as a defender of strong episcopacy and as the author of the constitution of the MEC, 1808, with its Third Restrictive Rule protecting the itinerant general superintendency. This constitution was adopted without modification when the MECS was formed in 1845, and it has been only slightly modified to the present.

In the controversy that arose in the 1820s over the question of electing presiding elders, Soule took the position that these elders were an extension of the episcopal office and should, therefore, be appointed only by the bishops. When himself elected to the episcopacy in the midst of this controversy in 1820, he became the first person in the history of the denomination to refuse ordination. He was convinced he could not serve when, in his judgment, the constitution had been violated by the decision to elect presiding elders. He did, however, accept election four years later when the matter had been resolved.

It is ironic that Soule, born in Maine, senior bishop of the MEC, and longtime resident of Lebanon, Ohio, at the age of sixty-three became the champion of the MECS. Soule's decision to affiliate with the southern branch, however, was consistent with his views on the episcopacy. The traditional understanding of that office in the southern church was compatible with his own and with his interpretation of the constitution itself. He was an active bishop in the southern church for a decade.

Bibliography

A: *Sermon on the Death of the Rev. Francis Asbury* (New York, 1816); *Sermon on the Death of the Rev. William McKendree* (Cincinnati, 1836).

B: *DAB* 17, 404–5; *CM* 814; *EWM* 2, 2199–200; *JLFA*; *LMB* 515–30; *MB* 169–70; Horace M. DuBose, *Life of Joshua Soule* (Nashville, 1911); Norman W. Spellman, *The General Superintendency in America Methodism* (Ph.D. diss., Yale University, 1961).

STILWELL, WILLIAM M. (1790?, Jamaica, NY–9 August 1851, Astoria, NY). *Career:* joined New York Conference of the MEC, 1815; appointed to Newburg, Ulster, Delaware, and Schnectady, 1815–18; Asbury and Zion ME African-American Churches, New York City, 1819–20; withdrew from the MEC to form the Methodist Society in the City of New York, 1820; pastor of independent Methodist Church, New York City, 1826–50?.

William Stilwell was born and raised on Long Island, NY. Through the influence of his uncle, Samuel Stilwell, a prominent leader in New York state politics and trustee of John Street Methodist Church, William early decided to become a Methodist minister. Admitted on trial into the Methodist Conference in 1815, he was first appointed to circuits along the upper Hudson River Valley.

In 1819 he returned to the city to lead Zion and Asbury Churches, two large (791 members reported in 1819) and restless African-American churches in New York City. The next year Stilwell spearheaded a major schism in New York Methodism.

The schism was rooted in a situation that extended back to the beginning of Methodism in New York City. From Wesley's day Methodist church buildings became the property of the denomination, held in trust by elected trustees who administered the church's business in accordance with the church's book of discipline. In New York City this pattern was not carefully followed. The trustees of John Street Church, for example, preferred to be governed by their original charter of 1766, which gave ownership and control to their local trustees rather than to clergy, bishops, or the denomination. The ministers in the city favored the Discipline, whereas the members of the six congregations in the city were divided.

When in 1820 the New York Conference sought action by the state legislature to bring all Methodist churches under the regulations of the trust clause in the Discipline, Stilwell hired a schoolroom as a place of worship and there on 16 July preached and gave notice that he had withdrawn from the MEC and invited all who wished to join him in forming a new Methodist denomination. A hundred discontented Methodists joined him on the spot, and within weeks the new church was incorporated as "The Methodist Society in the City of New York." Stilwell's congregation quickly grew to three hundred members. A lot was purchased near the rented premises, and a new brick church erected and dedicated before the year was out.

To guide the "reformed" Methodists a new Book of Discipline was published in 1821; the new text agreed with the old, except there was no provision for bishops or presiding elders and no trust class for church property. In governance the new church was intensely democratic: All ordained ministers, itinerant or local, were members with vote in the annual conference, along with two lay delegates from each congregation. Every lay member, female and male, had a vote in congregational meetings and every question was decided by a majority vote.

By pamphlet and other means Stilwell sought to spread the word of resistance and encouraged secessions in other communities. By 1824, when city membership topped three hundred, two additional churches were opened in New York City. "Reformed" Methodist churches were also organized on Long Island and in upstate New York, as well as in Connecticut, New Jersey, Pennsylvania, and Ohio, and for a time they associated together.

Stilwell used the 1820 New York Conference directive to instill in the African-American members a feeling of uncertainty, leading them to fear that they might lose their own religious liberty and eventually their property to the white church. When the Asbury and Zion Churches failed in 1821 to get approval from the bishop or the annual conference for ordination and the organization of a black conference, they turned to Stilwell for guidance. On 17 June 1822 Stilwell and two other "Stilwellite" clergy ordained three elders and six deacons for Zion Church, renamed African Methodist Episcopal Zion (AMEZ) Church, and James Varick was elected bishop of what would become the second independent black Methodist denomination. Stilwell's other church, Asbury Church, decided to join Richard Allen's Philadelphia-based AME Church.

Questions of connectional unity versus congregational autonomy persisted in Stilwell's Methodist society. Some preachers and laypersons believed that each church should be independent and have a permanent minister. Others, though agreeing that they did not want to be ruled by bishops, wanted the churches to be connected and the ministers to be part of an itinerant system. The founding church in New York City declared its independence from the association in 1826 and chose Stilwell as permanent pastor. The fragile association of connectional-minded reformers struggled along into the 1840s, while one church after another either joined the newly organized MPC or returned to the Methodist Episcopal fold.

While the association dissolved, Stilwell's independent congregation thrived. As late as 1846 his congregation numbered over three hundred members and in 1847 built a new church on First Street near First Avenue. Here Stilwell passed the rest of his ministerial career in supreme ecclesiastical independence. He died in 1851 and the church died with him.

Both Stilwell and the secession were controversial and have been evaluated differently by historians according to their denominational bias. Writing from the perspective of the MEC in 1892, Seaman editorialized, "The case is especially instructive in respect to the unwisdom of seeking the reform of supposed abuses or the correction of infelicities in the affairs of the Church by going out from its communion" (*Annals of New York Methodism*, 231). Historian of the MPC Edward J. Drinkhouse, writing in 1899, stressed that Stilwell was persecuted by his brethren and constrained finally to withdraw from the church. William J. Walls, bishop of the AMEZ Church, observed in his 1974 history, "Reverend William Stilwell proved to be a shepherd among our people, so that he won their confidence" (*The A.M.E. Zion Church*, 75).

Bibliography

A: *A Collection of Hymns for Worship* (New York, 1821, 2d ed., 1825); *Discipline of the Methodist Society as Adopted in the City of New-York, 16th of July 1821* (New York, 1821; 3d ed., 1851); "The Methodist Society," in I. Daniel Rupp, *An Original History of the Religious Denominations at Present Existing in the United States* (Philadelphia, 1844), 423–42.

B: *CBTEL* 9, 1028 (Stilwellites); *CM* 833–34 (Stilwellites); *HAM* 1, 625–29; Edward J. Drinkhouse, *History of Methodist Reform* (Baltimore, 1899); Samuel A. Seaman, *Annals of New York Methodism* (New York, 1892), pp. 215–29; Samuel Stilwell, *Historical Sketches of the Rise and Progress of the Methodist Society in the City of New York* (New York, 1821); William J. Walls, *The A.M.E. Zion Church: Reality of the Black Church* (Charlotte, NC, 1974).

STOCKTON, WILLIAM SMITH (8 April 1785, Burlington, NJ–20 November 1860, Burlington, NJ). *Career*: bookseller, Trenton, NJ, 1809?–15?; bookseller, Easton, PA, 1815?–22; superintendent of welfare programs, city of Philadelphia, 1825?–43.

William Smith Stockton's parents were among the earliest Methodists in Burlington, NJ, whose home was the gathering place for religious meetings. Stockton was educated in the local public schools and early developed a taste for reading and writing. Following a youthful conversion experience he joined the MEC and as a young man was appointed leader of a class of African-American Methodists in his neighborhood. Following marriage to Elizabeth S. Hewlings in 1807, he moved to Mount Holly, New Jersey.

In the 1820s Stockton took a leading part in the temperance reform movement, publishing a little book on the subject in 1821, four years before the American Temperance Society was formed in 1825. In the next decade he became an ardent antislavery man. But his chief claim to fame was the heroic role he played in the 1820s and 1830s in the reform movement that gave rise to the Methodist Protestant Church. To give voice to the reformers who were protesting the government of the MEC, he founded the *Wesleyan Repository and Religious Intelligencer* in 1821. In its first issue he pledged open debate. For three years Stockton's *Repository* was the principal forum for reform ideas. Views for or against the existing church discipline were welcomed. Articles on the election of presiding elders, lay representation in the conferences, conference rights for local preachers, episcopal powers, constitutional change, and trials and appeals of ministers and members were accepted. Contributing far more than most was the editor, who was careful to use a variety of pseudonyms.

After 1822 Stockton lived in Philadelphia, where he became an advocate of the poor and prison reform and editor for a time of the *People's Advocate*. Stockton first superintended Philadelphia's old almshouse on Spruce Street, which was immortalized by Longfellow in his *Evangeline*. In 1835 he helped plan and superintend the innovative Blockley Almshouse in suburban Philadelphia, an immense complex that housed two thousand of Philadelphia's poor who worked on farms or in house industries, hospitalized the sick, and cared for the mentally ill in a "lunatic asylum." Stockton abolished punishments by shower-baths, the lancet, and the whip and ended chaining of the insane.

During this time Stockton was an active member of St. George's ME Church but grew increasingly unpopular with its pastors and lay leaders as he pressed the reform agenda. With other reform-minded Methodists in the city he organized the Union Society, which soon grew to some eighty members. The society was dissolved after the expulsions in Baltimore in 1827. The next year Stockton was expelled from St. George's Church with other reformers who later organized the MPC. With his son Thomas he was a member of the Reform Convention of 1828 and the organizing General Convention of the MPC in 1830.

In 1826 Stockton began publishing the first collected works of John Wesley in America (a reprint of Benson's second London edition of 1809–12) and in 1844 purchased the exclusive American copyright for John Whitehead's revisionist lives of John and Charles Wesley, reissuing them in 1845 in handsome style with steel engravings and introductions by his son.

Stockton retired at age seventy-five to his native Burlington, New Jersey, in 1860 and died from complications of a wagon accident shortly thereafter.

Bibliography

A: "Methodist Protestant Church," in Charles Buck, *A Theological Dictionary* (Philadelphia, J. Kay, 1831); *Seven Nights; or, Several Conversations, Containing Arguments from Reason, Scripture, Facts, and Experience between Individuals of
Different Denominations* (Philadelphia, 1821); *Statements Published by S. K. Jennings and W. S. Stockton in a Controversy Regarding the Periodical Entitled "Mutual Rights and Christian Intelligencer"* (Baltimore, 1827); *Truth versus a Wesleyan
Methodist and Other Objectors* (Philadelphia, 1820).

B: *EWM* 2, 2256; *Lamb's Biographical Dictionary* 7 (1903): 223–24; *Methodist Protestant* (Baltimore) 1 December 1860; *Public Ledger* (Philadelphia) 23 November
1860; Thomas H. Colhouer, *Sketches of the Founders of the Methodist Protestant
Church* (Pittsburgh, 1880), 2: 29–33; Edward J. Drinkhouse, *History of Methodist
Reform* (Baltimore, 1899); Charles Lawrence, *History of the Philadelphia Alms-
houses and Hospitals* (Philadelphia, 1905); Thomas C. Stockton, *The Stockton Family of New Jersey* (Washington, DC, 1911).

STRAWBRIDGE, ROBERT (1732?, Drumsna, County Leitrim, Ireland–August 1781, near Towson, Maryland). *Career*: Methodist lay preacher in Ireland,
about 1755–61; in Maryland, about 1762–81.

Robert Strawbridge, one of the earliest apostles of Methodism in America,
was the son of a farmer in County Leitrim, Ireland. Methodist preachers came
to his Roman Catholic hometown in 1753, and John Wesley visited in 1758 and
1760. Strawbridge converted to Methodism and soon began to preach. His cham-
pionship of the Protestant message and ways of Methodism aroused opposition
from his Catholic neighbors, which drove him to the county of Sligo, where he
joined a Methodist society and continued preaching. During the next few years
he seems to have lived in several different places, preaching and working as a
house builder.

Precisely when or why Strawbridge came to North America we do not know.
Most authorities date his immigration about 1760. By the early 1760s he had
settled in the fertile valley of Sam's Creek in Frederick County, near Baltimore,
Maryland. The area had been retrieved from the Indians and a good road had
been built to the county from Baltimore. Shortly after coming to Maryland,
Strawbridge began to preach to his neighbors in his own house near New Windsor, first rented, then purchased on March 1773. Credit for the first-known Methodist convert in America, however, goes to Elizabeth Strawbridge rather than
to her husband. One day, in her husband's absence, a Quaker neighbor, John
Evans, had a serious conversation with Elizabeth and she became converted.

Following Methodist custom Strawbridge organized a class meeting in his
home. For a time the class alternated between meeting in the Strawbridge home

and in the more elegant home of John England, from whom Strawbridge had purchased the farm. On many occasions Strawbridge moved his meeting outdoors. With ordained ministers in short supply, Strawbridge began to administer the sacraments as well as to preach. Documentation exists for baptisms as early as 1762 or 1763. Strawbridge built a log meetinghouse about 1764 in a large meadow a mile from his home. A second Methodist chapel was built near Aberdeen, Maryland, in 1769.

With the aid of neighbors who looked after his farm and family, Strawbridge expanded his ministry, itinerating throughout Maryland, including the Eastern Shore area. Strawbridge helped form Methodist classes; later congregations in Baltimore (1763), Georgetown, Washington, DC, and Leesburg (1766), as well as several towns in Fairfax County, Virginia. He also worked with John King and Robert Williams in Maryland. In the early 1770s Strawbridge preached as far north as Trenton, New Jersey, and at St. George's Church in Philadelphia and at Martin Boehm's* home near Lancaster, Pennsylvania. An impressive list of gifted persons began to preach as a result of Strawbridge's ministry. Slaves, too, heard him gladly; some were converted and a few began to preach.

When Wesley missionaries came to America in fall 1769, Strawbridge was at first inclined to cooperate with them and to conform to Wesley's Discipline. He visited Joseph Pilmore in Philadelphia not long after his arrival. In 1773 he and his Maryland associates deeded at least six meeting houses to the Methodists. But when Strawbridge was ordered to stop administering the sacraments, he simply went on administering them to his people as he always had.

In 1773 Strawbridge, together with three other preachers, including Francis Asbury,* was appointed to the large Baltimore circuit, but his name was dropped from the conference minutes in 1774, probably because of his unyielding attitude on the sacraments. His name reappeared in the minutes for 1775, being appointed to serve at Frederick. That was the last time his name appeared in the minutes. His break with the conference had become final.

Apparently this exclusion did not discourage or embitter Strawbridge, for he continued his work and became the permanent pastor at Sam's Creek until his death in 1781. In 1776 he moved his family to the farm of Charles Ridgely in the upper part of Long Green, Baltimore County; Ridgely presented him the use of it during his life. While making his ministerial rounds, in the summer of 1781, Strawbridge died and was buried on the farm of John Wheeler, near Towson, Maryland.

The large crowds who assembled to hear Francis Asbury preach when he began to travel through Maryland in the 1770s and continued following him are explained partly because the people knew he was John Wesley's representative to America, but more importantly because many of them were enthusiastic about Methodism, having been converted under the persuasive preaching of Strawbridge. The Strawbridge home near Windsor, Maryland, still stands. A tablet commemorates its importance for Methodism. The house was designated a historical shrine in 1940, and a replica of the log meeting house has been erected.

Bibliography

B: *AAP* 7:3–4; *CM* 836; *DAB* 18, 132–33; *EWM* 2, 2262–63; *HDM*; Frederick E. Maser,
   Robert Strawbridge, First American Methodist Circuit Rider (Rutland, VT, 1983).

SUMMERS, THOMAS OSMOND (11 October 1812, Dorset, England–6 May
1882, Nashville, TN). *Career*: Admitted on trial to the Baltimore Conference,
MEC, 1835; ordained deacon in 1837, elder in 1839; minister at Augusta, Baltimore, and West River, Maryland, 1835–40; missionary in Texas (Galveston
and Houston), 1840–43; minister in Tuscaloosa, Livingston, and Mobile, AL,
1843–46; assistant editor, *Southern Christian Advocate* (Macon, GA), 1846–50;
book editor for the MECS, Nashville, 1850–81; editor, *Sunday School Visitor*,
1851–56; editor, *Quarterly Review of the MEC, South*, 1858–81; editor, *Christian Advocate*, Nashville, 1868–78.

Thomas Summers was born near Corle Castle, Isle of Purbeck, Dorset, England. Orphaned in childhood, Summers lived with his grandmother and then with
his aunt under the guardianship of three men appointed by a Presbyterian church.
Although he had little formal education, Summers educated himself. He was a
good penman and accountant, however, and easily found employment. In his late
teens he entered a period of intense religious turmoil that led to his break with the
Calvinists and their central doctrine of God's predetermining will.

During this time of turmoil he migrated to America (1830), where he experienced a religious conversion, and in 1832 he joined the Ebenezer ME Church
in Washington, D.C. Within a few years Summers felt called to the Methodist
ministry, and in 1835 he was admitted on trial to the Baltimore Conference. He
was appointed first to the Augusta circuit in the Shenandoah Valley of Virginia,
and then in 1839 to the West River circuit in Maryland. His entry into the
ministry prompted an intense period of study, during which he taught himself
a wide range of subjects.

In 1840 Summers accepted a call to missionary work in Texas and became
the only minister serving the Galveston–Houston area. His 1844 marriage to N.
B. Sexton in Tuscaloosa, Alabama, where he had been newly stationed, further
strengthened his ties to the southern branch of Episcopal Methodism, which was
in the process of becoming independent. During the 1840s Summers served
churches in Alabama while taking responsibilities at the denominational level.
He served as secretary for the General Conference of 1845 at Louisville, Kentucky, that formed the MECS. He chaired the committee that compiled a new
hymnal and joined the editorial staff of the *Southern Christian Advocate*. In
1846 Summers began editing all the church's Sunday school publications, a
practice he would continue for the next twenty-four years. In 1850 he began a
thirty-two-year role as secretary of the MECS quadrennial General Conferences,
during which time he also served as book editor of the church, building his
catalogue at the rate of more than a hundred titles a year.

In 1855 Summers moved to Nashville, where he lived for the rest of his life,
except for several years during the Civil War. During the early years of the war

Summers offered the services of his press to the Confederacy, editing the *Confederate Almanac* and publishing tracts and testaments for soldiers. When Nashville fell to Union forces, Summers fled to Alabama, where for three years he preached to black and white congregations. Returning to Nashville in the summer of 1866, Summers resumed his highly productive career, beginning with his appointment as editor of the *Christian Advocate* (1866–78). In addition to his work on periodicals and Sunday school books, the church's Books of Discipline and hymnals, prayer books, and catechisms, Summers wrote or edited hundreds of books on a wide range of religious subjects. Through his writing and editing he gave direction to the MECS that lasted well into the twentieth century.

From the beginning of his ministry Summers worked to recover Wesley's commitment to liturgy. He oversaw the reprinting of Wesley's *Sunday Service*, edited a collection of prayers, published a *Wesleyan Psalter*, and in 1870 developed a standard order of worship for the MECS. His book on baptism was widely read since publication in 1852 and was required reading for ministerial candidates from 1878 until 1902.

Summers held all the major editorial posts of the church. A highly versatile intellectual, Summers was southern Methodism's most prolific editor-author and was equally at home in the idiom of the religious newspaper or the scholarly journal. His abilities were further acknowledged when in 1874 he was appointed professor of systematic theology and the following year dean of the theological faculty at the newly created Vanderbilt University. He held the deanship for the rest of his life. His lectures at Vanderbilt were edited by John J. Tigert and published in 1888 under the title *Systematic Theology*.

Summers attended the opening of the 1882 General Conference in Nashville, where he was again elected secretary, but he served only one day. He died before the conference adjourned and was buried on the Vanderbilt University campus.

Bibliography

A: *Baptism* (Nashville, 1852); *Biographical Sketches of Eminent Itinerant Ministers* (Nashville, 1858); *Catechisms of the Methodist Episcopal Church, South* (Nashville, 1860); *Commentary on the Acts of the Apostles* (Nashville, 1874); *Commentary on the Gospels*, 4 vols. (Nashville, 1869–72); *Commentary on the Ritual of the MEC, South* (Nashville, 1873); *The Golden Censer: An Essay on Prayer* (Nashville, 1874); *Holiness: A Treatise on Sanctification* (Nashville, 1850); *The Sunday School Teacher; or, The Catechetical Office* (Richmond, 1853); *Systematic Theology: A Complete Body of Wesleyan Arminian Divinity*, 2 vols. (Nashville, 1888); *The Sunday Service of the MEC, South* (Nashville, 1867); *Wesleyan Psalter* (Nashville, 1855).

B: *DAB* 18, 207–8; *Daily American* (Nashville) 6 and 8 May 1882; *EWM* 2, 2275–76; *NCA* 13 May 1882; *RLA* 456; Oscar P. Fitzgerald, *Dr. Summers: A Life-Study* (Nashville, 1884); E. Brooks Holifield, *The Gentlemen Theologians* (Durham, NC, 1978); Thomas Langford, *Practical Divinity* (Nashville, 1983); L. Edward Phillips,

"Thomas O. Summers, Methodist Liturgist of the Nineteenth Century," *MH* 2/4 (July 1989): 241–53; James P. Pilkington, *The Methodist Publishing House: A History*, 2 vols. (Nashville, 1968–89); William N. Wade, *History of Public Worship in the MEC and MEC, South, from 1784 to 1905* (unpublished Ph.D. diss., University of Notre Dame, 1981).

SUNDERLAND, LAROY (22 April 1804, Exeter, RI–15 May 1885, New York, NY). *Career*: joined New England Conference of the MEC, 1824; ordained deacon in 1826, elder in 1828; appointed to Methodist churches in Massachusetts and Connecticut, 1824–33; leave of absence, became antislavery activist, 1833–36; editor, *Zion's Watchman* (NY), 1836–42; withdrew from the ministry of the MEC, 1840; evangelist for the occult, 1842–85.

LaRoy Sunderland was born in Exeter, Rhode Island, educated in the town's common schools, and early in life was apprenticed to a shoemaker. At a Methodist revival in 1822 he was converted and the following year began to preach in Walpole, Massachusetts. After studying for a time at Day's Academy in Wrentham, Massachusetts, he joined the New England Conference in 1824 and soon made a name for himself as an evangelist.

Next to preaching, his greatest interest was in education, especially for the ministry. Convinced Methodism needed to improve the quality of its ministers, he formed the Junior Preacher's Society and in 1834 published a landmark essay on theological education in *Methodist Magazine and Quarterly Review*. In the 1830s Sunderland took a leading role in another crusade in New York and New England—the emerging slavery question. He was an associate of Orange Scott,* a leading Methodist abolitionist, and by 1834 had risen to enough prominence within the antislavery ranks of Methodism to preside at the formation of the Methodist Antislavery Society in New York City. The initial document of the slavery debate among Methodists, "An Appeal on the Subject of Slavery Addressed to the Members of the New England and New Hampshire Conferences," published in Boston's *Zion's Herald* on 4 February 1835, was written by Sunderland and four other Methodist ministers. In it they insisted "that Methodists be true to John Wesley and their *Discipline* by urging laws for the immediate destruction of the flagrant 'sin' of slavery." During these years Sunderland also published two antislavery tracts, the *Antislavery Manual*, which set forth the legal definition of slavery and then proceeded to show what that definition meant in actual practice by depicting the barbarities of the system, and *Testimony of God against Slavery*, which wrung timely morals from biblical allusions to the evil.

Due to the active hostility of the bishops, the church press, and the church's governing General Conference, in 1836 the church's Antislavery Society founded *Zion's Watchman* in New York City and made Sunderland its editor to press the case for abolition. The *Watchman* gave voice to Methodist abolitionists whose views the church's official newspaper, the *Christian Advocate*, refused to publish. Sunderland himself unleashed a steady barrage of editorials attacking the MEC generally and the bishops in particular for permitting pro-slavery discussion in the southern conferences while muzzling antislavery talk in the northern conferences.

Within five years Sunderland bore the ordeal of five ecclesiastical trials and one civil trial because of his outspoken views on slavery as reflected in his fiery newspaper. Charges against him ranged from slander to immorality. The church's highest lawmaking body, the General Conference, went so far as to change its rules in order to make him amenable to ecclesiastical discipline, and he successfully sued for libel in the courts. Finally in 1842 he withdrew with other "radicals" and signed their call for the formation of a new church, without bishops and against slavery, called the Wesleyan Methodist Connection of America.

Sunderland, however, did not join the new denomination. During his last years he became an evangelist for the occult. The bitterness of his persecution and the acerbity of his resistance had left their mark upon his loyalties. Moreover, he had long been convinced that his early success as a revivalist had been due to hypnotic powers. Conversion, he concluded, was a natural, not a miraculous, phenomenon and religion itself was a fraud. Caught up in the restless reformism of the 1840s, Sunderland drifted away from organized religion and supported successively Mesmerism, Grahamism, and faith-healing, and he invented a faith of his own, which he called Pathetism. His Methodist friends hoped for a deathbed reconversion, but Sunderland reportedly died cheerfully facing an end that to him had no hereafter.

Bibliography

A: *Antislavery Manual* (New York, 1837; 2d ed., 1837; 3d ed., 1839); "An Appeal on the Subject of Slavery," *ZH* Extra, 4 February 1835; *Biblical Institutes; or, A Scriptural Illustration of the Doctrines, Morals, and Precepts of the Bible, with Notes and Questions* (New York, 1834); *Book of Health for the Million, with Practical Remarks on Bathing, Diet, Exercises, Disease, and the Water Cure* (Boston, 1847); *Book of Human Nature, Illustrating the Philosophy (New Theory) of Instinct, Nutrition, Life, with Their Correlative and Abnormal Phenomena, Physiological, Mental, Spiritual* (New York, 1853); *Book of Psychology* (New York, 1853); "Confessions of a Magnetiser" Exposed (Boston, 1845); *The Dynamic Cure without Medicine* (Boston, 1863), ten-plus printings; "Essay on a Theological Education" *MQR* 16/4 (October 1834): 423–37; *History of the United States of America* (New York, 1834); *Ideology*, 3 vols. (Boston, 1885–87); *Manual of Self-Healing by Nutrition without Medicine* (Boston, 1862); *Manual of the Nutritive Cure* (Boston, 1856); *Mormonism Exposed and Refuted* (New York, 1838); *Pathetism: Man Considered in His Form, Life, Sensation, Soul, Mind, Spirit; Giving the Rationale of Those Laws Which Produce the Mysteries, Miseries, Felicities of Human Nature* (Boston, 1847); *Pathetism, New Theory of Mind* (Boston, 1851); *Pathetism with Practical Instructions* (New York, 1843); *The Testimony of God against Slavery* (New York, 1835; 2d ed., 1836; 3d ed., 1839); *Theory of Nutrition* (Boston, 1855); "This Life a Time of Probation," sermon 13, *The Methodist Preacher* 1 (September 1830); *The Trance and Correlative Phenomena* (Chicago, 1868).

B: *CA* 4 June 1885; *DAB* 18, 222; *NCAB* 5:354; J. R. Jacob, "LaRoy Sunderland: The Alienation of an Abolitionist," *American Studies* 6/1 (April 1972): 1–17; Edward D. Jervey, "LaRoy Sunderland: Zion's Watchman," *Methodist History* 6/3 (April 1968): 16–32.

T

TAYLOR, WILLIAM (2 May 1821, Rockbridge County, VA–18 May 1902, Palo Alto, CA). *Education:* rural schools. *Career:* local preacher, 1842–45; admitted to the Baltimore Conference, 1845; pastoral assignments in Maryland and Virginia, 1845–48; missionary to San Francisco, CA, 1849–56; preaching, Canada to raise money, 1856–63; missionary evangelist to Australia (via Europe), 1863–66; South Africa, March–October 1866; England, West Indies, British Guiana, Australia, and Ceylon, December 1866–October 1870; India, November 1870–spring 1875; South America, 1875–84; elected missionary bishop for Africa, MEC, 1884; Africa, 1884–96; retirement, 1896–1902.

William Taylor was nineteenth-century Methodism's missionary to the world. After his election as a missionary bishop, he was given oversight of the entire continent of Africa. Taylor preached for seven years in the Baltimore Conference and then was assigned as a missionary to California. He arrived in San Francisco, with a prefabricated chapel, in 1849 to begin a unique and successful ministry that included the establishment of the Seaman's Bethel Mission. In seven years thousands heard him as he preached in his church, in the plaza, on the wharf, and in any other place where he could find an audience. He was independent and entrepreneurial, traits that led him into conflict with the organized missionary structures of the denomination. During his lifetime he published seventeen books that helped provide a living for his family and support for his missions. A shortage of money took him from California to Canada, where he heard stories of Australia and set sail in May 1866 to begin a mission there. His success and contacts in the British Empire led him to preach in South Africa, England, Barbados, and British Guiana.

Some of his most successful missionary service was in India, to which he was led by his contacts in the British Wesleyan Methodist Church. He organized a MEC in Bombay in May 1872 and found himself in conflict with both American Methodism and English Methodism. His goal was to organize an indigenous, independent church without dependence on an overseas missionary agency. In 1872 these congregations petitioned the General Conference to be organized into the Bombay Conference, to which all ministers and missionaries serving outside of the India Conference would belong. Taylor was designated its superintendent.

Taylor left India in 1875, fully expecting to return to the United States, but his next field of service was South America. Between 1877 and 1884 he made three trips to that continent. Once again his desire to establish missions independent of foreign support and control brought him into conflict with the Missionary Society. In 1882 he was informed by the General Missionary Committee that his missions were "out of order" and that he should relinquish control of them to the church.

In an interesting irony, the MEC in 1884 elected him a missionary bishop on the first ballot, and "California Taylor" became "Bishop of Africa." This work of twelve years would take him to the end of his active service. By now the church was willing to encourage self-supporting missions, and Taylor saw his election as a vindication of his concept of the Pauline method of missions. He refused to accept his salary from the Missionary Society because he did not want to be responsible to the society and because he believed the General Conference that elected him should provide his support from the Episcopal Fund. He took forty persons with him to Liberia and eventually established missions in Angola, Congo, and Mozambique. His report to the General Conference of 1888 was a glorious triumph. Exhausted and broken in health, Taylor was retired by the General Conference of 1896 and spent the balance of his life in retirement in California.

Bibliography

A: (selected) *California Life Illustrated* (New York, 1858); *Christian Adventures in South Africa* (New York, 1867); *The Election of Grace* (London, 1868); *The Flaming Torch in Darkest Africa* (New York, 1898); *Four Years' Campaign in India* (New York, 1876); *Model Preacher* (New York, 1859); *Our South American Cousins* (New York, 1878); *Reconciliation, or How to Be Saved* (New York, 1867); *Seven Years' Street Preaching in San Francisco* (New York, 1857); *Story of My Life* (New York, 1895); *Ten Years of Self-Supporting Missions* (New York, 1882).
B: *DNB* 18, 345–46; *DCIA* 1162; *EWM* 2, 2317–18; *MB* 175–76; Goodsil F. Arms, *History of the William Taylor Self-Supporting Missions in South America* (New York, 1921); David Bundy, "Bishop William Taylor and Methodist Mission: A Study in Nineteenth Century Social History," 2 pts. (*MH* July and October 1989); O. von Barchwitz-Krauser, *Six Years with William Taylor in South America* (Boston, 1885); Edward B. Davies, *The Bishop of Africa* (Redding, MA, 1885); Leon L. Loofbourow, *Circuit Riders of 1952: Isaac Owen and William Taylor* (San Francisco, 1952); John H. Paul, *The Soul Digger; or, Life and Times of William Taylor* (Upland, IN, 1928).

THOBURN, JAMES MILLS (7 March 1836, St. Clarisville, OH–28 November 1922, Meadville, PA). *Education:* Allegheny College, 1857. *Career:* taught school briefly, admitted to the Pittsburgh Conference, 1858; missionary service in India, 1859–63; returned to India, 1865, serving in Garhwal (1865–67), Moradabad (1868), Sambhal (1869), Rae Bareilly (1870), Lucknow (1871–73), and Calcutta (1874–88); founded the *Indian Witness*, 1871; founded churches in Rangoon, 1879, and in Singapore, 1884–85; elected missionary bishop for South Asia, MEC, 1888.

The Thoburn name is synonymous with MEC missions in India and South Asia. James Mills Thoburn was the first bishop of the denomination to reside in India, and the bulk of his ministry was there. His sister, Isabella, was a driving force behind the education of women in India. James was sent by the Missionary Society to India in 1859, and only a short time after he was admitted to the Pittsburgh Conference. Joining forces there with William Taylor to promote church growth and evangelism in India, Thoburn also founded the *Indian Witness* in 1871 and established churches with William F. Oldham in Burma and later in Singapore. When the Philippines opened in 1898, Thoburn went there.

William Taylor persuaded him to move to the missions in Calcutta in 1874. Following Taylor's pattern of the Pauline Method, he undertook the work without salary from the Missionary Society. His work among Europeans and Anglo-Indians in the city established him in their society as the most influential religious figure in India. He was elected a missionary bishop for southern India on the first ballot at the General Conference of 1888 and served until his retirement in 1908.

Bishop Thoburn did almost as much to educate and raise the awareness of Methodists in America to the needs and opportunity in India as he did for the churches there. One writer said that he "put India on America's heart." Altogether, he spent half a century there.

Returning to America, following the death of his first wife in October 1862, he brought with him a Hindu boy who accompanied him wherever he went. The boy, Harkua, became as well known as the missionary himself.

Thoburn's sister, Isabella (1840–1901), became well known for her work to educate the women of India. It was her influence that sent James back in 1865 when he was tempted to remain in the United States with his young son. Isabella Thoburn died in the cholera epidemic of 1901 in Lucknow, where now the women's college of Lucknow University bears her name. Thoburn's second wife, Anna Jones, a medical doctor, assisted him the missions after their marriage in 1882.

John R. Mott described Thoburn as "possibly the greatest ecclesiastic of the nineteenth century." He is richly deserving of the tribute. In addition to his missionary labors, Thoburn was the author of numerous books and articles.

Bibliography

A: (selected) *The Christian Conquest of India* (New York, 1906); *The Christless Nations* (New York, 1895); *The Church of Pentecost* (Calcutta, 1901); *India and Malaysia* (Cincinnati, 1892); *India and Southern Asia* (1907); *Life of Isabella Thoburn* (Cincinnati, 1903); *Light in the East* (Chicago, 1900); *Missionary Addresses* (New York,

1888); *My Missionary Apprenticeship* (New York, 1884); *WCA*, ''Wayside Notes: An Autobiography,'' 4 January–27 December 1911.

B: *DAB* 18, 418–19; *EWM* 2, 2334–35; *MB* 177–78; Guy D. Garrett, *The Missionary Career of James Mills Thoburn* (Ph.D. diss., Boston University, 1968); William F. Oldham, *Thoburn, Called of God* (1918); W. H. Crawford, *Thoburn and India* (New York, 1909).

V

VINCENT, JOHN HEYL (28 February 1832, Tuscaloosa, AL–9 May 1920, Chicago, IL). *Education*: academies at Milton and Lewisburg, PA; Wesleyan Institute, Newark, NJ. *Career*: Methodist Episcopal minister, northeastern PA, 1851–53; transferred to New Jersey Conference, 1853; ordained deacon in 1855, elder in 1857?; appointed pastor in Franklin, NJ, 1853–55; Irvington, NJ, 1855–57; transferred to Rock River Conference, Joliet, IL, 1857–58; Mt. Morris, IL, 1859–60; Galena, IL, 1860–62; Rockford, IL, 1862–64; Trinity, Chicago, 1864–66; general agent, Sunday School Union, MEC, 1866–68; corresponding secretary, 1868–88; bishop, Buffalo, NY, Topeka, KS, and Zurich, 1888–1904.

John Vincent was the son of Mary Raser and John Himrod Vincent, descendent of a Huguenot family. His father was a farmer, miller, postmaster, and superintendent of a Methodist Sunday school. Although born in the South, Vincent moved to Pennsylvania with his family in 1837 and grew up near Lewisburg, where he attended local high schools and became a school teacher. Around 1850 he was licensed as a preacher in the MEC and appointed to a circuit that included several small congregations in central Pennsylvania. Relocating to northern New Jersey, he continued to preach, and after completing the required course of reading in 1857, he was ordained. Later that year he transferred west to the Rock River Conference, which covered Chicago and northern Illinois. Here he successively served churches in Joliet, Mt. Morris, Galena, Rockford, and Chicago. During the Civil War he engaged in war relief work with the United States Christian Commission.

Vincent was largely self-educated. To compensate, he spent the rest of his life studying, teaching, and devising self-education schemes for himself and others. His real career began in 1866 when he moved from Chicago to New York to head the Sunday School Union of the MEC. The Sunday school movement was just emerging as a popular force in American Protestantism, and Vincent had already put several innovative ideas into practice. As early as 1855 he had organized a class to study the history and geography of the Holy Land as an aid to understanding the Bible. Two years later he organized the first class to train Sunday school teachers, and in 1861 he held the first Sunday school teacher's institute and authored his first Sunday school textbook, *Little Footprints in Bible Lands*. He labored mightily to overcome the conservative forces who opposed the use in the Sunday school of any literature other than the Bible.

Vincent established a popular *Sunday School Journal* and a companion teacher's magazine that introduced a new system of study in leaflet form, which led within a few years to uniform lessons for all Protestant denominations. Vincent's Berean lesson leaves reached a circulation of over two million. For young people Vincent organized the Oxford League (forerunner of the Epworth League) for the study of Methodist doctrine and history.

Vincent's push to professionalize the Sunday school and its faculty led to an invitation by businessman Lewis Miller to the Chautauqua campgrounds in western New York. The campgrounds, owned by the Erie Conference of the MEC, were offered to Vincent as a spot to hold a summer Sunday school teacher-training institute. Such an interdenominational training session was held in 1874. It became an annual event, growing to include activities throughout the summer and eventually giving birth to one of the greatest experiments in adult education. In 1878 the Chautauqua Literary and Scientific Circle was organized as a four-year correspondence course of study. The Chautauqua University opened in 1883, and the movement involved hundreds of thousands of people annually as it diffused through local Chautauquas around the country.

In 1888 Vincent was elected a bishop of the MEC. He served first in Buffalo, New York, which kept him close to Chautauqua. He remained the chancellor at Chautauqua until 1898, when he turned the office over to his son. Vincent served four years as bishop in Topeka, Kansas, before undertaking supervision of Methodism's churches in Europe headquartered in Switzerland in 1901. He retired from the episcopacy in 1904.

Bibliography

A: ''Autobiography,'' *NWCA* 58 (6 April–2 November 1910); *The Chautauqua Movement* (Boston, 1886); *The Church at Home: A Manual for Family Worship and Home Training* (New York, 1893); *The Church and Its Officers* (New York, 1872); *The Lesson Commentary*, with Jesse L. Hurlbut (New York, 1881–88); *Lesson Compend* (New York, 1875); *Little Footprints in Bible Lands* (New York, 1861); *The Modern Sunday School* (New York, 1882); *The Revival and after the Revival* (New York, 1883); *A Study in Pedagogy for People Who Are Not Professional Teachers* (New York, 1890); *Sunday School Institutes and Normal Classes* (New York, 1872).

B: Anne M. Boylan, *Sunday School: The Formation of an American Institution* (New Haven, CT, 1988); *Chicago Daily Tribune* 10 May 1920; *CA* 20 May and 17 June 1920; *DAB* 19, 277–79; *EWM* 2, 2429–30; *HDM*; *NCAB* 24:378; *NYT* 10 May 1920; *RLA* 987; *Sunday School Journal* 52 (September 1920): 523; Edward A. Trimmer, *John Heyl Vincent, an Evangelist for Education* (unpublished Ph.D. diss., Columbia University, 1988); Walter N. Vernon, *The United Methodist Publishing House: A History*, vol. 2 (Nashville, 1989); Leon H. Vincent, *John Heyl Vincent: A Biographical Sketch* (New York, 1925).

W

WHATCOAT, RICHARD (23 February 1736, parish of Quinton, Gloucestershire, England–5 July 1806, Dover, DE). *Education:* apprenticed, 1749–57. *Career:* exhorter, class leader, steward, 1758–69; entered the Methodist ministry, serving in England, Ireland, and Wales under the supervision of John Wesley, 1769–84; ordained and sent to America, 1784; itinerant preacher and presiding elder, 1785–1800; bishop, MEC, 1800–1806.

Richard Whatcoat, along with Thomas Coke* and Thomas Vasey, was ordained by John Wesley and sent to America to organize the Methodists there. Reared as an Anglican, Whatcoat began his association with the Methodists in 1758 and in 1769, upon the recommendation of John Pawson, was received by Wesley into the conference. Francis Asbury,* with whom he was destined to be intimately associated in America, was admitted two years earlier. Whatcoat served in England, Ireland, and Wales prior to coming to America in 1784. He was thirty-three when he began his work in Oxfordshire; his last appointment in England was at Norwich.

The invitation to go as a missionary to America seems to have taken Whatcoat by surprise, and the decision to ordain him both deacon and elder reflected Wesley's conclusion that the Methodists in America needed both an independent organization and the sacraments. He arrived to begin his work in November 1784. The decision was soon made to gather the preachers in a general conference at Baltimore in December for the purpose of organizing the MEC. Wesley's plan was accepted; Coke and Asbury were elected to the episcopacy. Following the so-called Christmas Conference, Whatcoat took up the work of an itinerant preacher. His appointment for 1785 was presiding elder of the Baltimore and Frederick circuits. The next year he went in the same capacity to the Kent, Talbot, Dorset, and Dover circuits, where he remained for the next three years.

In 1786 Wesley wrote Thomas Coke expressing his desire that Whatcoat be made a bishop, but the conference, influenced by James O'Kelly,* refused to accept the recommendation. Their reluctance was based partly on his lack of experience in America, and the fear that if Whatcoat were elected Wesley might recall Asbury to England. Wesley had, in fact, expressed his wish that Asbury should return. The larger issue, however, was the extent of Wesley's power over the church in America. Not only did the conference refuse to elect Whatcoat; they also removed Wesley's name from list of persons with authority in the 1787 minutes.

During the years up until 1800, when he was elected to the episcopacy, Whatcoat preached in the middle states from New York to North Carolina and often accompanied Asbury on his tours requiring travel in all conditions for thousands of miles. He served for extended periods as a presiding elder in Virginia, Maryland, Delaware, and in congregations in Philadelphia and New York. After his election as a bishop, Whatcoat was regarded by Asbury as a junior or assistant bishop rather than his equal. They traveled together until September 1801, when they separated for a brief period. Whatcoat's labors from 1803 on were confined largely to the middle states.

The rigors of the work of a bishop proved too much for Whatcoat, who was sixty-four at the time of his election, and he died in the home of Richard Bassett in 1806. He was a kind and humble man whose knowledge of scripture was well known. Asbury said at his death, ''A man so uniformly good I have not known in Europe or America.'' His influence on the church in America is difficult to measure, since he was so overshadowed by Asbury, but it was undoubtedly significant.

Bibliography

A: *To the Members of the Methodist Episcopal Church in Philadelphia* (Philadelphia, 1801).
B: *AAP* 7, 92–101; *CM* 934–36; *DAB* 20, 36; *EWM* 2, 2546–47; *JLFA*; *LMB* 107–26; *MB* 193–94; standard histories of Methodism, including Bangs,* Lee,* and Stevens; Sidney B. Bradley, *The Life of Bishop Richard Whatcoat* (Louisville, 1936); Benjamin St. James Fry, *The Life of Rev. Richard Whatcoat* (New York, 1852); William C. Larrabee, *Asbury and His Coadjutors* (Cincinnati, 1853); William Phoebus, *Memoirs of the Rev. Richard Whatcoat* (New York, 1828).

WILLARD, FRANCES (28 September 1839, Churchville, NY–18 February 1898, New York, NY). *Education*: B.A., Northwestern Female College, Evanston, IL, 1859. *Career*: school teacher in Illinois, Pennsylvania, and New York, 1860–67; travel in Europe, 1868–70; president, Evanston College for Ladies, 1871–73; dean of women, professor of English and art, Northwestern University, 1873–74; secretary, WCTU on state and national levels, 1874–77; president, National WCTU, 1879–98; president, World WCTU, 1891–98 (in England 1892–96).

Frances Willard was born in upstate New York. She got her first schooling surreptitiously from her mother, a school teacher, while her father was away serving the state legislature. When she was seven years old, the family moved to Janesville, Wisconsin. Since there was no Congregational church there, the family joined the MEC. Greatly admiring her older brother, Oliver, she followed him to college, entering Northwestern Female College in Evanston, Illinois, in 1852. Unlike her brother, she could neither vote nor preach (he had by that time become a student at Garrett Biblical Institute, the Methodist seminary in Evanston). She graduated with honors in 1859. The next year she had a bout with typhoid fever that led to a religious conversion, as a result of which she formally joined the MEC.

For the next seven years Willard taught school. During these years she became engaged to Charles Fowler (later a bishop in the MEC), but the engagement was suddenly broken off and she never married. In 1865 she became corresponding secretary of the American Methodist Ladies Centennial Association and then assumed the burden for the association's goal of raising money to build a dormitory at Northwestern University. The speech she wrote for the dedication was eloquently read by a man, as women were not generally allowed to speak before mixed audiences at the time.

In 1871 Willard became president of Evanston College for Ladies, associated with Methodist related-Northwestern University, and hence the first American woman to head a college. Unfortunately, the Chicago Fire that year burned the assets of the school's major financial backers, and Charles Fowler, by then the president of Northwestern University, annexed the school to the university. When Fowler stripped Willard of her control of the school, she resigned in 1874. She threw herself into work for the Association for the Advancement of Women but was soon caught up in the enthusiasm of the women's crusade against saloons. With the help of John H. Vincent,* evangelical women from a number of churchly backgrounds formed the Woman's Christian Temperance Union (WCTU) in 1874.

Though not a temperance crusader, Willard saw the possibilities of the new organization for changing women's status. She was elected the first corresponding secretary and began her rise to control. An earnest and compelling speaker, she was able to draw crowds, make headlines, and enlist support from local church women. She refused a salary and lived on lecture fees. Increasingly she put the WCTU behind the suffrage movement, in opposition to the union's first president, Annie T. Wittenmeyer. In 1877 Willard became editor of *Our Union*, the WCTU's widely circulated paper, and immediately opened its pages to the advocacy of suffrage. In 1878 she became president of the Illinois WCTU and the following year gained the national presidency, a position she held for the rest of her life.

In her first presidential address, Willard announced her controversial "Do Everything" policy. She directed the organization to press for reforms not only regarding alcohol but also labor, welfare, public health, race relations, and voting. During her presidency thirty-nine departments were established to deal with a broad range of social problems from suffrage to white slavery. Under her direction the WCTU became the largest women's and women's rights organization in the country.

In 1888 Willard was one of five women elected as delegates to the General Conference of the MEC. When they arrived at the conference, however, they ran into opposition organized by Bishop Fowler and James Buckley, editor of the influential New York–based *Christian Advocate*. Willard and other women delegates were never seated, though the same conference adopted a resolution praising women for their temperance work.

In 1892 when a coalition of farmers' alliances, labor unions, and prohibition and woman's suffrage groups failed to form a national reform party in which women would take an active role, Willard sought rest and solace in England with a friend, Lady Somerset, a devout Methodist who was president of the British WCTU. She spent most of the next four years brooding in England, where she joined the Christian Socialists and began saying that poverty was the primary cause of intemperance, and education rather than prohibition its major cure. Willard's increasingly radical views and prolonged absences added to the long-standing dissatisfaction of many WCTU rank and file with her emphasis on politics. When Willard returned to the United States in 1897, an acrimonious WCTU annual meeting reelected her president, but her health was failing. She died on the road in a New York City hotel early the next year at the age of fifty-eight.

Following her death, Willard's private secretary, Anna Gordon, wrote a glowing biography, and the WCTU promoted memorials in the form of streets, parks, and buildings around the United States. In 1905 the State of Illinois placed her statue in the rotunda of the Capitol in Washington, DC, and in 1910 she was elected to the Hall of Fame for Great Americans.

Bibliography

A: *Glimpses of Fifty Years* (Chicago, 1889); *Nineteen Beautiful Years* (Chicago, 1886); *Woman and Temperance* (Hartford, CT, 1883); *Women in the Pulpit* (Chicago, 1889); *A Woman of the Century*, ed. with Mary A. Livermore (Buffalo, NY, 1893); *Writing Out My Heart: Selections from the Journal of Frances E. Willard, 1855–1896*, ed. by Carolyn De Swarte Gifford. (Urbana, IL, 1995).

B: *DAB* 20, 233–34; *DARB* 607–8; *EWM* 2, 2564–65; *HDM*; *NAW* 3, 613–19; *NCAB* 1: 376–77; *NYT* 18 February 1898, 1; *RLA* 504–5; Ruth Bordin, *Frances Willard, A Biography* (Chapel Hill, NC, 1986); Mary E. Dillon, *Frances Willard: From Prayers to Politics* (Chicago, 1944); Anna Gordon, *The Beautiful Life of Frances E. Willard* (Chicago, 1898); Lydia J. Trowbridge, *Frances Willard of Evanston* (New York, 1938).

WILLING, JENNIE FOWLER (22 January 1834, Burford, Ontario–6 October 1916, New York, NY). *Career*: public school teacher, occasional preacher, and evangelist in New York and Illinois, 1849–74; professor of English, Illinois Wesleyan University, Bloomington, IL, 1874–89?; corresponding secretary, Northwestern Branch WFMS, 1870–84; editor, *Our Union* (WCTU), 1875–76; officer, Woman's Home Missionary Society, 1884–94; principal, New York Evangelical Settlement House and Training School, 1895–1910.

Jennie Fowler was born in Ontario. Her mother was the daughter of one of the founders of Methodism in Canada, and her father was a Canadian patriot who lost his property in the rebellion of 1837. After taking refuge with relatives in New York, Horatio Fowler in 1842 moved his family to a farm near Newark, Illinois. There Jennie grew up with two brothers, one of whom, Charles Henry, was briefly engaged in Frances E. Willard and later became president of Northwestern University and a Methodist bishop. Jennie received little formal schooling. Her natural curiosity, as well as her mother's example of reading, spurred her on to a program of self-education so that at the age of fifteen she was able to begin teaching in the village school.

At nineteen (1853) she married William C. Willing, who soon gave up practicing law to enter the Methodist ministry. Willing held several pastorates in his native New York state. He then transferred to the Rock River Conference in northern Illinois, where he moved from one town to another, serving as presiding elder in the Rockford, Joliet, and Chicago Districts while Jennie became publicly active in church. Willing arranged a local preacher's license for his wife in 1873, turning over to her all but nominal control of one Methodist church. Over the years she continued to preach and, on occasion, conducted revival meetings.

Since girlhood Mrs. Willing had written essays, some of which appeared in church periodicals. Her published books and pamphlets, as well as her many stories and articles, stressed themes of uplift, self-help, and holy living. The Evanston College for Ladies, of which Frances Willard was president, honored her for her work with an honorary bachelor's degree in 1872. Two years later she was appointed professor of English at Illinois Wesleyan University in Bloomington, Illinois, and her husband was given a law professorship there.

Mrs. Willing had already become involved in the suffrage movement in Illinois, being chosen recording secretary of the Chicago convention that formed the Illinois State Suffrage Association in 1869. At the same time she took leadership in foreign missions, promoting the Woman's Foreign Missionary Society by forming a branch chapter in Chicago and another in St. Louis a year later. For the next fourteen years, as corresponding secretary of the Chicago-based Northwestern Branch, she was responsible for organizing and coordinating the work of the society from Ohio to the Pacific coast. She attended annual meetings of the society's national executive committee, wrote articles for its paper, *The Heathen Women's Friend*, and traveled widely across the Midwest organizing societies in local churches. A third cause to which she devoted considerable energy was intemperance. In 1874 she campaigned for stricter license laws in Bloomington, giving public lectures in the evenings after her classes. That summer, while attending a training course for Sunday school teachers at Chautauqua, New York, she met other temperance reformers. With the encouragement of John Vincent,* the women set out to form a national women's temperance organization. Together with two friends, Willing issued a call for a national women's temperance meeting to be held in Cleveland, Ohio. Delegates from seventeen states met in Cleveland in November 1874 and organized the Woman's Christian Temperance Union. Willing declined national office but agreed to edit the union's first newsletter, the *Woman's Temperance Union*, and for several years served as president of the Illinois WCTU.

Internal conflict over the role of Methodism's Woman's Foreign Missionary Society led her to transfer her efforts to the cause of home missions. When the Woman's Home Missionary Society was formed in 1880, Mrs. Willing became the only paid staff person who traveled widely organizing regional and local branches and was a frequent contributor to its new magazine, *Woman's Home Missions*. She later headed the society's Bureau for Spanish Work from 1886 to 1890 and the Bureau for Immigrants from 1890 to 1894. When her husband was transferred to a church in New York City in 1889, Mrs. Willing turned her attention to the plight of immigrant girls, founding a settlement house in "Hell's Kitchen" and establishing Methodist training schools for settlement work in New York, Boston, and Philadelphia.

She died in New York City in 1916 at the age of eighty-two, leaving her estate to be divided equally between the WCTU and the Methodist evangelistic training school program.

Bibliography

A: *A Bunch of Flowers for Girls* (Chicago, 1888); *Chaff and Wheat* (Cincinnati, 1896); *Diamond Dust* (New York, 1880); *A Dozen Be's For Boys* (Boston, 1888); *From Fifteen to Twenty-Five* (Chicago, 1885); *God's Great Women* (Louisville, KY, 1910?); *How To Win Souls* (Boston, 1909); *The Little-Book Man* (New York, 1894); *The Lure of Korea* (Boston, 1913?); *On American Soil; or, Mormonism, the Mohammedanism of the West* (Louisville, KY, 1906); *The Only Way Out* (Boston, 1881); *The Potential Woman* (Boston, 1886); *A Prince of the Realm: Lessons from the Life of Rev. W. C. Willing, D.D.* (New York, 1895); *Rosario*, with Mrs. E.J.M. Clemens (Chicago, 1882); *Through the Dark to the Day: A Story of Discipline* (Cincinnati, 1868); *To Cairo and Back by Way of the Holy City* (New York?, 1905).

B: *CA* 9 November 1916; *CM* 952–53; *NAW* 3, 623–25; *NYT* 7 and 27 October 1916; Frances E. Willard, *Woman and Temperance* (Hartford, CT, 1883), 147–53; Frances E. Willard and Mary A. Livermore, eds., *A Woman of the Century* (1893); *Standard Encyclopedia of the Alcohol Problem* 6 (1930): 2855–56; Joanne Carlson Brown, *Jennie Fowler Willing, Methodist Churchwoman and Reformer* (unpublished Ph.D. diss., Boston University, 1983) and "Shared Fire: The Flame Ignited by Jennie Fowler Willing," in *Spirituality and Social Responsibility*, ed. Rosemary S. Keller (Nashville, 1993), 99–116.

WINANS, WILLIAM (3 November 1788, Chestnut Ridge, PA–31 August 1857, Wilkinson County, MI). *Education:* no formal education but later acquired one of the largest private libraries in the Southwest. *Career:* admitted to the Western Conference in 1808; circuits in Indiana and Kentucky, 1808–10; volunteered for service in Mississippi District, 1810; missionary to New Orleans, 1813; joined MECS, 1845.

A southern leader, William Winans served for almost half a century in the Mississippi Conference. He was a powerful legislator and debater. Self-educated and an avid reader, he acquired one of the largest private libraries in the Southwest, and he spoke and wrote correctly and with force. It was Winans who was the leader of the southern coalition at the General Conference of 1844, one of nine persons appointed to the committee that drew up the Plan of Separation, chaired the southern delegates at the Louisville Convention in 1845 at which the MECS was organized, and called its first General Conference to order in 1846. McTyeire described him in the debates at the 1844 General Conference as speaking ''in Italics,'' and claimed he ''wore no cravat.''

Bibliography

A: *A Series of Discourses on Fundamental Religion* (Cincinnati, 1855), reprinted (Nashville, 1891).

B: *CM* 957; *EWM* 2, 2575–76; Ray Holder, *William Winans: Methodist Leader in Antebellum Mississippi* (Jackson, 1977); Rex Paxton Kyker, *William Winans: Minister and Politician of the Old South* (Gainsville, 1957).

A CHRONOLOGY OF AMERICAN METHODISM

1703	John Wesley is born.
1720	Wesley goes up to Christ Church, Oxford.
1726	Wesley is elected a fellow of Lincoln College, Oxford. Philip William Otterbein is born in Dillenburg, Germany.
1729	"Holy Club" appears at Oxford University.
1735	Wesley leaves England to minister to colonists in Georgia; meets Moravians; remains in Georgia from early 1736 until late 1737.
1738	Wesley preaches "Salvation by Faith" and experiences assurance of salvation by faith during a Moravian prayer meeting in Aldersgate Street, London. He visits Moravian communities in Germany, reads Jonathan Edwards's "narrative" of the revival in New England, and publishes extract from the "Homilies" of the Church of England.
1739	Wesley begins field preaching, forms first Methodist societies in Bristol and London, and with Charles publishes first collection of *Hymns and Sacred Poems*. Wesley establishes Kingswood School.
1744	Wesley calls the first conference of his preachers in London.
1745	Francis Asbury is born.
1752	William Otterbein, Reformed pastor, comes to America and settles in Lancaster, Pennsylvania.
1758	Mennonite Martin Boehm receives assurance of salvation.
1759	Jacob Albright, to be reared Lutheran, is born near Pottstown, Pennsylvania.
1760	Methodist people begin to arrive in American seaports.
1769	Wesley sends the first two Methodist preachers to America.
1771	Francis Asbury arrives in America.

1773	First conference of Methodist preachers in America meets in Philadelphia.
1774	Wesley publishes *Thoughts upon Slavery*; Otterbein assumes Baltimore pastorate.
1777	Richard Allen is converted while still a slave.
1784	Methodist Episcopal Church (MEC), which organizes during Christmas Conference in Baltimore, ordains bishops and preachers and adopts Wesley's hymnbook and prayerbook.
1789	Otterbein calls first conference of United Brethren; MEC establishes publishing house.
1791	John Wesley dies; Jacob Albright experiences peace with God.
1792	First General Conference of Methodist preachers meets; Wesley's prayerbook is "laid aside"; O'Kelly schism over episcopacy occurs. African-American Methodists from St. George's Church leave to form first separate black Methodist church in Philadelphia, Bethel Church.
1796	Albright begins his preaching ministry among the Pennsylvania Germans.
1800	Church of the United Brethren in Christ organizes.
1801	The Great Revival in the West begins. Methodists adopt camp meetings.
1803	Albright's followers hold their first conference.
1807	Newly formed Methodist connection organizes and in 1816 takes the name Evangelical Association.
1808	The MEC adopts a constitution and elects the first native American preacher bishop, William McKendree. Albright dies.
1810	Jesse Lee publishes *A Short History of the Methodists in the United States of America*.
1812	First delegated General Conference (MEC) meets.
1815	Church of the United Brethren in Christ holds the first General Conference.
1816	African Methodist Episcopal (AME) Church organizes in Philadelphia. Asbury dies. The first course of study for preachers is adopted, and the first General Conference of Evangelical Association convenes.
1818	*Methodist Quarterly Review* begins publication.
1819	Missionary Society of the MEC forms and the mission to Native Americans begins.
1820	Black Methodists in the New York area form the African Methodist Episcopal Zion (AMEZ) Church. Methodists debate the roles of bishops, superintendents, and laity.
1826	*Christian Advocate*, first official weekly, begins publication.
1827	Methodists form the Sunday School Union.

1830	Methodist Protestant Church is founded.
1833	First American Methodist missionary, Melville Cox, is sent to Africa (Liberia).
1834	Jason Lee leads an expedition that explores the Williamette Valley in Oregon and founds the first Methodist mission and first farming settlement.
1835	First Methodist mission to South America opens in Brazil.
1839	New England Methodists found first "Biblical Institute" to train preachers; it later becomes Boston University School of Theology.
1842	Radical abolitionists exit to form the Wesleyan Methodist Church.
1844	Methodists North and South agree to separate over disagreement on the twin issues of slavery and episcopacy. Indian Missionary Conference organizes in Oklahoma.
1846	Methodist Episcopal Church, South (MECS), holds its first General Conference. MEC sends its first missionaries to China.
1855	Christ Church, Pittsburgh, erects one of the first gothic revival "cathedrals."
1859	Southern Methodists organize first Spanish mission in Texas.
1864	MEC grants full clergy rights for African-Americans; separate black annual conferences form.
1865	Palmyra Manifesto calls for continuance of the MECS.
1866	MEC forms Freedmen's Aid Society. Drew Theological Seminary, the first graduate professional school for training preachers, is founded.
1866–72	Lay representatives join clergy in the MECS General Conference and the MEC General Conference, respectively.
1867	National Camp Meeting for the Promotion of Holiness organizes.
1869	First independent women's missionary society forms in the MEC. First woman local preacher, Maggie Newton Van Cott, is accepted in the MEC.
1870	Colored Methodist Episcopal Church is organized for newly freed black Methodists in the South.
1872–74	MEC and MECS make program boards accountable to General Conference, thus establishing general agency structure.
1874	Woman's Christian Temperance Union organizes and elects Annie T. Wittenmeyer first president; Frances E. Willard succeeds her in 1873.
1876	MECS and MEC reestablish fraternal relations at Cape May Conference. Matthew Simpson publishes *Cyclopaedia of Methodism*.
1880	First test case on the ordination of women comes before the MEC General Conference. Anna Howard Shaw is ordained by the Methodist Protestant Church.

1881	First Ecumenical (now World) Methodist Conference meets in London.
1885	Henry G. Appenzeller begins Methodist mission to Korea.
1888	MEC adopts office of deaconess.
1889	MEC establishes Epworth League, first youth organization.
1890s	Holiness "come-outers" establish denominations.
1900	Women gain full laity rights (MEC).
1905	Methodists North and South adopt common hymnal, order of public worship for Sundays, and catechism.
1907	Methodist Federation for Social Service organizes.
1908	MEC adopts first Social Creed.
1912	MEC establishes episcopal areas and financial apportionments.
1913	MEC begins Wesley foundations on college and university campuses.
1920	MEC elects first black bishops, Robert E. Jones and Matthew W. Clair.
1922	Evangelical Church is formed, uniting the Evangelical Association and the United Evangelical Church. MECS gives full laity rights to women.
1935	Common Methodist hymnal is adopted by Methodist Episcopal, Methodist Episcopal, South, and Methodist Protestant Churches.
1939	MEC, MECS, and Methodist Protestant Church unite to form the Methodist Church, establishing a segregated Central Jurisdiction for African-Americans as "price" of unity.
1944–48	Crusade for a New World Order, first successful quadrennial campaign, garners Methodist support for United Nations.
1946	Evangelical United Brethren Church forms, uniting the Evangelical and United Brethren churches. Methodist layman John R. Mott receives Nobel Peace Prize. Order of St. Luke, a liturgical and sacramental fellowship, organizes.
1951	World Methodist Council organizes. Methodist Publishing House begins publication of *Interpreter's Bible*.
1956	Women gain full clergy rights in the Methodist Church.
1966	Evangelical Methodists launch the Good News movement.
1967	Margaret Henrichsen becomes the first woman district superintendent. Methodists begin dialogue with Roman Catholics.
1968	The United Methodist Church (UMC) unites the Methodist Church and the Evangelical United Brethren Church; ten million strong (5.5 percent of the U.S. population), the new church establishes commissions on religion and race, archives and history. Black Methodists for Church Renewal forms.

1970	UMC establishes the Commission on the Status and Role of Women. Hispanic American Methodists form MARCHA, and Native American Methodists form caucus.
1971	Asian-American Methodists found caucus.
1972	United Methodism's first General Conference reorganizes national structure and adopts new statements on social principles and doctrinal standards. Caucuses abound. UMC elects first Asian-American bishop, Wilbur Choy.
1975	Gay and lesbian Methodists establish Affirmation. Publication begins of modern critical edition of Wesley's works.
1980	Marjorie Matthews becomes the first woman bishop. UMC membership down to 9.6 million.
1984	UMC elects Elias Galvan first Hispanic bishop.
1986	UMC bishops issue pastoral letter on peace.
1992	Hae Jong Kim becomes first Korean-American bishop.

BIBLIOGRAPHIC ESSAY

GENERAL RESOURCES

The basic bibliographical guide, particularly for United Methodism, is *United Methodist Studies: Basic Bibliographies*, Kenneth E. Rowe, comp. and ed., 3d. ed. (Nashville: Abingdon Press, 1992), a volume revised every five years. Also by Rowe and essential for identifying and locating Methodist titles is the *Methodist Union Catalog, Pre-1976 Imprints* (Metuchen, NJ: Scarecrow Press, 1975+), 7 vols., A-K published to date. For topical treatment, see also "Bibliographies" in *Encyclopedia of World Methodism*, ed. Nolan B. Harmon (Nashville: United Methodist Publishing House, 1974), 2: 2721–66, and in *History of American Methodism*, ed. Emory Bucke (Nashville: Abingdon Press, 1964), at the end of each of the three volumes. For archival material, see the multivolume work by Homer L. Calkin, apparently to be continued by his wife, *Catalog of Methodist Archival and Manuscript Collections* (Alexandria, VA: World Methodist Historical Society, 1982+). For ethnic and black Methodism see C. Jarrett Gray, Jr., comp., *The Racial and Ethnic Presence in American Methodism: A Bibliography* (Madison, NJ: General Commission on Archives and History, United Methodist Church, 1991). For Methodist women, consult Susan M. Eltscher, ed., *Women in the Wesleyan and United Methodist Traditions: A Bibliography* (Madison, NJ: General Commission on Archives and History, United Methodist Church, 1991). On the holiness movement, see William C. Miller, *Holiness Works: A Bibliography*, rev. ed. (Kansas City, MO: Beacon Hill Press, 1986), and Charles E. Jones, *A Guide to the Study of the Holiness Movement* (Metuchen, NJ: Scarecrow Press, 1974).

Specializing in British Methodism but also useful for American topics is Clive Field, "Bibliography of Methodist Historical Literature, 1974" (and succeeding years), since June 1976 published annually in the *Wesley Historical Society Proceedings*. See also Laurie E. Gage, *English Methodism: A Bibliographical View* (Westcliff-on-Sea, Essex, England: Gage Postal Books, 1985). On the Wesleys see especially Betty M. Jarboe, *John and Charles Wesley: A Bibliography* (Metuchen, NJ: Scarecrow Press, 1987); Frank Baker, "Unfolding John Wesley: A Survey of Twenty Years' Study in Wesley's Thought," *Quarterly Review* 1/1 (1980): 44–58; Richard P. Heitzenrater, "The Present State of Wesley Studies," *MH* 22 (1984): 221–31; Richard Green, *The Works of John and Charles Wesley*, 2d rev. ed. (New York: AMS Press, 1976; reprint of the 1906 edition); and Frank Baker, *A Union Catalogue of the Publications of John and Charles Wesley* (Stone Mountain, GA: George Zimmermann, 1991; reprint of the 1966 edition).

Three useful bibliographical essays by Frederick A. Norwood are "Historical Study in Methodism [1988]," *Lutheran Historical Conference* 13 (1990): 173–93; "Methodist Historical Studies 1930–1959," *Church History* 28 (1959) 391–417; 29 (1960): 74–88; and "Wesleyan and Methodist Historical Studies, 1960–1970: A Bibliographical Article," *Church History* 40 (June 1971): 192–99. Reprinted in *Methodist History* 10 (January 1972): 23–44. See also Henry D. Rack, "Recent Books on Methodism," *Epworth Review* 7 (January 1980): 82–88; Kenneth E. Rowe, "Methodist History at the Bicentennial," *Methodist History* 22 (1984): 87–98.

Three encyclopedias are invaluable: Nolan B. Harmon, ed., *Encyclopedia of World Methodism*, 2 vols. (Nashville: United Methodist Publishing House, 1974); John McClintock and James Strong, *Cyclopedia of Biblical, Theological, and Ecclesiastical Literature*, 12 vols. (New York: Arno Press, 1970; reprint of the 1867–87 edition, still standard for the nineteenth century); and Matthew Simpson, *Cyclopedia of Methodism* (New York: Gordon Press, 1977; reprint of the 1876 edition, also useful for the nineteenth century).

Among the general surveys for North America are the following: Emory C. Bucke, ed., *History of American Methodism*, 3 vols. (Nashville: Abingdon Press, 1974); Frederick A. Norwood, *The Story of American Methodism: A History of the United Methodists and Their Relations* (Nashville: Abingdon Press, 1974) and ed., *Sourcebook of American Methodism* (Nashville: Abingdon Press, 1983); Joseph E. Sanderson, *The First Century of Methodism in Canada*, 2 vols. (Toronto: William Briggs, 1908); William W. Sweet, *Methodism in American History*, rev. ed. (Nashville: Abingdon Press, 1953; first published in 1933), and *Religion on the American Frontier, 1783–1940: The Methodists, A Collection of Source Materials* (New York: Cooper Square, 1964; reprint of 1946 edition). For the Evangelical and United Brethren traditions, consult J. Bruce Behney and Paul H. Eller, *The History of the Evangelical United Brethren Church* (Nashville: Abingdon Press, 1979). Wade C. Barclay, *History of Methodist Missions*, 4 vols. (New York: Board of Missions, Methodist Church, 1949–73), comprehends much of the history of American Methodism in detailing its national and world outreach.

Two collections of essays are important: Russell E. Richey, Kenneth E. Rowe, and Jean Miller Schmidt, eds., *Perspectives on American Methodism: Interpretive Essays* (Nashville: Kingswood Books/Abingdon Press, 1993), and Russell E. Richey and Kenneth E. Rowe, eds., *Rethinking Methodist History* (Nashville: Kingswood Books, United Methodist Publishing House, 1985). The Kingswood series has become an important medium for studies of American Methodism and quite a number of the Kingswood titles provide general assessments, among them Richard P. Heitzenrater's *Mirror and Memory: Reflections on Early Methodism* (Nashville: Kingswood Books, 1989). Among the collections examining women's experience of Methodism are Rosemary Skinner Keller, ed., *Spirituality and Social Responsibility: The Vocational Vision of Women in the Methodist Tradition* (Nashville: Abingdon Press, 1993); Rosemary Skinner Keller, Hilah Thomas, and Louise Queen, eds., *Women in New Worlds: Historical Perspectives on the Wesleyan Tradition*, 2 vols. (Nashville: Abingdon Press, 1981–82). Another collection, particularly important for assessing long-term patterns in Methodist theology, is Thomas A. Langford, ed., *Doctrine and Theology in the United Methodist Church* (Nashville: Kingswood Books, 1990), which sets 1972 and 1988 doctrinal statements in historical context.

For overviews of American Methodist theology, see Langford's *Practical Divinity: Theology in the Wesleyan Tradition* (Nashville: Abingdon Press, 1983) and *Wesleyan Theology: A Sourcebook* (Durham, NC: Labyrinth Press, 1984). See also Donald W. Dayton, *The Theological Roots of Pentecostalism* (Grand Rapids, MI: Francis Asbury Press of Zondervan Publishing House, 1987); Dale E. Dunlap, *Methodist Theology in Great Britain in the 19th Century* (Ann Arbor, MI: University Microfilms, 1968, unpublished Ph.D. diss., Yale University, 1956); Robert E. Chiles, *Theological Transition in American Methodism, 1790–1935* (Lanham, MD: University Press of America, 1984; reprint of the 1965 edition); Albert C. Outler, *Evangelism in the Wesleyan Spirit* (Nashville: Tidings, 1971); the several sections in *HAM* devoted to the topic; Thomas C. Oden, *Doctrinal Standards in the Wesleyan Tradition* (Grand Rapids, MI: Francis Asbury Press of Zondervan Publishing House, 1988); Theodore C. Runyon, ed., *Wesleyan Theology Today: A Bicentennial Consultation* (Nashville: Kingswood Books, 1985). Another work, important for understanding an understudied aspect of Methodism, is E. Brooks Holifield, *Health and Medicine in the Methodist Tradition* (New York: Crossroads/Continuum, 1986).

THE BRITISH BACKGROUND

The basic work on the founding era and on Methodism in eighteenth-century Britain and Ireland is Richard P. Heitzenrater, *Wesley and the People Called Methodists* (Nashville: Abingdon Press, 1995). Other standards include Frank Baker, *John Wesley and the Church of England* (Nashville: Abingdon Press, 1970); Rupert E. Davies, *Methodism*, 2d rev. ed. (London: Epworth Press, 1985), the best compact survey; and Rupert E. Davies and Gordon Rupp, eds., *A History of the Methodist Church in Great Britain*, 4 vols. (London: Epworth Press, 1975–87). See also Leslie F. Church, *The Early Methodist People* (London: Epworth Press, 1948) and *More About the Early Methodist People* (London: Epworth Press, 1949), and John M. Turner, *Conflict and Reconciliation: Studies in Methodism and Ecumenism in England, 1740–1982* (London: Epworth Press, l985). For Celtic Methodism see Frederick Jeffery, *Irish Methodism: An Historical Account of Its Tradition, Theology, and Influences* (Belfast: Epworth House, 1964); Wesley F. Swift, *Methodism in Scotland: The First Hundred Years* (London: Epworth Press, 1947); and Norman E. Taggart, *The Irish in World Methodism, 1760–1900* (London: Epworth Press, 1986).

For early Wesleyanism in its social and political context, see W. R. Ward, *Faith and Faction* (London: Epworth Press, 1993) and *The Protestant Evangelical Awakening* (Cambridge: Cambridge University Press, 1992); Gerald W. Olsen, ed., *Religion and Revolution in Early Industrial England: The Halevy Thesis and Its Critics* (Lanham, MD: University Press of America, 1990); Gordon Rupp, "Evangelical Revival" in his *Religion in England, 1688–1791* (Oxford: Clarendon Press, 1986), 325–490; John D. Walsh, "Origins of the Evangelical Revival," in *Essays in Modern English Church History*, ed. G. V. Bennett and J. D. Walsh (New York: Oxford University Press, 1966), 132–62; David Hempton, *Methodism and Politics in British Society, 1750–1850* (Stanford, CA: Stanford University Press, 1984).

Collections of Wesley works abound but the starting point now should be Richard Heitzenrater, ed., *The Works of John Wesley*, bicentennial edition (Oxford: Clarendon Press, 1975–83; Nashville: Abingdon Press, 1984–), projected in thirty-five volumes.

This version replaces the older standards: *The Works of John Wesley*, Jackson edition, 1829–31 (Grand Rapids, MI: Baker Book House, 1978); *The Journal of the Rev. John Wesley*, ed. Nehemiah Curnock, 8 vols. (London: Epworth Press, 1909–16); *The Letters of the Rev. John Wesley*, ed. John Telford, 8 vols. (London: Epworth Press, 1931); *Explanatory Notes upon the New Testament* (Grand Rapids, MI: Baker Book House, 1987); *Explanatory Notes upon the Old Testament*, 3 vols. (Salem, OH: Schmul Publishers, 1975).

For Charles Wesley, see *Charles Wesley's Earliest Sermons*, Thomas A. Albin and Oliver A. Beckerlegge, eds. (London: Wesley Historical Society, 1987); *The Journal of Charles Wesley*, 2 vols. (Grand Rapids, MI: Baker Book House, 1980; reprint of the Jackson edition of 1849); *Poetical Works of John and Charles Wesley*, 13 vols. (Salem, OH: Schmul Publishing Co., 1992; reprint of 1872 George Osborn edition); *The Unpublished Poetical Writings of Charles Wesley*, S. T. Kimbrough and Oliver A. Beckerlegge, eds., 3 vols. (Nashville: Kingswood Books, 1988–92).

On Charles also see Frank Baker, *Charles Wesley's Verse: An Introduction*, 2d ed. (London: Epworth Press, 1988); S. T. Kimbrough, Jr., ed., *Charles Wesley, Poet and Theologian* (Nashville: Kingswood Books, 1991); John R. Tyson, *Charles Wesley on Sanctification: A Biographical and Theological Study* (Grand Rapids, MI: Francis Asbury Press of Zondervan Publishing House, 1986).

Among the many treatments of the Wesleys, special mention should be made of Richard P. Heitzenrater, *The Elusive Mr. Wesley*, 2 vols. (Nashville: Abingdon Press, 1984); Henry Rack, *Reasonable Enthusiast: John Wesley and the Rise of Methodism* (London: Epworth Press; Philadelphia: Trinity Press International, 1989); Henry Abelove, *The Evangelist of Desire: John Wesley and the Methodists* (Stanford, CA: Stanford University Press, 1991); Ted A. Campbell, *John Wesley and Christian Antiquity: Religious Vision and Cultural Change* (Nashville: Kingswood Books, 1991); Randy L. Maddox, ed., *Aldersgate Reconsidered* (Nashville: Kingswood Books, 1990) and *John Wesley: Practical Theologian of Responsible Grace* (Nashville: Kingswood Books, 1993); Martin Schmidt, *John Wesley: A Theological Biography*, 3 vols. (Nashville: Abingdon Press, 1962–73); Kenneth E. Rowe, ed., *The Place of Wesley in the Christian Tradition*, rev. ed. (Metuchen, NJ: Scarecrow Press, 1980).

EIGHTEENTH-CENTURY AMERICAN METHODISM

The views of one of our co-authors, Russell E. Richey, are expanded in somewhat different directions in *Early American Methodism* (Bloomington, IN: Indiana University Press, 1991). A volume long awaited is Dee Andrews, *Religion and the Revolution: The Rise of the Methodists in the Middle Atlantic, 1760–1800* (Princeton, NJ: Princeton University Press, forthcoming). Companion social histories are William H. Williams, *The Garden of American Methodism: The Delmarva Peninsula, 1769–1820* (Wilmington, DE: Scholarly Resources, 1984), and Gary Nash, *Forging Freedom: The Formation of Philadelphia's Black Community, 1720–1840* (Cambridge: Harvard University Press, 1988). Important as both an early assessment and a firsthand account of American developments is Jesse Lee, *A Short History of the Methodists* (Rutland, VT: Academy Books, 1974; reprint of the first published history of Methodism in America, 1810). A British angle on American developments and an insistence on continuities between British and American developments are provided by Frank Baker in *From Wesley to Asbury: Studies in*

Early American Methodism (Durham, NC: Duke University Press, 1976). Robert E. Cushman, in *John Wesley's Experimental Divinity: Studies in Methodist Doctrinal Standards* (Nashville: Kingswood Books, 1989), also provides a vigorous argument for American fidelity to Wesley's theology. On German Pietism see Stephen L. Longenecker, *Piety and Tolerance: Pennsylvania German Religion, 1700–1850* (Metuchen, NJ: Scarecrow Press, 1994).

NINETEENTH-CENTURY METHODISM

A number of recent works on American society or American religion accord a central role to American Methodism. Notable among these are Nathan O. Hatch, *The Democratization of American Christianity* (New Haven, CT: Yale University Press, 1989); C. C. Goen, *Broken Churches, Broken Nation: Denominational Schism and the Coming of the Civil War* (Macon, GA: Mercer University Press, 1985); Terry D. Bilhartz, *Urban Religion and the Second Great Awakening: Church and Society in Early National Baltimore* (Rutherford, NJ: FDU Press, 1986); and Richard J. Carwardine, *Evangelicals and Politics in Antebellum America* (New Haven, CT: Yale University Press, 1993). Three older works remain indispensable for the same reason—Richard Carwardine, *Trans-Atlantic Revivalism: Popular Evangelicalism in Britain and America, 1790–1865* (Westport, CT: Greenwood Press, 1978); Donald G. Mathews, *Religion in the Old South* (Chicago: University of Chicago Press, 1977); and E. Brooks Holifield, *The Gentlemen Theologians: American Theology in Southern Culture* (Durham, NC: Duke University Press, 1978).

A. Gregory Schneider in *The Way of the Cross Leads Home: The Domestication of American Methodism* (Bloomington: Indiana University Press, 1993) applies some of the broader themes directly to the assessment of nineteenth-century Methodism. Related discussions of changes in American Methodism, particularly of its revivalistic style, are detailed above in the notes on the camp meeting. In that regard, see also Ellen Jane Lorenz, *Glory Hallelujah: The Story of the Camp Meeting Spiritual* (Nashville: Abingdon Press, 1980).

The efforts to hold onto that revivalistic style and to resist acculturation, efforts constitutive of the holiness movement, are described in Melvin E. Dieter, *The Holiness Revival of the Nineteenth Century* (Metuchen, NJ: Scarecrow Press, 1980); by Donald W. Dayton in *Discovering an Evangelical Heritage* (Peabody, MA: Hendrickson Publishers, 1988; reprint of the 1976 edition) and in *The Theological Roots of Pentecostalism* (Metuchen, NJ: Scarecrow Press, 1987). A very different view, from the preceding one and rendered from the MEC or Methodist perspective, is provided by John L. Peters, *Christian Perfection and American Methodism* (Grand Rapids, MI: Francis Asbury Press of Zondervan Publishing House, 1985; reprint of the 1956 edition with a new foreword by Albert C. Outler). See also Charles E. Jones, *Perfectionist Persuasion: The Holiness Movement and American Methodism, 1867–1936* (Metuchen, NJ: Scarecrow Press, 1974); and for the institutionalizations of the holiness impulse see Ira Ford McLeister, *Conscience and Commitment: The History of the Wesleyan Methodist Church of America*, 4th rev. ed. (Marion, IN: Wesley Press, 1976); Leslie Ray Marston, *From Age to Age a Living Witness: A Historical Interpretation of Free Methodism's First Hundred Years* (Winona Lake, IN: Light and Life Press, 1960); Timothy L. Smith, *Called unto Holiness: The Story of the Nazarenes, the Formative Years* (Kansas City: Nazarene Publishing

House, 1962); Paul W. Thomas, *The Days of Our Pilgrimage: The History of the Pilgrim Holiness Church* (Marion, IN: Wesley Press, 1976); Francine E. Walls, *The Free Methodist Church: A Bibliography* (Winona Lake, IN: Free Methodist Historical Center, 1977). Timothy Smith's *Revivalism and Social Reform: American Protestantism on the Eve of the Civil War* (New York: Peter Smith, 1976; reprint of 1957 edition) argues for wider influence of holiness. Essays in Leonard I. Sweet, ed., *The Evangelical Tradition in America* (Macon, GA: Mercer University Press, 1984), locate holiness within the larger evangelical movement. For later phases see Vinson Synan, *The Holiness–Pentecostal Movement* (Grand Rapids, MI: William B. Eerdmans, 1972).

For Methodism, slavery, sectionalism, and the Civil War, see also Donald G. Mathews, *Slavery and Methodism: A Chapter in American Morality, 1780–1845* (Westport, CT: Greenwood Press, 1978; reprint of the 1965 edition); Donald G. Jones, *The Sectional Crisis and Northern Methodism: A Study in Piety, Political Ethics, and Civil Religion* (Metuchen, NJ: Scarecrow Press, 1979); Reginald F. Hildebrand, *The Times Were Strange and Stirring* (Durham, NC: Duke University Press, 1995); Katharine L. Dvorak, *An African-American Exodus: The Segregation of the Southern Churches* (Brooklyn, NY: Carlson Publishing, 1991); and Clarence E. Walker, *A Rock in a Weary Land: The African Methodist Episcopal Church during the Civil War and Reconstruction* (Baton Rouge: Louisiana State University Press, 1982).

Other important treatments of African-American Methodism are Harry V. Richardson, *Dark Salvation: The Story of Methodism as It Developed among Blacks in America* (New York: Doubleday, 1976); Grant S. Shockley, ed., *Heritage and Hope: The African-American Presence in United Methodism* (Nashville: Abingdon Press, 1991); Will B. Gravely, "African Methodisms and the Rise of Black Denominationalism," in *Rethinking Methodist History*, ed. Russell E. Richey and Kenneth E. Rowe, and in *POAM*; Gravely, "The Rise of African Churches in America: Re-examining the Contexts, 1786–1822," in *African American Religious Studies*, ed. G. S. Wilmore (Durham, NC: Duke University Press, 1989), 301–17; Carol V. R. George, *Segregated Sabbaths: Richard Allen and the Rise of the Independent Black Churches, 1760–1840* (New York: Oxford University Press, 1973); George A. Singleton, *The Romance of African Methodism* (New York: Exposition, 1952); William J. Walls, *The African Methodist Episcopal Zion Church* (Charlotte: A.M.E. Zion Publishing, 1974); Lewis V. Baldwin, *"Invisible" Strands in African Methodism: A History of the African Union Methodist Protestant and Union American Methodist Episcopal Churches, 1805–1980* (Metuchen, NJ: Scarecrow Press, 1983); David H. Bradley, *A History of the A.M.E. Zion Church, 1796–1968*, 2 vols. (Nashville: A.M.E. Zion Publishing House, 1956–60); Othal L. Lakey, *The History of the C.M.E. Church* (Memphis, TN: C.M.E. Publishing House, 1985); William E. Montgomery, *Under Their Own Vine and Fig Tree: The African-American Church in the South, 1865–1900* (Baton Rouge: Louisiana State University Press, 1993).

TWENTIETH-CENTURY METHODISM

Southern Methodism's history, including its struggles over race, are well covered in Robert Watson Sledge, *Hands on the Ark: The Struggle for Change in the Methodist Episcopal Church, South, 1914–1939* (Lake Junaluska, NC: General Commission on Archives and History, 1975). For the larger Methodist picture, consult the general works cited above and Dwight W. Culver, *Negro Segregation in the Methodist Church* (New

Haven, CT: Yale University Press, 1953). A number of the general studies cited above cover the 1939 union. For that of 1968, see Paul Washburn, *An Unfinished Church: A Brief History of the Union of the Evangelical United Brethren Church and the Methodist Church* (Nashville: Abingdon Press, 1985).

A number of works cover the various Methodist peoples, with special emphasis upon twentieth-century developments. Among those covering African-American Methodist experience, in addition to those cited above, are C. Eric Lincoln and Lawrence H. Mamiya, *The Black Church in the African American Experience* (Durham, NC: Duke University Press, 1990), and William B. McClain, *Black People in the Methodist Church: Whither Thou Goest?* (Nashville: Abingdon Press, 1984). On Asian-American Methodists see Artemio R. Guillermo, ed., *Churches Aflame: Asian Americans and United Methodism* (Nashville: Abingdon Press, 1991); Arlo W. Andersen, *The Salt of the Earth: A History of Norwegian-Danish Methodism in America* (Nashville: Parthenon Press, 1962); Paul F. Douglass, *The Story of German Methodism: Biography of an Immigrant Soul* (New York: Methodist Book Concern, 1939); and Roy I. Sano, *From Every Nation without Number: Racial and Ethnic Diversity in United Methodism* (Nashville: Abingdon Press, 1982). Also see Justo L. Gonzalez, ed., *Each in Our Own Tongue: A History of Hispanic United Methodism* (Nashville: Abingdon Press, 1991), and Homer Noley, ed., *First White Frost: Native Americans and United Methodism* (Nashville: Abingdon Press, 1991).

Much of the rich texture of twentieth-century Methodism is accessible through biographical treatments. See bibliography in that section of this work and also in the first Rowe item. See also below the works cited under various topics, including especially Social Thought and Action and Women and Methodism.

EDUCATION

Various dimensions of Methodism's educational venture are covered in the following: Sylvannus M. Duvall, *The Methodist Episcopal Church and Education up to 1869* (New York: Bureau of Publications, Teachers College, 1928); Charles E. Cole, ed., *Something More than Human: Biographies of Leaders in American Methodist Higher Education* (Nashville: General Board of Higher Education and Ministry, United Methodist Church, 1986); Jack Boozer, *Edge of Ministry: Chaplain Story, United Methodist Church, 1945–1970* (Nashville: Board of Higher Education & Ministry, United Methodist Church, 1984); Beth A. Bowser, *A History of the University Senate in the Methodist Episcopal Church, the Methodist Church and the United Methodist Church* (Ph.D. diss., University of Akron, 1990; Ann Arbor, MI: University Microfilms International, 1990); Frank Lloyd Dent, *"Motive" Magazine: Advocating the Arts and Empowering the Imagination in the Life of the Church* (Ph.D. diss., Columbia University, 1989; Ann Arbor, MI: University Microfilms International, 1989); Terrell E. Johnson, *A History of Methodist Education and Its Influence on American Public Education* (Ph.D. diss., Southern Illinois University at Carbondale, 1989; Ann Arbor, MI: University Microfilms International, 1989). For Methodist theological education consult Gerald O. McCulloh, *Ministerial Education in the American Methodist Movement* (Nashville: General Board of Higher Education and Ministry, United Methodist Church, 1980), and Glenn T. Miller, *Piety and Intellect: The Aims and Purpose of Ante-Bellum Theological Education* (Atlanta: Scholars Press, 1990). For works covering the several United Methodist theological schools consult the Rowe bibliography mentioned at the first part of this essay.

Very full description of the literature on the Sunday school can be found above in the sections devoted specifically to that topic. In addition, see Cawthon A. Bowen, *Child and Church: A History of Methodist Church School Curriculum* (New York: Abingdon Press, 1960). The basic history is John Q. Schisler, *Christian Education in Local Methodist Churches* (Nashville: Abingdon Press, 1969). See also Grant S. Shockley and Ethel R. Johnson, *The Christian Education Journey of Black Americans* (Nashville: Discipleship Resources, 1985).

ARCHITECTURE

On Methodism and church architecture, see Paul Neff Garber, *The Methodist Meeting House* (New York: Board of Missions and Church Extension, Methodist Church, 1941); James F. White, "Early Methodist Liturgical Architecture," *Motive* 18 (1958): 12–13, 19–20, also his *Protestant Worship and Church Architecture: Theological and Historical Considerations* (New York: Oxford University Press, 1964) and his joint work with Susan J. White, *Church Architecture: Building and Renovating for Christian Worship* (Nashville: Abingdon Press, 1988).

SPIRITUALITY, WORSHIP, AND DISCIPLINE

On these topics see especially *Wesleyan Spirituality in Contemporary Theological Education: A Consultation Held October 17–19, 1987* (Nashville: Division of Ordained Ministry, General Board of Higher Education and Ministry, United Methodist Church, 1987); Robin Maas, *Crucified Love: The Practice of Christian Perfection* (Nashville: Abingdon Press, 1989) and "Wesleyan Spirituality, Accountable Discipleship," in *Spiritual Traditions for the Contemporary Church*, ed. Robin Maas and Gabriel O'Donnell (Nashville: Abingdon Press, 1990), 303–31; and Steve Harper, *Devotional Life in the Wesleyan Tradition* (Nashville: The Upper Room, 1983). On the Methodist class meeting and its place in Methodist spirituality and discipline, see the several works by David L. Watson, *Class Leaders: Recovering a Tradition* (Nashville: Discipleship Resources, 1991); *The Early Methodist Class Meeting: Its Origins and Significance* (Nashville: Discipleship Resources, 1985). On the love feast and its place in early Methodism see Frank Baker, *Methodism and the Love Feast* (London: Epworth Press, 1957).

On Methodist hymnody, consult S. T. Kimbrough, Jr., *Lost in Wonder: Charles Wesley: The Meaning of His Hymns Today* (Nashville: The Upper Room, 1987); also two works by John E. Rattenbury, *The Evangelical Doctrines of Charles Wesley's Hymns* (London: Epworth Press, 1941) and *The Eucharistic Hymns of John and Charles Wesley* (London: Epworth Press, 1948; rev. ed., Cleveland, OH: Order of St. Luke Publications, 1990). For American Methodist hymnody, see Samuel J. Rogal, comp., *Guide to the Hymns and Tunes of American Methodism* (New York: Greenwood Press, 1986), a reference guide to the 3,901 hymns and tunes included in six major Methodist hymnals, 1878 to 1964; James I. Warren, *O for a Thousand Tongues to Sing: The History, Nature, and Influence of Music in the Methodist Tradition* (Grand Rapids, MI: Francis Asbury Press of Zondervan Publishing House, 1988); and Carlton B. Young, *Companion to the 1989 Hymnal* (Nashville: Abingdon Press, 1992), the basic work.

Methodist preaching is treated implicitly, if not explicitly, in general works on the movement. For more self-conscious discussion, see Merrill R. Abbey, *The Epic of United*

Methodist Preaching: A Profile in American Social History (Lanham, MD: University Press of America, 1984); Jon Michael Spencer, *Sacred Symphony: The Chanted Sermon of the Black Preacher* (New York: Greenwood Press, 1988).

Methodist worship is covered in William N. Wade, *A History of Public Worship in the Methodist Episcopal Church and the Methodist Episcopal Church, South, from 1784 to 1905* (Ph.D. diss., University of Notre Dame, 1981; Ann Arbor, MI: University Microfilms International, 1981), and in James F. White, *Protestant Worship: Traditions in Transition* (Louisville, KY: Westminster/John Knox, 1989), 150–70. The standard works on Methodist liturgies are Nolan B. Harmon, "John Wesley's 'Sunday Service' and Its American Revisions," *Wesley Historical Society Proceedings* 39 (June 1974): 137–44, and *The Rites and Ritual of Episcopal Methodism* (Nashville: Publishing House of the Methodist Episcopal Church, South, 1926). See also Richard J. Cooke, *History of the Ritual of the Methodist Episcopal Church, with a Commentary on Its Offices* (Cincinnati: Jennings & Pye; New York: Eaton & Mains, 1900). On marriage and funeral rites, see Karen B. Westerfield Tucker, *"Till Death Us Do Part": John Wesley's Services of Marriage and Burial and Their Development in the Methodist Episcopal Church* (Ph.D. diss., University of Notre Dame, 1992; Ann Arbor, MI: University Microfilms International, 1992). On African-American worship, consult William B. McClain, *Come Sunday: The Liturgy of Zion* (Nashville: Abingdon Press, 1990). Especially helpful for twentieth-century developments are Hoyt Hickman, *Companion to the Book of Services [1984]* (Nashville: Abingdon Press, 1989) and *United Methodist Worship* (Nashville: Abingdon Press, 1991), and Heather M. Elkins, *Living on Borrowed Time: The Christian Calendar in 20th Century United Methodism* (Ph.D. diss., Drew University, 1991; Ann Arbor, MI: University Microfilms International, 1991).

THE SACRAMENTS

On the sacraments, see items on worship mentioned above plus Paul S. Sanders, *An Appraisal of John Wesley's Sacramentalism in the Evolution of Early American Methodism* (unpublished Ph.D. diss., Union Theological Seminary, New York, 1954) and "The Sacraments in Early American Methodism," *Church History* 26 (1957): 355–71; Rob L. Staples, *Outward Sign and Inward Grace: The Place of Sacraments in Wesleyan Spirituality* (Kansas City: Beacon Hill Press, 1991); Ole E. Borgen, "Baptism, Confirmation and Church Membership in the Methodist Church before the Union of 1968: A Historical and Theological Study," *Methodist History* 27 (1989): 89–109, 163–81; Gayle C. Felton, *This Gift of Water: The Practice and Theology of Baptism among Methodists in America* (Nashville: Abingdon Press, 1992).

SOCIAL THOUGHT AND ACTION

Methodism's social witness is covered in general works and in the histories of Methodist thought noted above. More explicit treatments of this topic include Walter G. Muelder, *Methodism and Society in the Twentieth Century* (Nashville: Abingdon Press, 1961); Richard M. Cameron, *Methodism and Society in Historical Perspective* (Nashville: Abingdon Press, 1961); and the synthetic work by Georgia Harkness, *The Methodist Church in Social Thought and Action* (Nashville: Abingdon Press, 1972). A number of works are helpful with respect to twentieth-century developments, among them Donald

K. Gorrell, *The Age of Social Responsibility: The Social Gospel in the Progressive Era, 1900–1920* (Macon, GA: Mercer University Press, 1988) and "The Social Creed and Methodism through Eighty Years," *Methodist History* 26/4 (July 1988): 213–28; and *On the History of the Methodist Federation for Social Service/Action* (special issue of *Radical Religion*, vol. 5, 1980). On Methodist women's remarkable social witness see the works on women's history cited above, plus Ruth Bordin, *Woman and Temperance* (Philadelphia: Temple University Press, 1981); John Patrick McDowell, *The Social Gospel in the South: The Woman's Home Mission Movement in the Methodist Episcopal Church, South, 1886–1939* (Baton Rouge: Louisiana State University Press, 1982); Jacquelyn Dowd Hall, *Revolt against Chivalry: Jessie Danie Ames and the Women's Campaign against Lynching* (New York: Columbia University Press, 1979); Betty J. Letzig, *Expressions of Faith* (Cincinnati: Service Center, United Methodist General Board of Global Ministries, 1990), a study of the social welfare institutions of the National Division of GBGM; and Thelma Stevens, *Legacy for the Future: History of Christian Social Relations in the Woman's Division of Christian Service, 1940–1968* (Cincinnati: Board of Global Ministries, United Methodist Church, 1978).

WOMEN AND METHODISM

The basic work on American Methodist women is Jean Miller Schmidt, *Grace Sufficient: A History of Women in American Methodism* (Nashville: Abingdon Press, forthcoming). Another work of considerable range is Nancy A. Hardesty, *Women Called to Witness: Evangelical Feminism in the 19th Century* (Nashville: Abingdon Press, 1984). A considerable collection of Methodist women's publications, particularly from the nineteenth century, were brought together by Carolyn D. Gifford in a multivolume series by Garland Publishing. Other useful items include Donald K. Gorrell, ed., *Woman's Rightful Place: Women in United Methodist History* (Dayton, OH: United Theological Seminary, 1980); Ethel W. Born, *By My Spirit: The Story of Methodist Protestant Women in Mission, 1879–1939* (New York: Women's Division of the General Board of Global Ministries, 1990); Ann Fagan, *This Is Our Song: Employed Women in the United Methodist Tradition* (New York: Woman's Division, General Board of Global Ministries, United Methodist Church, 1986), a history of the Wesleyan Service Guild; Rosemary Skinner Keller et al., eds., *Methodist Women, A World Sisterhood: A History of the World Federation of Methodist Women* (Cincinnati, OH: World Federation of Methodist Women, 1986).

PUBLICATION AND COMMUNICATIONS

The basic study is James P. Pilkington (vol. 1) and Walter N. Vernon (vol. 2), *The Methodist Publishing House: A History*, 2 vols. (Nashville: Abingdon Press, 1968–88). For a comparable study of the institution in the Evangelical United Brethren tradition, see John H. Ness, Jr., *One Hundred Fifty Years: A History of Publishing in the Evangelical United Brethren Church* (Nashville: Abingdon Press, 1966). On communications, see Edwin H. Maynard, *Keeping up with a Revolution: The Story of United Methodist Communications, 1940–1990* (Nashville: United Methodist Communications, 1990).

MINISTRY: DEACONS, ELDERS, AND BISHOPS

Historical works on the several forms of ministry include Mary E. Moore, Rosemary Keller, and Gerald Moede, *The Diaconate in the United Methodist Tradition* (Nashville: Division of Diaconal Ministries, General Board of Higher Education and Ministry, United Methodist Church, 1986); Frederick A. Norwood, *Church Membership in the Methodist Tradition* (Nashville: Abingdon Press, 1958); Dennis Campbell, *The Yoke of Obedience: The Meaning of Ordination in Methodism* (Nashville: Abingdon Press, 1988); E. Dale Dunlap, "The United Methodist System of Itinerant Ministry," in *Rethinking Methodist History*, 18–28; Richard P. Heitzenrater, "A Critical Analysis of the Ministry Studies since 1944," *Occasional Papers Issued by the United Methodist Board of Higher Education and Ministry* no. 76 (1 September 1988), and *POAM*, 431–47; E. Brooks Holifield, *A History of Pastoral Care in America: From Salvation to Self-Realization* (Nashville: Abingdon Press, 1983); Gerald O. McCulloh, ed., *The Ministry in the Methodist Heritage* (Nashville: Department of Ministerial Education, Board of Education, Methodist Church, 1960). Works covering episcopacy are detailed quite fully in that section.

POLITY

Also discussed in full in both the first and second sections of this work are the several works on polity. See also the Rowe bibliography cited first.

INDEX

abolition. *See* slavery
Adkins, Leon M., 249
Advocate. *See Christian Advocate*
Affirmation, 158
African-American Methodists, 73, 77;
   bishops, 46; catechisms for slaves,
   185–87; Central Jurisdiction, 143–44,
   154; colleges, 217; formation of
   separate churches, 84, 90–91; racial
   segregation in 1939 reunification, 146;
   racial segregation in MECS, 122; sepa-
   rate ordinations, 87. *See also* bishops,
   African-American; clergy,
   African-American; women,
   African-American
African Methodist Episcopal Church
   (AME), 90
African Union Church, 90
agencies. *See* boards
Albright, Jacob, 91–92
Allen, Richard, 77, 84, 87, 90
American Conference, 4, 73
American Methodism, 3; independence
   from British leadership, 4, 69–70
Ames, Edward, 121
Anderson, William K., 249
Andrew, James Osgood, 30, 36–37, 51,
   111
annual conference, 29, 80 n.32; annual re-
   ports, 125; authority, 31, 141; bounda-

ries, 126; bureaucratic structure, 93–94;
   clergy education, 140–41; conference
   size, 126; fraternal aspect, 141; frontier
   expansion, 92–93; membership, 83;
   regulated by General Conference, 86;
   supervision of clergy, 87, 141. *See also*
   laity, conference representation
architecture: Akron plan, 213–15, 232;
   Gothic style, 213; public school model,
   232
Armstrong, James L., 54
Articles of Religion, 223, 226, 239–40
Asbury, Francis, 24, 51; arrival in America, 3; as bishop, 8–9, 12–13; the
   Council (1789–90), 9; encouragement
   of revivals, 88; episcopal powers, 8–9;
   as General Assistant, 3–4, 79 n.23, 80
   n.29; and general conference, 6, 21; as
   general superintendent, 7–8, 73; influence on episcopal office, 11–12, 43;
   and quarterly conferences, 67, 88; relationship with fellow bishops, 13; Sunday school, 170–72; and Thomas Coke,
   8; view of clergy marital status, 87

Baker, Osmon C., 178
Baltimore Union Society, 105
Bangs, Nathan, 102, 109, 170, 181–82

About the Authors

JAMES E. KIRBY is Professor of Church History at Southern Methodist University's Perkins School of Theology. His interests are in the history of Methodism and the American nineteenth century. He is currently working on a biography of Bishop William C. Martin, President of the National Council of Churches in 1952.

RUSSELL E. RICHEY is Associate Dean for Academic Programs and Professor of Church History at The Divinity School at Duke University. His most recent books include *Early American Methodism* (1991) and *Reimagining Denominationalism* (1994).

KENNETH E. ROWE is Professor of Church History at Drew University Theological School and Librarian of the United Methodist Archives and History Center. He is the author of *United Methodist Studies: Basic Bibliographies* (1992), of the multi-volume *Methodist Union Catalog* (1975–) and co-editor with Richey of *Perspectives on American Methodism* (1993).